THE JEWS IN POLAND AND RUSSIA

Forgetting leads to exile, remembering is the path to salvation.

ISRAEL BEN ELIEZER, THE BA'AL SHEM TOV

The Jews are not a historical nation
They are not even an archaeological nation
The Jews are a geological nation
With fissures and breaks
And layers of burning lava
One has to measure their history with another measure.

YEHUDA AMICHAI

And I went back to my childhood years, to the days that perished under the sediment of forgetfulness. With a tremendous effort of memory, I raised the Atlantis that seemed to have been lost and drowned for ever.

JULIAN STRYJKOWSKI

THE LITTMAN LIBRARY OF JEWISH CIVILIZATION

Dedicated to the memory of
LOUIS THOMAS SIDNEY LITTMAN
who founded the Littman Library for the love of God
and as an act of charity in memory of his father
JOSEPH AARON LITTMAN
יהא זכרם ברוך

Get wisdom, get understanding:
Forsake her not and she shall preserve thee
PROV. 4: 5

The Littman Library of Jewish Civilization is a registered UK charity
Registered charity no. 1000784

THE JEWS IN POLAND AND RUSSIA

VOLUME I

1350 to 1881

ANTONY POLONSKY

Oxford · Portland, Oregon
The Littman Library of Jewish Civilization
2010

The Littman Library of Jewish Civilization

Chief Executive Officer: Ludo Craddock
Managing Editor: Connie Webber

PO Box 645, Oxford OX2 0UJ, UK
www.littman.co.uk

Published in the United States and Canada by
The Littman Library of Jewish Civilization
c/o ISBS, 920 NE 58th Avenue, Suite 300
Portland, Oregon 97213-3786

A catalogue record for this book is available from the British Library

Library of Congress cataloging-in-publication data

Polonsky, Antony.
The Jews in Poland and Russia / Antony Polonsky.
p. cm.
Includes bibliographical references and index.
Contents: v. 1 1350–1881
1. Jews—Poland—History. 2. Jews—Russia—History.
3. Poland—Ethnic relations. 4. Russia—Ethnic relations. I. Title.
DS134.53.P65 2009
305.892′40438—dc22 2008054390

ISBN 978-1-874774-64-8

Publishing Co-ordinator: Janet Moth
Production: John Saunders
Design: Pete Russell, Faringdon, Oxon.
Copy-editing: Laurien Berkeley
Proof-reading: George Tulloch, Arlene Polonsky, Joyce Rappaport
Index: Sarah Ereira
Typeset by Hope Services (Abingdon) Ltd
Printed in Great Britain on acid-free paper by the
MPG Books Group, Bodmin and King's Lynn

This book is dedicated to the memory of

SHIMON DUBNOV
(1860–1941)

and

MAJER BAŁABAN
(1877–1942)

Pioneers in the study of the history of the Jews of Poland–Lithuania and Russia who perished in the Holocaust

ACKNOWLEDGEMENTS

IN PRODUCING THIS BOOK I am greatly indebted to the students and faculty of Brandeis University, and particularly those in the Department of Near Eastern and Judaic Studies and the Comparative History programme, from whom I have learned so much. In the more than twenty years that I have been chairman of the editorial committee of *Polin: Studies in Polish Jewry* I have worked closely with many of the leading scholars in the field of east European Jewry and have profited enormously from their work. I have also benefited greatly from the periods I spent as a visiting professor at the University of Warsaw, the Institute for the Human Sciences (Vienna); the University of Cape Town, and the Jagiellonian University (Kraków); as Skirball Visiting Fellow at the Oxford Centre for Hebrew and Jewish Studies, as Honorary Research Fellow at University College London; and as Ina Levin Invitational Fellow at the United States Holocaust Memorial Museum.

I have consulted many individuals on different aspects of this work. I list them here in alphabetical order, and apologize that I do not have space to describe in more detail the many ways in which they have assisted me: David Aberbach, Eliyana Adler, Allan Amanik, David Assaf, Irina Astashkievich, Karen Auerbach, Arnold Band, Jakub Basista, Steven Bayme, Michael Beizer, Eleonora Bergman, Michael Brenner, Michael Brown, John J. Bukowczyk, Richard Butterwick, Anna Cienciała, Toby Clyman, Mike Cohen, Hugh Denman, Curt Dunagan, Glenn Dynner, Todd Endelman, ChaeRan Freeze, David Frick, Klaus-Peter Friedrich, Michał Galas, Arthur Green, the late Avraham Greenbaum, Leo Głuchowski, Chris Gniewosz, John-Paul Himka, Brian Horowitz, Gershon Hundert, Dovid Katz, Adam Kaźmierczyk, Ellie Kellman, Sophie Kemlein, Padraic Kenney, Victoria Khiterer, Reuven Kimelman, Maria Klanska, Toralf Kleinsorge, the late John Klier, John J. Kulczycki, Sarunas Liekis, Dominic Lieven, Jacek Maj, Krzysztof Makowski, Jerzy Mazur, Vladimir Melamed, Joanna Michlic, Allen Nadler, Ben Nathans, Charles van Onselen, Philip Pajakowski, Yohanan Petrovsky-Stern, Jan Piskorski, Simon Rabinovich, Ada Rappoport-Albert, Benjamin Ravid, David Rechter, Monika Rice, David Roskies, Moshe Rosman, Szymon Rudnicki, Jonathan Sarna, Vassili Schedrin, Jan Schwarz, Naomi Seidman, Eugene Sheppard, Joseph Sherman, Inna Shtakser, Leonid Smilovitsky, Shaul Stampfer, Michael Steinlauf, Daniel Stone, Roman Szporluk, Adam Teller, Magda Teter, Jerzy Tomaszewski, Steve Velychenko, Piotr Wandycz, Jonathan Webber, Ted Weeks, Brett Werb, Marcin Wodziński, Piotr Wróbel, Joshua Zimmerman, and Steven Zipperstein.

The form and content of this book owe an enormous amount to the constant assistance and advice I have received from my publishers, the Littman Library of Jewish Civilization. I should like to thank, above all, the directors Mrs Colette

Littman and her son Roby, and also the managing editor, Connie Webber, the chief executive officer Ludo Craddock, and the publishing co-ordinator Janet Moth. Laurien Berkeley copy-edited the volume to her usual high standard; George Tulloch checked the Slavonic languages and assisted in preparing the maps; Zosia Sochańska assisted in checking the Polish and checked the Yiddish; Philippa Claiden checked the rabbinic and Hebrew material; and Pete Russell designed the book's text and jacket. I have also been greatly assisted in bringing it to publication by Joyce Rappoport.

This book has benefited from grants from the Foundation of Jewish Culture, who awarded me the Ganz-Zahler prize to help defray the costs of publication; the Memorial Foundation of Jewish Culture, from whom I received an international fellowship which enabled me to take time off from my teaching; and from Sigmund Rolat. I am enormously indebted to all of them.

My greatest debt is to my wife Arlene, who has not only consistently supported me in the sometimes onerous tasks of research and writing but has provided wise advice and counsel at every stage in the creative process. Obviously, in the last analysis, this work reflects only my own opinions and preoccupations.

November 2009 A.P.

CONTENTS

MAPS

TABLES

NOTE ON TRANSLITERATION

THE transliteration of Hebrew in this book reflects consideration of the type of book it is, in terms of its content, purpose, and readership. The system adopted therefore reflects a broad approach to transcription, rather than the narrower approaches found in the *Encyclopaedia Judaica* or other systems developed for text-based or linguistic studies. The aim has been to reflect the pronunciation prescribed for modern Hebrew, rather than the spelling or Hebrew word structure, and to do so using conventions that are generally familiar to the English-speaking reader.

In accordance with this approach, no attempt is made to indicate the distinctions between *alef* and *ayin*, *tet* and *taf*, *kaf* and *kuf*, *sin* and *samekh*, since these are not relevant to pronunciation; likewise, the *dagesh* is not indicated except where it affects pronunciation. Following the principle of using conventions familiar to the majority of readers, however, transcriptions that are well established have been retained even when they are not fully consistent with the transliteration system adopted. On similar grounds, the *tsadi* is rendered by 'tz' in such familiar words as barmitzvah, mitzvot, and so on. Likewise, the distinction between *ḥet* and *khaf* has been retained, using *ḥ* for the former and *kh* for the latter; the associated forms are generally familiar to readers, even if the distinction is not actually borne out in pronunciation, and for the same reason the final *heh* is indicated too. As in Hebrew, no capital letters are used, except that an initial capital has been retained in transliterating titles of published works (for example, *Shulḥan arukh*).

Since no distinction is made between *alef* and *ayin*, they are indicated by an apostrophe only in intervocalic positions where a failure to do so could lead an English-speaking reader to pronounce the vowel-cluster as a diphthong—as, for example, in *ha'ir*—or otherwise mispronounce the word.

The *sheva na* is indicated by an *e*—*perikat ol*, *reshut*—except, again, when established convention dictates otherwise.

The *yod* is represented by *i* when it occurs as a vowel (*bereshit*), by *y* when it occurs as a consonant (*yesodot*), and by *yi* when it occurs as both (*yisra'el*).

Names have generally been left in their familiar forms, even when this is inconsistent with the overall system.

The transliteration of Yiddish follows the YIVO system except for names of people, where the spellings they themselves used have been retained.

The transliteration of Russian and Ukrainian follows that of British Standard 2979:1958, without diacritics. Except in bibliographical and other strictly rendered matter, soft and hard signs are omitted, and word-final -й, -ий, -ый, -ій in names are simplified to *-y*.

NOTE ON PLACE NAMES

POLITICAL connotations accrue to words, names, and spellings with an alacrity unfortunate for those who would like to maintain neutrality. It seems reasonable to honour the choices of a population on the name of its city or town, but what is one to do when the people have no consensus on their name, or when the town changes its name, and the name its spelling, again and again over time? The politician may always opt for the latest version, but the hapless historian must reckon with them all. This note, then, will be my brief reckoning.

The least problematic are those places that have a widely accepted English name, which I shall use by preference. Examples are Warsaw, Kiev, Moscow, St Petersburg, and Munich. As an exception, I maintain the Polish spelling of Kraków, which in English has more often appeared as Cracow.

Most other place names in east central Europe can raise serious problems. The linguistic and contextual diversity encountered cannot adequately be standardized by editorial formula, and in practice the least awkward solution is often to let subject matter and perspective determine the most suitable spellings in a given context. The difficulty is well illustrated by Galicia's most diversely named city, and one of its most important, which boasts four variants: the Polish Lwów, the German Lemberg, the Russian Lvov, and the Ukrainian Lviv. In this volume I have opted for Lviv.

A particular difficulty is posed by Wilno/Vilnius/Vilna, to all of which there are clear objections: until 1944 the majority of the population was Polish; the city is today in Lithuania; 'Vilna', though least problematic, is an artificial construct. My preference will be to use the common English form 'Vilna' until its first incorporation into Lithuania in October 1939, and 'Vilnius' thereafter. Thus, in this first volume of this three-volume work, I shall use Vilna throughout.

MAPS

1. THE KINGDOM OF POLAND AND THE GRAND DUCHY OF LITHUANIA, 1350

Derived from Rowell, *Lithuania Ascending*

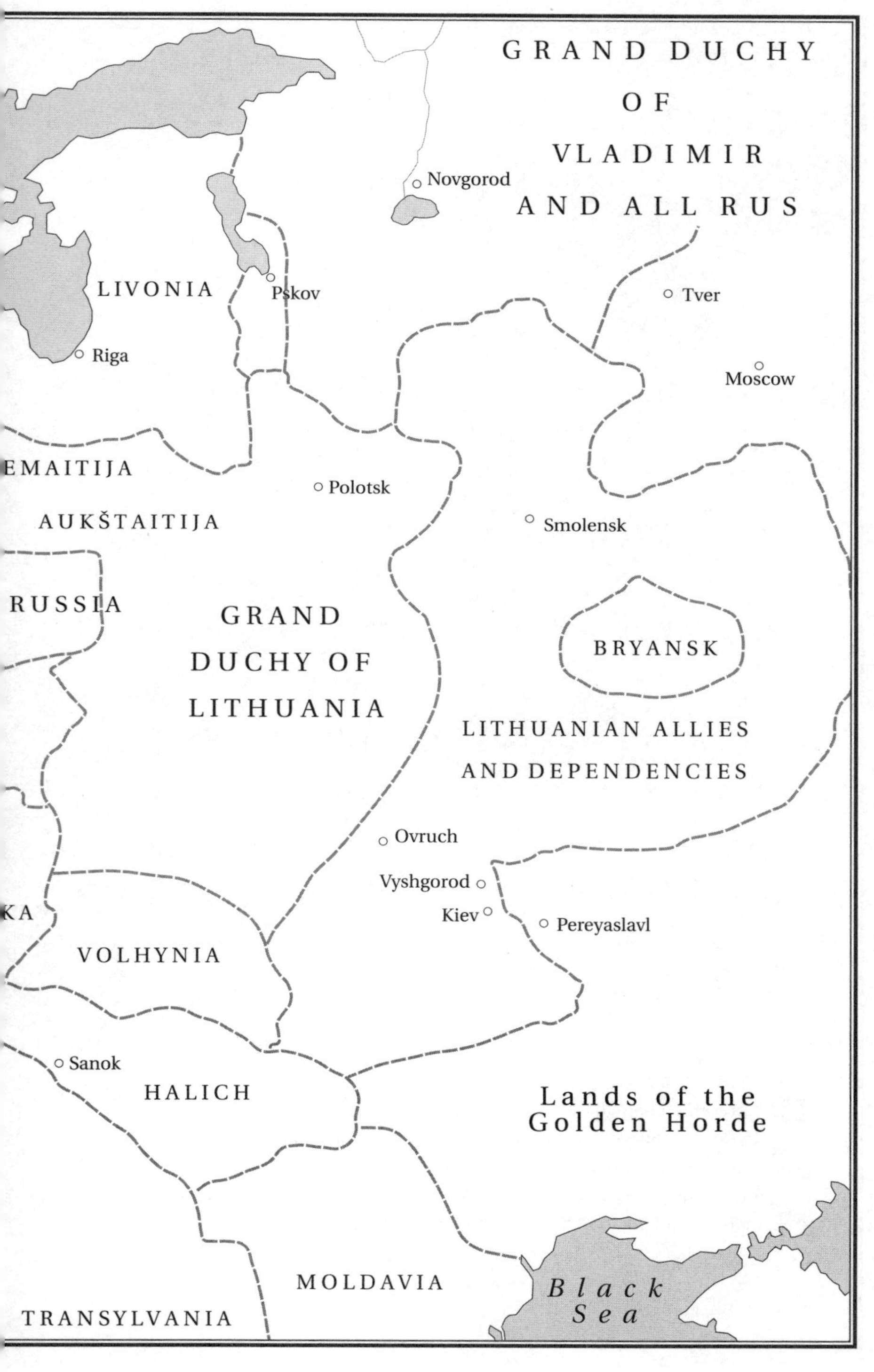
GRAND DUCHY
OF
VLADIMIR
AND ALL RUS
Novgorod
LIVONIA
Pskov
Tver
Riga
Moscow
EMAITIJA
Polotsk
AUKŠTAITIJA
Smolensk
RUSSIA
GRAND
DUCHY OF
LITHUANIA
BRYANSK
LITHUANIAN ALLIES
AND DEPENDENCIES
Ovruch
Vyshgorod
KA
Kiev
Pereyaslavl
VOLHYNIA
Sanok
HALICH
Lands of the
Golden Horde
MOLDAVIA
Black
Sea
TRANSYLVANIA

Baltic Sea
Słupsk
Gdańsk
Marienburg
STATE OF THE TEUTONIC ORDER
Szczecin
BRANDENBURG
Berlin
Toruń
MAZOVIA
Gniezno
Płock
Poznań
WIELKOPOLSKA
Kalisz
Głogów
Wrocław
Świdnica
MAŁOPOLSKA
Prague
Kraków
Racibórz
Wieliczka
KINGDOM OF BOHEMIA
Boundary of Kingdom of Poland c.1370
Territories inherited by Kazimierz the Great in 1333
Territories annexed to the state by Kazimierz the Great
Piast principalities tributary to the Holy Roman Empire
Piast principalities tributary to the Kingdom of Bohemia
Independent duchy of Bolko II, Duke of Świdnica
0
100
200
300 miles
0
100
200
300
400
500 km

2. POLAND UNDER KAZIMIERZ THE GREAT, 1370
Derived from Zamoyski, *The Polish Way*
GRAND DUCHY
OF LITHUANIA
Varsaw
Chełm
Sandomierz
Bełz
Lviv
RUTHENIA
Halich
PODOLIA
Kamenets-Podolsky
KINGDOM
OF HUNGARY
PRINCIPALITY
OF MOLDAVIA
(Polish fief)

SWEDEN
GOTLAND
ÖLAND
Baltic Sea
BORNHOLM
LIVONIA
to Polish Livonia
to Polish Livonia
oRiga
KURLAND
oMittau
ŻMUDŹ
WILN
Wiłkomi
Kowno
Troki
TROKI
EAST PRUSSIA
WARMIA
PRUSSIA
BRANDENBURG
Gdańsk
Oliwa
Elbląg
Malbork
Marienwerder
Grudziądz
Chełmno
Fordon
Bydgoszcz
Toruń
Inowrocław
Gniezno
Brześć Kujawski
Płock
Gostynin
Drezdenko
Poznań
Warsaw
Grodno
Nowogró
Słonim
N O
Brześć Litewski
Łęczyca
Rawa
Kalisz
Sieradz
Biała
Wieluń
Piotrków
Kozienice
Radom
Zwoleń
Parczew
Lublin
(Land of Chełm)
Chełm
Włodzimierz
Łuck
Częstochowa
Sandomierz
Siewierz
Kraków
Oświęcim
Zator
Bochnia
Wieliczka
Nowy Targ
Nowy Sącz
Czorsztyn
Sanok
Przemyśl
Lwów
Bełz
Tarnopo
Halicz
Spisz
HABSBURG DOMINIONS
1
2
3
4
5
6
7
8
9
10
11
12
13
14
15
16
17
18
19
20
0
50
100
150
200 miles
0
100
200
300 km

3. POLAND–LITHUANIA, 1771
Place names are given in their Polish form as these were official at the time
Derived from H. Kaplan, *The First Partition of Poland*
POŁOCK
Połock
Uła
WITEBSK
Witebsk
Smolensk
Orsza
Mścisław
Mohylew
MŚCISŁAW
Mińsk
MIŃSK
RUSSIA
Rochaczew
Słuck
Boundary of Poland, 1771
Boundary between Lithuania and the Korona
Province boundaries
The provinces of the Korona
1 Malbork
2 Pomorze
3 Poznań
4 Gniezno
5 Inowrocław
6 Chełmno
7 Brześć Kujawski
8 Płock
9 Mazowsze
10 Podlasie
11 Kalisz
12 Sieradz
13 Łęczyca
14 Rawa
15 Kraków
16 Sandomierz
17 Lublin
18 Ruś and Ziemia Chełmska
19 Bełz
20 Wołyń (Volhynia)
21 Kiev
22 Podole (Podolia)
23 Bracław
21
Kiev
Żytomierz
Nowy Konstantynów
Winnica
22
Bar
Bracław
23
Kamieniec Podolski
Bałta
OTTOMAN EMPIRE

Baltic Sea
Windau
Riga
COURLAND
Libau
Mittau
Memel
Kovno
Königsberg
Vilna
1793
EAST PRUSSIA
Danzig
Elbing
WARMIA
WEST PRUSSIA
Marienwerder
Stettin
NEW EAST PRUSSIA
Grodno
1772
Bydgoszcz
BRANDENBURG
Toruń
Volkovysk
Białystok
Łomża
1795
Noteć
Gniezno
Ciechanów
Vistula
Frankfurt
Wyszogród
Płock
Poznań
Brest-Litovsk
Bug
SOUTH PRUSSIA
Łęczyca
WARSAW
Kalisz
SAXONY
Neisse
SILESIA
1793
Pilica
Breslau
Radom
Lublin
Chełm
Oder
1795
Częstochowa
Vladimir
Sandomierz
GLATZ
1795
Bełz
Kraków
Vistula
1772
GALICIA
Lviv
Teschen
Neustadt
Przemyśl
Dniester
Halicz
1768–9
Eperjes
ZIPS
HABSBURG MONARCHY
VIENNA
Danube
0 50 100 150 miles
0 100 200 km
Territories lost to
Russia
Prussia
Austria
Boundary between the Korona and the Duchy of Lithuania

4. THE PARTITIONS OF POLAND

Derived from Lukowski, *The Partitions of Poland*; Kieniewicz (ed.), *History of Poland*

5. THE GRAND DUCHY OF POZNAŃ 1815–1914

Derived from Kulczycki, *School Strikes in Prussian Poland*

POMERANIA
WEST PRUSSIA
WEST PRUSSIA
BRANDENBURG
RUSSIAN POLAND
SILESIA
Bydgoszcz
Poznań

0 10 20 30 40 50 60 miles
0 20 40 60 80 100 km

Bydgoszcz district
- ○ Bydgoszcz (urban)
- 1 Bydgoszcz (rural)
- 2 Chodzież
- 3 Czarnków
- 4 Gniezno
- 5 Inowrocław
- 6 Mogilno
- 7 Strzelno
- 8 Szubin
- 9 Wągrowiec
- 10 Wieleń
- 11 Witkowo
- 12 Wyrzysk
- 13 Żnin

Poznań district
- ○ Poznań (urban)
- 14 Babimost
- 15 Gostyń
- 16 Grodzisk
- 17 Jarocin
- 18 Kępno
- 19 Kościan
- 20 Koźmin
- 21 Krotoszyn
- 22 Leszno
- 23 Międzychód
- 24 Międzyrzecz
- 25 Nowy Tomyśl
- 26 Oborniki
- 27 Odolanów
- 28 Ostrów
- 29 Ostrzeszów
- 30 Pleszew
- 31 East Poznań
- 32 West Poznań
- 33 Rawicz
- 34 Skwierzyna
- 35 Szamotuły
- 36 Śmigiel
- 37 Śrem
- 38 Środa
- 39 Września
- 40 Wschowa

6. GALICIA, 1850–1914
Derived from Magocsi, *Galicia*
GERMAN EMPIRE
SILESIA
HUNGARIA
CARPATHIAN
Kielce
Częstochowa
Vistula
San
Tarnobrzeg
Nisko
Mielec
Kolbuszowa
Oświęcim
Chrzanów
Kraków
Podgórze
Wieliczka
Brzesko
Bochnia
Dąbrowa
Tarnów
Ropczyce
Rzeszów
Pilzno
Łańcut
Przeworsk
Jarosław
Biała
Wadowice
Myślenice
Żywiec
Limanowa
Nowy Sącz
Nowy Targ
Dunajec
Grybów
Gorlice
Jasło
Krosno
Strzyżów
Wisłok
Brzozów
Sanok
Lesko
Dobromyl
Poprad
Košice
Uzhhorod
Tisza
Lubl
Galicia (Rus) before 1772
International borders, 1850
Boundary between Hungarian Kingdom and Austrian crownlands
Austrian crownland boundaries
Boundary between west and east Galician judicial districts
Approximate Polish–Ukrainian ethnolinguistic boundary
0 20 40 60 miles
0 20 40 60 80 100 km

RUSSIAN EMPIRE
VOLHYNIA
PODOLIA
BUKOVINA
KINGDOM
ITAINS
C
I
A
Volodymyr-Volynsky
Lutsk
Rivne
Sokal
Rava Ruska
Kaminka Strumylova
Brody
Zhovkva
Lviv
Zolochiv
Horodok
Bibrka
Peremyshlyany
Rudky
Zboriv
Zbarazh
Ternopil
Skalat
Sambir
Berezhany
Drohobych
Rohatyn
Zhydachiv
Terebovlya
Stryi
Pidhaitsi
Husyatyn
Buchach
Kalush
Dolyna
Chortkiv
Stanyslaviv
Borshchiv
Tovmach
Bohorodchany
Horodenka
Zalishchyky
Nadvirna
Kolomyya
Pechenizhyn
Snyatyn
Kosiv
Chernivtsi
Styr
Horyn
Buh
Seret
Zbruch
Dniester
Stryi
Prut
Cheremosh

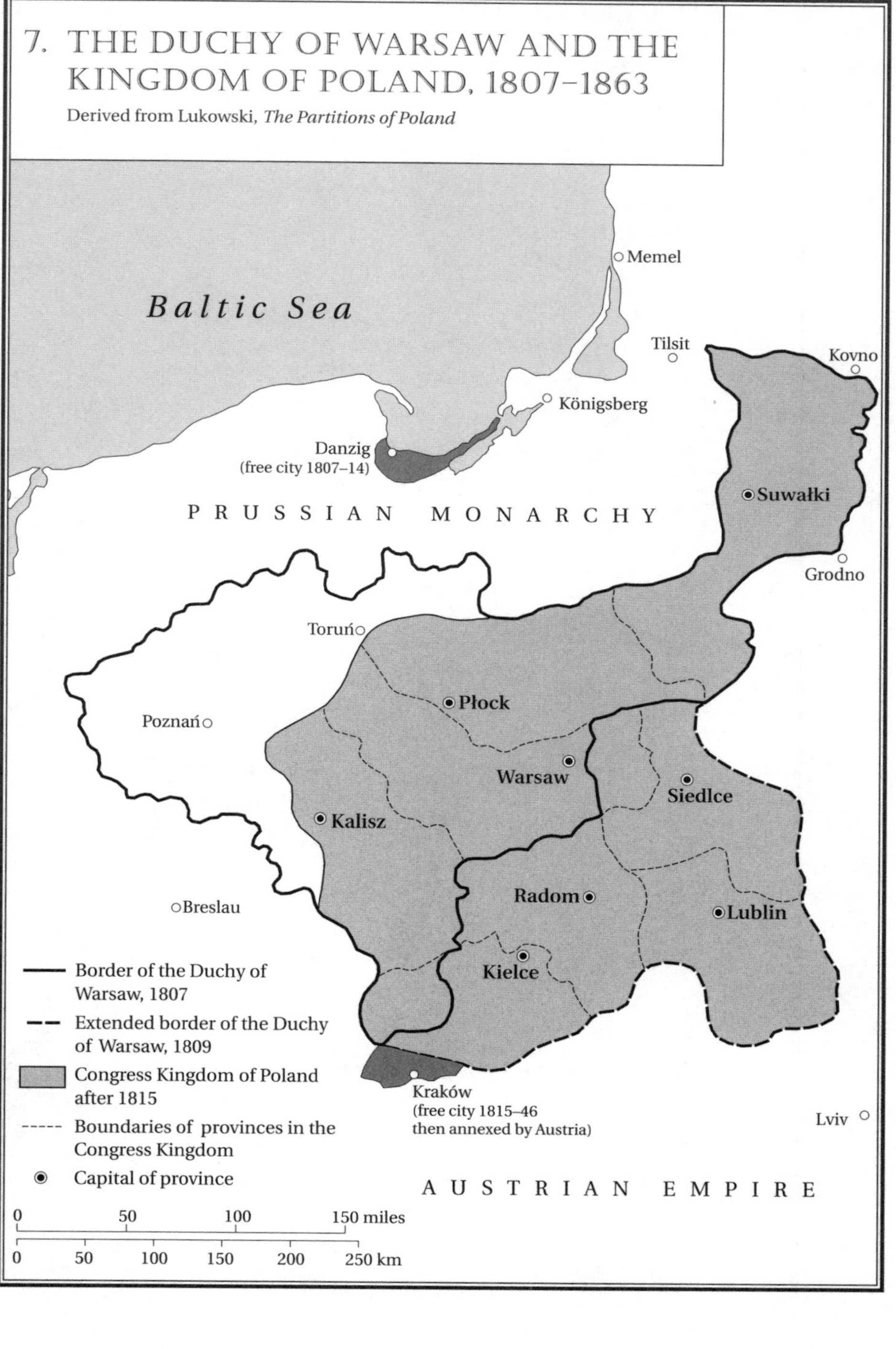
7. THE DUCHY OF WARSAW AND THE KINGDOM OF POLAND, 1807–1863
Derived from Lukowski, The Partitions of Poland
Baltic Sea
Memel
Tilsit
Kovno
Königsberg
Danzig
(free city 1807–14)
PRUSSIAN MONARCHY
Suwałki
Grodno
Toruń
Płock
Poznań
Warsaw
Siedlce
Kalisz
Radom
Lublin
Breslau
Kielce
Border of the Duchy of Warsaw, 1807
Extended border of the Duchy of Warsaw, 1809
Congress Kingdom of Poland after 1815
Boundaries of provinces in the Congress Kingdom
Capital of province
Kraków
(free city 1815–46
then annexed by Austria)
Lviv
AUSTRIAN EMPIRE
0
50
100
150 miles
0
50
100
150
200
250 km

NORWAY
SWEDEN
FINLAND
OLONETS
Baltic Sea
ESTLAND
St Petersburg
ST P'BURG
NOVGOROD
LIVLAND
KURLAND
Riga
PSKOV
TVER
KOVNO
VITEBSK
MOSCOW
Moscow
PRUSSIA
VILNA
SMOLENSK
KALUGA
GRODNO
MINSK
MOGILEV
TULA
KINGDOM OF POLAND
OREL
CHERNIGOV
KURSK
VOLHYNIA
Kiev
KIEV
POLTAVA
VORONEZH
AUSTRIA
PODOLIA
KHARKOV
BESSARABIA
KHERSON
EKATERINOSLAV
Nikolaev
TAVRIDA
OTTOMAN EMPIRE
Sevastopol
Black Sea

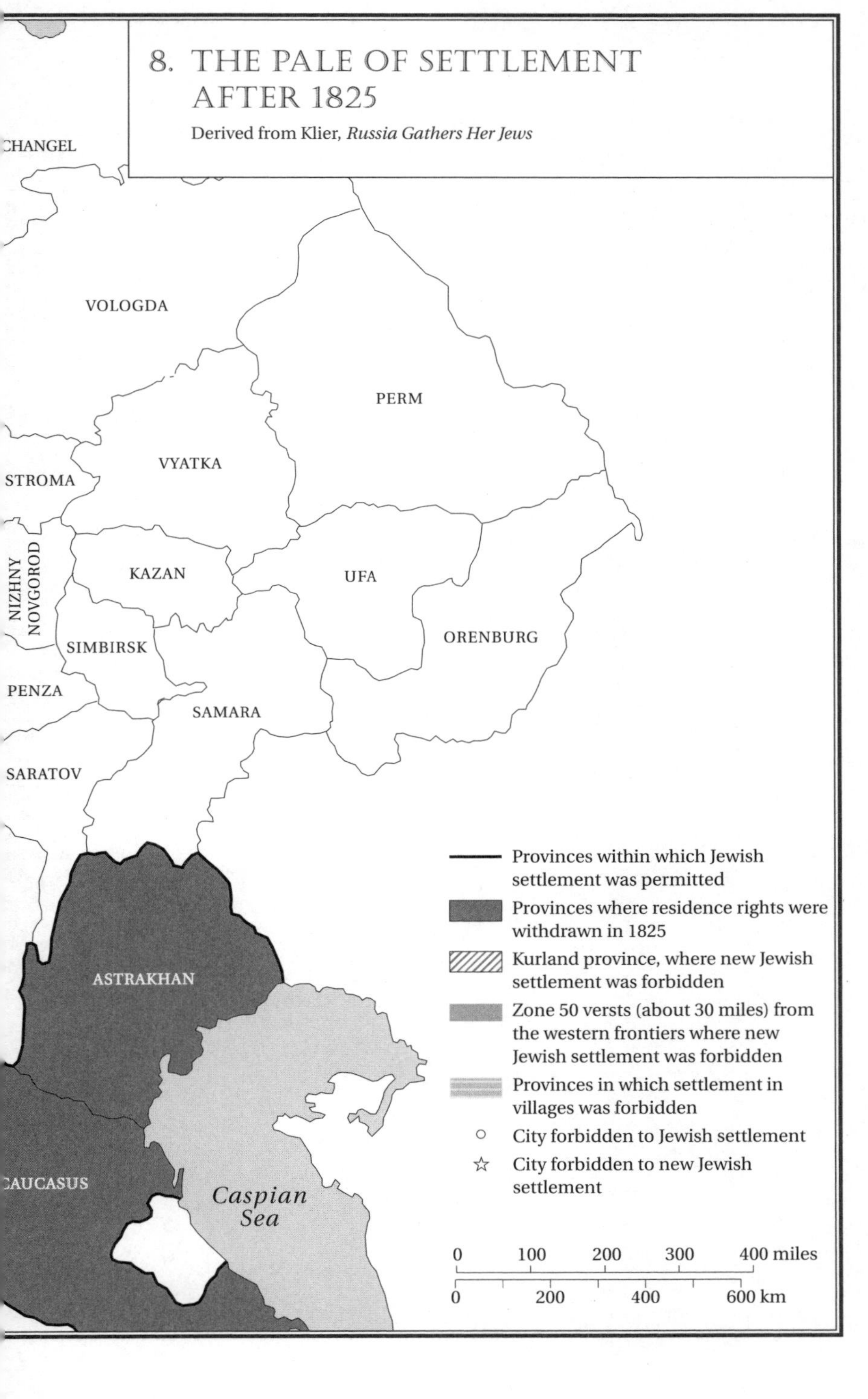
8. THE PALE OF SETTLEMENT AFTER 1825
Derived from Klier, *Russia Gathers Her Jews*
CHANGEL
VOLOGDA
PERM
VYATKA
STROMA
NIZHNY NOVGOROD
KAZAN
UFA
ORENBURG
SIMBIRSK
PENZA
SAMARA
SARATOV
ASTRAKHAN
CAUCASUS
Caspian Sea
Provinces within which Jewish settlement was permitted
Provinces where residence rights were withdrawn in 1825
Kurland province, where new Jewish settlement was forbidden
Zone 50 versts (about 30 miles) from the western frontiers where new Jewish settlement was forbidden
Provinces in which settlement in villages was forbidden
City forbidden to Jewish settlement
City forbidden to new Jewish settlement
0 100 200 300 400 miles
0 200 400 600 km

GENERAL INTRODUCTION

Hayim Nahman Bialik, the Hebrew poet, in a letter written in early January 1906 to the Yiddish writer Shalom Aleichem, observed, 'No country is better for [the Jews] than Russia . . .'.[1] He was entitled to think so. In the 130 years prior to his letter, hasidism had developed within the tsarist empire as a major religious revival, its mitnagdic opponents had created the great Lithuanian yeshivas, Hebrew and Yiddish literature had flourished, and new political movements, above all Zionism and Jewish socialism, had emerged and transformed the Jewish political landscape.[2]

However, within little more than a decade the Bolshevik Revolution had taken place and Stalin's subsequent seizure of power destroyed the basis of organized Jewish life in Russia and its empire until it was restored with the collapse of the Soviet Union.

In his introduction to the collaborative history *The Jews in Reborn Poland* (*Żydzi w Polsce odrodzonej*), published in 1932 and 1933, Ozjasz Thon, rabbi of the Tempel in Kraków and chairman of the Jewish parliamentary club in the Sejm (the Polish parliament), asked, 'What is the role of Polish Jewry today; what is its mission?' He continued: 'Both quantitatively and qualitatively its mission, which it will soon take up, is to assume the leadership of world Jewry.' This was a task which he believed it alone was capable of undertaking, given the spiritual and material devastation of Soviet Jewry and the lack of freedom in which it lived, and the loss by American Jewry, under the pressure of assimilation, of its specific Jewish character. Polish Jewry possessed the 'genuine' character of Russian Jewry, but also, according to Thon, lived in the freedom enjoyed by American Jews. He foresaw a splendid future for the Jews of Poland:

> Polish Jews in the past have on occasion determined the character of world Jewry. There were moments when the genius of the Jewish people reached its full flowering in Poland. I am convinced that events are again creating a situation in which in Poland there will emerge one of the great centres of the Jewish spirit.[3]

Yet within seven years Poland had ceased to exist, partitioned between Nazi Germany and the Soviet Union, and the destruction of Poland's huge Jewish community was about to commence.

1 Letter of 3 Jan. 1906 to Shalom Aleichem, in Bialik, *The Letters of H. N. Bialik*, ii. 9.

2 On this, see Lederhendler, 'The Jews in Imperial Russia', 18.

3 Thon, 'Wstęp', 17–18.

These passages illustrate the basic themes I examine in this work: in the first place, the enormous importance of the history of the Jews of Poland and Russia in the history of the Jewish people and the development of Jewish religious traditions. That the Jews of this area would come to assume such significance within world Jewry was by no means self-evident. During the nineteenth century Germany was seen as the pattern for successful Jewish modernization, and many German Jews, like Heinrich Graetz, who himself came from the lands of former Poland–Lithuania, frequently referred to 'the demoralized and barbarous state' of the Jews there. Even in the twentieth century the area was often seen as the repository of unchanging and eternal Jewish authenticity, in spite of the multifaceted Jewish civilization which had developed there.

The second basic theme is that of the danger of reading history backwards. It is difficult to write the history of the Jews of eastern Europe without being aware of the devastating impact on their lives of twentieth-century integral nationalism, Nazism, and communism. Yet Bialik, writing at the time of a major pogrom wave and on the eve of the cataclysms of the First World War and the Bolshevik Revolution, could still envisage a future of enormous promise for his community. So too did Thon in the face of rising Polish nationalism and the threat of Hitler's coming to power in Germany.

Bialik and Thon thought of Polish and Russian Jews as separate entities, and certainly this was one of the consequences of the developments of the nineteenth and early twentieth centuries. Yet in the middle of the eighteenth century there was a strong sense of the common character of all Jews who lived in the Polish–Lithuanian Commonwealth. What I have tried to do in this book is both to describe this common character, along with the regional differences which existed in Poland–Lithuania, and then to outline how the impact of the partitions of the Commonwealth led to very different developments under Prussian, Austrian, and Russian rule. Similarly, I have tried to analyse the impact on Jewish life after the First World War of the emergence of the national states of Poland and Lithuania and the establishment of Bolshevik power in most of the former tsarist empire.

This is the first of a series of three volumes that will tell this history. The present volume deals with Jewish life in pre-modern Poland–Lithuania and with the attempts of the governments of the region from the middle of the eighteenth century to transform the Jews from members of a transnational community united by faith and culture into subjects or citizens of the countries in which they lived, and the Jewish response. The second volume examines the rejection by the tsarist government after 1881 of the politics of Jewish integration and the emergence of new forms of Jewish politics in response to the crisis this created. The third volume examines the period from the outbreak of war in 1914 to the renewed conflict in 1939, as well as the tragic impact on the area of Nazism and the Second World War, the slow and incomplete recovery of Jewish life after 1945, and the more promising revival after 1989–91.

The history of the Jews of the former Polish–Lithuanian Commonwealth is an important topic of study because it is from these lands that the majority of world Jewry, whether in the State of Israel or in the diaspora, trace their roots. The Jewish past in these lands is well established in Jewish collective memory. But with the opening of the archives in the former Soviet Union and eastern Europe and the vast amount of research which has taken place in the last two decades in Israel, North America, and Europe, there is a need to produce a new synthetic account which will correct the overly sentimental and also the excessively negative view of this past, both of which are prevalent. It is my hope that this will enable us better to appreciate from where the Jews have come and how much has been achieved by them on the path to the modern world.

PART I

JEWISH LIFE IN POLAND-LITHUANIA TO 1750

INTRODUCTION

BY THE MIDDLE of the eighteenth century the Jewish community of Poland–Lithuania had become the largest Jewish community in the world and a centre of Jewish intellectual and religious life. This development was the result of a fundamental transformation of the geography of the Jewish world between 1200 and 1550. From the twelfth century the position of the Jews in the Arab world began to deteriorate, while at about that time in western Europe a series of expulsions occurred, starting with that from England at the end of the twelfth century and culminating in the forced conversion of part and the emigration of the remainder of the largest Jewish community in western Europe, that in Spain. As a result, Jews were now concentrated in three small and two larger communities.

The three smaller communities were to be found in Italy, in the German states including that of the Habsburgs, whose rule extended to some largely non-German territories, such as Bohemia, Moravia, and Hungary, and in the port cities of the Atlantic coast of Europe. Italy at this time was not subject to a single ruler, and Jews were found in the Papal States, in the Republic of Venice, in the Grand Duchy of Tuscany, and in the smaller states of the north. The Jewish community had a mixed character: some of its members were descendants of the earliest Jewish settlers in the peninsula, some had moved there from the German lands from the twelfth century on, and some were immigrants from the Iberian peninsula. Perhaps 40,000 Jews lived in Italy by the end of the eighteenth century.

Germany at this time was also politically divided. On the eve of the French Revolution there were more than 300 states in German-speaking Europe, ranging from great states like the Habsburg empire, Prussia, and Saxony to free cities like Hamburg, Frankfurt am Main, and Lübeck. Jews were found in these free cities as well as in tiny principalities and medium-size and large states. When they were expelled from one area they were able to move to another. In the middle of the eighteenth century there were about 70,000 Jews in central Europe.

Jews were also able to settle in many of the ports which developed with the growth of transatlantic commerce from the sixteenth century. They were mostly the descendants of conversos who returned to their Jewish faith after leaving Spain. Their communities, which were to be found in Bordeaux, London, Amsterdam, Hamburg, Copenhagen, and elsewhere, also became magnets for the Jews from the Ashkenazi world.

The bulk of world Jewry was to be found in the two large communities of the Ottoman empire and the Polish–Lithuanian Commonwealth, the subject of this book. The sixteenth century had seen a great expansion of the Ottoman empire, which finally conquered Constantinople, the capital of Byzantium, in 1453. Under the new name of Istanbul it became the capital of the empire, which now extended over most of the Middle East, North Africa, and the Balkan peninsula. Although the situation of Jews under Islam was not always significantly better than in Christendom, the Turks were an exception. They welcomed Jewish settlement, particularly from the Iberian peninsula. They were prepared to make use of the Jews as administrators and tax farmers and saw their position as traders with connections all over the Mediterranean as a useful asset. The situation of the Jews in the Ottoman empire was less favourable in the eighteenth century than earlier, but the community still numbered around 350,000 with substantial concentrations in Istanbul, Salonika, Adrianople, Baghdad, and elsewhere.

The union in 1569 of the Kingdom of Poland and the Grand Duchy of Lithuania, which had previously been linked dynastically, created one of the largest states in Europe. Jews first settled here in significant numbers in the fifteenth and early sixteenth centuries, invited in by the Polish kings. From the mid-sixteenth century, with the increasing political and social dominance of the nobility (*szlachta*), which owed its prosperity to the trade in grain down the Vistula and other rivers to the Baltic, Jews came to settle in the small towns which the nobles established. A 'marriage of convenience' developed between the Jews and their noble protectors, and the Jewish population of Poland and Lithuania expanded rapidly from around 25,000 in 1500 to perhaps 150,000 in the middle of the seventeenth century and nearly three-quarters of a million by 1750.

In this part I first examine the place of the Jews in the life of Poland–Lithuania and then go on to analyse the autonomous structure of the community. The location of Jewish life—the nature of Jewish existence in the royal towns, in the noble towns, and in the countryside—and the Jewish role in the economic life of the country are then investigated. The part concludes with a description of the religious and spiritual life of the Jewish community. As the history of Poland and Lithuania might not be familiar to all readers, an appendix to the part gives an account of these two states before the dynastic union established in 1385 and then describes their further evolution until the accession of the last king of Poland, Stanisław August Poniatowski.

ONE

JEWS AND CHRISTIANS IN EARLY MODERN POLAND–LITHUANIA

When the gentiles had greatly oppressed the exiled Jews, and the Divine Presence saw that there was no limit and no end to the oppression and that the handful of Jews might, God forbid, go under, the Presence came before the Lord of the Universe to lay the grievance before Him, and said to Him as follows: 'How long is this going to last? When You sent the dove out of the ark at the time of the flood, You gave it an olive branch so that it might have a support for its feet on the water, and yet it was unable to bear the water of the flood and returned to the ark; whereas my children You have sent out of the ark into a flood, and have provided nothing for a support where they may rest their feet in their exile.' Thereupon God took a piece of Erets Yisrael, which he had hidden away in the heavens at the time when the Temple was destroyed, and sent it down upon the earth and said: 'Be My resting place for My children in their exile.' That is why it is called Poland (*Polin*), from the Hebrew *poh lin*, which means: 'Here shalt thou lodge' in the exile.

SHOLEM ASCH, *Kidush hashem*, 1919

What does this cunning race of serpents do here?
It greedily garners illegal profits
And oppresses the poor with unjust usury.
A worm does not destroy an oak in one fell swoop,
But eats it away slowly so that nothing is left but dust;
So too does rust consume unyielding iron,
The moth devour the cloth and the leech the human body.
Just so does the wandering Jew with his lawless arts
Bury his claws deep in the body of society,
Eats up and digests our riches
And takes possession of all the wealth of our country.

SEBASTIAN FABIAN KLONOWIC, *Roxolania*, 1584

THE EMERGENCE OF THE JEWISH COMMUNITY OF POLAND–LITHUANIA

THE EMERGENCE OF the Jewish community of Poland–Lithuania as the largest in the world was the result of the establishment of a new geography of the Jewish world which started at the end of the thirteenth century. This was primarily the consequence of the worsening situation of the Jews in the countries of western and central Europe, which led to their being driven out of England in 1290, their partial expulsion from France in 1306 and their total expulsion from the lands of the French monarch in 1394, their banishment from many German states and cities in the fifteenth and early sixteenth centuries and finally from Spain and the Spanish possessions in Italy between 1492 and 1510, and the forced conversion of the Jews in Portugal. At the same time, new opportunities opened up for Jews in the Kingdom of Poland and the Grand Duchy of Lithuania.

Where did the Jews of Polin come from, and what accounts for the rapid increase in the size of the community there? Although some nineteenth-century historians have exaggerated the degree to which the communities established in Poland and Lithuania had their roots in eastern (Palestinian, Byzantine, or Persian) Jewry, there seems little doubt that individual Jews from these countries did settle in Poland and in the Grand Duchy of Lithuania from the tenth century on.[1] Some of them came from the Khazar kingdom, whose ruler and aristocracy are held by some sources to have converted to Judaism in the eighth century. Kiev, on the main trade route through northern Europe from Spain to Byzantium and the Muslim caliphate, was also the home of a number of Jews. Certainly the Jewish presence in Kiev is well documented from the tenth century, when the Kievan Letter was written, a letter of recommendation written on behalf of one of its members by the local Khazarian Jewish community which was discovered in the Cairo Genizah documents.[2] Slavonic sources are relatively abundant: 'Khazarian Jews' went to Vladimir in 986–8, according to a legend included in the Russian Primary Chronicle, while the life of St Theodosius of the Cave Monastery of Kiev records that he held disputes with Jews.[3] A Jewish quarter and Jewish gates are mentioned in the Chronicle under the years 1124, 1146, and 1151, and also in the context of the riots of 1113. Recent philological research on East Slavonic medieval documents has revealed well-established cultural links between Jews and the local population and an involvement of Jews in the translation of sacred texts from a very early stage of the development of Slavonic written culture.[4] By this time the community was not exclusively Eastern in origin and included some Jews from Ashkenaz (Germany and north-eastern France). In Western Jewish sources we find references to the twelfth-century Moses of Kiev, a pupil of Rabbi Jacob b. Meir Tam (Rabbenu Tam, *c.*1100–1171), a leading French rabbinic scholar. He is mentioned in *Sefer hayashar*, in the responsa of Rabbi Meir

[1] On this, see Weinryb, 'The Beginnings of East European Jewry in Legend and Historiography'; see also id., *Jews of Poland*, 19–22. A more favourable view of the old Russian sources is taken by Birnbaum, 'On Some Evidence of Jewish Life and Anti-Jewish Sentiments in Medieval Russia'.

[2] For the dating of the Kievan Letter, see Golb and Pritsak, *Khazarian Hebrew Documents of the Tenth Century*; Poppe, 'Khazarian Hebrew Documents of the Tenth Century'.

[3] *Das Paterikon des Kiever Höhlenklosters*, 65.

[4] On this, see Toporov, 'K russko-evreiskim kul'turnym kontaktam i literaraturno-tekstovym svyazyam', 340–57, 392–412.

b. Baruch of Rothenburg (1215–93), and also, possibly, as 'Moses of Rus' in *Sefer hashoham* by Rabbi Moses b. Isaac Hanesiah (late thirteenth century).[5]

A Jewish presence in Volhynia which seems to have been mostly derived from Ashkenaz and which involved more than a mere trading post has been documented both in a Slavonic source—the Ipatevsky Chronicle, which under the year 1288 describes Jews weeping, 'as during the capture of Jerusalem, when they were led into the Babylonian captivity' on the occasion of the death of the Prince Vladimir Vasilkovich—and in several Jewish sources.[6] *Sefer hazekhirah* by Rabbi Ephraim b. Jacob of Bonn (b. 1132), which describes the persecution of Jews in western Europe during the Crusades, cites Rabbi Benjamin of Vladimir as visiting Cologne for the purpose of engaging in trade.[7] There also seem to have been students and scholars from Rus living in Toledo before the beginning of the fourteenth century. It thus seems very probable that there was a Jewish community at least in Vladimir and possibly also in Kholm (Chełm). These communities were included in the cultural realm of Ashkenazi Jewry and were connected to Ashkenazi yeshivas. However, they also appear to have had unique characteristics of their own, such as traditional names that were not typical of other Ashkenazi communities. They were for the most part small and isolated.[8]

From the second half of the twelfth century a Jewish community largely derived from the lands of Ashkenaz was also established in the Kingdom of Poland, although probably without local religious leadership. The following century a properly functioning communal structure was established there, creating a community which had connections with the German pietists (Hasidei Ashkenaz), who espoused an austere and revivalist form of Judaism (see Chapter 5). Some of these may even have moved to Poland.[9] Emigration to Poland continued in the next centuries as the situation of Jews in central Europe, particularly Bohemia and other Habsburg territories as well as Hungary, deteriorated with the expulsion of Jews from many towns and regions, including Mainz in 1420, 1438, and 1462, Austria in 1420–1, 1454, and 1491, Saxony in 1432, and Breslau and other Silesian cities in 1453–4.

The first serious attempt to estimate the size of the community at the end of the fifteenth century was made by Ignacy Schiper. He calculated that in the Kingdom of Poland there were around 18,000 Jews organized in fifty-eight communities, the largest of which were in Kraków, Lviv, and Poznań. An additional 6,000 Jews lived in Lithuania.[10] Bernard Weinryb has argued that these figures are

[5] See Ettinger, 'Moses of Kiev'.

[6] Quoted in Kulik, 'The Earliest Evidence on the Jewish Presence in Western Rus'.

[7] Haberman, *Anti-Jewish Decrees in Germany and France* (Heb.), 128.

[8] Kulik, 'The Earliest Evidence on the Jewish Presence in Western Rus'.

[9] Ta-Shema, 'On the History of the Jews in Poland in the Twelfth and Thirteenth Centuries' (Heb.); id., 'New Sources on the History of the Jews in Poland in the Twelfth and Thirteenth Centuries' (Heb.), 208.

[10] Schiper, *Istoriya evreiskogo naroda*, ii. 107 ff., 116 ff.; Schiper et al. (eds.), *Żydzi w Polsce odrodzonej*, i. 26–32.

greatly exaggerated and that the Jewish population of the Kingdom of Poland was more likely between 6,000 and 8,800, to which should be added a very small number of village Jews and an unknown number in Lithuania, making a total of 10,000 or 'very slightly more'.[11]

By now the community both in the Kingdom of Poland and in Lithuania was largely Ashkenazi in character, although some remnants of Jews from the East were still to be found. Until the early sixteenth century it was still dependent on the older centres of Jewish life in the German-speaking lands as well as those in Italy for providing rabbinic personnel and spiritual guidance.

Sephardi and Italian Jews did not settle in Poland in large numbers. Jewish legends about the establishment of the community in Poland dating from the sixteenth century—such as that describing the five illustrious rabbis Hiskiya Sephardi, Akiba Estremaduri, Immanuel Ascaloni, Natanel Barceloni, and Levi Baccari, who are said to have gone to Poland in 889 to meet Prince Leszek in order to persuade him to allow Jews to settle in Poland—clearly allude to some Sephardi and Italian settlement. Similarly, the legend of Saul Wahl, who was crowned king of Poland for a day in 1587 to prevent an interregnum, indicates an Italian connection, although it should be stressed that Italian Jews were not necessarily Sephardi (the Yiddish name Wahl means 'from Italy', and Saul Wahl is described as the son of a rabbi from Padua).[12] Names like Beyle (Ladino or Italian: Bella), Shprintse (Esperanza), Yente (Jentilla), and Simhah Bunem (Bonhomme) may also reflect some Sephardi or Italian settlement. The same seems to be the case with some Jewish surnames, like Abarbanel, Barbanel, Perec, Wloch, Bloch (literally 'Italian'), Wlochowicz ('from Italy'), and Sfard and Szpanir ('from Spain').

There was in Kraków in the sixteenth and early seventeenth centuries a group of well-educated and economically powerful Jews originally from Spain and Italy, including the families Wlochowicz, Kalahora, Morpurgo, Hadida, Rapoport, and Luria. Among them was the king's physician Isaac (also described as Isaac Hispanus), who aroused hostility among other Kraków Jews, probably because of his Sephardi origin.[13] A similar group established itself in Lviv, which had links with the Genoese and Venetian colonies on the Black Sea (principally Caffa and Killia) and also with the Ottoman empire. In 1474, for instance, Kazimierz IV Jagiellon (r. 1447–92) issued a special privilege for Italian and Spanish merchants allowing them to travel with convoys of slaves brought from the Crimea through

[11] Weinryb, *Jews of Poland*, 309–11.

[12] On these legends, see Bar-Itzhak, *Jewish Poland*; Weinryb, *Jews of Poland*, 17–19; id., 'The Beginnings of East European Jewry in Legend and Historiography', 443–5. For the general question of the settlement of Sephardim in Poland–Lithuania, see Shatzky, 'Sephardim in Zamość' (Yid.); Morgensztern, 'O osadnictwie Żydów w Zamościu na przełomie XVI–XVII w.'; id., 'Uwagi o Żydach sefardyjskich w Zamościu w latach 1588–1650'; and Guterman, 'Żydzi sefardyjscy na ziemiach polskich'.

[13] Weinryb, *Jews of Poland*, 93.

Poland.[14] Negotiations between Poland and Turkey during the reign of Zygmunt II August (r. 1548–72) were facilitated by Joseph Nasi, duke of Naxos, who settled his emissary and factor in Lviv. The town archive contains a number of references to Portuguese Jewish settlers linked with him from 1567. Between this date and 1635 there seems to have been in Lviv a Sephardi colony of around thirty merchants and their families. This community appears to have left Poland in the 1630s when relations between Poland and the Ottoman empire deteriorated seriously.[15]

The largest Sephardi settlement was located in Zamość, a private town founded in 1571 by Jan Zamoyski, the chancellor of the Kingdom of Poland and one of the leading figures in the Commonwealth. Among those he encouraged to settle there were Ruthenians, Armenians, Greeks, Germans, Hungarians, Italians, Scots, and Sephardi Jews. As early as 1586 a group of Sephardi Jews, responding to his calls, wrote to him asking for permission to settle in the town. Two years later Zamoyski issued a privilege for Sephardim who wished to settle there and create their own communal institutions. The new immigrants were entitled to own and sell land, were free to leave the city if they wished, and were given the right to build a synagogue and a *mikveh* (ritual bath) and establish a cemetery. They could wear the same clothing as non-Jews and could freely engage in trade in Zamość and in Poland subject only to the limitations of Polish law. They could also practise medicine and open pharmacies in Zamość provided they passed an examination at the Zamość Academy, a university-style institution established in the town.

By 1600 there seem to have been eleven Sephardi families in Zamość, who had come from Venice, Turkey, and Amsterdam. Full records do not exist, but at least an additional eighteen families settled there in the 1630s and 1640s. The community probably numbered in all fifty families (250 people) and it established a synagogue, two schools, and a cemetery. Most of its members seem to have left Poland during the wars of the mid-seventeenth century, although a few new settlers arrived in the late eighteenth century. However, they were unable to maintain a separate communal existence and merged with the Ashkenazi Jews who had settled in the town.

The Jewish population of Poland–Lithuania now began to grow rapidly. Prior to the Union of Lublin in 1569 approximately 3 million people lived in the Kingdom of Poland. With the union with Lithuania the population of the Commonwealth swelled to about 7.5 million, of whom more than a third were Eastern Orthodox. By the end of the sixteenth century there were perhaps 80,000 to 100,000 Jews out of a total population of nearly 8 million. By this stage there

[14] *Matricularum Regni Poloniae summaria*, no. 1245; I am grateful to Jerzy Mazur for this reference.

[15] Schorr, 'Zur Geschichte des Josef Nasi'; Kraushar, *Historia Żydów w Polsce*, 323; Bałaban, *Żydzi lwowscy na przełomie XVI i XVII wieku*, 460; and Morgensztern, 'Pośrednictwo Żydów w nawiązywaniu nieoficjalnych kontaktów dyplomatycznych między dworem polskim i tureckim w 1590 r.'

were fifty-one communities in Wielkopolska (the area around Poznań) and Mazovia, forty-one in Małopolska (the area around Kraków), eighty in Red Rus (the area around Lviv), Volhynia, and Podolia (south-eastern Poland), and twenty in the Grand Duchy of Lithuania.

The situation of the Jews in the royal towns, where they faced constant conflict with the burghers and hostility from the Catholic Church, particularly as the Counter-Reformation established itself in Poland–Lithuania, led many Jews to take advantage of the opportunities created by the Polish colonization of Ukraine, which had been transferred from the Grand Duchy of Lithuania to the Korona (the Kingdom of Poland). There they settled in the towns established by the great Polish magnates. Shmuel Ettinger has estimated that as early as 1569 Jews lived in twenty-four towns in Ukraine with a total Jewish population of 4,000. By 1648 they lived in 115 Ukrainian towns and numbered over 50,000.[16]

The number of Jews in Poland–Lithuania by the mid-seventeenth century is disputed. A higher estimate of 350,000 has been questioned by Gershon Hundert, who has argued for a figure of 150,000 out of a total population of 11 million.[17] Using a similar method, Weinryb has argued for the slightly higher figure of between 200,000 and 220,000, an estimate supported by Shaul Stampfer. This is in line with later population growth and is also consistent with modern scholarship, which has scaled down estimates of the number of Jewish casualties in the upheavals of the mid-seventeenth century. It is now estimated that at least 13,000 Jews died in the Khmelnytsky Uprising, which began in 1648, and more perished in the subsequent Swedish and Muscovite invasions.[18] Significant numbers may have fled the country. This fall in population seems to parallel the situation in the wider society. According to one estimate, the total population fell from 11 million to 7 million, while that of Warsaw fell by a half and of Kraków by two-thirds. Jerzy Topolski has estimated that the population of Mazovia shrank from approximately 990,000 before the war to 360,000 in 1662–3, a fall of about 65 per cent. The population of Wielkopolska fell by 42 per cent to 830,000 in the same period, and that of Małopolska by 27 per cent to 1.06 million. Topolski considers the effects of increased child mortality in the wake of the wars as the main cause of this decline.[19]

Jewish population losses were soon made good. By 1720 the Jewish population had risen to perhaps 375,000 and by 1764 to around three-quarters of a million out of a total population of between 12.3 and 14 million (5.35 per cent). By this stage the bulk of Jews lived in the eastern part of Poland–Lithuania. Only 12 per cent were to be found in Wielkopolska and 17 per cent in Małopolska, as against 27 per cent in the Grand Duchy of Lithuania and 44 per cent in Ukraine–

[16] Ettinger, 'The Role of the Jews in the Colonization of Ukraine (1569–1648)' (Heb.), 110–11, 119–24.

[17] Hundert, *Jews in Poland–Lithuania in the Eighteenth Century*, 21–5.

[18] These are the conclusions of Shaul Stampfer's as yet unpublished study of this problem.

[19] Topolski, 'Wpływ wojen połowy XVII wieku na sytuację ekonomiczną Podlasia', 324–8.

Ruthenia. Jewish urban concentrations were also to be found mostly in the eastern part of the country. Of the forty-four towns with a Jewish population of more than 1,000, four were in the west, seven in the centre, five in Lithuania, and twenty-seven in Ukraine–Ruthenia. One (Warsaw) was in Mazovia.[20] Half a century later the number of Jews living on the lands of the now non-existent Polish–Lithuanian Commonwealth had risen to perhaps a million. The rapid rise of the Jewish population continued throughout the nineteenth century until the impact of modern methods of contraception and an increase in the age of marriage among Jews. By the late nineteenth century, for which we have much more accurate statistics, the Jewish birth rate began to fall below that of the general population. (For these developments, see Volume II, Chapter 6.)

How is the increase in the size of the Jewish population to be explained?[21] It was widely commented on by contemporaries, often in highly exaggerated terms. Thus, Zygmunt II is said to have remarked to the bishop of Kraków in the middle of the sixteenth century: 'Tell me, my Lord Bishop, since you do not believe in sorcery, how is it only 16,598 Jews pay the poll tax, while two hundred thousand of them apparently live underground?'[22] The rise in the number of the Jews was explained thus by an unsympathetic observer, Sebastian Miczyński: 'None of them dies in war or of the plague . . . Moreover, they marry when they are twelve . . . and so multiply rampantly.'[23]

Most scholars who have examined this question agree that the Jewish population grew faster than the wider population throughout the early modern period. In seeking to explain this difference some have pointed to the commandment to 'be fruitful and multiply' (Genesis 1: 28), which is linked to the idea that Jews tended to have a relatively larger number of children. However, this commandment also applied to Christians and contraceptive methods were not widely used in either group. Other factors have also been used to explain the increase. Celibacy was not a feature of Jewish religious life, while the relative ease of divorce and the possibility of remarriage may have played a role. Jews suffered fewer deaths on the battlefield and may have been more resistant to diseases like plague because of the hygiene requirements of their religion (although scholars like Salo Baron, Weinryb, and Stampfer have disputed this), and may have been able to flee from epidemics because of their greater mobility, a consequence, in part, of the extent of the Ashkenazi world. Urban Jews had relatively better access to food, heating, and mutual support. Certainly Jewish *kehilot* (communal

[20] The figure of 750,000 is derived by Raphael Mahler from the Polish–Lithuanian census of 1764. For Mahler's views, see *Jews in Old Poland in the Light of Figures* (Yid.). Other important studies are Stampfer, 'The 1764 Census of Polish Jewry', and Guldon and Wijaczka, 'Jewish Settlement in the Polish Commonwealth in the Second Half of the Eighteenth Century'.

[21] This is a matter which has been extensively discussed. The most important contribution to this debate is the article by Hundert, 'Population and Society in Eighteenth Century Poland'.

[22] Quoted in Edwards, *The Jews in Christian Europe 1400–1700*, 123.

[23] Miczyński, *Zwierciadło Korony Polskiey*, quoted in Tazbir, 'Żydzi w opinii staropolskiej', 200.

organizations) stressed the importance of providing support for the poor, which may have limited the impact of outbreaks of disease (on this, see Chapter 2), as did the fact that at this period the Jews were probably part of the better-off section of the urban population. Jews may also have benefited from easier access to food in time of famine because of their contacts with Jewish traders and agents in agricultural goods. The rise in population was also caused in part by continued immigration, above all from central Europe. Jews were expelled from Brandenburg, Berlin, and Frankfurt an der Oder in 1510 and 1573, from Saxony in 1514, Erlangen in 1516, Bohemia in 1517, parts of Silesia in 1527, and Brunswick in 1557 and 1590.

Above all, the growth of the Jewish population was the product of natural increase. As Hundert has convincingly argued, the critical factor in explaining the difference between Jewish and Christian rates of population growth is the lower rates of infant and child mortality among Jews. Jewish society was probably less prone to illegitimacy, venereal diseases, and alcoholism, which increase the likelihood of infant mortality. Even more important was the Jewish ideal of early marriage, which was justified on both moral and religious grounds, and the facilitation of this practice through the *kest* system, whereby the parents, usually those of the bride, supported the young couple until they were ready for economic independence. Widespread demographic research has shown that mothers who give birth early to a surviving infant are likely to have large families. In Poland–Lithuania in the early modern period it seems to be the case that in Jewish society the women who were youngest when they successfully gave birth were usually to be found in wealthier households where, presumably, there was better heating, better hygiene, adequate food, and freer access to medical care than in poorer households.[24]

The practice of *kest* was probably limited to the wealthier stratum of Jewish society. The proportion of families able to practise *kest* diminished as the size of the Jewish community grew. At the same time the fact that the elite practised early marriage may have led to attempts by the rest of Jewish society to emulate them.[25] (On subsequent developments in this area, see Volume II, Chapter 6.)

The Jewish population certainly grew more rapidly than that of the country as a whole. While European urban populations in this period generally failed to maintain their numbers (although this was not true of rural populations, and the population of Poland–Lithuania is thought to have doubled between 1648 and 1764), it seems that the upper strata of the cities' populations were able to do so. As Hundert has argued, we need to undertake studies comparing the population histories of the urban patriciate and the upper strata of Jewish society. 'These

[24] Hundert, 'Population and Society in Eighteenth Century Poland'.

[25] Stampfer, 'Social Attitudes towards Early Marriage in Eastern Europe in the Mid-Nineteenth Century' (Heb.); Hundert, 'Jewish Children and Childhood in Early Modern East Central Europe', 89.

would tell us a good deal and not only about the structural integration of Jews in Polish society. They might enable us to determine if there indeed were actual distinguishing characteristics of Jewish population growth in this period.'[26]

What is clear is that the rate of growth of the Jewish population in the eighteenth century was greater than that of the population of the country in general but that it may not have been greater than that of the urban patriciate. This had important consequences. In the period when Poland–Lithuania was expanding and economically buoyant, it made possible the establishment of a new and dynamic community. In the period after 1648, with the decline of the burgher estate, Jews were able to establish themselves in areas of economic life not previously open to them. From the end of the seventeenth century, however, the Jewish population began to outstrip the economic opportunities available to them, a phenomenon which underlies a number of important developments within Jewish life, most notably the support for the growing hasidic movement among many young men without an obvious livelihood , as well as the increase in vagrancy and begging within the community. (On this, see Chapter 5 below, and Volume II, Chapter 6.)

THE JEWS AND CHRISTIAN SOCIETY

The Jews have sometimes been described as an 'estate', like the other self-governing estates, the nobility, the burghers, and the Church, into which Poland and Lithuania, like all the states of Western Christendom, were divided. This is at best a half-truth. It is of course correct that the Jews enjoyed wide communal autonomy, both at the local and at the national level, which I will examine in the next chapter. But they were also a pariah group, espousing a religion which was rejected as both false and harmful by the dominant Roman Catholic Church. The supersessionist claims of Christianity had been set out by St Paul and the essence of the position of the Church was formulated by St Augustine in the fifth century. It held that the Jews were to be tolerated in an inferior position in order to demonstrate the truth of Christianity. In his words:

> But the Jews who killed him and refused to believe in him . . . suffered a more wretched devastation at the hands of the Romans, and were utterly uprooted from their kingdom . . . They were dispersed all over the world—for indeed there is no part of the earth where they are not to be found—and thus by the evidence of their own scriptures they bear witness for us that we have not fabricated the prophecies about Christ . . . In fact, there is a prophecy given before the event on this very point in the book of Psalms, which they also read . . . 'Do not slay them, lest at some time they forget your Law; scatter them by your might.' And this is the reason for his forbearing to slay them . . . [so that the Church would have them] as witnesses to the prophecies which were given beforehand concerning Christ.[27]

[26] Hundert, 'Population and Society in Eighteenth Century Poland', 15–16.

[27] Augustine, *On the City of God*, book 18, ch. 46, p. 827. The reference is to Ps. 59: 11, 'Slay them not, lest my people forget: scatter them by Thy power and bring them down, O Lord, our shield.'

This position was codified as part of canon law at the Third and Fourth Lateran Councils in Rome in 1179 and 1215. Jews were now subject to a number of restrictions: they were required to pay tithes on properties they acquired, to wear clothes that would distinguish them from Christians, and to stay at home during Holy Week and the Easter holiday, so as not to 'profane' the Christian observances. They were not to hold public office or to employ Christian servants. The Church believed that the Jews had rejected God and been rejected by him: they were no longer 'chosen' or 'elect'. The Church, the new Israel, had superseded the old Israel. The Church had supplanted the Synagogue, an image reproduced in sculpture outside many cathedrals, most notably that in Strasbourg.

In western Europe the Christian understanding of Judaism and the anti-Jewish polemic developed in stages.[28] Initially attacks on Judaism stressed biblical exegesis, providing a Christian explanation for the Hebrew Bible and discussion about the principles of faith. Anti-talmudic polemics were a feature of the disputations at Paris in 1240 and at Barcelona in 1263, and in the fourteenth century, when the Talmud came to be seen as the basis of Judaism and fundamentally anti-Christian, a new and more menacing phase began. A little later the kabbalah was discovered and studied, which led to the beginning of Christian Hebraism, which sometimes involved calculations of the date of the Final Judgement and a renewal of polemics about enforced conversion of the Jews. All of these Christian constructions of Judaism were imported into Poland from the West in modified forms, and continued to exist side by side into the early modern period.

The Catholic Church in Poland consistently tried to implement the directives of the Vatican on Jewish matters. At the Provincial Church Council of Breslau in 1267 (which had jurisdiction over Gniezno, the seat of the primate of the Polish Church, in Wielkopolska) concern was expressed about Christian–Jewish contacts since 'the Polish land was still a new plant in the body of Christendom'.[29] As a result, it was laid down that Christians were forbidden to invite Jews to weddings and other feasts, to share meals with them, to dance with them, to buy their food, to go to the baths with them, or to frequent Jewish-owned inns. There were limitations on the rights of the Jews to lend money, and separate Jewish residential quarters had to be established. It was also decreed that there should be only one synagogue in every town. Jews should be compelled to wear horned hats, they were forbidden to employ Christian servants (which was also not permitted by the Third and Fourth Lateran Councils), and they were to stay indoors with their windows closed when the Holy Sacrament was carried past. Finally, they were prohibited from holding public office, particularly the office of customs or toll collector. These regulations were reinforced at the 1279 Synod of Buda (whose decisions also applied in Poland) and that of Mikołaj Trąba in 1420, except that a red cloth circle on a Jew's outer garments was substituted for the horned hat.

[28] Kalik, 'Polish Attitudes towards Jewish Spirituality in the Eighteenth Century', 77–8.

[29] Quoted in Teter, *Jews and Heretics in Catholic Poland*, 17.

These regulations appear to have been ineffective since Jews lived in Kraków and elsewhere in close proximity to Christians. There is no record of their actually wearing special markers on their clothes—indeed contemporary testimony seems to show that the opposite was the case. Thus, when Zygmunt I (r. 1506–48) wrote on 20 March 1535 to Ferdinand I of Bohemia and Hungary asking him to protect Jewish merchants travelling through his lands to Venice, Ferdinand wrote that this would be difficult since, whereas the Jews in his countries were required to wear distinctive clothing, this was not the case in Poland.[30] In addition they were entrusted with the leases of toll houses and of the Wieliczka salt mine. The prohibition on the employment of Christian servants also seems to have been disregarded, as does the ban on social contact.

The *ad limina* reports sent by the Polish bishops to the Vatican in the seventeenth and eighteenth centuries provide a great deal of information on the relations between the Church and the Jews.[31] Pope Sixtus V (1585–90), in his bull *Romanus Pontifex* of 20 December 1585, put all Catholic bishops under the obligation to inspect their dioceses and submit written reports to Rome. These give us a very clear picture of the point of view of the Catholic hierarchy on the Jewish presence in Poland. What they reveal is that, in the late sixteenth and first half of the seventeenth centuries, references to Jews were sporadic. They became more frequent in the second half of the seventeenth century, with many complaints about the increasing number of Jews and of their role in trade in the impoverished and devastated towns, particularly noble towns, after the wars of the mid-seventeenth century. The Jews are also criticized for taking inns on lease and for their financial connections with the nobility, above all with the magnates. Their effect on Catholic religious belief is said to be deleterious, and they are seen as encouraging the faithful to commit sacrilege when taking Holy Communion. There are also frequent complaints about the inability of the Church to make its legislation on the Jews effective, because of the links of the Jews with all strata of Polish society.

These complaints intensified in the eighteenth century. There were now accusations that the Jews were taking over houses situated near churches or in other places not meant for them or where up to now they had not lived. They were building new synagogues and establishing cemeteries, and settling on the estates of the nobility and even on those of the Church, particularly those of monasteries. Jews were also, contrary to the often repeated clerical prohibition, living under

[30] On this, see Pociecha (ed.), *Acta Tomiciana*, xvii. 485–6.

[31] The *ad limina* reports arose out of the obligation of residential diocesan bishops to visit the thresholds (*limina*) of the tombs of the Apostles Peter and Paul and to report to the Pope on the state of their dioceses. They have been examined in two recent studies: Kalik, 'The Catholic Church and the Jews in the Polish–Lithuanian Commonwealth in the Seventeenth and Eighteenth Centuries' (Heb.), and Teter, *Jews and Heretics in Catholic Poland*, and in Mueller (of the Catholic University of Lublin), 'Jews in the *ad limina* Reports of the Polish Bishops of the Seventeenth and Eighteenth Centuries'. See also Hundert, *Jews in Poland–Lithuania in the Eighteenth Century*, 57–78.

the same roof as Christians, which was having a harmful effect on the religious observance of the latter. Christians were working as wet-nurses for Jews and cooperating with them in business ventures. Jews were also accused of corrupting the morals of Catholics and inducing them to drink heavily, tempting them by means of music or other inducements into inns run by Jews, especially after they had left church services. The consequence was a decline in the observance of the sabbath and of Church holidays in the appropriate manner, a neglect of fasting, and the impoverishment of those tempted in this way. The large number of Jews in both larger and smaller towns, and the fact that they lived in many cases in the centre of those towns, where they were often held to behave 'offensively', posed a threat to the proper carrying out of Corpus Christi processions and to priests on their way to the sick with the Blessed Sacrament or going to administer the last rites to the dying. Jews were also undermining the economic well-being of Catholics by their growing monopoly of trade.

The Church hierarchy recognized that it was difficult to attack the position of the Jews since, in addition to their 'cunning', they enjoyed the protection and support of the nobility and of some monastic orders, who had strong economic ties with them. Indeed the fact that Jewish communities and councils owed Church bodies literally millions of zlotys was a crucial factor moderating the Church's implementation of anti-Jewish policies. Nevertheless, the bishops did attempt to reduce what they regarded as the harmful influence of the Jews. In 1751, for instance, the bishop of Kraków, Andrzej Stanisław Załuski, demanded from the Pope a 'constitution', or special papal 'breve', which would remind the Sejm of the Church regulations with regard to the Jews, and in particular the prohibition on their living near churches or in the centre of towns.

This led to Pope Benedict XIV (1740–58) addressing the Polish bishops in an encyclical on the Jews, *A Quo Primum*, on 14 June 1751, reaffirming the position of the Church.[32] In it he referred to the 1542 Council of Piotrków, which 'had prohibited the principle of freedom of conscience' and which, together with the other enactments of the Church, had made possible the defeat of Protestantism in Poland. He reminded the Polish episcopate of the decisions of the Synod of Breslau of 1267, and pointed out that the prohibitions which it had established were clearly being violated. Jews had been allowed to establish a dominant position in trade and commerce, particularly in alcoholic beverages. They should not be permitted to hold leases on villages or inns, nor to fine or otherwise punish Christians. Those who acted as agents of nobles 'ceaselessly exhibit and flaunt authority over the Christians with whom they live' and also lent large amounts of money to Christians, which gained them 'as many defenders of their synagogues and themselves as they have creditors . . . All these activities that are now allowed in Poland are forbidden.' The Polish clergy should observe the old regulations,

[32] On this, see Hundert, *Jews in Poland–Lithuania in the Eighteenth Century*, 59–64, and Teter, *Jews and Heretics in Catholic Poland*, 83, 89–90.

which would increase their authority on this matter in the society. They should not lease their lands or grant monopolistic rights to Jews, nor provide them with money and credits. 'Thus, you will be free from and unaffected by all dealings with them.'

Pope Benedict did, however, maintain the traditional position of the Church on the Jews, namely that the Jews should be tolerated in an inferior position, citing with approval the opposition of Bernard of Clairvaux (1090–1153) to the 'immodest and maddened zeal' of the Cistercian monk Radulf during the Second Crusade:

> The Jews are not to be persecuted. They are not to be slaughtered, they are not even to be driven out . . . In this matter as in all others, We adopt the same norms of action as did . . . our venerable predecessor . . .

Nevertheless, he qualified this statement by some remarks which suggested that the papacy was not unequivocally opposed to expulsion of the Jews:

> Innocent IV, also, in writing to St. Louis, King of France, who intended to drive the Jews beyond the borders of his kingdom, approved of the plan . . . 'Since We strive with all Our heart for the salvation of souls, We grant you full power by the authority of the letter to expel the Jews, particularly since We have learned that they do not obey the said statements issued by this See against them.'[33]

It is not clear how far this encyclical affected the behaviour of either the Church or the laity. What did occur, even before the letter, was an attempted intensification of the norms reasserted by the Counter-Reformation. Thus, the Synod of Lutsk in 1726 laid down that Christians were not to live or bathe with Jews, eat with them, or serve them. They were not to guard Jewish cemeteries, light or extinguish candles on Jewish holidays, eat matzah, or play the role of the villain Haman in plays performed at the Jewish festival of Purim. Similarly, Bishop Wacław Sierakowski of Przemyśl, on 10 July 1743, issued a decree forbidding the Jews to celebrate during Lent. Jewish weddings, whenever they were held, were not to be celebrated with processions with candles and torches, and when the bridal couple was escorted to the synagogue or marital house there was to be no singing, shouting, or discharging firearms. Christians should not have social contact with Jews and should not attend their weddings or dances. Jews were not to employ Christians to light candles in the synagogue or to play Haman during Purim. Jewish ceremonies were not to interfere with Christian ceremonies or processions. Jews committing such offences would be heavily fined, Christians excommunicated.[34] In addition, the episcopate attempted to break the links between the nobility and some monasteries and the Jews.

[33] Quoted in Hundert, *Jews in Poland–Lithuania in the Eighteenth Century*, 61.

[34] On these and other regulations, see ibid. 63–4; Goldberg, 'Poles and Jews in the Seventeenth and Eighteenth Centuries: Rejection or Acceptance', 252–7; Kaźmierczyk, 'The Problem of Christian Servants as Reflected in the Legal Codes of the Polish–Lithuanian Commonwealth during the Second Half of the Seventeenth Century and in the Saxon Period', and Schorr, *Żydzi w Przemyślu do końca XVIII wieku*, 41–2.

The information which circulated about the Jewish religion in Poland–Lithuania was of a very mixed character. In the eighteenth century polemical compositions based on the Bible alone appeared in Poland alongside the critique of the Talmud that was fuelled by the Frankist controversy (see Chapter 5). Christian commentaries on kabbalah and the Zohar and more specialized Hebraistic works reflecting deep understanding of Jewish law and religious practice appear at the same time as compositions rife with ignorance and prejudice concerning the Jewish religion (including magical explanations of various Jewish rituals).

Because of the large numbers of Jews in Poland, there was sometimes a quite sophisticated understanding of Jewish practice, as was the case in the writings of the monk Jan Kostka Wujkowski, who was genuinely interested in the Jewish roots of Christianity. Mostly the understanding of Judaism and Jewish customs was marked by considerable ignorance, which often led to accusations about the use of Christian blood or the desecration of the host, the bread used in the Christian Mass. This ignorance was not only a feature of popular literature but can also be found in compositions by clerics—sometimes even by those of high rank. One of the most widespread and popular sources of distorted information about Judaism in Poland was the encyclopedia by Benedykt Chmielowski entitled *Nowe Ateny, albo, Akademia wszelkiej sciencyi pełna* (The New Athens, or, The Compendium of All the Sciences, 1745–6; repr. Warsaw, 1966), in which can be found misinformed entries under 'Talmud', 'Judaism', and 'Sambation'.[35]

Information about Judaism of whatever type was used for propaganda purposes, either in anti-Jewish polemics or for missionary purposes. One new element in the mid-eighteenth century was that some Polish clerics saw in the development of the Frankist movement the beginnings of the 'conversion of the Jews' which would usher in the end of time, and this seems to have encouraged conversionary activity.

Pressures on the Jews to convert certainly increased in the eighteenth century.[36] In 1737 in the diocese of Vilna a religious order, the Mariawitki (Sisters of Maria Vitae—the living Mary), was founded by Fr. Szczepan Turczynowicz with the goal of converting Jewish women. It claimed to have converted 500 women in the following four decades. Jesuits in the diocese also intensified their missionary activity and claimed the right which had been revived by Pope Gregory XIII in 1584 to preach conversionary sermons in synagogues. This practice was also adopted by perhaps the most ardent eighteenth-century proponent of missionary activity to the Jews, the bishop of Lutsk and Brest, Franciszek Antoni Kobielski. He wrote to the general of the Dominican order in Rome requesting information

35 Kalik, 'Polish Attitudes towards Jewish Spirituality in the Eighteenth Century', 80–2.

36 On conversion, see Hundert, *Jews in Poland–Lithuania in the Eighteenth Century*; Teter, *Jews and Heretics in Catholic Poland*; ead., 'The Legend of Ger Zedek of Wilno as Polemic and Reassurance', esp. 259–63; and Lewalski, 'Szkic do dziejów misji chrześcijańskich wśród Żydów na ziemiach polskich w XVIII–XX wieku'.

on the methods the Dominicans had used to convert Jews, and in 1741 instituted the practice of preaching four times a year to the Jews of his diocese, who were ordered to 'receive with respect the priests who come to you with God's word and teaching in your schools [synagogues] and to listen to them'.[37] The results of his activity are unknown, but in his *ad limina* report for 1749 he informed Pope Benedict XIV that he had 'visited Jewish synagogues in all places . . . [and] preached pastoral sermons so that they may convert . . . God so blessed the worth of my pastoral care that many of the infidels were converted and baptized and the number of those receiving religious instruction . . . rises daily.'[38]

Bishop Kobielski's campaign does not seem to have been particularly successful, as he admitted in several letters. He also instituted measures to limit Jewish contact with Christians and, in particular, to forbid Jews to employ Christian servants. His zeal led the Jews of his diocese to complain to Rome. On 12 December 1752 the papal nuncio wrote to him asking him to ensure that Jews were not being oppressed and persecuted in his diocese and that 'those responsible must be punished and tried immediately so that priests will not become accustomed to permitting themselves to such hateful deeds towards this wretched people'.[39] The practice of Christian clergy preaching in synagogues was not widespread, but it does seem to have been followed by a number of other clergymen, including Fr. Wawrzyniec Owłoczyński, a Dominican who preached in Brest, and the Bernardine Fr. Wiktoryn Adrian Krzywiński.

Conversion to Judaism or reversion to Judaism by converts was treated by the Church as apostasy and until 1768 was punished by death. There was one exception to this: Jews who were forced to convert to Orthodoxy during the Khmelnytsky Uprising were given permission by King Jan II Kazimierz (r. 1648–68) to revert to Judaism. Given the criminal sanctions which were attached to conversion, there were considerable reservations in Jewish society against receiving any converts. Thus, Rabbi Solomon b. Jehiel Luria (Maharshal, 1510?–1574) took the view that, while earlier Jews had the power to accept converts even under Roman rule, 'now, we are not in a land of our own and are like slaves under the hands of our lords . . . should anyone accept him [a convert], he is a rebel responsible for his own life'.[40]

Nevertheless, there were a number of conversions to Judaism in Poland–Lithuania. Katarzyna Wejgl, who was burned at the stake in 1539 for 'falling into the perfidious and superstitious Jewish sect', was probably a Judaizer, the follower of a sect which imitated Jewish practices, or an anti-Trinitarian, rather than an actual convert to Judaism.[41] We do know of a number of eighteenth-century converts. The well-known case of the convert Walentyn Potocki, who was allegedly

[37] Quoted in Teter, 'The Legend of Ger Zedek of Wilno as Polemic and Reassurance', 259.

[38] Ibid. 260.

[39] Quoted in Hundert, *Jews in Poland–Lithuania in the Eighteenth Century*, 70.

[40] Quoted in Teter, 'The Legend of Ger Zedek of Wilno as Polemic and Reassurance', 244.

[41] Quoted ibid. 245. On Katarzyna Wejgl, see also Tazbir, *A State without Stakes*, 47, and Bałaban, *Historja Żydów w Krakowie i na Kazimierzu*, i. 125–7.

burned at the stake in Vilna in 1749 and whose death was commemorated in the Vilna Jewish cemetery, is clearly mythical.[42] We do, however, know of a number of eighteenth-century converts to Judaism. Among them was Maryna Wojciechówna, who in 1716 was arrested in Dubno for apostasy and, after renouncing Judaism, was beheaded instead of being burned alive. Another such convert in Dubno, Maryna Dawidowa, refused to recant and was burned at the stake after having had three pieces of her body ripped off, presumably as a symbol of the Trinity. In Vilna on 29 May 1753 the Lithuania Tribunal sentenced to death a Croatian, Rafal Sentimani, for apostasy. The execution took place outside the small town of Ilia on 2 June 1753. Before he was burned, Sentimani's tongue, which had uttered blasphemies, was ripped out, and afterwards his ashes were shot into the air through a cannon.[43]

Conversion for both Christians and Jews was the ultimate proof of the superiority of their faith. Certainly, the Jews reciprocated the contempt in which their religious beliefs were held by the Christians. As Hundert has put it, 'the norms of both the Church and the Synagogue were strongly segregationist in intent, and . . . each faith taught that the other was spiritually and morally inferior'.[44] The preacher and moralist Zevi Hirsch Koidonover (d. 1712), in his ethical tract *Kav hayashar*, argued strongly against any contact with the society of non-Jews, which he saw as 'full of idolatry, violence and drunkenness'.[45] Christians, lacking divinely taught ethics, were in the process of sliding steadily into chaos. A Jew could best save his soul by avoiding all contact with them. In the medieval period Ashkenazi Jewry had seen Christians as idolaters and, like the Christians, had set strong obstacles to Christian–Jewish interaction.[46] In Poland in the sixteenth century Rabbi Solomon Luria accepted the view of some earlier authorities who had argued that Christians were not 'idolaters' since they 'believe in Divine providence', a position also held by two of his Polish contemporaries, Rabbi David b. Manasseh Darshan and Rabbi Eliezer Ashkenazi, who had been educated, at least in part, in Mediterranean societies, where Jewish attitudes were perhaps less hostile towards non-Jews. This also seems to have been the position of Rabbi Mordecai b. Abraham Jaffe (1535–1612). These views were not universally accepted and it is also not clear to what extent they affected popular attitudes towards Christians.[47]

Yet one should not equate the position of the two groups. Legally the Christians were clearly in a dominant position, even though there were occasions

[42] This issue is fully discussed by Teter in 'The Legend of Ger Zedek of Wilno as Polemic and Reassurance', 237–45.

[43] On these cases, see ibid. 246–8 and Kaźmierczyk (ed.), *Żydzi polscy 1648–1772*, 187–9.

[44] Hundert, 'The Implications of Jewish Economic Activities for Christian–Jewish Relations in the Polish Commonwealth', 56.

[45] See Koidonover, *Kav hayashar*, ch. 76, 159*b*; ch. 82, 170*b*–171*b*; ch. 83, 172*a*.

[46] For these, see Katz, *Between Jews and Gentiles* (Heb.), 35–45.

[47] On this, see Fram, *Ideals Face Reality*, 28.

in Poland–Lithuania when this legal situation was at odds with the social realities. Moreover, along with the official Catholic teachings of contempt, a number of superstitions attached to the Jews in their character as a pariah people, which considerably worsened their position. Of these the most important were the belief that the Jews were responsible for spreading disease, and specifically the plague, which had devastated Europe in the fourteenth century; the belief that the Jews used Christian blood for ritual purposes and specifically for the making of matzah; and the belief that the Jews desecrated the host.

The Black Death appears to have had relatively little impact in Poland; indeed, this may be one of the reasons why the Jews who were being expelled from elsewhere in central Europe were able to settle there. But accusations of child murder and host desecration became well established in early modern Poland. The belief that some or all Jews engaged in these practices was widespread, as it was elsewhere in Europe. Fr. Stefan Żuchowski (1660–1716) of Sandomierz was one of the principal proponents of this myth. At the end of the seventeenth century he published a detailed account in verse, *Odgłos procesu przewiedzionego w trybunale koronnym R. P. 1698* (1700), of an alleged ritual murder in Sandomierz. According to Fr. Żuchowski:

> Let me tell the story of an unheard of and cruel crime.
> Of how the Jews consumed Christian blood like hungry dogs
> At the end of the celebrations of their holiday
> How they stabbed to death an innocent infant without blemish . . .
>
> The Jews have a secret law proclaimed to them by their false prophets
> And written down in their Talmud, that they should consume the 'Euicomen'.
> This is blood which has to be consumed in unsalted bread or dissolved in wine.
> Its purpose is to celebrate their feasts. They believe it purifies the spirit.
> If one of them has a suppurating abscess, they believe that it will only heal
> When they sprinkle on it innocent blood.
> In the same way they believe this syrup derived from an infant
> Cures the pain caused by the moon to those of either sex.
> They also give food with this blood to noble Lords, so that
> They will be more willing to look kindly on the affairs of the Yids.
> Thus, if fate so decides, a living child
> Has to pay with his life to provide this blood, think about this!
> They roll the body so that the blood comes out
> And saturates cloths ready for this purpose
> Or they strain it into suitable vessels.
> This they later divide among all of them assembled.[48]

Żuchowski took an active role in two trials for 'ritual murder', one in 1698 and the second in 1710–13. In the first, a Jew and the mother who had brought the

[48] S. Żuchowski, *Odgłos procesu przewiedzionego w trybunale koronnym R. P. 1698* (1700), quoted in H. Markiewicz (ed.), *Żydzi w Polsce*, 203.

accusation were both executed, and in the second, four Jews died under torture, the rabbi of the town died in prison, his young son was baptized, and four Jews were executed. Żuchowski's two books on these trials were widely quoted. The first, published in 1700, highlighted the extent to which economic rivalry lay at the root of many such accusations, opening with a lament for the economic decline of Sandomierz and denouncing the fact that the Jews not only had taken over all trade and commerce but also ruled the Christians. 'The kikes [*parchy*] hold the breweries, the distilleries and the taverns and measures in the towns.'[49] A series of paintings depicting the various threats to Christianity in the town, including Jews engaging in ritual murder, hangs in the Cathedral in Sandomierz to this day.

In 1758, when the views of the Enlightenment had already begun to influence Poland–Lithuania, Fr. Gaudenty Pikulski, another Catholic priest, basing himself on Żuchowski, could still assert that in Poland Jews needed 30 gallons of blood every year and required even more in Lithuania. He further claimed that the Talmud laid down that the Jews required a consecrated host twice a year for ritual purposes. He explained these needs by the distortions introduced by the 'accursed Talmudists' into the Jewish religion, which had then diverged fundamentally from the Law of God revealed to the Jews by Moses.[50] Similarly, according to Jędrzej Kitowicz, the author of *Opis obyczajów za panowania Augusta III*, a popular account of life and manners under the last Saxon king, 'Freedom cannot exist without the *liberum veto*, and nor can Jewish matzahs without Christian blood.'[51]

Accusations of ritual murder and of host desecration were an inevitable consequence of these beliefs. The garbled way in which Jewish rituals were interpreted often had tragic consequences. Thus, a Purim procession in which Haman in chains, possibly portrayed by a Christian, was led through the 'Jewish street' in Poznań and splashed with mud by Jewish onlookers was taken to be a parody of the Passion of Christ and led to a number of Jews being tried for desecrating the host. We do not know how the case turned out.[52] Nearly two centuries later, on 10 July 1743, the bishop of Przemyśl, Wacław Sierakowski, issued a ban on Christians taking part in such ceremonies. By this time, however, he was well informed regarding the nature of Purim and the Jewish commemoration of it.[53]

The first violence against Jews in Poland for allegedly killing a Christian child took place in Kraków in 1349 when local burghers, incited by the accusations of a local canon, attacked Jews in the town, for which a number of artisans were put on

[49] Quoted in Hundert, *Jews in Poland–Lithuania in the Eighteenth Century*, 74. See also Teter, *Jews and Heretics in Catholic Poland*, 113–17.

[50] Pikulski, *Złość żydowska przeciwko Bogu i bliźniemu, prawdzie i sumieniu na objaśnienie przeklętych talmudystów na dowód ich zaślepienia i religii daleko od Prawa Boskiego przez Mojżesza danego*. On Pikulski, see A. J. Zakrzewski, '*Złość żydowska* . . . Gaudentego Pikulskiego, czyli XVIII-wieczna encyklopedia antysemityzmu'.

[51] Kitowicz, *Opis obyczajów za panowania Augusta III*, 175.

[52] On this, see Węgrzynek, 'Sixteenth-Century Accounts of Purim Festivities'.

[53] 'Dekret biskupa Wacława Sierakowskiego, zawierający różne rozporządzenia obyczajowe i ceremonialne względem Żydów', doc. no. 136 in Schorr, *Żydzi w Przemyślu do końca XVIII wieku*, 205–8.

trial by the king. The first Polish legal accusation of ritual murder was made in 1547 in Rawa Mazowiecka, as a result of which a number of Jews were burned at the stake and others expelled from the town. According to a recent study of ritual murder trials by Zenon Guldon and Jacek Wijaczka, between 1547 and 1787 there were eighty-one cases of ritual murder: sixteen in the sixteenth century, thirty-three in the seventeenth century, and thirty-two in the eighteenth century.[54] This does not include the less frequent accusation of host desecration. Not all of these accusations resulted in trials and not all trials resulted in convictions. These conclusions upset the previously held view that there was an increase in the number of trials after 1648. What does seem true is that the influence of the clergy on such cases was greater after 1648. There are at least six cases at this time in which bishops were involved. The number of victims may also have been higher. In the eighteenth century more than 100 Jews and several non-Jews were executed for such offences. In addition, justice was more partial. Torture was consistently used to extract confessions, and after 1648 the goal of effecting conversions was more important. Thus, after a ritual murder trial in Zhitomir in May 1753, thirteen Jews were baptized after confessing under torture. Of the six Jews condemned, three converted, either to obtain an easier execution or to be spared.

Certainly, Jewish popular memory preserved a vivid image of these tragic and painful events. One of the earliest forms of popular Yiddish literature in Poland was the Yiddish popular ballad.[55] Not many of these have survived (we know of nine). One of the most striking is a song entitled 'Kidush hashem hameyuḥad shel reb mates vereb pinkhes vereb avrom' (The Martyrdom for the One God of Reb Mates, Reb Pinkhes, and Reb Avrom). In it the three individuals, who are accused of stealing church property or desecrating the host in three separate incidents (in Mościska, Tomaszów, and Kraków), all die the death of martyrs, refusing to apostasize. Other songs also depict accusations of various sorts (one of stealing ritual objects from a church, two of ritual murder, and one unspecified) in which innocent Jews die as martyrs. One describes the miraculous disproving of a ritual murder accusation in Poznań. All of these songs date from the second half of the seventeenth century.

Accounts of the remorse of false accusers also appear in Jewish traditions. Thus, the Jews of Tarnobrzeg, where twelve innocent Jews were judicially murdered in 1757, recorded in their *Yizkerbukh*, published in Tel Aviv in 1973, that after the twelve accused were burned, their principal accuser, Countess Rosa Konstancja Tarnowska, took some ashes of those consumed and attempted to disperse them in the waters of the Vistula. A wind blew ash particles into her eyes and, as a consequence, she became blind. Some time later the 'murdered' boy returned to

[54] Guldon and Wijaczka, 'The Accusation of Ritual Murder in Poland 1500–1800'. See also Hundert, *Jews in Poland–Lithuania in the Eighteenth Century*, 72.

[55] For these, see Turniansky, 'Yiddish "Historical Songs" as Sources for the History of the Jews in Pre-Partition Poland'.

Tarnobrzeg. In contrition, the Tarnowski family solemnly declared to the Jewish community that they would provide timber over the winters and flour for matzahs for the needy Jews of Tarnobrzeg in perpetuity. The vow was kept until the drought of 1927 (other accounts say the frosts of 1928) when Count Jan Zdzisław Tarnowski declared that the Jews were responsible for the drought. This, he asserted, freed him from the obligation to provide timber and flour. The following winter a fire broke out in the manor of the Tarnowski family and the count, taking this as a divine portent, reversed his decision and renewed his ancestors' oath.[56]

Similarly, after an alleged ritual murder in Zaslav in Volhynia in 1747, for which eight Jews were sentenced to horrible deaths by torture, Jewish legend has it that the owner of the town, Duke Paweł Sanguszko, who was also district governor of Kremenets, where the trial took place, was haunted by the ghosts of his victims. While driving through a 'Jewish street', he apparently screamed, 'Go away, go away, my victims. Stop being angry.' When representatives of the Jewish community in one of his towns complained that they could not obtain land for a cemetery, he immediately ordered that their request be granted.

The last known ritual murder trial in eighteenth-century Poland took place in Olkusz, near Kraków, and did not result in a conviction. The ending of these trials was the result, first, of the growing influence of the Enlightenment. The great Dutch jurist Hugo Grotius had as early as 1636 declared in response to a letter from a Polish Protestant, Jerzy Słupecki, that accusations that Jews used Christian blood were false and that testimony obtained under torture was worthless. Also important was the influence of the eighteenth-century papacy. In 1756 one of those accused in a ritual murder trial in Yampol, in Volhynia, Jakub Selek (Zelek), who had managed to escape from jail, was sent by the Council of the Lands to the Apostolic See to implore Pope Benedict XIV to protect Jews from ritual murder accusations. The document he carried with him detailed unjust charges made against the Jews, not only in Yampol, but also in Shepetovka, Zaslav, Zhitomir, and near Oster. The intervention was effective. The papal nuncio Cardinal Corsini di Visconti wrote to Henryk Bruehl, the first minister of the Polish court. Both Benedict XIV and the new Pope, Clement XIII (1758–69), condemned these trials, the latter on the basis of a report by Cardinal Lorenzo Ganganelli, who was to succeed him as Clement XIV (1769–74). According to them, 'there was no evidence that Jews need to add human blood to their unleavened bread [called] matzah'.[57] Similarly, when Rabbi Jonathan Eybeschuetz (1690/5–1764) of Altona, near Hamburg, prepared his refutation of the blood libel accusations of Frank, who had claimed in the course of the disputation organized by the Church between the Frankists and the rabbinate in Lviv that 'the Talmud teaches us that Christian blood is needed and whoever believes in the Talmud should demand it', he obtained the support of two prominent Christian scholars of the pre-

[56] Leeson, 'The Tarnobrzeg Blood Libel'.

[57] See Roth (ed.), *The Ritual Murder Libel and the Jew*.

Enlightenment. He seems to have intended to send his submission to the Royal Danish government, which was to forward it to the Church authorities either in Rome or in Lviv. We do not know whether it reached these higher authorities, or whether it had any significant impact. What is clear is that Fr. Mikulicz Mikulski, who orchestrated the Lviv disputation and who originally accepted the idea of the blood libel, began to hesitate, in part because of opposition from the higher Church authorities.[58]

In June 1775, in the course of a ritual murder trial in Warsaw in which all the accused were acquitted, the use of torture as a means of obtaining evidence was widely criticized. The following year it was abolished by the Sejm and no further trials were mounted before the final partition of Poland–Lithuania.

In addition to the problems they faced as the exponents of a despised and scorned religion, the Jews were also subject to periodic outbreaks of popular violence. In towns Jews were sometimes harassed by Jesuit students or local residents. Such incidents took place in Lublin, Lviv, Kraków, Płock, and Poznań.[59] The worst eruptions of anti-Jewish violence occurred in the eastern provinces of the Commonwealth, where the role of the Jews as the agents of the great Catholic (sometimes Greek Catholic) and Polish magnates aroused the hatred of the local Orthodox peasantry and Cossacks. Thus, during the Khmelnytsky Uprising and the wars which followed, the Jews were massacred not only by the Cossacks but also by the Swedes and Muscovites. Violence remained endemic in the Polish part of Ukraine in the late seventeenth and eighteenth centuries, much of it perpetrated by Haydamaks (*haidamaky*, outlaws), who went from banditry to opposition to Polish rule. Thus, in 1734, in the aftermath of the interregnum and the disputed election of King August III (r. 1734–63) under Russian control, Verlan, a Cossack officer in the private army of the magnate Jerzy Lubomirski, mutinied and organized Cossack-style units of some thousand peasants. He raised the standard of revolt against the Polish nobles, promising the removal of Polish lords, Jews, and Catholic institutions from Ukraine. This revolt was renewed in 1750 and was followed in 1768 by a much more extensive Haydamak revolt, the Koliyivshchyna, led by a Greek Orthodox peasant, Maksym Zaliznyak. At its height, it encompassed almost all of the Kiev and Bratslav provinces and most of Volhynia and required a combination of Russian and Polish troops to crush it. In the worst episode around 2,000 Jews were massacred in the town of Uman, when the local commander of the Polish garrison, Ivan Gonta, went over to the rebels.

As with the cases of accusations of ritual murder or host desecration, the Jews preserved a vivid memory of the violence to which they were subjected. As early as

[58] On this, see Leiman, 'Rabbi Jonathan Eibeschuetz's Attitude to the Frankists'.

[59] Tollet, 'Les Manifestations anti-juives dans la Pologne des Wasa (1588–1668)', in his investigation of such attacks in Poznań and Kraków suggests that they were economically motivated. See also Hundert, 'The Implications of Jewish Economic Activities for Christian–Jewish Relations in the Polish Commonwealth', 56 n. 4, on Kraków and Lublin.

1650 the Council of Four Lands decreed a fast to be observed on 20 Sivan, the day that the massacre occurred in Nemirov. This fast was observed in both Poland and Lithuania until the Second World War. There were also many songs which referred to these catastrophes. By 1649 a ballad had been written called 'The Misfortunes of the Holy Communities in the Land of Ukraine', while another song portrays the sufferings of the Jews in Lithuania and Belarus as well as in Lviv and Lublin during the Muscovite invasion of 1655. A further song chronicles the deeds of Gonta and the Haydamaks in Uman in 1768. In addition, there were many Yiddish translations of Nathan Nata Hannover's chronicle *Yeven metsulah*, describing the Khmelnytsky Uprising and the massacres which accompanied it, the first from 1677.[60]

The anti-Jewish violence took place in a general atmosphere of contempt and hostility. Most expressions of opinion about Jews by Christians in Poland in this period, much of it written by burghers rather than nobles, are unfriendly. A good example of the general attitude to Jews can be culled from the work of Sebastian Petrycy (1554–1626), a professor at the Jagiellonian University. In his reworking of book 7 of the *Politics* of Aristotle, *Rzeczpospolita Polska sposobem Arystotelesowym ułożona* (The Polish Commonwealth Examined According to the Principles of Aristotle; Kraków, 1605), he posed the question of whether it was desirable to allow Jews to remain in Poland–Lithuania. On the positive side, it could be claimed that they supplied money to people in need, paid high taxes, and as merchants paid most of the tolls and duties. In addition, they were generally peaceful. These benefits were, however, outweighed by their negative characteristics: they were blasphemers, desecrated the host, made use of Christian blood, bribed judges, seduced married women and virgins, and enticed Christians from their beliefs. As leasers of estates they oppressed Christians, and as merchants and artisans they deprived Christians of their livelihood.[61]

An even more hostile view was expressed by Sebastian Fabian Klonowic in his long poem *Roxolania*, written in 1584:

> Here in the muddy pools outside the city [of Lviv]
> You find the huts of the Jews, ragged like beggars,
> Each like a goat with a disorderly beard,
> With eternally pallid face and cheeks.
> Their synagogue throbs with a disorderly cry,
> One hundred voices shriek out the sabbath prayer,
> Their blind throng demands from God
> What they are taking from the world.
> You may ask: why should one allow a wolf into a flock of sheep? . . .
> Too late do kings see whence come the damaging wounds

60 On these developments, see Shmeruk, 'Yiddish Literature and Collective Memory'.

61 On Petrycy, see Hundert, 'Security and Dependence', 221.

From which our Republic groans,
Soon all the blood will be sucked from its body
And its life will be completely atrophied.
Let us turn our eyes away from this nation,
It is an unworthy act to curse—let us say farewell to the unbelievers
And return to the beautiful city
Which shines from afar.[62]

A somewhat more humorous but still malicious view of the Jews is to be found in the work of the satirical poet Jan Achacy Kmita (1560–1628).[63] In his *Jerycho nowe* (A New Jericho), published in 1615, he describes the advent of the Jewish messiah. Given the strength of the Turks and the unlikelihood of Jerusalem's being reconquered, this event would take place in Kazimierz, where the Jews had established a 'new Jericho' (*sic*). The Messiah would settle here and reward those who had treated the Jews well while punishing their tormentors. Jews would now take the place of the nobility, while the burghers would become peasants. The Jews would enact the laws and Christians would seek their protection. The fields around Kraków would be planted with onions and garlic and the Vistula widened as far as Wieliczka to accommodate the Leviathan. Poland would be so attractive to him that the Messiah would establish himself permanently there and abandon any attempt to return to Jerusalem.

Yet, paradoxically, the Jews in Poland–Lithuania had a strong sense of rootedness, which had a certain basis. In 1565 a visiting papal diplomat, Antonio Maria Gratiani, bishop of Amelia, reported:

In those principalities one still comes upon masses of Jews who are not disdained as much as in other such lands. They do not live here under pitiful conditions and do not engage in lowly pursuits . . . But rather they possess land, engage in commerce, and devote themselves to medicine and astrology . . . They possess considerable wealth and they are not only among the respectable citizens, but occasionally dominate them. They wear no special marks to distinguish themselves from Christians and are even permitted to wear swords and to go about armed. In general, they enjoy equal rights.[64]

The Jewish sense of security was reflected, first, in Jewish folklore,[65] as in the false etymology attributed to the name of Poland, which was referred to either as Po-lin, construed on the basis of a false Hebrew etymology as 'Here find a haven', or Po-lan-yah, similarly glossed as 'Here God rested'. This folklore recorded that when the Jews came to the country they found a wood, the forest of Kawęczyn, in which on every tree one tractate of the Talmud was incised. In his re-creation of this legend, Shai Agnon continued: 'And every man said to his neighbour, "We have come to the land where our ancestors dwelt before the Torah and revelation

[62] Sebastian Fabian Klonowic, *Roxolania* (1584), quoted in H. Markiewicz (ed.), *Żydzi w Polsce*, 17.

[63] On Kmita, see Michałowska-Mycielska, 'Jan Achacy Kmita'.

[64] Quoted in Hundert, *Jews in Poland–Lithuania in the Eighteenth Century*, 7.

[65] On this, see the references in n. 1.

were granted." '[66] The claim that Kazimierz the Great (r. 1333–70) had a Jewish wife by whom he had four children, two boys raised as Christians, two girls as Jews, is also probably mythical, but testifies to the sense of belonging which Jews felt. This sense of rootedness was often expressed by Jewish authors. Rabbi Moses Katz of Narol, who fled to Metz after the Khmelnytsky Uprising, described the country as 'Poland, the admirable, devoted to Torah and high purposes'.[67]

In a much quoted letter to a student who had decided to forgo a lucrative rabbinic career in Germany and return to Poland, Moses b. Israel Isserles (the Rema, 1525/30–1572), the outstanding rabbinic figure in sixteenth-century Kraków, wrote: 'Perhaps we ought to prefer a piece of dry bread in peace in these lands . . . where the hatred of Jews has not taken the dimensions of that in German lands. May God allow this condition to continue until the coming of the Messiah . . .'.[68]

His words were echoed by Judah Loew b. Bezalel (the Maharal, *c.*1525–1609), who served as rabbi of Poznań, which was probably his birthplace, from 1592 until 1597 before moving to Prague. Unlike earlier generations who had to observe the law under very difficult conditions, he wrote, 'now we sit in our homes, each person in tranquility and quiet'.[69]

This was also the view of the Karaite scholar Isaac b. Abraham Troki (*c.*1533–*c.*1594): 'The Kings and nobles of these lands, may God increase their well-being, love kindness and justice and do not wrong or oppress Jews living in their country.'[70]

These sentiments were repeated in the early seventeenth century by Rabbi Meir Ashkenazi of Lublin (b. 1597), who observed that in Poland Jews live under 'their vine and under their fig tree' and have children and grandchildren, an allusion to two biblical verses discussing idyllic times.[71]

This feeling survived the crisis of the mid-seventeenth century. In a penitential prayer after the Khmelnytsky massacres, Rabbi Yom Tov Lipmann Heller (1579–1654) referred to 'Poland, a country of royalty where we have dwelled from old in tranquil serenity', while in rabbinic responsa referring to the situation of the Jews in Poland it is frequently stated, 'They think that they have found dry land and that the exile is ended.'[72]

This was still the situation in the eighteenth century when Rabbi Jacob Israel of Kremenets still claimed that the Jews in Poland suffered persecution only in time

[66] In Agnon and Eliasberg (eds.), *Das Buch von den polnischen Juden*, 1.

[67] M. Katz, *Bakashah nifla'ah* (1667), quoted in Weinryb, *Jews of Poland*, 173.

[68] Isserles, *Responsa*, no. 95, quoted in Fram, *Ideals Face Reality*, 33–4.

[69] Judah Loew b. Bezalel, *Derekh ḥayim*, ch. 6, quoted in Fram, *Ideals Face Reality*, 32.

[70] Isaac b. Abraham Troki, *Ḥizuk emunah* (Ashdod, 1975), 156, quoted in Rosman, 'Jewish Perceptions of Insecurity and Powerlessness in 16th–18th Century Poland', 20.

[71] In Shabbetai b. Meir Hakohen, *Responsa* (Dessau, 1697), no. 1; see 1 Kgs. 5: 5, which speaks of times of peace and security, and Mic. 4: 4, a description of messianic times.

[72] Rabbi Heller's penitential prayer is published in Gurland, *On the History of Anti-Jewish Decrees* (Heb.), vii. 58.

of war or interregnum, when the authorities were distracted by the exigencies of the hour: 'Then men of violence, present in every society, gain the upper hand, plundering and settling scores with Jews. Normally, however, these wanton men were powerless to do as they wished for fear of the government, which has the power to save the oppressed from the hand of the oppressor and to root out evil from the country.'[73] According to the eighteenth-century mystic Phinehas b. Abraham Abba Shapiro of Korets (Korzec), 'In Poland, exile is less bitter than anywhere else.'[74]

This security was not absolute and there was a strong awareness of its fragility. Describing their situation in early modern Poland–Lithuania, Jews often cited the verse of God's promise to the Children of Israel from Leviticus 26: 44: 'Yet even when they are in the land of their enemies, I will not reject them or spurn them to destroy them and annul my covenant with them, for I am the Lord their God.'[75] As in medieval Europe, whose conditions were in many ways re-created in Poland–Lithuania, the Jewish elite took the view that toleration of the Jewish community was granted in exchange for the economic services it performed. Thus, Rabbi Benjamin Aaron b. Abraham Slonik (*c.*1550–*c.*1619), in one of his responsa (number 3), referred to an observation to this effect by the medieval German rabbi and talmudist Asher b. Jehiel (the Rosh, *c.*1250–1327), who later settled in Spain.[76] Isserles's wish 'May God allow this condition to continue until the coming of the Messiah' obviously expresses a degree of insecurity, which was set out more explicitly in his remark that Jews were able to maintain themselves in Poland–Lithuania

> Because unless God [had] left a remainder [of the Jewish people] in this land, God forbid Israel would become one who is cursed and damned like a faithless wife [see Num. 5: 11–31]. But with the help of Him who is wrapped in light, the heart of the king and his ministers is turned towards us that he wants us, thank God, as long as the announcers of darkness [informers] do not speak like the piercing of a sword [see Prov. 12: 18; BT *Ned.* 22*a*].[77]

This view was widely shared. When the Sejm or *sejmiki* (provincial parliaments) met, Jews said special penitential prayers beseeching God for mercy and asking that nothing harmful to the well-being of the Jewish people would result from the meeting.[78] The belief that it was important not to provoke the surrounding society is reflected in the importance Jews attached to their sumptuary legislation.

As Edward Fram has shown, Jewish religious practices in Poland also reflect this sense of vulnerability. Because they were afraid that parchment would be

[73] Jacob Israel of Kremenets, *Shevet miyisra'el*, ch. 56, 9.

[74] Quoted in Hundert, *Jews in Poland–Lithuania in the Eighteenth Century*, 7.

[75] See, for instance, Ber of Bolechów, *Memoirs*, 144, cited in Teller, '"In the Land of their Enemies"?', 431.

[76] Tollet, 'Merchants and Businessmen in Poznań and Kraków, 1588–1668', 23.

[77] Isserles, *Responsa*, no. 63, 289.

[78] Ashkenazi, *Seliḥot ufizmonim*, repr. in Halpern (ed.), *Minutes of the Council of Four Lands* (Heb.), no. 89.

stolen and defiled, some Jews claimed that they were unable to fulfil the biblical precept (Deuteronomy 6: 9) to put a *mezuzah* on their front doorpost.[79] Solomon Luria observed that Jews abandoned saying 'Birkat harehavah' (a blessing said in the street as mourners return from burying their dead) since they feared the effect this would have, given the 'wickedness' of the surrounding population.[80] Solomon b. Judah Leybush (d. 1591) hesitated to impose too strict a penance on an adulterous woman in 1582 since not only would this cause Christian neighbours to mock the Jews but it could cause 'misfortunes' for the whole community.[81]

Yet Jews were conscious of the difference between their situation in Poland and that elsewhere in Europe. The way they saw their position is best summed up in an allegory often used by them: The Jews came to Poland and began to make fires on a broad plain, which turned out to be the back of an enormous animal, and which, angered by the pain of the fires, began to move and threw them off.[82]

The Jewish sense of relative security and rootedness had a number of sources. In the first place the Polish–Lithuanian state was, to use modern and in some ways anachronistic terms, multi-ethnic and multi-religious. In spite of the differences from modern conditions, it is certainly the case that the Jews were not the only religious or social outsiders, or indeed the most numerous. In addition, the state and even more so the 'political nation' of the nobility was committed to the principle of toleration among different Christian denominations, however much this was attenuated, particularly after the growing strength of the Counter-Reformation in Poland–Lithuania. Thus, according to the General Confederation of Warsaw, adopted by the Sejm and senate in January 1573:

> And whereas in our Commonwealth there are considerable differences in the Christian religion, these have not caused disorders among people as detrimental as those that have begun in other kingdoms which we have observed; we therefore promise to one another, for ourselves and our descendants, for all time, pledging our faith, honour and conscience, that we who are divided by faith will keep peace among ourselves and not shed blood on account of differences of faith or rite, nor will we allow punishment by the confiscation of goods, deprivation of honour, imprisonment or exile, nor will we in any manner aid any sovereign or official body in such undertakings.[83]

In May of the same year a second Confederation aimed at reassuring an even wider circle:

> Since Turks, Armenians, Tatars, Greeks and Jews not only sojourn in Poland, but also reside there and [freely] move from place to place, they ought unreservedly to profess their

[79] Halevi, *Turei zahav*, 'Yoreh de'ah', 265: 5. Presumably the Jews feared that non-Jews would steal the *mezuzah*, not other Jews.

[80] Luria, *Yam shel shelomoh*, *Ket.* 1: 22.

[81] Solomon b. Judah Leybush, *Sefer piskei ushe'elot uteshuvot maharash milublin*, no. 58.

[82] Quoted in Hundert, *Jews in Poland–Lithuania in the Eighteenth Century*, 7.

[83] The document is to be found in the original Latin with an English translation in Biskupski and Pula (eds.), *Polish Democratic Thought from the Renaissance to the Great Emigration*, 131–6.

faiths, enjoy their liberties and benefit, so to say, from the same rights of citizenship [*una quasi civitate utantur*].[84]

The Jews also occupied a defined niche in Polish society, as was realized by the Jewish elite. They had been invited into Poland by the rulers, starting with Bolesław of Kalisz in 1264. By and large they were protected by the kings and by the charters which had been granted to them, which I will discuss in the next chapter. Even more important was the relationship between the Jews and the Polish nobility. One of the main features of Polish social history was the way the nobility gained overwhelming political and economic power. In 1539 legislation was passed in the Sejm giving owners of private towns (which by 1500 constituted 56 per cent of the towns in Poland[85]) the exclusive right to exercise jurisdiction over their Jewish communities, a right which was confirmed by King Zygmunt II August on 28 January 1549. This right had previously been exercised by the royal governors. This was the origin of the peculiar marriage of convenience between the Jews and the nobility.

According to Justus Decjusz (1485–1555), the chancellor to Zygmunt I and a well-known humanist: 'There is hardly a magnate . . . who does not hand over the management of his estates to a Jew . . . and more zealously protects them against any wrong, real or imaginary than he protects Christians.'[86] As a sixteenth-century Polish chronicle noted, 'Even if the Polish Diet would like to harm the Jews it would not be able to do so, because the king, the lords and the nobility are on their side. No Polish noble can do without a Jew.'[87] Another hostile witness, the early seventeenth-century priest Fr. Szymon Starowolski, complained that the Jews 'are a nation dear to many lords. Who has easiest access to the lord? The Jew. Who is most trusted at the manor house? The Jew.'[88]

The Jews frequently managed the estates of the nobility which they leased. They also acquired leases on mills, tolls, and taxes and on brewing and distilling. They played an important role in the vital grain trade down Polish rivers to the Baltic. In addition, they were the indispensable craftsmen of the rural economy in small towns and villages: carpenters, cobblers, tailors, tar-makers.

This marriage of convenience between the nobility and the Jews did not involve much mutual respect. The former looked on the Jews with contempt. Since they believed that 'only agriculture deserves to be called work' and that 'it is a sin and a shame to engage in trade', they regarded Jewish merchants, like Italian and German merchants, as swindlers, deceivers, and criminals. They valued above all physical strength, courage, and skill in battle, and despised the Jews as weak, cowardly, harmful, and parasitic. The diaries of noblemen are marked

[84] *Volumina Legum*, ii. 859, quoted in Baron, *A Social and Religious History of the Jews*, 34–5.

[85] Stone, *The Polish–Lithuanian State, 1386–1795*, 79.

[86] Quoted in Hundert, 'Some Basic Characteristics of the Jewish Experience in Poland', 31–2.

[87] Quoted in Weinryb, *Jews of Poland*, 51.

[88] Quoted in Tazbir, 'Images of the Jew in the Polish Commonwealth', 23.

by xenophobia, and particularly by a dislike of Jews.[89] The Jews for their part regarded their noble patrons as spendthrift and immoral. Yet, for a long period each needed the other, and this formed the basis for their relations. Since the nobles needed their Jewish agents, they granted many privileges to Jewish communities in the towns on their estates. The nobles also had the upper hand in relation to their leaseholders (arendators), but the typical leaseholder was conscious of his own power and 'by no means a cowering sycophant, but a man as much aware of his rights as his obligations'.[90]

The other constituent elements of Polish society were much less friendly towards the Jews. As I have already described, the Catholic Church in Poland was consistently hostile to the Jews, in accordance with the position of the Church as a whole. However, for a variety of reasons, the Church was unable to persuade either the king or the nobility to follow its rulings on how the Jews should be dealt with. The close economic ties which developed between the Church and the Jews, above all the loans made by Church dignitaries and monasteries to the various Jewish communities or *kehilot* (on this, see Chapter 4), further limited the desire of the leading members of the episcopate to take strong action against them.

The relationship between the Christian burghers and the Jews in the larger royal towns was also marked by persistent conflict and hostility. Trade was regarded as limited, and the competition of the Jews was seen by the burghers as inevitably working to their detriment. The burghers in one town even attempted to enlist support elsewhere. Thus, in 1521 the leading burghers in Lviv wrote as follows to their comrades in Poznań:

To our Honoured and Dear Friends, Peace and Blessing,

As is known to Your Honours, the unbelieving Jews have caused damage and destruction not only in our city but in others as well. Just as they have robbed our citizens and tradesmen of almost their entire livelihood, they do like damage also in other places. [They take] as much as their hands can grasp of the business of Christian tradesmen. As a result they alone are involved in trade: they have spread out among the villages and towns and permit nothing to come into the hands of Christians.

All this is contrary to the charter which was granted to them many years ago . . . We are aware that your honours have also had not a few troubles because of the Jews. We therefore urge your excellencies in the strongest terms to inform us of your willingness to join with us in opposition to the privileges which have been granted the Jews and join with us in asserting our common position before His Majesty in opposition to these Jews at the coming Sejm. Such an agreement between us against these Jews must result in an end of their privileges. It will be a benefit to our citizens and a blessing for our country . . .

THE CONSUL AND CONSULS OF THE CITY OF LVIV[91]

[89] On this, see particularly Partyka, 'Szlachecka silva rerum jako źródło do badań etnograficznych'.

[90] Rosman, *The Lords' Jews*, 131, 206–10.

[91] Halpern, *The House of Israel in Poland* (Heb.), ii. 236–7; Schiper, *Studya nad stosunkami gospodarczymi Żydów w Polsce podczas średniowiecza*, 350.

As is clear from this document, the disputes between Jews and burghers focused on the conflict between the rights which had been conferred by charter on the two groups. These conflicts were persistent and long-lasting, but they were also usually resolved by agreement. Thus, on 2 August 1609 the municipality of Kazimierz, across the river from Kraków, reached an agreement with the Jews of the town. It was highly specific in character and had nine points:

Jews may not manufacture vodka or beer; they are to purchase these from Christians in Kazimierz. They may resell them only to local Jews.
Jewish tavernkeepers must be registered with the *kahal*, which must submit the list to the guild of innkeepers.
Jews may have only eight butcher's stalls.
Jews are restricted to two bathhouses, a large one and a small one.
Jews are not to practise artisanry or to trouble Christian journeymen.
They may trade in furs but furrier work is to be done by Christian furriers.
Jews may not apply to powerful persons or royal officials against this agreement.
Jews have complete freedom to trade in Kazimierz and Stradom and they may rent shops and stalls in the Christian town. But disputes over rent fall under the competence of the officials of the town of Kazimierz.
Jews are to pay eighty zlotys annually to the magistrate in return for this agreement.

These were further elaborated in a subsequent agreement of 1615. Its most important provisions read:

2. Various goods which the Jews bring to Kazimierz or to their street and which, prior to shipping out again, they wish to weigh, must be weighed on the Kazimierz municipal scales. Only goods weighing up to one *kamień* may be weighed on the Jews' street.
7. Jews may not sell liquor or mead to Christians during the morning of [Christian] holy days . . .
8. Jews may have only eight butcher's stalls and sixteen master butchers. Violation is subject to a fine of twenty-four groszy. Meat deemed unfit by them may be sold to Christians.
9. Jews may not hire Christian servants to live in their houses on a yearly basis, men or women. Day work is permitted as long as the Christian returns to his home at the end of the day.
10. Jews may not import beer or mead from outside Kazimierz. For weddings and baptism parties and for domestic needs they may seek special permission from the mayor. Jews may import wine in barrels for sale to Jews or Christians. But they may sell wine on credit only to Jews.
11. No Jew can give work to a tailor or furrier but only to the guild master. If the guild refuses the work they may seek a non-guild craftsman. The penalty is confiscation of the goods involved—by the city if the action takes place in Kazimierz, by the royal administration if it takes place on the 'Jewish street'. Jewish tailors and furriers may make garments only for Jews.
12. Fish, hens, and geese and other things which are brought to the market—Jews are prohibited from going outside the marketplace to purchase them. They may, however, go

> to the villages to buy from a noble or a peasant, and they may purchase fish on the Vistula.[92]

Basic to the position of the burghers was the view that economic relations were a zero-sum game. If the Jews gained an advantage, this could only be to the detriment of the burghers.

More complex was the attitude of the peasantry, particularly in the Catholic parts of the country. Peasants and Jews lived in what has been described as a 'pattern of "distant proximity" based on continued economic exchange and mutual disdain'. Most Jews were economic middlemen—'pariah capitalists' filling a necessary but unpopular position between the two major strata in the Polish lands, the peasantry and the nobility.[93] Contact between Jews and peasants was primarily economic. On market days in the shtetls and during the week as travellers in the countryside, the Jews purchased agricultural produce from the peasants and sold them goods produced in the towns. In these circumstances other forms of contact which developed from this economic nexus persisted into the nineteenth century. These included consultation on medical matters, the role played by Christian servants in Jewish homes, and the mutual influence of the folk music of the two groups.

This interaction led to the creation of deep-rooted prejudices on both sides. The peasants despised the Jews for their lack of connection to the land and regarded them as 'treacherous and exploitative in nature'. At the same time, 'peasant perceptions of Jews also contained a detectable element of ambivalent, if not positive and admiring, evaluation, ascribed to the initiative, resourcefulness and intellectual cleverness of the Jewish traders'.[94]

The attitude of the Jews to their Christian neighbours was equally contemptuous and disdainful. They saw the peasants, to whom they felt greatly superior, as uncivilized and uncultured, primarily a source of material livelihood. The term *goy*, which, although meaning 'non-Jew', was taken to signify a peasant, 'meant people and things that were backward, ignorant, driven by corporeal, unrestrained instincts and physical aggression—everything (*goyish*) a Jew did not want to and should not be'. At the same time, 'the Jews' negative attitude toward peasants was accompanied by a feeling of pity resulting from their observation of the wretched conditions of the latter's existence—poorer even than that of the Jews'.[95]

The religious divide reinforced the wide gap between the two groups. The peasants saw the Jews as adherents of a religion which was not only false but deicidal and found Jewish religious practice bizarre and incomprehensible. To the Jews, Christianity was both idolatrous and hypocritical, since in their eyes it combined a call to 'turn the other cheek' with encouragement of violent antisemitism.

92 Bałaban, *Historja Żydów w Krakowie i na Kazimierzu, 1304–1868*, i. 200–4.

93 Morawska, 'Polish–Jewish Relations in America, 1880–1940', 71–6.

94 Ibid.

95 Ibid.

CONCLUSION

The situation of Jews in premodern Poland–Lithuania had a paradoxical character. On the one hand, they were the representatives of a despised minority whose religious beliefs were regarded not only as false, but as harmful to the society around them. On the other, they occupied a position in Polish–Lithuanian society which was recognized by law and which gave them a certain amount of economic leverage and security. The pioneer Jewish historians of the late nineteenth and early twentieth centuries, primarily Simon Dubnow, perhaps influenced also by pervasive Russian hostility to Poland–Lithuania, highlighted the negative attitude of the surrounding society, while stressing the importance of the Jews in achieving a wide degree of autonomy. More recent historians, such as Gershon Hundert, Moshe Rosman, and Adam Teller, as well as their Polish counterparts such as Adam Kaźmierczyk, have stressed the degree of security which Jews enjoyed. Contemporary observers certainly commented with surprise on the visibility of Jews and on their importance in the economic life of Poland–Lithuania.

Another paradoxical feature of Jewish life was that the Jewish community expanded considerably and became more important in Poland–Lithuania in the period of the Commonwealth's decline after 1648. In this sense, the increasing importance of the community was linked with the economic and social decline which Poland–Lithuania experienced in these years. What was most characteristic of the situation of the Jews in the Commonwealth was their marriage of convenience with the nobles and, in particular, with the magnates.[96] This was a reflection of the political and economic backwardness of Poland–Lithuania and meant that the situation of the Jews was inevitably threatened as the political, social, and economic hegemony of the noble estate was challenged and then undermined in the nineteenth century. As Hundert explains, 'the Jews' successful political strategy of the early modern period became a liability as political and economic conditions changed and they were left dependent for their livelihood and security on the crumbling old order'.[97]

[96] Rosman, *The Lords' Jews*, 210.

[97] Hundert, 'Some Basic Characteristics of the Jewish Experience in Poland', 32. See also Cała, *Wizerunek Żyda w polskiej kulturze ludowej*.

TWO

THE STRUCTURE OF JEWISH AUTONOMOUS INSTITUTIONS

'The sceptre shall not depart from Judah'—these are the Exilarchs in Babylonia . . . 'nor the ruler's staff from between his feet'—these are the descendants of Hillel who teach Torah to the people.

BT SAN. 5A, commenting on GEN. 49: 10

[The Council of Four Lands] is a fragment of redemption and a scrap of honour, proving that Almighty God in his great pity and lovingkindness had not deserted us.

The Memoirs of Ber of Bolechow (1723–1805)

IN THE PREVIOUS CHAPTER it was pointed out that there were two contrasting aspects of the position of the Jews in early modern Poland–Lithuania. On the one hand, they were a pariah group, tolerated in an inferior position, a status highlighted by the constant references to them in legal documents from the sixteenth century as 'unbelieving' (*infidus*, *perfidus*, or *incredulus*) and by the contempt in which they were held by most Christians. On the other, they were in many respects a corporation with the legal right to govern themselves as did all medieval corporations, whether those of an estate, like the nobility, or of a specific group, like the burghers of a particular town. In this context it should be stressed that freedom in the Middle Ages had a 'local rather than a universal character'.[1] The words 'liberty' and 'freedom' generally appeared in the plural form, as in the 'rights and liberties' of town, province, or estate which were granted by the sovereign and carefully recorded in charters. The rights and obligations of an individual were derived from participation in a given community: the abstract idea of individual 'human rights' was alien to medieval thinking.

The Jews were in the same position as other groups in society, possessing rights which were guaranteed to them by charters, whether general or applying to a specific region or town or to the institutions through which Jewish communal autonomy was exercised. The character of Jewish communal autonomy has given rise to a considerable literature. Jews have everywhere sought such autonomy since they established themselves in the diaspora. Its successful functioning was regarded as the key to the maintenance of Jewish life as reflected in the often cited adage from the Babylonian Talmud (tractate *Ta'anit*) 'O ḥevruta o mituta' ('Without

[1] Janowski, *Polish Liberal Thought before 1918*, 1.

community there is death') and it was given halakhic sanction. This right to self-administration for different religious groups was recognized in the Persian and Roman empires, in the Islamic world, and then in Western Christendom, where Jews emulated the 'institutional and legal patterns developed by the non-Jewish nations'.[2] Thus, there were assemblies of the Rhineland communities—Speyer, Worms, and Mainz—at the time of the Crusades and in Spain in the fourteenth and fifteenth centuries. However, although these assemblies took decisions and passed enactments, they did not become permanent institutions. It was only in Poland and Lithuania that central institutions of Jewish autonomy were established which operated continuously for 200 years from the second half of the sixteenth century until their abolition in 1764. These two bodies, the Council of the Lands in the Polish Kingdom and the Council of Lithuania, met, at their height, twice a year. They elected officers, such as the *parnas* (president of the council), the *shtadlan* (an advocate who represented the community before the king, magnates, Sejm, or courts), and officials who represented the council between assemblies and preserved the continuity of its activities.

The structure of Jewish autonomous life was undoubtedly impressive. According to Shmuel Ettinger, 'No wonder, therefore, that the Council of the Lands was regarded as the greatest expression of Jewish aspirations towards self-rule since the institution of the Gaonate came to an end.'[3] But it has also been idealized for political purposes. One of the goals of the new Jewish politics from the 1880s onwards, which stressed Jewish peoplehood, was to establish Jewish autonomy in the diaspora. The Council of the Lands and the Council of Lithuania were now seen as models to be emulated. Israel Halpern, who was responsible for a monumental edition of the minutes of the Council of the Lands, wrote in his introduction to this work, to which he devoted eighteen years of his life, that it was begun after the First World War, 'in the days of struggle for Jewish autonomy in Poland, when it seemed that there was a prospect of domestic Jewish government in the Diaspora'.[4]

JEWISH LEGAL RIGHTS

Like those of other medieval corporations, Jewish rights were defined by charter. Since Jews had no uniform legal status in Christendom throughout the Middle Ages, negotiating legal rights when settling in a new area was normal Jewish practice. Beginning in eleventh-century Germany, Jews sought written commitments from national, regional, and local powers that defined their rights and obligations with respect to the authorities. The first such charter granted in Poland was issued

[2] Baron, *The Jewish Community*, 22, 31.

[3] Ettinger, 'The Council of the Four Lands', 94. The heads of the academies of Sura and Pumbeditha (geonim) were the highest Jewish authority in Babylon between the 6th and the 11th centuries.

[4] Halpern (ed.), *Minutes of the Council of Four Lands* (Heb.), 8.

on 16 August 1264 by Bolesław the Pious, duke of Wielkopolska, to the Jews of his province. Subsequent charters were of several types: general charters applying to the whole country, regional charters, charters regulating the position of the Jews in individual towns, and charters which gave rights to specific individuals.[5] There is a problem of how these should be interpreted since they are prescriptive and it is not always clear how they worked in practice.

Since privileges not explicitly renewed by a sovereign's successor could be declared void, Jewish communities strove to have them reconfirmed by each successive monarch. Privileges could also be withdrawn. This situation was well understood by those hostile to the Jews and demonstrates how important the general charters were, both to the Jews and to their opponents. In 1454 Kazimierz IV briefly yielded to clerical pressure and rescinded the privileges he had granted in the previous year, while in 1606 John Felix Herboth of Dobromil wrote to the bishop of Kraków arguing that the charters given to the Jews were no longer valid because, among other reasons, they had not been renewed by Polish kings.[6]

Initially most of the charters guaranteeing Jewish rights were issued by the king or the grand duke. However, with the growing weakness of central government in Poland–Lithuania, particularly from the mid-sixteenth century, charters were also granted by great nobles. This was not a new phenomenon in Jewish history. In fifteenth-century Spain, for example, in border areas, where the king's authority was limited, authority over Jews on their lands was often assumed by local nobles.[7] Similarly, Jews benefited from the protection of the local landowner in the feudal enclaves of Pitigliano and Monte San Savino after the majority of their co-religionists in the Grand Duchy of Tuscany were confined in the ghettos of Siena and Florence in 1569.

The charters granted to the Jews were of different types, both general and specific. Of the general charters the most important was that granted by Bolesław the Pious in Kalisz in 1264, to which I have already alluded. It was modelled on the Austrian charter of 1240 and formed the basis for many subsequent enumerations of Jewish rights.[8] It was confirmed in a slightly altered form by Kazimierz the Great (r. 1333–70) and extended to cover the whole of Poland. It was again confirmed in 1453 by Kazimierz IV (r. 1446–92), son of the first Jagiellonian king of Poland, and it became part of the legal statutes prepared for King Aleksander Jagiełło (r. 1501–6) by his chancellor Jan Łaski in 1506, which,

[5] See Goldberg, *Jewish Privileges in the Polish Commonwealth*.

[6] On this, see Cygielman, 'The Basic Privileges of the Jews of Great Poland as Reflected in Polish Historiography'; and Fram, *Ideals Face Reality*, 25–6.

[7] Neuman, *The Jews in Spain*, i. 15–18.

[8] The charter of 1264 has not been preserved. But the introduction to the privilege granted by Kazimierz the Great in 1334 states that it is a confirmation of the earlier document (Weinryb, *Jews of Poland*, 339 n. 1). The privileges were collected by the Polish Chancellor Jan Łaski in 1506. For these general charters, see Schorr, 'Krakovskii svod statutov i privilegii'; id., 'Zasadnicze prawa Żydów w Polsce przedrozbiorowej'; Bałaban, 'Pravovoi stroi evreev v Pol'she v srednie i novye veka'; Gumplowicz, *Prawodawstwo polskie względem Żydów*; and Bloch, *Die General-Privilegien der polnischen Judenschaft*.

although they were never formally adopted, were applied as if they had been. This general charter also formed the basis for the charter issued in 1388 to the Jews of the Grand Duchy of Lithuania by Grand Duke Vytautas (Witold), the cousin of Grand Duke Jogaila (Jagiełło), which was confirmed in 1507 by Zygmunt I in his capacity as grand duke.[9]

The charter was obviously prepared for the king by the Jewish leaders, and reflected their desire to protect their position in five principal areas: exemption from the jurisdiction of the municipal authorities, economic rights, security, religious rights, and the character of the 'Jewish oath' which Jews had to take in court proceedings with non-Jews. Thus, under articles 8, 9, and 10 of the charter Jews were to be subject first to their own law and then to the law of the king, rather than to the law of the municipality.

These clauses meant that the Jews had the legal right to try cases between Jews according to their own law, although appeals in such cases were often heard in royal and later in magnate courts. In effect, Jews were exempt from the jurisdiction of the municipality in all areas except that of real estate owned by the municipality.

The economic rights conferred on the Jews were clearly specified in articles 1, 2, and 35, which laid down that in cases involving money or property 'no testimony of a Christian against a Jew is to be accepted unless there is a Christian and also a Jewish [witness]', and which gave Jews the right to pass unhindered through the territory of the duke. Jews could not be imprisoned for counterfeit without 'a warrant from us, or our Governor, or a high official'.

A number of provisions, in particular articles 14, 15, 20, 26, and 36, made clear how important for the Jews was the security of their community. They imposed severe punishments on those who murdered Jews, destroyed or damaged Jewish cemeteries, or attacked synagogues. Jews were given security against nobles to whom they had lent money, and Christian neighbours were obliged to assist Jews attacked during the night.

The right to practise their religion was of great concern to Jewish settlers and was alluded to in a number of clauses in the charter, as was specific condemnation of the blood libel:

33. In accordance with the order of the Pope, and in the name of our Holy Father, we absolutely forbid, from this time on, accusations that the Jews of our land use human blood, inasmuch as all contact with any blood is forbidden by their religion. And if any Jew is accused of the murder of a Christian child, this must be established by three Christian and three Jewish witnesses; only then will the Jew be incriminated and punished in accordance with the accepted penalty for this crime. But if he is proved innocent by these witnesses and by being guiltless of the crime, the Christian will suffer for his maliciousness the penalty which he sought to inflict on the Jew, and not without justice.

[9] For this, see Lazutka and Gudavičius, *Privilege to Jews Granted by Vytautas the Great in 1388*.

A final crucial issue was the nature of the oath which Jews would take in order to establish the truth of a statement, a right which was generally granted only to freemen. This was modelled on the edict of Duke Frederick of Austria and possibly also on that of the Czech king Ottakar II of March 1254.[10]

19. We decree: no Jew shall take an oath on their Torah except in important cases involving fifty units of silver or when they appear before us. But in smaller litigations he must swear before the synagogue, near the doors of that synagogue.

This was expanded in the revised version of the charter which was issued by Kazimierz the Great:

First, we decree that in any case involving money or property movable or immovable or in a criminal case touching the person or property of the Jews, no Christian may testify against the Jews in any case involving goods or immovable property touching, as mentioned, the life or property of these Jews. Such a Christian [may not testify] against Jews accusing one of them in any matter even [a] criminal [one], unless with two good Christians and two good Jews. And all this should not defame their humanity [*sua humanitate non essent infames*]. However, if accepting this the Christian proves his accusation against a Jew then he may punish the Jew according to the crime of which he has been accused . . . The two Christians mentioned must take an oath on a sacred crucifix as follows, 'May God and this sacred crucifix help us etc. . . .', according to the custom of Christians, while the Jews will take their oath on a copy of the Ten Commandments according to the custom of the Jews in cases involving more than fifty marks of pure silver. If the case involves less than the sum of fifty marks of pure silver then the Jews must swear their oath on the chain or *kolcze* which hangs on the door of the synagogue according to their custom. This is the formula, 'May God who illumines and guards the Books of Moses help us'. This will be the oath of the Jews and no other in all matters great and small grasping the chain, and this must be the direction given by the official or *woźny* or the functionary in charge.

These formulations were intended to preclude the way in which, in the German-speaking lands, the Jewish oath (*more judaico*) had from the thirteenth century increasingly been used to humiliate Jews. Here the oath often contained derogatory expressions and was administered in an insulting manner. The Jew taking the oath was required to stand on a pigskin or barefoot on a three-legged stool. If he faltered in pronouncing the oath, his testimony was declared invalid. These forms were clearly excluded by the two Polish charters, and the Jews obtained repeated confirmation (in 1551, 1553, 1576, 1580, 1585, and 1593) that they were not to be used in Polish courts.[11]

Some rights which were not specified in the Kalisz charter and other general charters were guaranteed in specific enactments. Among these was the right to slaughter cattle and sell those parts of the animal which Jews were not permitted

[10] Teimanas, *L'Autonomie des communautés juives en Pologne aux XVIe et XVIIe siècles*, 21.

[11] On the 'Jewish oath', see Weinryb, *Jews of Poland*, 39, and I. Lewin, 'The Protection of Jewish Religious Rights by Royal Edicts in Pre-Partition Poland'.

to consume (in the case of cattle, the hindquarters). This was conceded in a privilege granted by Kazimierz IV in 1453. According to this:

> Wherever the Jews have their residence in a city or town of our kingdom, they may slaughter for their use large and small cattle; and should a kind of meat, according to their custom, not correspond to their purpose and desire, they may sell it to the best of their ability, as they may wish.[12]

The Jews were also given the right to choose a rabbi, who was also empowered in accordance with Jewish law to issue judgments and enforce them with a ban of excommunication (*ḥerem*). According to a decree granted by Zygmunt II August on 13 August 1551:

> We, Zygmunt August, by the grace of God King of Poland, Grand Duke of Lithuania ... make this proclamation to all and every individual, to all who might need to know. Certain of our advisers have informed us in the name of our Jews of Wielkopolska that when their Rabbi or religious judge dies and the office is unfilled until we appoint another in his place there is much neglect. Therefore we have been requested, in the name of those Jews of Wielkopolska, to give them the right to choose by their unanimous vote and consent a Rabbi or judge who seems good and just in their eyes when that position becomes vacant because of the death of the previous occupant.
>
> We give him complete authority to judge, investigate, and sentence without appeal, all the Jews resident in Wielkopolska and the Duchy of Mazovia who are under his jurisdiction. Further, he may issue excommunications and impose punishments according to the custom and law of Moses in all matters related to religion. In addition we maintain and repeat what the Jews have themselves proclaimed before us: if any of the Jews dares to behave in a way which calls into question the sentence or excommunication imposed upon him by the Rabbi or the judge and other elders of the Jews, disregarding it for a period of one month, he shall be placed in our hands for capital punishment and his property shall be seized by our treasury.[13]

The state's support for the decisions of a rabbinic court was confirmed in a number of decrees, including those issued by Zygmunt I on 6 August 1527 and 12 December 1541 and that of Zygmunt II on 13 August 1551, discussed above. In all of these the king asserted that his government could not be indifferent to insubordination on the part of a Jew to a decision of his religious authorities. In cases of such insubordination, Jewish legal decisions would be supported by the state, provided the excommunication which followed was in accordance with Jewish law. The two earlier statutes provided for royal confiscation of property; that of 1551 went still further and imposed the death penalty on those condemned. What is not clear is whether such a sentence was ever carried out.[14]

[12] *Codex Diplomaticus Maioris Poloniae*, iii (Poznań, 1877), 88–94, no. 1368, quoted in I. Lewin, 'The Protection of Jewish Religious Rights by Royal Edicts in Pre-Partition Poland', 122.

[13] Cited in Hundert, 'Jews in Poland'.

[14] I. Lewin, 'The Protection of Jewish Religious Rights by Royal Edicts in Pre-Partition Poland', 130–4.

In addition to these general and specific charters, rights were frequently conceded to Jewish communities in individual towns. Here one needs to distinguish between royal towns—those subject to the king and the royal governor—and private towns, which were subject to their noble owners. In the case of royal towns, these rights were obviously granted by the king. The situation of the Jews was, however, complicated by the fact that the Christian burghers frequently negotiated special agreements with the Jews (on this, see Chapters 1 and 3).

Przemyśl offers a good example of the rights granted to Jews in royal towns.[15] They are contained in a number of documents. The first of these is the privilege of 29 March 1559, which was granted by Zygmunt II and sanctioned the settlement of the Jews in Przemyśl. In its preamble it is explained that the Jews have long lived on their own street in Przemyśl ('street' in this context means a small district), yet they have not yet been granted a privilege which would ensure them permanent domicile, peace, and legally guaranteed security. The privilege granted a number of rights to the Jews, including the right to dwell permanently in the town, to acquire houses from Christians on the 'Jewish street', to hold property in perpetuity, and to make use without any obstacle of the right to buy and sell goods and also to hold them like other burghers. In addition, the Jews were subject not to municipal jurisdiction but to the jurisdiction of the king and his *starosta*, the official who had administrative and judicial authority over the royal castle in a town and its surrounding region. They were to be judged according to the relevant statutes (the privilege of Bolesław and its reissue by Kazimierz III). In return the Jews were to pay 4 zlotys to the royal castle.

Three further privileges were granted by Zygmunt II August. The first, issued in 1562, freed the Jews from all taxes and duties except for the border tariff. It was not made clear for how long this was to last and it may be that it was only for a year in order to enable the community to establish itself. That issued in 1570 affirmed that the Jewish synagogue and cemetery were subject only to the royal court, while in a proclamation of 1571 the king calls on the municipal councillors not to impede Jews in their liberties or trading rights, nor to inflict any injury on their faith—on the contrary, to protect them from such harm and violence 'since together with you they are jointly responsible for the taxes of the town'.

A final royal privilege—described as a statute for the common good—was granted by King Stefan Batory in June 1576. According to its terms only the *pospólstwo* (electorate) could elect the officers of the *kehilah*. The governor was to confirm this choice. He could not impose a rabbi on the community; rabbis could only be elected by the *pospólstwo*. The remainder of the statute set out the internal structure of the community, providing for a judge of the Jews (*judex Judaeorum*), scribes, elders, and a teacher.[16]

[15] A history of the town to the end of the 18th century was written by one of the founders of modern Jewish historiography, Dr Mojżesz Schorr: *Żydzi w Przemyślu do końca XVIII wieku*. These charters are to be found on pp. 73–5, 78–81.

[16] Ibid. 83–5.

The rights granted by the king were frequently modified by agreements between burghers and Jews, often to the detriment of the Jews. An agreement of this type was concluded between the Jews and the burghers of Przemyśl on 12 June 1645.[17] There were similar agreements between the Jews and the burghers of Kraków of 2 August 1609 (see Chapter 1) and a series of agreements between the Jews and the burghers of Vilna (see Chapter 3).

The position in the private towns was more favourable to the Jews because of the weaker position here of the Christian burghers. As a result, their social status was higher and they did not have to contend with the economic competition they faced in larger centres or the hostility of burgher-controlled municipalities. Nobles sometimes made specific reference to religious toleration in order to attract Jews to towns on their estates. Thus, when Hieronim Sieniawski in 1576 founded a new township in Oleszyce, near Lubaczów, he included provisions in the charter he granted to the Jews specifying their equal rights:

> The Polish Crown flourishes with people of diverse estates, particularly in regard to their religious allegiance on the principle that no authority shall exercise power over faith, honour and conscience. We wish therefore to secure a peaceful life especially to those persons who have suffered persecution not because of any crimes or evil deeds, but for other reasons, so that they may enjoy all the liberties of the laws enacted by us.[18]

Most charters in noble towns were very specific. Thus, the charter granted to the Jews of Opatów, after reaffirming earlier privileges, continued:

> In the first place, they are entitled to build on their own grounds a synagogue, schools, a cemetery and a hospital. They may sell all types of alcoholic drinks in different measures, goods in various measures and practise other types of trade in their home and in places where booths are permitted. We prohibit the burghers from establishing any obstacle to Jewish trade. They are also permitted to slaughter all types of cattle and sell the meat freely.
>
> In relation to rents and taxes, they are to pay the same as all burghers. We will maintain the courts of their elders as before, with the right of free appeal to the court at our residence, as is set out in their earlier privilege.
>
> We thus, having listened carefully to the humble supplication they have made to us, deign to accept their just request and confirm all their rights both ancient and more recent granted by the princes our ancestors of blessed memory and while maintaining our feudal rights unimpeded, maintain, confirm and approve their request . . .[19]

Kings also sometimes supported Jews close to them. Thus, in 1528 Zygmunt I issued a personal charter in favour of Dr Moses Fischel, the nephew of Rabbi Jacob Pollak, and his wife, Esther. It read: 'You [the Jews] are never to coerce the above-mentioned Moses and his wife by excommunication or by other customs of your Jewish sect or by laws or by any other means whatsoever.' Rights were also conceded by the Crown to individual merchants, including some Jews. Individuals who were given the title of *faktor* (agent), *serwitor* (servant), and less

[17] Ibid. 147–52. [18] Baron, *A Social and Religious History of the Jews*, xvi. 125.

[19] Hundert, *The Jews in a Polish Private Town*, 160–1.

frequently *sekretarz* (secretary) were exempt from communal authority and subject only to that of the king. Thus, when King Michał Wiśniowiecki renewed the privilege of Mendel b. Szmul (Szmujlowicz) of Lviv as royal agent in 1671, he freed him from all except royal jurisdiction and specifically laid down that he and his family could not be held responsible for the debts of the *kahal* or of other Jews.[20]

THE LOCAL *KEHILOT*

At the centre of the rights which the Jews enjoyed was that to administer their communities themselves. In Poland–Lithuania there was a three-tier structure of Jewish self-government. The basic unit was the local community, the *kehilah* (Hebrew for a communal corporate body). The individual *kehilot* sent representatives to regional councils in the different parts of Poland and Lithuania. Above the regional councils were two national councils, the Council of the Lands in the Kingdom of Poland and the Council of Lithuania in the Grand Duchy.

The key unit in this structure was the local *kehilah*. Its significance in Jewish history has been well described by Lionel Kochan:

> It is the institution of the *kehillah* . . . that to each of these scattered settlements gives a degree of coherence and unity, over centuries of dispersion and migration. As an historical agent in its own right and as a sovereign power, the *kehillah* fulfils, relative to time and place, the Biblical promise that 'the sceptre shall not depart from Judah nor the ruler's staff from between his feet' (Genesis 49: 10). In all its multiple guises it originated in Talmudic times as a vehicle of self-government during the dispersion to Babylon and elsewhere and in this capacity evolved into the basic unit of Jewish history. It groups together the Jews of a specific locality. Amidst expulsion, migration and resettlement in Europe and the Americas, the *kehillah* strove to uphold some semblance of self-government.[21]

Jewish self-government was seen as serving both secular and religious functions. According to the regulations of the Kraków *kehilah*, enacted in 1595, those who exercised authority on its behalf had been chosen 'according to the prescriptions of our Torah and the statutes we have received from kings and other princes and rulers'.[22] The religious sanction which upheld the *kehilah* was set out in an ethical will written for his sons by Abraham b. Shabetai Sheftel Horowitz (1550–1615), a Polish talmudist who lived first in Kraków and then moved to Lviv, where he became judge of the *kehilah* and of the council of Lviv province:

> Take care not to quarrel with the *kahal* at any time, not over taxes, not over charitable contributions and not over office-holding—not over anything at all. If, however, it does seem that the *kahal* has significantly wronged you, then present your case calmly . . . And afterward, however the matter turns out, you must do exactly as they order . . . even if it seems to

20 Hundert, 'Security and Dependence', 41.

21 Kochan, *The Making of Western Jewry, 1600–1819*, 1.

22 Bałaban, 'Die Krakauer Judengemeinde-Ordnung von 1595 und ihre Nachträge', 309.

you the opposite of good sense. For the spirit of God is with the leaders of the people . . . the Holy One, Blessed be He, does not bestow greatness, stature and the office of leadership of the generation without first inspecting [their souls]. Therefore since the leaders of the generation hold office with the consent of the Omnipresent, Blessed be He, you are obliged to obey them in all they order . . .[23]

The *kehilah* was administered by the *kahal*, a body of between ten and twenty members. Each *kahal* had its own regulations. We have a copy of those for Kraków, and those for Vilna were seen before the Second World War by Israel Cohen and described in detail in his account of Jewish life in that city. In addition, a significant proportion of the minute book (*pinkas*) of the Poznań community has survived.[24] The *kahal* was headed by a *parnas* (president), a revolving office which changed hands every month or, in smaller *kehilot*, every quarter, and its responsibilities were very wide. It was responsible for all matters relating to religious observance, for the physical welfare of the community, including relief of the poor and care of the sick, orphans, and the aged, and for education.

In Vilna the responsibility for poor relief fell to the *tsedakah gedolah* (the great charity), an organization subordinate to the *kahal* which was administered by the wardens of the Great Synagogue on the synagogue courtyard (see Chapter 3). It distributed alms weekly to the local poor and also provided transport out of Vilna for the poor of other towns who had come there in the hope of improving their lot. It supplied flour for matzahs at Passover, paid for wet-nurses for orphan infants, furnished shrouds for those unable to afford them, and assisted householders in straitened circumstances. To fulfil these tasks it was financed by charitable donations from the synagogues, the *batei midrash* (houses of study), and the *minyanim* (groups for prayer) of the town. It also received two-thirds of the burial fees (in return for which it covered two-thirds of the cost of the upkeep of the cemetery), the other third going to the *ḥevra kadisha*, the charitable society which looked after the dead and dying. It also had some other sources of funding, including a tax on the grinding of flour for Passover, a tax on *etrogim* (citrons) bought for Sukkot, and a regular subsidy from the slaughterhouse.

The *kehilah* was also responsible for the maintenance of communal property and for the cleanliness and water supply of the Jewish quarter. In Vilna a subordinate body called *bedek habayit* (repairing of the house) was responsible for the maintenance of the Great Synagogue and other communal property, the cleanliness of the synagogue courtyard and the Jewish quarter, and the maintenance of water-pipes, canals, and baths. It was administered by four wardens appointed for three years by the *kahal*, who needed its approval for any important action. It paid the Dominican friars 200 gulden a year for permission to transport water from

[23] Quoted in Hundert, 'Security and Dependence', 25.

[24] For the Kraków regulations, see Bałaban, 'Die Krakauer Judengemeinde-Ordnung von 1595 und ihre Nachträge', 309–17; for Vilna, I. Cohen, *Vilna*, 114–33; for Poznań, Avron (ed.), *Minute Book of the Electors of the Community of Poznań* (Heb.).

their wells to the synagogue courtyard, where it served not only those who dwelt in the immediate vicinity but also those who lived farther off and did not have a well in their own courtyard. It also operated a ritual bath.

This body's main income came from an annual levy on householders, who were assessed according to their annual contribution to the *kehilah*. The various Jewish artisans' guilds were also obligated to pay a levy. From 1752 the body also received a contribution on the occasion of a wedding or circumcision in the community. In that year its income was further augmented by a grant of 1 per cent of the income the *kahal* received from its properties.

The *kahal* was also authorized by the Crown and the local municipality to exercise control over the economic life of the community, granting the right of domicile in the city and regulating the right to buy property and the right to work. It sought to establish the maximum rate of interest to be charged to non-Jews. According to the Kraków ordinances of 1595, this was to be 12 groszy per 100 zlotys per week, an annual rate of just over 20 per cent. In Poznań the *kehilah* elders decided on one occasion to ask the *av beit din* (the head of the rabbinic court) whether they could charge more interest than the rate of 31.2 per cent laid down by the Council of the Lands.[25]

The *kahal* exercised strict control over the institution of marriage. According to the Poznań communal records from the eighteenth century, the official rabbi was required to solemnize all marriages, and men from other communities required the permission of the *kahal* to marry in the town, making possible the scrutiny of their financial and moral character. Women could only marry if they were provided with a dowry of at least 400 zlotys. A quota for 'marriages among people of limited means' was established, which allowed six marriages a year for women who did not possess the requisite dowry. Domestic servants and other employees (*mesharetim*) could marry only with 'the consent of at least two-thirds of the communal administration'.[26] It also acted to limit competition between Jews in their dealings with the outside world. Thus, in Kraków in 1653 the court of the *kehilah* confirmed the right of a group of Jews to supply clothing to the Lubomirski family, laying down 'that no [other] man may do any business at all with the court of the lord named above, here or in any of his villages or any place he or his entourage may be, at fairs or not at fairs'.[27]

These and other commercial matters generally came before the *parnas*, or, if larger sums were involved, before all *roshim* (literally 'heads') and *tovim* (literally 'good men'), who in this way exercised a judicial function. This seems to have extended to matters of illegal competition, as well as the farming of taxes and the

[25] The economic activity of the *kehilah* is discussed in Hundert, 'Security and Dependence', ch. 2.

[26] Weinryb, 'Studies in the Communal History of Polish Jewry II', 113–14. For similar restrictions in Kraków, see Bałaban, 'Die Krakauer Judengemeinde-Ordnung von 1595 und ihre Nachträge', 329.

[27] F. Wettstein, *Treasures from the Minute Book of the Kraków Kahal* (Heb.), no. 28, 32–3; Bałaban, *Historja Żydów w Krakowie i na Kazimierzu, 1304–1868*, i. 306, quoted in Hundert, 'Security and Dependence', 45.

assignment of leases (arendas), an abrogation of rabbinic jurisdiction which seems to have been preferred by Jewish merchants although it was sometimes attacked by those who sought to uphold the judicial powers of the rabbinate. According to the rabbi Joseph Joske b. Judah Judel of Lublin (1659?–1706): 'They sit in judgment and degrade the study of our Torah, rendering sentences based on [their own] assessment, arbitrarily, perverting the law. In the majority of cases, the judgments of householders and the judgments of [rabbinic] judges are opposite; the guilty are pronounced innocent and the innocent guilty.'[28]

The *kehilah* had powers of taxation in accordance with which it imposed and collected taxes for the state and the municipality and levied taxes to maintain its own administration. In addition, it levied taxes for special purposes, such as ransoming prisoners of war or defraying the expenses of a *shtadlan*. In addition, it levied direct taxes on the sale of meat and on commercial transactions, and levied fees on dowries and funerals and for the use of the ritual bath and the official scale of weights and measures. Income was also derived from the sale of synagogue places and the annual fee paid by slaughterers (*shoḥetim*).

The revenues of the *kehilah* were used to fund its own activities and to pay the taxes due to Jewish provincial and national councils. It also regularly made gifts to prominent officials and churchmen, which in Kraków amounted to about 10 per cent of its disbursements. Another third went to pay taxes and an additional third to pay the debts it had contracted. We do not know how far this pattern was followed elsewhere.[29]

At the head of the *kehilah* was an executive. In Kraków the executive authority of the *kehilah* was vested in a board of twenty-three members (for this structure, see Chapter 3), in Vilna one of thirteen. In Kraków these were made up of four *roshim*, five *tovim*, and fourteen ordinary *kahal* members. The four *roshim* also held the office of *parnas* in rotation for a month at a time. They exercised considerable power, especially in judicial matters, tax collection, certifying Jewish artisans and tradesmen, fixing the communal budget, and for authorizing loans granted or taken out by the *kehilah*. In addition, the executive appointed specialized officers to carry out the functions with which it was entrusted: four auditors (whose business was to examine the *kahal*'s accounts), almoners, *dayanim* (judges), *ba'alei takanot* (drafters of regulations), and *shomerei takanah*, whose function was to supervise the observance of these regulations.

Kahal elections were not democratic in the modern sense. In Kraków the sitting members of the *kahal* and the executive officers met on the first intermediate day of Passover and placed the names of possible electors in a hat. First fourteen and then nine names were drawn. These people then selected five electors, who chose the *kahal* and its officers. This pattern was repeated in other communities. Thus, in Vilna the elections also took place on the first of the intermediate days of

[28] Joseph Joske b. Judah, *Yesod yosef* (Shklov, 1785), ch. 42, quoted in Hundert, 'Security and Dependence', 48.

[29] Hundert, *Jews in Poland–Lithuania in the Eighteenth Century*, 86–7.

Passover. The first stage of the election was carried out immediately after the morning service when the members of the *kahal*, the heads of the *asefah* (the communal assembly), the rabbi, the secretary, and the beadles (*shamashim*) assembled in the *kahal* chamber. Five members of the *asefah* were chosen by lot and were designated as electors with the responsibility of naming the thirteen members of the *kahal* as well as four auditors, four almoners, and two presidents of the *asefah*. The regulations which were common to most *kehilot* forbade them to elect relatives of the retiring *rashei hakahal* and the judges, although this did sometimes occur, as in Kraków in the 1640s. The entire proceedings had to be concluded in a single day. Four officers responsible for drafting laws and supervising their observance were elected before the new moon in the month of Kislev (generally December).

The candidates for office were required to possess appropriate qualifications. In Vilna they had to have been married at least ten years and to have made a special contribution to the *kehilah*'s treasury. According to an enactment of 1774, two of them had to pay 200 gulden each and two 100 gulden each, while a minimum payment of 50 gulden was required in the case of an almoner. Election to office was also based on a system of 'grades', a candidate being required to fill a post of the lowest grade before he was eligible for the next, the order of the hierarchy beginning with the almoner or judge, and then rising in the case of Vilna through the intermediate posts to *rosh hakahal*. Artisans, whose status was low in traditional Jewish society, were from the late seventeenth century usually excluded from those eligible to hold office.[30]

Under all these circumstances, it is not surprising that communal self-government was everywhere in the hands of the Jewish elite and that the proportion of those entitled to vote rarely exceeded 10 to 15 per cent of the adult male population and was frequently much lower. Regulations which sought to prevent the acceptance of office by relatives of existing office-holders as well as to prevent the election of relatives of the rabbi were often ineffective and there were frequent and bitter struggles for communal office, particularly in the eighteenth century.

Acting as a control on the activity of the *kahal* was a broader, more numerous group referred to as the 'leaders of the community' (*kenu'ei edah*), 'outstanding people' (*yeḥidei segulah*), 'those who belong to the assembly', or 'householders who pay taxes'. In Polish documents this group was referred to as the *pospólstwo* (the commonality). It was a group made up of those taxpayers (sometimes only a part of them) who did not hold office, and it also dealt with matters of broad concern to the community, such as the appointment of a rabbi or the passage of general legislation.[31]

In Vilna, where it was also called the *asefah* (assembly), or *asefat reḥash* (the 'rehash' assembly, a name derived from the initials of the three principal officers which it appointed, the rabbi, the *ḥazan* (cantor), and the *shames* (beadle)), it con-

[30] On this, see Hundert, 'Security and Dependence', 29.

[31] See Hundert, *Jews in Poland–Lithuania in the Eighteenth Century*, 83.

sisted of 120 members in 1750 and 196 in 1796. This increase occurred in spite of the efforts of the Council of Lithuania to restrict the number of its members to fifty. Five new members were admitted each year. The assembly met at least once every three months under the presidency of the *rashei asefah* (elders of the assembly).

The *kehilah* leadership was very conscious of the vulnerable position of the Jewish community. In all its actions it took as a basic principle the need to prevent actions by individuals which would provoke anti-Jewish hostility. This need governed the economic regulations of the *kahal* and also its sumptuary legislation, by which it sought to 'avoid envy' by 'costly display'. Thus, in Poznań in 1713 Jews were forbidden to wear silver buckles, silver belts, gold rings, lace, or gold and silver ornaments. Such displays were

> bringing misfortune to our holy community, particularly dresses and jewellery of the new style, which are strictly prohibited by the laws of the Gentiles. Our creditors, seeing Jews parade in royal garments ornamented with silver and gold, shout for justice in the *sejmiki* and in the courts, saying that obviously they can pay their debts to noblemen and to priests.[32]

Some of these prohibitions applied to women. In Poznań they were forbidden in 1734 to wear gold or silver, ducats, or coral. 'This applies to unmarried girls and even more to women; it is even forbidden for brides to ornament themselves.'[33] These prohibitions were frequently repeated, which must raise some doubt about their effectiveness. Infractions were usually punished by a fine.

Sumptuary legislation also served to maintain the prestige and status of the communal elite, who also obtained the best synagogue seats and honours. Particularly important in this small world were such honours as being called up first to bless the Torah on festivals like Simhat Torah and Shavuot.

There was also an awareness that if the *kehilah* was too obviously oligarchic this could lead to popular discontent and the breakdown of communal solidarity. Both the thirteenth-century halakhic authority Rabbi Asher b. Jehiel, and Rabbi Moses Isserles in sixteenth-century Kraków, upheld the idea that the wealthy should decide major issues but should avoid excessively antagonizing the majority.[34] This unwillingness to impose decisions on the majority was articulated first by Rabbi Joshua b. Alexander Hakohen Falk (*c.*1555–1614) in Poland and then by the Polish-born rabbi Menahem Mendel b. Abraham Krochmal (*c.*1600–1661), who was rabbi first in Prostějov and then in Kroměříž in Moravia. In one of his responsa, Rabbi Krochmal strongly asserted the need to take into account the interests of the poor and disfranchised minority, who otherwise 'would become

32 Avron, *Minute Book of the Electors of the Community of Poznań* (Heb.), no. 1965, 355–6, quoted in Hundert, *Jews in Poland–Lithuania in the Eighteenth Century*, 89.

33 Avron, *Minute Book of the Electors of the Community of Poznań* (Heb.), no. 2144, 395.

34 Shilo, 'The Individual versus the Community in Jewish Law in Pre-Eighteenth Century Poland', 231.

very resentful and in the end could secede from the community and cause bitter strife between the social strata'.[35]

Jewish communal self-government was further buttressed by the existence of *ḥevrot* (associations) created for specific purposes. The most important of these was the *ḥevra kadisha*, the 'holy society' responsible for caring for the dying, burying the dead, and maintaining the cemetery.[36] This was usually the first association to be created in a community and sometimes even preceded its formal establishment. Membership of the association was seen as a great honour and a religious duty, and was largely the province of the elite. By the middle of the eighteenth century in Vilna the main society, the 'great *ḥevra kadisha*', was made up of 260 members, with around 100 members of a sub-society, the 'small *ḥevra kadisha*', which was responsible for actual burials and was of lower status and principally composed of artisans. In addition, there was a group of 'pious women' who were responsible for the preparation for burial of women's bodies.

The entry of a new member to the society was a solemn occasion. After paying an entrance fee, he had his name registered in the minute book, was called up to the reading of the Torah at a service in the prayer house of the society, and was required to host a feast for the members. The executive board was composed of eight members: four *gaba'im* (wardens), two auditors, and two ordinary members, who were elected annually on the second of the intermediate days of Passover, the day after the election of the *kahal*. The election took the form of drawing names from an urn, with the proviso that the office of *gabai* could not be held for more than two consecutive years. Every three years seven *ba'alei takanot* were elected. In addition, the society appointed a *magid* (preacher), who was responsible for funeral orations, and a secretary. The latter was responsible not only for keeping the minute book and the accounts, but also for writing the inscriptions for tombstones and giving the address at the biannual feasts of the beadles.

The members of the small *ḥevra kadisha*—the beadles—were required to pay a membership fee like those of the large *ḥevra kadisha*. Some were permanent members, while others were elected only for limited periods. They were responsible for digging graves and other physical tasks connected with the actual burial and had their own secretary and minute book. They received no payment for their services but were often given gratuities, which they were obliged to pass on to a common fund for charitable purposes. Like the large *ḥevra kadisha*, they had their own place of worship.

The income of the *ḥevra kadisha* came from the weekly subscriptions of members, entrance fees of new members, burial fees (two-thirds of which went to the *tsedakah gedolah*), and the sale of burial plots. However, its expenditure—particularly on the upkeep of the cemetery as well as on the feasts of members—was

[35] Shilo, 'The Individual versus the Community in Jewish Law in Pre-Eighteenth Century Poland', 233. See also Ben-Sasson, *Thought and Conduct* (Heb.), 158, 229–31.

[36] On the *ḥevra kadisha* in Vilna, see I. Cohen, *Vilna*, 124–9.

generally in excess of its income so that it had to admit many new members and resort to the sale of honours, a practice which became increasingly frequent in the eighteenth century.

The high point of the year for the *ḥevra kadisha* was the annual banquet held on 15 Kislev. After the morning service, held in the Great Synagogue because the usual place of worship of the *ḥevra kadisha* was too small for all its members, ten members and ten beadles, together with the *magid*, went to the cemetery, where they offered up special prayers. In the evening, after a day-long fast, the members assembled for a ceremonial dinner, to which the head of the *beit din* (literally 'house of judgement') was invited and at which the *magid* delivered a theological discourse. The guests then sang a special hymn; in the late eighteenth century in Vilna they used an acrostic in Hebrew and Yiddish composed by Rabbi Mordecai b. Moses, who joined the society in 1770, which reflected on the fleeting nature of man's life on earth. It concluded:

> O man, in vain hast thou thy follies sown,
> For God on high the world doth judge alone,
> Where neither tears nor prayers can e'er atone.
>
> With food and drink and lusts thyself dost sate,
> And with thy tongue dost arrogantly prate,
> But deep below the earth will be thy fate.[37]

The beadles had two feasts of their own—one on the sabbath after Passover and the other on that after Sukkot. The *tsedakah gedolah* was obliged to provide money for these banquets and when they ceased to be held regularly the beadles began to neglect their duties. Special feasts were also held for the executive board of the *ḥevra kadisha* and a small number of guests. These occasions were crucial for cementing the solidarity of the group but were also responsible for its increasing indebtedness.

Ḥevrot were also established to provide religious education for the young, and especially for poor children and orphans. In Vilna the *ḥevrah talmud torah* was established for this purpose. Originally a department of the *kahal*, it soon became an independent body. It hired a teacher for its school, whose pupils were also given food and clothing, and supervised all the teachers in the various privately run schools in the community. The children were given a traditional education starting with the Pentateuch and moving on to the Mishnah, and went on the sabbath with young ushers (*belfer*) to pray in the synagogue. After the service there was usually a recapitulation of the lessons of the week, and at the end of the year there was an examination. The *ḥevrah talmud torah* was administered by a board of eight members and two wardens, who took part in the annual examination. It derived its income from the subscriptions of members, special donations and bequests, and a levy on teachers (*melamedim*), which amounted to about 6 per cent of their income.

[37] Quoted ibid. 128.

Another important area served by a *ḥevrah* was the obligation of looking after the sick, particularly those who could not afford to pay for such care. This was the province of the *bikur ḥolim* (visiting the sick), which maintained a shelter (*hekdesh*) for the sick, the infirm, and those unable to maintain themselves. In Vilna this *ḥevrah* employed a communal doctor, who also on occasion visited the sick in their homes.

Artisans were generally excluded from the principal *ḥevrot* because of their low status in Jewish society. They were also, for the most part, barred from membership of Christian artisan guilds. Consequently, they created their own *ḥevrot*, to regulate their trade, provide mutual support for their members, and train apprentices, and to perform religious functions which would gain prestige for their members. There were large numbers of these *ḥevrot*. Thus, in Vilna a record of income of the *bedek habayit* society dating from 1759 mentions *ḥevrot* of tailors, furriers, jewellers, tinsmiths, goldsmiths, glaziers, and candlestick-makers. Subsequently, guilds of butchers and musicians were also established. Only one Christian guild in Vilna, that of the barbers, admitted Jewish members, limited to two. From time to time the Jewish guilds made agreements with their Christian counterparts, primarily to control entry into a craft.

The members of an artisan *ḥevrah* were required to complete an apprenticeship of six years and to work for two years as journeymen before they were fully qualified. Every member had to pay an entrance fee, and provide a feast for his fellow members on entry to the guild and another when he married. After marriage an apprentice was considered a 'junior' for ten years and could only engage a limited number of apprentices and workmen. He then became a 'senior'. Particular trades were often restricted to a number of families, and sons and sons-in-law often followed in their father or father-in-law's footsteps.

Like other *ḥevrot*, guilds were headed by officers, usually a number of wardens and a committee. According to a decree of the Council of Lithuania of 1687, two of the wardens were to be elected from the guild and the other two appointed by the local *kahal*. As with Christian guilds, they combined secular and sacred functions and established separate prayer halls for their members. The religious activity of the guild was taken very seriously by its members. Thus, in Vilna in 1640 the tailors' guild donated an iron door for the Great Synagogue, and in 1674 the jewellers' guild presented an embroidered girdle for the Torah for Yom Kippur to the head of the *beit din*.

Two other important elements in the communal structure were the rabbinate and the *beit din*. (These two institutions are discussed in more detail in Chapter 5.) The rabbi was the religious head of the community and was referred to as Rav or *av beit din* (head of the *beit din*), denoting his primary official function, which was to serve as chief jurist and head of the judicial apparatus in the community.[38]

[38] On the functions of the rabbi, see Rosman, *The Lords' Jews*, 198–9, and Teller, 'The Laicization of Early Modern Jewish Society'.

Where there was a yeshiva, this was usually under his control. He had great authority, not only ecclesiastical but also secular. He took part in the meetings of the *kahal*, although he was not a member of the plenum, and no decision of any importance could be taken without his approval. Although he was a contract employee of the elders and had no independent standing apart from that derived from his personal charisma, he signed all important documents together with the elders. As the head of the *beit din*, he took part in many of its sittings. His seal was usually sought after the conclusion of contracts, wills, and deeds in order to give them the sanction of tradition, parallel to the Polish custom of having elections and budgets ratified by the seal of a higher authority.[39]

He preached only rarely—on the sabbaths before Passover and Yom Kippur, and on special occasions of celebration or distress. He enjoyed important honours: he was always called up third to the reading of the Torah; if he could sing, he would chant the additional service on Rosh Hashanah and the concluding service on Yom Kippur; he received the best *etrog* (citron), he presided at weddings, and was much sought after as a *sandak* (godfather at a circumcision). However, as he was appointed by the community, the question of where ultimate authority lay did sometimes arise.

The implementation of Jewish law was the responsibility of the *beit din*, comprising twelve judges, who were elected every year and sat in panels of three. They acted with the authority of the *kahal* and were concerned with all aspects of financial and business life, while the *kahal* dealt with cases of breach of the peace. The *beit din* legalized transfers of property and registered contracts for the sale of goods, *ḥazakot* (rights of priority), seats in the synagogue, promissory notes, and similar documents. It kept watch over weights and measures, and exercised a check on prices. Both the *kahal* and the *beit din* did their utmost to prevent Jewish litigants from going to a Christian court, and if any Jew resorted to such a court without the permission of the *kahal* he was liable to excommunication and other penalties. Nevertheless, Jews frequently did apply to Christian courts.

In Vilna the judges were divided into two groups, called the higher *beit din* and the lower *beit din*, although in important cases they sat in joint session. The president of the entire *beit din* was the rabbi. The senior group chose the *rosh beit din* (chairman of the *beit din*), who sometimes acted in place of the rabbi. The decisions of the court were recorded in its minute book by one of its members, the secretary and judge, who was also secretary of the *kahal*. Although new judges were elected every year, the larger communal assembly could also appoint judges for life or for definite periods. The judges were not given a fixed salary but divided among themselves and the *av beit din* the fees paid by the two litigant parties. In suits between Jews and Christians, if the plaintiff was a Christian, then there was a special court headed by a Christian judge, the *judex Judaeorum*, who was the

[39] For the position of the rabbinate, see Hundert, *Jews in Poland–Lithuania in the Eighteenth Century*, 84–6.

vice-governor or a deputy of his, but if the plaintiff was a Jew, then he appealed to the particular court to which the defendant was answerable. Other functionaries of the *beit din* were the beadles, who acted as messengers and court orderlies. Every month they chose by ballot a 'secret informer' (*rodef ne'elam*), who took an oath that he would not act against anybody contrary to Jewish law. This official, whose identity had to be kept an absolute secret, was regularly consulted by the beadles in regard to the punishment of individuals who had injured the community and where the secular authorities might object to the punishment imposed.

The bulk of the cases were civil, but some were criminal and in these the judges had at their disposal a range of penalties. These included fines, deprivation of the right of residence, the lash, imprisonment, and confinement in the stocks (*kuna*), usually located at the entrance to the main synagogue.

THE PROVINCIAL AND NATIONAL COUNCILS

The core of the autonomous system were the local *kehilot*. Above them were the provincial and national councils, which were initially established to apportion tax between different *kehilot*, while their other functions were added subsequently. A good indication of how the provincial assemblies worked can be gathered from the history of the Council of Wielkopolska.[40] It had at its disposal a clerk, tax assessors, and tax collectors. It is first mentioned in 1597, and we have records of its meeting throughout the seventeenth century and in the eighteenth century until 1733 in different towns of the province, including Poznań, Gniezno, Kalisz, Neustadt an der Warta, Jarocin, and Kobylin. Its functions included the election of the chief rabbi of Wielkopolska, who had extensive powers over the Jews of the area, the adoption of measures of protection against common dangers (above all ritual murder accusations), the collection of the poll tax and other levies needed for common welfare, the negotiation of loans for communal purposes, and the approval and subsidization of books.

A similar provincial council, the *va'ad medinat rusyah* (the council of the 'lands of Russia'), existed for the communities in the Mogilev, Mstislavl, and Vitebsk districts in the Grand Duchy of Lithuania. Like that in Wielkopolska, its principal function was the apportionment and collection of taxes among the Jewish *kehilot* in the area. In addition, it functioned as the highest legislative and judicial body for the Jews of the region, regulating economic activity, including the purchase and orderly transfer of leases, and adjudicating in disputes between *kehilot*, or between individuals and *kehilot*. One unusual feature was the key role in the council played by the provincial rabbi (*rav hamedinah*), who was the council's highest official. He directed the council's fiscal affairs between one meeting and the next, apportioning taxes and disbursing funds. He also exercised control over local rabbis, who were paid by the council. This power aroused some resentment, and

[40] On this, see *The Jewish Encyclopedia*, x. 141.

there are several recorded complaints to the local landowner (the Sieniawa-Czartoryski entail) and local courts about his alleged abuse of power. In 1746 the *kehilot* of Shklov and Kopys even briefly seceded from the council in protest at the way the tax burden had been apportioned.[41]

The national councils, the Council of the Lands for the Korona and the Council of Lithuania for the Grand Duchy, emerged in the late sixteenth century, the first recorded meeting of the Council of the Lands occurring in 1580 and that of the Council of Lithuania in 1623.[42] Originally there was one national council for the whole of the Commonwealth (Rzeczpospolita) and it is originally described as the Council of the Three Lands (Va'ad Shalosh Aratsot)—Poland, Rus, and Lithuania—or, more rarely, as the Council of the Five Lands—Wielkopolska, Małopolska, Rus, Lithuania, and Volhynia. In Polish documents it is sometimes referred to as 'Congressus Judaeorum' (the Council of Jews). In 1613 Zygmunt III Vasa (1587–1632) established separate tax assessments for the Jews of the Korona and those of the Grand Duchy, which led in 1623 to the establishment of a separate Council for the State of Lithuania (Va'ad Medinat Lita). This council was also sometimes referred to as the Council of the Three [Four or Five] Main Districts of Lithuania (Va'ad Shalosh [Arba or Ḥamesh] Medinot Rashiyot Delita)—Brest, Grodno, Pinsk, Vilna, and Slutsk.

After the establishment of the Council of Lithuania, the designation Council of Four Lands (Va'ad Arba Aratsot)—Wielkopolska, Małopolska, Red Rus, and Volhynia—became established for that in the Korona and figures exclusively in the documents of the seventeenth century. The term was still usually employed in the eighteenth century in spite of the fact that many more regions were now represented. The Council of Four Lands usually met biannually at the great fairs held in the spring in Lublin, which began on the Catholic holiday Gromnice (Candlemas) in February and lasted about a month, and from the beginning of the seventeenth century at that held in Jarosław towards the end of the summer. In exceptional circumstances meetings took place in other towns, as in Tyszowce in 1583 and Łęczyca in 1668. In the eighteenth century meetings also took place in Stary Konstantynów and Pilica. The Council of Lithuania, for its part, met biannually or triannually at Brest, Zabłudów, Seltsy, and also in some other places.

The number of delegates who attended the meetings of the Council of Four Lands seems to have varied. According to Nathan Nata Hannover (d. 1683), one representative was sent to the council from each *kehilah* and they were joined by

[41] On the secession, see Trunk, 'The Council of the Lands of Russia' (Yid.), 70–3. On this council, see ibid.; D. Fishman, *Russia's First Modern Jews*, 2–3; Mstislavsky [Dubnow], 'Oblastnye kagal'nye seimy v voevodstve volynskom i v Belorussii (1666–1764)'; Dubnow (ed.), *The Minute Book of the Council of Lithuania* (Heb.); and Marek, 'Belorusskaya sinagoga i ee territoriya'.

[42] For the Council of Four Lands see Halpern (ed.), *Minutes of the Council of Four Lands* (Heb.). For minutes of the Council of Lithuania, see Dubnow (ed.), *The Minute Book of the Council of Lithuania* (Heb.). In addition, see Rosman, 'A Minority Views the Majority', and Goldberg, 'The Jewish Sejm'.

the six leading rabbis of Poland.[43] The minute books of individual communities show that only the most important *kehilot* sent delegates to the council, while regional capitals (Poznań, Kraków, Lviv, and Ostróg) each sent two or even more. The signatures of fifteen to twenty-five delegates—though often the signatures of the six rabbis only—are usually found attached to the decisions of the council. The total number of delegates, together with the rabbis, seems usually to have been around thirty. The Council of Lithuania was somewhat smaller. It was originally composed of delegates from the three most important communities—Pinsk, Brest, and Grodno. Vilna began to send delegates in 1652 and Slutsk in 1691.

The relationship between the two councils is not entirely clear. Before the formal establishment of the Council of Lithuania, the Lithuanian delegates usually held preliminary meetings at Brest before taking part in the deliberations of the Council of the Lands, but the decisions taken there may not have been binding. There are also cases where the Lithuanian delegates did not feel themselves bound by the decisions of the Council of the Lands. After 1623 the Council of Lithuania soon established its full independence but also seems to have accepted a subordinate position to the Council of Four Lands, and where differences occurred, the authority of the latter seems to have prevailed. Thus, it was decided to place Tykocin, a town on the border of the Korona and the Grand Duchy, under the jurisdiction of the Council of Four Lands although formerly it had been regarded as part of Lithuania. Similarly, in a dispute between Tykocin and Grodno concerning the smaller neighbouring communities of Zabłudów, Gródek, and Choroszcz (Horodok and Khvoroshcha), these were assigned by the Council of Four Lands to Tykocin. In this case, however, the decision was not accepted as final by the Council of Lithuania.[44]

Polish Jews were very proud of their national councils. Nathan Nata Hannover has given a description of the functioning of the Council of Four Lands which is impressive, even if one takes into account that he wrote this in the aftermath of the Khmelnytsky Uprising in a work in which, as an exile, he idealized a lost world:

The representatives of the Four Lands had sessions twice in the year . . . at the fair in Lublin, between Purim and Passover, and at the fair in Jarosław in the month of Av or Elul (July–August). The representatives of the Four Lands resembled the Sanhedrin in the session chamber in the Temple of Jerusalem. They had jurisdiction over all the Jews of the kingdom of Poland with power to issue injunctions and binding decisions [*takanot*] and to impose penalties at their discretion. Every difficult case was submitted to them for trial. To make the task easier for themselves, the representatives of the Four Lands would select special judges from each land, who were called 'land-judges' [*dayanei medinah*] and who tried civil suits; while criminal cases, disputes over priority of possession [*ḥazakah*] and other difficult cases were tried by the representatives themselves [in full session].[45]

[43] Hannover, *Abyss of Despair*, 119.

[44] On these disputes, see Dubnow (ed.), *The Minute Book of the Council of Lithuania*, 278–89.

[45] Hannover, *Abyss of Despair*, 120.

Dov Ber of Bolechów (1723–1805), who was a delegate to the Council of Four Lands, saw in it 'a fragment of redemption and a scrap of honour, proving that Almighty God in his great pity and lovingkindness had not deserted us', while after the dissolution of the councils the preacher Hillel b. Ze'ev Wolf lamented, 'Without the Council, there is no-one to go to the lords of the land and the king to bow down and to make requests because of the weight of taxes and evil decrees.'[46]

We are able to investigate the activity of the councils from their minute books—that of the Council of Lithuania survived into the modern period and that of the Korona has been reconstructed by Israel Halpern and Israel Bartal. In addition, copies of the decisions of the councils have been preserved in the minute books of individual *kehilot*. The minutes of the councils were kept in rabbinic Hebrew, as were its resolutions. When they sought a wider audience for their enactments, these were read publicly in synagogues and were written in Yiddish.

The principal responsibility of the councils was to apportion the levy of the poll tax by individual communities, and it was for this reason that they were given the recognition and support of the state authorities, who described them as 'Jewish assemblies' (Congressus Judaeorum) or 'Jewish Sejms' in official documents. The Council of Four Lands apportioned the burden of the poll tax between its four constituent provinces, while the detailed apportionment of taxes within each province and each community was the task of the provincial councils (*va'adei hagalil*) and *kehilot*. By the eighteenth century, representatives of the Crown Treasury attended meetings of the council and exercised a supervisory role over their activities. They appointed Jewish trustees to report to them on the council's activities, in effect subordinating these bodies to the control of the Crown. In 1717, as part of the general financial settlement enacted by the Silent Sejm (see appendix to Part I), the global sum to be contributed by the Council of the Lands was fixed at 220,000 florins for Poland and 60,000 for Lithuania.

Like other parliamentary bodies which were originally convened to ratify taxation, the councils soon acquired additional functions. One of the most important of these was in the judicial sphere. Indeed even before the formal constitution of the Council of the Lands, rabbis from the principal *kehilot* seem to have convened to deal with disputed questions of Jewish law (on this, see Chapter 5). They usually dealt with conflicts between two *kehilot* or between an individual and a *kehilah*, and seem to have met in Lublin, the residence of Rabbi Shalom Shakhna b. Joseph (d. 1558), a leading scholar who had established a major yeshiva here and who was the father-in-law of Moses Isserles (see Chapter 5). As early as 1533 Zygmunt I of Poland characterized one of their decisions in a private case as that of the 'supreme court' for the Jews 'in accordance with their own law'.[47] In 1559 a

[46] Ber of Bolechów, *Memoirs*, 40; H. Wolf, *Heikel ben shaḥar*, 22*b*, quoted in Hundert, *Jews in Poland–Lithuania in the Eighteenth Century*, 13.

[47] Bershadsky (ed.), *Russko-evreiskii arkhiv*, i, no. 152.

meeting in Lublin of rabbis and *rashei yeshivot* (heads of yeshivas) of the 'Three Lands' gave approbation (*haskamah*) for the printing of the Babylonian Talmud in 1559 for use in Polish yeshivas. This was at a time when, although the Talmud had been removed by the papal curia from the index of prohibited books, to print it still needed formal consent from a Church censor appointed by the Holy Office or by the local bishop, a regulation which does not seem to have been enforced in Poland. There does, however, seem to have been a censor of Hebrew books in Kraków in the mid-seventeenth century.

The principal function of the court of the Council of Four Lands, which seems to have been made up exclusively of rabbis, was to settle disputes between *kehilot* over their respective boundaries, which had important implications for their tax burden and their income. It also dealt with conflicts over where a case should be tried, and acted as a court of appeal from the courts of the *kehilot* and regional assemblies. In 1594 the council passed an edict requiring rabbinic sanction for books published in Hebrew, and the court attached to it sometimes decided whether such sanction should be granted.

As bodies which were in some senses organs of the state, the councils felt obliged to support state policy. Thus, in 1580 the Council of the Lands confirmed the law forbidding Jews to engage in farming state taxes and customs duties in Wielkopolska, Małopolska, and Mazovia which had been adopted by the Polish Sejm in Piotrków in 1538, claiming that Jewish tax farmers and leaseholders, in their pursuit of gain, had given rise to accusations against Jews in general, and had excited the Christian populace against them. The council also gave its support to edicts forbidding Jewish settlement in specified areas (the privilege *de non tolerandis Judaeis*), reminding its co-religionists in 1669 of the prohibition on Jews settling in Warsaw. Such edicts were read publicly in all synagogues with the threat of excommunication for those who failed to observe them.

At the same time the councils saw themselves as bodies representing the entire Jewish community in Poland–Lithuania and attempted to put their case to the authorities, sending intercessors (*shtadlanim*) to Warsaw during the sessions of the Sejm in order to alleviate the tax burden on Jews and to ensure the maintenance of the rights they enjoyed. Lobbying was particularly important at 'Coronation Sejms', those held after the election of a new king, since, as we have seen, the new monarch was expected to confirm the rights and privileges granted to the Jews by his predecessors. The councils also attempted to combat anti-Jewish activity and in particular accusations of blood libel and host desecration. Such activities were expensive and were financed by special levies on the *kehilot*.

Much of the activity of the councils was concerned with the smooth functioning of the institutions of Jewish self-government. Communal harmony was considered of crucial importance because of the danger of malcontents appealing over the heads of the communal leadership to the king or prominent nobles or churchmen. Thus, at Tyszowce in 1583 the council laid down that the election of the *kahal* board and local rabbis should take place without recourse to the Christian authorities, and regulations were enacted in 1587, 1590, 1635, and 1640 condemning the use of bribes or the support of the Polish authorities to obtain a rabbinic post. In 1628 the Council of Lithuania laid down that 'No individual in any of the communities may go to the royal court in a town or in the country or to any of the assistants of the governor or to any government official without permission from the elders. Each community must be watchful in this matter.'

In a meeting in Jarosław in 1671 the council stressed the damaging effect on all Jews in the Commonwealth of a dispute which had arisen in the *kehilah* of Chełm, since such conflicts led to the intervention of 'nobles and priests', with serious implications for all Jewish communities. Accordingly, it authorized the leaders of communities and of regional councils to

> prosecute persons so intriguing and offending and to punish them with the ban of excommunication, with fines or with imprisonment . . . at the cost of the offenders . . . Such persons should never be nominated to any office in any community or district, nor should they have the right of *ḥazakah* [see Chapter 4] . . . since they have no pity on themselves, on the community or district, or on the whole of Israel . . .

The regulations dealing with economic life reflect the councils' desire to preserve communal harmony and avoid actions which could provoke non-Jewish hostility. Many decrees of the councils call for the prosecution of those who, by their activity, brought upon Jews the wrath of the government and of the Christian populace. Council decrees in 1671, 1677, and later prohibit Jews from leasing estates or other enterprises from Poles without the knowledge of the *kehilot* of which they are members. Merchants are ordered to deal honestly with the Christians and not to engage in unlawful practices which could harm the Jewish community. In 1607 the Council of the Lands had one of its members, the Lublin rabbi Joshua b. Alexander Hakohen Falk, draw up a series of detailed rules regulating Jewish economic activity, dealing with the granting of credit, the way interest was to be assessed, and the obligations incurred under promissory notes with the intention of curbing abuses.

This was also a concern of the Council of Lithuania, which passed an edict in 1623 enjoining communal leaders to expose any attempts at fraud they discovered on the part of Jews borrowing money or goods from a nobleman or leasing noble estates or other sources of income. If the person involved failed to respond appropriately, the communal leaders were to declare the transaction void 'in order that the Christians concerned may not suffer loss'.

The importance of avoiding conflict within the community is evident in the rules for the issuing of loans established by the Council of Four Lands of 1684. Under these the lenders of small sums were not to charge 'exorbitant interest' and the amount of interest was clearly specified:

Any loan of less than 100 and more than 50 zlotys is to be charged the interest rate fixed for 100 zlotys. Any loan of 50 zlotys or less is excluded from this regulation and one is not permitted to take more than half a 'gadol' [30 gadol = 1 zloty] from every Polish shak [2 zlotys]. Whoever exacts more than half [a gadal per] two zlotys is guilty of usury. What has gone before is done with, and from now on this reckoning applies and let there be peace.

Similar regulations were issued by the Council of Lithuania. A regulation of 1623 limited competition within the *kehilot*, making it clear that the law of monopoly was to apply in the case of a lease but only in the *kehilah* where the person who had contracted the loan lived. This arrangement did not apply to somebody who did not live in the *kehilah* (paragraph 74).

The importance of having a 'special overseer' for weights and measures in each *kehilah* was laid down in an edict of 1628, while in the same year a decree forbade the contracting of loans with non-Jews without the permission of the *kehilah*. Those seeking to borrow money from 'any non-Jew or nobleman' required the consent of the rabbi and at least one elder. If this were not obtained, the lender must be informed that the borrower was 'untrustworthy', and if the loan had already been concluded, the borrower was to be expelled from the *kehilah*.

Attempts were also made to control Jewish population movement. Thus, in 1673 a regulation of the Council of the Lands attempted to regulate migration from one Jewish community to another:

The heads [*alufim*, *ketzinim*, *roznim*] of the Pińczów community have appeared before us with the complaint and plea concerning their *kehilah*, where poverty is increasing from day to day, on account of persons arriving there from other *kehilot* and provinces in order to settle. Neither they nor their forefathers possessed any right of domicile here. For this reason the inhabitants who have resided there from time immemorial by virtue of their parents' domicile are unable to earn their livelihood because of the great burden they have to bear . . . hence we decree and concur in enforcing on behalf of the leaders of the Pińczów community, granting them the right to enact as they see fit, as is appropriate to the occasion and the turbulent time and in accordance with the state and situation in the *kehilah*, with anyone possessing the right to protest or prevent enforcement. Moreover, even if anyone had established his right of residence here long ago, and had moved to another province and community, and now wishes to resume residence and settlement here, they will still be entitled to control this as they see fit having full and complete power.

Itinerant beggars also concerned the Council of Lithuania. In a regulation of 1623 it laid down that

Beggars invading Lithuania and Russia [meaning Belarus], especially those who disguise themselves as scholars and pious persons while committing secretly various wicked acts, shall not be allowed to remain in any one community more than twenty-four hours.

The fear that informers might prejudice the situation of the Jewish community by recourse to the civil authorities was ever-present. In the month of Iyar (May–June) 1725 the Council of Four Lands issued the following proclamation against informers:

A solemn and terrible *ḥerem* [proclaimed by] shofar blowing and the extinguishing of candles is enacted against informers and slanderers who disclose Jewish secrets . . . at customs [barriers] and inform against individuals, thus leading to the confiscation of Jewish property by the nobles and clergy and also locally in respect of presumed ownership . . .

One of the main preoccupations of the councils was to uphold Jewish religious traditions. They attempted to provide supervision over the Jewish school system from the *ḥeder*s (elementary schools) to the yeshivas and they also acted as moral censors. Thus, in 1607 the Council of the Lands called for the dietary laws (*kashrut*) to be strictly observed, for Jews drinking in inns with Christians to be struck off the list of reputable members of the community and to be ineligible for office in the *kahal*, and for Jewish dress to differ from that of Christians. Modesty and moderation were to be observed in dress, especially by women. Jewish behaviour also concerned the Council of Lithuania, which in 1623 laid down that 'Every community shall carefully guard against card- and dice-playing, and offenders shall be fined and subjected to corporal punishment.'

The councils were also concerned with heresy, taking action against the Sabbatians and Frankists in the eighteenth century. An indication of the importance of the Council of Four Lands in the Jewish world beyond Poland–Lithuania is that it was consulted when Rabbi Jacob Emden of Altona (1697–1776) accused Rabbi Jonathan Eybeschuetz, the chief rabbi of Hamburg, Altona, and Wandsbeck, of being a secret Sabbatian.

Many of the decrees concerned social life. Thus, in 1623 the Council of Lithuania passed an enactment that

A young man who is not yet eighteen years of age who marries without his father's consent, or, if his father is dead, that of his relatives—such an action is legally null and void.

A decree of 1628 laid down:

Women who are involved in trade and whose business takes them into the homes of non-Jews may not enter such houses unless they are accompanied by their husband and one young man or married man.

A decree of 1627 regulated the issue of intestacy:

If a man should die without appointing executors in his lifetime, the court must seal his dwelling and his goods immediately after his death and make an accurate list of his possessions. [It must] appoint as executors upright men of wealth comparable to that of the deceased as provided by law. These men will supervise the estate for the orphans so that it bears fruit. The court must also appoint auditors to whom the executors will present their accounts.

Each of the Three Communities at the time of its elections must elect three 'Fathers of Orphans' who will receive an annual accounting from the executors and will record the sum belonging to each orphan in their minute book every year.

Another decree of the Council of Lithuania called on the three communities 'to arrange annually for the marriage of thirty poor girls, giving each a dowry of thirty gulden'.

By the early eighteenth century the two national councils were increasingly subordinated to the Crown, which diminished their prestige in Jewish eyes. The local *kehilot* also faced growing difficulties. Economic decline meant that their indebtedness increased significantly. This has led a number of scholars, most notably Israel Dinur and Raphael Mahler, to write of a 'crisis' in Jewish communal institutions occurring at this time. Yet the *kahal* did continue to operate effectively, and claims that 'the Jewish communal establishment was being run by strongmen, habitués of the nobles' courts and those with access to political influence . . . [turning] Jewish self-government into a fiction, a caricature' are exaggerated.[48] At the same time, the interference of royal officials, and even more of the noble owners of towns, increased significantly in the eighteenth century. Individuals with strong ties to noble courts now attempted with increasing success to emancipate themselves from communal control. Frequently, too, the noble owner of a town or his agent had to approve the judgments of communal courts and interfered in communal finances. An unquestionably hostile observer, Bishop Franciszek Kobielski, in an enforced conversionary dispute with the Jews of Brody in 1743, mocked their claim that they enjoyed extensive self-government and asserted that the prophecy 'The sceptre will not depart from Judah . . . until Shilo comes' had not been fulfilled (Genesis 49: 10):

> How abject is this sceptre—childish and comical—your [self-rule] and the freedom to observe the Jewish commandments are leased from Christian lords. Even the office of rabbi can only be held by someone who has purchased it, for life, or for a fixed time, leasing the rabbinate from a Christian lord. The position of communal elder, for life or for a fixed time, also costs a goodly sum. It is only after you have paid the Crown, the provincial governor [*wojewoda*], the lieutenant-governor [*podwojewoda*] and various other officials that you are able to enjoy your synagogues and to live a Jewish life . . .[49]

Nobles also often attempted, not always successfully, to prevent Jews from leaving towns in their possession. In addition, individual Jews now often made appeals from local Jewish courts to Crown courts or courts under noble control. There were also cases where the town owner appointed the communal leadership. According to a charter granted by Józef Potocki to the Jews of Kutów in 1715, two of the elders were to be elected and two appointed by the town owner.[50] The appointment of *kehilah* officials required ratification, and, on the estates of the Sieniawa-Czartoryski entail, the largest group of estates in eighteenth-century Poland–Lithuania with a Jewish population of over 30,000, 'Jews with close ties to the owner enjoyed a dominant position in the Jewish community.'[51]

There was also increasing conflict in local communities. This should not be seen, as it was by some Marxist historians like Raphael Mahler, as the outcome of

[48] Dinur, *As Generations Change* (Heb.), 100, 104. On the question of how critical was the situation of Jewish self-government, see Hundert, *Jews in Poland–Lithuania in the Eighteenth Century*, 98–118.

[49] Quoted in Hundert, *Jews in Poland–Lithuania in the Eighteenth Century*, 101–2.

[50] Goldberg, *Jewish Privileges in the Polish Commonwealth*, 142.

[51] Rosman, *The Lords' Jews*, 191.

conflict between the communal elite and lower-status artisans. Although artisans and similar groups did participate in such conflicts, they were usually the product of rifts within the elite in which one group sought wider social support. One such situation occurred in Leszno, the largest Jewish community in Wielkopolska, where in 1763 excessive taxation provoked a revolt of one section of the community supported by artisan guilds. This led to the intervention of the town's owner, August Sułkowski, who re-established the power of the communal elite. However, in 1792, shortly before Wielkopolska came under Prussian rule, the communal leadership conceded to the artisan guilds a degree of participation in local affairs. Similar conflicts took place in the mid-eighteenth century in Lublin, Dubno, and Šiauliai.[52]

CONCLUSION

Much of the interest in Jewish communal structures in Poland–Lithuania has concentrated on the history of the Council of the Lands and the Council of Lithuania. Important as these bodies were, the core of the system of Jewish self-government lay in the local *kehilot*. It was here that the tradition of Jewish self-government was developed, which gave to Jews the sense that they controlled the most important aspects of their life. It was a fundamental aspect of Jewish life in Poland–Lithuania and, in the royal and noble towns alike, gave the Jews their sense of rootedness. Medieval forms of corporatism were anathema both to governments inspired by the principles of the Enlightenment and to their liberal and constitutional successors. Yet in those places where some modernized form of Jewish self-government was retained, the transformation of the Jews from a religious and cultural community linked by a common faith into citizens or subjects of the countries where they lived was most successful. Similarly, the communal self-government which was exercised through the *kehilah*, for all its imperfections, is one important element in the democratic tradition of the State of Israel. In this sense, the legacy of Jewish self-government was one of the most fundamental legacies of the Jewish experience in Poland–Lithuania.

[52] On this general question, see Hundert, *Jews in Poland–Lithuania in the Eighteenth Century*, 99–118; on Leszno, R. Mahler, *Jews in Old Poland in the Light of Figures* (Yid.), i. 330–52.

THREE

JEWISH PLACES: ROYAL TOWNS AND NOBLE TOWNS

> The Polish Crown flourishes as it is composed of people of diverse estates, particularly in regard to their religious allegiance, on the principle that no authority shall exercise power over faith, honour, and conscience. We wish therefore to secure a peaceful life especially to those persons who have suffered persecution not because of any crimes or evil deeds, but for other reasons, so that they may enjoy all the liberties of the laws enacted by us.
>
> HIERONIM SIENIAWSKI, *Privilege granted to the Jews in Oleszyce*, 1576

BY THE MID-SEVENTEENTH CENTURY the Jewish community of Poland–Lithuania was the largest in Ashkenaz. A century later it was the largest Jewish community in the world with a population of over three-quarters of a million, and probably made up more than a third of world Jewry. In the two previous chapters the relations between Jews and Christians in Poland–Lithuania and the structure and character of Jewish communal autonomy have been described. This chapter will examine the locations of Jewish life in Poland and Lithuania.

There were four types of location. First, there were royal towns like Kraków, Vilna, Poznań, and Lviv, which were under the jurisdiction of the king or his governor (*wojewoda*) and, in smaller towns, the *starosta*. Then there were the 'suburbs' (areas outside the town walls not formally under the jurisdiction of the municipality) and *jurydyki* or *libertacje* (noble or clerical enclaves) of royal towns. Thirdly, there were the many towns established on the estates of the nobility; and finally there were the villages.

Royal towns were adversely affected by the growing economic and social dominance of the nobility in the Polish–Lithuanian Commonwealth, and in Polish urban history the mid-seventeenth century was not as important a turning point as it was in the realms of politics and culture. The movement of Jews from royal to noble towns had already begun in the late sixteenth century so that, in the words of the Polish economic historian Andrzej Wyrobisz, the seventeenth century in Poland–Lithuania was 'an age of small towns', by which he meant noble towns.[1]

1 For his views, see Wyrobisz, 'Materiały do dziejów handlu w miasteczkach polskich na początku XVIII wieku'; 'Rola miast prywatnych w Polsce w XVI i XVII wieku'; 'Small Towns in 16th and 17th Century Poland'; and 'Functional Types of Polish Towns in the 16th–18th Centuries'. On the history of Polish towns, see also Bogucka, 'Polish Towns between the Sixteenth and Eighteenth Centuries'; Ptaśnik, *Miasto i mieszczaństwo w dawnej Polsce*; Bogucka and Samsonowicz, *Dzieje miast i mieszczaństwa*

In addition, economic decline began in Poland in the late sixteenth and early seventeenth centuries, well before the Khmelnytsky Uprising in 1648. There was a minor recovery during the reign of Jan Sobieski (1676–96), but the nadir was reached in the first decades of the eighteenth century. From around 1720 a slow economic recovery began, which continued until the partitions.

JEWS IN THE ROYAL TOWNS

The royal towns date back to the earliest period of Polish recorded history, but they do not really become significant until the thirteenth and fourteenth centuries. The reign of Kazimierz the Great (r. 1333–70), who 'found Poland wood and left it brick', was particularly important in urban development. Many of these towns followed a common pattern of development which can be seen in Breslau (Wrocław), Kraków, Vilna, and Prague. The town was divided into two parts, one part being the seat of the local ruler (the *burg*, or *zamek*), which was often set on a hill or separated from the rest of the town by a river and dominated by the ruler's residence and the cathedral. The city proper was built around a central market square, where the wealthiest merchants resided, tradesmen conducted their business, and a large church was built to serve the merchants and artisans—in Kraków, the Church of the Virgin.

The burghers governed themselves and controlled their economic activities through an elected city council (*magistrat*) without interference from the local ruler. They also had their own courts, which dealt with criminal and some civil matters, and sometimes even had a police force. Their legal rights were based on German municipal law derived from the principal German mercantile centres like Lübeck, Magdeburg, and Nuremberg. A municipal government on this pattern was introduced in Toruń in 1231, Poznań in 1253, Danzig in 1255, Kraków in 1257, Breslau in 1261, Lublin in 1317, Warsaw in 1334, and Lviv in 1356. The charter granted to the burghers of Poznań by Duke Przemyśl and Duke Bolesław of Wielkopolska, for example, laid down the level of customs dues which the city was obliged to pay the Crown, and gave it control over the river Warta and its banks for a mile on each side of the city and over a number of villages near the town. The burghers were to enjoy the benefits 'of the law according to the forms of the city of Magdeburg, unchanged and unaltered'. The *wójt*, an official appointed by the duke, was to establish a court to resolve all disputes: no burgher could be obliged to appear before any other court to answer for a debt or any other matter. There was to be an annual fair, which would be free from ducal control. To ensure order in the city the duke would provide at his own expense four guards and two archers. The burghers were to establish a system of weights and measures and would receive half the proceeds of the fines of those who gave false

w Polsce przedrozbiorowej; and Gierszewski, *Struktura gospodarcza i funkcje rynkowe mniejszych miast województwa pomorskiego w XVI i XVII w.*

measure. Burghers were obliged to defend the country within its borders but did not have to serve abroad.[2]

The municipal governmental structure consisted of an executive and a judiciary, which were responsible to a larger assembly. In Lublin, for instance, there were three to five consuls, three to five magistrates, and an assembly which numbered at different times between twelve and forty members. The office of mayor was held in rotation by the consuls. The system was essentially oligarchic, and the franchise in the elections to the assembly, which were held every spring, was limited to the small group of burghers who were citizens of the town.[3]

The second half of the fifteenth and the first half of the sixteenth centuries was an age of urban expansion in east central Europe. By the mid-sixteenth century the population of Breslau, which was now a part of the Habsburg-ruled kingdom of Bohemia, had reached 100,000. The largest town in the Commonwealth was the port of Danzig, which had a population of 50,000. The other towns were somewhat smaller—Kraków (and the adjacent town of Kazimierz) had a population of perhaps 20,000–25,000, Lviv's population numbered around 25,000, that of Poznań around 20,000, that of Vilna perhaps 15,000, and that of Lublin somewhat over 5,000.

These and other royal towns were very adversely affected by the wars of the mid-seventeenth century, as a result of which, it is estimated, Kraków lost half its population and Lublin one-third. There was a recovery in the last three decades of the seventeenth century, but neither Kraków nor Lublin regained their lost population. One consequence of this was that the urban population of Poland fell from 25 to 16 per cent between 1600 and 1750, although this figure is deceptive since it depends on what is classed as a town, fails to take into account the growth of noble enclaves and 'suburbs' of royal towns, and reflects the growing importance of the much smaller private (noble) towns, many of which were little more than villages.[4]

It was partly in order to stem the flight from royal towns that the royal *starosta* induced the king in 1674 to issue an edict granting the freedom to sell and to trade in the royal towns of Chęciny, Chełm, and Kazimierz to 'people of all nations found in our dominions . . . Armenians, Greeks, and Jews now found there' or who might come in the future.[5] A similar decree had been issued in the previous year by the *starosta* of Nowy Sącz which resulted in the town renouncing the privilege it enjoyed *de non tolerandis Judaeis* (of not tolerating Jews).[6]

[2] See Franke (ed.), *Die Residenzstadt Posen und ihre Verwaltung im Jahre 1911*, 12–17.

[3] Ryabinin, *Rada miejska lubelska w XVII w.*, 2.

[4] Małecki, 'Le Rôle de Cracovie dans l'économie polonaise aux XVIe, XVIIe et XVIIIe siècles', 116–17; Stankowa, 'Zmierzch znaczenia Lublina'; Gieysztorowa, 'Research into the Demographic History of Poland', 12; Manikowski, 'Zmiany czy stagnacja?', 787. This issue is discussed in Hundert, 'Security and Dependence', 1–5.

[5] Quoted in Hundert, 'Security and Dependence', 7.

[6] Ibid. 8 and R. Mahler, 'Z dziejów Żydów w Nowym Sączu w XVII i XVIII wieku', 4–5.

Jewish life in pre-partition Poland–Lithuania was very much centred on the individual Jewish settlements, and, as we have seen, *kehilot* zealously protected their right to control who could live within them and to ban the settlement of undesirable outsiders. To understand the evolution of Jewish life it is necessary to look in detail at its development in individual towns, as has been done in a series of studies on Kraków, Lviv, Lublin, Poznań, Przemyśl, and Vilna.[7]

The size of the Jewish population of royal towns is difficult to measure. Although Kazimierz and Kraków were separate towns until 1800, sixteenth- and seventeenth-century Jews of Kazimierz generally referred to themselves as residents of Kraków. Majer Bałaban, citing the treasury book of Kazimierz, where Jews had begun to move in significant numbers after they were expelled from Kraków in 1495, states that there were 2,060 Jews in Kazimierz in 1578.[8] By 1764 this had risen to perhaps 4,150.

In 1578 approximately 1,500 Jews lived in Lviv, where there were two Jewish communities, one inside the town walls and one outside. At this time the total population of the town was perhaps 12,500.[9] By 1648 both natural population growth and immigration from western Europe had helped swell Lviv's Jewish population to maybe 4,800 of the approximately 25,000 residents. By 1764 their number had risen to 7,400, which made this the second largest Jewish settlement in Poland–Lithuania (the largest—8,600—was in the private town of Brody, owned in the second half of the eighteenth century by one of the many branches of the Potocki family, and the third largest—6,000—was in the town of Leszno, a private town in Wielkopolska owned by the Sułkowski family).[10]

In Poznań in 1567 Jews lived in approximately fifty of the over 400 houses in the town. By 1619 some 762 Jewish families were living in 141 homes. The total number of individuals may have been around 3,000.[11] By 1714 this seems to have fallen to around 2,500.

The Jewish population of Vilna in the early seventeenth century appears to have numbered around 3,000. By the end of the eighteenth century, according

[7] See e.g. Bałaban, *Historja Żydów w Krakowie i na Kazimierzu, 1304–1868*; id., *Żydzi lwowscy na przełomie XVI i XVII wieku*; id., *Die Judenstadt von Lublin*; Reiner (ed.), *Kroke, Kazimierz, Kraków* (Heb.); Schorr, *Żydzi w Przemyślu do końca XVIII wieku*; Teller, *A Confined Life* (Heb.); I. Cohen, *Vilna*.

[8] The view of Bałaban that the Jews were expelled from Kraków in 1495 set out in his *Historja Żydów w Krakowie i na Kazimierzu, 1304–1868*, 50–2, has recently been challenged by Wyrozumska, 'Did King Jan Olbracht Banish the Jews from Kraków?', 27–32, 36–7.

[9] E. Nadel-Golobic estimates the total population of Lviv between 1574 and 1591 at 12,344; see 'Armenians and Jews in Medieval Lvov', 352.

[10] See the table in Hundert, *Jews in Poland–Lithuania in the Eighteenth Century*, which is based on R. Mahler, *Jews in Old Poland in the Light of Figures* (Yid.), i. 62.

[11] Guldon and Wijaczka, 'Osadnictwo żydowskie w województwach poznańskim i kaliskim w XVI–XVII wieku', 66, 73. Tollet, 'Marchands et hommes d'affaires juifs dans la Pologne des Wasa (1588–1668)', 31–2, gives a higher estimate for the Jewish population.

to Raphael Mahler, the Jewish population had grown to around 3,900. A recent Lithuanian study has given the higher estimate of 6,000.[12]

In the royal towns the Jews generally lived in houses grouped together around a square or set of courtyards or along an alleyway—a pattern of settlement which had already been established in the areas of Germany from which most of them came, and which was often not the result of legislation but reflected rather Jewish self-interest and convenience. This area, often described as the 'Jewish street', which referred not to a single street but to a set of adjacent streets, was often enclosed by a wall with gates that could be locked at night. Jews had mixed feelings about having non-Jews in their midst. In 1558 the community in Luboml (about 25 miles east of Chełm) took the view that as long as Christians lived in their midst, there would be no danger of outsiders setting fire to the Jewish quarter for fear of killing Christians. Accordingly, the community forbade any Jew, on pain of excommunication, to purchase additional houses from non-Jews who lived within the Jewish area. This ordinance was strengthened in 1577 when it was enacted that anyone who had disobeyed it was to resell the property to non-Jews.[13] A contrary example is to be found in Sandomierz in the mid-seventeenth century, where local Jews feared the repossession by a non-Jewish creditor of a bankrupt Jewish debtor's home 'in the middle of the street of the Jews'. They feared that the presence of a non-Jew in the Jewish area would give them 'no rest' and that this individual might allow into his house priests and seminary students who would harass the community.[14] This was in accordance with the popular idea that keeping a non-Jew out of the Jewish community was as necessary as 'keeping a lion at bay'.[15] One of the leading local rabbis, Moses Isserles, claimed that no non-Jews lived in the Jewish section of Kazimierz although they did pass through the streets and controlled the gates of the town, while in 1582 Rabbi Solomon b. Judah Leybush noted that Jews in Chełm lived among 'non-Jews, our wicked neighbors and our enemies' while 'in the other holy communities '[Israel] is a nation that dwells alone' (Numbers 23: 9) and 'no foreigner mixes among them' (cf. Job 15: 19).[16] Other patterns of settlement also existed, as in Pinsk where several Jewish areas overlapped with those where Christians lived.

As we have seen, the situation of the Jews in the royal towns was dependent on the complicated balance of power between the king and nobles, on the one side,

[12] R. Mahler, *Jews in Old Poland in the Light of Figures* (Yid.), i. 62; Bumblauskas, *Senosios Lietuvos istorija 1009–1795*, 390.

[13] Joel Sirkes, *Responsa* (Kraków, 1631–40), no. 4, quoted in Fram, *Ideals Face Reality*, 22.

[14] Joshua Heschel, *Responsa* (Piotrków, 1902), vol. ii, no. 97.

[15] Joel Sirkes, *Responsa* (Kraków, 1631–40), no. 18. On this occasion Sirkes disagreed with the questioner's assumption. The non-Jew was only 'questionably a lion', not certainly one. The use of the metaphor 'lion' for a non-Jewish neighbour is talmudic in origin; see BT *BM* 108*b*; Fram, *Ideals Face Reality*, 23.

[16] Isserles, *Responsa*, no. 132, 512; Solomon b. Judah Leybush, *Sefer piskei ushe'elot uteshuvot maharash milublin*, ed. I. Herskovitz (Brooklyn, NY, 1988), no. 58, 16, quoted in Fram, *Ideals Face Reality*, 23.

who by and large supported the right of the Jews to establish themselves and to trade, and, on the other, the burghers and the Church, who were basically hostile to them. Nevertheless, the Jews succeeded in establishing permanent settlements in these towns, which, although small by modern standards, were the scene of intense religious and cultural activity. Towns such as Kraków (the home of people such as Moses Isserles), Lublin (with the talmudist Solomon Luria), Vilna, and Poznań were major centres of Jewish life. The largest Jewish centres in northern Europe, Prague and Amsterdam, were not much bigger. In 1638, for example, Prague had 7,815 Jewish inhabitants. These royal towns also contained Jewish 'sacred spaces', like the complex of synagogues in Kazimierz and Vilna.

These last two towns exemplify in many ways the character of Jewish life in the royal towns of Poland and Lithuania. Kraków had been the seat of the senior line of the Polish royal family from the twelfth century. It became the capital of the united Kingdom of Poland in the fourteenth century and retained this position until 1609, when the royal residence was moved to Warsaw. Kraków had acquired the status of a city on the German model in 1257. Its situation on the Vistula and on the trade route to Prague soon attracted an influx of immigrants from the German lands, including a number of Jews, who settled near the university. King Kazimierz made frequent use of Jewish bankers in the town, notably Lewka, son of Jordan. In 1335 he founded the rival city of Kazimierz, at that time separated from Kraków by branches of the Vistula, on what are today Dietl and Starowiślna streets, where Jews were also encouraged to settle.

The early history of the Jews in Kraków was marked by persistent conflicts with the Christian burghers and with the students at the university, the second to be founded in east central Europe, in 1364, after that in Prague. As early as 1369 the city council in Kraków complained to King Kazimierz that, because of the high interest rates demanded by the Jews, the urban patriciate and artisans were being impoverished. Jews were required to lend money to students at rates of interest low for the time (25 per cent), which did not prevent anti-Jewish rioting on the part of the students. Similarly, economic competition and religious difference led to frequent clashes with the burghers. In spite of these difficulties, the Jewish community prospered and its merchants developed commercial links with Breslau, Danzig, Lviv, and Constantinople. Conflicts with the Christian burghers did not abate; indeed, they were exacerbated by the activities of the fifteenth-century preacher Jan Capistrano. In 1485 the Jewish community of Kraków was forced to sign an agreement with the burghers severely limiting Jewish commercial activity, and in 1495 the Jews were finally forced out of the town and settled in Kazimierz, although doubt has been expressed as to whether all the Jews did in fact leave Kraków. They did retain the right to maintain shops and stalls in a specific area of the town, Raszka Fischel was allowed to remain as the king's banker, and during the course of the sixteenth century royal dispensations were granted to individual Jews to live in the town.

At the end of the fourteenth century the Jews in Kazimierz began the construction of the late Gothic synagogue which was completed in 1407. It still stands at the bottom of Szeroka Street (Breitgasse), which became the centre of Jewish Kazimierz. By 1480 there is mention of a *mikveh* (bathhouse), a cemetery, and a marketplace. In the early sixteenth century Rabbi Jacob b. Joseph Pollack, who was born in Bavaria, founded the first yeshiva in the town, of which he remained head until his death in 1552. As early as 1503 he was appointed chief rabbi of Poland by King Aleksander. At this time the community was divided between the older settlers and newer immigrants from the Czech lands. (Władysław Jagiełło, king of these lands, was the elder brother of Zygmunt I, who became king of Poland in 1506; this facilitated links between the Czech lands and the Polish kingdom.) In 1553 a second synagogue was built, and four years later the Old Synagogue, built in late Gothic style, was remodelled by the Italian architect Mateo Gucci. Also in 1553, the Jews acquired additional land from the town of Kraków, and in 1564 the Jewish quarter was granted the privilege of preventing non-Jews from acquiring residential and business property there. Further agreements with the municipality increasing the area of the *oppidum Judaeorum* were concluded in 1583 and 1608. Early Jewish population figures are notoriously unreliable, but by 1570 the Jewish population of Kazimierz numbered around 2,000, making it probably the largest community in Poland.[17]

Poland now enjoyed new prestige in the Jewish world. In the fifteenth century a German rabbi had observed of the Jews of Kraków that they are 'not well-versed in Torah',[18] but only a few decades later the Jews of Istanbul were seeking direction in halakhah from Kraków. Kraków also became important in the systematization of this law. The *Shulḥan arukh*, a codification put together by Joseph Caro of Safed, was printed in Venice in 1565; it was reprinted in 1570–1 in Kraków (which was now becoming a major centre of Jewish publishing), with modifications relating to the Ashkenazi context by Isserles. Isserles was perhaps the most important Jewish intellectual figure in sixteenth-century Kraków, but the town possessed a number of other distinguished scholars, including Joel Sirkes (1561–1640) and Yom Tov Lipmann Heller, and had established itself as a major centre of Jewish intellectual and religious life (on this, see Chapter 5).

The Jews continued to prosper, and in 1609 their trading rights in Kazimierz were extended. This prosperity occasioned new conflicts with the local burghers which are reflected in the anti-Jewish polemics of Sebastian Miczyński. A Jewish furriers' guild was established in 1613, and one for Jewish barber-surgeons in 1639.[19] By 1644 six main synagogues had been established, the largest and most impressive of them being the Old Synagogue on Szeroka Street, the High and Kupa synagogues, built around the turn of the sixteenth century, and the Ajzik

[17] On these developments, see Krasnowolski, 'Architektura krakowskiego Kazimierza jako świadectwo historii'.

[18] 'Poland', in *Encyclopaedia Judaica*, xiii. 721.

[19] M. Wischnitzer, *A History of Jewish Crafts and Guilds*, 213–14.

Synagogue, built in the mid-seventeenth century. By this stage Kraków had become one of the most important Jewish religious and cultural centres north of the Alps, with an elaborate communal organization (on this, see also Chapter 2). As mentioned before, there were four *roshim*, five *tovim*, and fourteen *kahal* members. Every month the responsibility for administration was assumed by one of the *roshim*, who publicly took an oath to fulfil conscientiously his duties as *parnas haḥodesh* (president for the month). Other members of the communal elite took responsibility for tax assessment, supervision of charity, and the maintenance of order in the market. The hierarchical character of the communal organization is reflected in the Jewish court system, with its three divisions reflecting the amount of money involved in a case. Kazimierz was one of the principal communities in the Council of Four Lands and was head of the province of Małopolska. The various regulations for the government of the community were systematized in the ordinance of 1595.

Jewish Kazimierz was divided from Christian Kazimierz by gates, but these were only closed at night. The stratified character of the community was reflected in the buildings of the crowded Jewish quarter. The communal elite lived in the oldest part of the town, at the intersection of Szeroka Street and Żydowska Street (Jewish Street, today Józef Street). They built substantial Italianate terraced houses here, modelled on those of the Kraków patriciate. Thus in 1536 Jonasz b. Abraham concluded a contract with the royal architect Bartolomeo Berecci and his assistants Giovanni Gini and Filippo of Fiesole to construct a house (no longer standing) at 36 Józef Street. A similar house was built in 1559 for the royal minter Feliks by an individual described as Tomasz, *murator Italus*.

The poorer sections of the community, the artisans and those dependent on charity, lived in the basements of these town houses (those which have survived still have traces of plaster from this period) and in the areas incorporated into the Jewish town in 1583 and 1608. Here a labyrinth of small wooden houses was created, some of which survived until the end of the nineteenth century. A full description of the topography of the town is to be found in the inventory of its buildings compiled by Paul Żegota in 1653.[20]

After 1648 the community shared in the general economic decline of Kraków and was adversely affected by the growing religious intolerance. In 1663 one of its members, Mattathias Calahora, was accused of blasphemy and burned at the stake. The community was increasingly in debt, a reflection partly of the large sums which were being expended on communal defence. Yet at the same time its involvement in trade and crafts expanded. Jews were a significant element in most of the trading activities of Kraków, including furs and hides, wax, soap, salt, tobacco, haberdashery, and silver and gold. Jews also worked as goldsmiths and were actively involved in large-scale import–export trade and in the leasing of

[20] Krasnowolski, 'Architektura krakowskiego Kazimierza jako świadectwo historii', 4.

estates. This economic expansion went along with widening economic disparity in the community.

By the end of the seventeenth century the community was deeply in debt, which led to increasing conflict among members of the *kahal*. This came to a head in the 1690s when Zacharjasz Mendel Kantorowicz, a member of the *kahal* and a leader of the Council of Four Lands with close ties to the *starosta* of Kraków, was held responsible by the *kahal* for 7,000 zlotys of its debts. Using his links with the *starosta*, he was able to take control of the *kahal*. He proceeded to transfer these debts to other members of the *kahal* and may even have misappropriated some communal funds. His arbitrary rule aroused resistance which ultimately compelled him to flee to Pińczów.[21]

Vilna, the capital of the Grand Duchy of Lithuania, was also a major centre of Jewish life with its own unique characteristics. It is an important, if not wholly resolved, question how far this made it different from the towns of the Kingdom of Poland. Certainly, the population of the surrounding countryside was largely Lithuanian or Belarusian rather than Polish, which meant that, as in Lviv, there were Greek Orthodox and Greek Catholic believers to be found in the town in significant numbers. It is also unclear when the idea of the *litvak*—the highly intellectual rationalist known for his frugality—emerged as a specific feature of Jewish life here, but by the nineteenth century it was firmly established.

Vilna was founded by the Lithuanian grand duke Gediminas (1316–41) in the early fourteenth century and became the capital of the Grand Duchy of Lithuania, which joined Poland in a dynastic union in 1385 (see the appendix to Part I). The Lithuanian grand dukes encouraged Jewish settlement, and in 1388 Grand Duke Vytautas granted his Jewish subjects a charter similar in character to that granted to the Jews of Poland by Bolesław the Pious and confirmed by Kazimierz the Great. There are some early references to Jews in Vilna, but at this stage we are dealing with isolated individuals and not an organized community.

Jewish settlement was essentially the product of the early sixteenth century. By 1568 the Jewish community was ordered to pay a poll tax, and in 1573 the first synagogue was established. In the year 1648, on the eve of the Khmelnytsky Uprising, the total population of Vilna numbered around 15,000, with a Jewish population of around 3,000. The city was adversely affected by the political upheavals after 1648, and in August 1655 was occupied by Muscovite and Cossack forces. Most Jews fled, and those that remained mostly perished at the hands of the invaders. By 1662 the number of its inhabitants had fallen to 5,000, with barely 415 Jews. Rabbi Moses Rivkes (d. *c.*1671), a scholar from Vilna who succeeded in escaping to Amsterdam, wrote the following description of these events in his commentary on the *Shulḥan arukh*, entitled *Be'er hagolah*:

> Throughout the whole of Lithuania there then roamed bands of Russians and Cossacks, who devastated the cities and occupied among others Polotsk, Vitebsk, and Minsk.

[21] On this, see Hundert, 'Security and Dependence', 41–4.

Wherever the Cossacks appeared they, in their lust for spoil, seized all the belongings of the Jews, whom they slaughtered in masses. When the army, spreading alarm and terror, approached the gates of Vilna, the governor Radziwill, together with his troops, quickly fled, and many of the inhabitants of the city followed his example. On Wednesday, 24 Tammuz 5415, almost the entire Jewish community fled like one man: those who had horses and carts went forth with their wives, sons and daughters and some of their belongings, and others went on foot, carrying their children on their shoulders.[22]

However, by 1795, when the area came under Russian rule, the population of Vilna had recovered to around 15,000. In that year 3,613 Jews paid the poll tax and the total Jewish population was somewhere between 5,000 and 6,000.

In 1527 a charter granted to the burghers of Vilna empowered the municipality to bar Jewish settlement in the town, but the Jews appealed to the grand duke and the nobility to allow them to settle there, and in June 1593 received permission to establish a synagogue and a cemetery. Their rights were confirmed by two charters granted on 15 February 1633, on the coronation of Władysław IV (r. 1632–48), the first confirming the general privileges of the Jews in Lithuania granted by Grand Duke Vytautas in 1388 and the second setting out in some detail the rights which they were to enjoy in Vilna.[23]

This second charter allowed Jews to run shops dealing in woollen and cotton goods, carpets, goods from Turkey, spices, linen, glass, and iron, as well as other goods sold by small shopkeepers. They could also buy and sell silver, gold, and jewellery. They could engage in trade throughout the town, both retail and wholesale, and deal with both local tradesmen and travelling merchants. They could work as artisans in trades that had no guild, though Jewish tailors worked only for Jews, and not for Christians. They could work as tanners and furriers and buy and sell skins and furs in their houses and from stalls. They could also make and sell all kinds of alcoholic drinks, use the municipal scale to pay the established fees for weighing, and buy cattle in the city or the market, though only for their own needs and not for sale within or beyond the city. They could sell unredeemed pledges after a year and six weeks, without notice, at an officially assessed price. In addition, they were exempt from taxes on their cemetery and slaughterhouse, and had sole use of their bathhouse.

The charter also set out the areas where Jews were permitted to live, where they were required to buy or rent houses within fifteen years. The municipality was required to maintain the water cisterns in this area in return for payment. A Jew could take possession of the house of a burgher outside the Jewish quarter as compensation for a debt, but this could be redeemed when the debt was paid. The Jews were also to be permitted to build a stone synagogue, provided it did not look like a church or monastery and was not higher than other buildings in the area. Finally, the charter warned the burghers that any of their privileges which conflicted with the rights conceded to the Jews were void.

22 Quoted in I. Cohen, *Vilna*, 43.

23 For these developments, see ibid. 25–37.

A prominent role in securing the charter was played by two Vilna merchants, the brothers Samuel b. Moses and Eliezer b. Moses, who also managed to persuade the Sejm to pass a resolution in 1633 stating that, because of rising prices in Lithuania, and to help reverse the trend, Jews in Vilna should be permitted to trade in all goods, both in shops and in their houses. The burghers appealed to the grand ducal court against this resolution and the charter, claiming that these provisions were incompatible with their rights. The court refused to pass judgment on this issue, and King Władysław appointed a commission, which issued an ordinance attempting to reconcile the position of the burghers and the Jews.

The ordinance granted the Jews permission for the next ten years to open twelve shops on Żydowska Street (today blood libel and Žydų gatvė), in which they could deal in skins, furs, clothes, linen, woven stuffs, silver, gold, jewellery, and spices. Other commodities were subject to restrictions. Jews could buy rye only for their own use, they could buy salt and herrings only in large quantities from the burghers for further sale, and could sell hemp in the city only to burghers. They could trade in flax, fat, and mead throughout the city, use the municipal scale, and keep seals in their own shops. They could also buy cattle for slaughter, though not for sale, but they could sell the meat both to Jews and to Christians in the slaughterhouse near the synagogue. They could sell spirits, beer, and mead to Jews, both wholesale and retail, but only wholesale to Christians. Jewish artisans were barred from activities in which there was an artisans' guild, but could work as glaziers, jewellers, and furriers, and could undertake any artisan work for Jews.

Jews were allowed to live on both sides of Jatkowa Street (Butchers' Street, today Mėsinių gatvė), and buy houses in any part of Niemiecka Street (German Street, today Vokiečių gatvė), but they could not have gates leading onto the latter, though they could have windows overlooking it. They were forbidden to rent or buy houses outside the area assigned to them, but they could remain in such houses if they had owned them when the ordinance was published. The question of houses belonging to hospitals and situated within the Jewish quarter was referred to the bishop. Disputes over real estate were to be settled by the court in whose jurisdiction the property stood, but in civil and criminal cases they were answerable to the local court of the grand duke. Jews were exempt from the obligation to give lodging to visitors when the Supreme Tribunal was holding a session, even when the king was on a visit to Vilna. They were also exempt from all municipal taxes, but the community was required to pay the municipality 300 gulden a year in peacetime and 500 gulden during a war. The ordinance concluded with an exhortation to Jews and burghers to observe it carefully, and enjoined the municipality to protect the Jews from physical attack.

The burghers were not happy with the rights granted to the Jews, and the next century and a half was marked by constant conflict in the courts, which was finally resolved in 1783, in the last days of Poland–Lithuania, by a decision of the grand ducal court. This abolished the requirement that the Jews live in a specified area, on the grounds that since the Jews had greatly increased in number since 1633 it was no longer possible to confine them to the streets assigned to them. Accordingly, Jews should have the right to live and buy houses anywhere in the city and its suburbs, with the exception of two streets: that leading from Ostra Brama to the cathedral (now Aušros Vartų gatvė, Didžioji gatvė, and Pilies gatvė), and that from the Troki Gate to the Monastery of St John (now Trakų gatvė, Dominikonų gatvė, and Šv. Jono gatvė). If Jews already had houses in those streets they could keep them, but they could not build a new one there without the permission of the municipality. Since the Jews could now live anywhere in the city with this exception, they should be liable for the same rates as other citizens and their annual tax abolished. To ensure that they were fairly assessed for tax they were to appoint two representatives to the assessment commission. If they considered that they had been assessed unfairly, they could appeal to the court of the grand duke. Jews were to be responsible for one-third of the city's expenditure, this sum to be collected by the *kahal* and handed over to the municipality.

Jews were now to be free to engage in any kind of business activity. The *kahal* was to be responsible for seeing that all Jews were usefully employed and for expelling from the city those without work. New Jewish artisans would be examined by a board appointed by the municipality consisting of both Jews and Christians. The Jews were to be responsible for the cleanliness of their streets and houses.

The court's judgment of 1783 was accepted by both Jews and burghers. The Jewish side was so satisfied with the settlement that on the death in 1784 of the *shtadlan*, Aryeh Leib Meitess, the man principally responsible for putting the Jewish case, an inscription was put on his tombstone reading, 'It was he who wrought the great salvation for Israel in the year 5544 [1784] and saved the city by his wisdom.'[24]

Even before the settlement of 1783 some Jews lived outside the area laid down in the various agreements. Most, however, concentrated in multi-occupied houses in their own quarter, which had only one gate, at the corner of Niemiecka and Szklanna (today Stiklių) streets. The centre of this area was the *shulhof*, which has been described as follows by Israel Cohen:

> The heart of the Jewish quarter, from the time when the community first began to assume organic form in the fifteenth century until the present day, was the *shulhof* or synagogue courtyard. It derives its name from the Great Synagogue, which was the most important of the many buildings and institutions that clustered thickly around this quaint cloistral enclosure. It was shaped like the letter L reversed, and could be approached from the Żydowska through a huge iron gate, flanked by lamps on two stone pillars, or through a short alley from the Niemiecka. It was entirely surrounded by houses of prayer and study of varied size and different degrees of antiquity, and embodied within its limited ambit more of the memories and legends, and of the aspirations and sufferings of Vilna Jewry over a period of five hundred years than any equivalent piece of earth in any other Jewish

[24] Quoted in I. Cohen, *Vilna*, 83.

community in Europe. During the greater part of this period the *shulhof* was the focus of all the manifold activities of the community—religious, administrative, judicial, intellectual and social—and even in more recent times it continued to dominate its religious and cultural life.[25]

This area was the location of the main buildings of the community: the offices of the *kahal* and the courthouse of the *beit din*, as well as the *mikveh* and the slaughterhouse. It also contained the well from which the Jews of the surrounding area obtained their water.

The Great Synagogue, which occupied most of the horizontal line of the reversed L, was a striking building, particularly on the inside. It dated back to 1573, and, since Jewish sacred buildings could not be higher than nearby churches, it had a sunken floor in order to increase the internal elevation. Cohen, who visited the building in the 1930s, described it as follows:

> Legend has it that when Napoleon, who was so impressed by the Jewish aspect of Vilna that he exclaimed: 'This is the Jerusalem of Lithuania' stood on the threshold of this temple and gazed at the interior, he was speechless with admiration. It has the overwhelming grandeur of an edifice in the style of the Italian Renaissance and an awe-inspiring atmosphere. Four massive, equidistant columns support the vast stone-floored pile, and within them is the ornate, rococo *Almemar* (reading desk), with a beautiful cupola, which was built in the second half of the eighteenth century by Rabbi Judah ben Eliezer, the famous scribe and judge [*sofer vedayan*], commonly known as YeSoD.[26] The Ark, with doors of iron, is also of very handsome design. It was restored—according to an inscription below it—by the Society Bedek Habayit [public works department of the *kahal*]—presumably after one of the many fires in the middle of the eighteenth century. Above the Ark is a large tablet with the Commandments supported by the conventional lion and unicorn, also a gift of YeSoD.[27]

Among the other synagogues in the *shulhof* were the 'old *kloyz*' (prayer hall), which was supposed to date back to the middle of the fourteenth century, the 'new *kloyz*', the *beit midrash* founded by Rabbi Judah b. Eliezer (d. 1762) in the middle of the eighteenth century, and the synagogue built on the house of the Vilna Gaon (Elijah b. Solomon Zalman, 1720–97). In addition, there were many smaller *kloyzn* and *ḥeders*.

As was the case with all Jewish communities, Vilna possessed a highly developed system of self-government (described in the previous chapter). Leading the community were the great traders and bankers. The bulk of the community was made up, however, of smaller traders, pedlars, and artisans. A census taken by the *kahal* in 1784 reveals that the Jews were engaged in at least forty occupations, including tailors and cobblers, bakers and butchers, doctors and teachers, writers and musicians, shopkeepers and pedlars, masons and plasterers, glaziers and turners, tinsmiths and coppersmiths, jewellers and goldsmiths, fishermen and

[25] I. Cohen, *Vilna*, 102–3.

[26] An acronym of the three words *yehudah sofer vedayan*.

[27] I. Cohen, *Vilna*, 105–6.

brewers, as well as their own drivers, nightwatchmen, water carriers, and chimney sweeps. Certain crafts enjoyed particular favour, for there were 135 tailors, eighty-eight furriers, and fifty-nine jewellers. Artisans formed about 50 per cent of all those gainfully employed.[28]

Vilna was the home of many notable religious scholars from the late sixteenth century onwards. These included Rabbi Menahem Monash Hayes, Rabbi Moses b. Isaac Judah Lima (1605?–1658), Shabetai b. Meir Hakohen (1621–62), Aaron Samuel b. Israel Koidonover (*c.*1614–1676), Zevi Hirsch Koidonover, Moses Rivkes, and Ephraim b. Jacob Hakohen (1616–78). Their activities are described in Chapter 5.

Secular scholarship also developed, although more slowly, and Vilna was less of a centre in this respect than Kraków, seat of the second oldest university in central Europe. The one area of secular knowledge which developed in Vilna was medicine. The Polish kings had often favoured Jewish doctors, sometimes converts, like the converso Isaac Hispanus, who attended kings Jan Albert, Aleksander, and Zygmunt I in the first half of the sixteenth century. A Spanish exile, Joseph Solomon Delmedigo (1591–1655), held the position of personal physician to Krzysztof Radziwiłł (1585–1640) between 1620 and 1624. Born in Candi, in Crete, he was the son of a local rabbi and studied medicine in Padua, along with mathematics and astronomy as well as kabbalah. While in Padua, he became acquainted with the Jewish scholar Leone Modena (1571–1648) of Venice and adopted his rational and sceptical approach to religious issues. In Vilna he became friendly with a number of like-minded individuals, including Moses b. Meir of Metz, and the Karaite scholar Zerah b. Nathan of Troki.[29] Zerah b. Nathan addressed a number of questions on religious and scientific subjects to him, and his answers to them are embodied in his work *Elim*, which also contains seventy mathematical paradoxes; it was published in Amsterdam in 1629. After he left Vilna he served as rabbi to the Sephardi communities in Hamburg and Amsterdam and subsequently practised as the communal physician in the Jewish communities of Hamburg and Prague, where he lived from 1648 until his death in 1655.

The first Vilna Jew to follow in Delmedigo's footsteps and study medicine in Padua was Aaron Gordon, who was born in the mid-seventeenth century and who, on his return to Poland, was appointed physician to King Jan Sobieski, from whom he received a privilege exempting him and his family from *kahal* taxes and giving them the right to live anywhere in the city. In spite of this privilege, he played an active part in communal affairs and his signature can be found in the minute book of the Lithuanian Council in an entry dated 24 Av 5476 (July 1716). The Gordon family was subsequently to play an important role in the history of Vilna Jewry.

As in other royal towns, the situation of the Jews in Vilna deteriorated after 1648. The sense of being under pressure gave rise to the legend mentioned before

[28] Ibid. 100. [29] Fuenn, *Kiryah ne'emanah*, 73.

of the convert Walentyn Potocki, or Graf Potocki, of Vilna.[30] He is supposed to have converted to Judaism along with a noble friend, Zaremba, in Amsterdam. He eventually returned to Poland, where he was ultimately recognized and arrested. He refused to renounce Judaism, and in 1749, on the second day of Shavuot, was burned at the stake after his tongue had been ripped out, and his ashes were scattered in the area. Those who took part in his execution were said to have suffered divine punishment and Potocki was received into heaven by angels, Abraham, and the righteous. His 'remains' were reinterred in the mausoleum of the Vilna Gaon in the new Jewish cemetery in Šeškinė when his grave was among those destroyed by the closing of the old Jewish cemetery in Shnipishok (today Šnipiškės) in 1948–50. There is no historical basis for the story, although it does echo the actual persecution of several converts to Judaism, most notably the burning of Rafal Sentimani for apostasy in 1753. What it does reflect is increased Jewish insecurity in the face of the intensified Catholic conversionary effort which occurred in the eighteenth century.

By the middle of the eighteenth century Vilna, like other towns in Poland–Lithuania, had become the scene of growing conflict within the Jewish community as the office of rabbi fell prey to the sale of offices which became the norm in the Commonwealth at this time. Samuel b. Avigdor was appointed to this post because of a substantial payment to the *kahal* by his father-in-law, Judah b. Eliezer. After the latter's death the *kahal* began to put limits on Rabbi Samuel's attempts to place his followers on it, and on his extensive commercial activities. After a conflict lasting fifteen years Rabbi Samuel triumphed and was to have been reimbursed by the *kahal* for the fees he had lost, but the failure of the *kahal* to meet this payment led to a renewal of the conflict. Supporters of Rabbi Samuel claimed that they were defending the whole community against the excessive tax burden imposed by the elite. The conflict soon assumed wider ramifications, with the bishop of Vilna, Ignacy Massalski, supporting Rabbi Samuel and the conservative magnate Karol Radziwiłł, the governor of Vilna province, supporting the *kahal*. The long-drawn-out conflict finally ended in 1790 with an agreement between the terminally ill Rabbi Samuel and the *kahal*, who agreed to pay him damages and bury him with appropriate honours. After his death the *kahal* decided never again to appoint a communal rabbi and symbolically placed a large stone on the rabbi's chair in the Great Synagogue. The *kahal* itself, in spite of the abuses which the conflict had brought to light, remained unreformed.[31]

JEWISH ENCLAVES AND 'SUBURBS'

Danzig, Lublin, and Warsaw, as well as many lesser commercial centres like Jarosław, did not officially tolerate Jewish settlement within their town walls,

30 On this, see Teter, 'The Legend of Ger Zedek of Wilno as Polemic and Reassurance'.

31 On this conflict, see Klausner, *Vilna during the Period of the Gaon* (Heb.); I. Cohen, *Vilna*, 490–501; and Hundert, *Jews in Poland–Lithuania in the Eighteenth Century*, 112–17.

having been granted by the king the right *de non tolerandis Judaeis*.[32] However, although they may have been banned from establishing themselves within these towns, Jews were frequently allowed into them to trade and participate in fairs. In order to take advantage of this situation Jewish settlements developed in areas beyond the town walls (*sub urbe*). In addition, Jews settled in *jurydyki*, areas of the towns not under the jurisdiction of the municipality.

The size and character of these settlements varied. The largest and most significant was in Lublin. From at least 1518 Jews were forbidden to reside within the city walls and they established themselves in the 'suburb' of Podzamcze (literally 'under the castle'), which fell under the jurisdiction of the *starosta*. This made possible the establishment of a major community with imposing synagogues, a cemetery, and important scholars. In 1564 the Jews obtained from the king a charter guaranteeing them rights of inheritance over their houses and property in Podzamcze after their original privilege documents were lost in a fire. By 1570 there were sixty-nine Jewish houses in the suburb with a total population of around 1,000 Jews. They also seem to have established themselves within the town walls, since in 1676 the municipality passed a statute repeating the rule forbidding Jewish settlement. The Jews here also succeeded, after complicated litigation, in obtaining in 1693 the right of freedom to trade in the city and its suburbs, a matter which continued to be the subject of complicated lawsuits throughout the eighteenth century.[33]

Other Jewish settlements on the periphery of towns were somewhat smaller. In Danzig the king and nobles intervened to ensure that Jews could trade in the town during fairs and market days. Jews entered the town in such numbers on these occasions that in 1590 the Council of the Lands enacted legislation forbidding such merchants to provide pork for their non-Jewish employees.[34] Jews had the right to enter Warsaw during sessions of the Sejm and they also succeeded in establishing a permanent Jewish settlement in Praga, on the right bank of the Vistula opposite Warsaw. Smaller enclaves were created in Antokol (today Antakalnis) and Shnipishok outside the walls of Vilna, and on the outskirts of Kiev and Kamenets-Podolsky. In other towns, such as Opoczno and Nowy Sącz, until the relaxation of the prohibition on Jewish settlement, municipalities succeeded only in excluding Jews from the areas under their direct jurisdiction, and Jews settled on land under the control of the *starosta* or in *jurydyki*.

[32] On this, see Schiper, *Dzieje handlu żydowskiego na ziemiach polskich*, 26–7, and Goldberg, 'De non tolerandis Iudaeis'. The issue is also discussed in Hundert, 'The Role of the Jews in Commerce in Early Modern Poland–Lithuania', 253–4 and n. 18.

[33] On the situation of Jews in Lublin, see Bałaban, *Die Judenstadt von Lublin*, 55–62, and Hundert, 'Security and Dependence', 196–204.

[34] Hundert, 'Security', 118–24 and Echt, *Die Geschichte der Juden in Danzig*.

JEWS IN NOBLE TOWNS

In 1539 Zygmunt I withdrew his judicial authority over the Jews living in towns owned by nobles;[35] however, he still collected taxes from the Jews on private estates and offered Jews some measure of legal protection.[36] From 1563 he lost all control over lands owned by members of the nobility. Nobles were able to make their own laws, set up their own courts, and dictate the conditions of settlement for anyone who lived on their property. By the end of the sixteenth century, with the development of the manorial system, towns under private jurisdiction accounted for more than 60 per cent of all the towns in Wielkopolska and Małopolska.[37] The Jews began to move to private towns, particularly in Ukraine from the late sixteenth century. By the mid-seventeenth century probably three-quarters of the Jewish population lived in towns and villages owned by nobles. By the eighteenth century 70 per cent of the Jewish urban population of Lublin province lived in such towns.[38]

These became the shtetls (small towns) of Jewish myth. They have often been described in a highly abstract and idealized manner. A good example of such a description is that of Abraham Joshua Heschel, scion of a great hasidic family, who emigrated from Poland, first to Germany and then to the United States, and became one of the leading theologians of American Judaism. In his lament for the lost world of east European Jewry, *The Earth Is the Lord's*, published in 1946, he wrote:

> Korets, Karlin, Bratslav, Lubavich, Ger, Lublin—hundreds of little towns were like holy books. Each place was a pattern, a way of Jewishness . . . The little Jewish communities in Eastern Europe were like sacred texts opened before the eyes of God, so close were the houses of worship to Mount Sinai. In the humble wooden synagogues, looking as if they were deliberately closing themselves off from the world, the Jews purified the souls that God had given them and perfected their likeness to God . . . Even plain men were like artists who knew how to fill weekday hours with mystic beauty.[39]

Heschel's sentiments were echoed, although with a characteristic twist, by the Polish Jewish poet Antoni Słonimski, also the possessor of a distinguished Jewish lineage, who, in spite of his baptism as an infant, always considered himself a 'Jew of antisemitic antecedents'. In his 'Elegia miasteczek żydowskich' (Elegy for the Shtetls, 1947), he wrote:

35 *Volumina Legum*, i. 550–1.

36 See Halpern, *Jews and Jewry in Eastern Europe* (Heb.), 25–6.

37 The reasons for the development of the manorial system have been the topic of much historical debate; see Topolski, 'Sixteenth-Century Poland and the Turning Point in European Economic Development'. For a more complete breakdown of the percentage of royal and private towns across Poland, see Wyrobisz, 'Rola miast prywatnych w Polsce w XVI i XVII wieku', 19–24.

38 Manikowski, 'Zmiany czy stagnacja?', 787, and Hundert, 'Security and Dependence', 1–5.

39 Heschel, *The Earth Is the Lord's*, 89, 92, 93.

No more will you find in Poland Jewish shtetls—
Hrubieszów, Karczew, Brody, Falenica—
In vain will you seek in the windows lighted candles
And search for the sound of chants from the wooden synagogue.

The last scourings, the Jewish rags have vanished,
They sprinkled sand over the blood, swept away the footprints,
and whitewashed the walls with bluish lime
As after a plague or a great day of fasting.

One moon shines here, cool, pale, alien,
Outside the town, when the night lights up,
My Jewish kinsmen, with their poetic fancies,
Will find no more Chagall's two gold moons.

They have flown away, frightened by the grim silence.
No more will you find those towns
Where the cobbler was a poet,
The watchmaker a philosopher, the barber a troubadour.

No more will you find those towns where biblical psalms
Were linked by the wind with Polish laments and Slavonic ardour,
Where old Jews in the orchard, under the shade of cherry trees,
Wept for the sacred walls of Jerusalem.

No more will you find those towns where poetic mist,
The moon, winds, lakes, and the stars above,
Wrote in blood a tragic story,
The history of the world's two saddest nations.[40]

Examples of this sort of elevated nostalgia could easily be multiplied. They all depict a mythical shtetl only tangentially related to reality. In most descriptions towns and villages of very different types are indiscriminately lumped together, while the presence of non-Jews, always an important element in the life of these towns, is almost entirely ignored. Jews were certainly a major element in the population of these towns, and their noble owners went out of their way to encouraged Jews to settle in them, since they were seen as less demanding politically and socially than Christian burghers. Thus when Hieronim Sieniawski founded a new township in Oleszyce, near Lubaczów, in 1576, he included provisions in the privilege he granted to new settlers which gave equal rights to the Jews to practise their religion:

The Polish Crown flourishes as it is composed of people of diverse estates, particularly in regard to their religious allegiance, on the principle that no authority shall exercise power over faith, honour, and conscience. We wish therefore to secure a peaceful life especially to those persons who have suffered persecution not because of any crimes or evil deeds, but for other reasons, so that they may enjoy all the liberties of the laws enacted by us.[41]

[40] Słonimski, *138 wierszy*, 175–6.
[41] Quoted in Baron, *A Social and Religious History of the Jews*, xvi. 125.

Similarly, Tomasz Zamoyski protected the trading rights throughout Poland–Lithuania of the Jews of his town of Zamość, while Jerzy Lubomirski, the owner of Rzeszów, protected the Jews of the town who travelled to Breslau from being held liable for the debts of the Council of Four Lands to two Breslau merchants.[42]

It was in this way that the 'marriage of convenience' between the nobility and the Jews which developed from the mid-seventeenth century in pre-partition Poland–Lithuania came into existence. Jews began to manage the estates of the nobility through the system of leasing and became the indispensable traders and craftsmen of the rural economy, locating themselves in the small towns and villages of the noble estates. By the middle of the eighteenth century less than a quarter of the 750,000 Jews in Poland–Lithuania lived in towns under royal authority. Nearly three-quarters lived in towns and villages controlled by the local nobleman.

Detailed records left by the nobles' estate managers provide a clear picture of life in these towns. Such a record describes life in Opatów, a small town about 25 miles north-west of Sandomierz, which came into the possession of Paweł Karol Sanguszko when he and his wife inherited the town on the death of her brother Aleksander Dominik Lubomirski in 1720. According to the inventory prepared for him, the population at this time numbered 1,700: 1,000 Jews and 700 Catholics. They lived largely in separate areas, the town having been split in 1638 into Catholic and Jewish sections. The Jews certainly dominated the town economically and socially. They owned most of the more imposing houses, including all eighteen made of stone (the bulk of the houses were wood), and included sixteen of the nineteen merchants (the other three were probably Scots). The large majority of both the Jewish and the Catholic populations consisted of artisans, but here there was some complementarity. The principal Catholic artisan trades were shoemaking, baking, and furriery; among the Jews, baking, butchery, and capmaking. One Jewish leaseholder lived in the town.[43]

The charter granted to the Jews of Opatów in 1670 was very specific in the rights it bestowed, including those to establish the institutions necessary to create a community and to trade in a variety of fields (it is described in Chapter 2). Jewish life here was marked by vitality and energy, so that the Jewish predominance in commerce and artisanry exceeded the proportion of Jews in the town. The Church was unable to undermine the position of the Jews because of the protection they enjoyed from the town owner. Jewish society was very stratified and dominated by a small group of related merchants and leaseholders. Contrary to the view of older Jewish historians, most notably Dubnow, which characterized the owners of the towns as eccentric and arbitrary, the town owner of Opatów was quite rational in his behaviour, seeking what was best for the town. He also on occasion supported the Jewish inhabitants. In the early eighteenth century the Christian municipality complained to him that whereas, according to municipal

42 Hundert, 'Security and Dependence', 11.

43 Hundert, *The Jews in a Polish Private Town*, 1–8.

law, the Jews were forbidden to trade except on the 'Jewish street', 'they now brew beer and mead, sell wine, grain, salt, candles, meat etc., in our marketplace. They even sell pork which they do not eat.' The town owner rejected this complaint, telling the burghers that they must 'obey the law', which granted Jews the right to buy and sell any commodity anywhere in the town. 'The Jews who benefit from the rights and privileges of the town have equal rights with the burghers.'[44] The situation of the Jews in Opatów, in Gershon Hundert's view, demonstrates that Jews felt reasonably secure in Poland–Lithuania and that 'Poland was as much theirs as their neighbors'.' At the same time, he argues, 'there is no question that animus and tension were the governing qualities in relations between Jews and Christians. The historical issue is how this animus was expressed in relations between particular people and groups of people at particular times and in particular places.'[45]

Moshe Rosman's analysis of the history of the town of Medzhybizh (Międzybóż), which was among the fifteen largest Jewish settlements in mid-eighteenth-century Poland–Lithuania, paints a similar picture.[46] The town was part of the Sieniawa-Czartoryski entail, the largest concentration of estates in Poland during that period. These estates were personally managed by Elżbieta Sieniawska and included more than twenty towns, among them Shklov in Mogilev province (see Volume II, Chapter 6), some of which had a substantial Jewish population. Elżbieta Sieniawska actively intervened in the management of these towns, encouraging settlement, both Jewish and non-Jewish, and even lending money to merchants to facilitate their activities. The town, which was founded in the twelfth century and provided with defences against possible Tatar attack, was situated near the border in Podolia, midway between Lviv and Kiev, near the river Bug, on the line where Greek Catholicism gave way to Orthodoxy. Medzhybizh developed as the local headquarters for the Sieniawa-Czartoryski entail and also became an important trading centre. It suffered considerably during the upheavals of the mid-seventeenth century: it was devastated by the Cossack leader Bohdan Khmelnytsky, who occupied it four times, and it came under Turkish rule in 1672–6 and 1678–86, not finally returning to the control of the Sieniawa-Czartoryski family until 1687.

Medzhybizh did not regain its pre-1648 population of 10,000 during the eighteenth century, but by 1740 it was inhabited by 764 potentially taxpaying households (545 Christian and 219 Jewish), or approximately 5,000 people (about one-third Jews). It profited from the increase in economic activity in the early decades of the eighteenth century, and this renewed prosperity was reflected in the late 1730s in the building or restoration of the town's synagogue and Catholic and Orthodox churches. During this period, as Rosman has demonstrated, the value of the general lease of the town, which entitled its holder to the income derived from the manufacture and sale of liquor, various market and product

[44] Ibid. 135. [45] Ibid. 38. [46] Rosman, *Founder of Hasidism*, 63–83.

taxes, the operation of local mills, and customary payments from some of the guilds, increased considerably. However, economic growth was not uninterrupted and the town was adversely affected by natural disasters and the predations of Haydamak rebels and the Russian army, which occupied the area on a number of occasions. The 1740s saw something of an economic recession, with the price of village leases falling and a reduction in the amount of excise collected from self-employed Jews.

The Jewish community of Medzhybizh had been re-established after its destruction during the years following the Khmelnytsky Uprising, and by the mid-eighteenth century, when the town was home to one of the fifteen largest Jewish communities in Poland–Lithuania, it numbered 2,039. Between 1722 and 1740, while the town's population as a whole increased by 50 per cent, the number of Jews grew by 67 per cent. Jews owned the majority of the better, stone houses, as well as most of the stores on the marketplace. There was no closed Jewish quarter, and close to a third of the Jews had at least one Christian neighbour.

An analysis of the lists of office-holders between 1726 and 1743 seems to show that, although the communal organization of Medzhybizh conformed to the eighteenth-century pattern of a self-perpetuating oligarchy, there was more turnover and less repeat incumbency of offices than is revealed by Bałaban's analysis of Jewish office-holding in Kraków in the early years of the seventeenth century:

> The structure suggested by these numbers is of an oligarchy composed of several factions, probably based mainly on family ties. Each faction had to be accommodated, and therefore no single group could commandeer all the offices year after year, merely exchanging titles among themselves, as was the case in seventeenth-century Cracow. In Medzhybizh apparently, the offices had to rotate through the factions, a process that took several years.[47]

Jewish life was unquestionably marked by wide social distinctions, and hostility existed between ruler and ruled, rich and poor, elite and plebeians. The elite groups—factors who worked for the Polish administrators, leaseholders of the magnate's rights, the leaseholders of the collection of the *kahal*'s income, and the *kahal* itself—tended to overlap, which strengthened their position. At the same time there were significant divisions between these groups and, on occasion, the *kahal* was capable of standing up for the interests of the community, as did the *pospólstwo*, a body made up of all male householders whose level of taxation entitled them to participate in the political process but who were not currently holding office and who were charged with supervising the activities of the *kahal*.

Unlike the situation in Opatów, in Medzhybizh Jews tended to live side by side with Christians. This seems also to have been the case in other private towns such as Opole, Bełżyce, and Lubartów. An inventory of the town of Kraśnik from 1631 shows the Jews living in twenty-eight houses, of which nine were on the 'Jewish

[47] Rosman, *Founder of Hasidism*, 77.

street', where there were also three houses inhabited by Christians. Ten Jewish houses were to be found on the *rynek* (town square). The 1688 inventory of Opole showed most Jews living on the *rynek*, where there was an equal number of non-Jews. A similar pattern prevailed in Modliborzyce, Dobromil, Łańcut, Chyrów, Biłgoraj, and Sieniawa.[48]

JEWS IN VILLAGES

We have a less complete picture of the situation of Jews in villages in this period. According to the not wholly reliable census of 1764, nearly 27 per cent of the Jewish population lived in villages. Of these a significant proportion either maintained a house in a town or returned there when the lease they were administering ran out. Generally only one or two Jewish families were found in a village, and many villages in the western part of the country had no Jewish inhabitants.

On the basis of a census conducted in 1787, Antoni Podraza has calculated that over 37 per cent of the Jewish population of Kraków province lived in the country, as did 42 per cent in Sandomierz province and nearly 36 per cent in Lublin province. In Kraków province just over half of the villages had some Jewish inhabitants—generally a single family.[49] The percentage has been estimated to range from 19 per cent to 36 per cent as one moved eastward.[50] Village Jews were sometimes farmers, particularly dairy farmers, and also played an important role in distilling and inn-keeping. They were also involved in milling and in small-scale credit provision.

CONCLUSION

By 1764, of the sixteen largest Jewish settlements in Poland–Lithuania, ten were in private towns, including the largest, in Brody. In spite of this the royal towns, especially Kraków, Lviv, Vilna, and Poznań, remained important. These were the areas where Jews interacted with the surrounding society, where they had their sacred spaces, and where Jewish intellectual life was more sophisticated. Most private towns were much smaller, although some, like Zamość, Leszno, Brody, and Żółkiew (Zhovkva), were intended by their noble founders to compete with royal towns. They were mostly places where the Jews had more impact on the running of the town and controlled a greater proportion of its wealth. They were also generally much less sophisticated, and when new religious movements, especially hasidism, began to penetrate Poland–Lithuania, it was here that they found their greatest support. Village Jews were an important part of the community. Most, however, did not live all their lives in the countryside, and even when they lived in

[48] Hundert, 'Security and Dependence', 223–5; id., *Jews in Poland–Lithuania in the Eighteenth Century*, 30–1.

[49] Podraza, 'Jews and the Village in the Polish Commonwealth'.

[50] Weinryb, *The Jews of Poland*, 117.

villages, usually went for special occasions, sabbaths, and holidays to a nearby town.

In spite of the terrible destruction of the twentieth century, traces of all these Jewish spaces can still be found in Poland, Lithuania, Belarus, Ukraine, and Moldova. Unfortunately, only one rather late wooden synagogue has survived (in today's Lithuania), but many masonry synagogues are still standing—in Kraków a whole complex of them. The layout of many noble towns has been preserved, and in some of them, such as Tykocin and Szczebrzeszyn, and Kiejdany (Kėdainiai) and Mariampol (Marijampolė) in Lithuania, the complex of *kehilah* buildings also survives. How these relics of a lost world, whose survival is something of a miracle, are to be preserved, and to what use they should be put, are questions to which there are no easy answers.

FOUR

JEWS IN ECONOMIC LIFE

When we use the words 'Frenchman', 'Englishman', 'Spaniard', we include all of the inhabitants of France, England, and Spain, because each individual is a constituent part of those states. It is not the same in Poland, as I observed. The three classes that make up the inhabitants do not constitute a nation. The nation is made up exclusively of the nobility, called the *szlachta*. The second class, that is, the Jews, are foreign to the state and merely serve the material interests of the first class. The third class [the peasants] are simply the property of the first.

HUBERT VAUTRIN, *L'Observateur en Pologne*, c.1770–80

THE EVOLUTION OF THE POLISH–LITHUANIAN ECONOMY

UNTIL the late thirteenth century Poland and Lithuania were on the periphery of Europe and their larger economic significance was marginal. From the late fourteenth to the early seventeenth centuries there was a period of economic expansion, linked with the flourishing of the Polish grain trade. A period of economic decline with some interruptions began in the early seventeenth century and continued into the early eighteenth century, when a gradual recovery began.

In the years before 1300 Europe was only gradually recovering from the economic collapse caused by the barbarian invasions, the fall of the western Roman empire, and the conquest of the southern Mediterranean by the Arabs. At this time there were three main trading routes in northern Europe, one down the Dnieper from Scandinavia to the Mediterranean, one overland from the Atlantic through Germany and the Czech lands to the lands further east, and one connecting these two routes and going on to Moorish Spain. Although its volume was quite small, a variety of goods were involved in this trade: slaves from the Slavonic and Baltic lands, fur from Russia, salt from Pomerania, foodstuffs from Pomerania, Mecklenburg, and Holstein, and Frisian and Flemish cloth. Poland participated only minimally in this trade. Until the Tatar conquest the Khazar kingdom and the Grand Duchy of Kiev were much more important.

From the late thirteenth century a new period in Polish and Lithuanian economic history began. The catastrophic outcome of the Fourth Crusade, with its conquest and sack of Constantinople in 1204, signalled the decline of the Byzantine empire, and was followed by the Mongol invasion, which led to the disappearance of Kievan Rus. The Mongols established an economic sphere which ran from the Bug to the Yellow River. These years also saw the beginnings of German eastward expansion and agricultural colonization (see the appendix to Part I).

Poland was now the eastern border of the European world—the world of Christendom—and became a part of its developing economic system. The Mongol conquest of Kiev gave Lviv a crucial position in the trade route to the Genoese colonies of Kaffa (Feodosiya), in Crimea, and Kilia, on the Black Sea. Merchants from Kraków and Sandomierz established links with these towns, while Armenians, Jews, and Italians moved to Lviv, where they traded with the Black Sea ports, importing Chinese silk, Indian and Persian cotton, and spices such as pepper, ginger, and cinnamon. Some of these goods, as well as copper from the Kingdom of Hungary and furs, hides, and wax from Novgorod and Muscovy, went westward via the land route to Breslau, while the remainder, along with increasing quantities of grain and forest products, went north, particularly to Danzig.

By the end of the thirteenth century Poland was becoming an important trading partner, the source of goods which were needed and valued in the West. This was above all the result of the creation of the Hanseatic League, the subject of much recent historical research and some controversy. Originally, the Hansa could be defined primarily in negatives. It was not a league of cities, it did not have a legal status nor a constant number of members, and it cannot be described, as has sometimes been done, as a group of cities with common interests.

What then was the Hansa? It first referred to a 'union of merchants', a partnership which concluded agreements between its members. In time these agreements were confirmed by the cities in which the merchants resided. In the end it became a system which facilitated the cooperation of these different cities. It was now that some of the institutions which we regard as most characteristic of the Hansa began to develop: the Hanseatic councils, currency exchange for its members, and a common treasury to which money was contributed for various purposes. It was now, too, that family links began to develop between the burghers, extending from Flanders to the eastern Baltic coast. In addition, all members of the organization were given reciprocal privileges in member cities.

The Hanseatic League originated in the northern German city of Lübeck, and the alliance was made up of four groups of cities: the Wendish cities, of which Lübeck was the most important; those of Westphalia and Rhineland, which were dominated by Cologne; the Saxon cities, of which Brunswick was the most important; and those of Prussia and Livonia, in which cities linked with Poland, including Danzig, Kraków, and Breslau, were dominant

From the first half of the fourteenth century the Hansa became a major trading power. Its trade was primarily between East and West: Novgorod exported furs to the West, mainly to Flanders, receiving cloth in return. Already in the fourteenth century grain was being exported from the Baltic coast to Norway under the monopolistic control of the Hansa. In addition, from the second half of the thirteenth century Poland became the bridge between the towns of the Baltic coast and two other important economic regions: the Sudeten–Carpathian area, which was an important source of minerals, and Red Rus, which came under Polish sovereignty in the mid-fourteenth century and whose principal town of Lviv was a major source of Asian luxury articles such as spices, silk, embellished weapons, and jewels.

The Baltic coast now underwent an economic transformation. In the early thirteenth century, when Duke Swiętopełk of Pomerania granted a privilege to the merchants of Lübeck, he described his duchy as lying 'on the borders of Europe'. It was now a gateway to Europe.[1] At this stage the principal port on the lower Vistula was Elbing (Elbląg), a town founded by the Teutonic Knights. It was from here that traders went to Toruń, on the Vistula, where smaller trading centres developed at Płock and Warsaw. They then branched out in three directions: to Silesia and the Czech lands, with their capital of Prague, and then on to Nuremberg and Munich; to Poznań, and on across the Carpathians to Kassa (Košice) in Hungary; and to Kraków, which was an important source for copper, and then to Lviv, Kamenets-Podolsky, and Red Rus.

In 1309 the lower Vistula area was conquered by the Teutonic Knights. This did not interrupt the development of trade, and Danzig now emerged as the most important port on the southern Baltic. In 1411, when the Teutonic Knights swore feudal homage to King Władysław II Jagiełło after his victory at the battle of Tannenberg, Danzig was trading extensively in timber for ships, principally fir, spruce, and oak. In the second half of the century, after it finally came under Polish rule through the second Treaty of Toruń in 1466, it began to export what later became its staple, grain, which was sent as far as Portugal, Iceland, and Finland. Danzig's position was further strengthened in the early sixteenth century, when the increasing power of the nobility meant that Kraków and Toruń lost their staple right to offer for sale to local merchants any goods which passed through their towns. In 1557 all remaining obstacles to toll-free traffic on the Vistula were abolished.

Because of these developments, Danzig became a major trading entrepôt, with a population of 50,000 by the early seventeenth century. Among the goods which it exported were its staple, grain, wool, flax, leather, timber, metals such as iron, lead, and copper, salt, calamine, potash, tar, and pitch. The imported goods which passed through its harbour were equally varied. They included manufactured goods, and products such as sugar, spices, and fruits, fish, alcohol, coal, glass, and paper. It also emerged as the greatest shipbuilding centre in the Baltic, and even produced vessels for export to England and the Netherlands.

Danzig now became the main axis of Polish long-distance trade, handling around three-quarters of it. The main trade routes remained the routes to Silesia, Bohemia, and Germany in the south-west, which were the sources of fine cloth,

[1] On this, see Samsonowicz, 'Dom zboża'.

arms, and high-grade metalwork and tools, south across the Carpathians, and eastwards to Ukraine and Muscovy, the sources of cattle, leather, potash, saltpetre, and furs. Grain was central to this trade, but only a small proportion of the grain produced in Poland was exported. The inadequate records available suggest that between 1560 and 1599 an average of 44,000 tons of grain were exported per year, mainly rye, with some wheat, barley, and milled flour, barely 4 to 5 per cent of the total harvest, most of which was consumed in Poland–Lithuania.[2]

Danzig was also the channel through which many new developments reached Poland, including bills of exchange, double-entry bookkeeping, new types of naval craft such as the caravel, as well as the religious ideas of the Reformation. Two additional trade routes should be mentioned: that which went directly west from central Poland to Breslau, Leipzig, and Germany, and that which went south-east from Lviv to Turkey and Persia.

From the early seventeenth century a long period of economic decline began in Poland–Lithuania which continued until the early eighteenth century. The worsening climatic conditions from the 1590s intensified the mini-ice age which had begun in western Europe at the beginning of the fourteenth century, and initiated a period of economic decline which affected the whole of Europe and had a significant impact on Poland–Lithuania. The eastern part of the continent was also adversely affected by the shift in trade and communication routes to the states on the Atlantic littoral and their overseas empires. The increase in population began to slow, and the money supply contracted as the import of gold and silver from the New World diminished. This led to a fall in commodity prices, particularly for grain, with obvious implications for Polish exports, which were also undermined by increased agricultural production in England and the Netherlands.

The long period of war which began in 1648 also had its impact. Between 1648 and 1720 the population of Poland–Lithuania, even allowing for the diminution in its territory, fell by 30 per cent. The amount of land under cultivation fell by 50 per cent, and grain production dropped during the crisis of the mid-seventeenth century to two-thirds of its former level, recovering only slowly. Peasant landholdings fell in size as landowners sought to resolve their economic difficulties by the seizure of land and the increased use of unfree labour.

In these circumstances, the export of grain now played a much smaller role in Polish economic life, averaging 20,000 tons annually, the result partly of local conditions and partly of competition from European and Russian grain and American rice. Cities suffered particularly as a result of the long period of war and unrest, and the populations of Warsaw, Kraków, and Poznań fell by around half. Danzig also lost much of its former prosperity, although, like Warsaw, it recovered more quickly than other royal cities. These developments increased the importance of private (noble) towns, and by the middle of the eighteenth century towns such as Brody and Leszno were larger than most royal towns. By this time

[2] Stone, *The Polish–Lithuanian State, 1386–1795*, 75.

private towns made up two-thirds of all the towns in the Commonwealth and as much as four-fifths of those in the Ukrainian provinces.

A slow economic recovery began under the Saxons and gathered pace under Stanisław August Poniatowski (1764–95), the last king of Poland. This was partly based on an intensification of serfdom as peasants lacked the resources to rebuild their holdings and landlords made increased use of unfree labour. This process was accompanied by the greater concentration of land in very large estates. Landlords also exploited their monopoly of milling, brewing, and distilling, and the liquor trade came to make up as much as half of manorial revenues. At the same time, the second half of the eighteenth century saw the introduction of new and improved stockbreeding and cultivation techniques, as new crops like rapeseed, buckwheat, peas, and potatoes were introduced. There was also some replacement of labour service by rent, and attempts were made to stimulate industrial production.

During these years foreign trade also began to revive. Grain exports increased significantly, although they were to be adversely affected by the first partition of Poland. By 1768 grain exports through Danzig reached 114,000 tons, and by 1770, 124,000 tons, as high as any year in the previous century.[3] Polish trade through Breslau and Leipzig also increased in these years.

JEWS AS MINTERS, BANKERS, AND MONEYLENDERS

Jews became important in the economic life of medieval Poland and Lithuania and then of the Commonwealth as minters, bankers, and moneylenders. Their involvement with specie explains their expertise in minting, which was valuable to the emerging Polish state. Jews were frequently authorized to strike coinage for governments in the early Middle Ages. There appears to have been a Jewish minter in Milan in the tenth century; a number of German coins with Hebrew inscriptions have been found in the German lands from the early Middle Ages; while the early minters in Hungary seem also to have been Jews, particularly during the reign of the first Christian king of the country, Stephen (r. 997–1038), and his wife, Gisela, the daughter of a Bavarian duke and sister of the emperor Henry II. Between 1170 and 1220 Jews minted coins for Polish rulers in Silesia and Wielkopolska. In the nineteenth century 640 coins were discovered in a hoard with Hebrew inscriptions in twenty-five variants. They include the name of the king, a blessing or a request for good luck, and the name of the minter. Similar coins of Jewish origin with inscriptions in Latin have also been found. In the twelfth century Jews were employed as farmers of the mint and coiners, a few under Bolesław IV the Curly-Haired, prince overlord of the Polish lands between

[3] Ibid.

1146 and 1173, and a larger number under his successor, Mieszko III the Old, who was prince overlord in 1173–7 and 1198–1202.[4]

Minting by Jews remained significant in the following centuries, but was on a smaller scale, and it was finally prohibited by the Sejm in the mid-sixteenth century, a prohibition which had the support of both the Council of the Lands and the Lithuanian Council. After 1581 almost no Jews held minting rights. By the early seventeenth century the influx of debased coins from neighbouring lands made the local minting of coins unrewarding. Under Władysław IV Vasa (r. 1632–48) most regions of Poland–Lithuania ceased minting coins and minting was only resumed much later in the century.

It was as bankers and moneylenders that Jews were first invited into Poland, as is clear from the charters of Bolesław of Wielkopolska and Kazimierz the Great (mentioned in Chapter 2). The charter reissued by Kazimierz IV in 1453 begins with seven articles dealing with the treatment of pledges held by Jews for security for loans, and includes six further such provisions in the remaining thirty articles. Kazimierz himself had a Jewish banker, Lewko, and until the fifteenth century banking and moneylending for the Crown were still important Jewish occupations. From the early seventeenth century there seem to have been no large reserves of capital in the Jewish community, and from this time on no Polish Jew became a royal banker. August II Mocny (1697–1706) had a Jewish financier, Behrend Lehmann of Halberstadt, but he came from Saxony and his position was similar to that of other German court Jews of this period.[5]

At the same time, during the sixteenth and seventeenth centuries a number of Jewish royal factors were responsible both for raising money and for administering some royal assets such as the salt mines at Bochnia. They include Solomon Włochowicz in the mid-seventeenth century; Mendel b. Szmul, factor to King Michał Wiśniowiecki (r. 1669–74); Zacharjasz Mendel Kantorowicz, who, as we have seen, was involved in a major conflict with the Kazimierz *kahal* at the end of the seventeenth century; and Jakub Bezalel b. Nathan, factor to Jan III Sobieski (r. 1674–96).

Jews were also active as private bankers. The larger Jewish bankers and, in some cases, the *kehilot* borrowed large sums of money at low rates of interest from the nobility and then lent this at higher rates in smaller amounts.[6] Transactions of this type were particularly important in smaller towns. Thus in Zamość in the seventeenth century Jews borrowed almost four times as much from noblemen as they lent to them, and borrowed almost fifty times as much as they lent to clergy-

[4] On Jewish minters, see Z. Zakrzewski, *O brakteatach z napisami hebrajskimi*; Kupfer and Lewicki, *Źródła hebrajskie do dziejów Słowian i niektórych innych ludów środkowej i wschodniej Europy*; Suchodolski, *Początki mennictwa w Europie środkowej, wschodniej i północnej*; Kiersznowski, *Wstęp do numizmatyki polskiej wieków średnich*; and Gumowski, *Hebräische Münzen im mittelalterlichen Polen*.

[5] On this, see Hundert, 'Security and Dependence', 88. On Behrend Lehmann, see Schnee, *Die Hoffinanz und der moderne Staat*, ii, esp. 169–222.

[6] Hundert, 'Security and Dependence', 69.

men. In the case of burghers, the difference between loans and credits was slight but the proportion of loans increased in the course of the century. The greatest number of loans came from burghers, while those from the nobility tended to be larger, and the largest loans and credits were used for trading purposes. In all, Jews in Zamość borrowed 40 per cent more money than they lent. A similar situation prevailed in Kraśnik and Nowy Sącz. Interest rates, as was usual in the early modern period, were high, rising from 8 to 10 per cent on loans from nobles to as high as 15 per cent on those from burghers.[7]

Many Jewish merchants also engaged in pawnbroking and small-scale money-lending, particularly in smaller towns. Italians were also involved in this, so that the Polish word for pawnshop is *lombard*. In Bełżyce in the middle decades of the seventeenth century, as Gershon Hundert has shown, a number of Jews were engaged in moneylending and pawnbroking in small sums.[8]

Jewish moneylending was attacked by anti-Jewish publicists such as Sebastian Miczyński and in the *sejmiki*.[9] Private moneylending was also regarded with some disfavour by the organized Jewish community; in 1647, for instance, the Poznań *kahal* condemned the practice. In order to avoid competition among Jews and to use communal resources to guarantee the loans, much of this lending was undertaken by the *kahal* itself, and Jews sometimes lent money to the *kahal* for this purpose. Between 1640 and 1648, for instance, more than a quarter of a million zlotys were borrowed by the Kraków *kehilah*. It extended twenty-eight loans to twenty-one creditors: fifteen noblemen, five burghers, and a Jesuit church.[10] Similarly, in 1676 the *kehilah* of Lutsk lent a local monastery 600 Polish zlotys, the interest on which was 48 zlotys per annum, secured against the movable and immovable property of the community.[11]

The *kahal* developed special lending instruments, such as the *membran*, or *memran*, a form of letter of credit, and the *wyderkauf*, in accordance with which the principal of a loan was transferred permanently to the debtor, who obligated himself to pay the lender instalments expressed as capital, which may have been derived from Christian efforts to evade the canonical prohibition on lending money with interest. In the conditions of economic decline of the late seventeenth century such instruments became more common as lending became riskier. The *kahal*s found themselves increasingly indebted and began to borrow more to meet their obligations.

Lenders are everywhere unpopular, and the institutions of Jewish self-government tried to mitigate the harmful effects of this dislike for the community as a whole by exercising control over Jews making loans and regulating the level of

[7] Ibid. 69–71; Morgensztern, 'Operacje kredytowe Żydów w Zamościu w XVII w.'; id., 'Z dziejów Żydów w Kraśniku do połowy XVII w.', 34–5; R. Mahler, 'Z dziejów Żydów w Nowym Sączu w XVII i XVIII wieku', 18–19.

[8] Hundert, 'Security and Dependence', 66.

[9] For Miczyński's views, see his *Zwierciadło Korony Polskiey*.

[10] Hundert, 'Security and Dependence', 70–5.

[11] Galant, 'Zadolzhennost' evreiskikh obshchin v XVII veke'.

interest. Severe restrictions were introduced to make declaring bankruptcy a matter of last resort. A bankrupt person had to swear in front of an open ark that he was without resources and his wife had to make a similar declaration in front of the beadles. All of the property of a bankrupt was sold within six months for the benefit of the creditors, a sentence of excommunication was pronounced against him in the synagogue, during which his wife and children had to be present, he could be imprisoned if he failed to hand over his property, and he lost office in the community and the right of settlement. These provisions applied to a business bankruptcy; a person who went bankrupt because he provided a large dowry for his son or daughter was treated as a thief and subject to imprisonment for a year.[12]

Another important area of Jewish economic activity was tax farming, which had a long tradition in Poland.[13] In the fourteenth century Władysław II Jagiełło (r. 1386–1434) had a Jewish factor called Wołczko the toll farmer, 'in whose industry, circumspection and foresight' he had 'great confidence'.[14] Between 1452 and 1454 another Jewish tax farmer, Natko, served Kazimierz IV in Lviv and Gródek (Horodok).[15] Josko, a Jew of Lviv, served Aleksander Jagiełło (r. 1501–6). According to several decrees issued by the king, Josko held contracts as a tax farmer in Podolia, Halicz, Lviv, Sanok, Przemyśl, Bełz, and Chełm. In 1504 Aleksander exempted him and his family for three years from all taxes usually paid by Jews because of the losses he had sustained as a result of conflict in Red Rus. In 1507 Zygmunt I confirmed Josko's will, which left all his possessions to his widow, Golda. In 1518 Golda's residential rights in Lublin were confirmed. She was to be exempt from all Jewish taxes, except for an annual contribution of 10 marks.[16]

The leasing of the many internal toll stations in Poland to Jews was also common in the sixteenth century. According to the king's secretary in 1516: 'At this time, the Jews are valued more and more highly; there is hardly a toll or tax which is not controlled by Jews or over which they do not strive to gain control.'[17]

Jewish tax farming was strongly opposed by the nobility in the sixteenth and seventeenth centuries. In 1538 the Sejm passed a resolution:

> We herewith prescribe and ordain that henceforth and for all future times, those in charge of the collection of our revenues must be without exception members of the landed nobility, professing the Christian faith . . . We decree that it be unconditionally observed that no Jew be entrusted with the collection of state revenues in any land, for it is unseemly and it runs counter to divine law that such persons be allowed to occupy any position of honour and to exercise any public function among Christian people.[18]

[12] Halpern (ed.), *Minutes of the Council of Four Lands* (Heb.), and Hundert, 'Security and Dependence', 82–5.

[13] On this, see Weinryb, *Jews of Poland*, 58–64, and Baron, *A Social and Religious History of the Jews*.

[14] 'Poland', in *Encyclopaedia Judaica*, xiii. 718, and Baron, *A Social and Religious History of the Jews*, xvi. 17.

[15] 'Poland', in *Encyclopaedia Judaica*, xiii. 718.

[16] Baron, *A Social and Religious History of the Jews*, xvi. 279–80.

[17] Quoted in Weinryb, *Jews of Poland*, 51.

[18] Quoted in Baron, *A Social and Religious History of the Jews*, xvi. 280.

These prohibitions were repeated in 1562 and 1565 with the aim of providing employment in this area for the lesser nobility. However, they were not successful. The nobility even sought the support of the Council of the Lands. As we have seen, at its first session in 1580 it declared:

Conditions in these lands require strengthening, especially with reference to men so greedy to secure profits and get rich from large and vast leases that we fear they will cause immense danger to the majority. Therefore, we have unanimously agreed that anyone calling himself a Jew shall have no dealing with the leasing of the *czopowe* [liquor tax] in Wielkopolska, Małopolska, and Mazovia, either from the king, may His Majesty be exalted, or through officials under any subterfuge whatsoever.[19]

This prohibition was upheld by rabbinical responsa. Rabbi Joel Sirkes explains that Jews would otherwise be 'in great jeopardy because of the outcry of the gentiles in many localities that Jews dominate them and behave towards them like kings and lords'.[20]

Nevertheless, Jews continued to hold tax leases. In the early seventeenth century, when asked to adjudicate a dispute over whether a Jew who held a lease from a nobleman was bound to pay tax to a Jewish toll collector on the Vistula (nobles were exempt from such tolls), Rabbi Sirkes observed that 'there are many Jews who are toll collectors for the king, collecting duties from freight transported [on the river] on the basis of the king's law'.[21]

Tax leases were particularly common in Red Rus. Thus in 1636 a Polish official appointed by the provincial council of Wisznia tried and failed to get better terms for the lease of the liquor tax from a certain Roza Nakhmanowicz; her son obtained a similar lease from the town of Lviv in the 1630s and 1640s. Similarly, in 1633 Samuil Borowicz of Zolochiv contracted to collect the liquor tax for the Lviv council.[22] These were, however, exceptional, and from the late sixteenth century virtually no Jews held leases on taxes or tolls. The situation may have been somewhat different in the Grand Duchy of Lithuania. According to a decree passed by the Council of Lithuania in 1627, 'Our eyes behold . . . that great danger may come from customs [posts] if they fall into the hands of non-Jews. God forbid . . . everything hangs on customs posts being in the hands of Jews for in this way Jews have the advantage.'

Another aspect of Jewish economic activity was the leasing of estates or parts of estates such as mills or distilleries. The monarch himself at times leased estates to Jews. Thus, Władysław II leased some of his villages to Wołczko the toll farmer. This practice was continued until the eighteenth century and was frequently found in border areas. In 1740 Hayim b. Moses held the lease of the town of Opole. The kings also let out on lease the valuable salt mines of Bochnia, which

[19] Halpern (ed.), *Minutes of the Council of Four Lands* (Heb.), 2.

[20] Joel Sirkes, *Bayit ḥadash hayeshanot* (Ostróg, 1834), responsum 61, quoted in Baron, *A Social and Religious History of the Jews*, xvi. 280.

[21] Quoted in Hundert, 'Security and Dependence', 122.

[22] Quoted in Baron, *A Social and Religious History of the Jews*, xvi. 140.

aroused considerable resentment. Indeed there was an accusation of host desecration in Bochnia, which led to the expulsion of the Jews. In addition, the Council of the Lands condemned the leasing by Jews of mints and salt mines. Yet we know that in the mid-seventeenth century Solomon Włochowicz was supervisor of the royal revenues from Wieliczka. He was succeeded by his son Joseph.[23]

As the centre of gravity of Polish political and economic life shifted from the Crown to the great nobles and the large majority of Jews found themselves in private towns owned by the nobles, leasing by this group became more important. The leasing system now became a central aspect of the noble–Jewish 'marriage of convenience'. The Jews attempted to control competition for the granting of leases, which would have driven down their profitability by means of the *ḥazakah* (acquired right or monopoly). This usually laid down that if a Jew held a lease for three years and met all his obligations to the landlord, no outsider was to interfere with his continuing the leasehold until the end of his life. After his death his heirs were to hold the lease until the end of the contracted period; then any Jew was free to seek the lease. A Jew might also bid for the lease if the original Jewish tenant failed to meet his obligations to the landlord or if he had already been replaced by a Christian tenant for at least one year. The terms of the *ḥazakah* varied in different areas, and it was not always enforceable by the community.

Leasing by nobles took a number of forms. First, there was the practice of leasing out a whole estate to a Jewish leaseholder. It was more common in the sixteenth century than later, when lesser nobility began to replace Jews in this function, and was rare after 1648. During the eighteenth century, despite the fact that magnates hardly ever entrusted Jewish agents with the running of entire estates, the Jewish influence in the rural economy grew significantly. These years saw an increase in serfdom, and more peasants were compelled to perform labour dues rather than pay rent for their land. This meant that the Jews became the principal source of cash in the eastern part of the country and consolidated the economic ties between themselves and the nobility.

It also led to a great expansion of the practice of concluding with Jews leases of a more limited character. These included leases on dairy farming, as is clear from a regulation of the Council of the Lands of 1607, and on forests and the production and sale of forest products. Most important was the leasing of the production and sale of alcohol (*propinacja*). This included both the brewing of beer and mead and the distilling of vodka, which was introduced into Poland and Lithuania in the sixteenth century and whose consumption became increasingly widespread in succeeding centuries.[24]

23 Hundert, 'Security and Dependence', 40.

24 On the involvement of the Jews in the liquor trade, see Hundert, *Jews in Poland–Lithuania in the Eighteenth Century*, 36–42; Stone, *The Polish–Lithuanian State*, 304–5; Goldberg, 'The Jew and the Rural Tavern' (Heb.); Lukowski, *Liberty's Folly*, 27; and Topolski, *Gospodarka polska a europejska w XVI–XVIII wieku*, 39.

In the eighteenth century the production of alcoholic beverages came to a significant degree to supplant grain export as a source of revenue on noble estates. The price of both beer and vodka rose more rapidly as consumption, particularly of vodka, increased and also brought a more rapid return. Income from the sale of vodka rose as a percentage of the income of royal estates from 6.4 per cent in 1661 to 40 per cent by the late eighteenth century. It was even more significant on private estates. On the Zamoyski estates, which in the late eighteenth century included ten towns, 220 villages, and a population around 100,000, and whose annual income was 1 million florins, sales of liquor were responsible for between 30 and 46.2 per cent of revenue and were highly rewarding, yielding a profit of 124 per cent. According to Józef Czartoryski, his distilleries were 'mints as it is only through them that in years of plenty we may convert our grain into cash'.[25] The nobles preferred to entrust this trade to Jews because they had the capital necessary to develop it and because they could be trusted to handle alcohol since they did not consume it to excess.

The trade in alcohol was particularly important in the eastern part of the Commonwealth, especially in Ukraine, where the Jews were concentrated. Here, unlike the situation in the western part of the country, Jews dominated this branch of the economy. According to one estimate, as many as 30 per cent of the Jews of the Commonwealth were involved in the production, distribution, and sale of beer, mead, and vodka on behalf of their noble lessors.

Not surprisingly this involvement in a trade which had a clearly deleterious effect on the life of the peasantry aroused criticism, particularly as the impact of the Enlightenment came to be felt in Poland–Lithuania. In 1768 the Sejm passed a resolution forbidding Jews to keep taverns without permission from the local municipality. This seems for the most part to have been ignored by the nobility but did lead to some diminution in the number of Jewish innkeepers.

JEWS AS MERCHANTS AND TRADERS

Trading was the principal Jewish occupation in Poland. Even before the establishment of the Polish state, a key role in the foreign trade of the Polish lands was played by a group of Jewish merchants known as the Radhanites, who were based in Mesopotamia. Their role was described in the middle of the ninth century by Ibn Khurdadhbe, head of the caliph of Baghdad's postal and intelligence service.[26] According to him, they operated along several routes stretching from the lands of 'Firanja' (France or possibly Italy) and 'Andalus' (Spain) to China, and their trading connections extended from their base in the Abbasid caliphate to the Arabian peninsula, North Africa, Egypt, Palestine, Syria, and the northern parts of India. They also traded in Constantinople, Antioch, and the Slavonic lands beyond

[25] Quoted in Hundert, *Jews in Poland–Lithuania in the Eighteenth Century*, 37.

[26] Ibn Khurdadhbe, *Kitab al-masalik wa'l-mamalik*.

Byzantium, and in the lands of the Khazars on the lower Volga. They knew Arabic, Persian, Greek, Frankish, Spanish, and Slav languages. They took from the West slaves, brocade, furs, and swords and exchanged them in China for musk, aromatic wood, camphor, and cinnamon. Their trading activity was possible because of a chain of Jewish communities which stretched from Spain to China. Recent scholarship has confirmed almost all aspects of Ibn Khurdadhbe's account. According to Mordechai Gil, 'there is no reason whatsoever to change anything in the text of Ibn Khurdadhbe which describes the routes of the Jewish merchants from Radhan and the goods carried by them'. However, 'They were no association, nor organization, nor group, they only had in common their country of origin.'[27]

The growing importance of trade can be seen if we compare the charter granted by Bolesław of Wielkopolska in 1264 with that of Kazimierz IV in 1453. While the original privilege provided in article 12 only that no one should interfere with a Jewish traveller or his merchandise and that Jews should not pay a higher toll than burghers in any town, articles 45 and 46 of the new charter were much more explicit:

> In addition, we decree that all the Jews living in our kingdom may secure, acquire, and trade freely and without impediment or arrest any merchandise or other goods, no matter by what name they are called, in the same way as the Christians residing in our kingdom. And if one of the Christians should prevent the Jews from doing what has been described or interferes in any way with their trade, this is done contrary to all of our royal statutes, and by so doing the Christian will incur our great wrath.
>
> Likewise, we decree that any merchant, or anyone else, who sells goods at the annual fairs or in the weekly markets must sell his goods both to Christians and to Jews. If he does otherwise and the Jews file a complaint, then the goods he has brought to sell will be seized for us and for the Governor.

The crucial role played by Jews in Polish trade was widely commented on by contemporary observers. George Carew, in his *Relation of the State of Poland and the United Provinces of that Crown around 1598*, observed that 'almost all trade is in their hands'.[28] His views were echoed a century later by a French traveller, Monsieur l'Abbé F.D.S., who remarked, 'You should know that in the kingdom there is a class of Jews without which the Poles would assuredly die of hunger, since they are most enterprising and hardworking',[29] and by the chevalier de Beaujeu, who wrote that 'They control the commerce of Poland and constitute nearly one-third of the inhabitants of the kingdom, without mentioning that they are the richest.'[30] According to Archdeacon William Coxe, writing in the 1780s,

[27] Gil, 'The Rhadhanite Merchants and the Land of Radhan', 323. See also Lombard, *Espaces et réseaux du haut Moyen Âge*, and Kowalski (ed.), *Relacja Ibrahima ibn Jakuba*.

[28] Quoted in Hundert, 'Security and Dependence', 117.

[29] *Relation d'un voyage de Pologne, fait dans les années 1688 et 1689, par Mon-sr l'Abbé F.D.S.*, quoted in Hundert, 'Security and Dependence', 117.

[30] Beaujeu, *Mémoires*.

'The number of Jews is now prodigious and they have in a manner engrossed all the commerce of the country; yet this state of affairs must not be attributed solely to the edicts of Casimir in their favour, but to the industry of those extraordinary people, to the indolence of the country and oppressed condition of the peasants.'[31]

How far are such comments accurate? Any discussion of the role of Jews in the trade of Poland and Lithuania in the early modern period must start with an analysis of the character of the burgher estate there. It should be stressed that the modern concept of nationality did not really exist in the Commonwealth, or, indeed, elsewhere in Europe. The 'nation' was synonymous with the nobility, which was sharply distinct from other social groups such as the burghers and peasantry. The Jews, as we have seen, were a special case, combining characteristics of an estate with those of a pariah group. The burghers were also not all Polish, in the sense that, like the Jews, many of them came from outside Poland. This phenomenon of a non-native intermediate stratum is of course quite common in agrarian societies—one could cite the examples of the South Asians in East Africa, the Lebanese in West Africa, or the Chinese in South-East Asia.

The largest group within the burgher estate was the Germans; in Kraków, for instance, German was the language of the courts of law until the beginning of the fourteenth century. In the sixteenth century the leading burgher there was Jan Boner, originally from Nuremberg, and other prominent burghers of German origin were Kasper Ber, a mining entrepreneur and minter, Paweł Kaufman, who manufactured tiles and metal wire, and Leon Fogelweder, a supplier to the court of Władysław IV in the middle of the seventeenth century who was connected with the Fuggers, the great Augsburg banking family. By this stage the Polonization of this group was proceeding rapidly, and from 1537 sermons were no longer preached in German in the Church of the Virgin. There were also a considerable number of Dutch merchants particularly in Danzig. Italians too were an important element within the burgher estate. King Stefan Batory's banker Sebastian Montelupi was Italian, as was the cloth merchant Marco Antonio Frederici. According to Gabriel Krasiński, writing in the mid-seventeenth century, Italians were 'even worse than the Jews'.[32] Other significant elements were the Scots, and the Armenians, who were particularly prominent in Lviv.

The organization of the burgher estate had many features in common with the system of Jewish autonomy described in Chapter 2. Thus the Italians in Kraków organized a confraternity with its own chapel and kept their records in Italian until 1745, while the Armenians in some towns of south-eastern Poland were able to obtain a degree of autonomy similar to that of the Jews. They were subject to a court made up of Armenian elders which was headed by an official described as

[31] Coxe, *Travels into Poland, Russia, Sweden and Denmark*, 3 vols. (London, 1784), i. 193, quoted in Hundert, *Jews in Poland–Lithuania in the Eighteenth Century*, 19.

[32] Quoted in Hundert, 'Security and Dependence', 114.

the Armenian judge, a position held originally by an Armenian but subsequently by the town bailiff.[33] A similar autonomy was enjoyed by the Scots, a significant number of whom were active as merchants in Poland–Lithuania from the late sixteenth century and whose number was estimated in 1616, with some exaggeration, by William Lithgow, a traveller from Scotland, at 30,000. In 1659 Scottish merchants in Warsaw reached an agreement with the municipality according to which they were to pay a fixed annual sum in return for the right to maintain shops in the market square.

We do not have an accurate account of how Scots merchants were organized. In the early seventeenth century Abraham Young, a captain in His Majesty's Scots Foot, reported to Zygmunt III that the Scots in Poland–Lithuania were organized in private guilds and societies which held tribunals at fairs and which were supervised by the 'Chief Scots Diet' held at Epiphany in Toruń. They settled disputes among themselves and were also responsible for collecting taxes. According to two other Scots who testified to the king on this occasion, 'Having lived here in Poland for many years, we do know that the Scots have their laws and statutes, according to which they elect four persons every year, who try them, publish decrees, and punish the guilty by fines or imprisonment, lending this money to other Scots and taking usury for it.'[34]

In Vilna the representatives of the four 'nations'—the Poles, the Lithuanians, the Ruthenians, and the Germans—took it in turn to be head of the various city guilds. It should also be stressed that in the period from the sixteenth to the eighteenth centuries loyalties were essentially local, as was citizenship, and burghers thought of themselves as linked above all to their town of residence, zealously enforcing their right to exclude outsiders.

Partly because of its origin outside Poland and Lithuania, the burgher estate was always in a subordinate position to the nobility, and from the early sixteenth century only Danzig, Kraków, and later Vilna and Lviv were represented in the Sejm, and then only as observers. Its economic decline was more gradual but was already evident by the beginning of the seventeenth century. One of its consequences was that many of the more prosperous burghers returned to their places of origin. From the late sixteenth century the burghers did undergo a degree of Polonization, but as a group they were much weaker in the early eighteenth century than they had been in the late sixteenth century. It was only under Stanisław August in the eighteenth century, and in particular during the Four Year Sejm (1788–92), that the Polish burgher class demonstrated a significant degree of unity and political mobilization (see Chapter 6).

A second issue which needs to be taken into account in assessing the role of Jews in the economic life of the Polish–Lithuanian Commonwealth is the larger

[33] On these groups, see Hundert, 'Security and Dependence', 114–16 and Weinryb, *Jews of Poland*, 72.

[34] Quoted in Hundert, 'Security and Dependence', 59. On the Scots generally, see ibid. 53–9 and Steuart (ed.), *Papers Relating to the Scots in Poland 1576–1793*.

question of the emergence of capitalism and the role played by Jews in Europe in the transition from a largely agrarian economy to one based on trade and industry. We now know that this was a very long-drawn-out process which started with the revival of long-distance trade in Europe from the end of the twelfth century and accelerated in the late eighteenth century with the technological advances which then occurred. The transition was neither as rapid nor as complete as was assumed by earlier scholarship, best exemplified in T. S. Ashton's classic work which presented the industrial revolution as starting in England in 1760 and being virtually complete seventy years later.[35]

The question whether there is a link between the Protestant Reformation and the development of capitalism has been much debated. It has not been wholly resolved, but certainly some aspects of Protestant theology do seem to have given a greater validation to the pursuit and accumulation of wealth.[36] The same argument was used by Werner Sombart in relation to the Jews in early modern Europe in a work not free of antisemitic elements.[37]

There are also other serious objections to Sombart's thesis in the context of Poland–Lithuania. There is, first, the question (which has also been raised in relation to the debate about the influence of Protestantism on the economic changes of the early modern period) whether Jewish values favoured the acquisition of wealth. There is certainly some evidence that Jewish values were not hostile to material enrichment. According to Haim Hillel Ben-Sasson, although there is no explicit reference in the sources to an ethos which required an individual to increase his wealth, certain writings of the period do suggest that such an ethos was compatible with Jewish teaching.[38] Ben-Sasson states,

> Clearly, what Weber says about the power of religious teaching to encourage economic activity by endorsing it and ensuring a 'psychological reward' for its pursuit is true of the Jews . . . It would appear that the psychological reward of *certitudo salutis* [certainty of salvation] was given to wealthy [Jews] in the teaching . . . of certain rabbis . . .[39]

This view that the wealth and authority of the communal elite was an indication of providential divine blessing can be found in the teachings of Moses Isserles, Solomon Luria, and their students, as well as of some other rabbis. In addition, lending money at interest was certainly not regarded as illegitimate.

But there were also countervailing views. Certainly, within the Jewish elite, rabbinical and scholarly pursuits had more prestige than trade and commerce. In addition, although Jewish values were not antithetical to the acquisition of wealth, there were some qualifications because of the value given to asceticism in the religious traditions of Ashkenaz and because of the strong fatalism inherent in Jewish belief and exemplified in the view that the fate of humanity was decided each year on the high holidays. The medieval ethical treatise *Ḥovot halevavot* of

[35] Ashton, *The Industrial Revolution in England 1760–1830*.

[36] Tawney, *Religion and the Rise of Capitalism*.

[37] Sombart, *Die Juden und das Wirtschaftsleben*.

[38] Ben-Sasson, *Thought and Conduct* (Heb.).

[39] Ibid. 89.

Bahya b. Joseph ibn Pakuda (eleventh century), written in medieval Spain, circulated widely in Poland–Lithuania. It advocated a life of pious self-deprivation and the renunciation of worldly pleasures.

There is also the question whether the Jews in Poland–Lithuania accumulated significant fortunes. Wealthy burghers in the Commonwealth tended to buy land and sought to aspire to the lifestyle of the aristocracy, to which a number of them, notably the Morsztyns, Szembeks, Wodzińskis, and Montelupis (under the Polish name of Wilczogórski), were elevated, and their capital thus tended to be dissipated. Under these circumstances, one might have expected a small group of very wealthy Jews to emerge, similar to the court Jews of central Europe. This does not seem to have been the case. In Poland–Lithuania, according to Hundert, 'there were some very successful Jewish merchants during the seventeenth century and despite the precariousness of commercial enterprise in that period, some succeeded in bequeathing substantial legacies to their children'.[40] But it was rare for wealth to remain in a family for more than three generations. As we have seen, no native Polish Jew acted as a royal banker after the early sixteenth century, and when Polish kings had Jewish bankers these came from abroad, sometimes from Hamburg, such as Daniel Abensur, 'resident' (financial agent) to Jan Kazimierz, and Daniel Levi, who performed the same function for Jan Sobieski. Sobieski also had a Jewish agent in the Netherlands named Simon de Pool, who conducted business there on his behalf.[41]

There were certainly some very wealthy Jews. A good example from the middle of the seventeenth century was Isaac b. Jacob of Kraków (Reb Eisik Reb Jekeles, d. 1653), who traded in silks and precious metals. In the period between 1640 and 1648, operating with his son Moses, he succeeded in obtaining credits of over 180,000 zlotys. He was a member of the Kazimierz *kahal* from 1608 to 1653, and obtained permission from Władysław IV in 1638 to build the Ajzik Synagogue, the most imposing in Kazimierz. He was an elder of the Council of the Lands in 1617, and may have been a member for a longer period. His wife, Breindl, was the sister of Rabbi Abraham Rapoport (1584–1651). Another wealthy merchant in Kraków at this time was Samuel b. Jacob (Jakubowicz), who, acting with his brother and son, incurred liabilities between 1640 and 1647 of over 55,000 zlotys.[42]

However, as Hundert has shown, great Jewish fortunes were rather exceptional in Poland–Lithuania at this time.[43] The greatest of these, particularly from the mid-seventeenth century, were accumulated by agents of the great nobles, and these were inevitably very vulnerable to changes of fortune. Among the wealthiest of these agents were Jakub Bezalel b. Nathan, factor to Jan Sobieski, who

[40] Hundert, 'Security and Dependence', 62.

[41] On this, see Hundert, ibid. 88; Kellenbenz, *Sephardim an der unteren Elbe*, 397, 400; and Fuks, 'Simon de Pool—faktor Króla Jana Sobieskiego w Holandii'.

[42] On these, see Bałaban, *Historja Żydów w Krakowie i na Kazimierzu, 1304–1868*, i, and Hundert, 'Security and Dependence', 63–9.

[43] Hundert, 'Security', 63, 88.

entrusted to him the collection of all royal tariffs in Podolia and Ukraine; Yisrael Rubinowicz, who acted as general manager for Elżbieta Sieniawska and was responsible for collecting the rent and taxes on her estates, administering contracts with nobles, townspeople, and peasants, and intervening with local authorities in her name; and Shmuel Itsakowicz (Samuel b. Isaac), estate manager for Anna Radziwiłł and her son Hieronim Florian Radziwiłł.[44] These positions aroused great envy and hatred, and the wealth accumulated in this way could be easily lost. Bezalel was attacked in the Sejm in 1593 and accused of a range of crimes, including desecration of the Christian religion, while Itsakowicz was accused of defrauding his employers and was forced to assign his entire fortune to the Radziwiłłs to escape imprisonment.

What did distinguish Jews was the ability to raise large capital sums, either as individuals or through the *kahal*, from noblemen, other merchants, and, to a lesser extent, from the higher clergy and monastic institutions. Jews and burghers clearly shared, with significant qualifications, a positive attitude to the accumulation of wealth. In earlier chapters the relations between the Jews and Christian burghers were described as generally hostile—the burghers regarding any Jewish competition, in a situation which they perceived as a zero-sum game, as causing them loss. However, there were also many cases of partnerships and business relationships which transcended the religious divide. Merchants often travelled together. Some Jewish preachers, most notably Zevi Hirsch Koidonover in his *Kav hayashar* of 1705, raised their voices against Jews who patronized the taverns of non-Jews, where they drank with them. Often Jewish merchants, for greater security, also dressed like non-Jews. Some even shaved their beards. According to Koidonover: 'As a result, sometimes they are not recognizable as Jews, and when asked their names, will reply with a non-Jewish cognomen. And if sometime one was travelling on the road with some notable non-Jews who did not know he was a Jew, he sinned by eating *treif* food and drinking unkosher wine.'[45] In the preacher's view, drinking with non-Jews carried a further danger: it could lead to 'pollution' by non-Jewish women.

Certainly, some Jews aped the lifestyle of the wealthy burghers and the nobility. Sebastian Miczyński in his anti-Jewish polemic of the first half of the seventeenth century attacked a certain Lewek Moszkowicz, who travelled 'like a nobleman' with a pair of footmen. In 1651, when one Aaron b. Isaac of Drohobych was accused of having four footmen, he replied that he only had two. It may be that these two cases are examples of habits picked up from their noble masters by Jewish factors.[46]

[44] On these individuals, see Stone, *The Polish–Lithuanian State, 1386–1795*, 301–2; Hundert, *Jews in Poland–Lithuania in the Eighteenth Century*, 43–4; Rosman, *The Lords' Jews*, 154–84; and Kaźmierczyk, 'The Case of Jakub Becal, King Jan III Sobieski's Jewish Factor'.

[45] Koidonover, *Kav hayashar*, 171*a*, quoted in Hundert, 'Security and Dependence', 227. It is possible that Koidonover is here referring to German Jewish merchants.

[46] See Miczyński, *Zwierciadło Korony Polskiey*, quoted in Hundert, 'Security and Dependence', 228.

Business partnerships between Jews and non-Jews were forbidden by Jewish law and by the local *kehilot*, which constantly issued denunciations and sentences of excommunication against those who revealed 'the secrets of Israel' to merchants or noblemen. A similar hostility to such partnerships existed on the Christian side. According to Miczyński, 'whoever forms partnerships with Jews . . . should know that he will always suffer losses . . . If you are taken in by the sincerity of a Jew, only betrayal and fraud will await you.'[47] This view was given the support of canon law and was strongly supported by the Jesuits who came to Poland with the Counter-Reformation.

In spite of the obstacles, business partnerships between Jews and Christians certainly existed, and some have been recorded. In 1656 a court in Bełżyce heard a dispute between a Jew, Joseph, and a Christian, Wojciech Rozdziałków, who had formed a partnership for the purchase and treatment of malt. Other recorded cases include those of Samuel, a Jew from Sandomierz, who formed a partnership with a Scot named Wilhelm to export hides on a large scale through Danzig, and of two brothers, Israel and Abraham b. Moses Bogaty of Kraśnik, who formed a partnership with Stanisław Farfar to float grain downriver to Danzig.[48]

Typically these were not partnerships between equals engaged in the same activity. Few Jewish merchants were very wealthy, and Jews who engaged in commerce were, by and large, 'second-order' merchants. The greatest traders were Italians, Germans, and Scots. They often used Jews as suppliers of raw materials for export or as distributors of imported goods. Jews frequently obtained capital and credits from them as well as from noblemen. There was also a rough division of foreign trade between different elements of the merchant stratum. Like the Italians, Germans, and Scots, Jews as traders benefited from their international connections, particularly in the German-speaking lands and also in Bohemia, Italy, and the Ottoman empire.

The most important long-distance and international trading centre was the port of Danzig, through which in the mid-seventeenth century nearly three-quarters of the exports of Poland–Lithuania, measured both in weight and in volume, passed.[49] This was essentially carried on by the magnates themselves. The local merchants in Danzig were Germans and Scots, and trade to the West was handled mainly by the Dutch. Trade down the Vistula and other rivers, which consisted primarily of grain but also involved hides, textiles, wax, wine, metals, and timber and timber products, was organized in a flotilla of rafts headed by a skipper. He was responsible for supervising the crew, selling the cargoes, paying the tolls, and bringing the flotilla back home.

[47] Miczyński, *Zwierciadło Korony Polskiey*, quoted in Hundert, 'Security and Dependence', 89.

[48] On these, see Hundert, 'Security and Dependence', 230–1.

[49] On the Danzig trade, see ibid. 118–30; Rosman, 'Polish Jews in the Gdańsk Trade in the Late 17th and Early 18th Centuries'. There is a large literature on the role of Danzig in the international trade of Poland–Lithuania. On this, see Hundert, 'Security and Dependence', 118 n. 1.

Danzig firms shipped the goods out of Poland and sold imports to the skippers. They took Polish commodities to Scandinavia, the Netherlands, England, France, Iberia, Italy, and the New World. What role did Jews play in this trade? From 1454 Danzig had a privilege, which gave it the right to refuse trading rights to foreigners, including Jews. In 1616 Jews were formally forbidden to reside in Danzig, although they were still allowed to visit the port. Nevertheless, Jews did play a significant if secondary role in the Danzig trade. They were not involved in the large-scale export of commodities from Danzig, which was in the hands of the Dutch and to a lesser extent of the Scots and English. Some of this trade was underwritten by Sephardim from Amsterdam and Hamburg. One of these was Samuel de Lima from Hamburg, who was a factor to the Danish king and who became factor to Władysław IV. He settled in Danzig between 1638 and 1654 and had extensive contacts with Polish and Jewish merchants.[50]

Jews played only a small role in transporting and selling grain, forest products, or minerals, the principal components of the trade down the rivers to the Baltic. This was controlled by nobles, particularly after 1648. There had been some Jewish participation before 1648. Those Jews who sold grain were usually brokers. They dealt with the less wealthy magnates and the richer peasants. They sold grain locally and sometimes transported it overland to Breslau and Leipzig. The trade in luxury goods was also largely in the hands of nobles. According to the autobiography of Solomon Maimon (1754–1800), 'The shaffers, that is the nobles . . . undertook the navigation and the purchase and delivery of goods for the high nobility.'[51]

Rafts were not always full, and, as a result, smaller merchants, primarily Jews, often sought capacity for themselves, transporting linen, skins, natural products, and crafts. They brought back cloth and tools for sewing, luxury foods, salt, fish, metal utensils, and some chemicals. Again, to quote Maimon, 'My father had once shipped in a vessel of Prince Radziwiłł some barrels of salt and herrings which he had bought.'[52] Jews dominated this section of the Danzig trade. Moshe Rosman has investigated the role of Jews in the Vistula fleet of the Sieniawski family. In the period 1695–1726 Jews took more types of goods (eleven types, as against three for small Christian merchants) and paid 50–90 per cent of the freight fees. A typical Jewish merchant paid four times as much as his Christian counterpart. Magnates needed to attract Jewish merchants to fill their fleets and made every effort to accommodate their Jewish customers. Boats were not loaded on Jewish holidays, and often adjusted their schedules at Jewish request. Thus, in 1716 a non-Jewish merchant on a raft complained that one of the reasons why the flotilla was delayed for weeks in Danzig was that the Jews persuaded the skipper to wait for more boats bringing merchandise they could buy. In the same year the

[50] On de Lima, see Kellenbenz, *Sephardim an der unteren Elbe*, 76–87, and Hundert, 'Security and Dependence', 101.
[51] Maimon, *An Autobiography*, 20.
[52] Ibid. 35.

Czartoryskis' administrator reported that, owing to the Jewish holidays, the estate was late in settling the accounts of that year's expedition.[53]

Thus in the Danzig trade the Jews did not deal in bulk commodities. They controlled the trade in what were the magnates' secondary items: linen, hemp, flax, wax, tallow, skins, and handicrafts. These products could not be handled in bulk. They were bought up by Jewish merchants and pedlars and transported on the rafts. Jews also bought imports such as sugar, spices, dyes, metal utensils, and cloth. These were not intended for the magnates, but for other merchants or their customers. The Jews were thus the link between the big import–export trade and the local markets. This contributed significantly to the viability of the trade.

A second major sector of international trade was the trade westward with Germany, which developed as trade through Danzig declined.[54] This was an area where Jews were particularly prominent and benefited from the close ties between the Jews of Poland–Lithuania and the different Ashkenazi communities in Germany, Bohemia, Austria, and the Netherlands. The trade was principally conducted at the fairs of Breslau, Leipzig, and Frankfurt. Jewish participation in this overland trade was more significant than in that on the Vistula. Already from the early seventeenth century Jews from both Wielkopolska and Małopolska were to be found in Breslau, and by 1700 two-thirds of the trade through Silesia was in Jewish hands. From the late seventeenth century Jews also began to attend the Leipzig fairs, whose importance grew at the expense of Breslau, and by the middle of the eighteenth century Polish Jews controlled east European trade there. By the last quarter of the eighteenth century the discriminatory taxes imposed on them had been done away with and Jews, including traders from Leszno, Brody, Shklov, Dubno, and Berdichev, constituted nearly 90 per cent of the merchants from Poland–Lithuania at the Leipzig fairs. The goods exported from the Commonwealth included hides, wax, furs, grain, wool, saltpetre, and oxen, which were exchanged for textiles, hardware, and precious metals.

Jews were also actively involved in the importation of wine and copper from Hungary. In the luxury trade with the East, Lviv remained a major centre, with Jews dominating trade with Turkey and Armenians pre-eminent in that with Persia.

Jews also played an important part in local trade. They attended the various fairs held in such towns as Lublin, Jarosław, Łuków, Gniezno, Toruń, and Danzig, where much business was conducted and where the prohibitions on Jewish settlement did not apply.[55] A Jewish preacher contrasted the frenzy with which Jews pursued their activities at such fairs with the nobles' desire to enjoy themselves: 'When he comes to the fair [the Jewish merchant] hurries about buying here and

[53] Rosman, 'Polish Jews in the Gdańsk Trade', 115–16.

[54] On the overland trade, see Hundert, 'Security and Dependence', 94–100, 102, 130–40; id., *Jews in Poland–Lithuania in the Eighteenth Century*, 34–5; Wolański, *Związki handlowe Śląska z Rzeczypospolitą w XVII wieku*; and Freudenthal, *Leipziger Messgäste*.

[55] On the activity of Jews at fairs, see Hundert, 'Security and Dependence', 104–9.

running there to every corner lest the short time pass and the merchants depart and nothing be left for him to purchase. The noblemen, on the other hand, when they come to the fair spend their time in vain pursuits, dining, gambling and making merry.'[56]

The fairs at Lublin and Jarosław were also the meeting places of the Council of the Lands, and they facilitated communication between Jews from all over Poland–Lithuania. 'Marriages were arranged, learned rabbis consulted on matters of *Halakha* and gave their approbation to monographs and commentaries while their students took the opportunity to study in local Yeshivas.'[57]

Jewish merchants also acted in concert. According to a hostile observer:

> when some goods arrive in Poland the Jews immediately purchase it all . . . First they send it to other Jews in the cities and towns for a low price, and the worse goods, after all the Jews have been able to satisfy their needs, they sell to the Christians after it has passed through their hands and for a three-fold price.
>
> Similarly at the fairs and especially the main ones such as Łęczyce, Łowicz, Poznań, Gniezno, Toruń, Lublin, Lwów, Jarosław and Kraków, they travel in groups that few Christians are seen among them. They gather together no small sum of money and by sorcery obtain goods from foreign merchants . . . Wishing in everything to harm the Christians they come early to the fairs (because they have nothing else to do) and rent the best places for display of goods, keeping one and renting another to Christian merchants or artisans for large amounts . . .[58]

Jews were sometimes attacked at fairs, as occurred in Lublin in November 1620 and Lviv in May 1664. This led the individual *kehilot* and the national councils to levy fees from merchants attending such fairs, money which was used to win the support of key noblemen, officials, and churchmen in the towns where the fairs were held. The Poznań *kahal* in the early eighteenth century sent officials to fairs attended by merchants from its community to collect the tax on the transactions they concluded there (the *perdon*, or *berdon*), which was used for these purposes.[59]

Jews also participated extensively in local trade. The privilege granted to the Jews of Parczew in 1569 specified that they could trade in hides, oil, and wax, that granted to the Jews of Zwoleń mentioned hides, tallow, and wax, and that in Opole in 1674 hides, cloth, linen, grain, tallow, and wax. Similarly, the agreement between the municipality of Jaworów and the Jews of 1641, which was confirmed by the king, laid down that they could trade in hides, wool, spices, wax, tallow, and mohair. These commodities certainly seem to have been traded largely by Jews.[60]

[56] Ephraim of Łęczyca, *Olelot efrayim* (Lublin, 1590), pt. A, no. 6, art. 18, 14*a*, quoted in Hundert, 'Security and Dependence', 107.

[57] Ibid. 105.

[58] Miczyński, *Zwierciadło Korony Polskiey*, 27–8, 32–3, quoted in Hundert, 'Security and Dependence', 109.

[59] Avron (ed.), *Minute Book of the Electors of the Community of Poznań* (Heb.), no. 220 (1633), 46; no. 311 (1637), 63.

[60] On these charters, see Hundert, 'Security and Dependence', 148.

In late seventeenth-century Lublin, where the documents reveal a once major commercial centre which 'had become merely a market place for the surrounding region',[61] the Jewish share of the town's trade seems to have been between 36 and 40 per cent. Jews monopolized the trade in furs, saltpetre, and pepper, and were dominant in the trade in aniseed, raisins, wool, sugar, tobacco, and oil. In some areas where the Jews were dominant, such as oil, sugar, pepper, and prunes, their involvement was limited to local (retail) commerce, which would suggest that, as elsewhere, Jews tended to be merchants of the second order. Jews do not seem to have traded significantly in cloth, goods from France, Brabant, Turkey, and Nuremberg, citrus fruit, silk, or metals such as tin, copper, and iron. They also did not deal in wine, possibly because they were excluded by custom from this trade by non-Jewish merchants, although they dominated the trade in mead. In addition, they frequently acted as local suppliers of raw materials and imported goods which they bought from first-order merchants, frequently Italians or Scots.

It is not clear how typical the situation in Lublin was. Hundert speculates that Jews hesitated to aspire to the status of first-order merchants because of the resentment and hostility this might arouse. In addition, given the rising power of the nobility, Jews with such economic ambitions preferred to seek the position of factor to a great magnate. What is clear is that by the end of the eighteenth century the involvement of Jews in local trade had grown significantly. By this time, of 473 merchants in the private town of Rzeszów, 412 were Jews. In the royal town of Przemyśl the figure was 111 of 137. In the eighteen largest towns around Przemyśl and Sanok, over three-quarters of the merchants were Jews. In the country as a whole the figure was probably between 50 and 60 per cent.[62]

JEWISH ARTISANS

Another major sphere of Jewish activity was as artisans. Jews were active in all spheres of artisanry in both royal and noble towns. They played a particularly important role in the clothing and food trades and in working precious metals. In Vilna artisans made up nearly 50 per cent of those gainfully employed in the second half of the eighteenth century. Among the artisan trades there, as we have seen, were tailors, cobblers, bakers, butchers, masons and plasterers, glaziers and turners, tinsmiths and coppersmiths, jewellers and goldsmiths, fishermen, brewers, water carriers, and chimney sweeps.[63] In the noble town of Opatów, Jews were particularly prominent in the baking, butchery, and capmaking trades, and in Medzhybizh we know of the existence of Jewish tailors, furriers, butchers, bakers, and jewellers, and a goldsmith.

Generally speaking, artisans had a low social status. In Medzhybizh, for instance, none of the office-holders on the *kahal* in the mid-eighteenth century

[61] Hundert, 'Security and Dependence', 150. For Lublin trade, see ibid. 149–85.

[62] Hundert, *Jews in Poland–Lithuania in the Eighteenth Century*, 33–4.

[63] I. Cohen, *Vilna*, 100.

was an artisan with the exception of Michel the goldsmith, who was *ne'eman* (trustee) in 1739 and 1740 and whose trade enjoyed a degree of prestige.[64]

CONCLUSION

Contrary to Roman Rybarski's view that Jews were significantly responsible for the decline of Polish trade,[65] it was the downturn in the Polish economy from the late sixteenth century which led to the Jews filling the important gaps in the economic structure caused by the progressive weakening of the burgher estate. At the same time, although many Jews profited from the economic recovery of the eighteenth century, the increase in the size of the community led to greater stratification and to the growing impoverishment of large sections of Jewish society. The economic difficulties of the community were reflected in the growing indebtedness of the *kehilot*. In this sense, even before attempts were made to 'reform' the Jewish social structure from the second half of the eighteenth century, there was a sense that the earlier prosperity and stability of the community was being undermined by economic developments.

[64] Rosman, *Founder of Hasidism*, 79.

[65] Rybarski, *Handel i polityka handlowa Polski w XVI stuleciu*.

FIVE

RELIGIOUS AND SPIRITUAL LIFE

When the Baal Shem had a difficult task before him, he would go to a certain place in the woods, light a fire and meditate in prayer—and what he had set out to perform was done. When a generation later the 'Maggid' of Meseritz was faced with the same task he would go to the same place in the woods and say: We can no longer light the fire, but we can still speak the prayers—and what he wanted done became reality. Again a generation later Rabbi Moshe Leib of Sassov had to perform this task. And he too went into the woods and said: We can no longer light a fire, nor do we know the secret meditations belonging to the prayer, but we do know the place in the woods to which it all belongs—and that must be sufficient; and sufficient it was. But when another generation had passed and Rabbi Israel of Rishin was called upon to perform the task, he sat down on his golden chair in his castle and said: We cannot light the fire, we cannot speak the prayers, we do not know the place, but we can tell the story of how it was done. And, the story-teller adds, the story which he told had the same effect as the actions of the other three.

GERSHOM SCHOLEM, *Major Trends in Jewish Mysticism*

JEWISH RELIGIOUS TRADITIONS

RELIGION played a central role in the lives of the Jews of Poland–Lithuania in the early modern period, as it had continued to do in Jewish history generally since the end of a significant Jewish presence in the land of Israel after the Arab conquests. The nineteenth-century Jewish historian Heinrich Graetz described it as 'a history of suffering and of religious literature', while Salo Baron entitled his monumental unfinished work *A Social and Religious History of the Jews*. There has been a tendency to write this history statically—to see normative Jewish religious practice as unchanging from the period of the Mishnah and Talmud. In addition, historical investigation is complicated by the absence in Jewish religious tradition of a clearly formulated creed. The attempts to formulate such a credal statement, like that of Maimonides (the Rambam, 1135–1204), who sets out thirteen basic principles of the Jewish faith, or those of other Spanish Jews, such as Hasdai Crescas (d. 1412?) and Joseph Albo (fifteenth century), can only be seen as deviations from this norm and are not regarded by normative believers as binding, although much of the religious establishment did accept them as such.

The great scholar of Jewish mysticism Gershom Scholem once wrote that 'Judaism cannot be defined according to its essence, since it has no essence.'[1] Yet it is possible to outline the main elements which make up the Jewish religious tradition. In the first place, Judaism is a religion of law, a law which it is believed was laid down by God for Israel and all mankind. This law is composed of the Written Law, found in the five books of the Pentateuch, and the Oral Law, which was subsequently written down and is contained in the Mishnah and Talmud. Together they constitute the basis of halakhah (literally 'the way'), the prescriptive part of Jewish tradition which defines the norms of behaviour and religious observance on the basis of the interpretation of the law. It is this aspect of Jewish religious practice which explains the importance of the rabbinate. Rabbis were above all needed to elucidate points of halakhah. The authority to rule in halakhic matters had been passed on to them from earlier generations in a chain that was believed to go back ultimately to the talmudic sages and from there to the revelation to Moses on Mount Sinai.[2]

While some areas of the law, such as the prohibition on adultery and consanguineous sexual relationships, remained constant throughout the ages since they were unequivocally set out in the Pentateuch, in post-talmudic communities, like medieval Ashkenaz, halakhah developed considerably. In Ashkenaz, under the influence of the rulings of *posekim* (rabbinic scholars who decide issues of law) such as Gershom b. Judah (Rabbenu Gershom, *c.*960–1028), Rashi (Solomon b. Isaac, 1040–1105), Rabbi Jacob b. Meir Tam (Rabbenu Tam, *c.*1100–1171), and Rabbi Asher b. Jehiel (the Rosh, *c.*1250–1327) and his son Rabbi Jacob b. Asher (the Tur, 1270?–1340), considerable effort had been made to adapt the laws set out in the Bible and the Babylonian Talmud to the entirely different conditions of Christian medieval Europe, especially in the areas of commerce and trade. This often required considerable skill and ingenuity, since rabbis in the post-talmudic age could not simply alter rules set out in Scripture or modify talmudic decrees to meet the needs of their day. As Edward Fram has pointed out in his important study of the way halakhah was interpreted in Poland between 1550 and 1650, 'Jewish laws were considered binding even if the factors that had motivated their enactment had vanished.' At the same time, some change was often necessary since, 'if rabbis failed to integrate modern life into the framework of the law, they threatened to render the latter irrelevant and undermine its authority. Thus in each generation and in every locale rabbis had to interpret the law in light of the needs of those who lived by it.'[3]

Alongside the halakhic core of Judaism, there developed two other aspects of the religious tradition, the attempt to reconcile normative Jewish belief with a

[1] Scholem, 'What Is Judaism?', 114. For a recent attempt to define this essence, see Satlow, *Creating Judaism*.

[2] This issue is interestingly described both by Heinrich Graetz in his 'The Structure of Jewish History' and by Jacob Katz in his book *Divine Law in Human Hands*.

[3] Fram, *Ideals Face Reality*, 2.

philosophical understanding of the world and with a specific Jewish mystical understanding of the world. The essence of the encounter of Judaism and philosophy has been clearly articulated by Isaac Husik, the author of the classic work on medieval Jewish philosophy:

The philosophical movement in mediaeval Jewry was the result of the desire and the necessity, felt by the leaders of Jewish thought, of reconciling two apparently independent sources of truth. In the middle ages, among Jews as well as among Christians and Mohammedans, the two sources of knowledge or truth which were clearly present to the minds of thinking people, each claiming recognition, were religious opinions as embodied in revealed documents on the one hand, and philosophical and scientific judgments and arguments, the results of independent rational reflection, on the other. Revelation and reason, religion and philosophy, faith and knowledge, authority and independent reflection are the various expressions for the dualism in mediaeval thought, which the philosophers and theologians of the time endeavored to reduce to a monism or a unity.[4]

This attempt to reconcile revealed religion with philosophy was more a feature of the Sephardi than of the Ashkenazi world. It did not end with the Middle Ages but has continued until our own time. It is, however, the case that in the premodern period, even when philosophical enquiry was valued, it did not possess the authority of halakhah. This was because, while most Jewish philosophers did attempt to reconcile revelation with reason, their form of enquiry did not favour the former. In addition, they were not bound by earlier precedent and made use of sources of secondary importance in halakhah.

Alongside the interest in philosophy, there was, from the beginnings of the establishment of rabbinic Judaism in the first centuries of the common era, a strong mystical tradition. Its scholarly recovery in our time has been the work of Scholem and his pupils, many of whom, while acknowledging their debt to him, have proceeded to revise most of his basic theses. Scholem saw this tradition as the main reason for the vitality of Judaism over the centuries. As he put it:

During the course of my studies, I have always swung between two poles of interest, which I must admit have not always been expressed with full subtlety and richness in my published work. The one pole—call it my exoteric side—was my scholarly interest in the literature of Jewish mysticism, in both its historical and philosophical-theoretical aspects . . . The other pole of my attention has not been emphasized or recognized to the same degree in my numerous publications over the course of half a century, even though it was no less important to me—namely, as a person who saw and sees Judaism as a living organism, constantly renewing and changing, taking on one form and casting off others, without being subjected to any fixed or predetermined definition. I refer to my interest in the imaginative world of the mystics . . .[5]

According to Scholem, 'Jewish mysticism in its various forms represents an attempt to interpret the values of Judaism in terms of mystical values. It concen-

[4] Husik, *A History of Mediaeval Jewish Philosophy*, p. xiv.

[5] Scholem, 'Understanding the Internal Processes', 47.

trates upon the idea of the living God who manifests himself in the acts of Creation, Revelation and Redemption.'[6]

This mystical tradition goes back to the period of the emergence of rabbinic Judaism, to the concepts of the *merkavah* (chariot) and *heikhalot* (heavenly halls) which attempted to describe the dwelling place of God, which was understood to have a mystical significance. The strength of the tradition rested on a number of factors. At one level, it could be seen as a reaction against the legalistic conventions of normative Judaism. Although mystics were not often openly antinomian, they gave a different and cosmic explanation for the observance of Jewish law. It was a necessary part of the process of *tikun* (repair), of repairing the damaged nature of God's universe and hastening the coming of God's kingdom on earth. With its idealization of the Shekhinah, or Divine Presence, which had a feminine character, the mystical tradition can also be seen as a reaction to the exclusion of the 'feminine principle' from mainstream Jewish tradition.

The most important aspect of Jewish mysticism took the form of kabbalah (tradition), which made its appearance in Provence in the twelfth century, where it may have been influenced by the Cathar heresy with its gnostic elements stressing the existence of an evil power in the universe in conflict with the Divine. There are also proto-kabbalistic elements in the thinking of Judah Halevi (*c.*1075–1141), the Spanish Jewish poet, in particular in his philosophical work the *Kuzari*. This tradition reached its height in thirteenth-century Spain, where a particularly important role was played by the anti-rationalist critique of the views of Maimonides by Nahmanides (the Ramban, 1194–1270).

The classic work of Spanish kabbalistic mysticism was the pseudo-epigraphic *Sefer hazohar* (the Zohar), which was said to have been written by Simeon b. Yohai, a mystic who lived in second-century Palestine. In fact it was for the most part the work of Moses de León (1240–1305), a Castilian kabbalist, written in the years 1280–6. According to the Zohar, the Divine Presence is incorporated in ten manifestations (*sefirot*). These act as intermediaries between God and the world he has created. They are part of God, but are present in the world. By their actions human beings can influence these manifestations and thus act to assist the Divine. This kabbalistic theology was further developed in an early fourteenth-century work whose author is unknown, *Ma'arekhet ha'elohut*. Alongside the Divine, there was a parallel system of evil, described as 'the other side' (*sitra aḥara* in Aramaic, the language in which the Zohar was written).

Two distinct types of kabbalistic practice developed in the following centuries. There was, on the one hand, an esoteric kabbalist school whose members were above all concerned with mystical union with God, and, on the other, those who practised a kabbalah which sought a more popular audience. After the expulsion from Spain a number of different kabbalistic centres emerged. In North Africa a school closely linked with the original Spanish kabbalists was preserved, while in

[6] Scholem, *Major Trends in Jewish Mysticism*, 10.

Italy the influence of Renaissance thought led to the introduction of Neoplatonic elements. The most important centre was to be found in the Ottoman empire. Here there was contact between Spanish exiled mystics and followers of local mystical traditions. These kabbalists stressed the ecstatic components of the mystical tradition, the transmigration of souls, the identification of cosmic cycles, and the calculation of when the 'End of Days' would come. The main centre was in Jerusalem and later in Safed, in upper Galilee, where it underwent a two-stage development. The key figure in the first generation of Safed mystics was Moses b. Jacob Cordovero (1522–70), who summed up his views concisely in *Pardes rimonim*. A more ecstatic form of mysticism was practised by his disciple Isaac b. Solomon Luria (the Holy Ari, 1534–72). The Safed kabbalists had a considerable influence in Europe, even among some non-Jews, although recent scholarship has tended to downplay the far-reaching claims of Scholem. In the mid-sixteenth century the Zohar was published in Mantua and Cremona, and in 1570 *Sefer reshit ḥokhmah* by Elijah b. Moses de Vidas (sixteenth century), a disciple of Cordovero, was published in Venice. It aimed at a wider audience than some of the more esoteric works of the mystics.

Linked with mysticism, but also separate, was messianism. This was certainly a central feature of the Jewish religious tradition, embodied in the wish 'Next Year in Jerusalem' expressed at the Passover *seder*. There were two versions of the messianic idea in Jewish life, the apocalyptic and the gradualist, the one foreseeing the messianic event as initiating an entirely new order of life, the other seeing it as merely bringing about the restoration of Jewish sovereignty in the land of Israel.

Messianism flourished in specific conditions. It seems to have surfaced when cataclysmic events occurred in the non-Jewish world, which were often seen as the battle of Gog and Magog expected to precede the coming of the messiah. The influence of *gematriyah* (numerology), in which special significance was ascribed to the numerical value of specific Hebrew words (as in Latin, letters were also used as numbers), led to special significance being attributed to certain dates because of the letters of the Hebrew alphabet with which they were represented. This was one of the links between messianism and mysticism, which was permeated by gematriological thinking. Catastrophic events in the Jewish world also seem to have increased messianic expectation, although there has been some argument about its extent, both after the expulsion from Spain and after the disaster which befell the Jewish community in Poland–Lithuania in the middle of the seventeenth century.

One additional factor should be mentioned in the religious tradition of the Jews of Poland–Lithuania: this is what Polish Jewry derived from the specific religious inheritance of medieval Ashkenazi Jewry, in which the overwhelming majority had its roots. By the early modern period the Ashkenazi world from Amsterdam to Kiev and beyond had many common features, although there was a strong awareness of the different traditions of the particular areas in which it could be found. The religious and cultural patterns of this world had developed in the urban centres of the Holy Roman Empire and also in northern France, places not totally isolated from the Sephardi world. There were continuing contacts between them, both during the Middle Ages and after the expulsion from Spain, with the establishment of a Sephardi diaspora in the port cities of the Atlantic littoral of Europe, especially in Amsterdam.

The basic religious pattern of Polish Jewry was heavily influenced by the group of religious thinkers of the thirteenth century referred to as the Hasidei Ashkenaz (the pietists of Ashkenaz). From this group there was derived a stress on personal humility, which went beyond resignation and was rather a refusal to respond to the humiliation with which they were frequently confronted. There was also a strong ascetic tradition—a downplaying of the pleasures of this world in anticipation of those of the next. Indeed the question of reward and punishment in the afterlife was a central element in the world-view of the Hasidei Ashkenaz. The importance of submitting to the divine will or heavenly law was constantly stressed, and it required that one should go beyond the literal requirements of Jewish law. Finally, there was a deep preoccupation with personal salvation. Fear of God should lead one constantly to question the level of one's commitment to carrying out His will. The performance of penances to atone for sin was another legacy of the Hasidei Ashkenaz. In addition, in halakhic questions this tradition was sometimes interpreted as requiring the rejection of leniency in legal matters.[7]

JEWISH RELIGIOUS LIFE IN POLAND–LITHUANIA TO 1648

In the history of Jewish religious life in Poland–Lithuania the mid-seventeenth century constitutes a major turning point. In the period before 1648 the Jewish community grew rapidly and became one of the main religious centres of the Jewish world. This was, to a considerable degree, the consequence of the work of a remarkable group of sixteenth-century rabbis. The emergence of a professional rabbinate was a late development in Jewish history. Until the thirteenth century rabbis were not paid for their services and it was only in the following century that it became the usual practice for communities in Ashkenaz to engage professional rabbis. The professionalization of the rabbinate was probably the result of the impoverishment of the communities of northern France and Germany and the disappearance of a class of independently wealthy scholars who could serve as rabbis. By the fifteenth century the concept of appointing a rabbi and paying for his services had become widely accepted.[8]

7 Hundert, 'Some Basic Characteristics of the Jewish Experience in Poland', 30.

8 On the development of the rabbinate, see Schwarzfuchs, *A Concise History of the Rabbinate*; Shulman, *Authority and Community*; and Teller, 'The Laicization of Early Modern Jewish Society'.

By this period two types of professional rabbi had developed. There was firstly the town rabbi, who was appointed by the *kahal* and whose salary was paid from community funds, although it could be supplemented by income from fees. This came from a number of sources, including payment for judging litigation, for officiating at weddings and authorizing divorce, for drafting documents of sale, partnership, or gift, for accepting and validating testimony, for administering oaths to women in order to enable them to claim their rights of dowry, and for authorizing ritual slaughterers and answering questions submitted by them. In addition, the community would sometimes build a home for the rabbi. In smaller towns without an independent yeshiva the rabbi was also head of this body. Then there was the scholar who took up residence in a town without an official appointment and established a yeshiva of his own. The rabbi who was a *rosh yeshivah* (principal of a yeshiva) depended on his yeshiva for his authority and for his income, and especially on the support of a wealthy patron and, later on, the fees paid by his students, although he might also be paid by the *kahal*. In a larger community the town rabbi was usually more powerful than the *rosh yeshivah*, although if the latter was a particularly well-known and respected scholar, this situation might be reversed.

The contract of a town rabbi was for a fixed term. Rabbi Joel Sirkes writes in a responsum from the early seventeenth century of 'these lands [Poland–Lithuania] where congregations customarily engage rabbis for specific periods'.[9] Initially, contracts were usually for three years. By the eighteenth century a small but growing number of rabbis achieved *de jure* life tenure, but this does not seem to have been a widespread phenomenon and contracts continued be drawn up for a maximum of six years. Thus, Rabbi Yom Tov Lipmann Heller, describing the various positions he had held in the first half of the seventeenth century, alludes to three-year agreements in each case, with the exception of a four-year period in Vladimir.[10] Even in the seventeenth century tenure was not always secure. In 1623 the Lithuanian Council declared that notice was not necessary in cases when communities chose not to renew the rabbi's contract.[11] In 1628, however, the council reversed this ruling and required that six months' notice be given. Without such notice, a rabbi's contract was automatically renewed.[12]

Some communities did try to terminate rabbinical contracts before their expiry date, but a decision by Rabbi Moses Isserles declared this to be against Jewish law. Since the institution of the professional rabbinate was relatively new, Rabbi Isserles based his decision on the conduct required towards a teacher, saying that the same rules governing contractual arrangements with teachers applied to rabbis, since rabbis were teachers and derived their basic authority from this function.[13]

9 Quoted in Shulman, *Authority and Community*, 67.

10 Yom Tov Lipmann Heller, *Megilat eivah* (Vilna, 1900), 11*b*–14*b*, quoted in Shulman, *Authority and Community*, 68.

11 Dubnow (ed.), *The Minute Book of the Council of Lithuania* (Heb.), 10, no. 48.

12 Ibid. 39, no. 171.

13 Isserles, *Responsa*, no. 50, quoted in Shulman, *Authority and Community*, 68.

The sixteenth century saw a significant change in the position of the rabbinate in the Polish lands. Adam Teller has argued that 'The declining power of the central authority and the corresponding rise in the status of the nobility in Poland was mirrored by a decline in the power of the centralized rabbinate in favour of the individual communities and the refashioning of the rabbinate as a form of semi-honorary post like those held by the Polish nobility.'[14] Nevertheless, the obligations of the rabbi were wide-ranging and his prestige and authority could be considerable. His most important function was to decide matters of Jewish law. In the area of halakhah, his decision was of great weight, even if Jews could and often did prefer non-Jewish courts over Jewish courts, a practice which became more prevalent in the eighteenth century. Within the Jewish legal framework, even the Council of the Lands could not challenge a rabbi if he could provide a legal basis for his decision. Thus Rabbi Meir b. Gedaliah of Lublin (1558–1616) challenged a decree of the council on the basis that it was not in accordance with Jewish law.[15] The rabbi could use his authority to force litigants to appear before him for judgment. As *rav demata* (local officially appointed rabbi), he was the head of the *beit din* (rabbinic court) of the local *kehilah*. The members of that *kehilah* were obliged to accept the decisions of their court and could not go elsewhere. It is true that lay Jewish judges established by the *kehilah* could also summon local residents. A litigant could, however, reject a lay judge in favour of a more 'learned' or competent court, even if this meant travelling to another community. Rabbi Isserles ruled that, when a rabbi issued a summons, the litigants could not go elsewhere for judgment except by mutual consent.[16] This involved an extension of the powers which the rabbinate had possessed earlier in Germany.

The authority of a highly respected *posek*, who made decisions concerning practical halakhah, often extended far beyond his town's boundaries, particularly if he was the head of a yeshiva. In that case, he was usually regarded as authoritative by all his students, wherever they settled. Rabbis were usually reluctant to interfere in the local decisions of their students, but did respond to their questions and were relied upon by them to adjudicate difficult points of law.

In addition, the rabbi was the spiritual head of the local community and was consulted on most matters of communal government. The nature of the relationship between the rabbi and the community which appointed him was complex, as was the relationship of the rabbinate to the national and regional Jewish communal bodies. During the high Middle Ages in Ashkenaz, rabbis had served on the communal bodies which ran Jewish life. By the fifteenth century they were generally excluded from the leadership of Jewish communal self-government in many of the bigger communities in the German-speaking lands, a pattern which was

[14] Teller, 'The Laicization of Early Modern Jewish Society', 349.

[15] Meir b. Gedaliah, *Responsa Maharam Lublin* (Brooklyn, NY, 1961), quoted in Shulman, *Authority and Community*, 71.

[16] Isserles, *Responsa*, no. 17, quoted in Shulman, *Authority and Community*, 71.

repeated in Poland–Lithuania, both at the local and at the national level. Nevertheless, their prestige and influence was very great.[17] The Jewish community of Poland–Lithuania was what Jacob Katz has termed a 'traditional society' built on the values it had received from the past, and there was no serious challenge to the position of the rabbinate. According to Rabbi Hayim b. Bezalel (*c.*1520–1588), the brother of Rabbi Judah Loew of Prague, speaking of Poland, where he was born, 'throughout these lands, but for the rabbi, no one will move hand or foot to issue decisions of law in his locality'.[18]

The laymen who ran the institutions of Jewish self-government were extremely unwilling to challenge the authority of the rabbinate. At the level of the local *kehilah* the rabbi often intervened against abuses in the running of local affairs. Rabbi Benjamin Slonik (*c.*1550–after 1620), in a responsum, deals with a case in which a rabbi intervened because a *kehilah* delayed an election.[19] On another occasion he compelled the elected assessors to carry out a tax assessment. At the local level the rabbi often supervised the distribution of charity funds and of the proceeds of fines imposed by the rabbinic court.[20]

The laymen who sat on the regional and national Jewish councils frequently made use of the authority of the rabbinate and helped to confirm it. Thus it became the practice of members of the regional councils, the intermediate branch of the system of Jewish autonomy which emerged first in Mazovia and Wielkopolska, and by the mid-seventeenth century also in the eastern portion of the country, to appoint a chief rabbi, generally the rabbi of the principal town in the region, who presided over a regional court (see Chapter 2).

Rabbis do not seem to have taken part in the meetings of the Council of Four Lands, but met separately to exchange ideas and deal collectively with difficult problems of halakhah.[21] Problems which they were unable to resolve there and then were delegated to one of those present for a more considered ruling. Rabbi Sirkes records that when the meeting of rabbis in Lublin in the spring of 1632 was unable to reach a decision about a particular divorce, it was decided that he should reach a final ruling later, which would bind all those present.[22] The rabbinate depended on the lay leadership to support its rulings. Thus Rabbi Joshua Falk looked to the communal leadership to disseminate his rulings on usury. Falk also objected to one family owning a lease for a tavern and living alone in an isolated village, since the wife would be exposed to temptation and danger when her husband was away on business. This led the council to prohibit a single family from administering such a lease: instead it should be held by two Jewish families who could then live together.[23]

[17] See Breuer, 'The Status of the Rabbinate in the Administration of the *Kehilot*' (Heb.), 47–54, 61, 62, 65–6.

[18] Quoted in Shulman, *Authority and Community*, 64.

[19] Slonik, *Responsa*, no. 7, quoted in Shulman, *Authority and Community*, 68.

[20] Dubnow (ed.), *The Minute Book of the Council of Lithuania* (Heb.), 27, nos. 109, 110.

[21] Luria, *Responsa*, no. 65, quoted in Fram, *Ideals Face Reality*, 43.

[22] Sirkes, *Responsa*, no. 91; Fram, *Ideals Face Reality*, 43.

[23] Fram, *Ideals Face Reality*, 45.

The Council of the Lands also sought to use the prestige of the rabbinate to uphold its authority in matters of social conduct. In 1607 the council authorized Rabbi Falk to write a pamphlet setting out its rulings, which were aimed at strengthening religious observance.[24] The pamphlet warned community rabbis to guard against violation of halakhah. It dealt with kosher slaughter, calling for care in the examination of slaughtering knives and requiring that the rabbi periodically examine slaughterers to ensure their knowledge of the law. Rabbis were further warned to advise women to be sure to soak and salt meat themselves and not to delegate the task to non-Jewish maidservants. In addition, the pamphlet warned against Jews attending the parties of non-Jews, where they might drink non-kosher wine, or leaving their women unchaperoned. A later ordinance of the Lithuanian Council called upon the rabbis to assist the local Jewish leadership in preventing excessively lavish wedding feasts.[25]

The rabbi had other important communal functions. He solemnized weddings and his permission was required for others to do so.[26] On such occasions, and also at circumcisions, he would be invited to give an address. He was responsible for ensuring that food sold in the town was kosher and that Jews did not violate the sabbath by trading or asking non-Jews to undertake forbidden tasks.

For the most part the rabbinate was, until the middle of the seventeenth century, an effective institution. Inevitably it was subject to abuses, and some efforts were made to control them. Rabbi Slonik set out the procedure to be followed when a rabbi acted dishonourably by advising a relative to renege on a contractual obligation. His fellow rabbis were first to admonish him privately and, if this failed, to denounce him publicly. If these efforts failed, the malefactor could be further censured at one of the fairs where the Council of the Lands met, as occurred at the Jarosław fair of 1611 and the Kremenets fair of 1612.[27]

Those who sought to enter the rabbinate were not always suitably qualified. According to Rabbi Solomon Luria, writing in the sixteenth century, some rabbis would ordain men who were improperly and insufficiently prepared for the rabbinate for the sake of an ordination fee.

> For our many sins, the ordained are proliferating and the learned are diminishing, and the arrogant are increasing, and not one of them knows his place. And as soon as he is ordained he begins to rule, and to gather young men by offering bribes, like the overlords who hire servants to run before them . . . and there are some (so-called) sages who do not understand even one discussion of Talmud . . . but are only 'sage' in years . . . who rule over communities and over the learned, excommunicating and permitting [that which is forbidden] and ordaining (so-called) students who never studied before them, but who only pay for the privilege . . . [of ordination]. And even sometimes, when we do find sharp minds, they often do not study sincerely . . . but engage in casuistry to aggrandize their fame.[28]

[24] Shulman, *Authority and Community*, 68.

[25] Dubnow (ed.), *The Minute Book of the Council of Lithuania* (Heb.), 27, 32–3, nos. 109, 128.

[26] Ibid. 11, no. 52.

[27] Shulman, *Authority and Community*, 70.

[28] Luria, *Yam shel shelomoh*, ch. 8, no. 58, quoted in Shulman, *Authority and Community*, 74.

A consequence of the prestige and power of the rabbinate was intense competition for rabbinic posts. Such a case of conflict came before Rabbi Isserles, who attempted to make peace between two rabbis who sought the same position. One of them took the case to a Polish court, a violation of Jewish law even were it to have been done by a layman. Bribery was also employed to obtain rabbinic posts. According to Rabbi Joseph Katz (Joseph b. Mordecai Gershon Hakohen of Kraków, 1510–91):

For it is known that many now have achieved prominence who are wise only in their own eyes, and who have not learned even half of what they ought, and who seize an academy by means of monetary bribes. It is not enough that they distort the meaning of the lessons in their lectures, and once used to mistakes, persist in them, but also, since they have become so-called masters, questions of what is permitted and forbidden come before them, and because they are embarrassed [to ask], they decide by guesswork [by dreaming], usually seizing the stricter interpretation . . .[29]

This may have been partly an imitation of the almost universal practice in Poland–Lithuania of the purchase of state office. Certainly, by 1587 the situation had deteriorated so markedly that the Council of the Lands laid down that no rabbi should attempt to buy a rabbinic position through loans or gifts, offered either personally or through intermediaries, nor should any rabbi attempt to renew his contract 'by means of gold or silver'.[30] Three years later the decree was reaffirmed, this time with the signatures of thirty leading rabbis appended, and this was repeated in 1597, 1640, and 1641. The Lithuanian Council was also alarmed by the practice of bribery, and in 1628 passed a statute affirming that the rules for appointment to the rabbinate which were current in Poland also applied in Lithuania.[31]

Abuses also occurred in the levying of fees for hearing court cases. Rabbi Sirkes claimed that these fees encouraged certain judges to rush their deliberations and make hasty decisions in order to increase the number of cases. In addition, cases were sometimes split into smaller units, so that separate fees could be charged for each.[32] These abuses led to attacks on the rabbinate. There were also cases where threats from powerful laymen, whether physical or political, were used to intimidate members of the rabbinate.[33]

Nevertheless, in general in this period the rabbinate was highly respected. A central role in the training of rabbis was played by the yeshiva. In 1567 King Zygmunt II August granted the Jewish community of Lublin permission to open a yeshiva, which was described in the charter as a 'high school for instructing men

[29] Joseph Katz, *She'erit yosef* (Kraków, 1767; repr. New York, 1984), responsum 19, quoted in Shulman, *Authority and Community*, 75.

[30] Quoted in Shulman, *Authority and Community*, 75.

[31] Dubnow (ed.), *The Minute Book of the Council of Lithuania* (Heb.), 43, no. 207.

[32] Sirkes, *Bayit ḥadash hayeshanot* (Ostróg, 1834), responsum 51, quoted in Shulman, *Authority and Community*, 75.

[33] Thus Solomon Luria refers to a certain layman who aroused universal fear; Luria, *Responsa*, no. 33, quoted in Shulman, *Authority and Community*, 73.

of that religion' (*gymnazium ad instituendos homines illorum religionis*). A synagogue was attached to the yeshiva, and its head, described as the rector, was granted extensive powers both over his students and in the community. Four years later Zygmunt granted a similar charter to 'the learned Solomon of Lviv, whom the Jewish community of Lviv and the whole land of Rus have chosen for their *senior doctor*', conferring upon him the right to open schools in various cities, 'to train the students in the sciences'.[34]

Yeshivas were soon established in many other towns and became the key institution in Jewish learning.[35] Having completed elementary education, a minority of young Jewish males continued to study at yeshivas, some of which were supported by a local community while others were financed by a private individual. Students here (*bakhurim*) completed their basic study around the age of 18, when they became *ḥaverim* and were now able to study on their own without supervision. Most left the yeshiva, some to become active in trade or commerce and others to become religious functionaries or even rabbis in smaller communities. Those who remained in the yeshiva, described as *lomedim*, continued to study, usually in a *beit midrash* (house of study), supported by the community, or in a privately endowed *kloyz* (prayer room). After a number of years the *rosh yeshivah* could grant them the title of *moreinu*, equivalent to rabbinic ordination, which conferred the right to be a communal rabbi, halakhic judge, or even *rosh yeshivah*.

The function of *rosh yeshivah* was sometimes performed by the local rabbi and sometimes by a man specially selected for the post. Generally speaking, it was only in smaller communities that the two functions were combined. In the more important centres the *rosh yeshivah* was an independent dignitary who possessed considerable authority.

The functioning of the yeshivas of Poland–Lithuania was described highly favourably by Simone b. Isaac Simhah Luzzatto (*c.*1583–1663) in the 1630s,[36] and in even more glowing terms by Nathan Nata Hannover:

> throughout the dispersions of Israel there was nowhere so much learning as in the Kingdom of Poland. Each community maintained yeshivot, and the head of each yeshivah was given an ample salary so that he could maintain his school without worry, and that the study of the Torah might be his sole occupation. The head of the yeshivah did not leave his house the whole year except to go from the house of study to the synagogue. Thus he was engaged in the study of the Torah day and night. Each community maintained young men and provided for them a weekly allowance of money that they might study with the head of the yeshivah. And for each young man they also maintained two boys to study under his guidance, so that he would orally discuss the Gemara (Talmud), the commentaries of

[34] Dubnow, *History of the Jews in Russia and Poland*, i. 115.

[35] On the development of yeshivas, see Assaf, *Poland: Chapters in the History of the Jews of Eastern Europe and their Culture*, nos. 5–6: *Torah and Learning* (Heb.); Reiner, 'Wealth, Social Position and the Study of Torah' (Heb.); id., 'Changes in the Yeshivas of Poland and Germany in the Sixteenth and Seventeenth Centuries' (Heb.); and Rosman, 'Innovative Tradition'.

[36] On this, see Shmeruk, 'Students from Germany in Polish Yeshivas' (Heb.), 304–5.

Rashi, and the Tosafot [additions to the law], which he had learned, and thus he would gain experience in the subtlety of Talmudic argumentation. The boys were provided with food from the community benevolent fund or from the public kitchen . . .

There was scarcely a house in all the Kingdom of Poland where its members did not occupy themselves with the study of the Torah. Either the head of the family was himself a scholar, or else his son, or his son-in-law studied, or one of the young men eating at his table. At times, all of these were to be found in one house . . .[37]

Given these conditions, it is not surprising that in the century before 1648 Polish Jewry produced a whole pantheon of sages and scholars, some of whom have already been referred to. At this time there were close links between the different parts of the Ashkenazi world, especially between Prague, one of the largest and most active Jewish centres in northern Europe, and Poland. The varied nature and high quality of the men who made up this group is a testimony to the multifaceted and rich religious life of Poland–Lithuania. The first of the important Polish rabbis was Jacob b. Joseph Pollack, who was born in Bavaria, and who in 1494 founded a yeshiva in Kraków, which he headed until 1522. His most important pupil was Rabbi Shalom Shakhna b. Joseph, who established a yeshiva in Lublin which became a major centre for talmudic study, and Shakhna's work was carried on by his principal students, his son-in-law Rabbi Moses Isserles and Rabbi Solomon Luria.

Moses Isserles was the most important figure in sixteenth-century Jewish Kraków. His father was a successful businessman who set up his son as head of his own yeshiva in Kazimierz. He had extensive links within the rabbinic elite of Ashkenaz and not only married Rabbi Shakhna's daughter but was related to Meir b. Isaac Katzenellenbogen of Padua (1473–1565) and Solomon Luria. In addition to his skill in halakhah, he was a warm defender of philosophy and believed that something could be learnt from Aristotle, once his work had been filtered through Maimonides. 'It is better', he claimed, 'to study philosophy than to err through the kabbalah.' He was very interested in astronomy and was the teacher of David Gans of Prague (1541–1613), the author of one of the first Jewish works of history in the modern period to attempt to explain the non-Jewish world. At the same time Isserles did not totally reject kabbalah and tried to reconcile its teachings with the knowledge he had acquired from his second-hand reading of Aristotelian philosophy. The other major talmudic scholar of his generation was Solomon Luria. A fiercely independent individual and a sharp social critic, he scorned those rabbis who, in his view, did not properly investigate the complexities of halakhah. Although he opposed the more rationalist views of Isserles, he was more flexible in his interpretation of halakhah.[38]

The next generation saw an even greater number of significant Jewish scholars. Among them was Joshua Falk (1555–1614), who became head of the yeshiva in

[37] Hannover, *Abyss of Despair*, 110–16.

[38] On Isserles's relationship to secular knowledge, see D. Fishman, 'Rabbi Moshe Isserles and the Study of Science among Polish Rabbis'.

Lviv and was actively involved in the work of the Lviv Council, as, from 1619, was Joel Sirkes (1561–1640), the rabbi of Kraków. Mordecai b. Abraham Jaffe (b. Prague 1535, d. Poznań 1612) was a pupil of both Moses Isserles and Solomon Luria. Head of the Prague yeshiva in 1561, when the Jews were expelled from Bohemia, he went to Vienna, where he studied astronomy. In 1582 he become rabbi of Horodno and in 1588 rabbi of Lublin and a major figure in the Council of the Lands. In 1592 he again became rabbi of Prague and in 1599 was appointed rabbi of Poznań.

An indication of the way Poland was now a central part of the religious life of Ashkenaz can be seen in the life of another prominent rabbi, Yom Tov Lipmann Heller (b. Wallerstein 1579, d. Kraków 1654).[39] While chief rabbi of Prague he was put on trial in 1629 for slandering the Christian religion and condemned to death, a punishment which was commuted to a large fine. In 1632 he left Prague and moved to Nemirov (Nemyriv) in Ukraine, and in 1635 he became rabbi of Vladimir. Subsequently, in 1643, he became rabbi of Kraków, where in 1648 he succeeded Joshua Hoeschel b. Joseph (1578–1648), as *rosh yeshivah*. Like Isserles, he was interested in mathematics and philosophy, but also wrote a kabbalistic treatise which was close in spirit to Cordovero's *Pardes rimonim*. In addition, he praised Azariah de Rossi's rationalist work *Meor einayim* about. A Hebrew grammarian, he also wrote an astronomical treatise about the moon. Another of his works was a Yiddish translation of the treatise 'Oraḥ ḥayim' of the *Shulḥan arukh*. His most influential work was the *Tosafot yom tov*, a commentary on the Mishnah. In addition, he composed three penitential prayers (*seliḥot*) on the Khmelnytsky massacres.

Vilna, the capital of the Grand Duchy of Lithuania, was also the home of many notable religious scholars. Among them was Rabbi Menahem Monash Chajes, the second person to hold the post of rabbi of the city. He was the son of Isaac b. Abraham Chajes (1538–*c.*1615), rabbi of Prague and himself a renowned scholar. Prior to his move to Vilna, Rabbi Menahem Chajes held the posts of rabbi in Turobin and Szydłów. He was rabbi of Vilna from 1617 to 1636, during which period he gave his approbation to an edition of the *Tsene rene*, the commentary in Yiddish on the weekly Torah portion intended for women written by Rabbi Jacob b. Isaac (Jacob Ashkenazi, 1550–1626?). Three of his sons succeeded to the rabbinate.

Rabbi Moses b. Isaac Judah Lima (*c.*1605–1658) was probably the descendant of Spanish exiles. He went to Poland from the Netherlands and was the fourth rabbi of Vilna. He studied at the yeshiva of Rabbi Joshua Falk in Kraków, and as a young man of 20 became rabbi and head of the yeshiva in Slonim. In 1655 he was appointed rabbi of Vilna, where his father-in-law, Rabbi Zanvill, lived and where he served until his death. He was the author of a commentary on the *Shulḥan arukh* which was published posthumously.

[39] He is the subject of a recent biography, Davis, *Yom Tov Lipmann Heller*.

Shabetai b. Meir Hakohen (1621–62) was perhaps the most outstanding of Vilna's scholars in the seventeenth century. He studied in Kraków and Lublin, and when quite a young man was appointed a member of the Vilna *beit din* under Rabbi Moses Lima. He established his reputation at the early age of 26 with his commentary entitled *Siftei kohen*, on the section 'Yoreh de'ah' of the *Shulḥan arukh*, in which he challenged many of the decisions of his predecessors and the opinions of his contemporaries. In 1646 he returned to Kraków, where, in the following year, he published his work on the second part of the *Shulḥan arukh*, which was widely praised. He struck out on a path of his own in his interpretation of talmudic law, and although his views aroused the hostility of some of his contemporaries, such as David b. Samuel Halevi and Aaron Samuel b. Israel Koidonover, the majority accepted his work as of the highest authority and applied his decisions to actual cases as the final word on the laws in question. During the Khmelnytsky Uprising he sought refuge for a time in Prague, where he probably wrote his account of the massacres, *Megilat ayefah*,[40] as well as some penitential prayers for 20 Sivan, the date of the massacre in Nemirov, one of the worst Jewish massacres. He remained outside Poland, being appointed as rabbi first in Dřešín and then in Holleschau (Holešov) in Moravia.

The emergence of Poland–Lithuania as a major centre of Jewish religious life was both facilitated and transformed by the development of printing, a widespread European phenomenon at this time.[41] The beginnings of Jewish printing in Poland were not particularly auspicious. The Halicz brothers, who established the first Jewish publishing house in Kraków in the 1530s, converted to Christianity, and the Jewish community was compelled by a commission established by Zygmunt I to purchase the entire stock of Jewish works which they had produced, mostly prayer books.[42] By the second half of the century two major Jewish printing houses were in existence, that of Isaac b. Aaron of Prosnitz in Kraków and one in Lublin. In addition, in 1566 Zygmunt II granted to one Benedict Levita of Kraków the right to import Jewish books. As papal censorship became more rigorous, the ability of the Polish presses, which were not subject to it, to compete with the more established presses of Prague and Venice became greater, and from the end of the sixteenth century local editions came to dominate the Polish Jewish book market.

Neither Jacob Pollack nor Shalom Shakhna left behind much in the way of written work. This situation changed in the next two generations when many significant halakhic and mystical studies were produced, and were much more widely distributed because of the new technology. Printing made it possible for readers to spend more time studying texts, rather than copying them, and made available a much larger range of works. As Edward Fram has observed, 'More Jews had

[40] An allusion to Jer. 4: 31 ('For my soul fainteth before murderers').

[41] On the impact of printing, see Reiner, 'The Ashkenazi Elite at the Beginning of the Modern Era', and Rosman, 'Innovative Tradition'.

[42] Shulman, *Authority and Community*, 6.

access to rabbinic texts at the beginning of the seventeenth century than at any time in the age of manuscripts.'[43] The importance of printing should not be exaggerated—printed books were expensive and not always readily available—but religious works of all sorts were now much more widely disseminated within the Jewish community of Poland–Lithuania. These works have also been preserved for posterity in much larger numbers.

One of the most important ventures was the printing of the Talmud. The first complete printed edition had appeared in the 1520s, when Pope Leo X, who thought that this would aid missionary work among the Jews, granted to Daniel Bomberg, a Christian printer from Amsterdam, permission to print the entire work. (Various individual volumes of the Talmud had already been published by Soncino, and perhaps others as well.) Bomberg had his printing shop in Venice, the capital of European typography. This first printing, which was assisted by Jewish scholars, went through three editions and was followed by another complete edition produced by the Venetian printer Giustiniani. Most of these volumes were not used for missionary purposes but found their way into Jewish hands, a fact which alarmed the Pope, who made several attempts to control the printing of the Talmud through his ambassador in Venice. In the end, in 1553 Pope Julius III ordered the confiscation and burning of the Talmud. This prohibition was also enforced by Julius III's successor Pope Paul IV, and the Talmud was included in the first index of forbidden books issued during his pontificate by the Congregation of the Inquisition.

The Talmud was discussed at the Council of Trent in its final sessions (1563), and in the following year the papal curia published a revised index of prohibited books, in which the Talmud was again included. At the same time it was agreed that it could be treated as a tolerated book provided that the title 'Talmud' was removed, along with sections which 'insulted' the Christian faith. To publish the Talmud, printers would need to receive formal consent from a Church censor appointed by the Holy Office or by the local bishop. In this new situation, neither Christian nor Jewish printers in Italy were prepared to print any tracts of the Talmud. It was printed, however, in Poland, Turkey, and Basel (part of the Swiss Confederation from 1501), and soon became the most popular printed Hebrew book in Poland in the sixteenth and seventeenth centuries.[44] The first Polish edition of the Talmud was produced in Lublin in 1559, and subsequently over a hundred editions were printed in Kraków in this period and about sixty in Lublin. We do not know the number of copies printed, but if each edition numbered between 300 and 500, then some 48,000 to 80,000 copies of the Talmud were produced in Poland at this time. This clearly contributed to the emergence of a religious culture dominated by halakhic concerns. The communal institutions of Polish Jewry were eager to control the spread of the printed word. In 1603 the

43 Fram, *Ideals Face Reality*.

44 Pilarczyk, 'Printing the Talmud in Poland in the Sixteenth and Seventeenth Centuries'.

first *haskamah* (approbation) by the Council of the Lands for printing a book was issued, and this power to license printed works was firmly exercised. The council invested the rabbinate with authority over printed material, threatening to close any printing press and excommunicate any printer and his associates who dared to print Jewish books without a rabbinic approbation or a licence from the council.

In the first half of the sixteenth century the Ashkenazi tradition of commentary became established in Poland, as did the principles of halakhic exposition. During the later Middle Ages yeshiva education had been characterized by individual scholars transmitting the canonical texts together with their interpretations to their pupils. 'The individualization of canonical texts by those who taught them explains why the manuscript era produced multiple recensions of the same work, such as the *Mordekhai* [a canonical work summarizing aspects of halakhah] of Rabbi Samuel, the *Mordekhai* of Rabbi Samson, the Rhenish *Mordekhai*, and the Austrian *Mordekhai*.'[45] This method of instruction was radically altered by printing, which established a permanent form of the canonical texts—the Talmud and the commentaries. In addition, a much wider range of works was now available: 'books by medieval Sephardic scholars who had previously been only names or occasional citations. Maimonides, Nahmanides, Saadiah Gaon, Don Isaac Abrabanel, Rabbi Isaac Arama, Rabbi Abraham ibn Ezra, Rabbi David Kimhi, Rabbi Solomon ibn Adret, Rabbi Bahya ibn Pakuda, and many others could now be studied directly and in depth.'[46] It was now much more practicable to attempt the codification of halakhah. This was first attempted within the Sephardi world. Polish Jewry also played a role in the codification of halakhah and its reduction to a manageable form.

In 1564 Joseph Caro, one of the principal scholars at Safed, published the digest of Jewish law entitled the *Shulḥan arukh*. It was composed of four sections: 'Oraḥ ḥayim', which dealt with daily commandments, the sabbath, and the festivals; 'Yoreh de'ah', which set out the law on kosher slaughter, dietary laws, forbidden practices, burial, and mourning; 'Even ha'ezer', which organized material on marriage; and 'Ḥoshen hamishpat', devoted to civil law and civil procedure. It was printed in Venice in 1565 and reprinted in Kraków in 1570–1 and 1578–80.

Caro based his work on three authorities, Isaac b. Jacob Alfasi (the Rif, 1013–1103), who lived in North Africa, Maimonides (Rambam), who wrote his code in Egypt, and Asher b. Jehiel (the Rosh), the son of one of the Hasidei Ashkenaz who had settled in Spain at the beginning of the fourteenth century. As a result, Caro's compilation did not take into account halakhic decisions and customs which had developed in Ashkenaz since the time of Asher b. Jehiel. It was in order to deal with this defect that the work was modified for Ashkenazi conditions by Moses Isserles, who had already been involved in a codification project, which he abandoned when he learned of Caro's work. He described what he had done with a metaphor. *Shulḥan arukh* in Hebrew means 'The Set Table'. He

[45] Rosman, 'Innovative Tradition', 239. [46] Ibid.

explained that he had prepared a table cloth (*Mapah*) for this table. His role was summed up in the rabbinic opinion 'In all the lands of Ashkenaz, we accept and obey the words of our master, Rabbi Moshe Isserles.'[47]

This acceptance did not come immediately and Isserles's innovations were resisted by more conservative scholars, including Rabbi Solomon Luria, Rabbi Sirkes, and Rabbi Aaron Land of Poznań. Codification radically changed the way the Talmud was studied. 'The objective was no longer to understand how the text formed the foundation for a particular area of halakhah; instead, it was to uncover the subtleties of the text itself: its logic, its internal consistency, the relationship between various passages even if they were ostensibly unconnected, and the contradictions entailed by competing interpretations of the text.'[48] *Pilpul* (close analysis), which had long been an element in yeshiva pedagogy used to sharpen analytical skills, now became a central element in talmudic analysis, sometimes leading to highly fanciful interpretations. At the same time codification meant that a student could now much more easily master the enormous and complex mass of material which made up the Talmud.

The Polish masters of halakhah both consciously and unconsciously reshaped Jewish law and practice in a number of fields.[49] Most modifications were introduced in the field of trade and commerce. Here rulings weakened the prohibition on the handling of wine by non-Jews, regulated competition among Jews in bidding for leases, extended the possibility of the transfer and payment of personal debts by letters of credit (*memranim*), and widened the scope of bankruptcy laws. Changes in matters of personal law were less frequent, although a more relaxed attitude was adopted towards the problem of allowing deserted wives to remarry by certifying the death of the absent husband. Permission was also granted to hold weddings on the sabbath in cases where there was little other choice.

These developments led to the emergence of a new attitude to Polish Jewry. In the fifteenth century, Polish rabbis had enjoyed little prestige.[50] Yet by the end of the sixteenth century Jews in Italy, Germany, Bohemia, Moravia, Amsterdam, and even Istanbul were seeking direction on halakhic questions from Poland–Lithuania.

The more widespread accessibility of printed books and the greater number of books available also transformed popular religious culture. The sixteenth and early seventeenth centuries saw the publication of a large number of biblical commentaries, both in Hebrew and in Yiddish, which expanded on that of Rashi. Of these the most widely available was *Keli yakar* (Lublin, 1602) by Ephraim Solomon b. Aaron of Luntshits (Łęczyca, 1550–1619). These commentaries concentrated on the Pentateuch and books such as Ruth and Esther, and were

[47] Quoted in Barnavi (ed.), *A Historical Atlas of the Jewish People*, 142.

[48] Rosman, 'Innovative Tradition', 244.

[49] This is the main subject of Fram's valuable study.

[50] 'Poland', in *Encyclopaedia Judaica*, xiii. 721.

thus intended not so much for scholars as for those who wished to understand better the weekly Torah portion or the biblical books connected with such festivals as Shavuot and Purim. There was also a more widespread diffusion of books of moral exhortation, ethical wills, and codes of conduct.

These exegetical and moralistic preoccupations were also catered to by preachers (*darshanim*), who became an established feature of the Jewish communities of Poland–Lithuania. They, rather than the rabbi, gave the weekly sermon usually devoted to the Torah portion and spoke at weddings, funerals, and communal events. Some were permanent officials, while others were hired only for a week or several weeks.

In addition, the development of printing seems to have accelerated the change in the position of the cantor (*ḥazan*) in religious life, since much of the early Hebrew book production in Poland took the form of prayer books, which now became increasingly standardized.[51] This reduced the ability of the cantor to improvise freely and deviate from the text of the prayer book and placed more stress on his ability as a musical performer. In medieval Ashkenaz the cantor was frequently a religious poet, composing liturgical poetry, and also performing at public functions, such as pronouncing the ban of excommunication when necessary and deciding the order of honours to the Torah, as well as calling up the congregants so honoured. Most of these functions were now eliminated, and the cantor's major function became that of leading the congregation in prayer. Whereas, previously, understanding the meaning of the prayers and the ability to compose new ones, coupled with Torah learning and piety, had been the most important qualities sought in a cantor, musical talent now became paramount, and other qualities were sacrificed to it. Thus Rabbi Slonik, in one of his responsa, criticized the many ignorant cantors who were in positions because of their excellent voices rather than because of their piety and scholarship.[52] This view was expressed even more strongly by Rabbi Solomon Luria:

> The law requires that the rabbi should choose the cantor from among his students, but should the rabbi dare to exercise this right, his recommendation would be rejected by the congregation. It would be futile for the rabbi to protest. The communities retain for themselves and withhold from the rabbi the power of appointment in order that the cantor should remain accountable to them alone and free from the control of the rabbi. As a consequence, the piety of the reader is subordinate to a pleasant voice and clear diction.[53]

A common complaint about cantors was that, carried away by their desire to demonstrate their musical talents, they prolonged the length of services excessively. The Council of Lithuania of 1623 limited the number of melodies a cantor could sing to three on an ordinary sabbath and four on a special sabbath.

[51] On this, see Shulman, *Authority and Community*, 76–81.

[52] Slonik, *Responsa*, no. 6, quoted in Shulman, *Authority and Community*, 77.

[53] Luria, *Yam shel shelomoh*, no. 49, quoted in Shulman, *Authority and Community*, 77.

No special melodies were permitted before the Shema, the central section of the morning service proclaiming the unity of God.[54]

Rabbi Slonik, in a responsum, criticizes the ignorance of many cantors and the length of their services but also the source of the melodies they employed, which he claimed were borrowed from popular songs and the theatre:

> From month to month and from week to week new melodies are sung which our forefathers never heard nor wanted to hear, for they are borrowed from churches and theatres! Yet no one seems to care. The longer the cantor sings the better they like it. Even if he knows not one law or prayer or Torah reading.[55]

Halakhah was perhaps the central concern of the Polish rabbis in this period, but they were also interested in both philosophical investigation and mysticism. There were major differences within the rabbinate, in some ways similar to the conflict between Maimonides and Nahmanides, on the value of philosophical enquiry. Those who were most interested in the study of newly available subjects were Moses Isserles and Abraham Horowitz, while Solomon Luria had a higher regard for traditional methods of investigation. Certainly, philosophical enquiry did not reach the levels which had been attained in Spain, and it may be that the catastrophe of Spanish Jewry led to a feeling that such enquiry was in some way illegitimate. Rabbi Luria observed with some indignation in one of his responsa that 'I myself have seen the prayer [*sic*] of Aristotle copied in the prayer-books of Yeshivah students.'[56] The prevalence of such views is confirmed by Joseph Solomon Delmedigo (1591–1655), the Cretan-born mathematician and astronomer of Sephardi origin, who spent four years in Vilna between 1620 and 1624 as a court physician to Prince Krzysztof Radziwiłł. According to him, the Jews of Poland–Lithuania 'are opposed to the sciences . . . saying the Lord has no delight in the sharpened arrows of the grammarians, poets and logicians, nor in the measurements of the mathematicians and the calculations of the astronomers'.[57]

At the same time the intellectual elite of Polish Jewry was closely linked with communities in areas like Prague and northern Italy which were centres of the Renaissance. This has led some to ask whether there was an Ashkenazi Renaissance. There were certainly contacts between Polish Jews and the Italian world, as is demonstrated by Rabbi Heller's interest in Azariah de Rossi's *Meor einayim*. There were also some contacts with the Protestants, who in the second half of the sixteenth century commanded the allegiance of more than a quarter of the Polish nobility. This led to the emergence of a small Jewish apologetic literature. The more radical Protestant groups, particularly the Unitarians, were often

[54] Dubnow (ed.), *The Minute Book of the Council of Lithuania* (Heb.), 12, no. 62.

[55] Slonik, *Responsa*, no. 6, quoted in Shulman, *Authority and Community*, 108.

[56] Dubnow, *History of the Jews in Russia and Poland*, i. 120.

[57] Ibid. 134. It should be pointed out that David Fishman has shown that the Jews of Kraków did show some interest in astronomy in the 16th century, although of a rather traditional kind.

attacked by their Catholic opponents for their Judaizing tendencies. Their leading theologians, Szymon Budny and Marcin Czechowic, attempted to demonstrate their distance from Judaism by engaging in oral disputes with Jews and attacking Jewish beliefs in their works. Most of the Jewish responses have not been preserved, if they ever existed. One that has come down to us is a short work by Jacob of Bełżyce with a reply by Marcin Czechowic, *Odpis Jakóba żyda z Bełżyc na Dyalogi Marcina Czechowica: Na który zaś odpowiada Jakobowi żydowi tenże Marcin Czechowic* (Lublin, 1582).[58]

The most effective anti-Christian polemic was that of the Karaite scholar Isaac b. Abraham Troki. At this time relations between Rabbanite Jews and Karaites in Poland–Lithuania were close, and the Karaites seem to have regarded themselves as Jews and to have been so regarded by Christian society. Isaac Troki served both the Karaite and the Rabbanite communities in his native town for several years as *dayan* and *shofet* (judge and magistrate), and when he speaks of himself and his Karaite co-religionists, he uses the phrase 'we Jews'. In one respect the religious culture of the Karaites differed from that of the Rabbanites. Joseph Delmedigo testifies to the fact that men of secular culture and what he regarded as genuine learning could be encountered only among the Karaites; they were not to be found among the Jews (that is, the Rabbanite Jews), for these 'knew nothing except for the Talmud, and contented themselves with talmudic study'. The Karaites, however, were 'open to secular sciences and interested in them'.[59]

Isaac's *Ḥizuk emunah*, a sophisticated analysis of the contradictions in the Gospel narratives and the differences between the faith of Jesus and his followers and that of the Christian churches, was initially circulated in manuscript form, both in its original Hebrew version and in German and Spanish translations. It was first published with a Latin translation and with other Jewish anti-Christian polemics by the Christian Hebraist Johann Christoph Wagenseil, who wished to make Christian missionaries better acquainted with Jewish arguments. This did not prevent its being used by Voltaire and other members of the Enlightenment in their anti-Christian polemics. According to Voltaire, 'Not even the most decided opponents of religion have brought forward any arguments which could not be found in the "Fortification of the Faith" by Rabbi Isaac.'[60]

In *Ḥizuk emunah* Isaac made extensive use of both Christian and Jewish sources. The Christian sources show his wide knowledge, while his extensive use of Jewish sources constitutes another testimony to the links between the Karaites and the Jewish community.[61] These Jewish texts include not only the Bible and Talmud, but also medieval and later biblical commentaries like those of David b.

[58] On Jewish–Christian debates, see Rosenthal, 'Marcin Czechowic and Jacob of Bełżyce', 81–6.

[59] Joseph Solomon Delmedigo, 'Sefer novelot ḥokhmah', in his *Sefer ta'alumot ḥokhmah*, ii (Basel, 1631), 6*a*, quoted in Mann, *Texts and Studies in Jewish History and Literature*, 676 n. 105*a*; id., *Sefer elim* (Amsterdam, 1629), 131; Geiger (ed.), *Melo Chofnajim*, 14*ss*; cf. introd., ibid., p. xxxii.

[60] Quoted in Dubnow, *History of the Jews in Russia and Poland*, i. 138.

[61] Schreiner, 'Isaac of Troki's Studies of Rabbinic Literature'.

Joseph Kimhi (*c.*1160–*c.*1235), Isaac b. Moses Arama (*c.*1420–1494), and Isaac b. Judah Abrabanel (1437–1508), historical works such as the anonymous *Sefer yosipon* and Abraham ibn Daud's *Sefer hakabalah*, and philosophical works such as the *Sefer ha'ikarim* of Joseph Albo.

Although some interest in historiography developed among Jews in Prague and Italy, there is much less to be found in Poland. One exception is Nathan Nata Hannover's record of the Khmelnytsky massacres *Yeven metsulah*, which contains a sophisticated account of the Polish–Lithuanian crisis of the mid-seventeenth century. Even here, however, historical analysis is combined with messianic expectation, although they are kept separate and the first is clearly dominant. Yet the work concludes, after thanking those who gave shelter to the exiles from Poland: 'May their merit be counted for us and for our children, that the Lord should hearken to our cries and gather our dispersed from the four corners of the earth and send our righteous Messiah, speedily in our day. Amen, Selah.'[62]

One aspect of the European Renaissance was a revolution in pedagogy, which also had some effect on the world of Ashkenaz, especially in Prague. This is perhaps reflected in the disputes over *pilpul*, which was strongly opposed by a number of rabbis, including Solomon Luria, Judah Loew b. Bezalel of Prague, and Isaiah b. Abraham Halevi Horowitz (b. Prague *c.*1565, d. Tiberias 1630). In the view of Rabbi Loew, this form of argumentation was intellectually dishonest, and destroyed the character and perverted the values of yeshiva students. He even went so far as to assert that dishonest argumentation could lead to dishonest behaviour.[63] This form of reasoning was also strongly attacked by the preacher Rabbi Ephraim Solomon, who had been head of the yeshivas of both Lviv and Prague. According to him:

> The whole instruction at the yeshivah reduces itself to mental gymnastics and empty argument called *hiluk*. It is dreadful to contemplate that some venerable rabbi, presiding over a yeshivah, in his anxiety to discover and communicate to others some new interpretation, should offer a perverted explanation of the Talmud, though he himself and every one else be fully aware that the true meaning is different. Can it be God's will that we sharpen our minds by fallacies and sophistries, spending our time in vain and teaching the listeners to do likewise? And all this for the mere ambition of passing for a great scholar! . . . I myself have more than once argued with the Talmudic celebrities of our time, showing the need for abolishing the method of *pilpul* and *hiluk*, without being able to convince them. This attitude can only be explained by the eagerness of these scholars for honours and *rosh yeshivah* posts. These empty quibbles have a particularly pernicious effect on our yeshivah students, for the reason that the student who does not shine in the discussion is looked down upon as incapable, and is practically forced to lay aside his studies, though he might prove to be one of the best, if Bible, Mishnah, Talmud, and the Codes were studied in a regular fashion.[64]

[62] Hannover, *Abyss of Despair*, 121.

[63] Shulman, *Authority and Community*, 88.

[64] Dubnow, *History of the Jews in Russia and Poland*, i. 119.

Mystical enquiry and mystical practice were much less controversial. Many of the leading halakhists were deeply interested in mysticism and did not see any contradiction in this. Some may have seen mysticism as something which should be the preserve of the elite and not available to the masses. According to Rabbi Slonik, who refers in one of his responsa to 'a secret wisdom of great holiness': 'Even though there is a great secret of the mysteries of the Torah connected with this matter, as is well known to scholars of the true wisdom . . . nevertheless there is need to give a sound explanation and clear understanding according to the *peshat hanigle*, the "open" exposition.'[65]

The development of printing enabled the rapid spread of mystical books, and in the early seventeenth century a special brand of Polish mysticism began to emerge. The first important mystics were Samson b. Pesah Ostropoler (d. 1648) and Nathan Nata b. Solomon Spiro (1585–1633), who were particularly concerned with demonology and messianism. The most important of the Polish mystics during this period was Isaiah Horowitz. After his move to Kraków, he studied with Solomon b. Judah Leybush and in 1590 became a judge at the Council of the Lands, where he condemned bribery to obtain rabbinic office. In 1621 he emigrated to Erets Yisrael, where he settled in Jerusalem. It was after this move that he completed *Shenei luḥot haberit*, which in an abridged form became the most widely distributed kabbalistic text in Poland, where popular mysticism soon acquired a large following.

There is a link between mysticism and messianism. During the period before 1648 messianic impulses appear to have been relatively weak in Poland, perhaps owing to the relative security which Jews enjoyed in this period. Indeed some religious figures linked this feeling of security with a fall-off in religious observance. What is striking in the period to the middle of the seventeenth century is the relative internal harmony of the community. The prestige of the rabbinate was solidly established, the balance between halakhic investigation, philosophic enquiry, and mysticism did not pose any serious problems, and the disruptive effect of messianic events was easily contained. In addition, in spite of accusations of host desecration and ritual murder, and periodic calls for the expulsion of the Jews, the security and stability of the community seemed assured.

JEWISH RELIGIOUS LIFE IN POLAND–LITHUANIA AFTER 1648

The second half of the seventeenth century saw the beginning of a new era in the religious life of the Jews of Poland–Lithuania. The relative security of the community was severely shaken by the major upheavals which began with the Khmelnytsky Uprising in 1648 and culminated in invasions of Poland–Lithuania by Sweden and Muscovy, which were accompanied by extreme brutality and

65 Shulman, *Authority and Community*, 187.

massive loss of life. Although contemporary chronicles considerably exaggerated Jewish casualties, these were possibly at least 13,000, which would have constituted between 6 and 8.5 per cent of the community. There was also a significant westward flight of Jews, included leading scholars such as Rabbi Shabetai Hakohen and Aaron Koidonover.

Jewish life did recover in the second half of the seventeenth century and Polish yeshivas remained important centres for Jewish scholarship, attracting students from the whole of Ashkenaz, but they were never able to attain their former eminence.[66] Traditional society continued and developed new themes in rabbinic thought, but the real historical development of the age was now more in the direction of mysticism and messianism.

Given their theological universe, inevitably some Jews claimed that Polish Jews were being punished for the iniquities of their generation. As Nathan Nata Hannover wrote poignantly: 'What can we say, what can we speak, or how can we justify ourselves? Shall we say we have not sinned? Behold, our iniquities testify against us. For we have sinned, and the Lord found out the iniquity of his servants. Would the Holy One, blessed be He, dispense judgment without justice?'[67] Some Polish Jews, such as Berechiah Berakh b. Isaac Eisik (d. 1663) and the preacher Bezalel b. Solomon of Kobryn attempted to list the transgressions which had caused the catastrophe, but most confined themselves to lamenting the 'great sin' of forsaking the Torah and the Commandments.[68]

Edward Fram cites a characteristic case of a Jew from Ukraine who migrated to Pińczów, a town near Kraków. Sometime before the Khmelnytsky massacres he came to a rabbinic court and admitted to having had 'bad thoughts' that led to masturbation. He also confessed to having been naked with an unclothed married woman, although they did not have sexual intercourse. The two rabbis who heard his admission offered him an unspecified penance, which he appears to have accepted. After the Khmelnytsky Uprising he made a second appearance before a rabbinic court. The anti-Jewish violence seems to have heightened his sense of guilt, since he came back to the court in the belief that his penance had been too light and that not only did his sin remain but it had been responsible for the massacres of 1648. He requested the court to impose a stricter punishment that would expiate his sin and neutralize its consequences for the Jewish people.[69]

Calls for repentance were widespread. At least two editions of a popular penitential manual were printed in Kraków, with an approbation by Rabbi Aryeh Leib b. Zechariah, the rabbi of the town.[70] Similarly, the Lithuanian preacher and

[66] Rosman, 'Images of the House of Israel as a Centre of Torah after the Catastrophes of 1648' (Heb.).

[67] Hannover, *Abyss of Despair*, 109.

[68] Berechiah Berakh, *Zera berakh*, ii, introd., and Bezalel b. Solomon the Preacher, quoted in Katz, *The 'Shabbes Goy'*, 83.

[69] P. Wettstein, 'The Past Revealed through Old Minute Books' (Heb.), 614–16, quoted in Fram, *Ideals Face Reality*, 62–3.

[70] Scholem, *Sabbatai Sevi*, 593.

kabbalist Rabbi Judah Leib Pukhovitser of Pinsk relates how he had been approached by several people 'whose hearts had been touched by the fear of God' and who wished to have penances imposed on them for sins they had committed in their youth. Originally they had wished to perform all the mortifications and fasts 'prescribed in the [book] *Roke'aḥ* [by Eleazar of Worms] and in the Lurianic writings', but they soon realized that if they did the full penance prescribed for each transgression, they would never be able to bear all the rigours and expiate all their sins. In order not to discourage penitent sinners, Rabbi Pukhovitser advised them to do the penance of mortification three times for each category of sin (instead of doing a full penance for each sinful act), 'and the great luminaries, the learned heads of the rabbinic courts and the heads of the rabbinic academies of the holy congregations in Lithuania assented to my suggestion'.[71]

This climate of repentance created a mood favourable to messianic expectation, and many Jews saw in the suffering and martyrdom the community experienced in the mid-seventeenth century the 'birth pangs of the messiah'. We do not know how widespread was the support in Poland for the messianic pretender in Turkey, Sabbatai Zevi. As Scholem has shown in his magisterial account of his career, Sabbatai Zevi argued that the massacres of 1648 were the beginning of the era of redemption, and announced in Smyrna that an unknown Jewish martyr, one Abraham Zalman, had been the messiah of the tribe of Joseph. Like the thirty-six righteous of Jewish legend, who maintain the world unknown to anyone, the unknown martyr–messiah had also fulfilled his mission in obscurity. The prophecy of Zevi's close supporter Nathan of Gaza that 'there will be no slaughter among the uncircumcised, except in the German lands' could also be seen as a promise of retribution for the Jews of Poland–Lithuania, who were part of Ashkenaz.[72] In a later version which Nathan rewrote in 1666 and dispatched to several countries, he asserted that in Poland alone vengeance would be wreaked on non-Jews 'to avenge the blood of our martyred brethren'.[73]

How much of this was known in Poland–Lithuania? As Scholem has pointed out, 'the available evidence regarding the diffusion of the movement in Poland indicates that very little was known about Sabbatai's personality or the actual events connected with him'.[74] Indeed the extent of the following for Sabbatai Zevi formed the subject of an important exchange between Bernard Weinryb and Michael Stanislawski, in which Stanislawski convincingly dealt with Weinryb's objections to Scholem's sources.[75] Scholem himself had cited a Yiddish source published in Amsterdam by a local Jew, Leyb b. Ozer, who testified to the welcome which the news of Sabbatai's proclamation of his own messiahship in 1666 had in Poland–Lithuania after the devastations of the mid-century: 'for we, the Jews in this bitter exile, love to hear good tidings of comfort and salvation, and *especially in Poland* where evil [hatred] of the Jews and the [oppression of] exile are

[71] Scholem, *Sabbatai Sevi*, 595–6. [72] Ibid. 592. [73] Ibid. [74] Ibid.

[75] See in particular Stanislawski, 'The State of the Debate over Sabbatianism in Poland'.

exceedingly great, and every day brings new persecution and harassment'.[76] Some Polish Jews appear to have been expecting a messianic event. Thus, Rabbi Jacob b. Solomon of Lobsenz proclaimed the upheavals in Poland between 1648 and 1656 to have been a 'preparation for the coming of Sabbatai Sevi'.[77]

Garbled versions of what was happening seem to have reached Poland–Lithuania. Early in 1666, as is documented in German reports, rumours began to circulate in Poland that the Grand Turk had placed a royal crown on Sabbatai's head and had made him ride on horseback at his right-hand side. 'And on the day that he came [to Constantinople], the earth shook and quaked, and he entered the royal court riding on a lion . . . and more of this kind.'[78] Another possible source of rumour was the agents of the Polish aristocracy in Amsterdam, which was an entrepôt for much of the Polish grain exported from Danzig.[79]

The impact of the news of Sabbatai Zevi's messianic claim is also reported in an account by the Greek Orthodox archimandrite Johannes Galatowski:

> Not long ago, in 1666, the Jewish heresy raised its head in Volhynia, Podolia, in all the provinces of Little Russia, in the Duchy of Lithuania, in the kingdom of Poland and the neighbouring countries. They raised on high their horn and their insolent obstinacy, they hoisted the flag of backsliding and insolently blew the trumpet of victory. At that time an impostor called Sabbatai Zevi appeared in Smyrna, who called himself the messiah of the Jews and drew them to his side by false miracles. He promised the Jews to bring them out of their exile among the nations, and to restore unto them Jerusalem and the kingdom of Palestine. . . . The foolish Jews rejoiced, and expected that the messiah would take them to Jerusalem on a cloud. Whenever a cloud appeared over some city, they would boast before the Christians and say that the messiah would soon take them to dwell in Palestine and in Jerusalem. At that time they fasted several days in the week because of the messiah, and some fasted the whole week. They gave no food even to their little children, and they immersed themselves in winter under the ice while reciting recently invented prayers. Many Jews died during the winter because of their immersions in the severe cold. They went to their synagogue every day and held services. Even some fools among the Christian masses acted and thought like them.[80]

There are some indications that the messianic expectations led some Jews to believe that they would soon be able to take revenge for their sufferings and that this seems to have provoked anti-Jewish violence in a number of places, including Pinsk, Vilna, and Lublin in 1666, which was also a year which in the Christian calendar aroused messianic expectations. Bałaban cites a royal decree of Jan Kazimierz of 4 May 1666 which forbade the Jews to carry portraits of the

[76] Scholem, *Sabbatai Sevi*, 591. Leyb b. Ozer's account has been published in Hebrew: *An Account of Sabbatai Zevi*.

[77] Scholem, *Sabbatai Sevi*, 592.

[78] Sasportas, *Tsitsat novel tsevi*, 75, quoted in Scholem, *Sabbatai Sevi*, 592.

[79] These are cited by Majer Bałaban in 'Sabataizm w Polsce', 38–43, quoted in Scholem, *Sabbatai Sevi*, 593.

[80] Johannes Galatowski, *Messiasz prawdziwy* (Kiev, 1672; Ruthenian edn., Kiev, 1669). It is referred to in Bałaban, 'Sabataizm w Polsce', and in Shneur Zalman Rubashov (Shazar), 'K istorii sabbatianstva v Pol'she (O knige, tsitiruemoi I. Galyatovskim)'.

messianic pretender and enjoined the local authorities to keep the matter under control and protect the Jews from hostile mobs:

This is already the second time that it has come to our ears that reckless people in their scheming plots, aiming to ruin the non-believing Jews of our kingdom and seeking booty, have caused the news to spread recently among the people that the Church has given permission and the royal courts of justice have issued decrees—forgeries—to all people to oppress and destroy [such] Jews; and as a result disturbances have broken out, persecutions, plunderings, and bloodshed in various places, as is known to all.

And at this same time the Jews too have become impudent, have brazenly and fanatically risen up, and are broadcasting among the people as a true, clear, and certain teaching, the false rumour that [has come] from foreign countries concerning a certain messiah, and asserting this to simple people by means of printed reports and various painted images. In certain places, in which these heretical [*niewierni*] Jews are found, the results of their caprice are already to be seen, and yet another greater disturbance approaches, that threatens to put these same Jews in peril and distress, in order to make room for the plundering of their properties and possessions by means of these forgeries.[81]

The king ordered all printed pictures, pamphlets, and broadsheets to be destroyed.[82] The Roman Catholic bishop of Przemyśl, Stanisław Sarnowski, wrote in a pastoral letter of 22 June 1666 that as a result of 'a new superstition that has arisen among them' the Jews 'are carrying about some printed reports in public processions through the markets and streets, on account of some false belief that has been revived among them, that do harm to the honour of the Faith, and false images as well'.[83] News of this scandal had reached the bishop from many towns and villages in his diocese in central Galicia. There are also references in a poem by Wacław Potocki to the 'new Jewish messiah'.[84]

Echoes of the crisis of 1666 can also be found in Jewish sources. In a halakhic enquiry, which he sent to Rabbi Isaac b. Abraham of Posen (d. 1685), who had been appointed the rabbi of Vilna in 1664, Rabbi Zevi Hirsch Horowitz, rabbi of three communities in the Zamut (Žemaitija) region of Lithuania (Kėdainiai, Vižainis (Wiżajny), and Biržai) and first head of the Zamut yeshiva, asked for information about what he referred to as the 'renewal'. He requested copies of all the reports that had reached Vilna and offered to pay whatever was required to copy them. Rabbi Isaac, after dealing with the halakhic query, added in a final sentence: 'As for the renewal, I have nothing to say but that which the rabbi of

81 Cf. Bałaban, 'Sabataizm w Polsce', 82–7; the text in Bałaban is somewhat corrupted. I am grateful to Adam Kaźmierczyk for providing me with a more accurate text from the Akta Grodzkie Lubelskie; id., *Historja Żydów w Krakowie i na Kazimierzu, 1304–1868*, i. 45. As Lenowitz points out in 'The Struggle over Images in the Propaganda of the Frankist Movement', 106–11, the text of this decree as it appears in the two works cited by Bałaban not only contains some errors but the two versions differ from each other as well.

82 The royal order was discovered by Bałaban (*Historja Żydów w Krakowie i na Kazimierzu, 1304–1868*, i. 44–5), in the archives in Lviv.

83 Ibid. 43.

84 Ibid. 37. The poem was first published by Brückner in W. Potocki, *Ogród fraszek niewypłewionny*.

Jassy has written to me and which is surely also known to Your Reverence. Mayest thou delight thyself in great peace forever.'[85]

The enquiry may have been provoked by the belief that Vilna was being affected by messianic fervour. Certainly, adherents of Sabbatai Zevi had made the pilgrimage to Gallipoli, including a talmudic scholar, Rabbi Abraham Kokesh. Rabbi Abraham subsequently visited his family in Amsterdam, to whom he recounted, weeping bitterly, 'how he had eaten meat and other dainties with Sabbatai Zevi on the Ninth of Av, and drunk wine with him, while musicians were playing and Turks were dancing before them with their sticks, as is their wont when they make merry'. When he asked Sabbatai why he allowed the fast of the Ninth of Av to be violated, the latter explained that the name Sabbatai Zevi could be mystically read as an acrostic signifying 'On the Day of the Ninth of Av Sabbatai Zevi shall not fast'.[86] One of the strongest messianic enthusiasts in Vilna, Joshua Heshel b. Joseph Zoref (Heshel Zoref, 1633–1700), a silversmith, was to become the chief exponent of Sabbatianism in Poland–Lithuania in the following generation. Some of his writings were later to be praised by the founder of hasidism, Israel b. Eliezer, usually known as the Ba'al Shem Tov (the Besht, *c.*1700–1760), who does not seem to have been aware of their Sabbatian character.[87]

More or less simultaneously a scribe in Kraków dedicated a parchment volume containing the readings from the Prophets for the whole liturgical year to the Remu synagogue in Kraków, dating its title page 25 Sivan 5426 (29 June 1666), and appending a short messianic prayer of five lines in which Sabbatai's name is mentioned five times in acrostic.[88]

A number of Polish Jews travelled to meet Sabbatai in Gallipoli, both as individuals and as representatives of their communities. The most important of the representative groups was that sent by the community of Lviv. It included Rabbi Isaiah, known as Isaiah Mokhiah (the Reprover), the rabbi of Komarno, son of David Halevi, rabbi of Lviv, and the former's stepson Rabbi Aryeh Leib b. Samuel Zevi Hirsh. About the beginning or middle of March they left Lviv for Constantinople but did not reach their destination until July. They became fervent supporters of the messianic pretender, recounting

> the glory which they had beheld, and the abundance of gold, silver, precious cloth, and ornaments, and the royal apparel which he was wearing every day, and the multitudes that were attending on him, and the honour shown him by non-Jews, who would not touch any of the Jews who came to visit him. They also brought a letter from the messiah . . . to their aged father, the Rabbi David, and the whole of Poland was in agitation and the fame thereof was heard in all those parts, and their faith was greatly strengthened.[89]

85 This is preserved in the responsa of Zevi Hirsch Horowitz. See Scholem, *Sabbatai Sevi*, 598.

86 Leyb b. Ozer, MS Shazar, fo. 54*a*; see Scholem, *Sabbatai Sevi*, 599.

87 Rosman, *Founder of Hasidism*, 157–8.

88 A facsimile of the title page can be found in Bałaban, *Historja Żydów w Krakowie i na Kazimierzu, 1304–1868*, ii, facing p. 64.

89 Sasportas, *Tsitsat novel tsevi*, 77, quoted in Scholem, *Sabbatai Sevi*, 600.

Rabbi Moses Segal of Kraków, writing on 8 October 1666 (the day before Yom Kippur, and about one month after Sabbatai's renunciation of his faith and conversion to Islam, news of which had not yet reached Poland), mentions this delegation in a letter to his brother-in-law Rabbi Meir Isserles in Vienna. He stresses that his account was but 'a drop in the ocean, for who can write all the wondrous things which they told',[90] but leaves no doubt that he himself, like the rabbi of Lviv, firmly believed in the messiah. According to Leyb b. Ozer, the two emissaries also made a written report on their embassy, which he probably made use of in his memoir.[91]

Another Polish Jew who made the pilgrimage to Sabbatai was the preacher Berechiah Berakh of Kraków, who gave a detailed account of his visit and stated that he 'went out from him with a glad heart'.[92] All these reports probably do not add up to widespread uncritical messianic fervour in Poland–Lithuania, but they certainly show that the Sabbatian crisis made its impact there, as it did in the entire Jewish world. The shock of his apostasy caused considerable disillusionment.

The late seventeenth and eighteenth centuries were characterized by a number of new phenomena on the religious landscape of Polish Jewry: the persistence of Sabbatianism, the activities of a new and more sinister messianic pretender in the form of Jacob Frank, the emergence of a major religious revival linked with the Ba'al Shem Tov and his adherents, and a revitalization of the rabbinic tradition by the Vilna Gaon, Elijah b. Solomon Zalman, and his followers. In the older historiography these developments are seen as the result of the political and economic decline of Poland–Lithuania, which culminated in the partition of the country in the second half of the eighteenth century. These views have been challenged in recent years by historians such as Moshe Rosman and Gershon Hundert. They have shown that the Jewish population losses of the mid-seventeenth century were quickly made good, and that by the middle of the eighteenth century the Jewish community of Poland–Lithuania had increased to 750,000. They have also demonstrated that the long period of economic decline which began in Poland–Lithuania in the 1620s came to an end in the 1720s and 1730s, and that Jewish involvement in economic life became more extensive in the eighteenth century.[93] Some issues do remain, however. Although there was some economic recovery, it did not create opportunities for all Jews in the situation of a rapidly rising population. This inevitably led to a significant generational conflict, with a large percentage of younger Jewish men unable to find gainful employment. Competition for rabbinic posts became more bitter, leading to violent controversies, of which that in Vilna in the second half of the eighteenth century was probably the most notorious (on this, see Chapter 3). These almost certainly

[90] Sasportas, *Tsitsat novel tsevi*, 79, quoted in Scholem, *Sabbatai Sevi*, 601.

[91] Leyb b. Ozer, MS Shazar, 16, quoted in Scholem, *Sabbatai Sevi*, 601.

[92] Ibid., quoted in Scholem, *Sabbatai Sevi*, 602.

[93] Rosman, *The Lords' Jews*; id., *Founder of Hasidism*; Hundert, *The Jews in a Polish Private Town*; id., 'The Contexts of Hasidism'.

contributed to undermining the enormous prestige the rabbinate had enjoyed in the sixteenth and early seventeenth centuries.

In addition, although the relative security of the Jewish community was re-established, the situation was far from that existing before 1648. In the first place, the increasing strength of Counter-Reformation Catholicism made more precarious the situation of all non-Catholics, including Jews. There may not have been more trials in the period after 1648 for desecration of the host or ritual murder, but they were more erratically conducted (often by the local nobility, rather than the Crown) and convictions seem to have been more frequent.[94] The Commonwealth was also plagued by foreign invasion in the Great Northern War and the War of the Polish Succession, and for much of the century was subject to constant depredations from foreign armies. Outbreaks of civil unrest were also numerous, particularly the revolts of the Haydamaks in Polish Ukraine. Inevitably the Jews suffered, probably disproportionately, from these developments.

In this situation it is not surprising that there occurred what Jacob Katz has described as 'a general shift in religious values . . . beginning in the latter part of the seventeenth century'.[95] This was above all the result of the popularization of kabbalistic and mystical religious concepts, which had previously been confined to a small and esoteric circle, but which now gained a much greater following with the growth in printing and distribution of popular and often inexpensive kabbalistic tracts. Written in easily understood language, they guided the reader through prayer services and rituals associated with the life cycle, to which were attributed a cosmic and mystical significance. Through them, as Hundert has argued, 'the individual could feel privy to the esoteric realm and attain the conviction that he was indeed acting in accordance with God's will'.[96]

One important aspect of Polish kabbalah was, according to Scholem, the degree to which its adherents were preoccupied with the theory of evil and 'all matters connected with the world of devils and spirits . . . What is surprising here is the degree to which they were fascinated with this field and the sharp personal grasp of evil [*kelipoth*].'[97]

The most important of the kabbalistic writings was Isaiah Horowitz's *Shenei luḥot haberit*, mentioned above. This was first published in Amsterdam in 1649 and five further editions appeared before the end of the eighteenth century. Between 1681 and 1792 twenty-three editions of an abridgement by Jehiel Michal Epstein appeared, while fifteen editions of a Yiddish abridgement were published between 1743 and 1797, which also included material from other kabbalistic books.[98] Another significant book in the popularization of kabbalah was the prayer book *Sha'arei tsiyon*, edited with mystical annotations by Nathan Nata

94 On this, see Guldon and Wijaczka, 'The Accusation of Ritual Murder in Poland 1500–1800'.

95 Katz, *Tradition and Crisis*, 190.

96 Hundert, 'Jewish Popular Spirituality in the Eighteenth Century'.

97 Scholem, *Sabbatai Sevi*, 602.

98 Vinograd, *Thesaurus of the Hebrew Book* (Heb.).

Hannover, of which more than forty editions were published in the eighteenth century, making it by far the most popular specialized prayer book of the period.[99] Jehiel Epstein included material from the prayer book in his digest of the *Shenei luḥot haberit*.

These are not the only examples. The sermons of the time, drawn from materials found in the popular publications, demonstrate an increasing preoccupation with esoteric matters generally associated with kabbalah. *Ḥemdat yamim*, a homiletic and ethical work permeated by Lurianic kabbalah, which was almost certainly written by a Sabbatian, was published in at least sixteen different editions between 1670 and 1770. Its popularity is only one indication of another important phenomenon, the existence of a Sabbatian religious subculture in Poland–Lithuania, as in other parts of Ashkenaz. Others may be the positive reference to Heshel Zoref, one of the principal Sabbatians in early eighteenth-century Poland–Lithuania, in *Kav hayashar*, the ethical treatise of Zevi Hirsch Koidonover, which was widely distributed during the period,[100] and the popularity of Elijah b. Solomon Abraham Hakohen of Smyrna's *Shevet musar*, although in neither case were the Sabbatian views of the individuals involved widely known. A religious guide dealing with sin, temptation, and repentance, *Shevet musar* is especially significant for its description of the tsadik, the holy man who was to become a central element in the hasidic movement. The book strikingly foreshadows the later hasidic embodiment of this concept. It lists the forty-two holy names of the tsadik, and among his various characteristics names his knowledge of the 'esoteric secrets' of the heavens, his defence of the people of Israel, his ability to prevent war, epidemic, and famine, and his ability to bring down the 'divine plenty [*mamshikh shefa*] to his followers. He is able to plead in the heavenly court and obtain the annulment of evil decrees and redeems souls through his acts of correction [*tikunim*] and his mystical devotions [*kavanot*].'

As Hundert has pointed out, most of this material is not new and 'can be traced to Talmudic sources, medieval ethical literature, or to the sages of sixteenth century Safed'. Yet the fact remains, as he concludes, that, although 'the concept of the *tsadik* as described here in one of the most popular and influential books of the eighteenth century does not correspond precisely with the version actually institutionalized in Hasidism, enough is shared for this fact to be suggestive indeed'.[101] Nevertheless, Moshe Idel is probably correct in arguing that hasidism was not greatly influenced by the kind of Lurianic ideas set out in the *Shevet musar*.

Of course, non-mystical texts were also widely distributed, but although they were not kabbalistic in character, they too maintained the tone of repentance and contrition which marked the religious life of the Polish Jewish community after the catastrophe of the mid-seventeenth century. The classical ethical treatise

[99] 1st edn. Prague, 1662.
[100] Koidonover, *Kav hayashar*, ch. 102.
[101] Hundert, 'Jewish Popular Spirituality in the Eighteenth Century', 93–4.

Ḥovot halevavot by Bahya b. Joseph ibn Pakuda went through twenty-seven editions between 1670 and 1797, including seven with Yiddish translations.[102] It called for a life of pious self-deprivation, advocating voluntary separation from the material world. The anonymous *Orḥot tsadikim*, an ethical work in the ascetic penitential spirit of Hasidei Ashkenaz, was published thirty-one times in the late seventeenth and early eighteenth centuries.

These works could not, however, rival the popularity of those which disseminated kabbalistic ideas. This had a number of important consequences for the character of religious observance. Carrying out the commandments of the law now had a cosmic meaning, affecting the hidden divine realm, and advancing or retarding progress towards redemption. Careful and proper observance became, therefore, a matter of fateful significance. This system of understanding erased the differences in degree and weight between the fulfilment of one Commandment and another. Moreover, one had to be conscious of this while performing the Commandment or reciting the prayer. This consciousness was ritualized by the kabbalists in the form of *kavanot* (mystical devotions), which are devotional formulas preceding observance or recitation and intended to focus the mind of the devotee on the symbolic connotation of the act about to be performed or the prayer about to be recited. For the kabbalists, 'performance of a commandment without *kavanah* virtually lost its religious significance'.[103]

A new importance attached to the kabbalistic elite. As Katz has pointed out, 'Henceforth, traditional Jewish society contained not one elite but two.'[104] The rabbinic elite did retain some of its traditional prestige, and rabbinic positions were eagerly sought after, sometimes leading to bitter and protracted disputes, like that provoked in the second half of the eighteenth century by the appointment of Samuel b. Avigdor to the post of rabbi of Vilna (see Chapter 3). This was partly because of the financial benefits derived from holding rabbinic office. It has been calculated that in large towns the salaries of rabbis exceeded those of municipal officials and all except those of the wealthiest leaseholders. In addition, the rabbi received a fee for the various religious services he administered, such as marriages and divorces. By now appointment to the post of rabbi often required the consent of the noble town owner or royal governor and this frequently required a cash payment. These payments were often quite large—one is recorded in Zhovkva of 350 ducats (6,300 florins)—and the fact that this meant that rabbinic office was open to sale inevitably reduced its prestige. In addition, rabbis in private towns were frequently treated as if they were part of the noble-controlled administration. They were used to uphold the authority of the town's owner and their fees were set by his representative. According to the preacher David b. Isaac Hakaro: 'The office of instruction [the rabbinate] has been so corrupted in some places that the rabbinate has become an agency for tax collection.

[102] Ibid. [103] Katz, *Tradition and Crisis*, 191. [104] Ibid. 192.

In many places [control of] the rabbinate has been taken away from Jews and they have no say in it.'[105]

As a result, alongside the rabbinic scholar there now emerged a new type of kabbalist, distinct from those who had wandered from place to place, looking (often unsuccessfully) for support from rich Jews. This new group was felt to be as worthy of respect as the rabbinate and equally entitled to public support. Individual mystics and small groups of kabbalists appeared in numerous communities. They devoted themselves to the study of esoteric doctrine, prayed separately in their own *kloyzn* (prayer rooms), and were thought to benefit the community that supported them by their special access to Heaven.[106] They not only prayed separately but also made use of the Lurianic prayer book (*nusaḥ ha'ari*) and, following a custom established in Safed, met for the third meal on the afternoon of the sabbath, wearing white robes. One of their particular concerns, derived from their preoccupation with Lurianic kabbalah, was that ritual slaughter should be carried out in the most meticulously scrupulous manner.

These circles also maintained the penitential tone which prevailed after 1648. They called for the avoidance of 'frivolity', advocating instead constant mourning over the exile and a continuous flight from sin. A believer should be dour, serious, and sober. This was well expressed in Mordecai b. Samuel's *Sha'ar hamelekh*, which was first published in 1762 and went through nine editions in the next thirty-five years.[107] In Hundert's words, 'the sort of spiritual world reflected in his writing is one that venerates a perpetual pious asceticism characterized by much mournfulness, a certain precision, and urgent calls for repentance'.[108]

As we have seen, although the rabbinic elite saw itself as set above the masses because of its learning, it also saw its role as a public one, teaching, judging, and preaching. The situation of the kabbalists was different. In Katz's words, 'the kabbalist elite saw itself as divided from the masses by a wide chasm even in the practical sphere. The only relationship possible between them and the masses was one of *shlihut* (agency or proxy). The few were transformed into exacting performers of the precepts on behalf of the many.'[109] Because of this, they were supported by the communities directly or through exemption from taxation. In the eyes of the community, they were precious, exceptional individuals (*yeḥidei segulah*) and 'servants of God'. In this context, the importance of Elijah b. Solomon Abraham Hakohen's characterization of the tsadik becomes all the more significant.

[105] Hakaro, *Ohel raḥel*, 15*a*, quoted in Hundert, *Jews in Poland–Lithuania in the Eighteenth Century*, 108. For the question of the rabbinate in general at this time, see ibid. 85–6, 108–9; Kaźmierczyk, *Żydzi w dobrach prywatnych w świetle sądowniczej i administracyjnej praktyki dóbr magnackich w wiekach XVI–XVIII*, 137–42, 200–2.

[106] Reiner, 'Wealth, Social Position and the Study of Torah' (Heb.); Hisdai, 'The "Servant of the Lord" in the Generation of the Fathers of Hasidism' (Heb.).

[107] Mordecai b. Samuel, *Sha'ar hamelekh*.

[108] Hundert, 'Jewish Popular Spirituality in the Eighteenth Century'.

[109] Katz, *Tradition and Crisis*, 194.

Connected with this kabbalistic elite but also separate from it were the many faith healers—*ba'alei shem* (masters of the Name, i.e. people able to cast spells using the name of God). Popular kabbalah and its prayers and rituals 'included both ancient Jewish traditions and folk ideas about averting danger and healing sickness that were by no means confined to Jews'.[110] These *ba'alei shem* cured disease, physical and spiritual, through the use of the secret names of God, the employment of amulets and charms, as well as numerology. They were familiar with the 'other side' of creation (that controlled by evil forces), and since it was widely believed that illness was caused by demons, exorcism played a large part in their cures. Among the leading *ba'alei shem* were Benjamin Beinish Hakohen (*c.*1690–*c.*1775) of Krotoszyn, in Wielkopolska, who described how he achieved his cures in his book *Sefer amtaḥat binyamin* (Wilhelmsdorf, 1716); and Joel b. Uri Heilperin (1690–1755) of Zamość, also known as Joel Ba'al Shem Tov, whose reputation extended beyond Poland to Germany and Palestine and who not only attracted many seeking help to his native town, but also travelled widely to minister to those in need. As Hundert has pointed out, 'the standing of the *baalei shem* in the cultural hierarchy was not a lowly one . . . [they] were consulted and honoured by all sections of Jewish society and were not particularly associated with the rustic and backward'.[111]

This new spiritual climate constitutes the background to the two major developments in the religious life of Polish Jewry in the eighteenth century: the messianic movement associated with the enigmatic figure of Jacob Frank and the emergence and development of hasidism. Jacob Frank has not, like his precursor Sabbatai Zevi, yet found his Gershom Scholem. This is primarily the result of the fact that Frankism was an even more disturbing and disruptive phenomenon than Sabbatianism and did not hesitate to adopt openly anti-Jewish positions, including accusing the Jews of the blood libel. Even Scholem, who was clearly fascinated by Frank, wrote that Frankism was the 'most terrifying' phenomenon in the whole of Jewish history. At the same time, the movement has also been seen in recent years as the forerunner of subsequent attempts to overcome the Jewish–Christian religious divide.

What made possible Frank's career was the persistence of Sabbatian beliefs in Poland–Lithuania after Sabbatai Zevi's conversion. These Sabbatians, many of whom had previously been part of the burgeoning kabbalistic circles, were compelled to hide their true beliefs. The more radical were attracted by the idea, expounded by Sabbatai Zevi himself, that one could achieve salvation through sinning and then repenting. Among the later adherents of the movement were Heshel Zoref, who moved from Vilna to Kraków, where he acquired a considerable following; Moses b. Aaron Hakohen, who later converted to Christianity and

[110] Hundert, *Jews in Poland–Lithuania in the Eighteenth Century*, 137.

[111] Ibid. 153. On the phenomenon of *ba'alei shem*, see ibid. 142–53; Rosman, *Founder of Hasidism*; and Etkes, *The Besht*.

became a professor at the University of Uppsala; and a group around Hayim b. Solomon Malakh of Kalisz and Judah Hasid Halevi of Szydłowiec, who emigrated to Jerusalem in 1700 in expectation of the resurrection of Sabbatai Zevi. Sabbatian sympathizers seem to have been particularly numerous in Podolia, which was under Ottoman rule from 1672 to 1699.[112] Sabbatian beliefs were also tolerated in wider circles. An indication of this is the popularity of the mystical work *Ḥemdat yamim*. Although this was not universally recognized at the time, its wide circulation testifies to the fact that in some circles there was 'rather a benign attitude to the failed Sabbatean movement and its teachings'.[113]

The basic facts of the career of Jacob Frank (1726–91) as a messianic pretender are well known. He was born in Podolia, the son of a prosperous merchant, and himself engaged in trade. His business affairs took him to the Ottoman empire, where he appears to have had contact with Sabbatians and become a follower of Barukhyah Russo of Salonika (d. 1720). Russo, who had converted from Judaism to Islam and in 1716 had proclaimed himself the Divine Incarnation, wanted to combine syncretically Judaism, Islam, and Christianity in order to create a single religion of the end of time (*dat hadosha legamre*). His followers were called in Judaeo-Spanish *konyosos* (initiates). In December 1755 Frank moved back to Podolia, where he was originally seen as an emissary from the *konyosos*, but quickly gained the support of many of the Sabbatians in Polish Ukraine, where he may also have been influenced by Russian Orthodox sectarians.

In April 1756 Frank was forced to leave Poland after he had been exposed as a Sabbatian. He and a group of followers then converted to Islam and established a new 'camp' of Muslim converts. Together with his closest followers, Frank was excommunicated by a rabbinical assembly convened at Brody in June 1756, and this ban was confirmed by the Council of the Lands in Konstantynów in September. The rabbinic establishment then turned to the Roman Catholic Church hierarchy, seeking its support to 'extirpate heresy'. This proved a serious mistake, since it enabled Bishop Dębowski of Kamenets-Podolsky to assert his right to investigate these claims and assert his authority over Jewish matters. At this point Frank decided to enter the Roman Catholic Church, but his followers would not follow his lead.

In 1757, having obtained safe conduct for himself and his followers as Turkish subjects from the Polish king, he returned to Poland. He was again taken under the wing of Bishop Dębowski, who in June 1757 organized a staged disputation between Frank and his followers and a group of rabbis and leaders of nine communities in Red Rus, who were described as 'talmudists'. The rabbis were compelled to attend under threat of corporal punishment. The outcome was a foregone conclusion. Bishop Dębowski, having declared Frank and his followers

[112] On Sabbatianism in Poland–Lithuania, see Hundert, *Jews in Poland–Lithuania in the Eighteenth Century*, 153–6, and Galas, 'Sabbatianism in the Seventeenth Century Polish–Lithuanian Commonwealth'.

[113] Hundert, *Jews in Poland–Lithuania in the Eighteenth Century*, 125.

victorious, ordered the burning of the Talmud in Lviv, where he had become archbishop. Dębowski's death soon after ended his campaign and exposed the Frankists to the wrath of their Jewish opponents; Frank again fled to Turkey.

In December 1758 Frank returned to Poland–Lithuania, having sent a letter to the new archbishop of Lviv claiming that the Jews used Christian blood in the preparation of matzah and agreeing to convert to Christianity. A second debate was now staged in Lviv, but although this found for the Frankists in most respects, it failed to conclude that the Talmud required the Jews to use blood in their rituals. Frank now carried out his promise to convert to Catholicism, together with approximately 600 of his followers. It soon became apparent that his conversion was part of his larger messianic plan, and he was arrested and confined in the monastery at Częstochowa. It was here that he finally modified his doctrine, recognizing Jasna Góra as the 'true Zion Mountain'—the place of the ultimate revelation which would precede the End of Days. He held to a form of this doctrine until his death.

In recent years a considerable amount of research has been conducted into the character of the Frankist phenomenon. As is the case with most aspects of Jewish mysticism, this research, which was undertaken in the nineteenth century by Heinrich Graetz, Majer Bałaban, and Alexander Kraushar, was revitalized by Gershom Scholem, who saw the movement as a 'radical and extreme' branch of Sabbatianism and who discovered manuscripts of Frank's *Księgi Słów Pańskich* (The Words of the Lord) in the Jagiellonian Library during his visit to Kraków in 1959.[114] Subsequently, additional manuscripts have been found in Kraków and Lublin and have been edited by Hillel Levine and Jan Doktór.[115]

As Doktór, the pre-eminent Frank specialist in Poland, has shown, not all of Frank's disciples chose to follow in his footsteps and enter the Roman Catholic Church.[116] Many retained their Jewish or Muslim faith, in spite of his urgings to convert, which had now become the key to his messianic strategy. Of Frank's Jewish followers, for the most part only those who had been exposed as Sabbatians chose to convert in 1759. Of the remainder, some of those in Poland may have been won over by the burgeoning hasidic movement. The Czech and German Sabbatians, who had assured Frank that they would 'join the holy faith' (that is, accept his teaching), abandoned him rather than become Catholics. Nevertheless, they recognized him as the messiah after his death, when Eva Frank and her brothers relinquished this requirement.

There were also Jewish crypto-Christians at Eva Frank's court in Offenbach. According to one of them, Moshe Porges, he and his colleagues officially remained Jews, but shaved their beards and went to the Roman Catholic church

[114] On Gershom Scholem's visit to Poland, see Galas, 'Die Mystik der polnischen Juden in Gershom Scholems Arbeiten', 97, 99.

[115] Levine (ed.), *The Chronicle* (Heb.); Doktór (ed.), *Rozmaite adnotacje, przypadki, czynności i anekdoty Pańskie*.

[116] Doktór, 'The Non-Christian Frankists'.

each Sunday in the uniform of Polish uhlans. They followed the typically Frankist strategy of concealing their true beliefs. In Jewish circles they did not reveal their baptism, while at Offenbach they concealed the fact that they still considered themselves Jews. We do not know whether they participated in the Catholic sacraments, but this seems likely. Another of them, Nathan Kassovitz, had persuaded Porges that one could follow the messiah in various ways and that public conversion was not necessarily desirable for all his supporters since it might alienate some of them.

The failure of the messianic hopes the Frankists placed in the year 1800 undermined their position. In 1800, on Yom Kippur, a solemn ban of excommunication was proclaimed against them. Nevertheless, members of the *edah kedushah* (holy congregation), as they described themselves, survived this crisis, and a number of memoirs from the early nineteenth century describe their beliefs.

The Muslim converts in Turkey and Wallachia who had converted with Frank were not persuaded of the need for yet another conversion. Many of them, including Frank's father-in-law, Tova, decided to remain Muslim. At the end of 1783, when the messianic event expected by Tova did not materialize, Frank began a campaign to attract the Muslim converts. Nevertheless, they took the decision not to go to Poland and not to convert to Catholicism. As the price of retaining their links with Frank, they demanded that he accept their continuing to profess Islam and that he modify his preaching at Częstochowa, which argued that salvation was open only to Catholics. Reconciliation with the Muslim Frankists required a certain doctrinal foundation. Frank argued that secret conversion would enable them to follow the road of salvation opened by him without abandoning Turkey and Islam. It is worth noting that in the last of Frank's Offenbach lectures they are treated quite differently from the way they had been a few years before in Brno: they were no longer competitors but equal partners of the Polish Frankists in the task of salvation.

We do not know exactly what role Frank assigned to the Muslim Frankists in his messianic plans. There are two possibilities. The first is that he treated their remaining in Islam as a mission of salvation analogous to his own mission in Christianity, that is to give concrete form to the Shekhinah that was hidden in both religions. More likely he may have seen Islam as a refuge for believers fearing persecution, in which case they should secretly adopt the saving truth of Christianity. Muslim converts seem to have been present at the Offenbach court until 1800. On the failure of the messianic expectations of that year they returned to the Balkans, and disappear from view. It may be that they settled in Salonika, where a Sabbatian centre persisted until at least 1914.

The Sabbatian controversy had European-wide ramifications, the most striking of which was the conflict between Rabbi Jacob Emden and the rabbi of the Three Communities (Altona, Hamburg, and Wandsbeck), Jonathan Eybeschuetz. There seems to be no basis for Emden's accusations, which were repeated by Heinrich

Graetz, that Eybeschuetz failed to condemn Frank's claim that the Jewish Passover ritual required Christian blood. In fact, Eybeschuetz wrote an effective refutation of Frank's arguments and was able to win support for his views from two leading Christian scholars, the distinguished professors of theology and oriental languages at the University of Halle, Christian Benedict Michaelis (1680–1764) and Johann Salomo Semler (1729–91).[117]

The emergence and development of Frankism forms an important element in the background to the rise of hasidism, which has been variously described as 'a movement of Jewish spiritual revival which began in southeastern Poland during the second half of the eighteenth century and came to be characterized by its charismatic leadership, mystical orientation, and distinctive pattern of communal life'[118] and 'an outbreak of radical immanentist mysticism in eighteenth-century Ukrainian Judaism'.[119] Our understanding of the emergence and development of hasidism has developed rapidly in recent years as scholars have adopted a much more critical approach to the sources. It has become apparent that the earliest sources, in particular some of the authenticated sayings and early letters of the Ba'al Shem Tov (or Besht), the initiator of the movement, raise relatively few problems of interpretation. This is also true of the material which can be found in the Polish archives, primarily those of the Sieniawa-Czartoryski estate, which owned the town of Medzhybizh, where the Besht spent the last twenty years of his life. However, this is not the case with the hagiographic material, whether in the form of the sayings of the Besht which were recorded later or the account of his activities, as recounted in *Shivḥei habesht* (In Praise of the Ba'al Shem Tov), and those of his successors. This material, among the most characteristic and attractive produced by the movement, is concerned with teaching a moral lesson, and cannot be seen as historical in the modern sense. Legends about the Besht arose from the very start of his preaching. Care and skill is needed to extract the kernels of historical evidence which are to be found in it. In addition, the role of editors and the way the material was modified in subsequent editions needs to be carefully analysed.

As a result of recent research we know a great deal more about the Besht and his activities in Medzhybizh.[120] As Rosman has shown, the town was no rural backwater. It had a population of 5,000, of which 2,000 were Jews, and was one of the fifteen largest Jewish towns in Poland. (For more details on the history of the town, see Chapter 3.)

The Besht was invited to come to Medzhybizh as the resident kabbalist, healer, and leader of the *beit midrash*, which made him a man of substance with a reputation. There was already a circle of kabbalists and mystics in the town, of which he became the most prominent. Rosman has documented from the archives of the

[117] On Michaelis, see *Allgemeine deutsche Biographie* (Leipzig, 1875–1912), xxi. 21, 676; and on Semler, see Cross (ed.), *The Oxford Dictionary of the Christian Church*, 1239.

[118] Rapoport-Albert, introduction to *Hasidism Reappraised*, p. xvii.

[119] Green, 'Early Hasidism', 442.

[120] See in particular Rosman, *Founder of Hasidism*, and Etkes, *The Besht*.

Sieniawa-Czartoryski estate that he lived in a house belonging to this community and was exempt from tax. Some of his associates received a weekly stipend from the *kahal* budget. He is described in the documents as a *kabbalista* and a *doktor*.[121] The same documents show that he employed a number of men, including the *pisarz balszema* (the Ba'al Shem's scribe). In addition, two members of the *beit midrash* were sponsored by the Medzhybizh community with 1 or 2 zlotys per week.[122]

It is clear from the work of Rosman and others that the Besht was a respected member of the Jewish community and that he did not see himself as a radical or as called upon to support the lower orders against the communal oligarchy. He was also not interested in creating anything more than a small circle of like-minded mystics. As Rosman puts it:

> the Besht was much more a representative of existing religious, social, political, and even economic realities than he was an innovator. He was certainly no rebel against the establishment, whether religious or social. He fit into the institutions of his time and conformed to the behavior patterns expected of the type of holy man he was.[123]

There were many circles of mystics in eighteenth-century Poland–Lithuania, led by charismatic figures. What was different about the Besht? This is more controversial. A number of elements can perhaps be isolated. In the first place he seems to have modified in a significant manner the concept of the tsadik, who was transformed in hasidic thought from the 'average, more or less pious Jew, the righteous person who has been approved by the celestial court in the days between New Year and the Day of Atonement . . . [into a] religious superman, the leader of his community, and the mediator between the divine and the human realms', a development which was linked with the kabbalistic concept of the ninth manifestation of the Divine Presence (known as 'tsadik') in the system of divine emanations, which brought divine power to the earth.[124]

How far did the Besht himself contribute to this later development? One aspect of this change was the way the Besht transformed the concept of the *ba'al shem*, the 'master of the Holy Name', or 'master of the Holy Names [of God]', who was the inheritor of 'the ancient Jewish mystical and magical tradition of the theology of names, a doctrine developed and transmitted by the *hekhalot* literature and further modified by the *hasidei* Ashkenaz in the twelfth and thirteenth centuries'.[125] In the earliest Ashkenazi *ba'al shem* tales, those of Rabbi Samuel Hehasid, we find 'a modest, sin-fearing Jew who used Holy Names only in rare and very specific cases', such as *kidush hashem* (martyrdom) and the creation of a golem—but never for material or selfish purposes. Subsequently, in the cycle of tales about Rabbi Judah the Pious (Judah b. Samuel Hehasid, *c.*1150–1217) and Adam Ba'al Shem, we encounter a *ba'al shem* similar to the Renaissance magicians

121 Rosman, *Founder of Hasidism*, 165. 122 Ibid. 166. 123 Ibid. 174.

124 Grözinger, 'Tsadik and Ba'al Shem in East European Hasidism', 160.

125 Grözinger, 'The Names of God and the Celestial Powers'. The *heikhalot* literature attempted to describe the dwelling place of God, which was understood to have a mystical significance.

of Christian society such as Dr Faustus and Pan Twardowski in Kraków. In the Polish–Lithuanian environment of the seventeenth and eighteenth centuries *ba'alei shem*, who were held in high esteem in Jewish society, were primarily healers who used spells to cure disease or exorcize evil spirits. They also dealt with the widespread fear of sin and ritual impurity, treating what we would regard as spiritual and psychological illness. In this context the Lurianic tradition, with its concept of the transmigration of souls, enabled the *ba'al shem* to intervene and to direct transmigrating souls towards their necessary cleansing and atonement. The Besht inherited this ability (as did other *ba'alei shem* of his time), and his use of it is documented extensively in *Shivḥei habesht*.

The new feature of the Besht's concept of the *ba'al shem* was derived from the mystical tradition of the *heikhalot*—the ascent to the celestial palaces. In Karl Grözinger's words, 'Unlike the ancient *hekhalot* mystics, the Besht did not ascend to heaven simply in order to see the Divine and to receive celestial knowledge of present and future events'; he also used these heavenly journeys above all 'to plead before the bar of the celestial court for his fellow Jews'.[126] One result of this new function, which emerges clearly from the *Shivḥei habesht*, is a change in the character of the spells cast. Instead of using the divine names, the Besht employed prayer and readings of sacred texts, which were more appropriate to his goals. He abandoned the formulaic use of spells in favour of prayer and mystical contemplation.

Another new element in the teaching of the Besht was its anti-asceticism, very different from the pessimistic and sin-laden atmosphere which was a feature of the religious culture of Polish Jewry. In a letter to his close associate Jacob Joseph of Polonnoye (d. 1782), who he felt was fasting excessively, he wrote:

> you should not put yourself in danger like this. For this is an act of melancholy and of sorrow and God's Presence will not inspire out of sorrow, but only out of the joy of performing the commandments . . . every morning when you study, attach yourself to the letters with total devotion to the service of your Creator, blessed be He and blessed be His Name, and then they will soften the verdicts with their root and lift the verdicts from you.[127]

In the Besht's view, evil differs from good only by degree in the hierarchy of holiness. As a result, the sinner is not completely rejected by the compassionate God, but always has the potential for self-improvement. Indeed, an evil impulse is not wholly evil. It carries within it the possibility of redemption if it can be redirected to become a force for good.

One example, examined by Hundert, is the Besht's attitude to the problem of how to atone for seminal emission (*keri*), a matter whose importance was clearly becoming more pressing with the rapid growth in the Jewish population and the increase in the number of young men.[128] In Hundert's words, this issue 'attracted

[126] Grözinger, 'Tsadik and Ba'al Shem in East European Hasidism', 167.

[127] Quoted in Rosman, *Founder of Hasidism*, 115.

[128] On this, see Hundert, 'Jewish Popular Spirituality in the Eighteenth Century', 99–103.

almost obsessive attention during the late seventeenth and eighteenth centuries'. According to the *Shulḥan arukh*, a person guilty of 'slaughtering [his generative] seed' is guilty of a sin more serious than all the sins of the Torah, a view which can also be found in the Zohar. These views were very different from those expressed in the Mishnah and Talmud, which saw seminal emission as the result of the work of female demons for which the person affected was not responsible. The sixteenth-century Safed mystics and their followers in Europe accepted the seriousness of the offence, but for the most part held that forgiveness was possible if extraordinary acts of penitence were undertaken. This was also the position of Isaiah Horowitz in his *Shenei luḥot haberit*, and of the *Shevet musar*.

The Besht's views were very different. According to Dov Baer, the Maggid of Mezhirech (d. 1772), 'The Besht . . . said: One should not worry over an impure accident, an involuntary seminal emission that occurred without impure thoughts.' The emission expels an evil spark that must be extinguished.[129]

The Besht also stressed the importance of prayer, which would enable the individual to achieve union (*devekut*) with God. For this union, intensity of feeling rather than learning was what was crucial. Ecstatic enthusiasm (*hitlahavut*) was the goal—the experience of spiritual exultation as the soul is elevated towards God. Arthur Green defines this change as 'a focusing of Judaism on worship—a sense that the simple prayer life . . . is the very centre of Judaism'.[130] This later became central to hasidism and clearly owes a great deal to the personal faith and religious practice of the Besht.

However, in spite of this stress on prayer rather than study, the Besht's teaching should not be seen as anti-intellectual—a revolt against the excessive legalism of rabbinic Judaism led by charismatic, populist, and barely educated figures—a view which was most strongly advanced by Simon Dubnow. It attracted men with great scholarly gifts such as Jacob Joseph of Polonnoye and Shneur Zalman b. Barukh of Lyady (1745–1813). Among many of its early adherents were yeshiva students and members of the scholarly elite. To them one of the attractions of the movement was its rejection of the characteristic forms of talmudic argument in Poland. One saying attributed to Jacob Joseph was 'It is easier for [me] to say ten *hilukim* than to recite one *shemoneh esreh* prayer [the central morning prayer].' The Besht's charge in *Shivḥei habesht* that the rabbis were inventing 'false premisses' was probably also intended to refer to textual casuistry.[131]

How far did the Besht see himself as a messianic figure, as has been claimed, for instance, by Benzion Dinur? In Scholem's dialectical view, hasidism was the 'latest phase' in the history of Jewish mysticism, and as such was related to the two immediately preceding stages, Lurianic kabbalah and Sabbatianism. 'Lurianic

[129] *Or torah* (Korzec, 1804), 'Re'eh' and *Magid devarav leya'akov* (Korzec, 1784), 38*b*; cf. *In Praise of the Ba'al Shem Tov* (1970 edn.), no. 209.

[130] Green, 'Early Hasidism', 445.

[131] Dov Baer b. Samuel of Linits [Luninets], *In Praise of the Ba'al Shem Tov* (Heb., 1814 edn.), 16*d*, quoted in Etkes, 'The Study of Hasidism', 453.

Kabbalism, Sabbatianism and Hasidism', he wrote, 'are after all three stages of the same process.'

Lurianic kabbalah aimed to capture the imagination of the masses; it succeeded because it enabled the common folk to express their yearning for redemption. Sabbatianism, however, tried to realize those yearnings 'in our time' and therefore culminated in catastrophe. Hasidism, in Scholem's view, was a sequel to both in that it attempted 'to make the world of Kabbalism . . . accessible to the masses of the people'. However, in order to do so it had first to relieve Lurianic kabbalah of its messianic 'sting'. This hasidism proceeded to do by replacing the Lurianic messianic ideal of *tikun* (reform of the world) with the mystical ideal of *devekut* (communion with God), thereby neutralizing the acute messianic element that pervaded both Lurianic kabbalah and Sabbatianism.[132] This explains what Scholem referred to as the 'neutralization' of the messianic element in hasidism.

If one discounts the Hegelian superstructure, Scholem was probably right to argue that hasidism was not a messianic movement, since it did not strive to accelerate the messianic redemption, while retaining the traditional belief in the messiah. A letter from the Besht to his brother-in-law, with its account of his conversation with the messiah, cannot be taken as evidence of any messianic urge in early hasidism. Moreover, although the letter was circulated in various earlier versions, the form in which we have it today remained concealed for many years in the possession of Jacob Joseph of Polonnoye, who had received it from the Besht in 1751 but revealed it only in 1781, when he included it in his book *Ben porat yosef*.

If Scholem's thesis of the neutralization of the messianic element in the Besht's teaching has received widespread acceptance, the same cannot be said for his arguments on the intellectual links between him and the Sabbatians. Scholem stressed that the origins of hasidism lay in Podolia, an area known for its large number of Sabbatians. In his view, the 'founder of Hasidism and his first disciples, therefore, must have been fully aware of the destructive power inherent in extreme mystical Messianism . . . They were active among the same people whom Sabbateanism had tried [to convert] . . . and it is by no means impossible that there was at first a certain passing over of members from one movement to the other.'[133]

Scholem also argued that there were clear similarities between hasidic and Sabbatian concepts of 'the ideal type of man to which they ascribe the function of leadership'. The 'ideal leader of the community' was no longer a rabbinical scholar of halakhah, as envisaged by rabbinic Jewry, but rather 'the illuminate . . . the prophet'.[134] This formulation overlooks the clear differences between the hasidic doctrine of the tsadik and Sabbatian ideas. Avraham Rubinstein has commented on the complexity of this relationship: 'Certain Sabbatean notions reverberated in the teachings of hasidism. But the intensity of the reverberation and

132 Scholem, *Major Trends in Jewish Mysticism*, 325–50.

133 Ibid. 330–1.

134 Ibid. 332–3.

the compensating effect of the complex of other influences on hasidism still await proper investigation and clarification.'[135]

The argument that hasidism originated in the same geographical areas as Sabbatianism has also come under fire. Michael Silber has shown that the regions in which proto-hasidism emerged were not those in which there were significant numbers of crypto-Sabbatians. Indeed, the reverse seems to have been the case: the Besht and his circle sought followers in areas where there were few Sabbatians.[136] There also seem to be few personal links between the last Sabbatians and this group. In this sense, the emergence of hasidism can be seen as a response to the dangers that the mystical circle in Medzhybizh saw in the Sabbatian movement.

Two other features of the Besht's teaching and practice also seem to stand out. Unlike other mystics, he was concerned with the salvation not only of himself and his small circle, but of all Israel, as in his interventions over such matters as Haydamak attacks on Jews, religious persecution including ritual murder accusations, and epidemics. In Ada Rapoport-Albert's words, 'Hasidism is distinguishable from all other schools of Jewish esoteric spirituality and mysticism in having fused together two diametrically opposed poles of human experience: intensely personal, reclusive, mystical flight from the world, and robust involvement in mundane human affairs.'[137] Finally in the proto-court created around his extended family we can see the beginnings of the court of the individual tsadik, which was such a characteristic feature of hasidism.

On his death in 1760 the Besht left behind him only a small circle of followers. It was they, and above all Jacob Joseph of Polonnoye and Dov Baer, the Maggid of Mezhirech, who were responsible for the emergence of the hasidic movement and for its rapid expansion, which is examined in Volume II, Chapter 8.

CONCLUSION

In no sector of Jewish life was the importance of the mid-seventeenth-century turning point in the history of Poland–Lithuania more important than in religion. Until 1648 there was a harmonious balance in Jewish religious theory and practice between halakhah, secular study, and mysticism. The period after 1648 paved the way for the emergence of a popular mysticism which led to the emergence of a kabbalistic religious elite alongside the older rabbinic one. Sabbatian ideas remained important in Poland–Lithuania and provided the soil from which such divergent phenomena as the messianic movement of Jacob Frank and what later became hasidism were to emerge. At the same time the spiritual awakening linked with Israel b. Eliezer, the Ba'al Shem Tov, which had its roots not only in

[135] Rubinstein, 'Between Hasidism and Sabbatianism' (Heb.), 188–9.

[136] Silber's findings are discussed in Etkes, 'The Study of Hasidism', 458.

[137] Rapoport-Albert, introduction to *Hasidism Reappraised*, p. xxii.

the popularization of kabbalah but in the growing importance of faith healers, brought many new and valuable elements to the Jewish religious tradition. Even though the view that hasidism was a populist revolt against excessive rabbinic concentration on literal observance of the law can no longer be accepted, this last religious movement to emerge in an almost entirely Jewish environment did speak in a new and moving way to the average Polish Jew.

CONCLUSION

WHAT DID the Jews of Poland–Lithuania bring with them as they began to encounter the new political and economic ideas which were to transform the lands in which they lived around the middle of the eighteenth century? In the first place, because of the size of the community and its sense of rootedness and security, its members possessed a strong sense of their own worth and the value of their religious traditions. They found in their religion assurance that their present sufferings would be transformed by a messianic event which would overturn existing social realities and recognize their true worth. In Gershon Hundert's words:

> The circumstances under which they lived . . . created a mentality which acted as a filter through which the new cultural, political and economic currents had to pass. That mentality both buffered Jews and buttressed their defences. And when in the nineteenth century, certain important aspects of this context broke down, the vast majority of these Jews were armored against trauma and splitting—psychological reversals of loyalty—by the mentality that had been formed earlier. Self-affirmation and a feeling of Jewish superiority and solidarity dominated the spectrum of self-evaluation of eastern European Jews.[1]

This self-confidence was linked with the institutions of Jewish communal autonomy. Although these were both oligarchic and male-controlled, they gave to all sections of the community a sense that they participated in its running and had a stake in its success. The transformation of Jewish society was most successful in those areas, such as Prussian Poland, where the communal structures were reformed rather than done away with. Elsewhere the breakdown of the mechanisms of self-government was painfully felt. Speaking at the Kovno conference in 1909, the Russian Jewish activist Genrikh Sliozberg observed, 'Unfortunately, we have neither a community structure nor a communal organization', and saw the rebuilding of such a structure as a pressing need.

A key element in the Jewish sense of security in premodern Poland–Lithuania was the alliance of convenience with the nobility, particularly after 1648. However, one of the principal developments in the social history of the lands of the Polish–Lithuanian Commonwealth after the partitions was the undermining, and in most places the end, of the social and economic hegemony of the nobility. The attitude of the nobility to 'their Jews' was certainly paternalistic and patronizing, but their support for them did provide the Jews with a niche in society. It

[1] Hundert, *Jews in Poland–Lithuania in the Eighteenth Century*, 239–40.

proved very difficult for the Jews of the area to find an appropriate place for themselves in the social system once the power of the nobility came to an end.

The last legacy of Poland–Lithuania was less beneficial. The anti-Judaic traditions developed here by writers such as Fr. Stefan Żuchowski and Fr. Gaudenty Pikulski were readily taken up in the tsarist empire in the nineteenth century and provided the basis for much of the Judaeophobia of important sections of the Russian bureaucracy. The renegade Polish Catholic and antisemitic writer Hipolit Lutostański, for instance, drew much of the material for his influential book on the blood libel from these works.[2] Nevertheless, in spite of such hostility, Jews were the only significant non-Christian group tolerated in Western Christendom and they flourished in the Polish–Lithuanian Commonwealth.

[2] Lyutostansky [Lutostański], *Vopros ob upotreblenii evreyami-sektatorami khristianskoi krovi dlya religioznykh tselei, v svyazi s voprosami ob otnosheniyakh evreistva k khristianstvu voobshche.*

APPENDIX

THE POLISH–LITHUANIAN BACKGROUND

> The Polish nobility are eager for glory, keen on the spoils of war, contemptuous of danger and death, inconstant in their promises, hard on their subjects and people of the lower orders, careless in speech, used to living beyond their means, faithful to their monarch, devoted to farming and cattle-breeding, courteous to foreigners and guests, and lavish in hospitality, in which they exceed other nations.
>
> JAN DŁUGOSZ, *Annales*, 1480

> You should know that Poland is made up of different provinces which are like individual kingdoms. It is so extensive that if you wanted to traverse the space from the extreme limits of Lithuania, which border on Muscovy, to the foothills of the Carpathians, you would need a whole month. And in another direction, calculate how far removed is the mouth of the Dnieper on the Black Sea from the Baltic coast. Therefore I ask: when the representatives of so many peoples, who differ in their past and in their level of prosperity and who are not linked by bonds of family or relationship, is it possible, I ask, when their representatives meet in the Sejm that they can be inspired by a single common idea?
>
> ANDRZEJ M. FREDRO, *Przysłowie mów potocznych*, 1664

The Kingdom of Poland and the Grand Duchy of Lithuania to the Union of Lublin 1569

When Jews found their way to the area at the end of the tenth century, Poland and Lithuania were still separate states. They were linked dynastically in 1385 when Jogaila (Jagiełło), the grand duke of Lithuania, married Jadwiga, the last ruling Polish monarch descended from the Piast dynasty. She was the daughter of Elisabeth, daughter of King Władysław I Łokietek (r. 1320–33) of Poland, who married Louis, king of Hungary, a member of the Angevin dynasty. Jogaila was crowned king of Poland in 1386, and in 1392 recognized his cousin Vytautas as grand duke of Lithuania, while retaining the title of *supremus magnus dux Lithuaniae*. The two states were now linked dynastically, and after 1447, when Kazimierz IV Jagiellończyk (Kazimieras I Jogailaitis) finally accepted the Polish throne, they were ruled by a common monarch (except for a hiatus in 1492–1501). In 1569 the two states were united constitutionally, creating the Polish–Lithuanian Commonwealth, one of the largest political units in Europe with an area of nearly 4 million square miles. After a period of flourishing, its internal problems led to a major crisis in the middle of the seventeenth century. This was overcome, but attempts at reform came too late and the country was partitioned by its three neighbours, Austria, Prussia, and Russia, in 1772, 1793, and 1795, and disappeared from the map of Europe (see Maps 1, 3, and 4). It is obviously impossible to deal in any detail with the evolution of Poland–Lithuania during the first seven centuries of Jewish settlement, but a few general observations may help to orient the reader to the general context in which Jewish life developed.[1]

Until the dynastic union the Kingdom of Poland and the Grand Duchy of Lithuania had developed on somewhat different lines. The Polish state, which was consolidated in the tenth century, received Christianity from the West when in 966 its ruler, Mieszko I, was baptized. This decision had momentous consequences, since it made the state part of the developing civilization of Western Christendom rather than of the world of Eastern Orthodoxy with its centre in Byzantium. Mieszko's successor, Bolesław I, obtained the permission of the emperor Otto I to create an independent Polish ecclesiastical organization, and in 1025 took the title of king, significantly elevating the status of his country. In the century following the death of Bolesław III Krzywousty in 1138, the breakdown of the system of primogeniture led to the division of the country. A sense of the unity of the Polish lands remained in spite of the difficulties which successive rulers faced in re-establishing a single government. At the same time the weakening of the power of the central royal authority allowed landowners, both ecclesiastical and lay, to obtain 'immunities'—the exemption of their estates from taxes, services, and the legal jurisdiction of the state, the beginning of the empowerment of the noble estate, or *szlachta*.[2]

The entry of Poland into Western Christendom occurred at a time of cultural development and political innovation: the Benedictine, Cistercian, and Dominican orders established themselves in the country and brought with them Romanesque and then Gothic architecture. It was also a period of economic expansion, agrarian colonization, and the development of new agricultural techniques, above all the use of the wheeled plough needed to till the heavy clay soils of the area and the crop rotation involved in the three-field system, which produced surpluses for sale to local towns and abroad. The boom in agriculture was accompanied by the development of the mining of gold and silver in Silesia and salt in Małopolska. The country also became much more integrated into the

[1] There are many useful accounts of the history of pre-partition Poland–Lithuania. Of those in English one might mention Reddaway et al. (eds.), *The Cambridge History of Poland*; Gieysztor et al. (eds.), *History of Poland*; Davies, *God's Playground*, i; Zamoyski, *The Polish Way*; Knoll, *The Rise of the Polish Monarchy*; Rowell, *Lithuania Ascending*; Sedlar, *East Central Europe in the Middle Ages, 1000–1500*; Stone, *The Polish–Lithuanian State, 1386–1795*; Fedorowicz et al. (eds.), *A Republic of Nobles*; Dembkowski, *The Union of Lublin*; Lukowski, *Liberty's Folly*.

[2] On medieval Poland, see Manteuffel, *The Formation of the Polish State*; Grudzinski, *Boleslaus the Bold . . . and Bishop Stanislaus*; Knoll, *The Rise of the Polish Monarchy*; and Halecki, *Jadwiga of Anjou and the Rise of East Central Europe*.

European trade system, and towns like Wrocław, Poznań, and Kraków received charters recognizing their right to self-government.

The German empire emerged as a major power and a transmission belt for new ideas and technologies, with obvious implications for the states on its eastern border. German eastward expansion increased significantly from the twelfth century. This expansion took the form partly of peaceful colonization, both rural and urban, which led to the Germanization of a number of areas previously inhabited mainly by Slavs. It was also the result of the actions of crusading orders, of which the most important was that of the Knights of the Sword, or Teutonic Knights (their official title was the Order of the Hospital of the Blessed Virgin Mary of the German House of Jerusalem), who re-established themselves in eastern Europe after the failure of their crusading activities in the Middle East. The Pope authorized the order to convert the heathen, and in 1228 Conrad of Mazovia, under pressure from the pagan Lithuanians, Prussians, and Jatvingians, peoples speaking similar Baltic languages, sought the order's aid. In response they established by force a territorial base in the lands of the Prussians, later known as East Prussia. This was given legal justification by the Golden Bull of the emperor Frederick II which authorized them to retain and govern the territories they had conquered.

In spite of German pressure, the Polish state, unlike that of the Czechs, was not incorporated into the Holy Roman Empire. In addition, although one of the Polish dukes, Henry II (the Pious) of Silesia, died at the battle of Legnica in 1241, when Małopolska and Silesia were conquered by the Mongols, the country was not retained by them, mainly because it lay too far west. In this respect its fate differed from that of Rus. This was the start of a period of economic and cultural growth. The unity of the state was partially re-established in the mid-fourteenth century (though without Silesia and Pomerania and with widespread autonomy in Mazovia) under Władysław I Łokietek, who came to the throne in 1320, and consolidated under Kazimierz III the Great (r. 1333–70). Kazimierz's slogan was 'One king, one law, one currency', and he organized the unification and codification of the legal systems of Małopolska and Wielkopolska. In 1364, to train administrators for his reunited kingdom, he founded the University of Kraków, modelled on that in Bologna and the second, after Prague, to be established in the Slav lands of Western Christendom. It preceded that in Heidelberg, founded in 1386. He was also able to establish a solidly based currency, the Kraków grosz, which stimulated trade with the outside world. These years also saw the beginnings of Polish eastward expansion into the realm of Orthodoxy with the occupation between 1340 and the 1360s of the greater part of Halich and Volhynia, successor duchies of Kiev (see Map 2). The Black Death, which devastated western and central Europe from 1348, does not seem to have affected Poland severely, partly because the region was protected by climate and low population densities. Kazimierz died without heirs, leaving the kingdom to his cousin King Louis of Hungary, who was succeeded by his daughter Jadwiga in 1382. In 1384 the Hungarian-raised Jadwiga was crowned 'king of Poland'. By this time the country had a population of approximately 2 million.

The Grand Duchy of Lithuania had a very different history. It was the last pagan state in Europe and, under a group of very able leaders—Mindaugas (d. 1263), Gediminas (r. 1316–41), Algirdas (prince of Krevo and Vitebsk 1341–5, grand duke of Lithuania 1345–77), and Jogaila (r. 1377–1434)—it was able to expand from its Lithuanian (Balto-Slav) ethnic core into the area of Rus as Tatar power waned. The grand duke Algirdas transformed the grand duchy, moving its capital from Trakai to Vilna (Wilno, Vilnius) and defeating the Tatars at the battle of Blue Water in 1363. He subsequently took Kiev, the former capital of the Grand Duchy of Kiev, and incorporated large areas which had once been under its control. In them the former Rus nobility was allowed to preserve its Orthodox religion, its privileges, and control of local government. Although there was a certain amount of intermarriage between the ruling Lithuanian warrior caste and the great East Slav princely families, the grand duke and his court still retained their nature-worshipping pagan religion, which made the state vulnerable to the crusading activities of the Teutonic Knights. The Lithuanian rulers were divided on how to respond: those who ruled in the eastern, largely Slavonic, regions of the state favoured conversion to Orthodoxy and an alliance with Muscovy, whereas those in the Lithuanian ethnic core supported an alliance with Poland. In 1333 Aldona, daughter of the grand duke Gediminas, married Kazimierz, who had come to the Polish throne in 1330. The pro-Polish group ultimately won and, as a result, by the Treaty of Krevo (Krėva) in 1385, a dynastic union with Poland was arranged through the marriage of the grand duke Jogaila to the 12-year-old Jadwiga. Jogaila now took the baptismal name of Władysław II Jagiełło, the Lithuanian court accepted Western Christianity, and newly baptized nobles were granted extensive privileges. Although Chancery Ruthenian (*ruskii*), the language later called 'Old Belarusian' by philologists, remained the language of the court, the dynastic union was the start of a process as a result of which the nobility as a whole, including its Ruthenian and Orthodox component, became increasingly Polonized and most of its members adhered to the Roman Catholic faith. At the time of the dynastic union the population of the grand duchy was probably between 1.5 and 2 million, of whom under half a million were ethnic Lithuanians and the remainder Ruthenians.

The period between the conclusion of the Treaty of Krevo and the political union of Poland–Lithuania in a single state in 1569 was one of expansion and prosperity in both countries, linked, above all, with the development of the trade in grain and forest products along the Vistula, Niemen, and other rivers to the Baltic, centred on the port of Danzig. Indeed a recent history of Poland and Lithuania is entitled 'The Land of the Great Rivers'.[3] At a time when the

[3] Rogall (ed.), *Land der grossen Ströme*. On this, see also Kula, *An Economic Theory of the Feudal System*, chs. 2, 5; Krannhals, *Danzig und der Weichselhandel in seiner Blütezeit vom 16. zum 17. Jahrhundert*; Cackowski, *Gospodarstwo wiejskie w dobrach biskupstwa i kapituły chełmińskiej w XVII–XXVIII w.*

beginning of a minor ice age in the western parts of the continent was reducing crop yields significantly, Poland and Lithuania experienced unusually warm weather and began to produce an agricultural surplus. The demand for grain and timber stimulated trade generally and led to a significant growth in both mining and manufacturing. The dynastically linked states flourished particularly under the reign of Kazimierz IV Jagiełło, who was grand duke of Lithuania from 1440 and who reigned as king of Poland between 1447 and 1492, who attempted, not entirely successfully, to strengthen the power of the monarchy. They did succeed in defeating the Teutonic Knights at the battle of Grunwald in July 1410, which significantly reduced the order's power, although it remained in control of the lower Vistula. The union between the two states was tightened by the Union of Horodło in 1413, although there was still a strong faction in the grand duchy opposed to closer links with Poland. Conflict with the Teutonic Order soon resumed and was brought to an end, after further Polish–Lithuanian victories and revolts against the order in the towns of the area, by the second Treaty of Toruń in 1466. Under its terms Danzig (Gdańsk) and the area south of it, now referred to as Royal Prussia, was incorporated into Poland with far-reaching autonomy, including its own parliament, legal system, and mint. The remaining lands of the order remained under its control but as a fiefdom of the Polish Crown. This did not resolve the issue, and when in 1525 the grand master of the order, Albert Hohenzollern of Brandenburg, who had been elected in 1511, became a Lutheran, he was allowed to secularize its holdings, which became known as Ducal Prussia, in return for an act of homage to the Polish king. The hope that this would be followed by the incorporation of Ducal Prussia by Poland proved vain, and the area became the core of the Prussian state, to which the Hohenzollerns were granted the right of hereditary succession in 1563. In the course of the seventeenth century Berlin and Brandenburg were linked dynastically with Ducal Prussia, and by the middle of that century the Elector of Brandenburg, heir of the Hohenzollerns, was able to unite these disparate areas and establish the complete independence of Ducal Prussia from Poland–Lithuania. By the eighteenth century Prussia had become one of the European great powers and, as such, participated in the partition of Poland–Lithuania.

This was, however, still far in the future, and in the late fifteenth century the prospects for Poland and Lithuania looked bright. Humanism began to influence both states, particularly in the Polish capital of Kraków, where the university and court became centres of the 'new learning' under the impact of the Italian scholar Filippo de Buonacorsi, known as Callimachus. It was during these years that Jan Długosz produced his history of Poland and the sculptor and painter Wit Stwosz (Veit Stoss), who came originally from Nuremberg, produced his great masterpiece, the altar screen in the Church of the Virgin in Kraków. In the following decades Zygmunt I (king of Poland and grand duke of Lithuania from 1506 to 1548), who had encountered Italian humanism at the court of his brother

Władysław, king of both the Czech lands and Hungary, and his second wife, Bona, daughter of Gian Galeazzo Sforza, duke of Milan, promoted Renaissance art and architecture as well as modern economic principles, particularly in the management of the royal domains. It was at this time that Nicolaus Copernicus established himself at the University of Kraków. Vernacular literature flourished with the development of printing, the emergence of major poets such as Mikołaj Rej and Jan Kochanowski, and the translation of the Bible into Polish in both Catholic and Protestant versions. Many of Zygmunt's counsellors were affected by these developments, most notably his chancellor, Jan Łaski, who had an extensive correspondence with Erasmus.[4]

The impact of the Reformation was also felt. Rej, usually described as the father of Polish literature, was a Protestant, and the translation of the Bible into Polish was important in fostering Protestant ideas. Calvinism found considerable support among the nobility, so that by the mid-sixteenth century perhaps a quarter of the nobility had become Protestant, including many members of the Radziwiłł family in Lithuania, such as 'Black' Mikołaj Radziwiłł, chancellor and governor of Vilna. In some areas the percentage of Protestants among the nobility was significantly higher, rising to half in Małopolska and two-thirds in Wielkopolska. However, the formerly independent Duchy of Mazovia, which was fully incorporated into the Kingdom in 1529, remained staunchly Catholic. In the towns, with their significant German populations, Lutheranism also gained adherents, particularly in Royal and Ducal Prussia. The Calvinists and Lutherans, together with a more radical group, the Unity of the Brethren, or Bohemian Brothers, joined in the Agreement of Sandomierz of 1570 to defend their religious freedoms.

Support for the Reformation came partly from conviction; in particular, the importance of lay councils in the Calvinist Church was very attractive to sections of the nobility. In addition, anticlericalism was strong, fuelled by the size of the agricultural holdings of the Church and the support it had given to the Teutonic Knights and those opposed to the Hussite movement in the Czech lands. Some efforts were made to halt the spread of the movement, but they were not strongly supported by Zygmunt, who favoured the calling of a General Church Council to deal with widely recognized abuses. His son Zygmunt August (grand duke of Lithuania from 1529 and both king of Poland and grand duke of Lithuania from 1548 to 1572) was also unwilling to persecute Protestants and seems to have hoped, at least in the early part of his reign, to create a national Church which would include both Catholics and Protestants.[5]

[4] On the Renaissance in Poland, see Fiszman (ed.), *The Polish Renaissance in its European Context*; Segel, *Renaissance Culture in Poland*; and Halecki, *From Florence to Brest*.

[5] On the Reformation in Poland and Lithuania, see Kot, *Socinianism in Poland*; Tazbir, *A State without Stakes*; Völker, *Kirchengeschichte Polens*; Górski, 'Some Aspects of the Polish Reformation in the XVI and XVII Centuries'; Weintraub, 'Tolerance and Intolerance in Old Poland'; Musteikis, *The Reformation in Lithuania*; Pollard, *The Jesuits in Poland*.

At the same time the political and social power of the nobility, whose separate legal status had already been recognized by the end of the fourteenth century, was growing and was reflected in the limitations which it was able to impose on the king, whose powers during the reign of Jagiełło were still quite extensive. As in Hungary and the Czech lands, the nobility constituted a larger proportion of the population than in western Europe and included within its ranks all those with noble titles, from great magnates to landless nobles attached to their courts. Some estimates claim that it constituted as much as 8–10 per cent of the population but these are certainly too high, and a figure of 5–6 per cent is probably more accurate. However, in certain areas of the country the proportion of nobles was much higher. This was the case, for instance, in Mazovia, which was only incorporated into the Kingdom of Poland in the early sixteenth century, and where nobles constituted nearly a fifth of the total population.

What is not in doubt is the way the privileges of this stratum expanded progressively. Already in the fourteenth century Kazimierz III's successor, his nephew Louis I of Hungary (king of Poland in 1370–82), had ensured his succession by granting privileges to key nobles in 1355. These were extended to the whole nobility in the Privilege of Košice (Kassa) of 1374, which obliged the king to consult the nobility if he wished to increase taxes beyond a specified level. The change of dynasty strengthened the nobles' belief that Poland existed independently of the king. Jagiełło was thus induced to increase further the rights of the nobility, and in 1422, in the Privilege of Czerwińsk, he conceded the principle *neminem captivabimus nisi jure victum* (literally 'We will not imprison anyone without legal cause'), which laid down that the king could not arbitrarily imprison a member of the nobility or confiscate his property and established a judiciary independent of the executive. The heavy costs of the war with the Teutonic Knights compelled Kazimierz IV to concede the Statutes of Nieszawa of 1454, which gave local nobles organized in the provincial parliaments (*sejmiki*) the right to levy soldiers and to raise new taxes. These developments made necessary the creation of a central representative body, the Sejm, which met for the first time in 1493, although councils of this type probably date back to the late fourteenth century and some certainly met during the reign of Kazimierz IV. It was a bicameral body in which the representatives of the provincial parliaments made up the lower house and the king's appointees constituted the senate. Its rights were laid down in the *Nihil novi* regulations of 1505, by which the king promised that 'nothing new' would be enacted 'by us or our successors without the common agreement of the council and representatives of the lands'.[6] Even more important was the fact that royal appointments required the ratification of the Sejm.

6 Stone, *The Polish–Lithuanian State, 1386–1795*, 35. On the evolution of Polish parliamentarianism, see Górski, 'The Origins of the Polish Sejm'; Miller, 'The Polish Nobility and the Renaissance Monarchy'; Sucheni-Grabowska, *Monarchia dwu ostatnich Jagiellonów a ruch egzekucyjny*; Russocki, 'Le Système représentatif de la république nobiliaire de Pologne'; Gierowski, *Sejmik Generalny księstwa mazowieckiego na tle ustroju sejmikowego Mazowsza*.

The growing power of the nobility was reflected in a number of areas. In the first place, the towns of Poland and Lithuania now lost much of their political and social influence. After 1505 representatives of the royal towns—those directly subject to the Crown—no longer attended meetings of the Sejm, where their role had previously been marginal. Danzig, Kraków, and later Vilna and Lviv retained the right to speak without voting on urban matters, but in practice were prevented from doing so. The inferior social status of burghers was enshrined in law when, in 1496, the Sejm forbade the acquisition of landed estates by them and barred them from holding high office in Church or State. In addition, as a result of the Sejm constitution of 1539, which was confirmed by royal decree in 1549, towns on the estates of the nobility fell under the full control of their noble owners and lost the right to appeal against their decisions to the royal courts of the governor who served as royal administrator in the Polish provinces.

The nobility was also able to impose a form of neo-serfdom on most of the peasantry in the Kingdom of Poland in a series of enactments which began with the Statute of Warka (1423) and culminated in that of Piotrków (1496), which were further codified in the first half of the sixteenth century. This brought to an end the previously largely free status of the peasantry. The intermediate group of village administrators, the bailiffs (*sołtysi*), were compelled to sell to nobles villages they had established, the peasants' freedom to leave their lord's estate was curtailed, their obligations to work the lord's land increased, and they were subject to his absolute legal power. Although these laws could not always be fully enforced, by the end of the sixteenth century the situation of the peasantry, who were now obliged to work at least three days per week without pay on noble land, as well as make contributions in both money and kind, had deteriorated significantly.

Similar developments were occurring in Lithuania. In 1447 Kazimierz IV, in his capacity as grand duke, granted a charter to the Lithuanian nobles, who were still referred to as boyars, reflecting the persistent influence of the traditions of the former Rus principalities, confirming their rights and privileges and increasing the subordination of the peasantry to noble control. These privileges were further extended under the rule of Grand Duke Aleksander (1492–1506), who was king of Poland between 1501 and 1506.

From the Union of Lublin to the Khmelnytsky Uprising of 1648

A new period of Polish–Lithuanian history began on 1 July 1569, when a common Polish–Lithuanian parliament meeting in Lublin transformed the personal union of the two states into a 'Commonwealth of Two Nations' with a common monarchy, a single parliament which met in Warsaw and, after 1673, also in Grodno (Hrodna), and a customs union, although the two constituent parts of the union retained their own administrations, treasuries, law codes, and armies. The union, the product of growing threats to the grand duchy from the Ottomans and

Tatars as well as from Muscovy, also further accelerated the Polonization of the Lithuanian nobility, to whom the privileges of the Polish nobility had been extended shortly before the union, and was followed by the introduction of Polish forms of administration and, from 1697, the use of Polish as the official language.[7]

In 1573 Zygmunt II, who had ruled both states from 1548, died without issue and the crown became fully elective. The first king to be elected by the direct vote of the nobility was Henry of Valois, the brother of the king of France, who was shortly to be Henry III of France. He agreed to far-reaching limitations on the power of the monarchy in what became known as the Henrician Articles and their supplement, the *pacta conventa*, which were to last until the partitions. According to these, the newly elected king was required to conclude a contract with the nobility as the embodiment of the Polish nation by which his successor would be freely elected by the entire nobility, religious toleration would be maintained, and the Sejm was to meet on a biennial basis and was to be represented in the interim by a standing body of senators. The king could declare war, conclude peace, and summon the military levy only with parliamentary approval. Should the king fail to uphold his part of the agreement, the nation could renounce its allegiance to him. Although the negative impact of the Henrician Articles was only gradually to become apparent, this was a recipe for political breakdown. The political system reflected the view of the nobility that the Commonwealth was a re-creation of the political system of ancient Rome. This idealization of the political system, linked with the belief that the Commonwealth was the granary of Europe and its defender against eastern barbarism, masked any awareness of its administrative, financial, and military weaknesses. The power of the Crown was also further undermined by the rapid and undignified renunciation of it by Henry shortly after he had assumed it in order to become king of France.

The country also became less tolerant. From the end of the sixteenth century Poland–Lithuania came under the increasing influence of the Counter-Reformation. Zygmunt III Vasa (1587–1632), the son of Katarzyna Jagiełło and Johan Vasa, duke of Finland, was an ardent Catholic who had lost the Swedish crown because of his support for the Counter-Reformation and hoped to use Poland to regain it. He strengthened these ties with the Counter-Reformation by his marriage to Anna, sister of the Habsburg emperor Ferdinand. In 1564 the Jesuit Order was invited into the country by Cardinal Stanisław Hosius, who had been a papal legate at the Council of Trent, for which he had written a new confession of the Catholic faith. He undertook a sustained campaign to win over the Protestant section of the nobility. The number of Jesuit priests increased to around 1,000 by 1624 and ten years later there were forty-two Jesuit colleges in the country, with that in Vilna at their head. Stronger measures were used against non-noble Protestants and were tacitly accepted by the king. There were several executions for blasphemy or for slandering the Catholic Church, and mob attacks

[7] On this, see Dembkowski, *The Union of Lublin*.

on Protestant burghers took place in Kraków in 1591, Poznań in 1606 and 1616, Lublin in 1627, and in Vilna on a number of occasions.

The revived Catholic Church attracted some sympathy among reform-minded Orthodox clerics in Kiev, Lviv, and Lutsk, including Gedon Balaban, Orthodox bishop of Lviv, and Ipaty Potis, Orthodox bishop of Lutsk, and in 1596 the two churches were united at the Synod of Brest-Litovsk (Brześć), a move which was also the product of pressures from Rome and was intended to strengthen the Commonwealth against the rising power of the Grand Duchy of Muscovy. The Greek Catholic or Uniate Church which this union established retained its own liturgy and a married lower priesthood while acknowledging the supremacy of the papacy. It did win a certain amount of support, particularly as the Basilian Order, reformed on Jesuit lines, provided the new Church with a well-educated priesthood. However, it was rejected by most of the Orthodox laity of the Commonwealth including the great magnate Prince Kostyantyn Ostrozky (1526–1608). Followers of the Greek Orthodox Church continued to practise their faith, and a parliamentary bill of 1609 restored to it a quasi-legal status by allowing Orthodox nobles to continue to hold office. The union certainly stimulated attempts to revive and reform the Orthodox Church. From the 1620s the Orthodox Monastery of the Caves in Kiev began to publish religious books, and a monastic brotherhood was re-established here. A new Orthodox metropolitan was consecrated and he ordained several bishops. Władysław IV Vasa (r. 1632–48), son of Zygmunt and Anna of Habsburg, attempted to conciliate the Orthodox. He gave legal recognition to the Orthodox Church and appointed Petro Mohyla metropolitan of Kiev. In addition, he did not implement the provision of the Union of Brest-Litovsk which admitted Greek Catholics to the senate.[8]

These concessions came too late to undo the anger caused by the union. The attack on the Orthodox Church was most bitterly resented by the Cossacks, a group of frontiersmen and fugitives who had established themselves on the lower Dnieper in a self-governing entity in the region known as Zaporozhia (Ukrainian: Zaporizhzhya, 'land below the rapids'), headed by a hetman with a staff of adjutants, a chancellor, a quartermaster, and a judge (the word 'Cossack' is derived from a Turkic word for horseman, warrior or vagabond). From this base they had resisted Tatar slave-raiding incursions and mounted their own raids into the Ottoman empire. By the late sixteenth century, perhaps 5,000 to 6,000 Cossacks had established themselves at the *sich* (fortress) created below the rapids on the lower Dnieper. They were a formidable force, and a number of Polish kings, including Zygmunt II and Stefan Batory (r. 1576–86), had tried to enlist their support. In 1583 Batory had placed 500 Zaporozhians on a list which guaranteed them regular pay and this number was increased by the Sejm to 1,000 in 1590, but

[8] On these developments, Horak, 'The Kiev Academy—a Bridge to Europe in the Seventeenth Century'; Graham, 'Peter Mogila, Metropolitan of Kiev'.

he had refused this status to the remainder of those who sought to establish their free status on the lower Dnieper.[9]

The disaffection of the Cossacks was the more serious because just before the Union of Lublin the fertile provinces of Volhynia, Bratslav, and Kiev, formerly subject to the Grand Duchy of Kiev, passed from the Grand Duchy of Lithuania to the Kingdom of Poland. This laid them open to colonization by the great magnates such as the Potockis, Ostrozkys, Wiśniowieckis, and Sanguszkos, many of them converts from Orthodoxy to Catholicism. One aspect of this colonization was intensification of the burdens on the peasantry, including those on 'unregistered' Cossacks, who were now subjected to the same process of progressive enserfment which had earlier occurred in Poland. The estates of the largest of the magnates, Jeremi Wiśniowiecki, who converted to Roman Catholicism in 1633, were worked by nearly a quarter of a million serfs. The magnates also founded as many as 200 towns, in which they settled considerable numbers of Jews, who often administered their estates, collected taxes, and provided credit to both nobles and peasants. In addition, many Jewish merchants and artisans established themselves in the region.

From the Khmelnytsky Uprising to the Accession of Stanisław August Poniatowski in 1764

These developments created a potent mix of religious, social, and ethnic tension in the south-eastern part of the Commonwealth, where Cossack discontent frequently led to resistance to Polish rule, culminating in the great uprising which began in 1648 and initiated a new and less successful period in the history of Poland–Lithuania. Already in 1594 a serious Cossack rebellion, which lasted over two years, had broken out under the leadership of Severyn Nalyvaiko. It was savagely repressed, and tension continued to mount, particularly as the number of Cossacks in Polish service increased. For the moment the crisis was postponed by the outbreak of war between Poland and Turkey in 1619. Initially the Poles were defeated at the battle of Cecora (Ţuţora) in September 1620 but won a great victory at Chocim (now Khotyn, in Ukraine), largely due to the assistance of a large number of Cossacks under Hetman Petro Konashevych-Sahaidachny. By now the number of people who could be described as Cossacks had risen to nearly 50,000. The rulers of Poland–Lithuania sought to regulate their status, and in 1625 the Polish hetman Stanisław Koniecpolski placed 6,000 Cossacks on a government

[9] On the crisis of the mid-17th century, see Peleński, 'The Incorporation of the Ukrainian Lands of Old Rus' into Crown Poland (1569)'; Sysyn, *Between Poland and the Ukraine*; Kamiński, 'The Cossack Experiment in Szlachta Democracy in the Polish–Lithuanian Commonwealth'; *Harvard Ukrainian Studies*, 8/1–2 (June 1984), devoted to the Kiev Mohyla Academy; Stökl, *Die Entstehung des Kosakentums*; Martel, *La Langue polonaise dans les pays ruthènes*; Rudnytsky, 'Polish–Ukrainian Relations'; Havelock, 'The Cossacks in the Early Seventeenth Century'; Podlaski, *Białorusini, Litwini, Ukraińcy*.

register. The remainder were to be classed as townsmen or peasants. The situation remained unresolved and led to a new rebellion, which was crushed in 1637, following which parliament again fixed the number of registered Cossacks at 6,000. All other Cossacks would be compelled to accept peasant status. Cossack officers were now to be selected from the nobility, and harsh punishments were meted out to those who attempted to flee from Ukraine to the fortress in Zaporozhia. The opposition which this aroused was easily crushed, and ten years of superficial peace followed, partly the result of the close cooperation which developed between the king and Adam Kysil (1600–53), a prominent Orthodox nobleman.

Władysław's plans for a new war against Turkey raised hopes among the Cossacks since the king hoped to make use of them and was prepared to increase the Cossack register from 6,000 to 12,000 and remove Polish troops from the areas they controlled. However, the Polish nobility, fearing that the king would make use of the power he obtained by this agreement to make himself absolute, prevented any change in the situation of the Cossacks. This overreaction to the threat of 'tyranny' was typical of the nobility, since what the king wanted was to gain greater control over the army and its use. This unsettled situation was made still more explosive by the death of the king in May 1648, at a time when a Cossack revolt had already broken out under the leadership of an Orthodox Ruthenian noble and Cossack Bohdan Khmelnytsky, who had fled to the Zaporozhian Cossacks after a violent dispute with his Roman Catholic neighbour Daniel Czapliński. He then succeeded in persuading the Cossacks to expel the Polish garrison, elect him hetman, and stage an insurrection.

Khmelnytsky may have hoped to compromise with the rulers of the Commonwealth and establish for Ukraine a status similar to that of the Kingdom of Poland and the Grand Duchy of Lithuania with himself as hetman. The logic of events, and in particular his defeats at the hands of Jan Kazimierz and his generals, drove him into an alliance with Muscovy, and in January 1654 he submitted to Tsar Aleksey in the Pereyaslav Agreement. This was followed by the invasion of Poland–Lithuania by the Muscovites and the Swedes, as well as by troops led by György II Rákóczy, prince of Transylvania, and very nearly led to the partition of the country. The new king, Władysław's brother Jan Kazimierz Vasa (r. 1648–68), succeeded in rallying the country and expelling the invaders with the assistance of the Danes and Austrians. In the Treaty of Oliwa, concluded in May 1660, the territorial status quo between Poland and Sweden was restored and the Polish Vasa dynasty renounced their claim to the Swedish throne. The death of Khmelnytsky in 1657 led to the creation of the Union of Hadyach, with his successor Hetman Ivan Vyhovsky, which provided for Ukraine to be a third constituent element in the Commonwealth. This was, however, rejected by the pro-Russian faction among the Cossacks and probably would not have been acceptable to the Polish nobility, although it was ratified by the Sejm. Its collapse led to renewed war between Poland and Muscovy, which culminated in Ukraine on the east bank of the river Dnieper being ceded to Muscovy in the Peace of Andruszów (Andrusovo) in January 1667. Kiev was ceded for two years but remained under Muscovite rule thereafter, confirmed by the Treaty of Grzymułtowski in 1686. Zaporozhia was placed under a joint protectorate.

These catastrophic events ushered in an era of political and economic decline. Royal authority was now even further undermined, and in 1652 the first *liberum veto* was cast in the Sejm. The *liberum veto* was the exaggerated result of the search for consensus which characterized medieval parliaments. It enabled any member of the Sejm to reject a piece of legislation, abrogate all legislation already passed, and dissolve parliament. The attempt to reform the constitution and strengthen the monarchy by Jan Kazimierz in the last years of his reign failed utterly and led him to abdicate in disgust in 1668. Jan Sobieski (r. 1674–96) did succeed in defeating the Turks (although Podolia was only regained in 1699) but was unsuccessful in his ambitious plans to buttress monarchical authority. As a result, the state budget in the latter half of the seventeenth century amounted to barely 10–11 million zlotys, little more than 3 per cent of that of France or 4 per cent of that of England. The efforts made by August II, the Elector of Saxony, who held the Polish throne from 1697 to 1733, to augment the power of the monarchy were also frustrated by the opposition of the nobility and the Russians. August's failure had even more baleful consequences. At the Silent Sejm (*Sejm niemy*) of February 1717, which took its name from the fact that in order to avoid a *liberum veto* the delegates agreed not to allow any discussion, the Russian ambassador mediated between the king and the rebellious nobility. The effect of this was that Poland became effectively a Russian protectorate and that Russia gave a guarantee to preserve the unreformed Polish constitution, which severely restricted the power of the king and limited the size of the Polish army to 24,000 men. In practice, the number of men under arms was even less.

There was also growing religious intolerance, since one of the consequences of the foreign invasions by Lutherans and Russian Orthodox was to strengthen the identification of Polishness with a strongly Marian-centred Catholicism in which the Virgin Mary was enthroned as the queen of Poland. As a consequence of the ascendancy of the Counter-Reformation, the Bohemian Brothers, anti-Trinitarian Arians, were expelled from the Commonwealth in 1658 on the grounds that they had collaborated with the invading Swedes, and increasing restrictions were imposed on other Protestants.

The political and social crisis in Poland had a number of aspects. The most obvious was the weakness of the monarchy. The king was now largely powerless and there was no modern bureaucracy. The king's government had changed little since the late Middle Ages. It was this which led a contemporary to assert that 'the vast republic of Poland has fewer civil servants than the petty principality of Lucca'.[10] The Sejm had effectively ceased to operate. Of the eighteen Sejms

10 Quoted in Lewitter, 'Poland under the Saxon Kings', 366.

which met under August II, ten were wrecked by premature dissolution caused by the exercise of the *liberum veto*. Under August III (r. 1733–63) Sejms were filibustered between 1738 and 1748, and broken up by the *liberum veto* from 1750. Most of these filibusters and dissolutions were engineered either by Prussia or by Russia, which exploited the rivalry of the great noble families. No Sejm between 1736 and 1764 passed any laws. The king still had huge powers of patronage, which could make or break magnate families. However, the constitutional impasse prevented the king (or anyone else) from taking a decisive lead.

In addition, Poland–Lithuania was a battlefield from 1648 until well into the eighteenth century. In 1672 Ottoman armies allied with the hetman Petro Doroshenko invaded and conquered Podolia and much of right-bank Ukraine (the area still under Polish control), leading to war between Poland–Lithuania and Turkey. After a major victory at Khotyn, Hetman Jan Sobieski, later to be elected king, regained most of right-bank Ukraine but not Podolia. This returned to Poland–Lithuania after another war with Turkey, which commenced with the combined Polish–Imperial relief of the siege of Vienna in 1683 and ended with the Treaty of Karlowitz in 1699.

Between 1699 and 1717 the country was the scene of much of the Great Northern War and also of the revolt of much of the nobility against the plans of August II, to increase the power of the monarchy by going to war with Sweden in alliance with Peter the Great of Russia. The disputed royal election of 1733 was followed by two years of fighting between the Austrians and Russians, who had supported August III, the son of August II, and the French, who had upheld the claim of Stanisław Leszczyński. During this war the Austrians fought the French in Italy and Germany, while in the Commonwealth the Russians and Saxons (and their Polish allies) fought Leszczyński's supporters. This was Leszczyński's second bid for the crown, since he had been elected king with Swedish support in July 1704 by the opponents of August II and had only renounced his claim to the throne in 1713. During the Seven Years War (1756–63) both the Prussian and Russian armies freely marched across Poland.

The weakness of the monarchy was counterbalanced by the power of the great magnates, the Radziwiłłs and Sapiehas in Lithuania, the Zamoyskis and Czartoryskis in the Kingdom of Poland and the Zaslavskys, Wiśniowieckis, Potockis, and Koniecpolskis in Ukraine, who sometimes cooperated but were frequently bitter rivals. All aspects of political, social, and economic life were now dominated by the magnates, two to three dozen great families with huge landholdings in Ukraine and Lithuania who monopolized all the high offices in Church and State. As Alexander Brückner wrote of the reign of August III, the history of the Commonwealth had, in effect, become 'that of a handful of families and their quarrels'. Their wealth was enormous. In the middle of the eighteenth century, when the total public revenue of the Commonwealth amounted to 8 million florins, that of Michał Radziwiłł amounted to 5 million and that of Franciszek

Salezy Potocki to 3 million. Radziwiłł had his own private army, which numbered at least 2,000 soldiers, with foreign officers and its own cadet school (some estimates argue that at its height it reached 12,000).[11]

The smaller landowners and the landless nobility were now dependent on the magnates. The magnates controlled the local parliaments, which, with the increasing paralysis of the Sejm, became the main focus of political life. The magnates were often in the pay of foreign rulers. For much of the eighteenth century two great families fought for political influence, the Czartoryskis, who were by and large committed to the Russians and their Saxon protégés, although they had initially supported the candidacy of Stanisław Leszczyński in 1733, and who also developed some ideas of their own for reforming the Commonwealth, and the Potockis, who were the pro-French party.

Although the magnates were the key element in the Commonwealth, the main feature of its social life remained the dominance of the 700,000-strong nobility. The position of the peasantry had deteriorated even further since the end of the sixteenth century. Most peasants were now obliged to work three days a week without pay on the lands of their feudal lords, and the amount of money they were required to pay in taxes and service also increased in the eighteenth century. They were now entirely under the control of the manor. Until 1768 nobles theoretically had the right *jus vitae et necis* (of life and death) over their peasants and certainly seem on occasion to have been able to ensure that municipal courts imposed capital sentences. Serfs were entirely subject to manorial jurisdiction, except where a village was composed of settlers who had the right to resolve disputes by German law.

One consequence of the deterioration of the position of the peasantry was the increasing frequency of peasant revolts. These took place primarily in the right-bank area of Ukraine, which had remained in Polish hands after the Peace of Andruszów. Here social and religious divisions, for the peasantry were mostly Orthodox or Greek Catholic, created an explosive social mix. At the end of the war with Turkey in 1699 the Polish–Lithuanian parliament had ordered the disbanding of the Cossack regiments in right-bank Ukraine. In 1702 Semen Paly, a Cossack colonel there, led a revolt of 12,000 Cossacks in support of Charles XII of Sweden in the hope that he would be able to create a Cossack state in the area. The revolt was defeated but was followed by one on a much larger scale when Hetman Ivan Mazepa attempted, in alliance with Charles XII, to create a Cossack state on both sides of the Dnieper, believing that, together with Stanisław Leszczyński, the Swedish candidate for the Polish crown, it would be possible to revive the Treaty of Hadyach and make Ukraine a third constituent part of the Commonwealth. Charles XII's defeat put paid to these plans, but unrest contin-

[11] Lukowski, *Liberty's Folly*, 26–7. On the general political system at this time, see Konopczyński, *Le Liberum Veto*, pt. II; Olszewski, *Sejm Rzeczypospolitej epoki oligarchii 1652–1763*; Zielińska, *Walka 'Familii' o reformę Rzeczypospolitej 1743–1752*; Müller, *Polen zwischen Preussen und Russland*.

ued to simmer in the area. Cossacks fled to the Zaporozhian fortress or engaged in indiscriminate banditry. There was a further wave of rebellion led by *haidamaky* (Haydamaks, peasant rebels) when the tax exemption extended to peasants after the Seven Years War came to an end. Bands of peasants and outlaws attacked towns and estates, killing Roman Catholic and Greek Catholic priests, Polish nobles, and Jews. The most savage of these risings took place in 1768 under the leadership of a Zaporozhian Cossack, Maksym Zaliznyak. Peasant unrest was also widespread in Mazovia, and the Podhale region of the Carpathians was plagued by bandits, who began a major peasant uprising there in the 1750s.

The Republic also experienced severe economic decline. This was primarily the result of the wars which devastated the country between 1648 and 1717 and indeed for much of the later eighteenth century as well. As a consequence, the population fell by nearly a third, while the amount of land cultivated and of grain produced fell significantly. Between 1700 and 1719 grain exports were only 20,000 lasts (1 last = 3,000 litres). They rose to 31,000 between 1720 and 1762, but even then were still only one-third of the highest level of grain exports in the seventeenth century.[12] This was nevertheless the beginning of a sustained economic recovery which continued until the end of the eighteenth century.

The political and economic stagnation was accompanied by increasing religious intolerance, as the values of the Catholic Counter-Reformation became much more influential at all levels in the nobility. This had extremely deleterious consequences for all non-Catholics in the Republic. By the early eighteenth century there were approximately 200,000 Protestants in Poland–Lithuania. They were mostly German Lutheran colonists in the towns and countryside of western Poland. There were still about 1,000 noble Protestant families. The position of both these groups deteriorated significantly from the beginning of the eighteenth century. They were accused of collaboration with the Swedes during the Great Northern War, a repetition of accusations which had been levelled during the Swedish invasion of the Commonwealth in the mid-seventeenth century. They were subjected to further discrimination in the early eighteenth century. From 1717 Protestants were not allowed to restore old churches or build new ones, and in 1733 and 1736 they were excluded from the Sejm and from many offices of the state, and a number of Protestant churches were destroyed by the authorities. There were also some violent incidents. The worst of these took place in the town of Toruń, which had equal numbers of Lutherans and Catholics (the groups also reflected the ethnic division between Germans and Poles), but which was governed by the Lutherans because of their dominant position in the craft guilds. In July 1724 a mob, provoked by a student, broke into a Jesuit college and demolished a chapel. For their failure to prevent this act of profanation, the Lutheran mayor and his deputy were executed as well as seven rioters. It should,

[12] Lewitter, 'Poland under the Saxon Kings', 368.

however, be pointed out that after this date Lutherans continued to govern the town.[13]

The Orthodox, who numbered around 600,000, were a declining force in the Commonwealth. By now almost all the Orthodox nobility had been Polonized and converted to Roman Catholicism, attracted by the privileges of the Polish nobility and the superior schooling available to its scions. Orthodox peasants were put under strong pressure to convert to the Greek Catholic Church established by the Union of 1596. In 1702 all of the bishoprics of the Orthodox Church in Poland with the exception of that in Mogilev became Greek Catholic (Uniate). In 1708 the Orthodox Stauropigial confraternity in Lviv came under the control of the Greek Catholic Basilians.

The worsening situation of the dissidents was exploited by Poland's neighbours Russia and Prussia. According to the Perpetual Peace of 1686 between Russia and Poland, a treaty only finally ratified by the Polish–Lithuanian parliament under Russian pressure during the Great Northern War in 1710, the civil and religious rights of the Orthodox were guaranteed. From 1720 Peter the Great began to intervene on their behalf. The Russians were quite cynical in their use of this issue. In 1766 Panin wrote to Repnin: 'It is necessary to resolve the Dissident affair not for the sake of propagating our faith and that of the Protestants in Poland, but for the sake of acquiring for ourselves, through our co-religionists and the Protestants, a firm and reliable party with the right to participate in all the affairs of Poland.'[14]

Linked with the growing religious intolerance was cultural and educational decline. Whereas in the sixteenth century Polish education had been strongly affected by the humanist currents of the Renaissance, it now became increasingly obscurantist. Partly this was a consequence of the worsening position of the Protestants. At the end of the seventeenth century the Calvinist schools, which had constituted an important link with Western ideas, were forcibly closed. Lutheran schools remained, but were essentially German in character, although this was often combined with strong sentiments for the Commonwealth.

The other institutions of higher learning in the Commonwealth were in disarray. The Academy of Zamość, founded at the height of the Polish Renaissance, was now largely moribund, and the Academy of Vilna was little more than a Jesuit College. The venerable Jagiellonian University of Kraków was dominated by a syllabus which had not changed significantly since its establishment.

A key role in the education of the nobility was played by the Jesuits, who had been the main architects of the Counter-Reformation in Poland. According to Lucjan Lewitter, referring to the situation after 1648: 'They taught Latin grammar by rote, Latin poetry reduced to the level of metrical exercises, formal, mostly panegyrical Latin rhetoric and macaronic Polish; their moral education

[13] On this, see Salmonowicz, 'Protestanci i katolicy w jednym mieście', 68.

[14] Quoted in M. Markiewicz, *Historia Polski 1492–1795*, 657–8.

inculcated veneration for the *liberum veto*, belief in the natural superiority of the *szlachta*, ritualism, religious intolerance and unquestioning devotion to the Church.'[15]

Literature and scholarship were also in a poor state. There has been a revival of interest in the culture of Counter-Reformation Poland, and the verse of the period is now assessed much more favourably than a generation ago. But certainly, the political thought of eighteenth-century Poland–Lithuania was very far removed from what was developing in the West. A good example of Polish political thinking at this time is provided by the Jesuit tract *Domina Palatii, Regina Libertas*: 'The purgatory of freedom is better than the hell of despotism. Thanks to the protection of Providence, we keep falling and yet we rise, we keep perishing and yet we live. . . . With this anarchy of ours, we succeed as well as others with the most subtle distillations of government.'[16]

All this was summed up in the unthinking acceptance of the motto *Polska nierządem stoi* ('Poland survives through anarchy', or 'Poland lives by the absence of a central government'). Linked with this was the cult of Sarmatianism, the cultivation of the customs of the Polish country nobles in contrast to the allegedly decadent customs of the West.[17] The name 'Sarmatian' was a reference to the supposed ancestors of the nobility, the prehistoric tribe of the Sarmatii, and adherents of this view of the world stressed the importance of Poland as a Catholic bastion, *antemurale Christianitatis* (the rampart of Christianity).

Enlightenment ideas and calls for reform were not entirely absent even in the worst period of obscurantism between 1697 and 1763. A small group of republicans and patriots placed their hopes in Stanisław Leszczyński, who had been elected king in 1733 with the support of France, but who never took the throne.[18]

Some reform of the taxation system also emerged as a result of the political settlement ratified at the Silent Sejm in February 1717. As a result, Poland–Lithuania now had, for the first time, something approximating to a budget. There were a number of sources of revenue, including a tax on the income of tenants on the royal demesne, customs dues, and taxes on wine, which were leased out, and the poll tax imposed on the Jewish community, which was now increased. Government revenue now increased significantly and could be augmented by an additional poll tax, levied mostly on the peasantry, and through provender money, which was mostly due from royal and ecclesiastical tenants. At the same time the local parliaments lost the right to levy taxes.

Progress was also made in education. In 1737 the Theatine Order established the Collegium Varsoviensis for children of the nobility, which was similar in

[15] Lewitter, 'Poland under the Saxon Kings', 370.

[16] Ibid. 371.

[17] For a good account of the Sarmatian mentality, see Pasek, *Memoirs of the Polish Baroque*.

[18] On the impact of the Enlightenment, see Krasicki, *The Adventures of Mr. Nicolas Wisdom*; Rose, *Stanislaw Konarski, Reformer of Education in 18th Century Poland*; Hinz, 'The Philosophy of Polish Enlightenment and its Opponents'; Seidler, *The Polish Contribution to the Age of Enlightenment*.

character to the knights' academies in Italy. The schools of the Piarist Order were also modernized. The main role in this was played by Stanisław Konarski (1700–64), who had entered the order in 1715 and who was an ardent supporter of Stanisław Leszczyński in 1733. In 1740 he established the Warsaw Collegium Nobilium, which was intended to educate the sons of the magnates and the wealthy nobility. It was based on modern pedagogical principles, with a central role being assigned to modern languages, geography, mathematics, and natural science. New textbooks were created to make possible effective instruction in these subjects.

Konarski followed his success at the Collegium Nobilium with an attempt to reform the whole of the Piarist school system. His efforts also put pressure on the Jesuits to introduce significant reforms in the schools they controlled. Between 1749 and 1755 they founded five new colleges, which attracted a large number of students, especially in Warsaw. There were also some educational reforms in Vilna and Kraków. Konarski called for further political reforms in the Commonwealth and set out his ideas in the four-volume *O skutecznym rad sposobie* (On the Effective Means of Government, 1761–3). In this treatise he criticized the *liberum veto*, and called for radical reform of the Sejm and the establishment of new executive bodies.

The election in 1764 of Stanisław August Poniatowski, the candidate of the Czartoryski family, led to a new era in the history of Poland–Lithuania (on this, see Chapter 6). The Czartoryskis hoped to use their links to Russia to facilitate reform, but were largely frustrated by the opposition of the tsaritsa Catherine. This led to the emergence of the Patriot Party, headed by reformers such as Ignacy Potocki and Hugo Kołłątaj, who hoped to take advantage of the preoccupation of Russia with Turkey after the outbreak of war between the two countries in 1788 to force through reforms in alliance with Prussia. These circumstances made possible the adoption of significant reforms and a new constitution on 3 May 1791, but also provoked strong opposition from Poland's autocratic neighbours. They made use of Polish domestic opposition to the reforms to intervene to stop their implementation. The end result was partition and the disappearance of Poland as a state.

Conclusion

A number of themes emerge from this survey of the history of pre-partition Poland–Lithuania. The first is the importance of the Polish nobility and, above all, of the great magnates. By the eighteenth century they determined almost all aspects of social, economic, and political life, and account for many of the specific features of its evolution. The social hegemony of the nobility was to last until the second half of the nineteenth century in the lands which formerly made up the Polish–Lithuanian Commonwealth and still longer in Galicia (Austrian Poland).

Secondly, the importance of the turning point of 1648 cannot be overstated. Although the weaknesses of Poland–Lithuania were shared by a number of other European states, including Sweden and Spain, Poland's geographical position made it increasingly vulnerable to its predatory neighbours. This made reform more difficult to achieve and also led to an increasingly intolerant atmosphere, certainly until the middle of the eighteenth century.

The depth and bitterness of the Polish–Russian conflict is also clearly evident. It had begun as a conflict between the Grand Duchy of Lithuania and the Muscovite state and was a clash in the first place over the inheritance of the Grand Duchy of Kiev. The claim of Muscovy to these lands was first clearly articulated in 1480, when Ivan III, grand prince of Moscow, proclaimed himself sovereign of all the Rus principalities. The Poles also made claims to this area. At the beginning of the seventeenth century, during the 'Time of Troubles', a section of the Russian nobility had offered the throne of Muscovy to Władysław, the son of King Zygmunt III of Poland, on condition that he convert to Orthodoxy. The conflict was also one between the rival worlds of Orthodoxy and Roman Catholicism, a conflict which had grown in bitterness since the Fourth Crusade, at the beginning of the thirteenth century. Both Polish and Russian national myths saw their countries as unique and chosen for a special role, the Poles as the ramparts of Christianity and the Russians as the third Rome, the successor to Rome and Byzantium. In addition they were extreme embodiments of rival political systems: that of Poland–Lithuania, characterized by an extreme form of the liberty espoused by the estates in medieval Europe, and that of the tsarist empire, consisting of an autocratic and patriarchal state with no popular participation in government. The difference between the two states is well embodied in the way each understood the concept of 'democracy'. To the Polish elite this was the rule of the nobility, which was threatened by royal aspirations to despotism, to the Russians it meant taking into account the needs of the 'people', whose position was safeguarded by the autocrat and threatened by aristocratic self-interest. This antagonism forms a backdrop to many of the issues discussed in the following pages.

PART II

ATTEMPTS TO TRANSFORM AND INTEGRATE THE JEWS, AND THE JEWISH RESPONSE, 1750–1880

INTRODUCTION

THE MIDDLE OF THE EIGHTEENTH CENTURY was a major turning point in the history of the Jews in Europe. Under the influence of the philosophy of the Enlightenment, many rulers now began to initiate attempts, carried still further by their constitutional successors in the nineteenth century, to transform the Jews from members of a religious and cultural community into 'useful' subjects, or, where a civil society had been established, into citizens. This process was also a feature of the last years of the Polish–Lithuanian Commonwealth and was continued after the partitions by the governments which ruled the lands of the former Rzeczpospolita. In examining the way these developments affected the Jews of the Polish lands, it is important to emphasize that this was a process which was taking place all over Europe, as well as in America and Asia, and that the process of Jewish integration is part of a larger phenomenon, involving the emergence of representative government and the creation of an industrial economy. In addition, other social groups, most notably peasants, were subject to government attempts to transform them into 'useful' members of society.

For the process of Jewish integration to be successful, two conditions needed to be present: governments had to be willing to accept the Jews 'on certain conditions' as citizens, or in autocracies as 'useful subjects', and there needed to be a group of Jews who were willing to respond to the possibility of integration.

The terms for describing this process have often been vague and, as a result, it is necessary to define them more precisely:

Integration can be divided into two subcategories: political integration and social integration. Political integration involves the acceptance of some or all of the Jews as citizens with political rights. Social integration means their full participation in all aspects of the life of the society, political, economic, and social.

Emancipation, a term made popular by Marx and other political radicals, referred, by analogy to the position of slaves in the European overseas empires, to the abolition of restrictions affecting unfree peasants and Jews. Since the Jews were never slaves, it is more of a metaphor than a useful term of analysis, although it was widely used in the nineteenth century and subsequently.

Acculturation refers to the voluntary acquisition by Jews of some of the values and ways of behaving of the host society in which they lived. It is a twentieth-century term and was not used at the time.

Assimilation (Polish *asymilacja*) is a problematic term. It was defined by Ezra Mendelsohn as 'the Jews' efforts to adopt the national identity of the majority, to become Poles, Hungarians, Romanians "of the Mosaic faith" or even to abandon their Jewish identity altogether'.[1] More recently, both Mendelsohn and Michael Stanislawski have attacked the use of the concept and have argued that it has become little more than a term to describe the negative behaviour of those of whom the writer disapproves. It was certainly widely used in the nineteenth century and I have tried to employ it only where contemporary usage makes this necessary.

Civil improvement is an inadequate translation of the German *bürgerliche Verbesserung* (literally 'transformation into citizens'), which was first used by the Prussian civil servant Christian Wilhelm von Dohm in his pamphlet *Über die bürgerliche Verbesserung der Juden*, first published in 1781.[2] The equivalent term in Polish was *uobywatelnienie*. As a concept, it rested on the belief that the 'negative' characteristics of the Jews were the consequence of the conditions under which they had been forced to live in Christian Europe and would be alleviated by their transformation into citizens. As Dohm put it, drawing on the classic Enlightenment view of the law of nature, 'Nature has endowed the Jews with equal capacities to become happier, better people and more useful members of society.' In his view, the Jew was first and foremost a man, who could be a good citizen if he were offered suitable conditions.[3] Dohm argued that the Jews should enjoy the rights and duties of the other estates in Prussia, which would result in their rapid integration. More conservative thinkers held that, before they could be offered civic rights or citizenship, the Jews should demonstrate their worthiness of these rights by transforming themselves.

Around the middle of the eighteenth century the position of the Jews was roughly similar all over Europe. On the one hand, the Jews were a corporation, like other corporations. The local Jewish autonomous bodies (the *kehilot*) were also corporations. This autonomy had two sources: the inability of the medieval and early modern state to administer all aspects of society, and the desire of the Jews to control the organization of their own communities. At the same time the Jews were a despised minority, tolerated in an inferior position to attest to the truths of Christianity. This point of view was expressed by St Augustine when he adjured the Christians, 'Chastise them, but do not kill them.' Their pariah position was linked with a number of anti-Jewish superstitions which became widespread from the later Middle Ages: the belief that the Jews used Christian blood in the making of matzah, that they desecrated the host, and that they were responsible for the spread of disease, in particular bubonic plague.

[1] Mendelsohn, *The Jews of East-Central Europe*, 2.

[2] Dohm, *Über die bürgerliche Verbesserung der Juden*. On Dohm, see Barzilay, 'The Jew in the Literature of the Enlightenment'.

[3] Eisenbach, *The Emancipation of the Jews in Poland, 1780–1870*, 53–4.

Economically, the Jews were everywhere limited to intermediary occupations. They were barred from owning land and from government service. The most important of these intermediary occupations were moneylending and banking, trading, often on a very small scale, and leasing. In the two largest Jewish communities, those in Poland–Lithuania and in the Ottoman empire, there were also Jewish artisans, administrators of estates, mills, breweries, distilleries, and inns. In Turkey they were also employed in the state administration and used to facilitate contact with the outside world.

The attempt to transform the legal, social, and economic position of the Jews was part of the more general process which Karl Polanyi has described as 'the Great Transformation'.[4] This involved changes in the way society was organized as fundamental as those which occurred during the Neolithic revolution, which replaced hunter-gathering by settled agriculture. There were two aspects to this transformation: economic and political. We now know that the industrial revolution was the end of a much longer process which probably should be dated back to the effects of European overseas expansion from the fifteenth century. Its end result was urbanization, the development of industry, the increasing importance of the bourgeoisie, and the displacement of the landed aristocracy as the dominant economic and political stratum.

The political transformation was accomplished in two stages. The first was the end of 'divine right' monarchy and the philosophical discrediting of the religious character of the state, leading to the idea of religious toleration. It was John Locke, one of the most persuasive advocates of religious indifference, who argued that a Christian state was a contradiction in terms and that the government should be religiously neutral, except where a religion had harmful consequences for society. As he put it in his *Letter Concerning Toleration*: 'Nay, if we may openly speak the truth . . . neither pagan nor Mahometan nor Jew ought to be excluded from the civil rights of the commonwealth because of his religion. The Church commands no such thing.'[5]

Under these conditions, a new form of political legitimacy was needed and emerged in the form of enlightened autocracy. Yet though the political philosophy of the Enlightenment stressed the value of religious toleration and called for the abolition of discrimination against minority religions, including Judaism, it was also strongly hostile to all forms of particularism, including Jewish autonomous structures, which it regarded as feudal relics.

The second stage in the political transformation saw the development of representative government, that is of governments which were dependent on the support of the people, however defined, a process which resulted ultimately in the triumph of representative democracy, based on universal suffrage. This was a process which was to develop slowly and which was to encounter numerous obstacles and setbacks. Even before it was fully established the idea became widespread

[4] Polanyi, *The Great Transformation*.

[5] Locke, *A Letter Concerning Toleration*, 56.

that the state should represent the interest of the 'people', a concept which was first fully articulated during the French Revolution.

The various European governments, inspired by the political thought of the Enlightenment, sought the political integration of the Jews, their economic and social transformation, and the purification of their religion from 'medieval', 'barbaric', and 'anti-Christian' elements. The goal of political integration was most easily defined and went along with demands for the abolition of Jewish communal autonomy, which was regarded as backward and as preserving 'Jewish separatism'. The aim was clearly set out by Count Stanislas de Clermont-Tonnerre in the French national assembly in December 1789:

> The Jews should be denied everything as a nation and granted everything as individuals. They must be citizens . . . Every one of them must individually become a citizen; if they do not want this, they must inform us and we shall be compelled to expel them. The existence of a nation within a nation is unacceptable to our country . . .[6]

Economically, the advocates of Jewish integration called for the Jews to give up 'unproductive' occupations and to take up agriculture. Dohm felt that the Jews would make excellent small farmers and also called for all economic and fiscal regulations restricting Jewish activity to be abolished, so that Jews would have complete freedom to engage in handicrafts and commerce.

The call was also made for the reform of the Jewish educational system, so that Jews would learn the language of the country where they lived. While Dohm called for the Jews to be granted access to all types of schools, others felt that the Jews should be kept for a transitional period in schools of their own. Religious reform was to be left to the Jews themselves, although there was an expectation that some changes would be introduced, if not in doctrine, then in the form of services. In this respect, Moses Mendelssohn (1729–86), who argued on natural-law principles that Judaism was a variant of the natural religion of mankind, marked a great break in Jewish thinking.

How did the Jews respond to these new policies? A minority, particularly in western and central Europe, responded favourably. Moses Mendelssohn and the Berlin Haskalah (Jewish Enlightenment), which was derived from his ideas, are good examples. Some mitnagedim (opponents of hasidism) also expressed some sympathy for a reform of Jewish life. The majority of Jews were, however, deeply suspicious, including the Vilna Gaon, the most prominent of the mitnagedim. They believed that the integrationist ideologies were a new and more subtle attempt to convert them. This was the view of Moses Sofer (Hatam Sofer, 1762–1839), the rabbi of Pressburg (Bratislava), and of Rabbi Shneur Zalman of Lyady, one of the founders of Habad hasidism. In 1812 he expressed his views as follows:

[6] Debate on the eligibility of Jews for citizenship in the French National Assembly, 23 Dec. 1789, quoted in Mendes-Flohr and Reinharz (eds.), *The Jew in the Modern World*, 115.

On the first day of Rosh hashana, before the musaf service, I saw a vision. I was shown that if Bonaparte is victorious, the wealth of Israel will be restored, the hearts of Israel will however become distant from their Father in Heaven. If our Lord Alexander triumphs, even though the poverty of the Jews will be increased and indignity will continue to be their lot, the hearts of Israel will be gathered together and united with the Name of their Father in Heaven . . .[7]

Jewish responses differed in the different parts of Europe. In western Europe the Jewish population was small and constitutional government soon became established. The economic transformation of society proceeded rapidly, leading to the emergence of an industrial society and strengthening the position of the liberal middle class. There the Jews were soon emancipated and integrated, first politically, and then, rather more slowly and incompletely, socially. Great careers in politics were made by people like Benjamin Disraeli and Adolphe Crémieux and in economics by the Rothschilds.

In central Europe, Jewish communities were larger, constitutional government became established more slowly, and the industrial revolution only got under way in the 1850s. Jewish emancipation was also slower there, and was only completed in the Habsburg empire in 1868 and in the newly unified German empire in 1870. The process was accompanied by considerable opposition, and the Jewish leadership felt the need to justify their being granted civil rights. This desire to demonstrate their fitness for emancipation led to the emergence of new forms of Jewish religious life which became the Reform movement, led by Samuel Holdheim (1806–60), and the Conservative movement of Zacharias Frankel (1801–75). In response, a new form of neo-Orthodoxy was developed by Samson Raphael Hirsch (1808–88). Jews also attempted to demonstrate in a scholarly way that they had a worthy and impressive history, and, in the development of the Wissenschaft des Judentums (Jewish studies, or, more literally, the science of Jewry), pioneered the scholarly study of the Jewish past using the principles developed by the Göttingen School and Leopold von Ranke, who were among the initiators of modern investigation of the past.

The consequence was that the Jews achieved full political equality, but that social integration remained elusive. The bourgeoisie remained divided, with Jews, at least initially, predominating in its commercial and financial parts, while what was described as the *Bildungsbürgertum*, which provided the civil servants, teachers, and university professors, remained exclusively Christian.

In the lands of the Polish–Lithuanian Commonwealth, the largest concentration of Jews in Europe, the impact of modernization on the Jewish population was slower and more complex. It began before the partitions of Poland with the accession of the reforming last king of Poland, Stanisław August Poniatowski (r. 1764–95), when an ultimately unsuccessful attempt was made to modernize the archaic structure of the Commonwealth and also to begin the process of integrating

[7] M. Teitelbaum, *The Rav from Lyady* [Harav miliadi], i (Warsaw, 1910), 156, quoted in Mendes-Flohr and Reinharz (eds.), *The Jew in the Modern World*, 138.

its Jewish population. For the most part, however, the process took place in the absence of Polish statehood and was complicated by the attempts of the Poles to regain their lost independence. Between 1795 and 1815 the dominant figure was Napoleon, and within the Duchy of Warsaw, which he established, important changes were initiated in the position of the Jews.

The period between the Congress of Vienna in 1814–15 and the unsuccessful Polish uprising of 1863 was dominated by the Poles' attempt to improve their status within the three empires whose rule over the Polish lands was confirmed in 1815. The question of the extent to which the Jews could be enlisted to the Polish cause aroused considerable controversy and led to a brief Polish–Jewish 'alliance' in the run-up to the ill-fated Polish insurrection of 1863 in the Kingdom of Poland, which had been created at the Congress of Vienna as an 'independent' Polish state in dynastic union with the Romanovs. In Prussian Poland these years saw a successful endeavour to transform the Jews into Germans of the Mosaic faith, something which was also attempted, but with smaller results, by the centralizing Austrian liberals.

After 1863 policies of integration were continued in the Prussian-, Austrian-, and Russian-ruled areas of Poland. But it was only in the Kingdom of Poland, which retained vestiges of the autonomy which it had been granted at the Congress of Vienna, and to some extent in Galicia, that the integration of the Jews was seen as linked with their Polonization.

Within the tsarist empire, which after 1815 had the largest concentration of Jews in the world, policy towards the Jews was based on two principles. The first was that they were basically a harmful element, and needed to be controlled, particularly since they were concentrated in the western border areas, which had only recently been incorporated into the empire. At the same time there was the hope that the Jews could be transformed into useful subjects of the autocratic empire.

The key role in Jewish policy under Nicholas I was played by two bureaucrats, Pavel Kiselev and Sergey Uvarov, who under the influence of Enlightenment ideas were convinced that the Jews could be transformed in the way they believed had been undertaken by Napoleon. Their aims were to undermine Jewish autonomy, to promote secular education, and to use conscription to 'civilize' and 'Russify' the Jews.

The consequences of these policies, which were eagerly embraced by the small number of maskilim (supporters of the Jewish Enlightenment, or Haskalah) and Jewish reformers, was to stratify the Jewish community. The policies of the government gained the support of the maskilim and also of wealthy notables, who profited from the leasing of the excise and other taxes from the government. They bitterly alienated the large mass of the community and created a deep rift between it and its former leadership.

Jewish policy was not fundamentally modified under the more liberal Alexander II (r. 1855–81). He did relax the more punitive aspects of Nicholas's policies and encouraged a degree of integration, although he neither introduced a constitution, which would have brought the concept of citizenship into the empire, nor did away with most of the restrictions under which the Jews suffered. This was to provoke great disillusionment, particularly among the Jewish elite, which was now increasingly committed to integration, when, after 1881, the tsarist government abandoned any further attempts to transform the Jews into useful subjects and concentrated overwhelmingly on restricting their 'harmful' impact on the population, especially its rural section, among whom they lived. This initiated a new period in the history of the Jews of the area as a significant proportion of the Jewish elite abandoned the hope of integration and began to espouse political ideologies based on the concept of Jewish peoplehood.

SIX

THE LAST YEARS OF THE POLISH–LITHUANIAN COMMONWEALTH

Everyone admits that this splendid fabric of our republic *mole propria ruit* [is in a state of collapse], that it must be succoured, that it indeed cannot subsist much longer without a miracle . . . Are our walls secure? The gates are open on all sides, the enemy enters the innermost reaches of our land, imposes contributions, starts fires, and takes prisoners. How can a country subsist without justice in its law courts, without control in its councils, and without order in its polity?

STANISŁAW LESZCZYŃSKI, 1734

Our laws regarding the Jews are wrong. Their situation, outside a class, is wrong. It is wrong to place power over them in the hands of private individuals or special Jewish bureaucrats. It is wrong to consider them an evil nation and to offer them no fatherland. Worst of all is that we allow them to live with special laws and customs. Owing to this, they appear as a *corpus in corpore*, a state within a state; in view of the fact that Jewish laws and rites are different from ours, such a state of things gives rise to conflicts, confusion, mutual distrust, contempt, and hatred.

MATEUSZ BUTRYMOWICZ, February 1789

ATTEMPTS TO REFORM THE POLITICAL AND SOCIAL SYSTEM OF THE COMMONWEALTH

THE REIGN OF the last king of Poland, Stanisław August Poniatowski, who was elected in 1764, was characterized by an attempt, in accordance with the political principles of the Enlightenment, to reform the institutions of the Polish–Lithuanian Commonwealth. The need for radical change was widely recognized. According to the reformer Fr. Stanisław Staszic, writing in 1790, 'The whole of Europe is already in the eighteenth century [while] Poland is still in the fifteenth century.'[1]

Indeed Enlightenment ideas and calls for reform had not been entirely absent even in the period of Saxon rule between 1697 and 1763. The taxation system had been placed on a somewhat better footing as a consequence of the political settlement ratified at the Silent Sejm in 1717. Polish finances now had, for the first time, something approximating to a budget. There were a number of sources of

[1] Staszic, *Przestrogi dla Polski*, 192.

revenue, including a tax on the income of tenants on the royal demesne, customs dues, and taxes on wine, which were leased out, and the poll tax imposed on the Jewish community, which was now doubled. Between 1717 and 1764 the government's revenue amounted to 900,000 zlotys per annum. Of this, revenue from the Jewish poll tax made up 220,000 zlotys.

Increasingly, as the century wore on, the hopes of the reformers came to be centred on the Czartoryski family, which was one of the two dominant magnate groupings in eighteenth-century Poland–Lithuania following the marriage of August Czartoryski to Zofia (née Sieniawska), the widow of Stanisław Denhof, the palatine of Polotsk. The 'family' saw the best prospects for change in a close alliance with Russia, which, as a result of the Great Northern War, had become the hegemonic power in the Polish–Lithuanian Commonwealth.

The Czartoryskis gained their opportunity with the election of Stanisław August. He was the fourth son of Stanisław Poniatowski, whose marriage to Konstancja Czartoryska, the sister of the two leading members of the Czartoryski family, made him an important figure in the 'family'. His brother Michał Jerzy Poniatowski, the youngest of six sons and two daughters, became primate of the Roman Catholic Church in Poland–Lithuania in 1784/5. As the 'Russian' candidate, Stanisław August was elected with the help of the tsaritsa Catherine II, whose lover he had been before she ascended the throne. His character is a matter of much dispute. He was certainly a man of the Enlightenment, with a broad vision acquired both through his extensive travels in western Europe and during his period in St Petersburg, where he was sent in 1755 by his Czartoryski uncles in the entourage of the British ambassador, Sir Charles Hanbury Williams. Endowed with considerable charm and natural ability, he helped found *Monitor*, the principal journal of the Polish Enlightenment, and assembled around him a group of like-minded individuals who met at the Thursday dinners which he organized between 1770 and 1777, where the political and social affairs of the day were discussed. While he did show some persistence in advancing his views, he was not a heroic figure, as is shown by his yielding to the anti-reform forces in 1792. Opinions about him have shifted widely since his death in exile in St Petersburg in 1798. Immediately after the partitions he was widely reviled for this final capitulation to the Russians. His reputation revived in the period of positivism after 1863, when he was lauded for his reformist efforts, a view which was again adopted by some historians during the period of Gomułka's 'little stabilization' between 1956 and the early 1960s and more recently in a biography by the Polish Jewish writer Józef Hen, who refers to the king as his 'friend'.[2] In 1995 his body was reburied in Warsaw Cathedral, further recognition of his improved reputation. In recent years his reputation has again begun to decline.

During Stanisław August's reign the ideas of the European Enlightenment, whose influence had been almost negligible before 1760, became increasingly

[2] Hen, *Mój przyjaciel król.*

widespread in Poland. The conflict between the old patriarchal and rural way of life and that of the urban, mostly Warsaw-based, reformers was tellingly satirized in the poetry of Bishop Ignacy Krasicki. Foreign travel brought home to many younger members of the nobility how backward their country was. Newspapers such as *Monitor*, founded in 1765 and edited by two enlightened clerics, Fr. Franciszek Bohomolec and Bishop Krasicki, and modelled on the English periodical *The Spectator*, and *Pamiętnik Historyczno-Politiczny*, which appeared between 1782 and 1792 and was edited by Piotr Świtkowski, publicized the ideas of the Enlightenment. *Monitor*, in particular, put forward a modern version of citizenship, stressing the importance of 'obligations which are owed to our country'.[3] Some of the reformers also became Freemasons, but anticlericalism did not become a major feature of the Polish Enlightenment as it did in France, partly because the enlightened elite hoped to gain the support of the clergy in implementing the changes they sought.

There were different strategies for the achievement of reform. The king, who understood the strength of the Russians and who did not command the firm support of even the 'family', favoured slow change in cooperation with the Russian monarchy. The radicals, who by the latter years of Stanisław's reign had come to be called the Patriot Party, a label which they adopted to attack what they regarded as the king's slavish dependence on Russia, did not believe that Russia would acquiesce in reform and insisted that change of a fundamental character could only be forced through in defiance of Russia.

The strategy of gradual change had one major drawback: it was never clear whether it had the support of Catherine. She was prepared to permit some limited reforms, but also insisted that Russia be given the right to 'guarantee' the Polish constitution, which ruled out a drastic break with the past. In addition, she demanded that political equality be conceded to the Greek Orthodox (who were few in number) and Protestant nobility, believing that in this way she could create a dependable pro-Russian party within the Commonwealth. Indeed, it was her insistence on supporting the rights of the 'dissidents' (non-Catholics) after Stanisław August's election that sparked off the Confederation of Bar in 1768, a nationalist and clerical revolt among the nobility. This movement combined slogans from the seventeenth century stressing the Catholic nature of the country with some rather limited calls for the reform of the constitution and the institution of a more up-to-date political structure. It led to four years of confused fighting, a peasant revolt in Polish Ukraine, and a Russian–Turkish war, and was followed by the first partition of Poland at the hands of Russia, Prussia, and Austria.

The shock this provoked did stimulate some attempts at reform. When Pope Clement XIV dissolved the Jesuit Order in 1773, a National Education Commission was set up to take over its endowments and educational functions in Poland–Lithuania. In 1783 it promulgated a set of school statutes and was made

[3] Janowski, *Polish Liberal Thought before 1918*, 9.

responsible for all secondary education, higher education, and teacher training. By 1792 it administered seventy schools with a modernized curriculum which were attended by between 40,000 and 50,000 pupils. Although the manner in which former Jesuit property was sold off was highly corrupt, so that the endowment produced was smaller than anticipated and the number of teachers therefore inadequate, most scholars agree that the new schools constituted a major advance over those administered by the Jesuits. The commission also created a Society for Elementary Books, which produced much more up-to-date material for the schools and also contributed to the modernization of the Polish language.

It proved more difficult to carry out political reforms. These were opposed by Russia and hampered by the legislation of the Sejm of 1767–8, which had distinguished between immutable 'cardinal laws', *materiae status*, including taxation and the size of the army, whose modification required unanimity, and 'economic matters', which could be decided by majority vote. At the same time support for fundamental reform was growing among an enlightened minority in the Sejm. The use of the constitutional device of the confederation made it possible to evade the *liberum veto*, while new rules on procedure made the functioning of parliament more effective.

In these circumstances, a rudimentary central government began to develop. A Permanent Council made up of eighteen members of the senate (including ministers) and eighteen deputies elected by the lower house was established by the Sejm of 1773–5 to serve as an executive between parliaments. Under it sat five commissions (Foreign Affairs, Police or Public Order, Military, Justice, and Treasury), which were to administer the country. Intended as a check on royal power, the council came to be a useful tool in Stanisław's hands as he was able to fill it with his supporters. At the same time it found itself under constant pressure from the Russian ambassador, Otto Magnus Stackelberg, whose actions the king likened to those of a Roman proconsul.

The new administrative structure was significantly more effective. The Military and Treasury commissions, which were established for both the Kingdom and the Grand Duchy of Lithuania, circumscribed the powers of the hetmans (the commanders-in-chief) and the treasurers, who controlled the state and court finances. General Jan Komarzewski, the king's adjutant-general, also made some progress in modernizing the Polish and Lithuanian armies, which could now be used to implement government decisions, although financial constraints prevented the army from reaching the permitted level of 24,000 men. In 1776 the military commissions, which had come under the hetmans' sway, were controversially abolished and their powers given to the Military Department of the Permanent Council. The increased effectiveness of the now unified taxation system also led to a rise in revenues, which increased in scale from 1789, when the Four Year Sejm's new taxes took effect. Revenues rose from 12 million zlotys in 1776–7 to nearly 43.5 million in 1789–90.

Some specific reforms were also enacted. The fiscal powers of the local parliaments were restricted and they were bound by majority rule when electing deputies to the Sejm. In 1764 and 1768 the rights of the nobility and clergy over the towns they controlled were reduced, and in the latter year the landlord lost the right 'of life and death' over his peasants. In 1775 the nobility was permitted to engage in trade. In 1776 the death penalty for witchcraft was abolished, as was the judicial use of torture, which had until then been the rule in witchcraft and ritual murder trials.

There were also a number of attempts to foster economic development, which were, however, hampered by the harsh economic consequences of the first partition. Quite apart from the loss of territory which this entailed, it followed a period of civil strife and material destruction. In addition, the Polish–Prussian trade treaty of 1775 undermined trade down the Vistula and also protected Prussian industry from Polish competition. As a result there was a major decline in the trade between Poland and Danzig, which by 1776 was at only two-thirds of its 1770 level, while the number of ships calling at the port had fallen by half. In the same year grain exports were barely 37 per cent of their 1769 level. A more favourable treaty of 1781 mitigated the worst effects of this fall, but trade did not recover to its pre-partition level.

Against this background an attempt was made to develop Polish grain export through Russia, which had adopted a more liberal trade policy towards Poland–Lithuania after the first partition by establishing a system of canals linking the rivers Vistula and Niemen with the Dnieper. Access to the Black Sea was blocked by the Turks, and Stanisław August hoped, perhaps naively, to win Catherine's support for a joint campaign to capture the Crimea and the north shore of the Black Sea and to open it to trade.

Efforts were also made to foster industrial development but these were held back by Prussian competition and by the lack of a pool of free labour. The king himself established a blast furnace near Sambir and a clothing factory in the same area. He created the Belweder pottery in Warsaw and also tried to stimulate copper mining and marble quarrying. His example was followed by others, such as his brother Michał Poniatowski, who set up a linen mill near Warsaw. But all these efforts failed to do much to transform the overwhelmingly agricultural character of Poland.

By the late 1780s Stanisław had not succeeded in overcoming the fundamental weaknesses of the Polish state, but he had created a new climate of opinion and had by his use of patronage created a group of politicians loyal to him and committed to the principles of the Enlightenment. He had also established the core of an effective bureaucracy crucial for the implementation of reforms.

Stanisław's reforms did not command the support of many of the reformers. The magnate-led opposition attempted to outbid the king for Russian support, and turned to Prussia after being rejected by Catherine in 1787. It posed as the defender of traditional republican values, supposedly threatened by the king's monarchist ambitions and the cosmopolitan and metropolitan vices of Warsaw. Before 1787 there was little support for radical reform, whether republican or monarchist. The radicals' chance came as a result of developments on the international scene. In 1787 war again broke out between Russia and Turkey. By this stage Catherine's opposition to any collaboration, either in southward expansion or in permitting the reform of the Polish constitution, had severely undermined the strategy of reform in alliance with Russia.

The dominant group in the newly elected Sejm, which met in October 1788, saw Russia's involvement with Turkey as an opportunity. Its members formed a confederation with the goal of augmenting revenue and increasing the size of the army. Catherine acquiesced in this in order to ensure stability in Poland during the war with Turkey. Prussia now offered an alliance, withdrew the guarantee it had given of the Polish Fundamental Laws in 1768, and disclaimed any intention of interfering in Polish affairs. The king was persuaded to abandon his hoped-for anti-Turkish alliance with Russia.

The situation now developed very rapidly. In October 1788 the Sejm resolved to raise an army of 100,000 men, although this was later lowered to 65,000. In the same month the Military Department of the Permanent Council was abolished on the grounds that it had been imposed by the Russians and was replaced by a parliamentary commission—a reform which was a violation of both the Fundamental Laws of 1768 and the Treaty of Guarantee with Russia. However, Russia was at war with both Turkey and Sweden and in no position to intervene.

In January 1789 the Permanent Council itself was abolished and its functions were taken over by parliamentary commissions. In the spring Russia and Austria complied with the Polish demand that they remove their troops from Podolia, and in May the Poles attempted to win the support of the British, sending an envoy to London to explore the possibility of developing Anglo-Polish trade and bypassing the Prussian customs barrier.

The key to the whole situation lay in the Polish–Prussian alliance, which rested on very shaky foundations. Prussia originally had little interest in fostering reform in Poland, and its support of the anti-Russian party was dictated by its desire to gain control of Danzig and Toruń. Late in 1789 the situation changed, as Prussian–Austrian relations deteriorated and Prussia, under the influence of its foreign minister, Hertzberg, determined to attack Austria. This attack was planned for the spring and it made an alliance with Poland much more important. In return for the cession of Danzig and Toruń, the Prussians were now prepared to offer a significant lowering of their tariff barrier, and in March 1790 they concluded an alliance with Poland in which each country agreed to come to the other's aid if attacked.

The alliance was never solid. Although opposition leaders such as the king's cousin Adam Kazimierz Czartoryski and Ignacy Potocki had agreed in principle to concede Danzig and Toruń, it soon became clear that this was strongly opposed by most deputies. For the Prussians, the alliance with Poland was seen primarily as a means to put pressure on Austria. In July 1790 the conflict between Austria and Prussia was settled by negotiation at Reichenbach, which meant that Hertzberg's cherished scheme of obtaining Galicia from Austria, which could then be handed over to Poland in return for Danzig and Toruń, was no longer realistic. As a consequence, the diplomatic position of the Patriots in Poland, who were very naive in their understanding of the international situation, was much weaker than they realized.

During this whole period the process of reform in Poland had been gathering speed at a time when revolutionary change was also occurring in France. In September 1789 a parliamentary commission to reform the government was created. A large demonstration of burghers took place on 23 November 1789. This was followed in late 1790 by the ennoblement of several hundred prominent townspeople, and in April the following year a new law increased the rights of the royal towns. In September 1790 the territory of the Commonwealth was declared inviolable and the Russian guarantee of 1775 repudiated.

By November 1790 the parliament's two-year term was coming to an end, and a law was passed to extend it by two years and calling elections to supplement the number of deputies. Of the 180 elected, perhaps 120 favoured reform. In January 1791 Britain and Prussia demanded from Russia a guarantee of the status quo in Turkey. At the same time the British expressed a willingness to enter a political and commercial agreement with Poland, but only if Prussia also participated. This could only be ensured by the cession of Danzig and Toruń. There was, however, little public support in Britain for a war with Russia, and by the end of March the plan for a 'Russian armament', a Prussian–British–Polish alliance which would guarantee the newly won independence of Poland, had clearly failed.[4]

The king and the Patriots were aware of the weakness of their position and were thus forced into an alliance. They felt they had to act quickly if they were not to lose all. As a result, in what was in some ways an act of revolution they passed a new constitution in May 1791 which attempted to write into law the most important changes which had taken place in Polish political life since 1764. In this sense, it was related more to Polish conditions than to developments in France, although the influence of the Enlightenment and of events in Paris were clearly to be seen.

The provisions of the new constitution, which had been much revised by the drafters, particularly Ignacy Potocki, Hugo Kołłątaj, who until 1786 had been the reforming rector of the Jagiellonian University, and the king, in order to reconcile royalist and republican views, created a government consisting of three powers, the legislative, the executive, and the judicial (article 5). The legislature was to be composed of two houses, the chamber of deputies and the senate. The

[4] Anderson, *Britain's Discovery of Russia 1553–1815*, ch. 6.

former could discuss all proposals for general laws and resolutions concerning policy, especially those put forward by the king. All decisions were to be by majority vote, and though the 204 deputies were still to be elected by the local parliaments, they were no longer bound by their instructions. Landless nobles were now excluded from active participation in such bodies, which limited the influence of the great magnates. The right to form confederations, leagues of noblemen formed in an emergency to restore the Commonwealth to its 'pristine state', was abolished. The royal towns were to send twenty-four representatives to the chamber of deputies, but they were purely advisory and had no vote. The senate, the upper house, was made up of bishops, provincial governors, castellans, and some ministers. It had a suspensive veto on legislation.

The executive was made up of a cabinet which was given the name Guardian of the Laws, chaired by the king and composed of the primate, the marshal (speaker) of parliament, and five ministers (police, chancellery, foreign affairs, war, and treasury) appointed by the king. Decisions required the signature of both the king and one minister. Separate courts were established for nobles, burghers, and peasants. In earlier discussions it had been proposed to make the throne hereditary in the Saxon (Wettin) line after the death of the childless Stanisław August. The constitution, in accordance with Enlightenment principles, favoured political centralization. Although it did not abolish the separate status of the Grand Duchy of Lithuania, this was implied by the failure to mention the Grand Duchy except in the king's titulature. Stanisław August and Kołłątaj certainly hoped to move in this direction. However, the Zaręczenie Wzajemne Obojga Narodów (Guarantee of the Mutual Rights of the Two Nations) of October 1791 confirmed Lithuanian status while merging some commissions (a half or a third of whose members had to be Lithuanians).

The social clauses modified only partially the previous Roman Catholic and noble political monopoly. Roman Catholicism remained the dominant faith, but freedom of worship was guaranteed to adherents of other religions. The rights and privileges of the nobility were confirmed and declared unalterable. However, earlier legislation depriving landless nobles (407,000 out of 725,000) of their political rights was confirmed. The rights of the royal towns were increased, granting burghers limited political rights, and a special law was to be enacted concerning towns and townspeople within the dominions of the Commonwealth. The law on royal towns of 18 April 1791 was declared an integral part of the constitution. Serfdom was maintained, but peasants were now brought under the law and peasant contracts with landlords were made enforceable in state courts.

The situation of the reformers in Poland was now perilous in the extreme. They had alienated the Prussians, who considered that the scale of the reforms already introduced released them from the obligations of their treaty with Poland of March 1790. In early 1792 the Russians concluded peace with Turkey, and succeeded in persuading the Prussians that the re-establishment of their dominant position in Poland would not affect Prussia's interests adversely. In March 1792 Leopold of Austria, who was opposed to a new partition, died. His inexperienced successor, Franz, did not oppose the growing Russo-Prussian rapprochement at Polish expense. In April the Prussian envoy declared that his government did not consider itself bound to defend the new constitution.

The Russians were able to make use of the considerable domestic opposition to the changes which had taken place in Poland. The conservative opponents of the new constitution were encouraged to form a confederation at Targowica, and Russian troops entered Poland to support the confederates. The Prussians refused to assist the Polish government. Although the king now attempted to compromise with both the Russians and his domestic opponents, the die was cast. The Prussians and Russians were determined on a new partition, whose outline they agreed in January 1793. Austria agreed to forgo her share in return for Bavaria.

Under threat of force a Sejm was assembled at Grodno, the town in Lithuania where parliaments traditionally met, and was compelled to accept the new partition. All that was left of the country was a small Russian protectorate, with a population of 4 million and an area of 80,000 square miles. Some vestiges of the political changes since 1788 were retained, but after the high hopes aroused by the reform process a significant part of the Polish political elite was not prepared to accept this humiliation. Moreover, the Polish army was still in existence and hope was also encouraged by the successes of the French Revolution. A revolt broke out, led by Tadeusz Kościuszko, when attempts were made to reduce the size of the army. It had some initial victories and by April 1794 had cleared of foreign troops the entire territory left to Poland by the second partition. In May, however, the Prussians intervened, and by November they and the Russians had succeeded in crushing the revolt. After some internal debate Russia decided on a final partition. Its details occasioned considerable argument among those sharing out the spoils, but it was finally accomplished in October 1795 (see Map 4).

The Kościuszko rebellion had many novel features. Kościuszko himself, who was declared 'leader' (*naczelnik*) of the country, had been educated not only in Poland but also in France. He had also participated in the American Revolution and had a strong belief in the common man. In May 1794 he abolished personal serfdom by decree and reduced labour obligations by half to three-quarters, guaranteeing the peasants' right to the land they had worked under serfdom. He also attempted to win Jewish support for the uprising. His rebellion looked to France for help, less because of the affinities between the two movements than in the hope that the French could compel the withdrawal of Poland's enemies. The small group of 'Jacobins' in Warsaw were of little significance, and at this time the French were in no position to come to the aid of the Poles. Nevertheless, a sense of kinship with revolutionary France was created in Poland, which was to be important in the future. Some of the Jacobins were later to become important supporters of moderate reform both in the Duchy of Warsaw and in the Kingdom of Poland. Although all the efforts to create a more viable political system for Poland–Lithuania had failed and probably could not have succeeded, given both the internal and the external situation of the country, major changes in attitude had occurred which created the basis for more successful change in the future.

THE DEBATE ON THE POSITION OF THE JEWS IN THE LAST YEARS OF THE COMMONWEALTH

The period after 1764 was also marked by attempts to reform the position of the Jews and integrate them more fully into the wider society. This issue aroused considerable debate, similar to that which was taking place elsewhere in Europe at this time under the impact of Enlightenment ideas, although it had some individual features which were the result both of the differences between the political system of Poland–Lithuania and the more autocratic model which prevailed in Prussia and Austria, and of the specific social conditions in the Commonwealth.[5] The Polish discussion was framed by the arguments set out by Christian Wilhelm von Dohm, whose *Über die bürgerliche Verbesserung der Juden* aroused considerable interest in the Warsaw press and was first discussed in 1783 by Piotr Świtkowski in *Pamiętnik Historyczno-Polityczny*, two years after its publication. It was also influenced by the reforms in relation to the Jewish population which Joseph II had introduced in the Habsburg empire, including the formerly Polish area of Galicia.[6]

The discussion took three basic positions on the Jews. The first held that the Jews needed to be 'reformed'. They could be granted municipal (but not general civil) rights only when they had abandoned some of their 'harmful' characteristics and when their autonomous status, which made them 'a state within a state', had been abolished. A more sympathetic position held that Jews could only be expected to transform themselves if they were granted municipal citizenship, while the most hostile held that the Jews could not be reformed.

One of the most articulate exponents of the first view was Fr. Hugo Kołłątaj (1750–1812), a key member of the Patriot Party and advocate of the rights of the burghers, on whose behalf he prepared memorandums for the Sejm and the king.

[5] On the issue of Jews at the time of the Four Year Sejm, see *Materiały do dziejów Sejmu Czteroletniego (MDSC)*, ii, vi; Eisenbach, 'Prawo obywatelskie i honorowe Żydów (1790–1861)'; id., 'Wokół świadomości roli politycznej mieszczaństwa polskiego na przełomie XVIII i XIX w.'; id., *Z dziejów ludności żydowskiej w Polsce w XVIII i XIX wieku*, 28; and id., *The Emancipation of the Jews in Poland, 1780–1870*; Gelber, 'Żydzi a zagadnienie reformy Żydów na Sejmie Czteroletnim'; Goldberg, 'Pierwszy ruch polityczny wśród Żydów polskich'; id., 'From Intercession to Citizenship' (Heb.); Michalski, 'Sejmowe projekty reformy położenia ludności żydowskiej w Polsce w latach 1789–1792'; Rostworowski, 'Miasta i mieszczanie w ustroju Trzeciego Maja'; Verete, 'Polish Proposals for the Territorial Solution of the "Jewish Question" 1788–1850' (Heb.), 148–55, 203–13; Zielińska, *Walka 'Familii' o reformę Rzeczypospolitej 1743–1752*; Zienkowska, 'Citizens or Inhabitants?'; ead., 'The Jews Have Killed a Tailor'; ead., 'Reforms Relating to the Third Estate'; ead., *Sławetni i urodzeni*; ead., 'Spór o Nową Jerozolimę'; ead., 'W odpowiedzi profesorowi Arturowi Eisenbachowi'.

[6] For these, see Ch. 8.

Kołłątaj set out his views on the Jews in *Listy anonima* (Letters by an Unknown Hand) and, in more detail, in *Prawo polityczne narodu polskiego* (The Political Law of the Polish Nation).[7] He saw the position of the Jews as part of the problem of how to redress the grievances of the burgher estate. As a believer in the principle of natural rights central to Enlightenment political philosophy, he took the view that 'with regard to the Jews, as with regard to all people, the rights of man should be observed'. He also deplored anti-Jewish prejudice, arguing that 'opinions tolerated by the government should not be allowed to become the basis for private usurpations and for the inciting of hatred among people'. Yet he did not think that it would be right to grant municipal citizenship to Jews, even without the right to participate in municipal self-government. The Jews needed first to approximate to the norms of European behaviour.

As a consequence, Kołłątaj wanted the Jews to abandon their traditional mode of dress:

> All the Jews living or domiciled in the states of the Republic, with no exception, must shave off their beards and stop wearing Jewish dress; they should dress as the Christians in the states of the Republic do; the governor's commissions [which were responsible for law and order] should ensure that this provision is observed within a year of its being proclaimed law.[8]

In addition, Kołłątaj called for a restriction on the scope of Jewish autonomy, which 'turns them into a state within a state'. The *kehilot* should lose their powers and the rabbinate should have no jurisdiction except in religious matters. The holding of rabbinic office should be contingent on an ability to demonstrate a knowledge of the Polish language and secular subjects, including Latin, arithmetic, logic, and the 'law of nature'.

Jews should lose their separate legal status, and all civil and criminal cases should be tried by municipal or noble courts. They should also be placed under the jurisdiction of the towns, whose self-government was one of Kołłątaj's basic demands, and removed from the jurisdiction of the governors.

Jewish education should be placed under the control of the Commission of National Education and Jews should be encouraged to attend public schools. Knowledge of the Polish language should be a major goal of Jewish education. Like many reformers, Kołłątaj believed that the Jews were partly responsible for the degradation of the Polish village because of their role in purveying liquor. They should be forbidden to sell alcohol in the villages and should not be allowed to lease inns, breweries, or distilleries. They should be allowed to engage in trade, crafts, and agriculture 'according to their desire' but not 'to the detriment of the rights of the towns'. Jewish beggars should no longer be permitted to roam freely around the country.

[7] *Prawo polityczne narodu polskiego* was written in the critical years 1789–90.

[8] Ibid. ii. 318.

Views similar to those of Kołłątaj were held by Fr. Stanisław Staszic (1755–1826), another strong advocate of improvement in the position of the burghers. In his *Przestrogi dla Polski* (Warnings for Poland), written in 1791–2, he called for equal political rights for townspeople, demanding that their representatives be admitted as full members of the Sejm.[9] Like many Enlightenment thinkers, Staszic believed that much of what was wrong with the Jews was the result of their 'separatism' and 'exclusiveness'. In his view,

> any spirit of exclusiveness is the most pernicious and obstinate adversary of progress to civilization. . . . the spirit of exclusiveness is the most pernicious in an association of people; whenever exclusiveness arises, justice disappears, and where there is no justice, there can be no morals. The spirit of exclusiveness is the main obstacle at every step to civilization; though less visible, it is still the greatest barrier to unity, to the unification of nations. Throughout the history of mankind, the spirit of exclusiveness regarding land, birth, defence, religion, and trade has done humanity the greatest wrong.[10]

Given these views, it is not surprising that Staszic should have believed that 'agriculture and the towns will hardly be able to rise as long as the sale of liquor is in the hands of the Jews, as long as the Jews in the towns constitute a separate estate'. The Jews were the cause of the peasants' 'indolence, stupidity, drunkenness, and misery' and they 'suck the peasants' blood'.

During the debates of the Four Year Sejm, Staszic put forward a number of proposals relating to the Jews. He conceded that they should 'be given by the national government the same facility for earning money as all other inhabitants' with the exception of the right to sell liquor. At the same time Jewish autonomy should be done away with and the Jews should be subject to the general laws of the kingdom and, in particular, to the municipalities and their courts. Taking a leaf out of Prussian legislation, he called for the right of marriage among Jews to be contingent on the husband having a trade or being engaged in agriculture.[11]

A more sympathetic view of the position of the Jews was expressed in an anonymous pamphlet of 1785 entitled *Żydzi, czyli konieczna potrzeba reformowania Żydów w krajach Rzeczypospolitej Polskiej* (Jews, or, The Indispensable Necessity of Reforming the Jews in the Lands of the Polish Commonwealth).[12] Following Dohm, the writer observed that 'The Jew like any other man is born neither bad nor good, nor wise; he is born with the capacity of becoming the former or the latter depending on the circumstances of his life.' As a consequence, he held, 'As human beings, the Jews can become useful citizens.' If they were harmful to the country this was the result of their oppression over many centuries.

Legislation was the key to reform generally and specifically to the reform of the Jews. 'Our laws with regard to the Jews are bad . . . The results are that the Jews are not included in any estate, that authority over them is in the hands of either

[9] For his views, see Staszic, *Pisma filozoficzne i społeczne*.
[10] Ibid. ii. 198, 217.
[11] Ibid. i. 302–3.
[12] For this pamphlet, see *MDSC* vi. 79–93.

private persons or their own jurisdiction.' They had to pay special taxes and conclude agreements with municipal authorities to obtain the right of settlement. They were not admitted to the guilds in towns, encountered obstacles in pursuing useful crafts, and were not allowed to attend state-run schools.

Under these circumstances, it was not surprising that they were regarded as 'an alien nation, for whom our country is not a motherland'. The goal of government policy should be 'to make them citizens of this country', which meant incorporating them into 'the middle estate, the estate of burghers'. This was a call for civic enfranchisement. In his words: 'to include the Jews in the burgher estate means to grant them all the liberties and prerogatives in which our towns took and take pride; it means excluding them from any other authority and placing them under the rule and jurisdiction of the town. In short, all differences now existing between Jews and Christians should be abolished.'[13]

Once the Jews were included in the burgher estate, their special legal status would be ended and all special taxes abolished. The Jews would be given access to guilds and would be transformed into useful citizens.

Similar views were expressed in a shorter pamphlet by Mateusz Butrymowicz, a protégé of Michał Ogiński, the hetman of the Grand Duchy of Lithuania, a prominent member of the 'family', who was also probably the author of the anonymous pamphlet *Żydzi, czyli konieczna potrzeba reformowania Żydów w krajach Rzeczypospolitej Polskiej*, mentioned above. In *Sposób uformowania Żydów w Polsce w pożytecznych krajowi obywatelów* (How to Turn Polish Jews into Citizens Useful to the Country), which appeared in February 1789 and which reproduced the earlier pamphlet with some comments and critical remarks, he called for a transformation in the legal status of the Jews by granting them municipal citizenship.[14] A committee of the Sejm should draw up a suitable proposal, which could then be given legislative approval. Butrymowicz himself submitted such a proposal to the Sejm on 30 November 1789, which, while not including the Jews in the burgher estate, saw as its goal the inclusion of the Jews living in the lands of the Commonwealth in its national laws and customs. This was to be achieved by recognizing 'every man of this faith to be a freeman and not subject to any serfdom. . . . and a true citizen of the state, whether domiciled in a city, small town, or village, provided he is engaged in trade, handicrafts, or agriculture, or in study useful to the country'. Nothing came of this proposal.[15]

Another political writer who advocated the partial enfranchisement of the Jews was the radical Józef Pawlikowski (1768–1829), who later, at Kościuszko's request, wrote the pamphlet *Czy Polacy wybić się mogą na niepodległość?* (Can Poles Achieve Independence?). In a pamphlet entitled *Myśli polityczne dla Polski* (Political

[13] Ibid. 87.

[14] *MDSC* vi. 79–93.

[15] On this, see *MDSC* vi. 119–28; see also Eisenbach, *The Emancipation of the Jews in Poland, 1780–1870*, 77.

Thoughts for Poland), first published anonymously in September 1789, he called for the abolition of personal serfdom and reform in the government of the towns which would enable their representatives to sit in the Sejm.[16] In relation to the Jews, he called for an end to their special status, although he did not go as far as Butrymowicz in calling for them to be granted municipal citizenship. The Jews, like other townsmen, should have the right to engage without restriction in trade and handicrafts, be members of the municipal police, pay only the local municipal taxes, and be subject to municipal laws and courts. He rejected the view that the Jews were responsible for the economic decline of the country and the misery of the peasantry. The impoverishment of the country was the consequence of serfdom and the minimal commercial relations between town and country. At the same time, like Kołłątaj and Staszic, Pawlikowski wished to end what he regarded as the harmful Jewish participation in the sale of liquor, and called for them to be barred from inn-keeping and the leasing of breweries and distilleries.

Pawlikowski repeated the call made by the author of the anonymous pamphlet for the Jews to undertake military service. Both were probably influenced in this by the reforms of Joseph II, which for the first time in modern Europe imposed conscription on the Jews. Pawlikowski did have some reservations about Jewish military service. 'The Jews are citizens,' he wrote; 'they can also be soldiers, but the time is not yet ripe.' Until their moral reform was accomplished, the Jews should be exempted from the obligation to provide recruits, but they could serve in the armed forces as volunteers.

The view that the Jews were unreformable, and that the medieval canon law provisions of the Catholic Church should be maintained, also had a number of advocates. One of the most ardent was the editor of the conservative *Gazeta Warszawska* Fr. Stefan Łuskina. He generally defended the unreformed Polish constitution and the maintenance of the political monopoly of the nobility, attributing the ills of the country to the deleterious effect of the misguided principles of the Enlightenment, which had produced moral decline and a lack of respect for authority. Fr. Łuskina opposed any change in the status of the Jews and, in an article on 9 October 1790, poured scorn on the idea of Jews serving in the army.[17] This position was supported by the burghers, who continued in their traditional hostility to the Jews and were for retaining and even extending restrictions on their economic activity.

Hostility to the idea of a change in the status of the Jews was also expressed by Michał Czacki, a deputy from Chernigov in the Four Year Sejm. In the second half of 1790 he published a pamphlet entitled *Refleksje nad reformą Żydów* (Reflections on Reform of the Jews). His goal was, he claimed, 'to reform the Jews, to turn these people who are a burden to the country' into useful inhabitants. In fact, arguing

[16] Józef Pawlikowski, *Myśli polityczne dla Polski* (Warsaw, 1789), cited in Eisenbach, *The Emancipation of the Jews in Poland, 1780–1870*, 79–80.

[17] Eisenbach, *The Emancipation of the Jews in Poland, 1780–1870*, 66.

against Zalkind Hourwitz, the Polish Jew who had settled in Paris and had published a widely praised pamphlet in support of Jewish integration, he asserted that Jews could not at present be granted civic rights since they were not fit for citizenship because of their religious and national distinctiveness.[18]

In the 1950s and 1960s a six-volume documentary series entitled *Materiały do dziejów Sejmu Czteroletniego* (Documents on the History of the Four Year Sejm) was published in Poland. One volume, edited by the doyen of historians of Polish Jewry in the eighteenth and nineteenth centuries, Artur Eisenbach, was devoted to the Jewish issue. It includes a number of Jewish responses to the debate about the position of the Jews. The picture they give us is obviously distorted, since what has been included is almost exclusively material by Jews who were able to write in Polish. Inevitably this means that there are few pieces by those who opposed integration. In addition, the abolition of the Council of the Lands and of the Council of Lithuania in 1764 meant that there was no representative body which could claim to speak for all the Jews. Nevertheless, an interesting picture of Jewish public opinion on the status of the Jews in the last years of Poland–Lithuania does emerge. Generally speaking, while a small number of acculturated Jews accepted the view that only coercive measures could transform the Jews into citizens of a reformed Poland, others stressed the need for more sympathetic treatment of the community if it was to modify its behaviour in the way desired by the Polish radicals. Most Jews rejected forced acculturation and sought to widen the sphere of their economic activity, looking for support to their traditional allies among the nobility, many of whom were alarmed by the increasing assertiveness of the burghers.

Most of the Jewish responses to the debate address specific grievances such as prohibitions on residence or trade. Only a few deal with the general question of emancipation. Of those dealing with specific issues troubling Jewish communities, one of the most interesting is the characteristically entitled *Pokorna prośba od Żydów warszawskich i prowincyj koronnych do Najjaśniejszych Sejmujących Stanów* (Humble Request of the Jews of Warsaw and the Crown Provinces to the Most Noble Estates of the Sejm), prepared by delegates from the *kehilot* of a number of Polish towns in the autumn of 1789, at a time when the burghers were also formulating their views for submission to parliament.[19] The Jewish representatives obviously felt that, given burgher hostility to their position, they needed to defend their interests. In this memorandum they sought to ensure their rights of residence in Polish towns. They compared their situation unfavourably with that of Jews in neighbouring countries. They were willing, they claimed, to pay all 'just' taxes and fulfil their duties to the country, 'but in return we want this country to become our motherland; we want it to give us the freedom which will ensure

[18] Repr. in *MDSC* vi. 208–9.

[19] *Pokorna prośba od Żydów warszawskich i prowincyj koronnych do Najjaśniejszych Sejmujących Stanów*, in *MDSC* vi. 129–32.

that we remain alive and have the strength to pay the taxes which are our obligation'. The memorandum then proceeded to discuss some specific issues. It pointed out that there were three types of town in Poland, towns where Jews had the right to settle freely, towns where Jewish settlement was conditional on an agreement with the municipal authority, which generally required a financial payment, and towns where Jews were forbidden to settle. In the Kingdom of Poland, the manifesto argued, some 200 of the 301 royal or ecclesiastical towns barred Jewish settlement. The plenipotentiaries requested that these towns should allow a small group of Jews to settle and be granted the right of citizenship so that they could trade freely. In return for this concession, each of these families would pay a lump sum to the treasury and all Jews would be liable to general taxes. The memorandum also declared the willingness of the Jewish community to work with representatives of the burghers to limit imports, protect domestic industry, and increase trade.

There were also some who supported the transformation of Jewish life on the lines suggested by Dohm and his Jewish supporters in Prussia, although their numbers in Poland–Lithuania were much smaller. They included Eliasz Ackord, a Warsaw-based physician born in Vilna and trained in Germany, who in 1786 produced a German translation of the anonymous pamphlet *Żydzi, czyli konieczna potrzeba reformowania Żydów w krajach Rzeczypospolitej Polskiej*, discussed above, which he dedicated to the king. Similar views were expressed in a pamphlet published anonymously in 1791 by Mendel Lefin of Satanów, who had returned to Poland from France via Berlin at the end of the 1780s and who was a protégé of Adam Kazimierz Czartoryski. Entitled *Essai d'un plan de réforme ayant pour objet d'éclairer la nation juive en Pologne et de redresser par là ses mœurs* it was intended to influence the National Education Commission and called for the abolition of special taxes on Jews. In return, the Jews would transform themselves through a reform of their educational system, introducing Polish as a language of instruction, and encouraging productive work in handicrafts and agriculture.[20]

At the end of 1789 Zalkind Hourwitz's pamphlet *Usprawiedlenie czyli apologia Żydów* (The Justification, or, An Apology for the Jews) appeared in Warsaw, a shortened and loose translation of a pamphlet which had earlier appeared in Paris.[21] Hourwitz was a Polish Jew who had settled in France, where he had won a prize in a competition organized by the Royal Society of Arts and Learning in Metz. He argued for granting Jews the right of citizenship, and that they should be allowed to settle in towns, to purchase land, and engage in trade and handicrafts. Jewish autonomy should be done away with, along with the jurisdiction of the rabbinate.

[20] On Ackord, see Eisenbach, *The Emancipation of the Jews in Poland, 1780–1870*, 65; on Lefin, Sinkoff, 'Strategy and Ruse in the Haskalah of Mendel Lefin of Satanow', and ead., 'Benjamin Franklin in Jewish Eastern Europe'.

[21] Malino, *A Jew in the French Revolution*, 84–5; Zalkind Hourwitz, *Apologie des juifs en réponse à la question: Est-il des moyens de rendre les juifs plus heureux et plus utiles en France?* (Paris, 1789), cited in *MDSC* vi. 113–18.

Similar views were expressed by the Jewish lobbyist from Vilna Szymel Wolfowicz. In a pamphlet published at the beginning of 1790 he appealed to the Sejm not to neglect the problem of Jewish reform. 'When deliberating on the happiness of its own nation and planning a reform covering all parts of society, the Commonwealth should not forget the Jews . . .'. It should, on the contrary, determine 'in the holy book of laws [whether] they are to be happy and useful to the country, or not'. This should be achieved by granting the Jews citizenship, which probably meant municipal citizenship: 'In taking our Jewish nation under the protection of the law, give us a definite class of citizenship, so that you need not write a separate law of rewards and punishments for the Jews.'[22]

Another Vilna Jew, the physician Salomon Polonus, known as the Amsterdam doctor, put forward, probably in early 1792, a plan for Jewish reform; he also translated a number of French revolutionary pamphlets on the subject.[23] He was clearly influenced by the events that were taking place in France, beginning his observations as follows:

> If 50,000 Jews have convinced the French nation, this refined and enlightened nation of Europe, that . . . they will help their country with all their resources, if these Jews have been granted civic rights and have been put on an equal footing with Frenchmen, are there any reasons to doubt whether the nearly one million Jews in the Polish state will through enlightenment become happy and useful to their country?[24]

In order to achieve this Polonus made a number of proposals. Jewish officials, including rabbis, should be elected by the whole community, and the jurisdiction of Jewish courts confined to matters of religion. Rabbis should be educated in general disciplines and sciences in addition to rabbinic literature, and must know Polish, which was also to be taught in Jewish schools. In return the Jews should be permitted to live freely in all towns without restriction, engage in all forms of trade or craft, open factories, and be admitted to guilds. Jews should be liable for military service and should gradually be granted civic rights, which in this context meant municipal citizenship. In the first instance, these rights should be granted to those who had opened a factory or who had served in the army for five years. In addition, the government should issue a declaration affirming that, 'after twenty years, every Jew, without exception, will be granted civic rights, and that persons who distinguish themselves by their enlightenment and are making use of it to improve the nation should be granted citizenship now'.

We have fewer accounts of the views of those who espoused normative Judaism. The opinion of Rabbi Shneur Zalman of Lyady, who in 1812 expressed the view that a Russian victory over Napoleon would be preferable since Napoleon's revolutionary ideas would undermine Jewish religious belief, has already been mentioned. The consequences of the Frankist heresy were fresh in

[22] Szymel Wolfowicz, *Więzień w Nieświeżu do Stanów Sejmujących o potrzebie reformy Żydów*, in *MDSC* vi. 141–53.

[23] S. Polonus, *Projekt względem reformy Żydów*, in *MDSC* vi. 421–33.

[24] Ibid. 421.

the memory of the religious leadership of the community, and calls for the 'reform' or 'transformation' of the Jews were seen as a prelude to Christianization. The argument against the various proposals for reforming the Jews was put in a pamphlet by Rabbi Herszel Józefowicz of Chełm in February 1789.[25] He contested the view that the Jews were driving the peasants to drunkenness and that they pursued trade at the expense of handicrafts. The Jews were a positive element in the Commonwealth and they should be allowed to retain their traditional dress, and their autonomous *kehilot* and judicial system, and to maintain their own educational system.

CHANGES IN THE POSITION OF THE JEWS BEFORE THE FOUR YEAR SEJM

A number of important changes in the position of the Jews took place in the early years of the reign of Stanisław August. One of the most significant of these was a decline in the number of ritual murder trials and their eventual cessation. There were only three such cases between 1764 and 1795, one in Warsaw and two in Vilna. In all of these cases the accused were acquitted. This was partly the result of the abolition of the use of torture in the judicial system, but attitudes were also changing. When the king met Count Stanisław Wodzicki, later to be the first president of senate of the free city of Kraków, who made an accusation of ritual murder in Olkusz in 1787, he told him, 'I did not expect that you, who have received a higher education, should still believe in medieval fairy tales.'[26]

One aspect of the position of the Jews which was constantly discussed was the level of taxation. The eighteenth century had seen an increasing indebtedness on the part of the *kehilot* and a growing failure of the central institutions of Polish Jewry to tax effectively. There was considerable parliamentary dissatisfaction with the level of Jewish taxation, and some parliamentary deputies also claimed that the Jews held back some of the tax receipts they collected. In 1746, for instance, a deputy claimed that Jews in Małopolska collected 900,000 florins, but gave the treasury only 'a hundred and some tens of thousands',[27] while in 1752 another asserted that in their district assemblies Jews collected 1.2 million florins, of which only 200,000 reached the treasury.[28] It was also widely believed that the number of Jews was significantly higher than the official figures, which also lowered the yield of the poll tax.[29]

It was dissatisfaction with the way the Council of Four Lands and the Council of Lithuania administered the poll tax, along with Enlightenment hostility to

[25] H. Józefowicz, *Myśli stosowane do sposobu uformowania Żydów polskich w pożytecznych krajowi obywateli*, in *MDSC* vi. 98–105. [26] Wodzicki, *Wspomnienia z przeszłości od 1768 do roku 1840*, 203.

[27] *Diarjusze sejmowe z wieku XVIII*, ii. 122–3. [28] Ibid. iii. 69–70.

[29] 'O zniesienie Sejmu żydowskiego instabat', ibid. ii. 76, 78, 127, 160, 175–7, 180, 251; iii. 69–70, 78.

particularist jurisdictions, which led the Sejm to dissolve them as part of a reform of the system of financial administration in 1764.[30] The liquidation commission appointed by the Sejm which investigated the financial situation of the community showed how high was the Jewish level of indebtedness. The Vilna *kehilah* owed 832,000 gulden, that of Grodno 448,500 gulden, Pinsk 310,000 gulden, and Brest 119,700 gulden. The bulk of the Vilna *kehilah*'s debt was owed to the Jesuit Order, but loans were also outstanding to the Dominicans, the Friars of St Bernard, the Augustinians, the Carmelites, and the Basilians, as well as to individual laymen and priests.[31] Henceforth any 'congress' of rabbis and *kahal* elders was forbidden under penalty of a fine of 6,000 marks (1 mark = 48 groszy). It is true that in the eighteenth century both councils had been less active, with meetings taking place less frequently. Nevertheless, their abolition was bitterly resented by the Jews. Thus in its decree excommunicating the hasidim in 1772, the *kehilah* of Brody lamented that it was not possible to act as effectively against such 'evil-doers' as in earlier times.

> Then we had eminent sages and the leaders of the Council of the Four Lands who repressed them and made the public aware of their wickedness, until we were finally rid of them. Today, alas, the crown is removed from us and we are poor in men of true faith who could stand up to them and so they have sprouted again.[32]

Kehilah liquidation commissions were set up to assess the debts of the *kehilot* and to decide how they could be paid. The poll tax was now collected by the *kehilot* in cooperation with the government, and was raised in 1775 to 3 zlotys per family annually, although a proposal to raise it to 4 was rejected (previously a lump sum had been paid, based on an approximate estimate of 1 zloty per family).

The raising of the poll tax was the occasion for a more general debate on the Jews in the Sejm on 7 February 1775.[33] During this the call was made for Jews (and Karaites) to take up agriculture, and those who did so were promised exemption from the poll tax. This was one of the first times that the physiocratic belief was raised that only agriculture was a truly productive branch of the economy and that the 'reform' of the Jews would be accelerated if they took up this 'healthy' occupation. This was to be a frequent theme throughout the nineteenth century. At the same time the role of the Jews as purveyors of alcohol in the countryside, which was criticized by such writers as Kołłątaj and Staszic, was also attacked, another persistent leitmotif in discussion about the reform of the Jews.[34] These

30 Halpern (ed.), *Minutes of the Council of Four Lands* (Heb.), no. 43, p. xli.

31 I. Cohen, *Vilna*, 172–5.

32 Wilensky, *Hasidim and Mitnagedim* (Heb.), i. 46.

33 Ringelblum, 'A Debate about Jews in the Polish Sejm of 1775' (Yid.), 118–25.

34 Eisenbach, *The Emancipation of the Jews in Poland, 1780–1870*, 45; cf. Ringelblum, 'Projekty i próby przewarstwowienia Żydów w epoce stanisławowskiej', 3–9. Apparently, in 1776 legislation was adopted barring Jews from leasing distilleries or taverns, but only in the towns, not the villages: Gelber, 'The History of the Jews in Poland from the First Partition to the Second World War' (Heb.), 110 n.

attacks seem to have had some effect. According to one estimate, between 1765 and 1784 as many as half of all Ukrainian inns may have passed from Jewish into Christian hands.[35] The Sejm also resolved that Jews without the means to support a family should be prohibited from marrying, something which also figured in the Austrian and Prussian legislation of this period, although it is not known whether it was, in fact, implemented.[36]

The centralizing drive inherent in the Enlightenment was also evident in the draft legal code put forward by Jan Zamoyski with the king's support in the late 1770s, but never adopted because of parliamentary opposition. It would have established municipal control of noble and clerical *jurydyki* (judicial enclaves) in the towns, and would have allowed non-voting representatives of the towns to sit in parliament. Jews would be made subject to the jurisdiction of the municipalities, which would certainly have adversely affected their position, particularly those living in *jurydyki*. In addition, the legislation, on the lines of that adopted in Prussia and Austria, would have expelled indigent Jews from the Commonwealth and would also have barred those without means from marrying.[37]

THE FOUR YEAR SEJM AND THE JEWS

The Four Year Sejm (1788–92) attempted to reform all aspects of Polish life; thus, it is not surprising that it also attempted to regulate the position of the Jews. In June 1790 it set up a Committee for the Amelioration of the Jews, whose ten members included Hugo Kołłątaj, Mateusz Butrymowicz, Tadeusz Czacki, and Jacek Jezierski. The views of Kołłątaj and Butrymowicz have already been described. Czacki was *starosta* of Nowogródek between 1786 and 1792. His proposal for the reform of the Jews bears some similarity to that proposed by Catherine the Great (see Chapter 10). It envisaged the Polish government granting Jews the right to citizenship, guaranteeing them religious toleration, abolishing special Jewish taxes, and subordinating them to the general jurisdiction. What was new in his proposal was that the Jews were to be divided up and the different strata to be placed in the estate most appropriate for them. Thus Jews in towns would enjoy full civic rights and be elected to the municipality in proportion to their numbers, Jewish craftsmen and traders were to be admitted to merchant and craft guilds, and Jews who settled on the land would be able to purchase what they tilled.[38]

Jezierski, the castellan of Łuków, saw the Jewish problem largely in economic terms and was unsympathetic to burgher political aspirations. He opposed the

35 Stone, *The Polish–Lithuanian State, 1386–1795*, 304–5; Menahem Mendel of Vitebsk, *Likutei amarim*, pt. 2, letter 6, 9*b*–12*b*; Barnai, *Letters of Hasidim from Erets Israel* (Heb.), 117–24.

36 Gelber, 'The History of the Jews in Poland from the First Partition to the Second World War' (Heb.), 110. Cf. Halpern, *Jews and Jewry in Eastern Europe* (Heb.), 289–309.

37 On this, see Gekker, 'Proekty reformy evreiskogo byta v Pol'she v kontse XVIII veka', 207–9.

38 Czacki's proposals were published somewhat later, in a pamphlet entitled *O Żydach*. See also his *Rozprawa o żydach i karaitach*.

demands of the Warsaw guild and municipality that Jewish artisans be banished from the capital or indeed the country, which, in his view, ran counter to the principle of religious toleration and the interests of the state and the towns themselves. 'If this nation were reformed and refined, it would render a great service to the country and would augment our wealth. This nation has great industry, quick wits in handicrafts, and hands like everybody else; it could be useful in everything.'[39] He also contrasted the way Jews and burghers were calling for recognition of their rights: '. . . the Jews do not threaten us with rebellion, as the towns do, they are not impudently demanding a settlement but are humbly asking for it'.[40]

The context in which this committee operated needs to be understood. One of the key issues facing the Four Year Sejm was how to improve the position of the towns and raise the status of the burghers, since it was widely believed that one of the principal reasons for the weakness of the Commonwealth was the decline of the towns which had occurred since the mid-seventeenth century. In dealing with this the legislators had to take into account the strong hostility of the burghers to the Jews. This was particularly evident in Warsaw, where the burghers had long been conducting a campaign to prevent the rescission of the ban on Jewish settlement in the capital. The issue now became particularly inflamed since Jews enjoyed the right of residence in Warsaw during sessions of the Sejm and, given the length of the parliament elected in 1788, this had led to several thousand establishing themselves in the capital. Almost immediately after it had been convened a group of 300 Jews petitioned the Sejm for freedom to reside and work in the city. In return they claimed that they were willing to pay an extra annual tax of 3,000 ducats and make a one-time payment to the treasury of 180,000 zlotys.[41] In so doing they bypassed the hostile municipality, which provoked a strong response from the Warsaw city magistrate, who explicitly rejected the Jews' demands.[42] The Jews responded equally strongly. In *Wyłuszczenie praw wolnego mieszkania i handlu Żydom w Warszawie pozwalających, z odpowiedzi na pismo magistratu warszawskiego przeciw Żydom r. 1789 wydane* (An Exposition of the Rights to Free Domicile and Trade Granted the Jews in Warsaw in Response to the Letter of the Magistrate of Warsaw against the Jews of 1789), they set out in detail the Jews' right to settle and trade in Poland going back to the Privilege of Bolesław of Kalisz in 1264. The memorandum went beyond purely legal argument. It attacked the burgher claim that the Jews were responsible for the economic ruin of the country or that they lacked patriotism. The burghers, they argued, well knew that it was not the Jews who were responsible for Poland's economic decline, but wars, conflagrations, and the ravaging of the country under the Vasa kings. The Jews were also not responsible for the heavy indebtedness of the *kehilot*. 'Contributions and thousands of levies were imposed and exacted from the

39 *MDSC* i. 316, 329. 40 Zienkowska, 'Citizens or Inhabitants?', 41. 41 *MDSC* ii. 23 n. 1.

42 'Ekspozycja praw miasta Warszawy względem Żydów oraz odpowiedź na żądaną przez nich w tymże mieście lokacyą', in *MDSC* vi. 23–31.

kehilot . . . they had to pay heavily to whoever threatened them in this disarray and they still have to pay.'

The Jews' memorandum argued that the expulsion of the Jews, as demanded by the burghers, would constitute an irreparable loss for the country. What the Jews needed, it asserted, was not hatred but

> more consideration from the state authorities, not expulsion but an inevitable reform which, if it includes them in a definite estate and this way secures the fate of their offspring, if it does not forbid them to engage in trade, arts, and crafts and in this way includes them in society and puts them in contact with more enlightened and better-organized people, this nation will see its vices reformed . . . and, treated in a humane manner, will engage in industry and set to work . . . Having become citizens, it will kiss the soil which has become its motherland, will respect the paternal government, and the better it sees its happiness, the greater will be its love for this country and the greater its courage in its defence.[43]

Early in 1789 the burghers of Warsaw sent a long memorandum to the king and the Sejm in which they called for the rejection of the Jewish request that a small number of Jews be allowed to settle, on the grounds that 'the Jews have ruined Polish towns and deprived them of craftsmen'.[44] Their views were set out in a pamphlet by Michał Świniarski published in 1789 and entitled *Wiadomość o pierwiastkowej miast zasadzie w Polsce* (Information on the Fundamental Principles of the Towns in Poland),[45] which was sent to all members of the Sejm. According to Świniarski, the decline of the Polish towns had been caused by Jews and foreigners who had gained control over trade and handicrafts to the detriment of the country's economy. He called for the exclusion of the Jews from larger towns and foreign trade, and for their restriction to retail trade in small towns.

The townspeople of Warsaw continued throughout the sitting of the Four Year Sejm to play the principal role in the mobilization of burgher opinion. In March 1789 the Warsaw municipality appealed to its counterparts in the other larger Polish towns to send representatives to Warsaw in order to coordinate their campaign for burgher rights, and in the autumn a general programme was agreed which rejected the granting of municipal citizenship to the Jews. In October 1789, when the Sejm appointed a committee to decide on the level of municipal taxation, the different municipalities appointed delegates who were to prepare documentation and lobby senators and deputies in order to 'secure consideration for the towns from the Most Serene Estates'.[46] In addition, in both October and November 1789 the Warsaw municipality addressed memorandums to the Sejm, calling for the abolition of the *jurydyki* in Warsaw and demanding the maintenance of its old privileges, according to which those who did not possess municipal

[43] *MDSC* vi. 27–42; Eisenbach, *The Emancipation of the Jews in Poland, 1780–1870*, 83–4, 157; *MDSC* vi. 38.

[44] 'Ekspozycja praw miasta Warszawy', in *MDSC* vi. 22–31.

[45] Michał Świniarski, *Wiadomość o pierwiastkowej miast zasadzie w Polsce* (1789), in *MDSC* ii. 32–57, esp. 43–7.

[46] *MDSC* vi. 129–32.

citizenship should not be allowed to carry out trade, handicrafts, or the sale of liquor, and, in particular, that Jews be expelled from Warsaw and its suburbs.[47]

The position of the Lithuanian towns, where the Christian burghers were somewhat weaker and the Jewish townspeople more powerful, was less hostile to the Jews. In the middle of 1789 the burghers there submitted a memorandum to the Sejm calling for the different *kehilot*, in accordance with the law of 1768, to reach agreements with the towns where they were established and for Jews as 'municipal citizens' to be placed under municipal jurisdiction. The right to engage in foreign and domestic trade should be restricted to Christian and Jewish merchants owning real estate worth at least 6,000 zlotys.[48]

The agitation of the townspeople provoked the Jews to undertake lobbying to defend their interests. I have already alluded to the response of a group of Warsaw Jews to the magistrate's summary rejection of their request for permanent residence in the city. This was not the only Jewish intervention at this time. When, in the autumn of 1789, the burghers seemed to be threatening Jewish interests, the representatives of the Jews of Warsaw and other towns in the Kingdom of Poland submitted a request to the Sejm to defend their rights, a request the Sejm did not consider.[49]

The political mobilization of the burghers was now proceeding apace. Two hundred and ninety-four delegates from 141 towns assembled in Warsaw, and on 23 November 1789 they proceeded in carriages in black dress (this pomp further angered nobles) from the Warsaw city hall to the parliament to hand the king and the marshal a memorandum, written by Kołłątaj, setting out their demands.[50] These included a separate house of burgesses in the parliament, the abolition of *jurydyki*, freedom from arrest without due process, the right to own landed estates, and the abolition of the supervision of municipalities by royal governors. (Kraków submitted a separate, more conservative petition.) The townspeople did not limit themselves to verbal attacks on the Jews. Anti-Jewish riots took place in Warsaw on 22 March, 19 April, and 16 May 1790. The first two were on a small scale, but the last involved substantial violence and destruction of property. It began when a tailor named Fux began to attack Jewish workshops on Senatorska Street. When the main exit from the Gołubski Palace courtyard (where many workshops were located) was barred to him, he escaped through a side door. His brief disappearance sparked a rumour that the Jews had killed a tailor, and although an official of the Jewish community found Fux and paraded him through the streets, the riot took on a life of its own and provoked widespread destruction, not only in the Gołubski Palace, but also in the adjacent Pociejowski Palace.

47 *MDSC* ii. 154–8, 174–205.

48 'Prośba miast litewskich do Najjaśniejszych Stanów Rzeczypospolitej Sejmujących', in *MDSC* ii. 96.

49 Eisenbach, *The Emancipation of the Jews in Poland, 1780–1870*, 70.

50 'Memoriały miast' and 'Prawa miast polskich do władzy prawodawczej, wykonawczej i sądowniczej', in *MDSC* ii. 259–300, 340–51.

Violence was directed against Jews but was also aimed at the nobility, whose use of *jurydyki* to evade regulations on Jewish settlement was bitterly resented. Strong action was taken against those responsible, but it was clear how much resistance there was to a change in the Jews' position.[51]

The Jews seem to have been taken aback by the strength of burgher opinion. The *Humble Request* which they now submitted 'from the Jews of Warsaw and the Crown provinces' to the 'most noble estates of the Sejm', described above, asked only in very moderate language for free residence in the towns of the Kingdom of Poland. In return they promised an unspecified contribution to the treasury and assistance to factory owners in selling their goods.[52] They responded more strongly to the violence of May 1790 and to the publication at the same time of an openly anti-Jewish pamphlet calling for the hanging of 'a hundred Jews every year'.[53] On 30 May 1790 an anonymous open letter addressed to the delegates of the towns appeared in the *Journal hebdomadaire de la Diète de Varsovie*. It was probably the work of David Koenigsberger, a prominent Warsaw merchant originally from Silesia. Drawing on French revolutionary slogans, it claimed that Jews should be considered members of the third estate in the same way as Christians and that their natural rights should be respected.[54] At the same time a group of Warsaw Jews submitted a petition to the Sejm requesting that rights of citizenship be granted to 250 Jewish families. These two initiatives should be seen as the beginning of the emergence of the Warsaw Jewish bourgeoisie, later to play such an important role in the history of Jewish life in the capital. In spite of Koenigsberger's argument for bourgeois solidarity, paradoxically the strongest supporters of the Jewish right to reside in Warsaw remained such aristocratic owners of *jurydyki* as August Sułkowski and Adam Poniński.

The Sejm was also impressed by the strength of the burghers and on 8 December 1789 responded to their demands by agreeing that the legal status of the Jews should not be included in the proposed bill regulating the legal position of the royal towns. In the first draft of this law in April 1790 the section dealing with municipal citizenship and freedom of occupation guaranteed these rights to all 'who own property, irrespective of their birth, calling, trade or religion, with the exception of Jews'.[55] To this was added in the draft of 12 May 1791, 'where and what kind of domicile these will have will be decided by a separate law'. Similarly,

[51] In the 1980s a debate arose between the historians Artur Eisenbach and Krystyna Zienkowska over whether these riots were marked by 'modern' elements of an antisemitic character or were more similar to earlier attacks on Jews. On this, see Eisenbach, *Z dziejów ludności żydowskiej w Polsce w XVIII i XIX wieku*, 103–5, 314, and Zienkowska, 'Citizens or Inhabitants?', 40, and ead., 'W odpowiedzi profesorowi Arturowi Eisenbachowi'.

[52] *Pokorna prośba od Żydów warszawskich i prowincyj koronnych do Najjaśniejszych Sejmujących Stanów*, in *MDSC* vi. 129–32.

[53] *MDSC* vi. 235–8.

[54] *MDSC* vi. 588–90; Eisenbach, *The Emancipation of the Jews in Poland, 1780–1870*, 90–1; R. Mahler, *The History of the Jews in Poland* (Heb.), 450–1; Ringelblum, 'An Echo of the French Revolution' (Yid.).

[55] *MDSC* iii. 211.

the new constitution which Fr. Scipio Piattoli, the Italian secretary of the king, was drafting contained a statement in article 11 that the legal status of the Jews would be regulated by a special law.[56]

On 18 April 1791 the Sejm, after considerable deliberation, passed the law regulating the status of royal (free) towns in Poland–Lithuania. No attempt was made to regulate the position of private (noble and Church) towns, which amounted to nearly two-thirds of all urban settlements. Many of them were extremely small, but their inhabitants did constitute nearly half the urban population of the country and they were where the bulk of Jews lived. Town citizenship, which now conferred the right of *neminem captivabimus nisi jure victum*, the Polish equivalent of the right of habeas corpus, was open only to Christians. However, the specific exclusion of Jews was now abolished. Towns were to be able to send non-voting deputies to the Sejm. They would also sit on the three commissions (Treasury, Police, Crown) which dealt with urban affairs. The *jurydyki* were abolished and a common judicial system was established. This law, although a major step forward in the social evolution of Poland and in raising the status of the royal towns, adversely affected the position of the Jews since it placed them under the exclusive legal and political authority of the burghers in these towns. Indeed, all towns were now obliged to conclude agreements with their Jewish populations laying down the conditions of their residence and economic rights.[57]

Even before the bill was passed, the Jewish committee of the Sejm began to consider how Jewish interests could be accommodated with those of the burghers. In spite of differences within the committee, a proposal was finally agreed by August 1790. In its second article it asserted:

> In admitting the Jewish people to state citizenship and putting their persons and property under state control . . . we give them freedom to settle in all towns and to make use of the rights and liberties enjoyed by these towns and to own land under lease in perpetuity or for life or on surety or on lease; we allow them to carry on all kinds of commerce and to pursue any craft, manufacture, and profession without hindrance.[58]

These privileges were contingent on the ability to demonstrate the right of domicile, whether in a town or in the countryside. In addition, the proposed bill would have guaranteed religious toleration, reorganized the *kehilot*, regulated the functions of the rabbinate, and restricted Jewish mobility. It also called for a general census of the Jewish population and the regulation of the debts of the *kehilot*. Jews were to be forbidden to operate inns and taverns and from acquiring rural leases. In the towns they were to be subject to municipal authority, and in the countryside to the relevant local authority. In fact, in spite of the high-flown language of article 2, this bill did not envisage conferring on Jews municipal citizenship. Rather they would be allowed to become permanent inhabitants with

56 Leśnodorski, *Dzieło Sejmu Czteroletniego*, 184.

57 For this law, see Stone, *The Polish–Lithuanian State, 1386–1795*, 80.

58 *MDSC* vi. 222.

economic rights. They would now pay municipal taxes and would be subject to the municipality. These changes were not seen even by the more enlightened of the Jews as being in their interest. In any event, dissenting members of the committee prevented it from being presented to the Sejm.

The king and his secretary, Fr. Piattoli, remained interested in introducing legislation which would satisfy at least some Jewish demands, if only because of the hope that this would yield significant financial benefits for the Crown. Jews continued to press for their rights, often in a way which combined both old and new concepts. Thus, within a month of the ratification of the constitution of 3 May, a group of Jewish delegates called for Jews to have the right of domicile 'in all towns, even those where they have not lived before'. Jews with property in towns should be granted the same rights of citizenship as the other inhabitants. All royal and communal privileges granted to the Jews should be reaffirmed. No creditor should be allowed to seize and imprison the wife or children of his Jewish debtor.[59] Separate Jewish jurisdiction should be maintained so that Jews could resolve disputes among themselves.[60]

In the autumn of 1791 nearly 120 representatives from *kehilot* in Wielkopolska, Małopolska, and Lithuania went to Warsaw to lobby on behalf of a bill regulating the legal status of the Jews.[61] They brought with them written instructions approved by their communal elders, much like the burghers. A key role in this lobbying activity was played by the prominent Jewish bankers and merchants of Warsaw, such as the army supplier Samuel Zbytkower, the Simonses, David Koenigsberger, and Levi Schlesinger. They held talks with the king, Fr. Piattoli, Kołłątaj, and Aleksander Linowski, and attempted to counteract the activities of the burghers' representatives.

Under these circumstances, Fr. Piattoli tried to induce some of the more sympathetic members of the Jewish committee to put before the Sejm a modified bill which would be more acceptable to Jewish lobbyists. The committee drew up a bill, which was submitted to the Sejm on 30 December 1791 and which had the support of the king. Although Jacek Jezierski called for the bill to be adopted at this stage, it lacked the necessary backing. It was opposed by the influential marshal of the Sejm, Stanisław Małachowski, who refused to cooperate, arguing that 'at the present moment, when issues of greater importance are being considered, this question cannot be raised'.

The issue continued to be discussed in the increasingly tense atmosphere of 1792. The committee now sought the opinion of Jewish representatives from all over the country. The Jews also conducted negotiations with Piattoli. These seemed to go well, and in mid-January 1792 Piattoli proposed to the king that he summon the Warsaw city councillors and tell them that he had 'undertaken negotiations with the Jews in order to conclude a sensible agreement which would

[59] *MDSC* vi. 101–2. [60] *MDSC* vi. 272–6. [61] *MDSC* vi. 355–8.

produce harmony between the burghers' rights on the one hand and the rights of humanity and the interests of the state on the other'.[62]

In fact, the Jews were too optimistic. The new proposal did not give them the right to settle freely and buy property in towns, nor did it grant them municipal citizenship. In addition, it is clear from the correspondence between Fr. Piattoli and the king that the two men realized that the proposal was encountering serious opposition. Fr. Piattoli suggested to the king that a direct approach to Kołłątaj might bear fruit in that he might be able to win over the burgher representatives to support the bill by showing them that it would not adversely affect their interests. As a result, on 13 January Kołłątaj was appointed chairman of the Jewish committee, which was enlarged by the co-option of four additional members.

The apparent successes of the Jewish lobbyists alarmed the burghers. Jan Leszkiewicz, the mayor of Kraków, sent a letter to the representative of the towns of the Kraków region, Jan Jagielski. He instructed him to get in touch at once with the other representatives of the towns to initiate a joint action 'so that the Jews should on no account be given municipal citizenship and domicile or be allowed to carry on handicrafts and trade, but should remain in their separate distinct settlements and practise handicrafts and trade there with restricted freedom'.[63]

The burgher representatives succeeded in winning the support of Świtkowski, the editor of *Pamiętnik Historyczno-Polityczny*. In a pamphlet entitled *Życzenia patriotyczne względem reformy Żydów* (Patriotic Wishes with Regard to the Reform of the Jews) he asserted: 'To give them civic rights would mean the destruction of the burghers' rights and instead of elevating the position of the royal towns, which are now prospering, would completely devastate them.'[64]

Given the opposition of the burgher representatives, Fr. Piattoli now tried a new tack. In a memorandum to the king of 17 January 1792 he suggested that Stanisław make a direct approach to the representatives of the Warsaw city council. They should be told that the king 'has undertaken negotiations with the Jews in order to conclude a sensible agreement which would produce harmony between the burghers' rights on the one hand and the rights of humanity and the interests of the state on the other'.[65]

This did not succeed. The burghers' representatives could not be won over. Indeed, they now succeeded in having several of their number co-opted to the Jewish committee. When the bill was discussed in the enlarged committee, the articles ensuring religious toleration and granting citizenship to Jews came under strong attack. Fr. Piattoli was provoked to describe the amendments put forward by the burghers' representatives as 'dictated by prejudice and hatred, in brief, by the old ideas'.[66]

[62] *MDSC* vi. 318.

[63] *MDSC* vi. 409. See also Eisenbach, *Z dziejów ludności żydowskiej w Polsce w XVIII i XIX wieku*, 80–9.

[64] *MDSC* vi. 410–11.

[65] Piattoli to the king, 17 Jan. 1792, in *MDSC* vi. 318.

[66] Piattoli to the king, 23 Jan. 1792, in *MDSC* vi. 321.

Fr. Piattoli, frustrated in his hope for a major act of legislation, now decided to attempt to introduce a more moderate reform, which would also impose new taxes on the *kehilot*. Early in February, after talks with Fr. Piattoli, the Jewish representatives signed a declaration supporting the revised proposal, which they hoped would guarantee to the Jews

> the integrity of our religion, admission to state citizenship, practice of trade, the right to open factories and craft workshops and practise handicrafts, as well as freedom and the protection of the law over all the Jewish people as it is accorded to all the free inhabitants on Polish soil and all the freedom, without exception, enjoyed by Christians.[67]

However, what was no longer included in the proposal was the freedom to settle and buy property in royal towns and to enjoy the same rights and freedoms as burghers.

In a later version of the bill Fr. Piattoli reintroduced a clause on citizenship which specified vaguely that 'this people may obtain state citizenship'. It was to confer on Jews the right to settle and buy property in free towns and to carry on economic activity in both towns and villages. Furthermore, it was clearly stated that 'we want this people not to differ from or be an exception to all the inhabitants of our states'.[68]

A quid pro quo was expected from the Jewish representatives and was duly forthcoming in the form of a special contribution which would be taken from the revenues of the Jewish courts or from the fees charged in the kosher slaughter of cattle. This was to amount to 5 million zlotys annually, of which 1.5 million would go to the king, 2.5 million to the treasury, 500,000 to the needs of the army, and 500,000 to the settlement of *kehilah* debts. In advance of the passing of the bill, a promissory note for this sum was given to the king in January 1792.[69]

Under the circumstances, pressure was brought to bear on the Jewish committee to come up with an acceptable bill. It now proposed an 'Arrangement for the Jewish People throughout the Polish Nation'. This came much closer to what was acceptable to the burghers. 'State citizenship' was no longer to be granted to the Jews, who were only to be permitted to settle in those free towns in which they had already been conceded the right of domicile. Only here would they be allowed to purchase property, and engage in trade, handicrafts, and other economic activity. Here, too, propertied Jews could be granted municipal rights, but 'without the prerogatives of active citizenship', which meant that a Jew could neither be elected nor elect others to municipal office.[70]

In spite of the concessions to burgher opinion, the bill encountered strong opposition. On 2 May 1792 the king turned to the marshal of the Sejm for assistance in securing its passage. He explained that what was proposed did not

[67] *MDSC* vi. 392–5.

[68] 'Reforma Żydów', in *MDSC* vi. 486–91.

[69] *MDSC* vi. 347–55; for the declarations of the Jewish representatives, pp. 391–6. For their activitiy, see also Kalinka, *Ostatnie lata panowania Stanisława Augusta*, ii. 282.

[70] *MDSC* vi. 492–515.

conflict with the interests of the Polish nation and that if the legislation was not passed 'an intolerable burden would oppress my soul and blacken my name'.[71]

The committee continued to work on the bill in the first half of May. Małachowski was now lobbied from both sides. Fr. Piattoli explained to him that it was in the interest of the country to secure the extra millions which would be contributed to the state treasury. More important than financial considerations was 'the happiness of a million people' (the Jews). Kołłątaj, for his part, was now well aware that the bill did not possess sufficient parliamentary support to pass and was concerned to show that he had done what he could to assist its enactment. He explained to the marshal that he 'had been implored to speak on behalf of the Jewish proposal' and that the virtue of the bill was that it would 'relieve the king from debt'. At the very least, the bill should be given a reading in the Sejm. If it were rejected, 'at least, this will not be our fault'. In the event, when Jezierski and Kołłątaj submitted the bill to the Sejm on 29 May 1792, the last day on which it sat, their opponents shouted it down.[72]

As it became apparent that the bill had no chance of being passed, the Jewish representatives sought to secure their goals in a different way. Around 20 or 21 May they sent a memorandum to the Police Commission (whose powers had been established by the Sejm in June 1791 and which constituted an embryo Ministry of the Interior). The Jews had some hope of redress from the Police Commission because, according to article 5, section 7, of the bill, defining its responsibilities, it was laid down that the commission would 'abolish all monopolies, bribery, and privileges and will guarantee every man, whatever his estate, nationality, or religion, freedom to practise any trade, handicraft, or art without hindrance and without payment, with the exception of the taxes of the Commonwealth'. Section 8 affirmed that the commission would guarantee freedom of trade and industry.

The Jewish memorandum made a number of recommendations for safeguarding the position of the Jews in the royal towns. Disputes between Jews should be dealt with not by the municipal authorities but by civil or military commissions or noble courts; Jews should not be burdened with excessive taxation or with demands to billet soldiers; they should be allowed to employ Christian servants and farmhands; the whole Jewish population should be under the protection of the government.[73]

The Police Commission was not sympathetic to Jewish demands. It upheld the principle that the Jews were now to be subject to municipal jurisdiction. It did concede that, in accordance with the new constitution, Jews like all other people were entitled to protection under the legal principle *neminem captivabimus nisi jure victum*. This vague assurance did not satisfy the Jewish representatives, and at the beginning of June the delegates from Wielkopolska, Małopolska, and Mazovia appealed to the king-in-council to consider a number of requests. These included

[71] *MDSC* vi. 335. [72] Smoleński, *Ostatni rok Sejmu wielkiego*, 406.
[73] For the petition and the reply of the Police Commission, see ibid. 405.

requests that they be exempted from municipal jurisdiction and excessive taxation, and that the Jews be allowed to make a financial contribution in lieu of supplying young men for auxiliary military service. The council examined the petition, but did not make any recommendations and referred the matter to the Police and Military commissions.[74]

By now events were moving very fast, and any further action on Jewish reform was forestalled by the crisis which culminated in the second partition and the Kościuszko rebellion. The events of the previous four years had caused an unprecedented political mobilization among the Jews, and a Jewish committee had been established in Warsaw, by analogy with a similar burgher committee, to support the new constitution. It is thus not surprising that of all the Polish insurrections this was the one which received most Jewish support. Kościuszko himself appealed for Jewish (as well as for peasant) backing. He spoke in the synagogue in Kazimierz at the beginning of the revolt, expressing his sympathy for Jewish aspirations. Shortly afterwards, in the market square in Kraków, he declared: 'Honoured Gentlemen, everyone is equal when it comes to defence of the Commonwealth and therefore the Jew, the peasant, the nobleman, the priest, and the burgher have the same respect from me.'[75]

Little was done during the short period of the revolt to introduce new legislation in relation to the Jews, and the ticket tax which Jews who wished to stay overnight in Warsaw were compelled to pay was not rescinded.

Nevertheless, Jews made a major financial contribution to the rebellion, particularly in Warsaw. They were called up for military service and to build fortifications, and also participated in the citizens' militia. In addition, a Jewish light cavalry regiment was raised under Berek Joselewicz, who had been in France during the revolution as a merchant and army purveyor with his patron Bishop Ignacy Massalski and had returned to Poland–Lithuania in 1789 imbued with revolutionary idealism. Joselewicz was given the rank of colonel by Kościuszko himself. After his regiment was decimated in the defence of Praga against the Russians in November 1794, Joselewicz emigrated to Galicia and subsequently to Italy, where he entered the Polish legion of Henryk Dąbrowski. Following the creation of the Duchy of Warsaw, Joselewicz joined its army and was granted the rank of squadron leader. For his services he was awarded the Cross Virtuti Militari. He died in a clash with Austrian forces near Kock on 5 May 1809.[76]

74 'Prośba delegatów żydowskich z trzech prowincji do króla w Straży', in *MDSC* vi. 515–16.

75 Ringelblum, 'Dzieje zewnętrzne Żydów w dawnej Rzeczypospolitej', 75.

76 Bałaban (ed.), *Księga pamiątkowa ku czci Berka Joselewicza pułkownika wojsk polskich w 125-letnią rocznicę jego bohaterskiej śmierci (1809–1934)*; Ringelblum, *Polish Jews and the Kościuszko Uprising, 1794* (Yid.); Tomaszewski (ed.), *Żydzi w obronie Rzeczypospolitej*; Goldberg, *Jewish Society in the Polish–Lithuanian Commonwealth* (Heb.), 277–88; Gierowski, 'The Jews in the Kościuszko Insurrection'; Bauer, *Wojsko koronne powstania kościuszkowskiego*, 231–3; Anich, *Vosstanie i voina 1794 goda v litovskoi provintsii*.

CONCLUSION

The failure to pass a law regulating the position of the Jews during the Four Year Sejm had a number of causes. These included the unremitting hostility of the burghers and the relative weakness of those sectors of the Jewish community who favoured integration into wider society. Probably the bulk of Polish Jewry would have been satisfied with the preservation of their long-established legal and social position if this could have been achieved, perhaps with some small alleviation of the restrictions on Jewish residence. Some of the noble supporters of an enlargement of Jewish rights such as Jacek Jezierski were also probably more interested in restraining the influence of the burghers than in increasing that of the Jews. In addition, the radical political changes of the period after 1788 aroused much conservative noble opposition. The same people who saw the constitution of 3 May 1791 as a subversion of the long-established constitutional order of Poland–Lithuania were also against any changes in the traditional paternalistic relationship between themselves and the Jews on their estates. As Fr. Piattoli wrote to Kołłątaj in January 1792, 'Our most important and at the same time most difficult object which we have to deal with in the "Jewish project" is how to maintain those rights which nobles think are their right over the members of this nation who live on their estates.'[77]

An example of these views, in this case those of the governor of Lublin province Kajetan Hryniewiecki, can be found in the pamphlet he published in early 1790 in response to Butrymowicz's pamphlet. Hryniewiecki started by rejecting Butrymowicz's call to expel the Jews from the villages on the grounds that this was a prerogative of the nobility. It was anyway undesirable since it would lead to the collapse of the brewing and distilling industries. Fifty thousand people would be needed to staff the taverns in the countryside. Germans might be found in Wielkopolska and Mazovia, but in eastern Małopolska and Ruthenia there was no alternative to the Jews; serfs could not be used since they would drink the liquor themselves, and other Christian innkeepers could not be found. An end to the lease of taverns and other leases would so undermine the income of the nobility that they would be unable to pay taxes. Driving the Jews out would not solve the problem of drunkenness among peasants and would impoverish a large section of the Jewish community, which would be dependent on the charity of Jewish town dwellers, who were in no position to provide such assistance.[78]

However, the archaic world described by Hryniewiecki was clearly passing. The lands of Poland–Lithuania were set on the painful path of modernization, with inevitable consequences for its large Jewish population. In the attempts of subsequent decades to transform the Jewish population the experience of the reign of Stanisław was not to be forgotten, particularly since a number of the

[77] *MDSC* vi. 400. [78] *MDSC* vi. 153–68.

prominent members of the Patriot Party, among them Stanisław Staszic, were to play an important role in the political life of both the Duchy of Warsaw and the Kingdom of Poland. For the acculturating Jewish minority, and indeed for the community as a whole, the experiences of these years, both good and bad, were also to condition their subsequent responses to calls for the 'reform' of the Jews.

SEVEN

THE JEWS IN THE PRUSSIAN PARTITION OF POLAND, 1772–1870

THE HISTORY OF THE JEWS in the Prussian partition does not bulk large in Jewish collective memory, yet it is important for a number of reasons. This was the first area in the lands of the former Polish–Lithuanian Commonwealth where Jews achieved civil emancipation. Almost all restrictions on Jewish activity were done away with in the run-up to the revolution of 1848, and the remainder were abolished in 1869. It is generally held that integration—the transformation of the Jews into citizens of the respective countries where they lived, as Englishmen, Frenchmen, or Poles of the Mosaic faith—did not succeed on the Polish lands. However, by the middle of the nineteenth century most Jews in Prussian Poland did regard themselves as Germans of the Mosaic faith.[1]

A second reason for the importance of the Prussian partition in the history of Polish Jewry is that Berlin, the capital of Prussia, was the principal source of the Haskalah, the Jewish Enlightenment. It was primarily from Prussian Poland that the influence of the Haskalah spread to the rest of Poland (although one should not ignore the influence of the Seitenstettengasse synagogue in Vienna). Abraham Meir Goldschmidt (1812–89), the first preacher in the 'reformed' synagogue on Daniłowiczowska Street in Warsaw, came from Krotoszyn, in Prussian Poland. His successor, Marcus Mordecai Jastrow (1829–1903), came from Rogoźno and was educated in the Protestant (German) gymnasium in Poznań.

The success of the Haskalah has been attributed to the weakness of hasidism in this area. This has sometimes been explained as a result of the fact that the region was not affected by the Cossack rebellions of the mid-seventeenth and eighteenth centuries. Rabbinic authority may also have been better preserved there. Certainly what this meant was that, unlike the situation in the other areas of Poland–Lithuania, the hasidic alternative to rabbinic traditionalism, which was so effective in opposing the educational projects of the Haskalah elsewhere, was absent.

[1] On the history of the area, see Lowenstein, 'The Shifting Boundary between Eastern and Western Jewry'; Jersch-Wenzel, 'Zur Geschichte der jüdischen Bevölkerung in der Provinz Posen im 19. Jahrhundert'; Kemlein, *Die Posener Juden 1815–1848*; ead., 'Zur Geschichte der Juden in Westpreussen und Danzig (bis 1943)'; and Makowski, *Siła mitu*. There is a useful study of the development of Poznań in the 19th century by Alvis, *Religion and the Rise of Nationalism*.

Jews from Prussian Poland played an important role in German Jewish history. The area became a sort of Alsace-Lorraine for German Jews, a reservoir of more traditional and, in some ways, more nationally conscious Jews. Among those who came from this part were leading figures in Jewish studies such as Heinrich Graetz, Ismar Elbogen, and Eugen Taubler, the politicians Raphael Korsch and Eduard Lasker, religious figures such as the cantor Louis Lewandowski, responsible for the creation of the liturgy of Prussian Jewry, and Rabbi Leo Baeck, the Zionist activist Arthur Ruppin, and writers and historians such as Maximilian Harden, Ernst Hartwig Kantorowicz, and Ernst Jaffe.

PRUSSIA AND THE JEWS

Some knowledge of the history of the Prussian state is necessary if one is to understand the context in which the integration of the Jews in Prussian Poland took place. The rise of Prussia is one of the major themes of European history in the early modern period. Created out of one of the smaller German electorates, that of Brandenburg, and the remnants of the state of the Teutonic Knights, which had been compelled to do homage to Poland in 1525, Prussia established itself as one of the principal European states at the Treaty of Westphalia, which brought an end to the Thirty Years War in 1648.[2]

The founder of the country's power was Frederick William (r. 1640–88), the Great Elector. It was he who created a single administrative machine out of the military supply organization (Kriegskommissariat). His successor, Frederick I (r. 1688–1713), completed the administrative unification of the various parts of the state and established a single military and bureaucratic system. It was he who, for the first time, styled himself 'king in Prussia'. The power of the Prussian state continued to increase under his successors, Frederick William I (r. 1713–40) and, even more, Frederick the Great (r. 1740–86), who described himself in classic enlightened fashion as the 'first servant of the state'. It was Frederick the Great's ruthless pursuit of Prussian interests which led him to play a major role in the first partition of Poland.

Under Frederick William II (r. 1786–97) the country further extended its rule over much of Poland, including Warsaw. The over-centralized and autocratic nature of Prussia led to its devastating defeat in the battles of Jena and Auerstadt at the hands of Napoleon in 1806. By the Treaty of Tilsit the country was cut back to very narrow boundaries and lost almost all the Polish territory it had acquired from the partitions. The shock of defeat led to a major administrative reform, encouraged by Frederick William III (r. 1797–1840), which paved the way for

[2] For a good account of the tangled relations between Royal and Ducal Prussia and the Polish–Lithuanian Commonwealth, see Stone, *The Polish–Lithuanian State, 1386–1795*, and Friedrich, *The Other Prussia*.

Prussia's successful participation in the anti-Napoleonic coalition and its eventual victory at the battle of Waterloo in 1815.

Prussia was considerably enlarged at the Congress of Vienna in order to provide a check to a potential French revival, and gained important territories in the Rhineland, in western Germany. Under Frederick William IV (r. 1840–61) the country weathered the storm of the 1848 revolution but refused to place itself at the head of the German revolution, an offer scornfully rejected by the king with the phrase 'I will not stoop to pick a crown out of the gutter'. His successor, William I (r. 1861–88), and his redoubtable chancellor Otto von Bismarck used the military and economic power of Prussia to exclude Austria from Germany and to unite the remainder of the German lands under Prussian hegemony between 1864 and 1870.

Like Poland, Prussia was an estate society. The dominant position in society was held by the landed Junker class, who ruled over an unfree peasantry in a country with very few, economically insignificant towns. Yet there were important differences between the political organization of Prussia and Poland. The Prussian monarchy was much stronger than its equivalent in Poland, and its power was increased by the tradition of submissiveness to authority inculcated by the dominant Lutheran Church. The series of highly able electors and kings who ruled the country in the second half of the seventeenth and the eighteenth centuries succeeded in creating effective governmental institutions, a powerful army, and an effective civil service. The system was, however, still rigid and over-centralized, and political office was monopolized by the Junkers, weaknesses which became obvious in the confrontation with Napoleon.

Although the Prussian state was based on Lutheran principles, its rulers were among the earliest to accept that service to the state should be used as a criterion for assessing the worth of subjects. As a consequence, immigrants, including French Huguenots and Hungarian Protestants, were encouraged to settle in Prussia. The question of Jewish settlement was also scrutinized from the perspective of their value to the state. This point of view was evident in the Revised General Code of Frederick the Great enacted in 1750, which made a distinction between a more privileged group of 'protected' Jews and one that was merely 'tolerated'. Each group was subdivided. The small group of 'generally protected' Jews could settle in the area set aside for Jews with a special permit. They enjoyed the same rights as Christians and could also, in exceptional cases, acquire citizenship and pass their rights on to their children. 'Ordinary protected Jews' did not have the right to choose their place of residence, and their status could only be passed on to one of their children. 'Exceptional protected Jews' were permitted rights of residence only if they performed 'useful' functions, as physicians, opticians, painters, engravers, and members of similar occupations. A member of this class was allowed to bring one child with him provided the child had assets of at least 1,000 thalers. The privileged group was entitled to employ Jewish servants and to have at their disposal community functionaries, including rabbis. Tolerated Jews could only obtain the right of residence if they had the patronage of a protected Jew. Also included in this group were the children of protected Jews who could not inherit their father's status. Jews were not permitted to engage in occupations which might involve competition with burghers, including smelting gold and silver, the sale of cattle or hides except for their own use, the sale of wool, alcohol production except for kosher wines, and curing tobacco. They were permitted to deal in precious stones and metals, in luxury clothing, in horses, furs, wax and honey, tea, coffee, chocolate, snuff, and goods imported from Poland. They were obliged to pay a special tax in return for their exemption from military service and had to supply a quota of silver to the mint.[3]

In spite of these restrictions, a small group of prosperous court Jews developed in Berlin by the second half of the eighteenth century, including Scholim Pless, Daniel Itzig, and David Friedländer. Between 1798 and 1809 seven such families were naturalized. Linked with this group was a circle of acculturated Jews who had studied at German Protestant universities. It was in this environment that Moses Mendelssohn had established himself and created around him a group of like-minded Jews.[4]

JEWS IN THE AREAS INCORPORATED BY PRUSSIA AS A RESULT OF THE PARTITIONS

Prussia acquired relatively few Jews as a result of the first partition. The towns of Pomerania, which was then annexed, had enjoyed the privilege *de non tolerandis Judaeis* from the times of the rule of the Teutonic Knights. As a result there were only between 10,000 and 25,000 Jews in the new territories, mainly in the Netze district. Frederick instructed the governor of the area that 'the impoverished Jews in the countryside must be got rid of, one by one and without violence, [but] the well-to-do commercial Jews . . . are to be kept and engaged in trade with Poland'. By his death some 7,000 Jews had been expelled into the territories still under the control of Poland–Lithuania and further expulsions were planned, but these were halted by his successor on the grounds that they were neither humane nor feasible.[5]

The situation changed radically as a consequence of the second and third partitions. Prussia now acquired extensive Polish territories, including Warsaw, the former Polish capital. The Prussian view of their new Jewish subjects, who numbered between 125,000 and 150,000, was well summed up by the minister responsible for South Prussia, Otton Karl von Voss, in mid-1795: 'Jews in South

[3] On these regulations, see Breuer, 'The Jewish Minority in the Enlightened Absolutist State', 148–9, and Baumgart, 'Die Stellung der jüdischen Minorität im Staat des aufgeklärten Absolutismus'.

[4] On the court Jews, see Stern, *The Court Jew*, and Carsten, 'The Court Jews'.

[5] Hagen, *Germans, Poles, and Jews*, 46–7.

Prussia are more cultured than burghers in smaller towns and the peasantry. These considerations alone necessitate a different treatment of Jewish matters than in the old provinces, since in my view this nation is able to improve itself, and its members could become useful citizens of the state.'[6]

The position of the Jews was accordingly regulated on 11 April 1797 by a General Statute for the Jews of South and New East Prussia which was part of the attempt of the Prussian state to dismantle the Jewish corporate self-government which had characterized the Polish–Lithuanian Commonwealth. The decree reflected the Enlightenment desire to transform the Jews into 'useful' citizens through extensive state involvement in their affairs. It laid down that they were to be treated as a separate estate, a corporation not yet ready to avail itself of the municipal or state rights of citizens. Jewish autonomy was restricted to matters of religion, rabbinical jurisdiction was abolished, and rabbis henceforth were only to be admitted to court proceedings as experts when religious issues were raised. The election of the *kehilah* administration was abolished, and the municipal magistrates were to appoint Jewish officials to administer their communities under the control of the magistrates. In addition, the legislation aimed to end the Jews' intermediary role in the countryside and concentrate them in towns since their influence on the peasantry was held to be harmful. Jews were also to be encouraged to take up 'useful' occupations like farming and artisanry. They were required to adopt surnames and have a permanent place of residence and an occupation. These formalities had to be complied with to obtain state permission to marry.[7]

These drastic measures aroused significant Jewish opposition and led to a meeting of the regional Jewish communal body in Kleczew, which petitioned the king to modify their stringency.[8] As a result, many of the economic provisions were relaxed and Jews were allowed to engage freely in trade and handicrafts, in farming, in transport and other services, and in some liberal professions. In addition, they were aided by the abolition of guild restrictions. The *kehilot* also continued to function and to be elected as under Polish rule. The Prussian state did not yet have the ability to organize efficiently the taxation of the Jews in the new territories and was thus compelled to retain for a period the Polish practice according to which the Jews were assessed for special taxes which they administered themselves. As in Prussia generally, Jews also paid some other specifically Jewish taxes, including a provision tax to pay for the army since they were exempt from military service, and a 'toleration' tax and a ticket tax to enable them to remain in Warsaw.

The Prussian authorities refused to accede to the Jewish request that in legal matters Jews should not be subject to the civil courts. They made one exception to

[6] Quoted in Kemlein, *Die Posener Juden 1815–1848* (Polish edn.), 50–1.

[7] For this law, see Rönne and Simon, *Die früheren und gegenwärtigen Verhältnisse der Juden in den sämmtlichen Landestheilen des Preussischen Staates*, 292–302.

[8] L. Lewin, 'Ein Judentag aus Süd- und Neuostpreussen'.

this in the city of Poznań, where the community was granted its own court, organized as a royal tribunal, although with a government-appointed non-Jewish judge and a non-Jewish clerk, who had to be paid from the community's funds. In fact when the new municipal court began to operate in Poznań, its impartiality so impressed the local Jewish community that in 1802 the *kahal* asked the authorities to abolish the Jewish court, a request which the authorities rejected.[9] Jews in Poznań were accustomed to the hostility of the local municipality; they were therefore surprised in the following year when, after a disastrous fire, the authorities allowed Jews to settle anywhere in the city.[10]

Prussian rule also led to increased settlement of Jews in Warsaw itself, where the burghers were now less able to implement restrictions on such immigration. Among the Prussian Jews who moved to Warsaw was the founder of the 'reformed' synagogue established on Daniłowiczowska Street, Isaac Flatau, who was born in Złotów and lived in Danzig, and a number of key figures in the Warsaw banking community. Their presence in Warsaw and their identification with Prussian rule led to an anti-Jewish riot on the eve of Corpus Christi, 16 June 1805.

THE EMANCIPATION OF THE JEWS IN PRUSSIA

The emancipation of the Jews in the areas which remained part of the Prussian state after the Treaty of Tilsit in July 1807 was the result of a major attempt to reorganize the Prussian state and to rectify the defects in its structure which had been exposed by its defeat at Napoleon's hands. The reform movement, which was headed by the ministers Friedrich Stein and Karl August von Hardenberg, aimed to transform the estate character of Prussia and end the social hegemony of the Junkers.

A start was made on the emancipation of the serfs, but this was to prove a slow process because of the bureaucracy's desire to protect the position of the landed classes. It was not finally accomplished until the 1820s and it led to the characteristic three-tier structure of Prussian agriculture in the areas east of the river Elbe: the preservation of the position of the landed aristocracy, the emergence of a class of prosperous peasants, and the dependence of the system on a reservoir of landless agricultural labourers. The situation of the towns was also transformed. They were made self-governing, ruled by their citizens, and a uniform system of taxation was introduced which abolished the privileged taxation status of the nobles and the clergy. The end result of these reforms was the emergence of a new social order, which, while it left the nobility with important privileges, also created the foundations for the establishment of a civil society based on common citizenship and the rule of law.

9 Bloch, 'Judenwesen', 600 n. 3.

10 Jaffe, *Die Stadt Posen unter preussischer Herrschaft*, 56 ff., 73 ff.

It was these developments which paved the way for the emancipation of the Jews, a draft for which was prepared by State Minister Leopold von Schrötter on the instructions of Frederick William III and which led to substantial debate within the Prussian bureaucracy. The final version was prepared by Hardenberg and enacted in the law of 11 March 1812. This annulled all restrictions on Jews living in Prussia; they were henceforth to be regarded as native residents and state citizens and no longer treated as aliens. They were granted formal legal equality with other citizens, with the freedom to settle anywhere in the state, choose any trade, and purchase any type of property, including landed property. The special taxes paid by Jews were abolished and they remained liable only for the assessments of the *kahal*, which retained its charitable and religious functions but without any sanctions of its own. Jews were also now liable for military service, and the obligation to serve in the army was to be 'laid down in detail in an ordinance on military conscription' (article 16). The law did not introduce complete legal equality for the Jews. According to paragraph 9 the king reserved 'the right to set down in law at a future date the extent to which the Jews shall be admitted to public services and state offices', effectively barring Jews from most civil service positions.[11]

JEWS IN PRUSSIAN POLAND AFTER 1815

One of the most disputed issues at the Congress of Vienna was the future of the Polish lands. Alexander I hoped to incorporate into the tsarist empire all the territories which had been part of the Duchy of Warsaw established by Napoleon. This was strongly resisted, not only by Prussia, which hoped to regain some of the lands which it had lost at the Treaty of Tilsit, but also by the British, who were fearful of the growth of Russian power. In the event, the Prussians, who had retained Pomerania and Danzig throughout this period, were also given the Grand Duchy of Poznań (Posen) with certain guarantees for the rights of the Polish majority there. The Prussian state also included Silesia, which had passed from Polish sovereignty in the fourteenth century, first to the Czechs, then to the Habsburgs, and finally to Prussia in the middle of the eighteenth century after the War of the Austrian Succession.

The bulk of the Jewish population of Prussian Poland lived in the Grand Duchy of Poznań (see Map 5). In Pomerania there were only 2,809 Jews in 1816, although their number here increased in the nineteenth century, particularly in the port of Danzig. Prussian Upper Silesia was not thought of as Polish until much later in the nineteenth century. Its Jewish population in 1816 was 16,100.[12]

[11] On the Emancipation Edict, see Freund, *Die Emanzipation der Juden in Preussen unter besonderer Berücksichtigung des Gesetzes vom 11. März 1812*, i. 165, ii. 455–9, and Jersch-Wenzel, 'The Prussian Edict of 1812'.

[12] Paprocki, *Wielkie Księstwo Poznańskie w okresie rządów Flottwella 1830–1841*, 175.

The Grand Duchy of Poznań was an ethnically mixed area. In 1816 it had a population of 776,000, which rose to 1.1 million by 1831, of which 64 per cent were Poles and the remainder Germans and Jews. The percentage of Poles had fallen by 1871 to 57 per cent but had risen again by 1910 to 62 per cent. In 1816 the Jews, who then numbered 52,000, made up 6.7 per cent of the population and constituted 42 per cent of the Jewish population of Prussia. Their numbers rose in the first half of the nineteenth century, reaching nearly 80,000 in 1837. They then declined gradually, largely as a result of emigration to the Kingdom of Poland, the interior of Germany, and the United States, falling to under 27,000 in 1910. By this stage they constituted only 6.4 per cent of the Jews in Prussia. (See Table 7.1.)[13]

Table 7.1 The Jewish population of the Grand Duchy of Poznań, 1816–1871

Year	No.	% of whole population
1816	51,959	6.7
1821	59,723	—
1827	65,100	6.5
1837	80,000	—
1849	76,757	5.7
1871	62,000	3.9

Sources: Schiper, 'Żydzi pod zaborem pruskim'; Köllmann, 'Bevölkerungsgeschichte 1800–1920'.

The Jews were overwhelmingly urban. In 1816, 97 per cent of them lived in towns. These towns were, however, quite small. In that year Jews were to be found in one town with a population of over 10,000 (Poznań), thirteen medium-sized towns (3,000–10,000 inhabitants), and seventeen small towns (under 3,000 inhabitants). In fact, Jews were to be found in most towns of the province: in the first half of the nineteenth century they made up nearly a fifth of the urban population and in some smaller towns constituted as much as half of the population. The Jewish communities were small: nearly half of the Jews of the province lived in communities with less than 1,000 members. By 1848 the largest community—that in Poznań—numbered 7,359, only slightly less than in Berlin, where there were 8,348 Jews. Table 7.2 shows the distribution of the province's Jews in 1842–3.

The province remained largely agricultural throughout the nineteenth century. Only two cities had more than 10,000 inhabitants in 1849: Poznań (39,000 not including members of the military) and Bydgoszcz (13,000). The smaller towns stagnated. The non-Jewish urban population was more or less equally

[13] For these figures, Kemlein, *Die Posener Juden 1815–1848* (Polish edn.), 61–6, and Schiper, 'Żydzi pod zaborem pruskim (1772–1807, 1815–1918)'.

Table 7.2 Distribution of the Jewish population of the Grand Duchy of Poznań, 1842–1843

Size of community	**No. of communities**	**No. of members**	**% of Jewish population**
>2,000	5	18,949	25
1,001–2,000	15	21,807	28
501–1,000	26	19,488	25
201–500	41	12,669	16
<200	36	4,526	6
TOTAL	123	77,439	100

Source: Kemlein, *Die Posener Juden, 1815–1848* (Polish edn.), 65.

divided between Germans and Poles, with Germans occupying the higher positions in the social hierarchy.[14]

Prussian politics in the Grand Duchy was determined by three factors: the obligation under the Vienna settlement to maintain the 'special' (Polish) character of the area, the desire to modify the society of the Duchy on the lines of what was taking place in the rest of Prussia and shift it from an 'estate' to a civil society, and the hope that the province could be Germanized, which was felt to be implicit in the goal of ending its estate character. The principal concession to the Polish character of the province was the establishment of a local Sejm in 1823, similar to the assemblies to be found in other Prussian provinces. It met for the first time on 24 December 1827 and was made up of forty-four elected deputies and four nobles, who sat by virtue of their position. Of the members of this first Sejm, twenty-two were Poles and twenty-six Germans. Its functions were, however, only advisory, and the electoral system was organized to keep down the number of Poles. In the Sejm of 1845, for instance, there were twenty-five Poles and twenty-five Germans, and in that of 1854 there were seventeen Poles and thirty-three Germans.[15]

In order to move the area away from an estate society the Prussian government applied over quite a lengthy period the Prussian legislation of 1811 abolishing serfdom. In 1831 it also passed a law reforming the government of the towns on the lines of the changes which had already been introduced into Prussia east of the Elbe. These changes went along with attempts to strengthen the German character of the area, which aroused Polish resentment and occasioned a protest from the Sejm in 1830.

The Jewish policies of the Prussian authorities should be seen in the context of their broader goals. Thus, although the Emancipation Edict of 1812 was not applied to the province, the Jews were seen as a key element in the trade and industry of this largely agricultural region, an element which should be encouraged. As a result the Jews, who made up about 40 per cent of the traders and 15 per

[14] Bartys, 'The Grand Duchy of Poznań under Prussian Rule'.

[15] On these developments, see Wąsicki, *Ziemie polskie pod zaborem pruskim*.

cent of the artisans of the area, were explicitly permitted to engage in trade, crafts, arable farming, animal husbandry, and carting. They were subject to the earlier Prussian regulations requiring them to have a fixed place of residence and a settled occupation, and to take a surname. Commercial accounts were now to be kept in German or Polish and could no longer be recorded in Hebrew characters. Public schools were established for Jews, in which the language of instruction could be German or Polish. In addition, in accordance with the principles of the Berlin Haskalah, a new manual on the teaching of the Jewish religion for these schools was to be compiled in the German language, which would stress the obligations of Jews to their fellow subjects and towards 'the territory of the sovereign'. Jews were still compelled to carry documentary proof of their right of residence and remained subject to a number of special taxes. These regulations certainly constituted an advance on the situation of the Jews in the Polish–Lithuanian Commonwealth, although many found burdensome the increased surveillance of the civic authorities and the limitations on Jewish autonomy imposed by the regulations of 1797.[16]

There was an inherent contradiction in the approach of the Prussian government in its general policies towards the Jews after 1815 which also affected the situation in the Grand Duchy. On the one hand, it intervened actively in Jewish life in order to integrate the Jews. On the other, the reactionary principles which dominated the early post-Napoleonic years meant that integration of the Jews into the larger population was regarded as undesirable, and, accordingly, local authorities were instructed to avoid involvement in internal Jewish affairs, intervening only when public order was threatened. This meant that the *kehilot*, which were legally voluntary organizations, could not count on the state to support them in compelling their members to pay communal taxes, which caused a drastic deterioration in their financial situation.[17] By 1832 the situation was so bad in Leszno, the second largest Jewish community in the province, that all land and buildings owned by the *kehilah* had to be auctioned, including the cemetery, the synagogue, and the bathhouse.[18]

The growing financial crisis of the *kehilot* led the Prussian authorities to adopt a more radical policy towards the Jews of the Grand Duchy, which took the form of the Provisional Regulation on the Status of the Jews in the Grand Duchy of Poznań, issued on 1 June 1833.[19] Like the earlier legislation of Frederick the

[16] On these developments, see Eisenbach, *The Emancipation of the Jews in Poland, 1780–1870*, 198–200; Kemlein, *Die Posener Juden 1815–1848* (Polish edn.), 77–124; and Jersch-Wenzel, 'Juden zwischen Germanisierung und Polonisierung im 19. Jahrhundert in Posen'.

[17] Letter of Oberpräsident (Governor) Flottwell to Secretary of the Interior Brenn, 5 Oct. 1832, Geheimes Staatsarchiv, Berlin, I. HA, Rep. 90, no. 33, fos. 168–71, quoted in Kemlein, 'The Jewish Community in the Grand Duchy of Poznań under Prussian Rule, 1815–1848', 57.

[18] Heppner and Herzberg, *Aus Vergangenheit und Gegenwart der Juden und der jüdischen Gemeinden in den Posener Landen*, 600. The real estate was purchased by a Jew and given back to the community.

[19] Text in Rönne and Simon, *Die früheren und gegenwärtigen Verhältnisse der Juden in den sämmtlichen Landestheilen des Preussischen Staates*, 305–9, repr. in Kemlein, *Die Posener Juden 1815–1848*, 331–7.

Great, this divided the Jews into two categories: a more privileged group of 'naturalized' Jews and the remainder of the community, who were merely 'tolerated'. In order to achieve naturalization, a Jew had to fulfil a number of conditions. He had to have a record of good conduct, demonstrate a willingness to employ only the German language in all public affairs, and adopt a surname. In addition, he had to have had a fixed place of residence in the Grand Duchy since 1815, demonstrate his ability to support himself adequately through a profession, agriculture, or 'settled trade' (i.e. peddling was excluded), or show that he possessed land worth more than 2,000 thalers or had capital of over 5,000 thalers. In exceptional cases it was possible to qualify by 'serving the state in an appropriately patriotic manner'. As an example of what was understood by this, a case could be cited from the town of Września (Wreschen). Here an applicant claimed that 'he had prevented a Prussian cavalry regiment, together with its cashbox, from falling into the hands of the enemy in 1805' and asserted that proof of his action could be found in the royal Ministry of War.[20] In this case, the request of the petitioner was not acceded to, as his wealth did not meet the requirements of the law.

Privileged Jews were a small minority. The overwhelming majority of the Jews of the province (75 per cent in the 1840s) fell into the category of tolerated individuals, and enjoyed legal protection only as members of a religious community which had corporate rights and which was subordinate to the control of the state. They were still subject to restrictions on where they could settle, could not acquire immovable property, employ Christian servants, journeymen, or apprentices, sell alcohol, engage in peddling, or undertake unregulated artisan work.

The scope of Jewish autonomy was also made more specific in this legislation, which declared that tolerated Jewish communities (*Gemeinden*) were to be organized in the towns where the Jews lived. Membership was obligatory, and although these bodies carried out religious functions, further restrictions were imposed on the role of the rabbi. What the Prussian authorities had now decided to do was to take advantage of the high level of indebtedness of the *kehilot* and the inability of the community structure to deal with this to create new institutions that would make possible the transformation of the Jews of the province.[21] The Jewish communal bodies became corporations under public law, which gave them the power to use the authority of the state to collect the contributions owed to them by their members.[22]

The *Gemeinden* were to be administered, in accordance with the revised regulations for such bodies enacted in 1831, by a board responsible to an elected representative body, whose election was to be subject to government supervision.

[20] Jacobson, 'Das Naturalisationsverzeichnis der Stadt Posen', 3.

[21] For the origins of this regulation, see Kemlein, *Die Posener Juden 1815–1848*, 96 ff.

[22] Instruction of Oberpräsident Flottwell on 14 Jan. 1834 to the royal government of Poznań and Bydgoszcz to ensure the implementation of the decree of 1 June, repr. in Rönne and Simon, *Die früheren und gegenwärtigen Verhältnisse der Juden in den sämmtlichen Landestheilen des Preussischen Staates*, 309–14.

Their authority was explicitly restricted to the internal affairs of the community, and in all other respects Jews were subject to the local municipality. This new structure imposed on the Jewish communities important new obligations, to which both the acculturated minority and the more conservative majority responded enthusiastically. There was a high turnout for the first elections held under the new law and, in contrast to later elections, there was no difficulty anywhere in mobilizing the required two-thirds of all individuals entitled to vote.[23] The hope was widespread that compliance with the new regulations would ensure that full legal equality would be granted, as was clear from the speeches made when the new representative bodies were inaugurated.[24] In these elections the Jewish reformers, who were widely held to possess the necessary skills to negotiate with the Prussian authorities, won a leading role in most communities. This was the case in Poznań and Gniezno, and in Grodzisk (Grätz) the physician Marcus Mosse, who had moved there from Lausitz in 1835, was elected leader of the corporation in the elections of 1838.[25]

The first task the boards of the *Gemeinden* were faced with was settlement of the communities' debts. This took several decades and was impeded by high Jewish emigration from the province, which reduced the tax base. By mid-century, however, the finances of almost all the *Gemeinden* had been placed on a healthy footing. This was in spite of the fact that the largest contribution to their income came from the tax on kosher meat, an indirect levy whose yield could not be calculated in advance. Paradoxically, this led to the preservation of some traditional customs, as rabbis often declared imported meat non-kosher or banned its purveyors from the local synagogue.[26]

Since the tax on kosher meat was not sufficient anywhere to meet the corporation's needs, its members were required to make additional payments, which were calculated according to income and were noted in tax rolls in accordance with a decree of the minister of the interior. Members could contest their assessments by complaining to the Prussian authorities, but the community leaders could count on the support of the police in collecting the tax.[27]

The settlement of the debt problem was crucial to the successful functioning of the *Gemeinden* given the large number of functions, both old and new, with which they were entrusted. Perhaps the most important of these was the supervision of

[23] On the elections, see Kemlein, *Die Posener Juden 1815–1848*, 110 ff.

[24] For these, see *Zeitung des Grossherzogtums Posen*, no. 84 (11 Apr. 1834); Bamberger, *Geschichte der Juden in Schönlanke*, 16; speech by Moses Veilchenfeld, 7 Jan. 1834, Archiwum Państwowe w Poznaniu (APP), Akten der Stadt Santomysl, sygn. 45, fos. 67–75; speech by the representative Liebermann Speyer, 9 Apr. 1834, APP OPP, sygn. 9013, fos. 30–8, cited in Kemlein, *Die Posener Juden 1815–1848*, 250 ff.

[25] Kemlein, *Die Posener Juden 1815–1848*, 110–11, 210 ff.; Kraus, 'Marcus Mosse', 12–13.

[26] Report of the corporate community of Rogoźno (Rogasen) on 29 Aug. 1834 and 10 July 1835, in Jacobson, *Zur Geschichte der Juden in Rogasen*, suppls.; Report of Chief Rabbi Heymann Joel (ibid.).

[27] See the letter of the Secretary of the Interior to Oberpräsident Arnim, 27 Dec. 1841, in Rönne and Simon, *Die früheren und gegenwärtigen Verhältnisse der Juden in den sämmtlichen Landestheilen des Preussischen Staates*, 323.

the German-language school system which all Jewish children from the ages of 7 to 14 were obliged to attend. At these schools both secular and religious subjects were to be taught, and the *Gemeinden* were responsible for providing textbooks and clothing for the children of indigent parents. Teachers of religion had to pass a state examination, and the *Gemeinden* were also to ensure that, after completing school, young people should be given training in a 'useful trade', so that they did not become pedlars.

The new school system was a great success. As early as 1836, of 9,039 Jewish children of school age in the Poznań district, 1,804 were attending general state schools, as against 5,777 who were attending Jewish state schools, which employed 113 teachers. These were maintained by the *kehilot* and used German as their language of instruction. In the Bydgoszcz district 911 Jewish children (out of 3,270) were attending general state schools, while the remainder were attending the seventeen Jewish schools. By 1839 there were fifty-eight Jewish elementary schools in the province, and by 1847 there were seventy-two, which were attended by 71 per cent of school-age Jewish children. (Of the rest, 23 per cent attended Christian schools and 6 per cent did not receive any instruction.[28]) Thus, the bulk of Jewish children of elementary school age were educated in a Jewish (even if modernized) environment. This was crucial for the preservation of Jewish identity in the area and had much to do with the key role of Jews from the area in German Jewish life. Since the first period of Prussian rule Jewish youths had also been attending secondary school in Poznań, where from 1834 a Catholic high school had been established alongside the already existing Protestant one.[29]

Another crucial area assigned to the *Gemeinden* was the relief of poverty, since Jewish beggars were now prohibited from moving freely about the province. The obligation to care for the poor remained, and though after 1842 the city magistrates were legally obligated to provide for the indigent regardless of religion,[30] many of them were unwilling to take on this responsibility in relation to Jews, particularly when it had a religious dimension, as in the provision of matzahs to those who could not afford them.

Traditional Jewish *ḥevrot* (societies) also continued to operate, sometimes in a modernized, reformed manner. The most important of these remained the *ḥevra kadisha* (burial society). In the Poznań district in 1843, for instance, sixty-one of the seventy-five *Gemeinden* had burial associations; only some of the smaller communities with fewer than 350 Jewish inhabitants did not have one.[31] In addition, there were more than forty other charitable organizations charged with

[28] Figures in Kemlein, *Die Posener Juden 1815–1848*, 129 and 123–4, tables 10*a*, 10*b*.

[29] Laubert, 'Zur Entwicklung des jüdischen Schulwesens in der Provinz Posen', 313.

[30] The Law Concerning the Obligation for the Welfare of the Poor, 31 Dec. 1842, Gesetzsammlung für den Preussischen Staat, 1843, no. 2318.

[31] Kemlein, 'The Jewish Community in the Grand Duchy of Poznań under Prussian Rule, 1815–1848', 62. This documentation does not exist for the government district of Bydgoszcz.

supporting the sick and the poor, as well as an orphanage and a Jewish hospital, the Latzsche Krankenanstalt in Poznań.

A number of new organizations were also created, some with traditional goals, such as the women's association for the 'support of poor widows by helping them pay for housing' in Poznań, which was founded in 1834.[32] Others saw their task as supporting modern education, often of a vocational character. These included the Association of Jewish Daughters in Poznań, a women's society 'for the promotion of poor girls' schooling and their training in feminine handicrafts',[33] and the Association for the Training of Jewish Artisans in Ostrów Wielkopolski, both established in 1845.[34]

Religious life was slower to respond to the new situation and was marked by conflict between traditionalists and those more oriented to religious reform. Paradoxically, it was easier to push through changes in liturgy and religious practice in smaller communities, where there was often no rabbi or burial society. Essentially, religious life remained for the moment in the hands of the traditionalists, with the more reform-oriented controlling the school system and the modernized Jewish societies. This created a very specific community, which has been characterized by Sophie Kemlein:

> in this transitional region between western European and eastern European Jewry, there developed a unique mixture of traditional Jewish culture of the eastern Ashkenazic type, with the *minhag Polin* (religious traditions), liturgical music, and traditional foods of the eastern European Jewry on the one hand, and the cultural patterns of the acculturated western European Jewries, with the adoption of German language, secular education, and a bourgeois culture of social clubs on the other.[35]

The years to 1848 certainly saw a major change in the social structure of the Jews of the province. Because of the strict requirements for naturalization laid down by the 1833 legislation, ten years after the law had been passed less than a fifth of Jews in the province had been naturalized (18.3 per cent).[36] Even by then, however, knowledge of the German language had become common. A transformation was also taking place in occupational structure. Whereas at the end of the eighteenth century about one-third of the local Jewish population earned their living from artisanry and two-thirds from trade, by the middle of the nineteenth century just under one-third were still traders and the remainder were to be found in the liberal professions, in the services, as rentiers, or as day labourers and

32 See the club's report of Aug. 1842, APP, Police Presidency (PPP), sygn. 4673, fos. 28–30, quoted in Kemlein, 'The Jewish Community in the Grand Duchy of Poznań under Prussian Rule, 1815–1848', 62.

33 See Statut des Jüdischen Töchtervereins of 14 Apr. 1850, APP PPP, sygn. 4673, fos. 41–8, quoted in Kemlein, 'The Jewish Community in the Grand Duchy of Poznań under Prussian Rule, 1815–1848', 63.

34 *Der Orient*, 6 (1845), no. 10 (5 Mar.), 74.

35 Kemlein, 'The Jewish Community in the Grand Duchy of Poznań under Prussian Rule, 1815–1848', 65.

36 Silbergleit, *Die Bevölkerungs- und Berufsverhältnisse der Juden im deutschen Reich*, 9.

servants. About 10 per cent could be considered as members of the financial and commercial elite, while between 75 and 80 per cent were self-employed. Although poverty had not been done away with, it was much less widespread and the community as a whole was increasingly middle-class in character, while its traditional features were still evident in the smaller towns of the province.

The character of the Jewish population was also being transformed by emigration. After the erection of customs barriers with Russia in 1820, some Jewish merchants emigrated to the Kingdom of Poland in order to avoid losing their former markets in the east. In addition, at this time there was a significant movement of Jews from smaller or economically depressed towns into prospering cities like Poznań and Bydgoszcz, or into areas such as Kościan (Kosten) and Pleszew (Pleschen) where Jewish settlement had previously been forbidden.[37]

The passage of the Provisional Regulation on the Status of the Jews in 1833 permitted naturalized Jews to apply for settlement in other Prussian provinces, and a significant number now moved, especially to the cities of Berlin and Breslau.[38] Those who had not been naturalized moved further afield. Between 1835 and 1852 some 19,000 Jews left the area; 5,000 of them settled in the other provinces of the Prussian state, most of them in Berlin, while the remainder moved to England, France, and the United States, to which by 1870 as many as 30,000 Jews from the Grand Duchy had emigrated.[39] Though emigration did diminish the tax base and in the long run was destructive of communal stability, leading to both shrinkage and ageing of the community, initially it facilitated its embourgeoisement.

These changes stimulated a debate, similar to that which took place in the last years of the Polish–Lithuanian Commonwealth, on the issue of whether the restrictions still imposed on the Jews could be abolished. This was conducted among Prussian officials in the Poznań area, the local Polish nobility and townspeople, and the local Jews. It was also part of the larger debate in Prussia as a whole. The acculturated minority within the Jewish community became much more assertive in pursuit of their rights. Many had taken advantage of the availability of secular education, and a number of young Jews had studied medicine, philology, and law at Prussian universities. Unable to gain access to the civil service, the legal profession, or academic posts, they became fervent advocates of a change in the status of the Jews. They were also buoyed up by support from public and general Jewish backing for such a change.[40]

The Prussian civil servants responsible for the running of the Grand Duchy were, in general, of the opinion that the Jews could be 'reformed' and Germanized. There was some dissatisfaction with the slow working out in the rest

[37] Breslauer, *Die Abwanderung der Juden aus der Provinz Posen*, table A.

[38] Kemlein, *Die Posener Juden 1815–1848*, 180 ff.

[39] Ibid. 65 and Östreich, '*Des rauhen Winters ungeachtet . . .*', 75.

[40] On this, see Laubert, 'Zur Entwicklung des jüdischen Schulwesens in der Provinz Posen', particularly 313.

of Prussia of the Emancipation Edict of March 1812, but the predominant official view still supported a policy of gradual integration. The view of local officials is summarized in a report submitted in 1844 to the government of the Grand Duchy by the provincial Department for Spiritual, Educational, and Medical Affairs. It claimed:

The unsatisfactory situation of the Jews, in particular in the administrative district of Posen, results in part from the fact that the Jews do not enjoy full civil rights. It should be the duty of the legislator to work consistently for the 'denationalization' of the Jews. The Jews in Posen represent a larger proportion of the population there than in any other province. In some towns they are a majority; above all, trade and industry are in their hands, and since restrictions have been lifted, their numbers have increased significantly among the artisan class. On average, they are clearly superior to the Christians in intelligence and industriousness. Since the province of Posen still lacks a strong bourgeoisie, the Prussian state would gain much if it were to enlist the Jews and transform them into such a group, and thus fundamentally reform the political conditions in the province. The Jewish population is already, in appearance, of German nationality, the German language is the language of everyday use; the Jewish German jargon is more and more giving way to High German. Because of the improvement of the educational system, German civic education is becoming stronger and stronger; study of the Talmud is limited to a small circle of scholars and older Jews. The Hebrew language is already so neglected that in some communities a German text translation can be found in the prayer books alongside the Hebrew text. However, the specific moral and religious condition of the Jews in Posen is far from the goals we have sought, because of their poverty and the dirt and ignorance of the lower classes. The Edict of 1833 has not yet had as much influence as might have been hoped, because the time since its enactment is rather short. However, progress can be observed in the adoption of German, in attitudes and in education. Economic and occupational habits, especially those created by petty trading and the sale of alcohol, are still damaging the lower classes of the people, among whom the traditional religious viewpoint still dominates.[41]

Yet, although some officials saw the Jews as the basis for a German bourgeoisie in the province, there was also a reluctance to provoke burgher opinion excessively, particularly by acceding to Jewish demands for a greater share in the government of the local towns. As early as 1838 the governor of the Grand Duchy, Eduard von Flottwell, felt compelled to write to the minister of the interior that, 'Taking into consideration the special conditions in the province and the educational level and specific character of the Jewish population, I regard it as appropriate and necessary to limit the numbers of members of the Mosaic faith which town councils should accept. This percentage should be determined by local

[41] Deutsches Zentralarchiv, Abteilung Merseburg, Rep. 76-III, Sekt. 1, Abtl. XIIIA, No. 1*c*: Bericht der Regierung zu Posen ueber die Regulierung des juedischen Kultus- und Schulwesens an das Ministerium fuer Geistliche, Unterrichts- und Medizinalangelegenheiten vom Januar 1844, quoted in Jersch-Wenzel, 'Zur Geschichte der jüdischen Bevölkerung in der Provinz Posen im 19. Jahrhundert', 76–7.

conditions and should nowhere exceed one third.'[42] This point of view received the support of the central authorities.

Leading Polish circles in the Grand Duchy were not in favour of local Jews being granted equal rights. By an overwhelming majority the first provincial Sejm, which met in Poznań at the end of 1827, resolved that the Emancipation Edict of March 1812 should not be extended to the Grand Duchy. The resolution stated that, although 'public good [makes it necessary] to transform their present situation as soon as possible', the Jews did not at present deserve to enjoy civic rights because of their 'way of life', which involved an avoidance of physical work. The Sejm called for the conscription of Jews to the army, a ban on their involvement in the sale of alcohol and their employment of Christian servants, and their exclusion from public service and the pharmaceutical profession. Jews should also be forbidden to buy landed estates. The Sejm was against extending the division of the Jews into protected and tolerated classes adopted by Frederick and widened a few years later to include the Grand Duchy. Should the Jews demonstrate 'moral improvement', the Sejm was willing to return to the matter and submit new proposals to the king. Discussion was, however, adjourned for ten years.[43]

The Jewish issue again came up for debate in the Sejm on 6 August 1841. On this occasion it was resolved to petition the Prussian king to forbid the Jews to engage in petty trade and the sale of alcohol and to restrict the number of taverns in Jewish hands.[44] The matter was more extensively discussed at the next session of the Sejm in February and March 1845. This time the Jews of Poznań, Bydgoszcz, Gniezno, Skwierzyna, and several other towns called on the Sejm to grant them equal rights. The majority in the assembly, which was dominated by the nobility, led by Count Działyński and Count Skórzewski, came out in favour of granting the Jews qualified emancipation, arguing on the basis of the British example that it was best to proceed gradually and only give the Jews full equality once they had demonstrated that they were 'civilized' and had abandoned their 'separatism'. Accordingly, the Sejm proposed that the Emancipation Edict be extended to the Grand Duchy but called, in addition, for the Jews to be liable to conscription and for the maintenance of the ban on Jews selling alcohol. Full equality of rights should only be granted to Jews who had completed three years' military service, had completed secondary school or university, or were engaged in agriculture or handicrafts without the help of Christian servants, or whom the municipal authorities deemed worthy of enfranchisement.[45]

42 Quoted in Jersch-Wenzel, *Jüdische Bürger und kommunale Selbstverwaltung in preussischen Städten 1808–1848*, 164–5.

43 On this, see Laubert, 'Die Judenfrage auf den Posener Provinziallandtagen von 1827 und 1845', 34–6, and Żychliński, *Historia sejmów Wielkiego Księstwa Poznańskiego do r. 1847*, ii. 57 ff.

44 Żychliński, *Historia sejmów Wielkiego Księstwa Poznańskiego do r. 1847*, ii. 185.

45 Ibid. 316–18 and Laubert, 'Die Judenfrage auf den Posener Provinziallandtagen von 1827 und 1845', 38–40.

Some of the Polish liberals in the province, such as Wojciech Lipski, went rather further and called for the Jews to be granted equal rights with Christians. In their view intolerance was 'alien to the Polish nation'. They believed that the granting of full equality would awaken a sense of civic responsibility among the Jews. This position was strongly opposed by some of the principal Polish burgher and artisan organizations. They called for the strengthening of the Polish element in the towns and attacked the Jews, who they claimed had 'grown fat' at Polish expense and were supporting the German cause in the province.[46]

In Prussia itself support for Jewish equality was also growing stronger. In January 1845 the Prussian government introduced legislation lifting existing restrictions and allowing Jews in Prussia to engage in almost all trades and professions.[47] By the spring of 1847 pressure for general political change had built up considerable momentum and compelled the government to convene a United Parliament (Landtag) made up of representatives of all the provincial diets in the Prussian state. When it assembled, the government submitted to it a bill dealing with the status of the Jews, which would regulate Jewish autonomous status as well as Jewish representation in municipal government and access to the civil service. The Edict of 1812 was to be applied in all areas of Prussia except for the Grand Duchy of Poznań, where the regulation of 1833 was still to apply. This proposal aroused considerable debate. In the upper house, which represented the aristocracy, there was support for the limited proposals of the government, and indeed some argument against the modest suggestions for the opening of the civil service to Jews. In the lower house, however, which represented the three estates of the gentry, the towns, and the communes, there was support for the extension of the Emancipation Edict to the Grand Duchy and the naturalization and granting of civil rights to all Jews there. The lower house resolved that Jews should be appointed to all positions in the civil service with the exception of those of a religious character. Jews should be able to hold university professorships, but not be employed as judges.[48] In the event, the law of 23 July 1847 retained the division into naturalized and tolerated Jews in the Grand Duchy of Poznań, but naturalized Jews were now entitled to the same rights as other Prussian Jews.

This law also changed significantly the position of the rabbinate in Prussia. Although at the time of the Emancipation Edict of 1812 the Prussian secretary of state Leopold von Schrötter had argued that 'Because of the great influence which the rabbis have over the community, it is necessary to ensure that educated and, what follows naturally from this, tolerant people be elected as rabbis',[49] Prussian

[46] On this, see Jaworski, *Handel und Gewerbe im Nationalitätenkampf*, ch. 1.

[47] Freund, *Die Emanzipation der Juden in Preussen unter besonderer Berücksichtigung des Gesetzes vom 11. März 1812*, i. 250.

[48] On these developments, see Hamburger, *Juden im öffentlichen Leben Deutschlands*, 18–20; Toury, *Soziale und politische Geschichte der Juden in Deutschland 1847–1871*, 315; and Jersch-Wenzel, 'Conflicts in the Years before 1848'.

[49] Freund, *Die Emanzipation der Juden in Preussen unter besonderer Berücksichtigung des Gesetzes vom 11. März 1812*, ii. 246–7.

policy had been rather to undermine the authority of the rabbinate, which was seen as an obstacle to reform. This policy also reflected a degree of 'contempt for the spiritual claims of Judaism' in the administration.[50] As a result, in the early nineteenth century rabbis were not classed as clerics and their appointment did not require government confirmation as was the case with the Christian clergy.

The low status of the rabbinate was confirmed in the new law of July 1847, which was partly influenced by the advice given to the authorities by the Jewish reformer Leopold Zunz. This law reorganized the structure of Jewish communal bodies, which were referred to as *Synagogengemeinden* (synagogue communities), rather than the more insulting *Judenschäfte* (Jewish associations), as a result of the intervention of the United Landtag. It established a strong and well-organized community on the local level but did not acknowledge its religious purpose. An elected lay board exercised full control over all communal affairs and institutions and was solely responsible for representing the community to the outside world. The only mention of the rabbinate was in a clause forbidding unnaturalized foreign Jews to hold this office. The community was not required to employ what was described as a religious functionary to manage its religious life, although it was required to provide the services of a religious instructor for the young.

The government justified this legislation to the Landtag on the grounds that Judaism made no distinction between laymen and clergy and failed to recognize any supreme religious authority. As a result the powers and functions of rabbis did not correspond to those exercised by Christian clergy. Religious ceremonies did not require their presence, and their authority was dependent on the public confidence they were able to inspire.[51]

The removal of most of the restrictive laws applying to the Jews of the Grand Duchy occurred as part of the revolutionary upheaval of 1848. The law of 5 April 1848 abolished the division of the Jews here into the two classes of naturalized and tolerated, and created a single legal status for Jews throughout the Kingdom of Prussia. Some restrictions were reintroduced after the collapse of the revolution, but almost all were abolished by the law of the North German Confederation of 3 July 1869, passed in the wake of the successful first stage of the unification of Germany under Prussian leadership.

One of the main consequences of the process of Jewish integration in the Grand Duchy was that most Jews here identified strongly with German culture and in particular with the Prussian liberal tradition, to which they believed they owed the abolition of the restrictions on their freedom. This was already evident at the time of the passage of the legislation of 1833, which was greeted by the majority of Jews in the Grand Duchy with 'patriotic celebrations of joy'.[52]

[50] Schorsch, 'Emancipation and the Crisis of Religious Authority', 34.

[51] On this law and its origins, see Fischer, *Judentum, Staat und Heer in Preussen im frühen 19. Jahrhundert*, 151–90; Strauss, 'Pre-Emancipation Prussian Policies towards the Jews 1815–1847'; and id., 'Liberalism and Conservatism in Prussian Legislation for Jewish Affairs, 1815–1847'.

[52] Heppner and Herzberg, *Aus Vergangenheit und Gegenwart der Juden und der jüdischen Gemeinden in den Posener Landen*, 838.

It was even more apparent in 1848. After the outbreak of revolution in Berlin in March a Polish National Committee was set up in Poznań. Its goal was national independence for the whole of Poland and it sent a delegation to Berlin to seek control of the Grand Duchy. On 24 March the Prussian king accepted its demands, and the National Committee sent representatives to all sections of the province to organize the spontaneous risings which had occurred and to take control of the Polish military units which had been formed. The committee believed that independence would be achieved through a war of national liberation against tsarist Russia, preferably in alliance with the German revolutionaries now taking power. Ludwik Mierosławski, the commander of the Polish military forces, soon had nearly 9,000 troops under his command, and his confidence was buoyed by calls in early April from both the German pre-parliament (the body that supervised the calling of a national German parliament) and the Prussian parliament for the re-establishment of Poland.

The euphoria did not last. The local Germans, who had initially supported the revolt, were fearful of the consequences of Polish rule, while the radicals soon lost ground in Berlin as well. Neither the Prussian conservatives nor the king himself had any stomach for war with Russia and they were eager to renege on the concessions they had made to the Poles in the Grand Duchy. Without informing the new Prussian government, the king gave orders to General Friedrich August von Colomb, the commander-in-chief of the Prussian troops in the province, to disband the Polish military units. In April von Colomb declared a state of siege in Poznań and began a military occupation of the province. Attempts to reach a compromise with the Polish National Committee by dividing the province on ethnic lines failed, largely because of local German opposition, and in early May the committee and its military forces were compelled to capitulate. The new royal commissioner General Ernst Pfuel now declared martial law across the whole province, and early in June he established a new demarcation line limiting the area to be controlled by the Poles to the small principality of Gniezno. In late October the Prussian national assembly rejected even this proposition and refused to consider the division of the province.[53]

Initially a number of local Jews, like their German counterparts, supported Polish aspirations. On the evening of 22 March, at a joint meeting of Poles and Germans, two Poznań Jews, Eduard Katz and Joseph Samter, declared their support for the position of the Polish National Committee. Nearly 100 Poznań Jews joined the local national guard, making up 16 per cent of its enrolment. This situation was repeated over the whole province. Jews participated in meetings supporting the Polish cause, wore white and red ribbons, and joined the local citizens' guard and the Polish National Committee.[54]

[53] On these events, see Kieniewicz, *Społeczeństwo polskie w powstaniu poznańskim 1848 roku*; Rakowski, *Powstanie poznańskie w 1848 roku*; Schmidt, *Die polnische Revolution des Jahres 1848 im Grossherzogtum Posen*; Makowski, 'Das Grossherzogtum Posen im Revolutionsjahr 1848'.

[54] On these developments, see Biblioteka Poznańskiego Towarzystwa Przyjaciół Nauki: Rok 1848 w

The mood of fraternity did not prove lasting. As early as 22 March the Polish National Committee antagonized both Germans and Jews by failing to include them in the delegation it sent to Berlin. The following day the Germans established their own committee in Poznań, which included Jews. This was reorganized on 27 March and came out strongly against granting control of the province to the Poles. German national committees now mushroomed all over the province, demanding the incorporation of many areas into the united Germany which it was hoped would result from the revolution. Initially the local German leadership seemed prepared to accept the partition of the province on ethnic lines, but from early April it came out in favour of maintenance of the unity of the province under German rule and suppression of the Polish National Committee and its military units. Violent confrontations between Poles and Germans erupted in many places.[55]

In this conflict most of the Jewish elite took the German side, though the scale of Jewish involvement is difficult to establish. Two Jews, Eduard Katz and Siegmund Hantke, were members of the original twelve-member German committee established in Poznań. Towards the end of March, when the committee was enlarged, four Jewish merchants were co-opted onto it. In addition, Katz, as one of two representatives of the German citizens of Prussian Poland, actively campaigned in Berlin for the incorporation of the Duchy into Germany.[56] Jews also participated in public meetings organized in support of the Germans. However, in absolute numbers active Jewish support for the Germans was probably limited. As Krzysztof Makowski has argued,

> In reality, the Jews were active in the German movement on a larger scale only in Poznań and a few other cities in which there was a preponderance of Germans in the population. Furthermore, a closer analysis indicates that in each of these localities, only a handful of individuals were active, and these were mainly the representatives of the wealthier classes—the emerging bourgeoisie and intelligentsia.[57]

There was also some support for the Polish position among Jews. Replying to criticisms in *Gazeta Polska*, the main Polish newspaper in Poznań, of the Jews' pro-German stance, Joseph Samter observed:

> Believe me, Poles, the great number of Jews who believe that your cause is just do not deserve the accusations of *Gazeta Polska*. Brother citizens! Tell me honestly how you would like it if some writer cursed the entire Polish nation because some fool did something bad? I protest against your claim that we are generally your enemies; I honour the holiness and

Wielkopolsce, sygn. 60358 IV, quoted in Makowski, 'Between Germans and Poles', 73. See also Białyniak [Rzepecki], *W półwiekową rocznicę*, 35; Grot, *Orężny czyn poznańskiej Wiosny Ludów*, 6; Grześ et al., *Niemcy w Poznańskiem wobec polityki germanizacyjnej 1815–1920*.

55 For a more detailed discussion, see Kohte, *Deutsche Bewegung und preussische Politik im Posener Lande 1848–49*, 25 ff.; Grześ et al., *Niemcy w Poznańskiem wobec polityki germanizacyjnej 1815–1920*, 81 ff.

56 Wuttke, *Städtebuch des Landes Posen*, 240–9.

57 Makowski, 'Between Germans and Poles', 77.

justness of the Polish cause and genuinely wish that the Lord God never bestows on another nation the fate that we have had to bear.[58]

Certainly, as Makowski has shown, a number of Jews were to be found on the Polish side in the conflict. They included Marcus Mosse, who directed the defence of Grodzisk against the Prussian army, and Robert Remak, who was a member of the delegation to the king demanding the release of the Polish prisoners in the Moabite jail in Berlin. Jews also gave financial support to the Polish military units at Miłosław and joined Polish national committees in several localities. Of course, the number of Jews who adopted a pro-Polish stance was much smaller than those supporting the German position. It is also true that the traditional and unacculturated majority of the community was probably neutral in the conflict and was more concerned about survival in difficult conditions, which was also true of most Poles and Germans in the area. Fraenkel has published the diary of a Jewish printer from Krotoszyn who printed material for both sides and showed no emotional involvement with either.[59]

Jewish support for the German side is easy to understand. The Jewish elite had every reason to be grateful to the Prussian government for the changes which had taken place in Jewish life in the province, particularly since 1833. In addition, German political groups in 1848 went out of their way to include Jews. Polish representatives in the local Sejm had opposed the granting of full equality for the Jews before 1848, and the Polish National Committee did not show itself particularly sensitive to Jewish concerns.

Jews were also alienated by the anti-Jewish violence perpetrated by the Poles. Although it was sometimes exaggerated in reports, there were three major incidents of such violence (in Trzemeszno, Września, and Buk), which occurred during military operations. In all, Makowski has estimated that 'a few or perhaps a dozen Jews at most died at Polish hands in the Grand Duchy in April and May of 1848'.[60] Several dozen more were injured, and there were cases of Jewish shops and places of worship being broken into. In some cases the violence was a response to Jewish support for the German military. The violence in Trzemeszno followed accusations that Jews, together with local Germans, had shot several insurgents during a skirmish with the Prussian army. In a number of places, notably Leszno and Krotoszyn, Jews were accused of preventing the Poles from taking control in the first days of the movement. Jews were also attacked for removing Polish flags, inciting Prussian soldiers, and denouncing Polish activists. The violence and mutual suspicion this aroused further alienated Poles and Jews in the province.

[58] *Gazeta Polska* (1848), no. 16, 62. See also *Zeitung des Grossherzogtums Posen* (1848), no. 98, 564; and the correspondence of Jewish residents of the Grand Duchy of Poznań, in *Allgemeine Zeitung des Judenthums*, 2 June 1848, 357–8.

[59] Fraenkel, 'The Memoirs of B. L. Monasch of Krotoschin', 216.

[60] Makowski, 'Between Germans and Poles', 76.

The pro-German position of the Jewish leadership was criticized by pro-Polish Jewish activists both within the Kingdom of Poland and among those who went into exile after the 1830–1 uprising, notably by Leon Hollaenderski, and also by the Polish philosemite of Frankist origins Jan Czyński, the founder of the Polish Inter-Faith Alliance. The most eloquent exposition of this stance appeared in a letter written by Rabbi Dov Berush Meisels (1798–1870) on behalf of the Jews of Kraków to the Jews of Poznań appealing to them to show their 'patriotism' and support Polish national aspirations. The Poznań Jews replied on 22 May 1848 that they approved of the Kraków Jews' love of their motherland, but could not comply with their request. They continued, 'You probably know well that the sacred love of the motherland, the consciousness of being permanently linked with a nationality, neither can nor should be restrained by gratitude or by prospects of material and spiritual benefits.' They had been brought up, they claimed, in the German language and customs, and since they only used the German language, they felt linked to the Germans, even if they were sometimes treated unfairly. The sense of national ties, they argued, was like conscience; the love of the motherland was unselfish and sometimes thankless, but could not be stifled by religion or other factors. The letter concluded: 'If you have become Polonized in culture and customs and are joining the fight to liberate enslaved Poland, you will be able to appreciate our love of the German nation. Only he who loves his country can understand what love of the motherland is.'[61]

The growing identification of the Jews with the German minority in the province caused strong resentment among the Poles and widened the gap between Jews and Poles. Thus, on 14 April 1848 *Gazeta Polska* blamed the Jews for the rift. 'For material benefits, you have preferred a German education to a Polish one.' In an article of 20 May 1848, under the title 'Religion and Nationality', it stressed the identification of Polishness with Catholicism. 'Our entire history is marked by a religious attachment to the motherland and a religious sacrifice to the national cause.'

The sense of identification with the German cause was further strengthened when, on 27 December 1848, the revolutionary Frankfurt parliament, in which all the German states were represented, adopted the Declaration of Fundamental Rights of the German People. It was to be part of the constitution of the united Germany which it was hoped would emerge from the revolution, and established full legal equality for all. It provided that 'The enjoyment of civil or political rights shall be neither conditioned nor limited by religious confession' (para. 16) and that 'No religious association shall benefit from any state prerogatives before others. No state church shall exist henceforth' (para. 17).

The defeat of the revolution led to the Prussian government again asserting the Christian character of the state and barring Jews from many public offices.

[61] This exchange took place in the pages of *Der Orient*, 9 (1848), no. 22 (27 May), 173–4, and no. 23 (3 June), 181, and is reproduced in Eisenbach, *The Emancipation of the Jews in Poland, 1780–1870*, 365.

However, Jews still enjoyed the right to vote and to be elected.[62] After the establishment of the North German Confederation, Bismarck, who in 1847 had opposed the granting of equal rights to Jews, persuaded the parliament of the new confederation on 3 July 1869 to do away with all 'still existing restrictions on civil and political rights derived from the difference in religious confession . . . the qualification for participation in communal and provincial representative bodies and for holding public office shall be independent of religious confession'.[63] In practice, Jews, with few exceptions, were still excluded from the officer corps, higher administrative positions, the Foreign Ministry, and university professorships. Nevertheless, Jews, including those in Prussian Poland, now saw themselves as equal citizens of the German empire established after the defeat of France in 1870.

CONCLUSION

It has often been argued that the integrationist solution of the Jewish problem, the transformation of the Jews into citizens, did not work on Polish soil. The experience of the Jews in the Grand Duchy of Poznań is the exception, although the Jews were transformed not into Poles but rather into Germans of the Jewish faith. There were a number of reasons for this development: the eagerness of the Prussian government in the first half of the nineteenth century to integrate the Jews and to transform them into the bourgeoisie in this area, the Prussian reforms which transformed an estate into a civil society, and the fact that at the outset of this process the Jewish population constituted a significantly smaller proportion of the population than elsewhere in the Polish lands. Certainly, although it fell short of granting the Jews complete legal equality, the 1833 reform of Jewish communal self-government greatly facilitated the adaptation of the Jews of the province to modern conditions. Its success can be seen in the fact that it was extended to all Jewish communities in Prussia in 1847 and served as the legal foundation for the Jewish *Gemeinden* until their dissolution in 1939.

In the second part of the nineteenth century the conflict between the Polish majority and the German government, which was determined to Germanize the area, became the dominant feature of political and social life in the Grand Duchy. This created serious difficulties for the local Jewish population, with its allegiance to a liberal concept of the German idea. The Jews of the area reacted to the growing radicalization of the national conflict there, which was accompanied by expressions of antisemitism on the part of both Poles and Germans, by reaffirming their belief in liberal ideas as a way to bridge the gap between the two sides. Although by now mainly German by culture, they had little sympathy with the

[62] On this, see Baron, 'The Impact of the Revolution of 1848 on Jewish Emancipation'.

[63] Law Concerning the Equality of All Confessions in Respect to Civil Rights and Political Rights, 3 July 1869, repr. in Mendes-Flohr and Reinharz (eds.), *The Jew in the Modern World*, 153.

growing chauvinism of the local German political elite. Many Jews sought safety by fleeing the area, while a minority reacted by arguing that the Jews could not be expected to choose between the two nationalisms struggling for control, but should rather assert their own national separateness.

EIGHT

THE JEWS IN GALICIA TO THE MID-1870S

THE NAME GALICIA was derived from the medieval principality of Halich, one of the successor states of Kievan Rus. It was revived by the Habsburgs in the form of 'the Kingdom of Galicia and Lodomeria' (Lodomeria was the Latinized version of another Kievan successor state, Vladimir), which had once been claimed by the Hungarian Crown and which thus gave a spurious justification for the incorporation of the area into the Habsburg empire in 1772. The Jewish statistician Abraham Brawer, writing after Galicia had become part of the new Poland, observed, 'There are few areas for which diplomats drew maps with such unnatural and unhistorical borders as they did for Galicia.'[1]

This statement is undoubtedly valid, politically speaking, but, from the viewpoint of east European Jewish history, Galicia developed a distinct character and contained within its borders one of the largest concentrations of Jews in east central Europe. Its Jewish population grew from around 178,000 in 1772 (out of a total population of just over 3 million inhabitants) to 317,000 in 1850 (out of 4.7 million) and 811,000 in 1900 (out of 7.3 million), when Jews made up over 11 per cent of the total population.[2] By that date a significant proportion of the Jews still lived in the countryside—36.6 per cent by one estimate—and there seems to have been a remigration of Jews to the villages in the last quarter of the nineteenth century.[3] Jews were also a significant presence in cities and market towns, in at least seven of which they formed the majority of the population.

The territorial extent of Galicia varied considerably in the century and a half during which the area was under Austrian rule (see Map 6). The core of the province was the area of Red Rus, with its capital of Lviv (Lwów, Lemberg), which in the fourteenth century had passed from the rule of one of the princely successor states of the Grand Duchy of Kiev to the Polish Crown. The area of Małopolska around Kraków was incorporated into Austria as a consequence of the third partition of Poland but was then transferred to the Napoleonic Duchy of Warsaw in 1809. At the Congress of Vienna in 1815 the town of Kraków, with a small area around it, was made an independent republic under the protection of the three partitioning powers. Following the outbreak of revolution there in 1846, the area

[1] Brawer, *Galicia and its Jews* (Heb.), 11.

[2] 'Galicia', in *Jewish Encyclopedia*.

[3] Himka, 'Ukrainian–Jewish Antagonism in the Galician Countryside during the Late Nineteenth Century', 116.

was annexed by Austria and remained under Habsburg rule until 1918. Under the third partition the area around Lublin, including the town of Zamość, which became an important centre of the Haskalah, passed to Austria. In 1809 this area was also transferred to the Duchy of Warsaw, and in 1815 at the Congress of Vienna was not returned to Austria, instead becoming part of the Kingdom of Poland, an autonomous state in dynastic union with the tsarist empire. In 1809 the area around Ternopil (Tarnopol), another important centre of the Haskalah, became part of the tsarist empire but returned to Habsburg control in 1815. Bukovina, which had never been part of Poland, and whose population was largely Ukrainian and Romanian with significant Polish, German, and Jewish minorities, was part of the Galician administrative district until 1848.

There were a number of features specific to the process of Jewish integration in Galicia. In the first place, the German element in Galicia was much weaker than in either Prussian Poland or the Czech lands, and most Germans in the province, including those who were brought there as Habsburg officials, were rapidly Polonized. This, along with the gradual decline of German hegemony in Austria as a whole, meant that, although there was some support initially among the Austrian authorities and sections of the Jewish leadership for the 'transformation' of the Jews into Germans, or possibly Austrians 'of the Mosaic faith', ultimately the Jewish integrationists there came to favour a Polish orientation.

Secondly, unlike the Grand Duchy of Poznań, Galicia was a stronghold of hasidism. The Jewish reformers and integrationists found themselves in a bitter conflict with hasidim as well as other Orthodox opponents of the transformation of the Jews. Certainly, until 1848 the Austrian authorities were rather suspicious of the Galician maskilim (supporters of the Haskalah) and often supported local hasidim because of their social conservatism.[4] In addition, the economic backwardness of Austria, and in particular of Galicia, meant that the area was still largely agricultural at the end of the nineteenth century and was still dominated by the Polish nobility. As a consequence, although there was some reorganization of the economic structure of the Jewish community, the granting of equal rights in 1868 was not followed by social integration on a significant scale.

Finally, the mixed ethnic character of the region, with Poles dominant in the western part of the province but a minority in the largely Ukrainian eastern area, had a major impact on the situation of the Jews. From 1848 the Polish–Ukrainian conflict became increasingly important and from 1867 came to dominate most aspects of the political life of the area. The Jews, for the most part, after provincial autonomy was granted to the Polish nobility in the late 1860s, favoured an alliance with the dominant Poles. They were, however, concentrated in the largely Ukrainian eastern section of Galicia and had to take into account the growing strength of Ukrainian nationalism. One feature of the province was the way in which ethnic and religious divisions largely overlapped with social

[4] On this, see R. Mahler, *Hasidism and the Jewish Enlightenment*, 69–73.

divisions. In the eastern part of the province the landowners were almost exclusively Polish, although some of them were still Greek Catholic. The peasantry was almost exclusively Ruthenian (or Ukrainian, as they came increasingly to describe themselves after 1900). Intermediate occupations were in the hands of the Jews. In the western part of the province both the landowners and the peasantry were Polish, although national consciousness spread only slowly to this latter group. Table 8.1 sets out the national composition of Galicia.

Table 8.1 Galician population by nationality, 1825–1857

Year	Poles	Ukrainians	Jews	Total
1825	1,800,000	1,740,000	270,000	3,850,000
1846	1,994,802	2,441,771	335,071	4,875,149
1857	1,981,076	2,085,431	448,973	4,632,866

Source: Himka, 'Dimensions of a Triangle', 26.

THE CHARACTER OF THE HABSBURG STATE

In the sixteenth century through skilled statecraft, particularly during the reign of the emperors Charles V (r. 1519–56) and Ferdinand I (r. 1556–64), and a series of fortunate dynastic marriages, the Habsburgs became the most powerful dynasty in Europe. By 1648, however, their power had declined significantly. They had failed to impose their Counter-Reformation vision of the world on the whole of central Europe, and the Spanish and Austrian branches of the family were now going their own way. By 1713, of their western possessions only the southern Netherlands remained under Habsburg control. Nevertheless, the Habsburg rulers of Austria retained the position of Holy Roman Emperor, and Austria, Catholic and committed to the principles of the Counter-Reformation, remained the strongest state in central Europe.

At the same time it should be stressed that Austria, in spite of the position it held in the German lands, was not a 'German' state. Nationalism was basically a nineteenth-century phenomenon and it proved deeply disruptive to the heterogeneous Habsburg empire, composed as it was of very disparate elements. These included the Catholic and German Alpine valleys, Lower Austria with the imperial capital of Vienna, the Kingdom of Hungary, which had mostly been reconquered from the Turks in the eighteenth century, the Crown lands of King Wenceslas, Bohemia, Moravia, and Silesia, which had come to the dynasty by marriage, and Lombardy and the Austrian Netherlands.

Like both Prussia and Poland–Lithuania, the Habsburg empire was an estate society, with a dominant aristocracy ruling over a largely unfree peasant class (outside the Tyrol as well as in Lombardy and the Austrian Netherlands, both of which were to be lost in the nineteenth century). At the core of the empire, towns were mostly small and politically insignificant, and, although there was more of a central bureaucracy than in Poland–Lithuania, it was rather weak and ineffective.[5]

The loss of most of the rich province of Silesia to the Prussians in 1740 made clear the need for reform. This was begun under Empress Maria Theresa (r. 1740–80) and her ministers Prince von Kaunitz and Count von Haugwitz. The bureaucracy was now greatly extended and modernized, and some improvement was made in the position of the unfree peasantry. These reforms enjoyed considerable success and avoided antagonizing the powerful conservative forces in the empire. This was not the case under Maria Theresa's son Joseph II (who was co-regent from 1765 and ruled on his own from 1780 to 1790, and who was the brother of Marie Antoinette), who made a more radical attempt to transform the political and social structure of the empire. This provoked resistance, which ultimately threatened the whole project. Of all the rulers of larger states in the eighteenth century, Joseph best deserved the title of 'enlightened autocrat'. He introduced a new civil code in 1786 and a new criminal code the following year. He attempted, not wholly successfully, to end the fiscal immunity of the nobility, and, in order to diminish the power of 'private' interest groups and to encourage trade, attacked the privileged position of trading and artisan corporations. By the Edict of Toleration of 1781 he broke with the Counter-Reformation tradition of the Habsburg state and granted freedom to practise their religion to Lutherans, Calvinists, Greek Catholics, and Greek Orthodox, who accounted for perhaps a third of the 18 million inhabitants of the empire. At the same time he attacked the position of the Catholic religious orders, and in 1773 he suppressed the Jesuits.[6]

In 1786 Joseph limited serfdom in his domains, codifying the labour obligations of the peasants and reducing the amount of work they had to undertake on manorial lands to three days a week. Nobles were no longer permitted to evict peasants, and peasants were allowed to leave the village without the permission of the landlord, provided they informed the local authority. They could also make complaints to the local administration, which took control of manorial courts, depriving the landlords of their jurisdiction.

Joseph also hoped to 'reform' the Jewish population of his different lands. In 1785 there were 68,000 Jews in the Czech lands, 17,100 in Hungary, 212,000 in Galicia, and a handful in Lower Austria. In return for a guarantee of the right to practise their religion and to dwell securely in the empire, Joseph expected the Jews to diminish their 'separateness' and transform their educational system and occupational structure so that they would become 'useful and productive'

[5] On this, see particularly Kann, *A History of the Habsburg Empire, 1526–1918*; Evans, *The Making of the Habsburg Monarchy, 1550–1700*; and id., *Austria, Hungary and the Habsburgs*.

[6] For these developments, see Zöllner (ed.), *Österreich im Zeitalter des aufgeklärten Absolutismus*; Wangermann, *The Austrian Achievement, 1700–1800*; Macartney, *Maria Theresa and the House of Austria*; Szabo, *Kaunitz and Enlightened Absolutism, 1753–1780*; Beales, *Joseph II*; Blanning, *Joseph II*; and Karniel, *Die Toleranzpolitik Kaiser Josephs II.*

subjects.[7] Thus, on 18 October 1781 he issued an Edict of Toleration for Bohemia, for Silesia on 15 December 1781, for Lower Austria on 2 January 1782, for Moravia on 3 February 1782, and for Hungary on 31 March 1783.[8] His aims are summarized in the preamble to the Edict of Toleration he issued to the Jews of Lower Austria: 'As it is our goal to make the Jewish nation useful and serviceable to the state, mainly through better education and enlightenment of its youth as well as by directing them to the sciences, the arts and the crafts, we hereby grant and order . . .'.[9]

Joseph's reforms encountered strong opposition because of their attack on the privileged position of a large number of different groups, the nobility, the Catholic orders, and the urban burghers. Resistance grew in the Czech lands, in Hungary, and above all in the Austrian Netherlands, where by 1790, the year of Joseph's death, a revolutionary situation had developed. Joseph's successor, his brother Leopold II (r. 1790–2), managed to calm the situation somewhat, retaining most of his predecessor's reforms but abandoning his abolition of serfdom. However, growing fear of the impact of the ideas of the French Revolution led to the abandonment of any further change under Franz II, who ruled from 1792 to 1835. In the period after 1815 Franz and his principal minister, Prince Klemens von Metternich, a key figure at the Congress of Vienna, became the main bulwarks of the attempt to restore the pre-revolutionary order in Europe. Nevertheless, the tradition of a reformist and enlightened centralizing bureaucracy, the main legacy of Joseph II, remained powerful in Austria throughout the nineteenth century.

THE AUSTRIANS IN GALICIA

The initial policies adopted by the Austrians in the province which they had acquired from Poland, somewhat reluctantly, in 1772 were aimed at integrating Galicia into the modernized and enlightened state which Maria Theresa and, particularly, Joseph II were trying to create. A whole series of reforms were introduced with this goal in mind and created a situation very different from the extreme decentralization of the Polish–Lithuanian Commonwealth. The local parliaments were abolished, and elected municipalities, whose privileges were guaranteed by Magdeburg law, were done away with and replaced by bureaucrats appointed from Vienna. A consultative assembly of estates was set up in Lviv. It was made up of representatives of the magnates, the gentry (referred to in the legislation as 'knights'), and the clergy. After 1815 the town of Lviv was also

[7] On these developments, see particularly McCagg, *A History of Habsburg Jews, 1670–1918*, and Karniel, 'Das Toleranzpatent Josephs II für die Juden Galiziens und Lodomeriens'.

[8] Häusler, 'Toleranz, Emanzipation und Antisemitismus', 84 ff.

[9] 'Edict of Tolerance (January 2, 1782)', repr. in Mendes-Flohr and Reinharz (eds.), *The Jew in the Modern World*, 36–40.

represented by two deputies. The assembly was similar to other such bodies in the Austrian provinces and it was solely advisory in character, with the right to send petitions to the emperor.[10]

Real power in the province lay in the hands of the governor, appointed by the emperor. He ruled through his deputies, who headed the nineteen districts into which the area was now divided. The previously privileged position of the nobility was undermined. Nobles lost their tax-exempt status and their control of the judicial system. Control of their serfs was also now regulated by the state, although the abolition of unfree cultivation, introduced by Joseph II in 1781, was rescinded after his death. This established a tradition among the peasantry of seeing the emperor as their benefactor and protector, in spite of the fact that the establishment of Austrian rule also meant higher taxes and liability to military service.

As elsewhere in the empire, the Austrians introduced the principle of religious toleration. This was of enormous significance for the previously somewhat oppressed Greek Catholic majority in the province. The Austrians referred to the confession as Greek Catholic rather than as Uniate, hoping in this way to raise its status. In 1784 they established a university in Lviv and created a general seminary there to train Greek Catholic priests. In 1808 they re-established the Greek Catholic metropolitanate of St George in Lviv.

In 1785 the Jews of Galicia made up nearly 60 per cent of those in the Habsburg empire. Initially Maria Theresa was reluctant to intervene in internal Jewish matters since she was unwilling to provoke opposition to Austrian rule. Joseph, for his part, was determined to transform their position in accordance with his attempt to introduce into Galicia the same principles of the 'well-ordered police state' which governed his policy elsewhere in the empire.[11] In March 1785 he promulgated a law supplemented in May 1789 by a Jewish Ordinance for the Jews of Galicia similar to those which he had already issued to the Jews in Lower Austria, the Czech lands, and Hungary.[12] According to its preamble,

> The monarch has found it necessary and useful to annul the differences which legislation has so far maintained between his Christian and Jewish subjects and to grant the Jews living in Galicia all the rights and liberties which our other subjects enjoy. Galician Jews will therefore from now on be treated like all other subjects as regards their rights and duties.[13]

There were a number of aspects to Joseph's policies towards the Jews of Galicia. In the first place, most, though not all, restrictions on Jews were abolished. Jews were granted restricted civic (municipal) rights. These were, however,

[10] On these developments, see Szabo, 'Austria's First Impressions of Ethnic Relations in Galicia'; Glassl, *Das österreichische Einrichtungswerk in Galizien (1772–1790)*.

[11] On this, see Raeff, 'The Well-Ordered Police State and the Development of Modernity in Seventeenth and Eighteenth Century Europe', and id., *The Well-Ordered Police State*.

[12] On its origins, see Karniel, 'Fürst Kaunitz und die Juden', 22–3.

[13] Quoted in Bałaban, *Dzieje Żydów w Galicyi i w Rzeczypospolitej Krakowskiej 1772–1868*, 47.

dependent on the willingness of the burghers of the different towns to concede such rights. Moreover, the scope of municipal self-government under the new Austrian regime was somewhat restricted. Jews were, in addition, given limited freedom to settle in towns and were permitted to employ Christian servants.

Secondly, Joseph was determined to 'productivize' the Jews, in accordance with physiocratic principles. He was eager to promote Jewish settlement on the land, establishing in 1786 a Jewish agricultural colony in the village of Dąbrówka, near Nowy Sącz. At the same time he sought to exclude Jews from non-agricultural occupations in the countryside, such as inn-keeping, brewing, and distilling, and from leasing inns and the right to produce alcoholic beverages. Jews were, however, to be given unrestricted access to handicrafts and were allowed to be apprenticed to a Christian master. They were also given permission, as in Prussia, to open factories.

A series of measures were introduced to foster the 'integration' of the Jews. Perhaps the most important was compulsory school attendance. According to section II of the Edict of 5 May 1789, a school for young Jews was to be set up in every district. Jews were also permitted to attend German or Polish schools. The granting of a marriage licence and other rights were dependent on completing primary school. A Czech maskil, Naphtali Herz Homberg (1749–1841), was put in charge of the new Jewish school system. By 1806 there were over 4,000 students attending these schools, of which 107 had been established for boys and a much smaller number for girls; 150 teachers were employed in the system.[14]

Other integrative measures were also introduced. Jews were obliged to take surnames and to keep their official records in German. The scope of Jewish communal autonomy was also severely restricted. In 1776 Maria Theresa attempted to create a supra-*kehilah* organization in the form of a General Council for Jewry (Generaldirektion der Judenschaft), which was composed of representatives from six areas into which the province was divided. This did not fulfil the expectations of the authorities as a means of transforming the Jews and was abolished in 1789. The powers of individual *kehilot* were now significantly reduced. They were now to be responsible for supervising the religious institutions, for dispensing charity, and for administering the special taxes imposed on the Jews. The poll tax was abolished and replaced by a number of new taxes, a kosher meat tax (from 1784), a candle tax, a marriage tax (from 1787), and a residence tax to be levied on Jews from outside the province. Rabbis were deprived of their judicial power and the right to excommunicate members of the community.[15]

In the preamble to his Edict of Toleration for the Jews of Galicia, Joseph had proclaimed their equality in 'rights and duties'. One of the duties he now imposed on them was that of service in his army, the first time this had been undertaken in modern Europe. Responsibility for supervising the draft lay with the individual *kehilot*.

[14] On this school system, see Bałaban, *Dzieje Żydów w Galicyi i w Rzeczypospolitej Krakowskiej 1772–1868*, 56–81.

[15] Ibid. 35–55.

Joseph's successors, Leopold II (r. 1790–2), Franz II (r. 1792–1835), and Ferdinand II (r. 1835–48), maintained the restrictive and punitive aspects of his policies while playing down the positive and integrative elements. Franz limited the participation of Jews in local self-government and, under pressure from both Jewish and Catholic opposition, abolished in 1806 the school system established by Herz Homberg, a move which was followed by the collapse of most of the schools he had established. During his reign there were some half-hearted attempts at 'reforming' the Jews. Under the influence of the maskil Joseph Perl (1773–1839), some attempt was made to restrict the circulation of hasidic books and also to limit the wearing of traditional Jewish dress. The school Perl had established under Russian rule in Ternopil in 1813, in which Polish and German were the languages of instruction, was registered by the Austrians when they took over the area, and prospered in the next decades.[16] In addition, by the middle of the nineteenth century Jewish state schools, both primary and secondary, based on Haskalah principles and generally using German as the language of instruction, had been established in fourteen towns, including Lviv, Brody, and Przemyśl, with a total of some 3,000 students.[17] We have less adequate figures for Jewish attendance in state high schools (commercial schools and gymnasiums). Partial estimates give the number of Jewish students in commercial schools as twenty-one in 1853 and forty-nine in 1868. The number in gymnasiums, where the atmosphere was more tolerant, was higher: 260 in 1850 and 620 by 1869.[18] Data for attendance at the University of Lviv are fragmentary, but Jewish students in the faculties of law and philosophy numbered forty-two in 1851 and this figure had risen to fifty-one by 1869.[19]

Some further efforts were made to encourage Jewish agricultural settlement. A decree of 8 March 1805 permitted Jews to purchase land for their own use. The *kehilot* were instructed to help finance such purchases, which, it was hoped, would lead to the creation of 1,400 families of Jewish agricultural settlers. Little was achieved, however, mainly because of the backwardness of Galician agriculture and the persistence of unfree cultivation. By 1822, 840 Jewish families were recorded as deriving their living from farming, a number which fell to 440 by 1840.[20]

The emperor Leopold had in August 1790 replaced the obligation on Jews to serve in the army with a tax, but military conscription was reintroduced in 1804. Several thousand Jews served in the wars against Napoleon. They were even eligible for commissioned rank.[21]

[16] Friedmann, *Die galizischen Juden im Kampfe um ihre Gleichberechtigung 1848–1869*, 30.

[17] Ibid. 32–4, 150.

[18] Ibid. 33–4; Bałaban, *Dzieje Żydów w Galicyi i w Rzeczypospolitej Krakowskiej 1772–1868*, 188–9.

[19] Friedmann, *Die galizischen Juden im Kampfe um ihre Gleichberechtigung 1848–1869*, 35, table.

[20] Ibid. 17–19 and Eisenbach, *The Emancipation of the Jews in Poland, 1780–1870*, 47.

[21] Eisenbach, *The Emancipation of the Jews in Poland, 1780–1870*, 130–2; Bałaban, *Dzieje Żydów w Galicyi i w Rzeczypospolitej Krakowskiej 1772–1868*, 38.

At the same time the special Jewish taxes introduced by Maria Theresa and Joseph were maintained, as were restrictions on where Jews could live. Thus special Jewish quarters were maintained in Lviv, Sambir, Tarnów, Nowy Sącz, and Horodok, while the ban on Jewish settlement was maintained in Biała, Bochnia, Żywiec, Wieliczka, and Jasło. Because of burgher hostility, Jewish rights in the towns remained on paper and the Jews were also still subject to significant occupational restrictions. They were effectively barred from access to merchant and artisan guilds and from pursuing a number of occupations, including that of pharmacist (until 1832), brewer, distiller, and miller, and were not appointed to positions in the state, municipal, or judicial systems. Jews could also not be teachers in the state schools. The right to contract a marriage, as elsewhere in the empire, was restricted in 1810 to those who had passed an examination (administered in German) based on Herz Homberg's catechism Benei Zion.

One of the main features of Galician Jewish life in the early nineteenth century was the worsening economic position of the Jews and their growing impoverishment. This was partly because of the economic backwardness of Galicia. The partitions of Poland had had very adverse effects on the economic life of the region: Galician poverty (*nędza galicyjska*) was to become proverbial in the course of the nineteenth century. The province was now separated from the trade routes and markets of which it had formerly been a part and was cut off from the rest of the empire by the natural barrier of the Carpathian Mountains. After some minor initial investment in the area, the Austrian government came to the conclusion that the region should export agricultural products to the rest of the empire. Industry, until the late nineteenth century, when substantial oil deposits were discovered near Drohobych, was limited to a few textile mills, iron foundries, glassworks, and breweries. Agriculture, in which unfree cultivation was still the rule, also remained backward and productivity low.

Jewish poverty was exacerbated by the heavy tax burden imposed on the community and by the attack on a number of traditional Jewish occupations, such as inn-keeping, brewing, distilling, and milling. An Austrian government investigation in 1815 estimated that one-third of the Jewish population was composed of *luftmenshn*, people whose only source of income was irregular odd jobs. In the same year 4,000 of the 45,000 Jewish families in the province were exempted from the candle tax on grounds of poverty, and another 1,000 paid it at a reduced level.

One consequence of the impoverishment of the community was substantial emigration. The principal areas to which emigrants moved were the more developed parts of the Habsburg empire. It was at this time, for instance, that a very substantial number of Jews from Galicia moved to Hungary. Jewish emigrants also went to the Romanian principalities and, in smaller numbers, to the Kingdom of Poland. Some even managed to reach the later favoured destinations of western Europe and the United States.

Kraków was made into a free city under the protection of the partitioning powers. However, in the early nineteenth century it became something of a backwater. Memories of its great past as the historic capital of Poland and the place where the Polish kings were buried gave it a special significance in the Polish imagination, but it remained a relatively small town. In 1833 it had a population of 38,000, which grew to 50,000 in 1870, 85,000 in 1900, and 120,000 in 1910. This was considerably smaller than Lviv, which was also the provincial capital. The Jewish population increased from 8,500 in 1818 (28.6 per cent of the population) to 26,000 in 1900 and 32,000 in 1910. In the period of self-rule the Polish ruling elite of the free city was divided over the question of whether the Jews could be granted civil rights only after they had reformed their own society, or whether these changes would only be possible after the achievement of political integration. In 1817 a Statute for the Followers of the Law of the Old Testament (*starozakonni*) was enacted. It abolished the *kahal*, which it replaced with a Committee for Jewish Affairs, whose authority extended only to religious and charitable matters and which was composed of the rabbi, two other Jews, and a civil servant. The Jews were subordinated to the local administration and judiciary. Rabbis were still elected by the community, but had to demonstrate to the civil authorities their knowledge of Polish and German. Jews were not eligible to be elected to the house of deputies which governed the free city, and the restrictions on their place of residence which had been in operation before the partitions, and which meant they could not own property in Kraków itself, were maintained.[22]

JEWISH RESPONSES TO THE POLICIES OF INTEGRATION IN GALICIA

The effect of governmental policies aimed at integrating the Jews and transforming them into 'useful and productive citizens' of the Habsburg empire and the free city of Kraków was greatly to exacerbate the already existing divisions within the Jewish communities of the area. A minority, particularly in the more developed areas of the state, especially the cities of Prague and Vienna, was strongly committed to the idea of reform from above. They were also greatly attracted to the German language and German culture, which they saw as embodiments of universal, secular, and liberal values. A majority of the Jews, particularly in Galicia, where hasidism was becoming increasingly important, was strongly opposed to these policies. They were seen as merely a more subtle form of Christian evangelization, and those who supported them were believed to be motivated by base and material considerations.

[22] On this, see Bałaban, *Dzieje Żydów w Galicyi i w Rzeczypospolitej Krakowskiej 1772–1868*, 110, and Bartel, *Ustrój i prawo Wolnego Miasta Krakowa 1815–1846*.

It was in the first decades of the nineteenth century that hasidism came to dominate the religious life of much of Galicia. As described above, hasidism began as a small circle of disciples around the Ba'al Shem Tov (the Besht) in Medzhybizh, in Podolia. After his death the centre of gravity of the movement had moved to Mezhirech (Międzyrzec) in Volhynia, where the key figure was Dov Baer, the Maggid of Mezhirech. He sent his followers over the whole area of the former Polish–Lithuanian Commonwealth: Rebbe Menahem Mendel (1730–88) to Vitebsk, Rebbe Shneur Zalman to Lyady, and Rebbe Levi Isaac b. Meir (*c.*1740–1810) to Berdichev. (On these developments, see Volume II, Chapter 8.)

It was at this time that two major hasidic dynasties became established in Galicia. The first was linked with the court of Rebbe Elimelekh (1717–87), who established himself in Lizhensk (Leżajsk), in central Galicia. His disciples Jacob Isaac Horowitz, the Seer of Lublin (1745–1815), and Rebbe Israel b. Shabetai Hapstein, the Maggid of Kozienice (1733–1814), were to bring hasidism to the Kingdom of Poland. In Galicia, Rebbe Elimelekh's principal disciples were Naphtali Zevi of Ropshits (Ropczyce, 1760–1827) and Menahem Mendel of Rymanów (d. 1815).

The second major hasidic dynasty in Galicia was that of the Ruzhiner tsadikim.[23] This was founded by Rebbe Israel Friedman of Ruzhin (also known as Israel Ruzhin, 1797–1850) in Podolia, which from 1793 was part of the tsarist empire. In 1838 the *rebbe* was arrested with some eighty of his followers when two Jewish spies for the tsarist authorities were murdered. Rebbe Israel, who was accused of complicity in the murder, was eventually released from Russian captivity because there was insufficient evidence against him and managed to cross the border into Galicia. The Austrian authorities allowed him to settle in Sadagura, in Bukovina, which at this time was administratively part of Galicia.

The first Ruzhiner tsadik died in 1850 and was succeeded by his eldest son (who died within a year) and then by his second son, Abraham Jacob (1819–83), who was tsadik until his death. Another son, Rebbe Mordecai Shraga (1834–94), established a court in Husyatyn and a Ruzhiner outpost was also created in Chortkiv. The leadership of the Ruzhiner was acknowledged by one of the most important tsadikim in western Galicia, Rebbe Hayim b. Leybush Halberstam (1793–1876), the tsadik of Neisants (Nowy Sącz or Sanz). Two other independent hasidic dynasties, whose importance increased in the later nineteenth century, were established in Belz and Vishnits (Vyzhnytsya).

Why did hasidism so quickly become dominant in Galicia? Much of the recent research on the origins of hasidism has sought to discredit the older view of historians like Benzion Dinur that the movement should be seen as a form of social protest by the lower orders of Jewish society against their worsening general position and the increased stratification of Jewish society. It is certainly the case that

23 On the career of the Ruzhiner rebbe, see Assaf, *The Regal Way*.

the Besht was no social revolutionary and did not seek in any way to overturn the established order of Jewish society. Yet, in Galicia in the early nineteenth century, as in the tsarist empire and the Kingdom of Poland, hasidism appealed to those who saw no advantage for themselves in the policies which sought to transform and integrate the Jews. Many of them were poor, but the hasidic leadership also made a great effort to recruit the wealthier members of the community, particularly those who had not been able to take advantage of the limited opportunities for social advancement and recognition offered by the authorities. The new government activism, with its increased taxation and involvement in the internal affairs of Jewish life, was also a major factor in the popularity of hasidic religious revivalism. It strengthened the belief within large sections of the Jewish world that the integrationist project was merely a new and more cunning attempt to convert the Jews to Christianity. The rise of hasidism was also aided by the economic and political backwardness of Galicia. It was above all in the smaller towns and shtetls, bypassed by progress towards the emergence of a more market-based economic system, that the movement established its main strongholds.

Given this economic and political backwardness, it is not surprising that the forces which sought to integrate the Jews into the wider society and acquire civil rights for them were much weaker than the forces of religious conservatism. The Haskalah went through a series of transformations as it moved eastwards from Germany over the three generations in which its influence was dominant within the modernizing minority in the Jewish world. In the Galician context there were two separate groups of reformers whose position should be distinguished, although there was considerable overlap in their views of the world: the maskilim, or followers of the Haskalah, and the reformers, or integrationists. The maskilim took the view that a modernized and purified Hebrew should be the basis for the reform of the Jews. For the most part, they were politically believers in enlightened autocracy, sharing the popular Jewish distrust of the 'violent and anti-Jewish' masses. They bitterly opposed the rise of hasidism, which they saw as obscurantist and backward-looking, its leaders mostly confidence tricksters deriving a good living from exploiting the gullibility of their ignorant followers. Among the principal exponents of the Haskalah in Galicia were Naphtali Herz Homberg; Joseph Perl, the author of *Megaleh temirin*, a savage critique of hasidism; the philosopher Nahman Krochmal (Renak, 1785–1840), who attempted to combine the Hegelian concept of history as a succession of stages, each characterized by a dominant idea, with a modernized version of the Jewish historical mission; Isaac Erter (1791–1851), the writer of satirical works in Hebrew; and Solomon Judah Leib Rapoport (Shir, 1790–1867), later a rabbi in Prague.

The reformers were oriented to German political liberalism. They were not as interested in Jewish religious reform as the maskilim, although they did favour a modernized and more organized form of synagogue worship, such as had been instituted by Isaac Noah Mannheimer (1793–1865) in the Seitenstettengasse synagogue in Vienna. There a pulpit had been introduced alongside the ark to make it possible to give sermons in German, and a choir had been created and the liturgy given a more Western form by the famous cantor Solomon Sulzer (1804–90). In addition, a women's gallery made it possible for women to take part in the service more fully. The political orientation of the reformers was liberal: they believed that changes in the position of the Jews would be linked with the establishment of a representative and constitutional government responsible to an electorate which would initially be somewhat restricted. They also believed strongly in education, primarily in German, as the road to Jewish reform.

Both groups advocated petitioning the authorities. Thus on 30 June 1830 the representatives of the *kehilah* of Brody addressed a petition to the emperor.[24] In it they asked that Jews, who constituted 90 per cent of the town's population, be represented on the municipal council, that they should benefit from the town's revenues, and that Jews in the town should not be held responsible to the *kahal*. Petitions to the authorities became more frequent in the run-up to the revolution of 1848. After Kraków was annexed to Austria following the failure of the revolution of February 1846, the local Jewish leaders vainly petitioned the Austrian government plenipotentiary Count Deym to extend to the former free city the improvements in the status of Jews which had been granted to the rest of Galicia. In the same year the representatives of the *kehilot* in Lviv, Brody, Stanyslaviv, Ternopil, Stryi, and Sambir requested the Austrian authorities to abrogate special Jewish taxes and grant the Jews full civic rights.[25] It is the failure of these petitions which accounts for the widespread Jewish support for revolution in 1848.

The groups favouring the integration and transformation of the Jews also frequently set up associations to 'raise the moral and material well-being' of the local Jewish population. Such bodies were created in Lviv, Brody, Tysmenytsya, Stanyslaviv, and Rzeszów, and also in the free city of Kraków. These were often linked with Polish émigré circles and helped to publicize the ideas of Polish exile circles in the West.[26] It was in towns like these and also in Ternopil, where Joseph Perl had established his school when the town was under Russian rule between 1809 and 1815, where the reformers were strongest. The conflict between the supporters and opponents of Jewish integration was particularly bitter in Lviv, which, alongside a Westernized minority, also had a large Orthodox and hasidic population. Conflicts raged primarily over the school system. In 1831, after a number of objections by the provincial authorities, following Perl's intervention with Metternich, the emperor gave permission for the establishment in the town

[24] Bałaban, *Dzieje Żydów w Galicyi i w Rzeczypospolitej Krakowskiej 1772–1868*, 103.

[25] For these petitions, see Eisenbach, *The Emancipation of the Jews in Poland, 1780–1870*, 331, and Bałaban, *Dzieje Żydów w Galicyi i w Rzeczypospolitej Krakowskiej 1772–1868*, 137–40.

[26] Bałaban, *Dzieje Żydów w Galicyi i w Rzeczypospolitej Krakowskiej 1772–1868*, 136, 154, 160–1; id., *Historja Żydów w Krakowie i na Kazimierzu, 1304–1868*, ii. 680 ff.; and Friedmann, *Die galizischen Juden im Kampfe um ihre Gleichberechtigung 1848–1869*, 59.

of a Society for Spreading Useful Crafts among Israelites. In addition, many Jewish youths attended German primary and secondary schools, much to the disgust of the Orthodox. In 1840 the municipal authorities supported the integrationists' refusal to hold an election for the *kahal* under the old rules, and appointed a Board of Commissioners made up of German-oriented maskilim, including the lawyers Emanuel Blumenfeld and Oswald Menkes and the physician Adam Barach. In 1844 a modern synagogue, the Deutsch-Israelitisches Bethaus, was established. Its first rabbi, Abraham Kohn, died tragically in 1848 when he was poisoned by an Orthodox fanatic.[27]

The integrationists were also divided among themselves over whether to favour a German or a Polish orientation. Until the 1860s the German orientation, represented in the organization Schomer Israel (Guardian of Israel), was dominant. With the establishment of provincial autonomy under Polish control, the pro-Polish orientation of Agudat Ahim (Alliance of Brothers) gained ground. The principal organ for the expression of assimilationist and pro-Polish ideas was now the weekly *Ojczyzna*.

In Kraków the pro-Polish orientation dominated from the start. In 1830 a Jewish state elementary school had already been created in Kazimierz, and five years later a Jewish state *Realschule* was also set up. In 1837 these establishments were merged, becoming a craft and commercial school, which by 1849–50 had 375 pupils.[28] In 1839 a Society for the Spreading of Useful Crafts among the Israelites, modelled on the similar body in Lviv, was also set up. A small number of Jewish students attended the Jagiellonian University. In the academic year 1826–7 there were three such students. Their number rose to twelve in 1846–7, fifteen in 1850–1, and twenty-six in 1865–6, when they constituted 7.7 per cent of the student body.[29]

In 1831 an ardent Polish patriot, Rabbi Dov Berush Meisels, was elected communal rabbi and, although firmly Orthodox, saw his mission as the achievement of civil rights for the Jews. In 1840 the Kraków Society for Religion and Civilization was created. In its meeting place on Plac Nowy in Kazimierz it held religious services with a choir and sermon inspired by those at the Seitenstettengasse synagogue. A key role in this was played by Abraham Gumplowicz, a prominent merchant, who succeeded in persuading the senate of the free city to confirm the statute of the organization, after some delay, on 19 June 1843. Among its supporters were members of the Kazimierz Jewish elite.[30]

[27] On these developments, see Wierzbieniec, 'The Processes of Jewish Emancipation and Assimilation in the Multiethnic City of Lviv during the Nineteenth and Twentieth Centuries', 228–30, and Bałaban, *Historia lwowskiej synagogi postępowej*, 5–6.

[28] Bałaban, *Dzieje Żydów w Galicyi i w Rzeczypospolitej Krakowskiej 1772–1868*, 114.

[29] Bobińska (ed.), *Studia z dziejów młodzieży Uniwersytetu Krakowskiego od Oświecenia do połowy XX w.*, ii/1, tables 12, 17.

[30] On this, see Bałaban, *Historja Żydów w Krakowie i na Kazimierzu, 1304–1868*, 665–6.

JEWS AND THE REVOLUTIONS OF 1846–1848

The Habsburg empire was, along with France, one of the two main centres of revolution in Europe during the crisis of 1846–8. Here the revolution was characterized by a series of overlapping conflicts, by liberal calls for representative government, by peasant demands for the ending of the labour tribute, and by assertion of the right of national self-determination. These national aspirations were not uniform in character, since the demands of the 'historic' nations—the Germans, Italians, Poles, and Hungarians—for the reorganization of central Europe into national states sparked off a response for the recognition of their existence by the 'non-historic' nationalities—the Czechs, Slovaks, Romanians, Croats, and Ukrainians, who had been seen by the 'historic' nations as merely peasant tribal groups which they would ultimately assimilate.[31]

The Jews in the empire were, for the most part, strong supporters of the movement in Austria, Galicia, and Kraków for the establishment of a liberal, constitutional state. The Polish revolution, which had long been planned, broke out in Kraków and in western Galicia in early 1846. It soon proved disastrous, as the fearful and ignorant peasants turned on the revolutionaries and the local nobility, and, in a reaction resembling the *grande peur* in France in 1789, massacred the landowners. The rising was almost entirely confined to the Polish-speaking western areas of Galicia. Some peasants in mountainous areas, where labour services were not a source of conflict, did in fact support the insurrection. In all, perhaps 1,100 people were killed, 3,000 arrested, and 430 manor houses burnt. The Austrian local authorities were not responsible for instigating this massacre, but some officials, notably the district head of Tarnów, Josef Breinl, undoubtedly saw the peasants' hostility towards the nobles as a useful means of suppressing the insurrection. There was also some satisfaction among the higher authorities, although this sentiment was combined with fear at the uncontrollable character of peasant violence. The governor of Galicia referred to the development of the situation in Galicia as 'gratifying', while the archduke Louis observed that it was a sign of the 'good fortune' of Austria.[32] Certainly, this clear indication of peasant hostility demoralized the Polish revolutionaries and enabled the Austrians quickly to restore order and incorporate the free city into Galicia.

The revolution of 1846 was significant in another respect. On 23 February 1846 the Revolutionary Council issued an appeal 'To Our Israelite Brothers', which promised the abolition of all distinctions between Jews and other citizens, the first such act on the Polish lands.[33] In response, some 500 Jews, including

[31] On these developments, see Namier, *1848*; Macartney, *The Habsburg Empire, 1790–1918*; May, *The Hapsburg Monarchy, 1867–1914*; Kann, *The Multinational Empire*; Taylor, *The Habsburg Monarchy, 1809–1918*; and Polonsky, 'The Revolutionary Crisis of 1846–1849 and its Place in the Development of Nineteenth-Century Galicia'.

[32] Wandycz, 'The Poles in the Habsburg Monarchy', 77.

[33] For this, see Bałaban, *Historja Żydów w Krakowie i na Kazimierzu, 1304–1868*, ii. 667–8.

Józef Oettinger, Maurycy Warshauer, Jozue Funk, and Maurycy Krzepicki of the Society for Religion and Civilization, joined the insurrectionary army, which was also enthusiastically welcomed by Rabbi Meisels. There was widespread enthusiasm in the Jewish community for the uprising. Both Meisels and Krzepicki called on the Jews to support the revolution 'as befits the free and brave sons of the motherland'.[34] This did not prevent some of the more reactionary Polish émigrés, such as Wiktor Szokalski, a member of Adam Czartoryski's entourage in Paris, from accusing the Galician Jews of responsibility for the jacquerie which followed the outbreak of revolution in Kraków and Austrian Poland. Similar views were propagated in the principal newspapers of the Czartoryski group in Paris. According to *Dziennik Narodowy* and *Trzeci Maj*, the Jews had participated in the democratic movement to advance their own interests. The activities of Jews, as well as Frankists and other converts, were 'harmful to the nation' and Jews had also denounced revolutionaries to the authorities and even participated in the peasant violence.[35] At the same time there was an increasing acceptance on the part of those who went into exile after the 1830–1 uprising that equality would have to be granted to the Jews. On 5 October 1846 *Trzeci Maj*, while admitting that this would be difficult to accept, conceded 'that the Jews (*starozakonni*) are entitled to have the same civic rights as we have'.[36]

The humiliating collapse of the revolution and the incorporation of Kraków into Austria were followed by Austrian reprisals against those who had supported it. Some Jews were imprisoned and all restrictive anti-Jewish laws re-established. In addition, a fine of 50,000 florins was levied on the Jewish community.

When revolution broke out again in 1848, Galicia was not one of its main centres because of the disastrous events of 1846. In addition, the rapid action by the Austrian governor of the province, Franz von Stadion, in abolishing the *robot*, the labour tribute owed by the peasantry to the nobles, took the wind out of the sails of the revolution. Nevertheless, the collapse of the central government in Vienna did lead to calls for widespread local autonomy, and also saw the beginning of the Polish–Ukrainian conflict which in the future was to dominate the political life of the province. Poles were certainly an important element in the revolutionary parliament elected in June 1848, which sat first in Vienna and then, after the re-establishment of imperial authority there, in Kroměříž. The leading Polish liberal Franciszek Smolka was elected president of this parliament.

Jews were divided in their political stance during the revolution. Some took an active part in the political struggle, aligning themselves with the Poles. Others did not support the national aspirations of the Poles, and adopted a pro-Austrian position, fearing an increase in the strength of Polish antisemitism and an

34 On these developments, see Eisenbach, *Wielka Emigracja wobec kwestii żydowskiej, 1832–1849*, 397–8; Gelber, *Aus zwei Jahrhunderten*, 264; and Giller, *Historia powstania narodu polskiego w 1861–1864*, iv. 52.

35 On these views, see Eisenbach, *Wielka Emigracja wobec kwestii żydowskiej, 1832–1849*, 414–18.

36 Quoted in Eisenbach, *The Emancipation of the Jews in Poland, 1780–1870*, 328.

outbreak of anti-Jewish violence. In fact, there was much less anti-Jewish violence in Galicia in 1846 and 1848 than in other areas of Europe, including Alsace, western Germany, the Grand Duchy of Poznań, the Czech lands, and Hungary.[37] No anti-Jewish outrages took place during the jacquerie of February 1846, and, when anti-Jewish violence threatened in the spring of 1848, an appeal from the Polish National Committee in Lviv calmed the situation.[38] It is not clear why this was the case. The main antagonism, both in the western and in the eastern parts of the province, was between landlord and peasant, and it may be that at this stage the local Jews enjoyed a degree of trust in the villages which was not enjoyed by the landlords. This may explain the curious appeal made in a pamphlet addressed to Jews in the countryside issued in Yiddish in Lviv in June 1848: 'Your words', it claimed, 'are listened to by peasants . . . you should therefore see to it that there is peace between the lords and the peasants.' It went on to assert that the Jews should make sure that the peasants understood that they had received their land because of an initiative of the landowners, who did not want to fight the emperor. Artur Eisenbach has argued that this pamphlet owes its origin to the attempts of the followers of Czartoryski to win over the peasantry to the Polish cause in the aftermath of the debacle of 1846.[39]

Stadion himself also attempted to secure Jewish support by calling on the Austrian authorities in April 1848 to abolish all special taxes paid by Jews. Jews were among those who participated in the formation of a delegation from the towns of Lviv, Kraków, and Tarnów which called, in an address of 6 April 1848, for the summoning of a national assembly. It affirmed:

> [The] main and indispensable foundation [of this assembly] should be the representation of the nation, irrespective of class and religion. . . . The prosperity of states depends on a free and harmonious development of all national forces, on their being used for the common good. A genuine love of the motherland can only exist if the motherland makes no distinction between her children . . . It seems to us therefore that the classes and religions existing in the nation should be granted equal civic and political rights . . . [and] that all taxes connected with religion as well as religion-based exclusions and restrictions should be abolished.[40]

The revolution saw considerable political mobilization among the Jews of Galicia. Jews played an active role in the national councils established in Lviv and Kraków and joined the National Guards established in many Galician towns. In Lviv and Kraków separate detachments commanded by Jewish officers were established. A Yiddish weekly, *Lemberger yidishe tsaytung*, was established under

[37] On this violence, see Baron, 'The Impact of the Revolution of 1848 on Jewish Emancipation', 197–8, and Toury, *Soziale und politische Geschichte der Juden in Deutschland 1847–1871*, 290–5.

[38] Friedmann, *Die galizischen Juden im Kampfe um ihre Gleichberechtigung 1848–1869*, 64, and Kieniewicz (ed.), *Rok 1848 w Polsce*, 209–10.

[39] Bałaban, *Dzieje Żydów w Galicyi i w Rzeczypospolitej Krakowskiej 1772–1868*, 166; Eisenbach, *Emancipation of the Jews in Poland, 1780–1870*, 350.

[40] For this address, see Kieniewicz (ed.), *Rok 1848 w Polsce*, 225–9.

the editorship of Abraham Menahem Mendel Mohr (1815–68). Shortly before the opening of the parliament delegates from *kehilot* all over Galicia assembled in Lviv and drew up a memorandum demanding full equality.[41]

Jews were particularly prominent in the revolution in Kraków. On 3 May 1848 (the anniversary of the adoption of the Polish constitution of 1791) the members of the Kraków Society for Religion and Civilization issued an appeal. At this moment, when the peoples of Europe were freeing themselves from the 'oppression by tyrants', when the Jews too 'were being granted rights for which they had been waiting for such a long time', it was

> the duty of an Israelite to evoke in himself love for the motherland, to be permeated by patriotism for the country in which he was born, and awake among his co-religionists a holy zeal for the cause of freedom . . . We shall show the world that we have the Maccabees' blood in our veins, that our hearts, like the hearts of our forefathers, respond warmly to everything that is noble and sublime.[42]

In Kraków the Club for the Advancement of the Spiritual and Material Interests of the Jews met on 1 October and prepared a memorandum for submission to parliament calling for Jews to be granted full legal equality.[43]

Two Jews were elected to the Reichsrat in 1848, Rabbi Isaac Mannheimer (of the Seitenstettengasse synagogue in Vienna) from Brody and Abraham Halpern from Stanyslaviv. In a subsequent by-election Rabbi Meisels was elected from Kraków, by an electorate made up of both Christians and Jews. He expressed well the views of those Jews who supported more moderate Polish aspirations and the revolutionary constitution of April 1848:

> the future of our Polish motherland can only be secured through organic work [work to raise the economic, social, and cultural level of the country], not through the dissolution of society . . . Realizing the needs of humanity in its present phase, I am an ardent believer in the principles of freedom, in the development of political rights, in all citizens having a share in these rights . . . I regard these principles as the basis of a true democracy which, far from lowering everything, raises everything, which does not destroy but constructs and consolidates the new constitution by love.[44]

However, the Jewish identification with the Polish cause was bitterly resented by the emerging Ukrainian movement, whose leaders held the Jews responsible for the economic backwardness of the Ukrainian countryside and, as agents of the Polish nobility, for the oppression of the Ukrainian peasantry. On 19 June 1848 the Ukrainian political leadership declared itself unequivocally against the emancipation of the Jews.[45]

[41] On these developments, see Friedmann, *Die galizischen Juden im Kampfe um ihre Gleichberechtigung 1848–1869*, 64, and the document printed in *Historishe shriftn* (1929), 741–5.

[42] *Der Orient*, 9 (1848), no. 22 (27 May), 173–4, quoted in Eisenbach, *The Emancipation of the Jews in Poland, 1780–1870*, 364–5.

[43] Bałaban, *Historja Żydów w Krakowie i na Kazimierzu, 1304–1868*, ii. 684–5.

[44] Quoted in Eisenbach, *The Emancipation of the Jews in Poland, 1780–1870*, 355.

[45] Kozik, *Ukraiński ruch narodowy w Galicji*, 192–4, 203.

During the revolution the government conceded the principle of equal rights for the Jews. The extent to which the rhetoric of the revolution had affected Jewish attitudes can be seen in the behaviour of a group of Jews in Tysmenytsya and Zhovkva. In August 1848 they approached Franciszek Smolka, the president of the revolutionary parliament, asking for his support in their aspiration for full Jewish emancipation. In addition, they submitted a petition to the parliament arguing that it was the old governments and laws which had isolated the Jews from the Poles and that the restrictions imposed on the Jews had weakened the Jewish spirit of freedom. The revolutionary ideas of liberty, equality, and fraternity had now crushed superstitions and prejudices and awoken the Jews from their lethargy. The hour of salvation had struck for all people. Everyone, Christian or Jew, was entitled to equal rights, 'all the rights of Man', which were 'a noble principle of democracy', the foundations of the European temple of freedom. Only 'through an alliance of all religions can freedom stand up to the storms of the century and survive for ever'. Their goals, they concluded, were to raise the educational level of the Jews, encourage agricultural settlement, and increase the knowledge of Polish culture.[46]

Smolka must have been rather put out by the fervent democratic and integrationist zeal of the petitioners. He told them he supported their demands, but warned them, should they achieve legal equality, to use their new rights 'cautiously and with prudence, not to the disadvantage of the Christian population, for this would provoke a reaction and result in another restriction of their rights'.[47]

The petition from Tysmenytsya and Zhovkva was not the only one submitted at this time. Petitions were also sent to the revolutionary parliament in Vienna by leaders of many other *kehilot*. They argued that, although the government had now proclaimed the principle of equality before the law, the special taxes on Jews had not been abolished and anti-Jewish discrimination had been maintained in a number of areas of economic life. They called for the establishment of full legal equality and religious freedom.

The Jewish parliamentary representatives also spoke against the restrictive legislation affecting the Jewish community. When the question of the special Jewish taxes was discussed at the beginning of October 1848, Rabbi Mannheimer argued that their abolition should be enacted not so much because this was in the interests of the Jews as for the sake of the dignity of this legislative chamber. 'You are the parliament, the first constitutional national assembly. There is no doubt that the question whether you want to sanction this abnormal, inhuman tax must be solved here. Do you want to legalize this injustice?'[48]

[46] Widman, *Franciszek Smolka, jego życie i zawód publiczny*, 279, 870, 876, quoted in Eisenbach, *The Emancipation of the Jews in Poland, 1780–1870*, 345.

[47] Eisenbach, *The Emancipation of the Jews in Poland, 1780–1870*, 345.

[48] Friedmann, *Die galizischen Juden im Kampfe um ihre Gleichberechtigung 1848–1869*, 71.

In the event, on 5 October the parliament voted overwhelmingly, by 242 votes to twenty, to abolish all taxes levied on a particular group, including those on the Jews. Further discussion of the Jewish issue in parliament was forestalled by its dissolution by General Alfred Windischgrätz. However, the constitution promulgated by the new emperor, Franz Joseph I, on 4 March 1849 confirmed the principle of full equality before the law, and extended civil rights to Jews, including the right to settle anywhere in the country and to purchase any sort of property. In practice, however, most Jews in Galicia were still unable to receive municipal citizenship or to settle outside the Jewish quarter in a number of towns. Some, though not all, of the former legal restrictions were reintroduced after the revolution was crushed with Russian help in 1849. In particular, Jews were now barred from state service or from owning land, their rights of residence were restricted, and they were forbidden to employ Christian domestic servants.

The Austrian government had defeated the revolution by default because of outside intervention and the divisions within the revolutionary groups. Austria would never be as powerful after 1848 as it had been in the post-1815 period. The revolution had other important consequences. The violence of the conflict between peasants and nobles in western Galicia came as a devastating blow to Polish hopes, which had prevailed from the time of the emigration following the uprising of November 1830 in the Kingdom of Poland, of restoring Polish statehood by insurrection. It was now clear that the Poles would have to devote a long period to internal reform before the issue of independence could again be raised. The influence of those who opposed revolution and who sought compromise with the partitioning powers was greatly enhanced.

The revolution in Galicia also saw the emergence of a self-conscious Ukrainian (still calling itself Ruthenian) nationalism. During the revolution the main Ukrainian organization, the Supreme Ruthenian Council, had embarked on widespread political agitation and had collected thousands of signatures in support of its objectives.

At the same time the abolition of the labour tribute, celebrated each year in Ukrainian villages, ended the principal source of conflict in the countryside, both Polish and Ukrainian. However, the way that peasant emancipation was introduced meant that most peasant holdings were barely sufficient to provide subsistence. Disputes also continued over rights to common grazing land and to forests, where the 1848 Edict of Emancipation mostly favoured landlord interests. Ultimately only 0.2 per cent of woods and pastures went to peasants. The land question had thus not been resolved and returned to plague Galician politicians in the second half of the nineteenth century.

For the Jews, the years of the revolution had seen an unprecedented political mobilization. The declaration of the revolutionary government in Kraków in favour of Jewish equality, the campaigns for the revolutionary parliament, which were accompanied by expressions of solidarity between Christians and Jews, and the final achievement of equal rights, all aroused widespread enthusiasm. The disillusionment occasioned by the crushing of the revolution and the return of many of the old restrictions was therefore all the harder to bear.

THE FINAL ACHIEVEMENT OF EQUAL RIGHTS BY THE JEWS OF GALICIA

The re-establishment of the Austrian government's authority was followed by a decade of autocratic rule. The Polish political leadership in Galicia was divided. Count Agenor Gołuchowski, the provincial governor, argued that only complete and absolute obedience to the Austrians could help the Polish cause. He was distrusted by the Austrian centralist prime minister Alexander, Baron von Bach, but had some success with the emperor, particularly during the Crimean War, when Ruthenians were seen as potential allies of Russia.

These years also saw the emergence of a new political group, the 'young conservatives' based in Kraków. Known as the Stańczycy, they held moderate opinions and had strong ties to the landed nobility through their leader, Count Adam Potocki. Implacably hostile to the insurrectionary tradition, they rejected the leadership of the émigrés in Paris, and their anti-revolutionary sentiments were intensified by the disastrous 1863 uprising and its negative impact in Galicia. They saw the weakness and final partition of Poland–Lithuania as a consequence not of the nefarious behaviour of its neighbours but of defects in the state constitution, the weakness of the monarchy, and the political omnipotence of the nobility reflected in the *liberum veto*. Some also condemned the growing religious intolerance after 1648. They called for Poles to work for the modernization of Polish society in cooperation with the partitioning powers, and for loyalty to the Habsburg dynasty.

The Stańczycy expressed their views initially in pamphlets, taking their name from a series published in 1869 under the title *Teka Stańczyka* (The Notebooks of Stańczyk), which set out their political credo in the guise of observations by a sixteenth-century jester at the court of Zygmunt I. They also had their own daily, *Czas*, founded in 1848, and a number of their leaders, such as Józef Szujski (1835–83) and Michał Bobrzyński (1849–1935), were professional historians whose works buttressed the ideological position of the group. Szujski, a professor at the Jagiellonian University from 1869 and secretary-general of the Kraków Academy of Sciences, was the author of many works on pre-partition Poland, including *Historyi polskiej treściwie opowiedzianej ksiąg dwanaście* (An Overview of Polish History in Twelve Parts; Warsaw, 1880) and an essay characteristic of the group's view entitled *O fałszywej historii jako mistrzyni fałszywej polityki* (False History as the Mistress of False Politics), while Bobrzyński was also a professor of law and, for a time, governor of Galicia. His *Dzieje Polski w zarysie* (Outline

History of Poland, 1879) remains one of the best books on the subject even today, in spite of its strongly ideological character.[49]

Aristocratic circles in Lviv, headed by Prince Adam Sapieha, rejected collaboration and favoured rather the building up of Polish economic strength through a savings bank, a land credit society, an agricultural school, and railway construction. Finally, the bourgeois liberals, led by the veterans of 1848 Franciszek Smolka and Florian Ziemałkowski, upheld traditional liberal demands for equality and freedom. They were divided, however, over both strategy and tactics. Smolka wanted to join the Czechs and seek the transformation of Austria into a federal state. Ziemałkowski regarded this approach as utopian and sought rather to obtain small concessions in a manner similar to the Kraków conservatives.

In 1859, under pressure from foreign defeat, the Bach centralist system collapsed. The dynasty had two alternatives: it could bring the German middle class into government, which would preserve centralism, or it could form an alliance with regional aristocracies. The emperor Franz Joseph at first favoured the latter. Gołuchowski was thus called to Vienna as minister of state to devise a solution, which took the form of the October Patent (1860), which proposed a central Reichsrat and local diets to advise provincial administrations. It broke down because of opposition from the Hungarians, and Gołuchowski was dismissed. The February Patent, introduced a few months later, in 1861, made provision for a far more centralized system. Local diets, however, were introduced with relatively limited powers. In Galicia the electorate was divided into four estates: the first was made up of landowners and was granted forty-four seats; the next two represented towns and commercial–industrial chambers, and were assigned twenty-six seats; while the peasants were granted seventy-four seats, technically a majority. In practice, because of aristocratic influence and open voting, nobles were still able to dominate the political scene.

Throughout this period the Ruthenians hoped to achieve their objectives, of division of the province and control of the eastern part, with the help of the Austrian government, and thus favoured centralization. They were rewarded with the creation of two chairs in the Ruthenian language at the University of Lviv at a time when there was still no chair in Polish.

Polish attempts to gain autonomy were further set back by the widespread sympathy shown in Galicia for the 1863 uprising, and in February 1864 a state of emergency was proclaimed in Galicia. But attempts to reach a compromise continued and were accentuated when the situation in Austria changed radically after defeat at the hands of Prussia in 1866. The new system established in 1867 granted far-reaching autonomy to Hungary within the borders of the Crown lands of King Stephen. The only matters which were now decided jointly by the two parts of the empire (the Empire (Kaiserreich) of Austria and the Kingdom (Königreich) of Hungary—hence 'K. und K.') were foreign policy, the common

[49] For the views of the group, see *Stańczycy*.

tariff, and the administration of the army. In the Austrian, or Cisleithanian, part of the monarchy a constitutional system was introduced, and in it the dominant political role was taken by the German centralist liberals who were to rule in Vienna until 1878. The new government sought the support of the Poles, who were now granted wide-ranging autonomy in 1868. Under this system a Polish minister sat in the cabinet in Vienna, only a Pole could be marshal of the Galician nobility, and only a Pole could be provincial governor (*namiestnik*). The Ukrainians were now granted two seats in the provincial cabinet and one vice-governor. The Galician school system, including the universities of Kraków and Lviv, was now Polonized, together with the whole of the civil service and legal system.

The establishment of a constitutional government in Austria and the granting of Galician autonomy again brought the question of the granting of full legal equality to the Jews of the province to the fore. This led to a debate within the Polish elite in the province. Already a number of restrictions on Jewish activity had been done away with. From November 1859 Jews had been allowed to enter into marriage freely, while all restrictions on occupations open to Jews were abolished throughout the monarchy by legislation in 1859 and 1860. Jews were also now entitled to testify in court against Christians and to settle in the villages. Jews who had the requisite educational qualifications were also permitted to purchase land.

The Stańczycy were ambivalent about granting full legal equality to the Jews. A number of them, including the historian Walerian Kalinka, had opposed the new liberal regulations of 1859 and 1860. In a pamphlet issued in 1860 Kalinka had argued that the Jews exerted a harmful 'moral and material influence' on the peasants and 'perpetuated drunkenness in the villages' and were increasingly dominating Polish trade and industry.[50] His views were shared by another conservative, Henryk Schmitt, who argued that Jewish assimilation was for the moment impossible since the Jews constituted a 'religious–national sect' whose goals were at odds with those of Christian nations. Only if the Jews renounced their faith and nationality could they become members of the 'national Christian community' and good citizens.[51] Equal rights could only be granted if the Jews became 'enlightened' and were 'brought up differently', a process which would take many decades.

A more liberal position was taken by the leaders of the Stańczycy in the Sejm, Józef Szujski and Count Stanisław Tarnowski. Both had opposed the municipal regulations introduced in 1863 and 1866 by the Lviv city council which restricted the number of Jewish councillors to 15 per cent of the total. They also had close links with the Austrian government, in particular with the Galician governor, Gołuchowski, and were well aware of the implications of the new Austrian consti-

[50] Kalinka, *Dzieła*, 226.

[51] Schmitt, *Rzut oka na projekt bezwarunkowego równouprawnienia Żydów oraz odpowiedź na zarzuty z którymi dzisiejsi ich obrońcy przeciw narodowi polskiemu występują*, 56.

tution. If they did not extend the principle of legal equality to Galicia, it would be imposed on them from Vienna and would strengthen the pro-German and centralizing tendencies within Galician Jewry. In addition, in a reflection of their aristocratic view of the world, they believed that the Jews were an essential conduit to the villages. If the Jews could be won over, the countryside could be kept quiescent.

Strong opposition to the abolition of the remaining anti-Jewish legislation was expressed by the Podolacy (the Podolians), the ultra-conservative large landowners of eastern Galicia, who also opposed any concessions to the Ukrainians. A similar position was adopted by the small number of Ukrainian deputies. The Ukrainian political leadership, which was dominated by Greek Catholic priests, lacked political sophistication and was acutely conscious of the bitterness of the social conflict between Jews and peasants in the villages of eastern Galicia. In addition, anti-Jewish tendencies were strengthened by the dominance of the Russophile tendency in Ukrainian politics.

The debate in the Galician Sejm focused initially on the question of the rights to be accorded to Jews under the new municipal regulations. Those opposed to full legal equality claimed that it would be inequitable to grant full participation in municipal government to the Jews since the local Jewish communal bodies (*gminy*) would be responsible for Jewish education, whereas there would be no corresponding Christian authority. This would mean that Jews would be called upon to deal with purely Christian matters and, if they were in a majority, to decide them. In addition, given the large Jewish population in certain towns, they feared for their Polish character. As a result the Sejm passed a law granting Jews only restricted access to local government.

Under the constitution for Cisleithanian Austria enacted on 21 December 1867 all legal restrictions suffered by Jews were finally abrogated, while under the school law of 25 May 1868 the influence of the Catholic Church in the running of state schools was greatly reduced. In addition, a law of 3 May 1868 abolished the special oath Jews had to swear in court. In this new situation Governor Gołuchowski presented to the Sejm a new non-discriminatory law on municipal self-government. If it were not accepted, imperial legislation would be imposed to implement its terms. An additional incentive to action was the bitter hostility of the Ukrainians to the new autonomous Galician government, which made the Jews potential allies in administering the province. These issues were among the first to be debated by the newly elected Sejm, initially between 18 February and 2 March 1867, before the Austrian Reichsrat enacted the new constitution, and then again between 22 August and 10 October 1868. The strongest supporters of Jewish equality were the Democrats (the liberals of 1848), still led by Smolka and Władysław Gniewosz, who had forty members in the Sejm, of whom four were 'Poles of the Mosaic faith'. In his speech in the Sejm on 30 September 1868 Smolka claimed that granting equality to the Jews was 'a sacred national obligation imposed on future generations by the last Polish Sejm'. He concluded as follows:

There has been and there will be no more important issue [than the Jewish question] since 1848, when the problem of compulsory agricultural labour was solved. There is no issue that enters so deeply into our national and social relations as the Jewish question, whose successful resolution in the spirit of freedom and unrestricted equality will guarantee our future . . . We do not want to delay; we are not seeking any artificial, mystical means for solving this issue; we are writing no thick, obscure legal books, and if we are still not right before the law, if we do not intend to be good politicians, we are at least honest Christians, and we will not do to the Jews what we do not wish to be done to us. Therefore, gentlemen, let us pass the proposal once more without haggling and without amendments.[52]

Smolka's views were seconded by the Jewish deputies. Marek Dubs, representing Lviv, argued that it was the exclusion of the Jews from Polish society which hampered their assimilation. 'If you want the Jews to be loyal sons of this country, gentlemen, you must win them over for the national cause not by excluding them from some institutions, but by other means.' Another Jewish deputy, Oswald Hönigsman, was more blunt: 'One can safely say that in order to emancipate the Jews one must first emancipate oneself from prejudices and imaginary fears.'[53] At the conclusion of the debate the Sejm, with only four dissenters, resolved on 8 October 1868 to accept Gołuchowski's proposal and to request the government 'to remove all the former provisions concerning the special position of the Jews'.[54] This resolution was given imperial assent on 19 November.

CONCLUSION

The granting of legal equality was, of course, only the start of the process of Jewish integration in Galicia, which was to prove slow and incomplete. Galicia was politically and economically backward, and in the second half of the nineteenth century its politics came to be dominated by the increasingly bitter Polish–Ukrainian conflict. This caused serious problems for Jewish political strategy since the bulk of the province's Jews lived in its predominantly Ukrainian eastern part. Because of the bitterness that had accompanied the adoption of full legal equality, it was some time before the alliance between the Jewish political elite and the Polish ruling stratum in Galicia was consolidated. Once established, it was to last until the outbreak of the First World War, but from the beginning of the twentieth century it began to show increasing signs of strain.

[52] Friedmann, *Die galizischen Juden im Kampfe um ihre Gleichberechtigung 1848–1869*, 87.

[53] Ibid. 88.

[54] Friedmann, 'Die Judenfrage im galizischen Landtag', 473.

NINE

THE JEWS IN THE DUCHY OF WARSAW AND THE KINGDOM OF POLAND, 1807–1881

As a result of the three partitions of Poland at the end of the eighteenth century, and particularly as a consequence of the redrawing of the Polish boundaries at the Congress of Vienna in 1814–15, the tsarist empire absorbed within its borders the larger part of the Polish lands. The Russian partition was qualitatively different from the areas ruled by Prussia and Austria. It was here that the fate of Poland was decided, it was here that the principal political struggles took place, and it was here that the potential future capital of an independent Poland, Warsaw, was located.

As a result of these territorial changes the tsarist empire now contained the largest Jewish community in the world. Thus, in 1820 Jews made up 1.6 million of the empire's population of 46 million. The number of Jews rose rapidly in the nineteenth century, reaching 4 million in 1880 (out of 86 million) and 5.6 million in 1910 (of 130.8 million). This community was largely inherited from the Polish–Lithuanian Commonwealth, but it lived in two very different environments. The smaller part of the community (400,000 in 1820, 1.1 million in 1880) lived in the Kingdom of Poland (see Map 7). This was an autonomous, semi-constitutional state created at the Congress of Vienna to satisfy, at least in part, the national aspirations of the Poles. It was in dynastic union with the Romanovs and its autonomous status was severely restricted after the unsuccessful Polish uprising of 1830–1, and almost entirely done away with in the aftermath of that of 1863–4. It did, however, possess a constitution and a concept of citizenship, which meant that, in theory at least, there was a basis for the transformation of the Jews into citizens. The remainder of the Jews found themselves in the western part of the autocratic tsarist monarchy (the Pale of Settlement). This had only a weak and undeveloped version of the estate structure which had developed in Western Christendom during the Middle Ages, and was still essentially an autocracy of a patriarchal kind. It lacked any concept of citizenship.

The situation of the Jews developed very differently in the two areas. In the Pale of Settlement, the area to which the Jews were restricted, the tsarist government in the first half of the nineteenth century pursued policies aggressively designed to break up Jewish 'separatism', conscripting the Jews and attempting to

Russify a minority through special schools. Although in the 1860s these harsh measures were relaxed, the hoped-for abolition of the restrictions on Jewish civil rights never materialized, and after 1881, as a result of the wave of pogroms which followed the assassination of Tsar Alexander II, pogroms which they saw as provoked by Jewish oppression of the peasantry, the tsarist authorities made it clear that they had no intention of granting citizenship to their Jewish subjects. It was thus within the Russian Jewish community that concepts of autonomous Jewish self-identity, the basis of the new Jewish politics, were first articulated and where, with the development of modern Hebrew and of Yiddish as a literary language, the Jews in the area came increasingly to form a proto-nation, like the other emerging nations of the area, the Ukrainians, the Lithuanians, and the Belarusians.

In the Kingdom of Poland the pattern of Jewish politics was rather different. In the first half of the nineteenth century the Polish nobility, which even after the failure of the revolution of 1830–1 was the dominant force in the area, took the view that Jewish emancipation was conditional on the Jews abandoning their religious and social separateness, a development which was regarded as rather unlikely, or, at best, could be expected to take a very long time. The run-up to the insurrection of 1863 changed this situation as a competition to win the support of the Jews developed between the viceroy of the Kingdom, Count Aleksander Wielopolski, a Pole who was trying to introduce a measure of self-rule which would also be acceptable to the tsarist authorities, and those Poles calling for the re-establishment of the autonomy of the Kingdom. As a result the Jews of the Kingdom received their emancipation from Wielopolski on 4 June 1862. This was not rescinded after the failure of the uprising, and the Jewish elite remained committed to an integrationist view of the Jewish future, which they propagated through the weekly *Izraelita*.

The position of the Jews was weakened by the slow progress of acculturation. The educational system was in the hands of the Russian authorities, who were determined to prevent another Polish uprising and therefore were not willing to see either a universal system of primary education or one which could foster Polish national values. (It should be pointed out that at this time there was no universal system of primary education anywhere in the tsarist empire.) It was further undermined by the impact of the new Jewish politics which was developing in the Pale of Settlement and which was brought to the Kingdom both by the pamphlets and newspapers which it produced and by immigration from that area to the Kingdom of considerable numbers of Jews (the so-called Litvaks). The growth of antisemitism further increased the attractiveness of the new politics, suggesting that the hope of converting the Jews into 'Poles of the Mosaic faith' was an illusion.

Ultimate control in both the Kingdom of Poland and the Pale of Settlement was in the hands of the tsar and his government, and, inevitably, policies adopted in one affected those in the other. In addition, in both areas society was still largely agricultural, with a small class of landowners ruling over a mass of unfree cultivators. Towns were small and progress towards constitutional government slow. Not surprisingly, the abolition of restrictions on Jewish activity and the political and social integration of the Jews were also to proceed very slowly in both.

THE POLITICAL EVOLUTION OF THE KINGDOM OF POLAND

The Kingdom of Poland was the direct political successor of the Napoleonic Duchy of Warsaw, which in turn should be seen as the heir to the political traditions of the reformers of the Four Year Sejm. The Duchy of Warsaw was created by Napoleon on 22 July 1807 after his defeat of Prussia out of territory which the Prussian state had acquired in the partitions of Poland. It was enlarged in 1809 to include territory taken from Austria, and, had Napoleon been victorious in 1812, would presumably have been further expanded at Russian expense. It was a constitutional state in dynastic union with Napoleon's ally King Frederick Augustus of Saxony (1807–15). This was only one of the many links with eighteenth-century developments in Poland, which had two Saxon kings during the first half of the eighteenth century and where the constitution of 3 May 1791 established a hereditary monarchy which was to be entrusted to the Wettin dynasty of Saxony. Another link was the prominence in the Duchy's administration of reformers from the era of King Stanisław August (r. 1764–95), notably Stanisław Staszic, Dominik Krysiński, Wawrzyniec Surowiecki, Stanisław Kostka Potocki, and Julian Ursyn Niemcewicz, who were also later to be active in the Kingdom of Poland.[1]

The Duchy was short-lived, and for Napoleon it was primarily a source of soldiers and finance for his wars. However, it marked an important stage in Polish political evolution. It had a constitution similar to those established elsewhere in the Napoleonic empire and introduced the Napoleonic Civil Code, which effectively abolished serfdom, though not the obligation to perform labour service, with its establishment of the principle of equality before the law, a principle which was also enshrined in article 4 of the constitution of the Duchy.

The defeat of Napoleon saw Tsar Alexander I in a dominant position in most of the territory of the former Polish–Lithuanian Commonwealth. Alexander had been persuaded by his foreign minister, the Polish magnate Adam Czartoryski, to try to reach a compromise between the aspirations of the Poles and Russian national interests, and therefore attempted to maintain the basic structure of the

[1] On the Duchy of Warsaw, see Grochulska, *Księstwo Warszawskie*; Askenazy, *Książe Józef Poniatowski*; Davies, *God's Playground*, ii. 294–305; Wandycz, *The Lands of Partitioned Poland 1795–1918*, 3–65; Reddaway et al. (eds.), *The Cambridge History of Poland*, ii. 208–57; Handelsman, *Napoleon a Polska*; Zawadzki, *A Man of Honour*; Czartoryski, *Memoirs of Prince Adam Czartoryski*, 174–88.

Duchy of Warsaw. Pressure from Britain and Austria, worried about the growth of Russian power, forced him to relinquish the western parts of the Duchy, which became the Grand Duchy of Poznań. In addition, although a Polish-controlled educational system was created in the areas of the former Grand Duchy of Lithuania, promises to extend the borders of the Kingdom of Poland (sometimes called the Congress Kingdom, because it was established at the Congress of Vienna) remained unfulfilled. At the same time the Kingdom, which was dynastically linked with the tsarist monarchy, enjoyed complete self-government, with its own administration and army. Its constitution, modelled on that of the Duchy of Warsaw and drawing on that of 3 May 1791, was liberal, with an assembly whose electorate was larger than that of Restoration France, and former reformers played a significant part in its political life. According to article 2, the constitution guaranteed freedom of religion and affirmed that 'there shall be no distinction in the enjoyment of civil and political rights'.[2]

Nevertheless, the Kingdom of Poland failed to reconcile the Poles to Russian rule and within barely fifteen years it was the scene of revolution and an open Russo-Polish military conflict. Some have argued that this failure was inevitable. The high hopes aroused within sections of Polish society by the French Revolution and the Napoleonic Wars could not be satisfied by the petty statelet given to the Poles at the Congress of Vienna in 1815. In addition, the role of Constantine, the tsar's brother, who was Minister of War and commander-in-chief of the Polish army, and his adviser Nikolay Novosiltsev, the tsar's unofficial 'delegate and plenipotentiary', who had no interest in genuine consultation with the Polish political elite, undermined any hope of smooth political evolution from the start. Furthermore, from the early 1820s Alexander himself came under the influence of the reactionary climate of Restoration Europe. Others have held that it was his death in 1825, and the accession of his much more autocratic brother Nicholas I, which doomed the experiment. Certainly, the refusal of the Sejm to hand over Poles allegedly involved in the Decembrist uprising of 1825 which followed Alexander's death and the attendant crisis further undermined the political system of the Kingdom. Yet, in the event, the final outbreak of revolution owed much to accidental factors: discontent in the army, the small conspiratorial group of students inspired by the developing Romantic movement, and the example to discontented elements of revolution in Belgium and France. Ultimately, it was the unwillingness of the leaders of Polish society to clamp down on the rather limited revolt of November 1830 which led to the clash with Russia.

[2] Thackeray, *Antecedents of Revolution*, 16. Also useful on the Kingdom of Poland between 1815 and 1830 are Davies, *God's Playground*, ii. 306–33; Reddaway et al. (eds.), *The Cambridge History of Poland*, ii. 257–310; Leslie, *Polish Politics and the Revolution of November 1830*; Wandycz, *The Lands of Partitioned Poland 1795–1918*, 65–132; Kula and Leskiewiczowa (eds.), *Przemiany społeczne w Królestwie Polskim 1814–1864*; Bortnowski, *Kaliszanie*; Dyłągowa, *Towarzystwo Patriotyczne i Sąd Sejmowy 1821–1829*; and Tokarz, *Sprzysiężenie Wysockiego i Noc Listopadowa*.

There was no hope that in 1830, in the absence of significant foreign assistance, the revolutionaries could either prevail against the Russians, or, as some of the more conservative among them hoped, reach some accommodation with Nicholas I. The crushing of the revolt was followed by a period of repression. The Sejm and the Polish army were abolished, and the constitution replaced by an Organic Statute. The country was ruled by a viceroy, Ivan Paskevich, who held office for twenty-five years until his death. Although the lower levels of the bureaucracy were still Polish, the Administrative Council, which was effectively controlled by the viceroy, now also included some Russians.[3]

In a speech he made to a group of Polish notables in 1835 Nicholas pulled no punches about the nature of the regime he was establishing in the Kingdom:

> You have, gentlemen, two choices: either persist in your illusions of an independent Poland or live peacefully and as faithful subjects of my Government. If you cling to the maintenance of your dreams of Utopia, of a distinct nationality, of an independent Poland and of all these chimeras, you cannot help but draw great misfortune upon yourselves. I have created here the citadel of Alexander I and I can tell you that at the smallest sign of unrest, I will destroy the city, I will destroy Warsaw and you may be sure that it will not be I who will rebuild it.[4]

Following the uprising, between 7,000 and 8,000 people, a significant section of the Polish elite, went into exile in western Europe, mostly establishing themselves in France and Belgium, where they awaited the coming European revolution which would make possible the resurrection of Poland. They bitterly disputed among themselves the reasons for the debacle of 1830. The Right, which was led by Adam Czartoryski, and which had its headquarters at his residence in Paris, the Hôtel Lambert, saw itself as a sort of government-in-exile. It adherents took the view that the uprising had failed because it had inadequate foreign backing, and they sought to advance the Polish cause through diplomacy, exploiting the deep-seated Russophobia of western Europe. On the left the view was widespread that the revolution had failed because it had not been sufficiently radical: it had not offered anything to those groups which lay outside the political nation. If any future rising was to be successful, it would have to gain the support of the peasants, even now subject to a labour tribute, and the Jews, who were still exposed to a whole set of restrictive laws.

The long period of repression in the Congress Kingdom came to an end with the death of Nicholas I in 1855 and of Viceroy Paskevich in the following year,

[3] For the period from 1830 to the 1863 Uprising, see Walicki, *Philosophy and Romantic Nationalism*; Davies, *God's Playground*, ii. 275–93; Leslie, *Reform and Insurrection in Russian Poland 1856–1865*; Wandycz, *The Lands of Partitioned Poland 1795–1918*, 132–93; Kalembka, *Wielka emigracja*; id., *Towarzystwo Demokratyczne Polskie w latach 1832–1846*; Kieniewicz, *Powstanie styczniowe*; and id., *Między ugodą a rewolucją*.

[4] Quoted in Corrsin, 'Political and Social Change in Warsaw from the January 1863 Uprising to the First World War', 41.

and the accession of Alexander II. Alexander was no liberal but his intention was to introduce a series of long-overdue reforms into the tsarist empire, in particular the abolition of serfdom and the compulsory labour tribute. He did not intend to modify drastically the nature of Russian control in the Kingdom of Poland, warning a group of Polish aristocrats on a visit to Warsaw in May 1856, 'Point de rêveries, messieurs'. Nevertheless, he granted an amnesty to the Polish exiles of the earlier revolt who were still in Siberia, and he aimed to introduce a greater degree of consultation and a significant degree of devolution. He allowed the reopening of the Polish Medical Surgical Academy and invited the Polish landowning class, now organized in the Agricultural Society (Towarzystwo Rolnicze), to express its views on the problem of peasant emancipation in the Kingdom. The task of reforming the administration in the Kingdom was entrusted to the enigmatic and controversial figure Count Wielopolski, who in March 1861 was appointed director of the re-established Government Commission for Religious Beliefs and Public Education (Komisja Rządowa Wyznań Religijnych i Oświecenia Publicznego), replacing the unpopular Pavel Mukhanov, and, after a temporary dismissal, was given the post of viceroy in June 1862.

Wielopolski, a great magnate, was convinced that the Poles had nothing to hope for from the West. After the massacres which had followed the unsuccessful Polish revolt of 1846 in Galicia he had written an open 'Lettre d'un gentilhomme polonais à M. de Metternich'. In it he attacked Metternich as a 'crowned Jacobin' and accused him of inciting peasants to rise up and kill their rightful masters. Whatever one could say about the Russians, he argued, they did not disturb the natural order of society. Wielopolski was bitterly hostile to Polish insurrectionary tradition, which, he claimed, had brought only disaster to the Polish cause. He wanted to reform Polish society, ending the labour tribute of the peasantry and creating a prosperous agricultural system, such as was emerging in Prussian Poland. A Polish bourgeoisie would foster the industrialization of the country and would create the conditions for a civic society and a more broadly based Polish nation. Wielopolski favoured reform and integration of the Jews so that they could constitute a significant part of this bourgeoisie.

This was a bold and well-conceived scheme for the reform of Polish society. What led to its disastrous failure was Wielopolski's autocratic temperament and the lessons he drew from nineteenth-century Polish history, especially from the revolt of 1830. He was convinced that, if the Polish authorities had been prepared to take more drastic action earlier, the debacle of 1830 could have been prevented. Thus he placed little stress on winning over Polish opinion and was very soon faced with strong political opposition. The Whites, led by the large landowner Andrzej Zamoyski, were conservatives, and their support could probably have been gained with a greater degree of consultation. (Zamoyski's unwillingness to compromise was also the result of his contrasting reading of history. As the scion of an important noble family he was convinced that the aristocracy could preserve its influence in Poland only by avoiding too open collaboration with Russia. He had taken this lesson from the Confederation of Targowica, which included among its organizers one of his ancestors, Szczęsny Potocki.) The Reds were determined revolutionaries. In order to stop them threatening his position, Wielopolski introduced in late 1862 a system of conscription which he hoped would keep the troublemakers out of mischief. It did just the opposite, sparking off a revolt in the dead of winter in January 1863 and bringing together the ill-assorted and incompatible Whites and Reds in a hopeless military struggle against the tsarist empire.

The uprising, poorly planned and ill-coordinated, with no chance of foreign support, was crushed by the Russians after nearly sixteen months of sporadic guerrilla skirmishing. Its defeat, which was signalled by the execution of its leader, Romuald Traugutt, on 5 August 1864, ushered in a new period of Polish history. The repression which followed not only undermined what remained of Polish influence in the former eastern parts of the Polish–Lithuanian Commonwealth, but threatened the Kingdom of Poland, now called the Vistula region (Privislinskii krai), with Russification. Polish educational institutions, including the Main School (Szkoła Główna), the university re-established in Warsaw by Wielopolski, were shut down, the vestiges of local self-government were abolished, and the area was ruled by a Russian bureaucracy headed by a Russian governor-general. From 1867 Russian became the language of all levels of the bureaucracy and from 1878 it was also used in the courts. To ensure that there would be no further unrest, what was in effect a Russian army of occupation of 200,000 troops was stationed in the area. The tsarist government believed that the demand for Polish nationalism had real support only among the nobility, and it aimed to punish this group and win the allegiance of the peasantry, whose gratitude it hoped to obtain by the abolition of labour dues in 1864 and by granting freeholds under favourable conditions.

The devastating consequences of the 1863 uprising led to the insurrectionary tradition within Russian Poland being almost totally discredited. A new ideology, whose impact had already been seen in both Prussian and Austrian Poland, came to the fore, asserting that practical work 'at the foundations' was necessary before the Poles could seek more far-reaching goals like national independence. In the Kingdom of Poland this new ideology had a specific form. It called itself 'positivism', in imitation of the similar, scientifically based, pro-industrial, and secular movement which had emerged in western Europe under the influence of thinkers such as Auguste Comte and Herbert Spencer, and was in fact a Polish variant of the liberal ideology which was now dominant in western Europe and the United States. However, the conditions for the flourishing of this ideology—'capitalist development, commercial spirit, and a strong third estate'—were present to a much lesser degree than in those areas.[5] Positivism took from Western liberalism

[5] For a useful analysis of the problem of liberalism in the Polish lands, see Janowski, *Polish Liberal Thought before 1918*.

its favourable attitude to industrial development, which it saw as the key to overcoming the backwardness of Polish society and to extending the national idea to those groups such as peasants, Jews, and women who seemed for the most part to lie outside the conscious national community. Russification could only be resisted by painstaking day-to-day work to create the social and intellectual conditions in which the Polish national identity could survive and flourish.[6]

ECONOMIC DEVELOPMENT IN THE KINGDOM OF POLAND

One aspect of the evolution of the Kingdom of Poland which made it very different from the other areas of partitioned Poland was that in the nineteenth century it underwent something like an industrial revolution. By 1914 the two provinces of Warsaw and Piotrków were largely urban and among the more industrialized parts of Europe, producing textiles and metallurgical goods not only for the Kingdom but for the whole of the tsarist empire. However, given the sharp discontinuities which characterized the political history of the area in the nineteenth century, it is not surprising that the development of industry and the transformation of the agricultural system there should have been marked by a series of false starts and periods of stagnation. Under Prussian rule between 1792 and 1806 the area's agricultural character had been maintained, although the boom conditions caused by the Napoleonic Wars benefited the landowners. Under the Duchy of Warsaw the heavy taxes exacted by Napoleon and the problems caused by his Continental System, which involved an attempt to prevent exports to Britain, undermined the profitability of agriculture. At the same time the period saw the emergence of a largely Jewish group of army suppliers and finance houses under the control of such families as the Fraenkels, Epsteins, Laskis, and Kronenbergs, many of whom came from areas under Prussian rule, which were to form the basis of Warsaw's banking community.[7]

In the period between 1821 and 1830 Ksawery Drucki-Lubecki, minister of finance in the government of the Kingdom of Poland, attempted to promote the industrialization of the Kingdom.[8] It was he who, in cooperation with Rajmund Rembieliński, chairman of the government-created commission for the province

[6] For the period after the Uprising, see Davies, *God's Playground*, ii. 3–111, 178–239; Reddaway et al. (eds.), *The Cambridge History of Poland*, ii. 387–489; Blejwas, *Realism in Polish Politics*; Weeks, *Nation and State in Late Imperial Russia*.

[7] On economic development in 19th-century Poland, see Jedlicki, *A Suburb of Europe*; Kieniewicz, *The Emancipation of the Polish Peasantry*; Kochanowicz, 'The Polish Economy and the Evolution of Dependency'; Kostrowicka et al., *Historia gospodarcza Polski XIX i XX wieku*; Zientara et al., *Dzieje gospodarcze Polski do 1939*; Pietrzak-Pawłowska (ed.), *Uprzemysłowienie ziem polskich w XIX i XX wieku*; and Puś, *Przemysł Królestwa Polskiego w latach 1870–1914*.

[8] On this, see Jedlicki, *Nieudana próba kapitalistycznej industrializacji*.

of Mazovia, issued a decree in August 1820 supporting the development of the textile industry in Łódź and who, in addition, encouraged the settlement of weavers from the German and Czech lands in the central part of the Kingdom. He also attempted to create a metallurgical industry in Będzin, the area of the Kingdom adjacent to the Silesian industrial belt. The period saw a further development of the Warsaw banking community, which was now also involved in supplying the bloated army of the Kingdom, which absorbed almost half the budget of the small state. In the words of Jan Kosim, 'The greater part of this income [from the supply of the army] was acquired by the great Warsaw trading bourgeoisie: the Jakubowiczes, the Sonnenbergs, Loebensteins, Epsteins, Trzcińskis and Bansmerόws; next came the capital's financiers, such as the Epsteins, Samuel Leizor Kronenberg, Samuel Antoni Fraenkel.'[9]

The crushing of the 1830–1 insurrection was followed by a period of economic stagnation. In order to punish the Poles for their rebelliousness, a high tariff barrier was introduced between the Kingdom and the rest of the tsarist empire. Little was done to resolve the problem of compulsory labour service in the countryside, although in June 1846 the Russian viceroy of the Kingdom, Paskevich, under the influence of the peasant jacquerie in Galicia, did modify the conditions under which peasants were obliged to perform this service.

From the early 1840s the economy of the Kingdom began to recover, stimulated by the beginnings of railway building, the opening of the Russian market through the abolition of the tariff barrier in 1858, and the abolition of unfree cultivation in the Kingdom of Poland in 1864. The first major railway line to reach Warsaw ran from Vienna and Kraków; it was constructed between 1845 and 1848 and financed by the bankers Samuel Antoni Fraenkel and Herman Epstein. It was followed by the completion in 1862 of a line from Warsaw to St Petersburg via Białystok and Vilna. By now the two principal railway entrepreneurs in the Kingdom were Leopold Kronenberg, the model for the character Wallenberg in Isaac Bashevis Singer's novel *The Manor*, who took control of the Vienna–Warsaw railway in 1862, and Jan Bogumił Bloch, who was married to Kronenberg's niece. This relationship did not prevent the two men from becoming involved in a bitter commercial struggle over the building of the railway from Warsaw to Kiev and Odessa, which was constructed between 1871 and 1873.

By 1885 Warsaw's industrial district, the centre of the railway industry, employed 33,000 industrial workers, a quarter of those in the Congress Kingdom. Thirty per cent of these workers worked in the metallurgical industry, 26 per cent in textile production, and 21 per cent in food processing. Warsaw had become the junction where the European narrow-gauge railway lines met the Russian broad-gauge. The metal-working industry, the largest in the city, was dominated by three great firms (Rudzki, Borman and Szwede, and Lilpop, Rau, and Loewenstein), which by 1914 employed 31,000 workers. They produced iron and

[9] Kosim, *Losy pewnej fortuny*, 52.

steel products for the Russian market, especially rails, bridge materials, railway wagons, and industrial and farm machinery.

The end of the tariff barrier with the Russian empire and the abolition of the labour tribute in the countryside in the Kingdom of Poland, which created a much larger domestic market, led to the rapid growth of the textile industry, particularly in the city of Łódź but also in the surrounding area. By the beginning of the 1880s the industrial district in Łódź employed 42,000 industrial workers, of whom 36,000 were in the textile industry, the majority in cotton textiles and the remainder in wool. By 1886 the area employed 30 per cent of the industrial workers in the Kingdom of Poland, and 65 per cent of the textile workers. The two largest industrialists in the textile industry were the German Karol Scheibler and the Jew Izrael Kalmanowicz Poznanski. Other Jews prominent in the textile industry were Szaja Rosenblatt, Markus Silberstein, Maks Kon, and Abram and David Prussak. The development of the textile industry in Łódź has been vividly described in fiction, as in Władysław Reymont's *Ziemia obiecana* (Promised Land), made into a film by Andrzej Wajda, Sholem Asch's *Three Cities*, and Israel Singer's *The Brothers Ashkenazy*. The infrastructure of the town also began to develop. In 1866 it was connected to the Warsaw–Vienna railway, in 1869 the first gaslights appeared on its streets, and in 1898 an electric tram system was inaugurated, the first in the Kingdom of Poland.[10]

These developments were part of the larger process of industrialization and urbanization in the Kingdom of Poland. Between 1860 and 1870 industrial production in the area trebled, and in the period between 1870 and 1890 it increased fivefold. The growth of industry was accompanied by urbanization. The population of Warsaw increased rapidly in these years, from 223,000 in 1864 to 625,000 in 1897 and 885,000 by 1914, by which time Warsaw had become the third largest city in the tsarist empire. It remained the administrative and military centre of the Kingdom of Poland and, although Polish educational and cultural life was more developed in Galicia and political activity much less constrained, Warsaw retained the role of capital-in-waiting. The growth of Łódź was even more dramatic. In 1820 it had been a small town with a population of 767. This rose to 4,343 in 1831 and 32,427 by 1862. By 1897 its population had grown to 314,000, while the surrounding areas which were not yet incorporated into the town also contained several hundred thousand inhabitants.

THE JEWS IN THE DUCHY OF WARSAW

The position of the Jews was the subject of constant discussion, first in the Duchy of Warsaw[11] and then in the Kingdom of Poland, right up until the granting of full

[10] Shloegel, 'W poszukiwaniu "Ziemi Obiecanej"', 12.

[11] The best account of the position of the Jews in the Duchy of Warsaw is Stanley, 'The Politics of the Jewish Question in the Duchy of Warsaw, 1807–1813'.

legal equality by Wielopolski in June 1862. The parameters of the debate were similar to those in the last years of the Polish–Lithuanian Republic: whether the Jews should demonstrate their fitness for citizenship before they could be granted civil rights or whether it was only by granting such rights that the goal of political and social integration could be accomplished. A new element in the debates during the brief period of the Duchy of Warsaw was introduced by the treatment of this issue, first by the French national assembly in 1790 and 1791 and then by Napoleon. The French assembly granted equal rights to the Jews of France in two stages, first giving the status of citizens to the acculturated Sephardi Jews of southern France and then, after some delay and debate, on 28 September 1791, to the Ashkenazim, concentrated in eastern France, mostly in Alsace. Napoleon reverted to some of the more hostile views of the Enlightenment regarding the Jews, stressing the importance of 'improving' them and undoing the evil effects of long centuries of Christian persecution. Thus, in summoning the Sanhedrin, he sought to find a body which could undertake the sort of 'reform' of the Jews which he favoured. The key questions which he posed to this body were:

In the eyes of Jews are Frenchmen considered as brothers or as strangers?
Do the Jews born in France and treated by the law as French citizens consider France as their country?
Are they bound to defend it?
Are they bound to obey the laws and follow the directions of the Civil Code?[12]

When Napoleon finally came to deal with the Jewish issue in three decrees in March 1808, he diverged significantly from the unconditional equality granted in 1790 and 1791. The first two decrees conceded state recognition to Judaism and imposed on it the same organizational structure as the two other major creeds in France, subordinating it to the state and making it a tool of state control. The third decree, the *décret infâme*, required a Jewish lender to prove that any loan he made was not usurious. Jews were now presumed to be usurers unless they could prove otherwise. They were also limited in their right of residence, and new Jewish settlement in Alsace and Lorraine was forbidden. Jews were also not allowed, like other French citizens, to provide substitutes if they were conscripted. These regulations, which were in line with other attempts, such as those of Joseph II, to make Jewish integration possible by compulsorily 'reforming' them, were to remain in force for ten years. When they were reviewed in 1818, after the fall of Napoleon and the restoration of the Bourbons, they were allowed by the chamber of deputies to lapse.[13]

The constitution of the Duchy of Warsaw, introduced in July 1808 and inspired by French revolutionary principles, laid down that 'All religious worship is to be free and public' (article 21) and that 'All citizens are equal before the law'

[12] Quoted in Mendes-Flohr and Reinharz (eds.), *The Jew in the Modern World*, 126.

[13] On Napoleon and the Jews, see Delpech, 'L'Histoire des Juifs en France de 1780 à 1840', 12–15; *Le Grand Sanhédrin de Napoléon*; and R. Mahler, *A History of Modern Jewry 1780–1815*, 62–75.

(article 4). Theoretically this should have entitled Jews to vote and even to sit in the Sejm. Indeed the more acculturated of the Jews had placed high hopes in the revolution. When the French entered Poznań in 1806, the Jews there proclaimed a holiday and danced in the streets. The Jews of Warsaw even composed a hymn in honour of the emperor Napoleon.[14]

The Enlightenment bureaucrats of the Duchy were not willing to extend political rights to the Jews, holding that these could only be granted once the Jews had been suitably transformed. According to Dominik Krysiński, a liberal economist of Frankist origins and follower of Adam Smith, the way to 'civilize' the Jews was to turn their natural abilities to agricultural work.[15] The only significant defender of the Jews in these circles was Wawrzyniec Surowiecki, author of a book on the decline of Polish industry and towns, who, following Dohm, argued that the faults of the Jews were a consequence of the way they had been treated. They should be freed from most restrictions so that their 'industry, thrift, and expertise in all their callings' could be employed for the benefit of the country. Accordingly, Jews should be allowed to live in the cities, buy real estate there, and engage in all trades, crafts, and businesses. At the same time they should be forbidden to settle in the countryside unless they were engaged in handicrafts or agriculture and should be barred from running inns and taverns or lending money to the peasantry.[16]

The issue of the rights to which the Jews were entitled under the constitution of the Duchy was first raised by a Jewish petitioner, Arno Szmulowicz of Łomża province, who requested King Frederick Augustus of Saxony to confirm the earlier privileges which had been granted to the Jews in Poland–Lithuania. Frederick Augustus did not reply directly to this request. Instead, reflecting what he understood to be the principles governing the Europe which Napoleon was establishing, he responded by stating that in his view the constitution of the Duchy ruled out differentiating between citizens. This commitment to legal equality for the Jews caused consternation among his civil servants. Tadeusz Dembowski, the treasury minister, protested that 'accepting that the Jews are subject to the constitution should first be preceded by the Jews giving up everything which differentiates them from other citizens'.[17] The minister of justice, Feliks Lubieński, took the view that 'the question of giving [Jews] the rights of citizenship . . . must be postponed for some time' and suggested a law on the lines of that passed in France, suspending for ten years the civil rights of Jews.[18] Accordingly, early in 1808 the director of public administration in the province of Warsaw, Andrzej Michał Horodyski, ruled that Jews could not be granted the rights

14 Kandel, 'Hymn do Napoleona', 122–3.

15 Krysiński, Letter to Antoni Gliszczyński, 15 Sept. [1807], in Krysiński, *Wybór pism*, 11.

16 Surowiecki, 'O upadku przemysłu y miast w Polszce', in Surowiecki, *Wybór pism*, 207–8, 213–14.

17 M. Wischnitzer, 'Proekty reformy evreiskogo byta v Gertsogstve Varshavskom i Tsarstve Pol'skom (po neizdannym materialam)', 166–7.

18 Eisenbach, 'Prawo obywatelskie i honorowe Żydów (1790–1861)', 245–6.

guaranteed in the constitution since this would involve 'too great a change in the country'.[19]

Since the matter involved a major issue of principle, it was decided to elicit the views of the emperor himself. In September 1808 oral confirmation was obtained that Napoleon was not opposed to the Polish plan to limit the political rights of Jews, provoking Frederick Augustus to protest piously, 'I am devastated that I have been unable to do anything for this nation, but the emperor himself has given up—he for whom nothing is impossible.'[20]

In the same month the exclusion of any specific mention of the Jews in an election decree was justified by Jan Paweł Łuszczewski, minister of internal affairs (and between 1785 and 1795 a secretary to Stanisław August), who in a letter to the prefect of the province of Kalisz stated that 'the Ministry of Internal Affairs cannot permit that Jews—born it is true on our soil but in custom and religion foreigners—be entered in the book of citizens'. If the prefect were faced with any such request, he was to plead lack of instructions.[21] One month later, on 17 October 1808, an electoral law was passed suspending for ten years the right of Jews to vote in elections to the Sejm. Only the small group of Jews expressly admitted into political life by the king as a reward for their political or military services was not affected by this suspension.

This was not the only restriction on Jewish activity that was maintained or strengthened at this time. The minister of internal affairs, Łuszczewski, in an edict to prefects in 1808, instructed them to continue to implement the restrictive laws introduced by the Prussians, even if they contradicted the constitution and the Napoleonic Code.[22] Accordingly, in October 1809 the restrictions on Jewish residence in the central areas of Warsaw were again implemented with a small number of exceptions for the most prominent and wealthy Jews. Separate Jewish residential quarters were maintained in a number of towns, including Wschowa and Płock.

More general issues were discussed by a committee of the Council of State which was created to deal with Jewish issues. Here again different views were expressed. N. F. Wojda, a master of requests in the Council of State, accepted that the granting of political rights to the Jews should be postponed for ten years. The goal should be to raise their moral and cultural level, and if this had been achieved in a decade he saw no reason not to grant them political rights. To encourage this process, rights should be given to those who had adopted Polish dress or speech.[23] His views did not command widespread support in the committee. For Lubieński, the key issue was whether Jews should now be given the right to purchase real property—this

[19] Ibid. 248–9.

[20] Mencel, 'Prawa wyborcze ludności miejskiej w Księstwie Warszawskim i Królestwie Polskim', 277.

[21] Kallas, *Konstytucja Księstwa Warszawskiego*, 111–12.

[22] Eisenbach, 'Prawo obywatelskie i honorowe Żydów (1790–1861)', 249–50.

[23] M. Wischnitzer, 'Proekty reformy evreiskogo byta v Gertsogstve Varshavskom i Tsarstve Pol'skom (po neizdannym materialam)', 170.

was too urgent to be postponed until a general reform of the Jews. Accordingly, he persuaded Frederick Augustus to issue a decree on 19 November 1808 suspending the right of Jews to acquire landed estates 'until our further decision'.[24]

The failure of the government to live up to the principles enshrined in the constitution provoked a group of prominent Warsaw Jews to respond. In a petition of 30 November 1808 they asserted that the political rebirth of the Polish nation had not improved the position of the Jews in any way. They still could not acquire land or a house in the city, and they could not build factories there. Their daughters were not able to marry Jews from outside Warsaw since such Jews did not have the right to reside in the capital. Although Jews were allowed to carry on a trade, they were taxed heavily for this privilege. Jews, they asserted, should be treated no differently from the rest of the Polish population. The promise of equality, inherent in the constitution 'created by the great Napoleon', should be honoured. On 4 January 1809 the king, chastened by his earlier experience with a petitioner, replied in an evasive and discouraging manner.

This setback did not deter the petitioners. The following day they submitted a second petition, this time to the minister of justice, Lubieński.

> The undersigned have for a very long time tried by their moral conduct and identical costume to draw near to the rest of the population and are now sure that they are already worthy of civil rights. If the wish to serve the country in which they were born or live, if the desire to draw close to other inhabitants of this country by demonstrations of public morality and increased education, if, finally, true fulfilment of the responsibility imposed on them by the state and the government, make them worthy of the rights of citizens, then the undersigned have no doubt that they should be allowed the full enjoyment of [these rights].[25]

When the minister presented the petition to Frederick Augustus, he attached to it his written opinion. It was true, he conceded, that, according to the constitution, all subjects were equal before the law. This was not, however, synonymous with citizenship. Only those subjects who regarded the Duchy of Warsaw as their true fatherland could be considered to be full citizens. He continued:

> Is it possible for believers in the Mosaic law, if they follow their own commandments, to consider our country to be their only fatherland? Do they not aim to return to the land of their ancestors and view themselves at present as living in exile? Could they, feeling themselves alien in the countries they inhabit, enter into close contact with the native population? Many centuries have passed and they all still appear as sons of one country, in spite of their continuous residence in numerous lands. Even in those places where they have already received the rights of citizenship, they nevertheless seem to remain an alien and separate nation.[26]

[24] *Ustawodawstwo Księstwa Warszawskiego*, i. 159, no. 778.

[25] For this exchange, see Gessen, 'V efemernom gosudarstve', 28–9.

[26] M. Wischnitzer, 'Proekty reformy evreiskogo byta v Gertsogstve Varshavskom i Tsarstve Pol'skom (po neizdannym materialam)', 171.

Petitions were also presented by individual Jews. On 21 March 1809 Michał Rawski asked for his rights as a citizen to be recognized. He cited testimonies from a number of high government officials and stressed his honesty, wealth, and contributions to charity. Solomon Girsz, a banker from Inowrocław, a town in the western part of the Duchy which after 1815 was part of the Grand Duchy of Poznań, claimed citizenship on the grounds of his education in a Christian school, his adoption of Polish dress, his patriotism, and his contributions to charity. Neither evoked any response. Girsz was told that the government had not yet laid down 'the conditions through the observance of which individuals of the Mosaic faith could acquire the rights of citizens'. When asked when these would be established, he was told the time was still 'premature'.[27]

The government also maintained the taxes introduced by the Prussians, the kosher meat tax, the toleration tax, and the tax for permission to marry. Although the minister of justice, Lubieński, conceded that 'the Jews pay too many taxes' and did abolish the tax paid by Jews visiting Warsaw, the desperate financial situation of the Duchy prevented the abolition of the other taxes.[28]

Although Jews were not given rights of citizenship, they were obliged by decrees of 9 May and 10 November 1808 to serve in the army on an equal footing with Christians. One rabbi and one cantor in any community was granted exemption. All other Jewish men between the ages of 21 and 28 were subject to the draft. Evasion was punished with a fine of 1,000 zlotys, for which the local *kehilah* was responsible. Military service was very unpopular with the bulk of the Jewish population, although it was seen by the acculturated minority as an important path to citizenship. In a petition of 9 January 1809 a group of prominent Warsaw Jews declared that 'They want, like others, to submit to conscription; they want to pay taxes equally with other citizens and observe the laws laid down for the whole population. Finally, wanting simply to be full citizens, they are glad and willing to make a declaration of allegiance and to end their present unsatisfactory status.'[29]

By 1812 it had become easier to find peasant recruits but more difficult to feed and equip them. Accordingly, the minister of war, Józef Poniatowski, nephew of the last king of Poland, exempted the Jewish community from conscription in return for a payment of 700,000 zlotys. Poniatowski justified his decision on the grounds that, if Jews were barred for ten years from the rights of citizenship, they could not in equity be asked to serve in the army.[30] It is a sad commentary on the events of these years that, when Alexander's troops entered the Duchy in pursuit of Napoleon's Grand Army in 1813, they were welcomed by Jews in a number of towns, waving banners with the Russian emperor's monogram.[31]

[27] Gessen, 'V efemernom gosudarstve', 30–1.

[28] Askenazy, 'Z dziejów Żydów polskich w dobie Księstwa Warszawskiego i Królestwa Polskiego', 2–3.

[29] Handelsman, 'Prośba Żydów do Fryderyka Augusta'.

[30] Dubnow, *History of the Jews*, iv. 706–7.

[31] Tokarz, 'Miscellanea', 270–1.

THE JEWS IN THE KINGDOM OF POLAND IN THE FIRST HALF OF THE NINETEENTH CENTURY

The legal position of the Jews did not change significantly in the period between 1815 and 1830, in which the Kingdom of Poland still enjoyed far-reaching autonomy. Throughout this period the dominant view of the Polish political elite, still mostly consisting of aristocrats, some of them recently ennobled, and senior officials brought up on the ideas of the Enlightenment, remained that Jewish emancipation should be conditional on the Jews abandoning their religious and social separateness and becoming far more acculturated, becoming in effect 'Poles of the Mosaic faith'. They were sceptical about the chances of this occurring in a reasonable period of time and 'had a negative stance towards a group which, they believed, held on stubbornly to anachronistic traditions'.[32] Their views were expressed by the minister of education, Stanisław Potocki, who argued that 'The Jews form here a state within a state. They have their own courts, language, dress code, religion . . . their leadership mocks those governments which have sought for some time to civilize them.'[33]

This was also the position of Adam Czartoryski, one of the key figures in the Kingdom. Czartoryski had long been concerned with policy towards the Jews. In the early years of the century he had served on a number of committees convened by the emperor Alexander to draft a bill for the 'reform of the Jews'. In the years before 1815 Czartoryski also participated in discussions in the Russian Administrative Council and the Council of State, which was composed of the ministers of the Kingdom, on the appropriate policies to 'reform' the Jewish community.

On 25 May 1815 Czartoryski set out the principles on which the government of the Kingdom of Poland was to be based. According to paragraph 36, 'the Jewish people preserve their civil rights which they have enjoyed until now under the existing laws and rules. A special instruction will establish the conditions under which the Jews are able to enjoy more widely the benefits of civil life.'[34] In July of the same year Czartoryski created in the Kingdom of Poland a Committee for the Reform of Peasants and Jews to which Jews were not admitted even as advisers. The remit of the committee is an interesting reflection of the way the administrators of the Kingdom of Poland saw the problems posed by peasants and Jews as analogous.

Czartoryski's views were well expressed in his response to a law proposed in the early years of the Kingdom of Poland by the somewhat sinister figure Nikolay

[32] Stefan Kieniewicz, quoted in Beauvois, 'Polish–Jewish Relations in the Territories Annexed by the Russian Empire in the First Half of the Nineteenth Century', 82.

[33] S. K. Potocki, *Podróż do Ciemnogrodu*, 323–4.

[34] M. Wischnitzer, 'Proekty reformy evreiskogo byta v Gertsogstve Varshavskom i Tsarstve Pol'skom (po neizdannym materialam)', 174–5; Eisenbach, 'Les Droits civiques des Juifs dans le Royaume de Pologne', 39 ff.

Novosiltsev, the principal adviser of the viceroy of the Kingdom, the grand duke Constantine. In 1816 Novosiltsev, who had dealt with the Jewish community through his right-hand man, the converted Jew Leon Newachowicz, proposed to the Council of State a large-scale reform of the Jews. An educational system with Polish as the language of instruction would be established and would pave the way for the abolition of existing restrictions on Jewish economic activity. Those Jews not literate in Polish would be denied the right to marry or carry on a trade. Jewish communal autonomy would be abolished and Jews would be required to undertake military service. In addition, Jewish economic life would be restructured and Jews encouraged to take up agriculture. Jews who fulfilled the requisite criteria would be given full political and civil rights.[35]

In response to Novosiltsev's proposal, Czartoryski conceded that its goals were

> most salutary—the transformation of the Jews from useless and harmful members of society into good citizens attached to their country, to give them more enlightenment, namely the morality which they lack; in a word to make them civil Christians. . . . Such is the intended goal of the bill, and no responsible, enlightened government could strive towards any other in the reform of the Jews.

Yet, he claimed, he could not accept the clause conceding 'complete tolerance and equality for the Jews', in spite of the provisions guaranteeing the equality of all citizens, which the constitution of the Kingdom of Poland inherited from that of the Duchy of Warsaw, because 'there are few sufficiently enlightened and honest people among the Jews'. To grant them civil rights at present would be 'to reward them before they have become worthy'. In addition, 'it would be harmful to the vast majority of the inhabitants and the good order and life of the whole country'.[36]

Reform of the Jews, Czartoryski believed, was necessary. Its goal should be acculturation and the eventual assimilation of the Jews. In a letter to the tsar on 24 July 1817, he wrote:

> In your piety and wisdom, Your Majesty has wished to convert [the Jews] to Christianity. But this idea should be entrusted secretly to the government, as was set out in a memorandum on this subject that I presented in connection with another Jewish reform; otherwise this fine and godly idea cannot succeed. It must be hidden from the Jews; administrative measures must be introduced to begin to prepare them for conversion—they must become like Christians in civil terms. This matter cannot be addressed too soon, whether one looks at it from a humanitarian, political, or religious standpoint.[37]

[35] On Novosiltsev's proposal, see Gelber, 'The Jewish Problem in Poland in the Years 1815 to 1830' (Heb.); Gessen, *Istoriya evreiskogo naroda v Rossii*, i. 222–3.

[36] Śliwowski, 'Zagadnienie tzw. Projektu Nowosilcowa Kodeksu Karzącego Królestwa Polskiego', 124–5.

[37] Zbiory Czartoryskich w Krakowie, file 1283, quoted in Eisenbach, *The Emancipation of the Jews in Poland, 1780–1870*, 172–3.

Novosiltsev's proposal was rejected by the Council of State in late January and February 1817. In its place it drafted a bill for the 'organization of the Jewish people', for which Staszic and Kajetan Koźmian were principally responsible and which was finally accepted on 31 March. This called for the abolition of the *kehilot*, the regulation of the rabbinate, the adoption by Jews of surnames, tighter control over Jewish marriage, and the obligatory use of Polish in legal documents. Jews with sufficient capital who did not wear traditional Jewish dress and sent their children to state schools should be allowed to live outside the areas where Jews were required to live and conduct business there. This bill was ultimately rejected by the tsar in his capacity as king of Poland.[38]

There was some support for such changes within the small group of acculturated Jews. In 1815 a group in Warsaw describing itself as made up of 'distinguished Jews' and numbering forty families submitted a petition to Alexander I requesting him to differentiate between them and the unreformed mass of Jews, and to grant them rights which would accord with their achievements, wealth, and culture. This would induce wider circles to emulate them and would 'accelerate the process of civilizing the Israelites'.[39]

The Jewish question also became a matter for public debate in the Kingdom of Poland, a debate which was more extensive than that which accompanied the Four Year Sejm. Its tone was set by Stanisław Staszic in his pamphlet *O przyczynach szkodliwości Żydów i o środkach usposobieniu ich aby się społeczeństwu użytecznymi stali* (On the Reasons for the Harmful Character of the Jews and the Means to Render them Useful to Society), which saw their negative characteristics as resulting from 'the fact that this nation systematically isolates itself from other nations'. Jews were responsible for the downfall of Poland; they were multiplying rapidly and would soon be an eighth of the population. Since they could not be expelled from Poland, they had to be rendered less harmful by measures which would 'civilize' them.[40] The Jewish question was further debated at the Sejm which met in 1818. Deputies also worried about the increase in the number of the Jews and requested the government to submit to the next Sejm 'a project for the reform of the adherents of the Old Testament'. This should involve the reform of Jewish education.[41]

Others expressed still more negative attitudes concerning the Jews. In a dystopic novel written in 1817 (but published in 1838) entitled *Rok 3333, czyli sen niesłychany* (The Year 3333, or A Nightmare), Julian Ursyn Niemcewicz described a Warsaw of the future, renamed Moszkopolis after its Jewish ruler, which had

[38] Archiwum Główne Akt Dawnych, Warsaw (AGAD; Central Archives of Historical Records), Rada Stanu Królestwa Polskiego, vol. 103, 244–9, 262–9, quoted in Eisenbach, *The Emancipation of the Jews in Poland, 1780–1870*, 174–6.

[39] Petition of Dr Józef Wolff and Natan Glücksberg to Tsar Alexander I, dated Warsaw, 1 Dec. 1815, quoted in Askenazy, 'Ze spraw żydowskich w dobie kongresowej', 30–1.

[40] Staszic, *O przyczynach szkodliwości Żydów i o środkach usposobieniu ich aby się społeczeństwu użytecznymi stali*, 219–20.

[41] Sawicki, 'Szkoła Rabinów w Warszawie (1826–1863)', 245.

been taken over by a mafia of superficially modernized Jews.[42] His views reflected the widespread resentment at the wealth which had been accumulated by Jewish banking and commercial circles in the Kingdom of Poland and at the fact that this group of acculturated Jews, having been rebuffed by the Polish rulers of the Kingdom, had sought to intercede with the unpopular Novosiltsev.

When, in 1818, the ten-year limit set on the decision not to grant Jews civil rights in the Duchy of Warsaw came to an end, the Council of State under the leadership of the viceroy, General Józef Zajączek, a former Jacobin now turned conservative, induced Alexander to maintain the existing restrictions and called for the expulsion of Jews from the countryside, a measure which was only prevented by Novosiltsev's intervention with Alexander.[43] Jews, with a small number of exceptions, were still barred from living on the main streets of central Warsaw. Jewish quarters were also maintained in fifty-five other towns, and an additional ninety towns still possessed the right totally to exclude Jews. The levy imposed on Jews visiting Warsaw, which had been abolished in 1811, was reintroduced in 1826, and Jews were also barred from living within 30 miles of the frontier.[44] A tax on kosher meat was introduced, and further efforts were made to limit the involvement of Jews in the sale of alcohol. Although initially Jews were expected to serve in the military in the same way as other citizens, it was now decided to exempt them 'until such time as they be given the rights of political life'. In compensation for this exemption the Jews of the Kingdom outside Warsaw paid an annual recruitment tax of 600,000 florins, while those of Warsaw paid 700,000 florins.[45]

Some attempts were made to reform Jewish education, a goal which had the support of the Jewish reformers in the Kingdom, who called for the adoption by Jews of the Polish language and modern dress and the purification of Judaism from 'talmudic prejudices'. Thus, Dr Schoenfeld of Kalisz called for an educational reform which would 'dissuade the Jews from their egoism, so that, as Mosaic believers, they would no longer be a state within the state, but would belong to the people in whose country they live and would be called Poles'. This was also the view of two Warsaw maskilim, Abram Buchner and Samuel Hirszhorn, who in 1818 called for *ḥeder*s to be closed, talmudic learning to be forbidden, and compulsory attendance of young Jews in state schools.[46]

Calls for the reform of Jewish education had the support of the Government Commission for Religious Beliefs and Public Education and its ministerial head,

[42] On other occasions Niemcewicz expressed himself in a less hostile manner. On his view on the Jews, see Goldberg, 'Julian Ursyn Niemcewicz on Polish Jewry', 323–6.

[43] Eisenbach, *Kwestia równouprawnienia Żydów w Królestwie Polskim*, 30; Gessen, *Istoriya evreiskogo naroda v Rossii*, i. 222–3.

[44] The restrictions on the Jews are set out in the first chapter of Eisenbach, *Kwestia równouprawnienia Żydów w Królestwie Polskim*, and in id., 'Mobilność terytorialna ludności żydowskiej w Królestwie Polskim'.

[45] Gessen, *Istoriya evreiskogo naroda v Rossii*, i. 231; Eisenbach, *Kwestia równouprawnienia Żydów w Królestwie Polskim*, 36.

[46] Sawicki, 'Szkoła Rabinów w Warszawie (1826–1863)', 245–6.

Stanisław Potocki, who was to be dismissed in 1820 because of his anticlerical views and replaced by the more conservative Stanisław Grabowski. The first elementary state schools for young Jews were opened in the Kingdom of Poland in 1818. In 1820 there were already three such schools with 300 pupils, and in 1825 five with 432 pupils. The number of schools did not increase in the next fifteen years, but the number of pupils rose to 526 in 1864. Their small number was partly due to the suspicion of these schools within the traditional section of the Jewish population. As a result, the amount of religious education in them was restricted and in 1823 Hebrew was removed from the syllabus. A key role in the establishment of these schools was played by Jakub Tugendhold (1794–1871), who was born in Działoszyce and educated at the Polish gymnasium in Breslau, later moving first to Kraków and then to Warsaw.[47]

Other reforms followed. On 1 January 1822 the kahal was abolished and its functions were taken over by Jewish congregational boards (*dozory bóżnicze*, sometimes also called *gminy żydowskie*), established on 20 March 1821. They were composed of the community rabbi and his assistant and three elected 'overseers', who were assisted by a secretary and two assistants and whose competence was restricted to religious matters, the administration of synagogues, ritual baths, and kashrut, and the dispensing of charity, as well as control over the tax on kosher meat and the recruitment tax, which remained in force. These boards were ultimately responsible to the commissions which ran each of the eight provinces of the Kingdom (this number was cut to five in the 1840s and raised to ten in 1867). In the course of the nineteenth century the number of overseers was significantly increased in larger cities like Warsaw and Łódź. By 1856 there were in the Kingdom 346 such congregational boards.

To strengthen the congregational boards, on 28 March 1822 the Jewish associations, including the most important of them, the burial society, were also declared illegal. This reform was justified by the viceroy on the grounds that it would free the community from the 'arbitrary control' of its 'elders', although the main motive in introducing it was to extend government control over Jewish life. It was supported by the small number of Jewish reformers, who sometimes took control of these bodies, often in partnership with Orthodox and hasidic groups.[48] For the most part, the old *kehilah* establishment remained in control, and the best study of the issue comes to the conclusion that 'the abolition of the kahal should not be seen as a major turning point in the life of the Jews of the Kingdom of Poland and of their communal self-government. The Congregational Board was

[47] On the development of these schools, see *Z dziejów gminy starozakonnych w Warszawie w XIX stuleciu*, i: *Szkolnictwo*, 15 and nn.; Lewin, 'Pierwsze szkoły elementarne dla dzieci wyznania mojżeszowego w Warszawie w latach 1818–1830'; ead., 'The First Elementary Schools for Children of the Mosaic Faith in Warsaw 1818–1830'.

[48] Kośka and Lewandowska, *Materiały do dziejów Żydów na ziemiach polskich w XIX wieku w zbiorach AGAD*; Levitats, *The Jewish Community in Russia, 1772–1844*, 16–18; and Guesnet, *Polnische Juden im 19. Jahrhundert*, 223–9.

in fact the continuation of the kahal but with diminished powers.'[49] That this was the case was partly the consequence of the highly restrictive franchise, which limited the right to vote first to male householders and then, after 1830, to those who paid the requisite amount of tax to the government. Thus in the elections to the Warsaw Congregational Board of September 1851, 968 people were entitled to vote, of whom 614 did so.[50]

Communal elections were also marked by government intervention and considerable electoral abuse. It was only in the last third of the nineteenth century that 'progressives' were able to establish themselves in a strong position on such bodies, particularly in Warsaw and Łódź, but also in Częstochowa, Radom, and Zawiercie.

During this period the Jewish community in the Kingdom became increasingly differentiated. Hasidism now began to spread to the area around Lublin and south of Warsaw, and major hasidic centres developed in Kock, Przysucha, and Ger (Góra Kalwaria). By the middle of the nineteenth century hasidim also made up the majority of the growing Jewish population of Warsaw, where the number of small prayer halls, almost all hasidic, grew from 111 in 1827 to around 300 in 1879.[51] (On these developments, see Volume II, Chapter 8.) At the same time, in Warsaw and in a number of other towns, notably Zamość, a circle of maskilim and supporters of Jewish integration began to emerge. The circle of relatively acculturated Jews included financiers (among them the leaseholders of the kosher meat monopoly, until 1862 the principal source of income of the Jewish congregational boards), bankers, and army suppliers, most of whom were closely associated with the rulers of the Kingdom. In addition, it included medical doctors, whether educated in Poland or abroad, as well as contractors, goldsmiths, and other skilled craftsmen attached to the court.

The influence of the religious changes taking place in Germany now began to penetrate into the Kingdom of Poland. Thus, in 1842 Hayim Dawidsohn, the chief rabbi of Warsaw from 1839 to 1854, introduced the first confirmation of girls which, like those established by reformed Jews in Germany, resembled those held by Christians and took place at the end of the school year, in the Jewish case during the festival of Shavuot. Dawidsohn, like his successor Dov Berush Meisels, chief rabbi from 1854 to 1863, previously communal rabbi in Kraków, was in general sympathetic to the moderate Haskalah but strictly Orthodox in his practice. At the same time the conflict between the hasidim and the maskilim was much less bitter in the Kingdom of Poland than it was in Galicia or in the western provinces of the tsarist empire. After the government reform of 1821 the hasidim were soon represented in significant numbers on the congregational boards in many areas,

49 Szterenkac, 'Zniesienia kahałów i utworzenie dozorów bóżniczych (w pierwszych latach Królestwa Polskiego)', 71.

50 AGAD, CWWKP, 1727, 892–917, quoted in Guesnet, *Polnische Juden im 19. Jahrhundert*, 405.

51 Guesnet, *Polnische Juden im 19. Jahrhundert*, 353.

including Warsaw, but were obliged to work together with the more secularized members of the community so as to present a united front to the authorities. They played a role in the election of Chief Rabbi Dawidsohn, although they may have later been suspicious of his reformist impulses, and worked together quite harmoniously with Chief Rabbi Meisels.

More radical religious and social currents were also developing in the Kingdom. In Warsaw the 'progressive' Jews prayed in the synagogue established in 1802, during the period of Prussian rule, by a Jew from Danzig, Isaac Flatau. Some of them had been among those prominent Warsaw Jews who had sent a petition to the authorities in early 1809 requesting that they 'should be allowed the full enjoyment' of the rights of citizens. The synagogue they established was 'modern' in the manner of those then being established in Germany, and the arrangements for worship had a number of progressive features: there was a ladies' gallery, and a sermon, which at first was given in German and then, from the late 1850s, in Polish. These innovations aroused the hostility of the Orthodox, who referred to the institution contemptuously as 'the German synagogue'.[52]

One important organization which fostered the emergence of a significant group of acculturated and Polonized Jews was the Warsaw Rabbinic School.[53] It had a difficult birth. The idea of such a school had been accepted in principle in 1818 during Alexander I's visit to Warsaw. The idea of the minister of education, Stanisław Potocki, was for a Higher Israelite School (Wyższa Szkoła Izraelska), which would train rabbis and schoolteachers. Six years after its opening all candidates for the rabbinate would have to be its graduates. The job of drafting the proposal for the school was given to Abraham Stern, an Orthodox Jew trusted in the Jewish community and an outstanding mathematician highly regarded in official circles, and Adam Prażmowski, bishop of Płock.[54]

Stern submitted his proposal to the Commission for Religious Beliefs and Public Education in May 1818, probably influenced by his visit to the reformed yeshiva recently established in Fürth, in Bavaria. According to the proposal, all subjects, both religious and secular, were to be taught in the school. The teachers were to be men 'of impeccable conduct and morality, observing the religion of the people of Israel'. The emblem of the school was to be two clasped hands with the motto 'Love thy neighbour as thyself'. No teacher would be allowed to teach without prior examination by the school. The director of the school would be the

[52] On the history of this synagogue, see Guterman, 'The Origins of the Great Synagogue on Tłomackie Street'.

[53] On the history of this school, see Sawicki, 'Szkoła Rabinów w Warszawie (1826–1863)'; *Z dziejów gminy starozakonnych w Warszawie w XIX stuleciu*, i: *Szkolnictwo*; Borzymińska, 'Przyczynek do dziejów szkolnictwa w XIX wieku, czyli jeszcze o Szkole Rabinów'; and S. Lewin, 'The Warsaw Rabbinical Academy'. I have described the evolution of the school in 'Warszawska Szkoła Rabinów', and it is the subject of Finkelstein, 'History of the Rabbinical School of Warsaw from its Establishment in 1826 to its Closure in 1863'.

[54] On Stern, see Shatzky, 'Abraham Jaakov Stern', and Wodziński, *Oświecenie żydowskie w Królestwie Polskim wobec chasydyzmu* (Eng. edn.), 87–94.

spiritual leader of Polish Jewry. He would examine rabbis and assistant rabbis. No Hebrew book could be published without the prior approval of the school's director. One of his principal concerns would be the struggle with hasidism, something close to the heart of Stern, an inveterate mitnaged (opponent of hasidism). 'His obligation will be to take care that not only in the school but also in the whole of Poland, no mystical teaching, known in Hebrew as kabbalah, be given either in schools or in private homes . . . Similarly, he should ensure that all books with a mystical content be removed from the libraries of all communities.'[55]

Stern's proposal was rejected by the commission for two reasons. It paid too little attention to lay subjects and it gave the director too much power. Instead, the commission accepted the separately submitted proposal of Bishop Prażmowski. This devoted very little attention to the training of future rabbis. The goal of the school should be to struggle against obscurantism. The study of the Talmud was therefore excluded from the curriculum, although it is difficult to conceive how rabbis could be trained without it. There were many reservations about this proposal and it was only accepted because of the support of Stanisław Staszic, a key member of the Government Commission for Religious Beliefs and Public Education. In addition, it was decided that from the date of the opening of the school no one could become a rabbi without a prior examination in lay subjects and ethics by the Elementary Commission (Towarzystwo Elementarne).

The school was given approval in 1818. Given the tenor of government policy, it was seen by the majority of the Jewish community as a cunning attempt to introduce Christianity to the Jews and it was bitterly opposed. That it was not immediately established was due to both financial constraints and Jewish objections. The Jews were able to obtain support for their views from Novosiltsev, to whom they gave lavish bribes.

What led to the school's ultimate establishment was a new government initiative on the Jewish question. On 3 June 1825 an Old Testament Believers' Committee (Komitet Starozakonny) was set up, composed of senior civil servants below ministerial rank, with an advisory committee, chaired by a civil servant, made up of eleven Jewish representatives. The key role on it was played by a priest, Fr. Luigi Chiarini, who was professor of Oriental Studies at the University of Warsaw and known for his hostile attitude to the Jews. He was obsessed by the harmful effect which he believed the Talmud exercised over the Jewish masses. On 21 March 1825 the committee reported, very much in accordance with Chiarini's views:

The Jews have not changed in the course of centuries; they have always avoided work and are greedy. They have attempted to keep themselves apart from the people among whom they live. These traits are the consequence of their religion, which deviates from the law of

[55] Akta Komisji Rządowej Wyznań Religijnych i Oświaty Publicznej (WR i OP), fascicle 2438, vol. 1, quoted in Sawicki, 'Szkoła Rabinów w Warszawie (1826–1863)', 247–8. On the foundation of the school, see also Bero, 'Z dziejów szkolnictwa żydowskiego w Królestwie Kongresowym 1815–1830'.

Moses. The misshapen collection of rules, filled with deep obscurantism, fanaticism, and intolerance of the rabbis, is not worthy to be called a religion.[56]

The committee therefore proposed the creation of a rabbinic school to train rabbis who could be used to 'reform' the Jews, the establishment of a system of lay elementary schools for young Jews of both sexes, the tightening of censorship of rabbinic books, the translation of the Talmud into a European language so that 'its contents can be made available to those who were responsible for the reform' of the Jews, and the creation of a special chair at the university with the aim of 'training a certain number of Christians in the language and methods of the Talmud, so that having obtained a real understanding of the true spirit of Judaism they could then serve the government in the constant pursuit of a radical reform of the Jews'.[57]

It was in the spirit of these directives that the Warsaw Rabbinic School was established in 1826 for pupils of secondary-school age. In the previous year the Government Commission for Religious Beliefs and Public Education, as a result of renewed pressure from the Sejm, had agreed to provide 12,000 zlotys to fund such a school. It was not confident about how it should proceed and, as a result, handed over all the material to the newly created Old Testament Believers' Committee.

In January 1826, after a joint session of the Old Testament Believers' Committee and the Government Commission for Religious Beliefs and Public Education, the final plan for the school was produced. At the same time were published 'regulations for the examination and choice of rabbis until the school itself will be able to provide sufficient numbers of Israelites for this office'. The school was to be a central element in the policy of the committee of 'reforming the adherents of the Old Testament':

Only by the moral reform of the Jews in the Kingdom of Poland will it be possible to remove those harmful consequences to other classes of the population which are caused by the presence of the Old Testament believers in the Kingdom.

The Jewish population will only be of benefit to this land when as a consequence first of moral and then of administrative reform its members will be induced to undertake occupations which are useful to themselves and to the country: such an impulse will be imparted to the Jews by the Rabbinic School, which will educate youth free from superstitions, hard-working and upright, useful to themselves and to the country.[58]

In order to win the confidence of the Jews the posts of director, bursar, and visitor of the school were to be held by Jews, although there would also be a Christian inspector, who would be chairman of the school council.

The first years of the school were difficult. Abraham Stern, angry at the way his views had been disregarded, refused to accept the position of director, despite

[56] Sawicki, 'Szkoła Rabinów w Warszawie (1826–1863)', 248. [57] Ibid. 248–50.

[58] Akta Komitetu Starozakonnych, fascicle 21, quoted in Sawicki, 'Szkoła Rabinów w Warszawie (1826–1863)', 251–2.

urgings from some members of the government commission to explain his objections, with the hope that they could be allayed. He made it clear that he was unwilling to have anything to do with the running of the school, and would not agree to undertake the task, vital if the school was to have any credibility in the eyes of the bulk of the Jewish community, of teaching Talmud, for which limited provision was now made. He was particularly opposed to the prominent position held in the school by the young reformer Antoni Eisenbaum, who in his twenties was appointed bursar and was also the principal teacher of secular subjects. Stern's decision proved disastrous for the school. According to its most recent historian: 'Stern was the only person of his time whose secular education, Jewish religious loyalty and learning, attachment to Poland and high standing in Polish and Jewish society could have made the School work in the way it was intended.'[59]

In a further attempt to reassure the Jews, the chief rabbi of Warsaw or his deputy was given the right to ensure that Jewish law and practice were observed in the school. In addition, the task of teaching Talmud was assigned to an elderly Orthodox scholar, Meir Horowitz, who was also to hold the position of de facto head. Horowitz did indeed enjoy considerable respect in Jewish circles, but did not know anything about lay subjects. In addition, his refusal to discard traditional Jewish dress made him suspect in the eyes of the Polish bureaucrats, steeped in the philosophy of the Enlightenment, and of the younger and more impatient of the Jewish reformers.

This was certainly the case with Antoni Eisenbaum, who was from the outset the key figure in the school and remained its moving spirit during most of its existence until his death in 1852. He represented a very different strand of Jewish reform from that of Stern. Stern was interested not in politics or in Polonization, but rather in a moderate reform of Jewish life, improving the economic situation of the Jews and opposing large-scale religious change, while hoping to restrict the growing influence of hasidism in the Kingdom of Poland. Eisenbaum, whose knowledge of both Judaism and the Hebrew language was somewhat limited, was a determined reformer and Polish patriot. In the words of Agaton Giller, a former insurgent who was one of the first to write a history of the 1863 uprising, it was he who

> taught the Jews to love the land on which they were born and to fulfil towards that land the duties of a grateful son. He was convinced that the Jewish community could expect freedom of religion and equal rights from the Poles . . . [He] propagated the maintenance of the Mosaic tradition together with faithfulness towards Poland and the use of the Polish language among the Jews.[60]

Eisenbaum was editor of the short-lived *Dostrzegacz Nadwiślański* (The Observer on the Vistula), a bilingual paper in Polish and Germanized Yiddish

[59] Finkelstein, 'History of the Rabbinical School of Warsaw from its Establishment in 1826 to its Closure in 1863', 45.

[60] Giller, *Historia powstania narodu polskiego w 1861–1864*, i. 180.

which advocated Jewish acculturation and the transformation of the Jews into Poles of the Mosaic faith. In 1823 he wrote *Essais sur l'état des Juifs en Pologne et les moyens de les utiliser* (Essays on the Condition of the Jews in Poland and the Means of Making them Useful), which he submitted to Alexander I. He was convinced that once the Jews had created a 'civilized' elite, they would achieve equal status in the Kingdom, and was a strong believer in the importance of Jewish emancipation. He hoped that the promise of equality would attract the younger generation of Jews to the school and would overcome their religious scruples. It was thus a bitter disappointment to him when the authorities refused to allow him to establish the school permanently on Gwardia Street, in the centre of Warsaw, where he had hired suitable premises and which would have given symbolic emphasis to its integrationist objectives. This was a part of Warsaw where the Jews were not allowed to live, and accordingly the permanent location of the school there was forbidden by the Government Commission for Internal Affairs. The school was thus forced in 1828 to move to a house owned by the banker Józef Janasz at 959 Krochmalna Street. It remained there until 1838, when it moved to 2257 Nalewki Street, and moved again in 1846 to Gęsia Street, where it remained until its closure in 1863.

The uprising of 1830–1 saw the first significant involvement of Jews in Polish politics. The Warsaw bourgeoisie had been rather suspicious of the rebellion, sparked off by discontented military cadets and students and marked as it was in its first days by looting and rioting. As in France at this time, they attempted to control popular violence by setting up a National Guard. This was to be made up of wealthier citizens, who would bear the cost of their uniforms and equipment themselves and would maintain order in the capital. A number of the more acculturated Jews wanted to join this body, both to demonstrate their solidarity with Polish patriots and to justify their claim for civil rights by fulfilling their civil obligations. They included financiers, such as Samuel Kronenberg, Jakub Epstein, and two of the Toeplitzes, the bookseller Merzbach, a number of doctors, and Antoni Eisenbaum. General Józef Chłopicki, commander-in-chief of the revolutionary forces, agreed initially to their recruitment, although he was prepared to admit only those who were exempted from the exclusion of Jews from residential restrictions in Warsaw and elsewhere. Governor Antoni Ostrowski, commander of the National Guard, was prepared to take a more liberal position, but he encountered resistance from the Christian members of the Guard. As a result, he agreed to a rather unsatisfactory compromise: Jews could enlist provided they shaved off their beards. Most of the Jews who wished to enlist were not prepared to take this step. However, some were, and by the summer of 1831 over 300 had been enrolled. The remainder, numbering perhaps 1,400, were allowed to form a Civil Guard, in the words of Ostrowski, 'preparatory and transitory, less honorific than the National Guard itself, but close to it'.[61] In the final stages of the uprising, when there was a general mobilization, a large number of Jews, mostly from the poorer sections of the community, were conscripted into a Security Watch and took part in the final hopeless defence of Warsaw.

The revolutionary government did not introduce any changes in the status of the Jews, although civic rights were promised to those who completed ten years of military service or received decorations. In addition the ticket tax was abolished, while censorship of Jewish books lapsed when censorship was abolished for all publications. The Sejm, when it debated the question of Jewish recruitment in May 1831, resolved to quadruple the recruitment tax, while continuing to exclude Jews from conscription. The minister of war, Franciszek Morawski, remarked on this occasion that 'exotic shoots' should not be grafted onto the 'Polish tree' and that Poles should win their freedom without the 'aid of Israel'.[62] Jews were also adversely affected by the widespread spy mania which marked the latter stage of the uprising.

Nevertheless, the experience of serving in the National and Civil Guard greatly buoyed the confidence of those who underwent this experience. The impact of serving in these organizations is characteristically described by Hilary Nussbaum (1820–95), an assimilationist Jewish historian and graduate of the Warsaw Rabbinic School:

> Having put on short jackets [instead of the long *kapote* of the Orthodox], although military ones, and having shaved off their beards and side curls, once their service in the Guards was over they did not go back to wearing their former long coats, but detached themselves from their backward tribe. Dressed in the European fashion, they moved freely along all the main streets of the city, entered public gardens confidently, and, whether out for a stroll, at a meeting, or in any public place, they were not attacked by the Christian mob.[63]

MOVEMENT TOWARDS EMANCIPATION

The defeat of the 1830–1 uprising was followed by a generation of repression, and the centre of Polish political life now moved into the émigré community, primarily in France. Among those who were part of this Emigration were Synaj Hernisz and Izaak Horowic, students of the Warsaw Rabbinic School who had served as volunteers in the insurrectionary army. In the bitter debates over the

[61] On the role of Jews in the 1830–1 uprising, see Shatzky, *The History of Jews in Warsaw* (Yid.), i. 306–30; Gelber (ed.), *The Jews and the Polish Revolt* (Heb.); Schiper, *Żydzi Królestwa Polskiego w dobie Powstania Listopadowego*, and the critical review of this book by Shatzky, 'Jews in the Polish Uprising of 1831' (Yid.). There is also useful material in Lewandowski, 'Materiały do udziału Żydów w Gwardii Narodowej, Gwardii Miejskiej i Straży Bezpieczeństwa', and Węgrzynek, 'Ludność żydowska wobec powstania listopadowego'.

[62] Quoted in Finkelstein, 'History of the Rabbinical School of Warsaw from its Establishment in 1826 to its Closure in 1863', 70–1.

[63] Quoted in Kieniewicz, 'Assimilated Jews in Nineteenth-Century Warsaw', 174.

reasons for the failure of the revolt, the left wing of the Emigration criticized the conservatism of the revolutionary government and its failure to introduce measures which could have attracted the support of politically and socially disadvantaged groups like peasants and Jews. Thus, in November 1837 one of the leading figures in the Emigration, the historian Joachim Lelewel, issued a declaration which exhorted Polish Jews to participate in the struggle for independence and in this way to obtain civil rights. The declaration, which was in fact written by a Jew, Ludwik Lubliner, argued that the Jews in Belgium and France, who already enjoyed the rights of citizenship, were regarded as Belgians or Frenchmen and that the grievances of Polish Jews could only be assuaged 'when you unite with the Polish nation'. Then Poles by citizenship and Jews by religion, they would be equal in all areas of life.[64]

As Artur Eisenbach has shown, the democratic conspiratorial movement in Galicia, and in particular the Association of the Polish People and the Confederation of the Polish Nation, had a significant impact on Jewish youth there. Certainly, one of the first acts of the revolutionary government in Kraków in February 1846 was to proclaim the equality of the Jews (on this, see the previous chapter).

Activists within the Emigration repeated such exhortations in 1848. Leon Hollaenderski, for example, issued two appeals in Paris. The first, entitled *Głos Izraelity. Bracia Polacy!* (The Voice of an Israelite. Brother Poles!), was published on 2 April 1848; the second appeared four days later and was directed to the Jews. In the first pamphlet Hollaenderski expressed his profound conviction that the revolutionary upheaval would lead to the 'rebirth of an independent, free, unfettered, and happy Poland'. This rebirth was dependent on the unification of all social forces, irrespective of estate, religion, trade, or profession. The Poles should exert pressure on the clergy so that it would adopt a new attitude to the Jews: 'following in the footsteps of Christ, your Lord, and acting in the spirit of the law of humanity, they should stretch out a friendly hand to the Jews . . . [and] accept them with love and open-heartedness'. If this occurred, the Jews would respond 'with the strength of their spirit and thought'. The Poles needed to act in harmony with the mood of the time, follow the example of the reviving nations of Europe, and adopt as their slogans liberty, equality, and fraternity. In these conditions, the Polish motherland would become the mother of all its inhabitants. In his second appeal Hollaenderski called on the Jews to join the burgeoning revolutionary struggle in Europe. He appealed to Jewish teachers and rabbis to remind Jews of their duties to the motherland and in the name of these ideals to spare no effort to liberate Poland and ensure her freedom.[65]

[64] Lelewel, *Polska, dzieje i rzeczy jej*, xx. 259, quoted in Eisenbach, *Wielka Emigracja wobec kwestii żydowskiej, 1832–1849*, 314.

[65] Ibid. 443–6. On this, see also Duker, 'The Polish Political Émigrés and the Jews in 1848', 98–101.

At this time the conservative element of the Emigration in Paris, with Adam Czartoryski at its head, repeated his support for conditional emancipation of the Jews. In addition, as described before, full civil rights for the Jews were supported by the Polish revolutionaries in the Grand Duchy of Poznań and in Galicia, and were enacted by the revolutionary parliaments in both Prussia and Galicia, although there was also significant Polish–Jewish conflict in Prussian Poland.

However, in the repressive and reactionary atmosphere of the Kingdom of Poland under Nicholas I and his viceroy, Paskevich, discussion of the Jewish issue was impossible. Few initiatives were taken in relation to the Jews, although in 1844, following a similar step in the tsarist empire, conscription had been brought in. This was first proposed by the Administrative Council (Rada Administracyjna) at the end of the 1830s and was introduced by decree of the viceroy on 1 January 1844. The recruitment tax was now abolished, and in 1845 the Jewish community's quota of new recruits was set at 950. Jewish recruits were allowed to provide substitutes, who were usually compensated financially. At the same time the integrationist minority in the community may have tried to persuade conscripts to fulfil their obligations, seeing this as a stage in the achievement of legal equality, although such appeals do not appear in the press or in memorandums to the authorities. Certainly, the impact of conscription in disrupting Jewish communal solidarity was far less there than in the Pale of Settlement.[66]

Renewed attempts were made at this time to enforce the ban on burial societies. Thus in Lublin in 1847 the government ordered the local synagogue board to ensure that the burial society be dissolved, and members of the society were barred by the town administration from participating in Jewish communal government.[67] This and similar interventions do not, however, seem to have achieved their object. Restrictions similar to those in Russia on traditional Jewish dress were also introduced by Paskevich on 2 July 1846, confirming an earlier prohibition of 1824, and those who wore such clothing were subject to a fine. This prohibition was renewed on 1 January 1851, and two years later women were forbidden to shave their heads on marriage, but these restrictions do not appear to have been rigidly enforced. For the most part, the authorities of the Kingdom, concerned above all to avoid political upheaval, were now far less willing to provoke the Orthodox Jewish majority by advancing a strongly reformist agenda in relation to the Jews.[68]

At the same time the processes of acculturation and assimilation continued, particularly in Warsaw. The Warsaw Rabbinic School continued to play an important role in these developments, although the distrust of the community,

[66] On this, see Guesnet, *Polnische Juden im 19. Jahrhundert*, 183, and Goldsztejn, 'Służba wojskowa a Żydzi w Cesarstwie Rosyjskim i Królestwie Polskim do roku 1874'. I am grateful to Marcin Wodziński for the information on actual declarations of support for conscription.

[67] Guesnet, *Polnische Juden im 19. Jahrhundert*, 383–4.

[68] Ibid. 196–8.

the divisions in the faculty, and the unsatisfactory character of religious instruction provided there caused it to develop slowly. Enrolment was twenty-five in 1826 and by 1831 had risen to only eighty-three. Numbers in the school began to rise after the November uprising. This was partly because of the belief that students in the school would not be recruited into the army. When this turned out not to be the case, numbers fell to between 150 and 200. Enrolment was also restricted by the requirement that instruction was to be in Polish.

Because of the equivocal reputation of the school, pupils were unable to obtain rabbinic positions and most were forced to find employment in education or in mercantile occupations. The failure of the school to produce rabbis aroused considerable disappointment and was widely discussed. The Old Testament Believers' Committee thought that it was caused by poor organization. In a memorandum of 2 July 1833 it called for the school to be divided into two institutions. One would train teachers for Jewish elementary schools. Alongside it should be created a special rabbinical seminary. It was vital that this latter organization should have the confidence of the Jews. In order to ensure that this would be attained, the committee wanted to create a delegation made up of the four members of the advisory committee, four rabbis from Warsaw, with Solomon Zalman Lipschitz, chief rabbi of Warsaw (1819–39), at their head, and four rabbis from the provinces. This delegation would be responsible for creating the plan for a rabbinical seminary 'which, while fulfilling the needs of the government, would also provide the Jewish population with a guarantee that it would in no way violate the principles or observances of the Mosaic faith'.[69]

This proposal was rejected by the Government Commission for Religious Beliefs and Public Education because it would lead to the establishment of a special school system for the Jews. In its opinion, Jewish elementary schools should be organized in such a way as to make possible the entry of Jews into the public secondary school system. The Rabbinic School should be transformed into a purely pedagogic body which would train teachers.

In 1835 Meir Horowitz finally retired and Antoni Eisenbaum was appointed acting principal, enjoying full authority in the school. Accusations against him as a radical and an unbeliever continued. Eisenbaum faced continual opposition from the Jewish community and was also to find himself in conflict with the authorities. During the insurrection of 1830 he was arrested by the revolutionary government following denunciation, but was released after a month and served in the National Guard. He was again in difficulties in 1834, accused this time of imbuing his students with revolutionary fervour, and in 1836, when he was attacked as a Freemason. He was also criticized for borrowing money from students and providing inadequate food. Support for these accusations was also provided by Rabbi Lipschitz, who had been appointed visitor to the school in an attempt to

[69] Projekt z 2 VII 1833, fascicle 2448, quoted in Sawicki, 'Szkoła Rabinów w Warszawie (1826–1863)', 265.

make it more acceptable to mainstream Jews. A report was produced on this matter by the Old Testament Believers' Committee, one of its last actions before it was abolished (on 23 January 1837) as part of the administrative unification of the Kingdom of Poland and the tsarist empire. A criminal investigation subsequently cleared him and recommended he retain his post 'because of the persecution that he suffered during the revolution'.[70]

The remaining members of staff were bitterly divided on ideology between radical and moderate reformers. After Rabbi Lipschitz's death in 1839 he appears to have been succeeded by the new chief rabbi of Warsaw, Hayim Dawidsohn, but there are no records of his visiting the school. In a memorandum prepared for the Government Commission for Religious Beliefs and Public Education in 1850 Jakub Tugendhold claimed that for four years Dawidsohn had been unwilling to visit the school. Chiarini was appointed inspector of the school. The Jewish community vehemently objected to this, as did the Jewish Advisory Committee. Accordingly, the Old Testament Believers' Committee was forced to replace him with Count Wincenty Krasiński, while, in another attempt to demonstrate the bona fides of the school, the school administration drew up an elaborate plan for talmudic instruction over five years.

In spite of these difficulties, the dynamism and commitment of Eisenbaum contributed to the expansion of the school and to its influence in creating a small Polonized Jewish elite. By the end of 1836 thirty-six students had completed their education at the school and by 1843 the total number had risen to 305. Most found work in commerce or as schoolteachers. None was employed as a rabbi.[71]

The school also began to draw support from the Polish elite and from the progressive section of the Jewish community. This is illustrated by the increasing success of Eisenbaum in raising money for the school's library and chemistry laboratories. The principal donor of books to the library was Adam Czartoryski. The list of Jews who supported the library is a roll-call of the progressive and assimilationist sector of Jewish society at this time, and it also obtained significant support from the Jewish bankers in Warsaw.[72]

The 1830s and 1840s saw a slow rise in the number of acculturated Jews in Warsaw. In 1841 they succeeded in having the banker Mathias Rosen elected chairman of the Congregational Board. In this capacity his influence was limited, since most members of the board were much more Orthodox, but he did introduce some minor modifications in synagogue and cemetery ritual. The progressive synagogue established on Daniłowiczowska Street by Isaac Flatau flourished in these years. Abraham Meir Goldschmidt became the preacher there in the early 1840s. Eisenbaum was asked to train a choir for the new synagogue from

[70] Sawicki, 'Szkoła Rabinów w Warszawie (1826–1863)', 256–7.

[71] Archiwum Oświecenia, Warsaw, Akta dyrektora gimnazjum w Lesznie, fascicle 2, quoted in Sawicki, 'Szkoła Rabinów w Warszawie (1826–1863)', 259.

[72] Akta Komitetu Starozakonnych, fascicle 16, quoted in Sawicki, 'Szkoła Rabinów w Warszawie (1826–1863)', 261.

among the pupils of the Rabbinic School, where singing had been taught. Eisenbaum's aim was to transform religious services by making them more orderly and by establishing a liturgy which would be capable of inspiring the congregation by its beauty. The way had been shown by Noah Mannheimer in Vienna, using the editions of Jewish liturgical music prepared by Solomon Sulzer.

The language of the sermon at the Daniłowiczowska Street synagogue was German, which was not acceptable to the more patriotic of the graduates of the Rabbinic School. They wanted to establish their own synagogue in the school, which they did on Passover 1842. The preacher at the synagogue from 1850 was Isaak Kramsztyk (1814/16–1889), a graduate and teacher of the Rabbinic School. As long as the school was situated on Nalewki Street, the synagogue was situated within the school. When the school moved to Gęsia Street in 1846, there was no space for the synagogue. It was re-established in 1850 in an apartment house on Nalewki Street, while retaining its links with the school. This house was owned by Wolf Zelig Natanson, father of Henryk and Ludwik Natanson, who were later to play a prominent role in Warsaw Jewish life, and who, together with the adjacent apartment house owned by Stanisław Neuding, another prominent integrationist, played a large role in the propagation of Polonizing and integrationist views. It was here that the integrationist Association of Tradespeople was to meet in the 1850s, and from the 1860s it housed the editorial office of the integrationist weekly *Izraelita*. It was also the home of the prominent integrationist philanthropist Jenta Centnerszwer.[73]

The school was financed by the ticket tax, which Jews had to pay to stay in Warsaw. This had been reintroduced in 1826, but soon became inadequate to the activities it was required to finance. On the dissolution of the Old Testament Believers' Committee in January 1837, financial responsibility for the school passed to the Warsaw magistracy. Its requirements were met by the municipality from the ticket tax, but it never enjoyed enough financial support to undertake the more ambitious plans of Eisenbaum.

Throughout this period the Orthodox continued to criticize the Rabbinic School, and the Government Commission for Internal and Spiritual Affairs accepted the justice of some of these criticisms. Accordingly, the commission asked the Jewish Advisory Council, which had been kept in being after the dissolution of the Old Testament Believers' Committee, what measures needed to be taken to ensure that the school achieved its objectives. As a consequence, it was decided that new rabbis would be obliged to pass an examination set by the school. From now on the provincial authorities were not to authorize as a rabbi anyone who had not passed this examination.

Aron Sawicki, in his study mentioned earlier, found in the archives a record of nearly fifty such examinations, which were destroyed during the Second World

[73] The role of this housing complex as a 'core centre' of enlightened views is stressed by Guesnet, *Polnische Juden im 19. Jahrhundert*, 288–9.

War. They showed that, apart from religious knowledge, the rabbis were largely ignorant. However, there were no cases in which a rabbi was refused certification since the examination board could only state that the candidate had presented himself for examination. This led Eisenbaum to argue that either the examination was superfluous or it should specify whether a candidate was competent to take up a rabbinic post. The government agreed to establish such a requirement, but until Eisenbaum's death no new candidates presented themselves. Subsequently a fair number of certificates were issued attesting competence.[74]

The provincial authorities did try to insist that appropriately trained rabbis be appointed. Thus in 1841 the Government Council, the governing body in the Kingdom, demanded of the director of the Educational Commission in Kalisz province, Karwowski, that he put forward a suitably qualified rabbi for Sierpce. They later demanded the same for Warka, Piotrków, and Warta. Karwowski could not find suitable candidates and wrote that 'not only now, but also in the future there is no hope that students of the Rabbinic School will feel an inclination for the rabbinical calling'. He continued: 'The Rabbinic School is, in practice, an institution in which Jewish youth, through the acquisition of knowledge and some education, will be emancipated from obscurantism and prejudices. As a result, the graduate of the Rabbinic School finds himself in complete opposition to the opinions and way of life of the remainder of his unenlightened co-religionists.'[75]

Complaints continued as a result of the new regulations for licensing rabbis. As a result, the Government Commission for Religious Beliefs and Public Education created in 1850 a special committee to investigate the Rabbinic School and the Jewish elementary schools. Its conclusion was that the school should be retained and transformed into a modern rabbinical seminary. Only through the help of enlightened rabbis could one work effectively for the 'civilization' of the followers of the Old Testament. Although the Rabbinic School had not yet achieved this objective, with time its success would increase. The achievements of the school were already considerable 'since, as the number of its graduates increases, education is spread, the fanaticism of the Jews diminishes, and the number among them friendly to civilization and even more to Christians increases'. At the same time it was necessary to take steps to diminish the distrust most Jews felt for the Rabbinic School. The school should be changed into an educational establishment, with the name Main Israelite School (Szkoła Główna Izraelska). In this school the teaching of secular subjects should be restricted and more emphasis be placed on religious ones. After completing five classes, pupils who wished to enter the clergy should attend a special further year of training. All secular subjects should be taught in Polish. Apart from supervision by the Government Commission for Religious Beliefs and Public Education, the school should be subject 'in religious matters' to a council composed of Jews which would examine and approve all

[74] Archiwum Oświecenia, Warsaw, Akta dyrektora gimnazjum w Lesznie, fascicle 1, vol. 2, quoted in Sawicki, 'Szkoła Rabinów w Warszawie (1826–1863)', 267.

[75] Ibid.

teachers of religious subjects. In order to create a more favourable attitude to the school within the Jewish community, the regulation on rabbinical qualifications should be repealed.[76]

Eisenbaum also favoured reform of the Rabbinic School to transform it into an institution of tertiary education. Students would follow two tracks, philology and theology. The students of the philological section should be able to study in other institutions after they had graduated from the school and should be able to study for professions. The students of the theological section, who would have studied under Jewish teachers, would, as enlightenment spread among the Jews, acquire the confidence of the wider Jewish society and would be recognized as fit for rabbinical office.

The Rabbinic School was not the only force fostering the acculturation of the Jewish elite. Economic forces were also pushing in this direction. As we have seen, the first half of the nineteenth century produced the consolidation of the Warsaw Jewish banking elite, a closely knit plutocratic circle made up of about a dozen families, often related by marriage, though competing furiously on the stock exchange or in the pursuit of railway concessions. Some bankers, such as Zelig Natanson and Mathias Rosen, remained Orthodox Jews all their lives and were enthusiastic supporters of Jewish causes, but on the whole, conversion made steady inroads into this group, if not in the second then in the third and subsequent generations. Samuel Antoni Fraenkel was baptized as early as 1806, Leopold Kronenberg in 1845, Jan Bogumił Bloch and Stanisław Rotwand in 1851, Leo Loewenstein in 1857, Jan Epstein in the 1850s, to be followed by many other members of his family. Altogether, in the first half of the nineteenth century seventy leading bankers, industrialists, and merchants, fifteen printers, and twenty communal officials adopted Christianity. Believing that this was the only way to overcome the barriers against entry into Christian society, some of them converted first to Lutheranism, an indication both of the prestige of German cultural values and of Jewish reservations about the anti-Jewish elements in Catholicism.

Another index of assimilation within the Jewish elite was the growing interest in Freemasonry, which was spreading widely at this time. In the first years of the Kingdom of Poland there were thirty-two lodges with nearly 3,000 members and another 1,000 in the areas of Poland–Lithuania directly incorporated into the tsarist empire.[77] In the early 1820s the Warsaw Masonic lodge admitted several Epsteins, Leopold Kronenberg, and a few other financiers. Many members of the Jewish elite were also allowed to settle outside the predominantly Jewish quarter of Warsaw. By 1836 the number of families to whom this privileged status had been granted had risen to 124. Other privileges followed, including the right to buy noble estates and personal or hereditary nobility. By the end of the nineteenth century the daughters of these families were marrying Polish aristocrats. It should

[76] Akta Komisji Rządowej WR i OP, fascicle 2437, vol. 2, quoted in Sawicki, 'Szkoła Rabinów w Warszawie (1826–1863)', 268.

[77] Kukiel, *Dzieje Polski porozbiorowe, 1795–1921*, 184.

be stressed, however, that holding enlightened views, assimilation, and conversion were very much minority phenomena. The overwhelming majority of the Jews of the Kingdom of Poland remained unacculturated, speaking Yiddish among themselves, and were by now increasingly hasidic in religious belief and practice.

One group which was more integrated into Polish society, though it retained some distinctive traits, comprised the descendants of the followers of the eighteenth-century messianic pretender Jacob Frank, who had converted to Christianity in 1759 (see Chapter 5). Of the 600 or so of his followers who converted with him, thirty-eight families were ennobled by the Sejm in 1764, while the number of Frankist surnames has been estimated at between 100 and 140. These families—the Jarmunds, Krysińskis, Lewińskis, Łabęckis, Szymanowskis, and Wołowskis—still married largely among themselves. They had noble status and some of them played a prominent part in Polish political and cultural life. Dominik Krysiński, whose views on Jewish reform during the Duchy of Warsaw were discussed above, and Antoni Łabęcki were liberal lawyers and deputies in the Sejm from Warsaw in the 1820s. Frankists did, however, encounter suspicion because of their background. In 1831, for example, one of the Wołowskis was rejected as a member of the senate.[78]

Other Frankists were prominent in the uprising of November 1830. Aleksander Krysiński was the general secretary to General Chłopicki, and then aide-de-camp and representative of the commander-in-chief, Jan Skrzyniecki. On the left, he was attacked as the 'evil spirit' of the insurrection, a capitalist in league with St Petersburg. In the Sejm, Dominik Krysiński attacked the leadership of the insurrection and opposed the 'capitulators', while General Jan Krysiński commanded the fortress of Zamość and was the last to admit defeat, on 21 October 1831, seven weeks after the fall of Warsaw. Throughout the nineteenth century this group continued to play an important, if not completely accepted, role in Polish life.

Throughout the period after the uprising, strict censorship prevented any discussion of Jewish issues, while hostility to the improvement of the position of the Jews was provoked by the close links of some of the leading Jewish industrialists and financiers with the tsarist government. Those who profited from this connection—whether through leasing monopolies and credits from the Bank of Poland or through building railways—were bitterly resented. The greatest hostility was aroused by Jewish bankers. Zygmunt Krasiński, one of the leading figures of Polish Romanticism and the author of *Nieboska komedia* (The Undivine Comedy), a vision of proletarian revolution led by Jewish converts, wrote on 1 August 1836:

> It is not until you get there [Warsaw] that you will hear and understand what Poland is today, how fawning everyone is, how corruptible, how it is ten times worse to have Poles in office than the Muscovite; how the last shreds of honour are collapsing around the nation's

78 Kieniewicz, 'The Jews of Warsaw, Polish Society and the Partitioning Powers', 158–9.

ears, how the Jews and Germans are profiting from poverty and disgrace, how the Jews settle on the ruins of our palaces, how everywhere it is Jews and Jews only who have influence, power, means.[79]

Polish–Jewish relations began to improve in the later years of Tsar Nicholas I's reign. Like the Poles, the Jews, both the elite and the masses, had every reason to resent Nicholas's repressive and interventionist regime. Within the Jewish community the influence grew of those who believed that civil rights would only be obtained when a degree of acculturation to the Polish environment had been achieved. In this a significant role was played by the graduates of the Rabbinic School and by Eisenbaum himself. The Russian defeat in the Crimean War and the accession of the more liberal Alexander II in 1855 strengthened the view that major political and social changes were in the offing.

The Jews hoped that the new tsar would significantly relax the restrictions under which they still laboured in the Kingdom of Poland. The brutal rejection by the tsar of a petition from the Warsaw Jewish Congregational Board calling for changes of this type brought the Jews closer to the Poles, among whom agitation for the restoration of Polish rights was increasing. Relations between Poles and Jews were also, paradoxically, improved by the controversy in the Warsaw press in 1859 which subsequently became known as the 'Jewish war'. This was sparked off by an article in Warsaw's principal daily newspaper, *Gazeta Warszawska*, in which the editor, Antoni Lesznowski, attacked the Warsaw Jewish elite for 'lack of patriotism' in a particularly offensive manner. In the face of Jewish protests, Lesznowski sought the support of the Russian director of the Commission for Internal Affairs in the Kingdom of Poland, Pavel Chekhanov, who invoked censorship to prevent criticism of Lesznowski's views. This discredited the editor in the eyes of Polish patriotic opinion and led those circles to take a much more favourable view of the assimilated Jews who had been attacked by him. One of their number, the banker Leopold Kronenberg, who had been baptized in 1845 but who still took an active interest in Jewish affairs, was even able to buy the newspaper's main rival, *Gazeta Codzienna*, which, under its editor, the prolific author Józef Ignacy Kraszewski, became a firm advocate of Polish–Jewish understanding.[80]

The Jews were now the beneficiaries of a three-way struggle for their support. While the Polish opposition aimed to enlist them for the anti-tsarist insurrection they were planning, Wielopolski sought to make use of them in the restructuring of Polish society which he was hoping to achieve. They could form a significant part of the middle class. Rural society would also be transformed on the English or Prussian model. This version of 'organic work' would create a

[79] Krasiński, *Listy do Adama Sołtana*, 98, quoted in Kieniewicz, 'The Jews of Warsaw, Polish Society and the Partitioning Powers', 163.

[80] On this, see Eisenbach, *Kwestia równouprawnienia Żydów w Królestwie Polskim*, 272–7, and Bartoszewicz, *Wojna żydowska w roku 1859*.

society much more able, even without political independence, to maintain itself and defend its interests.

The Russian central government in St Petersburg was alarmed by the growing fraternization between Poles and Jews, and also sought to win over the Jews (as it was later to attempt with the peasantry) in order to weaken the hold of the Polish revolutionaries on the Kingdom of Poland. It was also suspicious of Wielopolski's own objectives, and the Russian-controlled police in the Kingdom closely monitored the approaches being made to the Jews and the dissemination of propaganda among them. On 12 May 1861 Valeryan Platonov, under-secretary of the Polish Council of State, wrote to Alexander II that, in the light of the proposed changes in the status of Jews in the Kingdom, 'it would seem useful to do something for the Jews; several proposals on the subject which are before the Jewish Committee [a body set up in the tsarist empire; see Chapters 11 and 12] could receive immediate implementation'. Count Kiselev, former chairman of the Jewish Committee and now Russian ambassador to France, and Dmitry Milyutin, the minister of war, both suggested cultivating the Jews as a counterweight to the Poles.[81]

Polish–Jewish fraternization was certainly a feature of the years immediately preceding the Polish insurrection of January 1863, even if it was limited to relatively small sections of the two societies. Jews participated in many anti-Russian protests in those years. Following the demonstrations of 25 and 27 February 1861, which led to the deaths of five protesters, two of them Jews, a city delegation was elected of twelve leading citizens of Warsaw. It included the chief rabbi, Dov Berush Meisels, who had also participated in the 1848 revolution in Kraków. On the 28th Meisels went to the palace of the leading Polish reformer, Count Andrzej Zamoyski, to sign an address to the tsar calling for the restoration of the 'rights of the Polish nation'. Zamoyski, who had previously opposed granting equal rights to Jews, spoke of the 'Old Testament believers' as 'our countrymen and brothers, the children of one land', while Meisels replied, 'And we too feel that we are Poles and we love the Polish land as you do.'[82] For the Polish reformers, the granting of equal rights to the Jews was a problem comparable to that of enfranchising the peasants. According to a prominent liberal, Karol Ruprecht, it was necessary 'to raise the peasant and the Jew to the dignity of a free person and a citizen . . . [because] the peasant and Jewish questions are the source of the rebirth of Poland'.[83]

[81] Eisenbach, 'Le Problème des Juifs polonais en 1861 et les projets de réforme du Marquis Aleksander Wielopolski', 149, and id., *Kwestia równouprawnienia Żydów w Królestwie Polskim*, 419, 422–5. For police reports on Polish agitation among Jews, see Tsentral'nyi derzhavnyi istorychnyi arkhiv (TsDIAU; Central State Historical Archive of Ukraine), Kiev, f. 442, op. 812, d. 4 (1862), ll. 56–7, 83–4; op. 811, d. 249 (1861–2), ll. 1–10, quoted in Klier, *Imperial Russia's Jewish Question, 1855–1881*, 147.

[82] Quoted in Kieniewicz, *Między ugodą a rewolucją*, 96–7. On Zamoyski's views on Jewish emancipation, Eisenbach, *Kwestia równouprawnienia Żydów w Królestwie Polskim*, 346–7, 390–1.

[83] Eisenbach, *The Emancipation of the Jews in Poland, 1780–1870*, 476; id., *Kwestia równouprawnienia Żydów w Królestwie Polskim*, 346–7, 390–401.

Both Meisels and Rabbi Marcus Mordecai Jastrow of the Nalewki Street synagogue also took part in the funeral of the five victims, which became another major political demonstration. Meisels himself issued an appeal to the Jews of Poland, reminding them of the persecution they had experienced in the Kingdom at the hands of the director of the Government Commission for Religious Beliefs and Public Education, Pavel Mukhanov, whom he compared to Haman, the enemy of the Jews in the book of Esther. The Poles, he claimed, had made clear their desire to grant the Jews equal rights; it was the duty of the Jews to support the Polish nationalist movement. Władysław Mickiewicz, the son of the poet Adam Mickiewicz, wrote of the Jews of Warsaw in a letter on 2 July 1861:

> The Jews here are the best in all of Poland. They sing national anthems in the synagogues. The sermons that are delivered there concerning love of the fatherland unite Poles and Jews in a single emotion, and the thought that Poland will arise awakens in the Jews the hope that their exile is coming to an end.[84]

This was the background to the acceptance by the tsarist government of Wielopolski's views on the Jewish question. Wielopolski had been dismissed from all his offices and recalled to St Petersburg in December 1861 when the initial reforms he introduced failed to allay Polish discontent. However, he persuaded Alexander that he could pacify the Kingdom with a more extensive programme of reforms, and as a result was appointed head of the Civil Administration of the Kingdom with increased powers. One of his goals was to grant full legal equality to the Jews, whom he saw as the core of a future Polish middle class. As he told a Jewish delegation in Pińczów in March 1861,

> Do not fear, gentlemen, that I share the contemporary view of those who call on you . . . to turn to agriculture. The agricultural sphere is an honourable one to which you may also want to aspire . . . but we already have too many farmers. What our country lacks is a 'third estate', whose seed has been planted by Providence in you and which will perish if neglected. Let us work together to foster and develop that seed.[85]

There was some opposition to Wielopolski's plans within the tsarist bureaucracy, both in St Petersburg and in Warsaw. On 22 November 1861 Platonov wrote to Alexander advising counter-measures:

> Marquis Wielopolski clearly wishes and hopes to merge the Jewish with the Polish population by means of the measures he intends for them, and to turn those who are actually Jews into Poles of the Mosaic Confession. I dare to suggest that such merging would be quite contrary to the interests and views of the government. The Jews, whose number exceeds 600,000, could easily be attracted to the side of the government which should not make Poles out of them, but leave them as Jews, with their religion, language, and nationality undisturbed.[86]

84 *Korespondencja namiestników Królestwa Polskiego z 1861 roku*, 128–9.

85 Quoted in Eisenbach, *The Emancipation of the Jews in Poland, 1780–1870*, 424.

86 Ibid. 507–8.

Wielopolski proved more persuasive and was able to convince both Alexander and the Jewish Committee in St Petersburg, which, after making some minor modifications, approved his programme of Jewish emancipation on 4 June 1862.[87]

As a consequence, by decree the viceroy abolished all the main restrictions on Jewish activity, in effect establishing the Jews as equal citizens. Jews were granted the right to own farmland and urban properties. All special Jewish taxes, including the tax on kosher meat, were abolished and Jewish congregational boards were authorized to levy a communal tax. All restrictions on residence and movement were abolished. Jews were permitted to serve as witnesses before a notary and their testimony was given equal status in court proceedings. The legal oath was modified to make it more acceptable to Jews, though Hebrew and Yiddish continued to be barred for all legal transactions. Subsequently, in 1866 Jews with university diplomas were allowed to become advocates and in 1876 were admitted to state posts. However, Jews were forbidden to be independent producers of alcohol, were not allowed to sell alcohol in villages, and could not be guardians of Christian children. The outbreak of the uprising in January 1863 prevented Wielopolski from introducing a reform of the Jewish communal structure, which would have established a version of the consistorial system in France which he believed would foster further Jewish reform.[88]

The new status of the Jews was confirmed by the underground National Government created after the outbreak of the insurrection. A proclamation of 22 June 1863 addressed to 'Brother Poles of the Mosaic faith' affirmed in somewhat archaic language: 'You and your children will enjoy all civil rights without exceptions and restrictions, while the National Government will ask, not about faith or descent, but about place of birth, Are you a Pole? And they will say about Poland . . . "that this man was born there, Selah"' (Psalm 87: 6).

These years also saw several attempts to reform the Warsaw Rabbinic School in order to make it more effective both in training rabbis and in creating a secular and progressive Jewish elite. In 1850 Jakub Tugendhold, at the request of Piotr Safiano, a member of the Government Commission for Religious Beliefs and Public Education, prepared a report on the Rabbinic School. He advocated creating a special rabbinic academy, alongside which a four-year *Realschule* would be created, where young Jews would study secular subjects which would prepare them for the teaching profession. The system of licensing rabbis would be abolished once the school produced a sufficient number of trained rabbis, when new entrants into the rabbinate would be restricted to graduates of the Rabbinic School.

In July 1852 Antoni Eisenbaum died at the age of 61. Even in death he proved controversial. In 1854 his supporters, mostly alumni of the Rabbinic School, wanted to erect a monument to him in the Jewish cemetery. It was to carry the

[87] Gessen, *Istoriya evreiskogo naroda v Rossii*, ii. 195.

[88] On the terms of the emancipation, see Guesnet, *Polnische Juden im 19. Jahrhundert*, 510–13.

inscription in Polish: 'To Antoni Eisenbaum, Principal of the Rabbinic School'. The Orthodox who controlled the cemetery as well as the congregational board objected to the use of Polish, and claimed that Antoni was not a Jewish name and that Eisenbaum had only been acting principal. It required the intervention of the Commission for Internal and Religious Affairs for the monument to be erected.

Eisenbaum was succeeded as director of the Rabbinic School by Tugendhold, who was more acceptable to the Jewish community in spite of his reputation as an opportunist, as demonstrated by his loyalism after the revolt of 1830–1. He was unable to introduce significant changes on the lines he had advocated in his report of 1850, but he did succeed in establishing three courses of study: a general introductory course and two special tracks, one rabbinic and the other pedagogic. The general course lasted four years, the rabbinic course an additional two years, and the pedagogic course only one. Students of the rabbinic course had to undertake, before graduation, a one-year internship with a rabbi. On completion of this internship and obtaining a certificate from the supervising rabbi, they were allowed to take their final examinations. Depending on their results, they would be eligible for the post of rabbi or assistant rabbi and would have preference over other candidates. Within ten years no one who had not completed the course at the Rabbinic School could be appointed to the post of rabbi or assistant rabbi.[89]

Again these changes failed to achieve their objectives and the position of the school was increasingly threatened. In the early 1860s Wielopolski, as director of the re-established Commission for Religious Beliefs and Public Education, prepared a project for the radical reorganization of all schooling in the Kingdom, creating a single system with access to a re-established university, the Main School in Warsaw. While not abandoning as a temporary expedient the establishment and maintenance of separate schools for Germans and Jews, the goal of the reform was a single system open to all those living in the Kingdom. The Jewish Religious Committee presented Wielopolski with a memorandum in which they argued that the Rabbinic School had failed in its goal. A rabbinic school, if it was to function successfully, 'must possess the confidence of the Jewish population, from whom rabbis must be selected and whom rabbis must serve. In its academic organization, it must be capable of training its students to be religious leaders.' The existing Rabbinic School was incapable of performing this function. Wielopolski, in planning a reform of the school, was influenced less by Tugendhold and the Jewish Religious Committee than by the preacher at the Daniłowiczowska Street synagogue, Marcus Mordecai Jastrow, who had been born near Poznań and had received his rabbinic training in Germany.[90]

Jastrow's plan was 'to move the Jews of the Kingdom from their present abnormal situation to a normal situation, to make them Poles of the Mosaic faith'. To

[89] Sawicki, 'Szkoła Rabinów w Warszawie (1826–1863)', 272; *Z dziejów gminy starozakonnych w Warszawie w XIX stuleciu*, i: *Szkolnictwo*, 110–11.

[90] Quoted in Sawicki, 'Szkoła Rabinów w Warszawie (1826–1863)', 273.

achieve this goal, religion should be taught in Jewish primary schools in Polish, since this would lead young people to think in Polish in those subjects which 'most engaged youthful fantasy'. The Rabbinic School should be abolished. Those who wished to enter the clergy should go to gymnasiums and obtain their religious education privately, as they did in Germany. Given that the school system was now organized on confessional lines, a seminary should be established for teachers of Hebrew and religion in elementary and secondary schools.[91]

On 13 March 1861 Wielopolski issued *A Project for the Reorganization of Educational Establishments in the Kingdom of Poland*, which was promulgated the following November. Article 75 dealt with the Rabbinic School. It abandoned any attempt to train rabbis and proposed transforming the school into a teachers' training college with a preparatory school for attending gymnasium, retaining extensive Jewish religious instruction, though somewhat more limited in scope than had previously been offered.

These plans fell victim to the growing political crisis. When, on 8 January 1862, in an attempt to calm the increasingly inflamed political atmosphere, a decree was issued opening the schools which had been closed because of the unrest, no mention was made of a Jewish teachers' training college. Over a year later, on 31 June 1863, in the midst of the uprising, the Rabbinic School was dissolved and its entire staff dismissed. The school was a casualty, like so much else, of the failure of Wielopolski to find a way to bridge the cavernous gap between the tsarist authorities and Polish society.

Altogether 1,209 students passed through the school. They remembered it with affection. Adolf Jakób Cohn, a former pupil, concluded his history of the school written in 1907 with a list of its pupils:

> This list would have been longer if we could have obtained information on those individuals who are spread across the wide world. Even though this was impossible, we are convinced that this fellowship of distinguished names will convince the reader that the school, founded eighty years ago, dissolved more than forty years ago, should be fondly remembered in the history of the civilization of the Jews of our country.[92]

Members of the school, like the rest of the acculturated Jewish elite in the Kingdom of Poland, were certainly caught up in the revolutionary fervour of these years. As early as 1859 a circle of students and alumni of the school was organized to discuss banned literature. Among the former students who were part of the various conspiratorial circles were Leon Wagenfisz and Maksymilian Unszlicht at the Medical Surgical Academy, and Aleksander Sochaczewski at the School of Fine Arts. As we have seen, Jews played a prominent part in the demonstrations in the two years before the outbreak of the insurrection in 1863, and, once it began, a number served in the revolutionary government, including Henryk Wohl, who was the director of its finance department, and Bernard

[91] Ibid.

[92] *Z dziejów gminy starozakonnych w Warszawie w XIX stuleciu*, i: *Szkolnictwo*, 117.

Goldman, who was the commissioner of the underground police organization in Warsaw and later an agent of the revolutionary organization in Breslau. Jews also served in the insurrectionary armies, including Izydor Heilpern, who fought under the revolutionary commander Marian Langiewicz, and Alexander Lande, who was wounded and probably killed in the battle of Radziłów, fighting under General Wysocki.[93]

At the same time the failure to create a modern institution training a professional rabbinate had very serious consequences for the evolution of Jewish life in the Kingdom of Poland in the nineteenth century. It was only in 1925 that the Judaic Institute was created, attached to the Tłomackie Street synagogue. The inability to establish a successfully functioning rabbinic school constituted a failure both of policy and of implementation. The goal should have been to create a university-level institution similar to those which appeared somewhat later in Germany, an aim not envisaged either by those committed to the radical transformation of Polish Jewry, like Eisenbaum, or by those more rooted in traditional Jewish values like Abraham Stern. The Polish educational bureaucracy had very little understanding of, or sympathy with, these issues, and the political upheavals which marked the period between 1815 and 1864 made the consistent implementation of policy impossible. These factors lie at the root of yet another of the many missed opportunities in Polish and Polish Jewish history.

FROM EMANCIPATION TO 1881

The 1863 uprising, poorly planned and ill-conceived, never had a chance of success, and its crushing by the Russians was followed by two generations in which all aspects of Polish national individuality were suppressed. As a consequence, the hope that achievement of national independence would usher in, as it had in Hungary and Italy, a new era of brotherhood and Jewish acculturation proved vain. Memory of the brotherhood of the early 1860s was to fade, though late in the nineteenth century it could still evoke nostalgia. In a poem by the sentimental patriotic poet Artur Oppman (1867–1932) the old Jew Berek Jawor, standing over the grave of his son who has perished in the uprising, tells his Polish interlocutor:

> My Eli disappeared like the light of an extinguished candle;
> Jehovah gave him a beautiful death.
> Do you remember, sir, Rabbi Meisels?
> Didn't you, sir, see Rabbi Jastrow?
>
> Those were good times. Then the Jew was a brother.
> You can see this, sir, clearly in the cemetery.
> Something has gone wrong with the world,
> Don't you agree, sir?[94]

[93] Gelber, *Die Juden und der polnische Aufstand 1863*, 219–32.

[94] Oppman, 'Berek Jawor', 483.

Full legal equality for the Jews of the Congress Kingdom was not rescinded after the uprising was crushed. Jews now had the right to settle anywhere in the Kingdom and purchase property. They could hold office and practise trades from which they had previously been barred. In addition, discriminatory taxes such as the kosher meat tax or the levy for living in Warsaw were now abolished. However, the Emancipation Edict of 1862 was not unopposed in Polish society, particularly after the remaining elements of Polish self-government were lost in the repression which followed the January insurrection. Józef Kraszewski, who as editor of *Gazeta Codzienna* had been a firm advocate of the integration of the Jews, expressed his resentment in 1868 at what he felt had been Jewish disloyalty:

> The insurrection collapsed in a welter of blood and the Jews, making use of their thousand-year-old experience, raised themselves over our corpses. But when they sacrificed us and abandoned us in an evil hour, only to save themselves, they shook our faith in them and dampened our love. The fact is that in the [Congress] Kingdom none of those who were rescued reached out their hands to help the drowning. What is involved here is a deal made with the [Russian] government, a commitment met with an unnecessary zeal. The country is in the hands of the Jews, who enjoy the government's backing. Only memories, embarrassing to both sides, remain of the brotherhood of 1861. Today, if we were to ask for equal rights with the Jews, there is no doubt we should not achieve our goal. When we who are perishing complain to the Jews, they reply coldly, 'You can perish'.[95]

This was still very much a minority view. The dominant intellectual tone was set by the Positivists, and among their cardinal political tenets was the view that the uprisings of 1830–1 and 1863 had failed because they had appealed to too narrow a circle of Polish society. Their views were expressed in *Przegląd Tygodniowy*, which appeared from 1864 to 1899, and in *Prawda*. One of their main aims was to incorporate into the nation those groups which had lain outside this circle or which had been at best marginal: the peasants, women, the Jews. Education, as well as self-education, was viewed by them as fundamental in achieving this goal, which they also hoped would foster the emergence of a middle class, now seen as the main repository of liberal values. The translation into Polish at this time of the Scottish author Samuel Smiles's tract *Self-Help, with Illustrations of Character and Conduct* (1859), which praised the Victorian values embodied in the 'gospel of work', strengthened the Positivists' view that social initiatives organized from below were the way to transform Polish society. In relation to the Jews they favoured a policy of assimilation and Polonization which would transform the Jews into 'Poles of the Mosaic faith'. In the words of the principal ideologist of Polish positivism, Aleksander Świętochowski, born in 1849, 'The maintenance of the present social isolation of the overwhelming majority of those who to whatever degree can be counted as members of the Jewish community will deprive our nation of an important element which could aid us in our struggle for survival.'[96]

[94] Oppman, 'Berek Jawor', 483. [95] Kraszewski, *Z roku 1868*, 273–4.
[96] Świętochowski, 'Klasyfikacja wyznaniowa'.

The Positivists' view that education was the means to achieve social integration and 'introduce the Jewish masses to the common norms of civilized life' was linked with the belief that the assimilation of the Jews would make it easier for Polish society to resist Russification. It also reflected their attempt to secularize Polish society and undermine religious obscurantism, whether Catholic or Jewish. In the view of the novelist Eliza Orzeszkowa, a determined advocate of Jewish integration who was close to the Positivists though she did not share all their views, the re-establishment of the traditions of tolerance and open intellectual exchange which had characterized Poland during the Renaissance would create a climate which would make possible a relatively painless integration of the Jews. She painted an idealized picture of sixteenth-century Poland, when the high level of culture attained by the ruling classes permeated the whole of society:

> the burgher became enlightened, enriched himself, worked steadily; the Jew learnt the language of the country, dressed as did its other inhabitants.
>
> I believe that all our social problems, including those with the Jews, will only be solved in a satisfactory manner when knowledge gives us the ability to think in a scientific, clear, and free way, and scientific, clear, and free thought teaches us to act energetically and intelligently.[97]

This view was shared by the most important moderate in the Positivist group, the novelist Bolesław Prus, who objected to the term 'Jewish question'. In his view this was a part of the wider problem of backwardness. 'Ignorance and the caste system lie at the basis not only of Jewish separatism . . . the peasants who squander money at taverns and fairs are as ignorant as the nobles who are bored in the theatres.' All these separatist tendencies will collapse 'under the pressure of education and progressive ideas'.[98]

Świętochowski was even more convinced that universal secular lay education would pave the way for the creation of a scientifically based industrial society, which would facilitate the integration of the Jews. In 1877 he wrote bluntly in *Przegląd Tygodniowy*, 'the Jewish question does not exist. There exists only the urgent need for compulsory education for Christians and Jews in order to break down their isolation and give them a common cultural and intellectual direction with the rest of humanity.'[99]

There were, however, some serious ambivalences in the attitudes of the Positivists, and, in particular, of Świętochowski, to the question of how to deal with the Jews. In the first place, although they believed that the Jews possessed those qualities such as thrift and industry which the Poles would have to acquire if they were to create an industrial society, they had serious reservations about the nature of such a society given their largely aristocratic origins. As early as the Vienna stock market crash of 1873 *Przegląd Tygodniowy* described stock exchanges as 'schools of fraud' and 'germs of demoralization'. On occasion they reverted to the eighteenth-century view that the Jews should be set to work on the land. They

[97] Orzeszkowa, *O Żydach i kwestyi żydowskiej*, 37.

[98] Prus, *Kroniki tygodniowe*, iii. 80.

[99] Świętochowski, 'Nie tędy'.

were divided on the extent to which they believed that the slow progress in assimilation and acculturation was the fault of the Jews themselves or of the hostility of Polish society to these processes, but, like their Enlightenment predecessors, they usually saw the root of the problem in 'Jewish separatism' and they expected the assimilated and acculturated minority within the Jewish community to take the principal role in breaking down this isolation. In addition, the position of the Positivists within the elite of Polish society was somewhat shaky. They were often opposed by the real economic and social elite and should be seen more as an embattled intelligentsia than an effective social force.

Their belief that the Jewish elite could undertake a fundamental transformation of Jewish society was also misplaced. This was probably a task beyond the power of this group, which understood well its social isolation and relative weakness. Certainly Positivist views found a ready echo within the group, which had been able to obtain a disproportionate influence by their success in gaining control of the Jewish congregational boards (sometimes still referred to as *kehilot*) in Warsaw, Łódź, and elsewhere in the Kingdom of Poland. These boards still retained control over many aspects of Jewish life, including education. The acculturated Jews demonstrated their growing self-confidence by the inauguration of the Great Synagogue on Tłomackie Street in 1878 and of a similar synagogue at the corner of Spacerowa (now Kościuszko) and Zielona streets in Łódź in 1883.

They also sought to propagate their views through the press. The weekly *Jutrzenka* (Dawn), founded in June 1861, at the height of Polish–Jewish revolutionary cooperation, under the editorship of Daniel Neufeld, a graduate of the Warsaw Rabbinic School, did not survive the post-insurrection repression. It was closed down in 1863 by the tsarist censors, and Neufeld was exiled to Siberia as a 'Jewish revolutionary'. Three years later it was succeeded by another weekly, *Izraelita*, which stoutly defended the integrationist position until it ceased publication on the eve of the First World War. Its first editor, Samuel Hirsh Peltyn (1831–96), who was born in Mariampol (now Marijampolė) in the province of Suwałki, was self-educated and moved to Warsaw in 1853. There he managed the bookshop and publishing house run by the Merzbach brothers, and between 1867 and 1868 worked on a short-lived Yiddish newspaper, *Varshoyer yudisher tsaytung*. Under his editorship, which lasted until shortly before his death, the weekly identified itself with the Warsaw Positivists and the principles of the European Enlightenment, opening its pages not only to Jews, but also to such Polish writers as Eliza Orzeszkowa and Maria Konopnicka.[100] Central to its view of the world was that what united the Jews was religion rather than a sense of nationhood. Jewish religious belief was compatible with reason, but needed to be reformed. 'For us as a religious community, development [*rozwój*] is necessary and this is possible only by means of strengthening the commonality that binds us together—

[100] On Peltyn, see the obituary written by his successor as editor, Nahum Sokolow, 'S. H. Peltyn—wizerunek literacki', *Izraelita*, 27 Oct. 1896.

religion—as well as those ties that link us with the rest of humanity—learning [*oświata*].'[101]

Izraelita echoed the views of the Positivists on the need for Jewish separatism 'to be undermined', calling in the first issue of 1872 for Jews to 'abandon . . . all signs of exclusivity'. It saw liberalism as the way to foster Jewish integration, and in August 1872 published an article, 'Swoboda i judaizm' (Freedom and Judaism), in which it traced the roots of the concept of individual liberty to the Hebrew Bible. At the same time, seeing its goal as the reform of Jewish society, it deliberately set out not to offend the conservative majority. In an article, 'What Should We Be?', Peltyn proclaimed, 'Let us be faithful sons of Judaism, propagators of its sublime truths, observing its humanitarian customs that are dictated by the highest love for humanity; let us raise our children in the pristine principles of faith and love, in a word, let us be Israelites . . .'. Outside the religious and spiritual sphere all difference should be abandoned: 'Away with all separatism . . . in thought, feeling, speech or deed! Here we are no longer Jews [*żydami*] but countrymen [*krajowcami*] in the complete, most essential meaning of the word.'[102]

Izraelita was dependent on the support of the Jewish financial elite, and its contributors held firmly to the view that economic development would pave the way for the emergence of the secular, tolerant, and modern society which they believed would make possible the integration of the Jews. In an article entitled 'Industry: The Source of Toleration', a contributor wrote:

People in commerce pay little attention to the religion of those with whom they deal. They are above all concerned about the real profits to be derived from such relations. The intellectual leadership provided by merchants and industrialists has already considerably weakened and will eventually completely efface the theological differences which have up to now divided individuals and peoples.[103]

Like the Positivists, the article assailed the religious conservatism of Jewish society, calling for the immersion of Jews in European culture and an end to 'Jewish isolation'. Yiddish was rejected as a debased 'jargon' and *ḥeder*s were attacked as backward and obscurantist. The difference between the Jewish integrationists and their Polish counterparts was clearly exposed over this latter issue. When, in 1879, *Izraelita* called for the modernization of the *ḥeder*, the liberal daily *Nowiny*, edited by Świętochowski, reacted scornfully:

We have examined the question of the typical *ḥeder* for the last fourteen years and now *Izraelita* expresses its doubts about the merging of the two tribes. We know the *ḥeder*, but we will never accept it, reformed or unreformed. Our only desire is that the citizens of one country should be brought up together so that their brotherhood will not be an empty word.[104]

[101] 'Indyferentyzm religijny', *Izraelita*, 1/6 (13–25 May 1866), 41–3.

[102] S. Peltyn, 'Czem być winniśmy?', *Izraelita*, 13/2 (30 Dec. 1877–11 Jan. 1878), 9–10. The term *krajowcy* rather than *Polacy* was probably dictated by the need to evade the censor.

[103] Quoted in Blejwas, 'Polish Positivism and the Jews', 28.

[104] Quoted in Prus, *Kroniki tygodniowe*, iv. 498.

This reproach seems to have stung Peltyn since, under the impact of the first pogroms in the tsarist empire following the assassination of Alexander II, he wrote in *Izraelita* on 27 May 1881 that *ḥeder*s should be closed by the state 'since only the strongest pressure would succeed in bringing the deeply reactionary mass of our co-religionists into forward motion'.

Izraelita soon acquired a unique place in both Jewish and Polish society, in spite of its relatively small circulation. In its first year its print run was only 330, and at its peak in 1901 this rose to only 1,300.

Enlightened religious views, if not the degree of acculturation favoured by *Izraelita*, were also supported by the Hebrew newspaper *Hatsefirah* (The Dawn), re-established in Warsaw in 1876 by Hayim Selig Slonimski (1810–1904), who had been principal of the rabbinic school, similar in character to that in Warsaw, which the tsarist government had set up in 1844 in Zhitomir (on this, see Chapter 11). It became a daily in 1886, and its influence extended far beyond Warsaw and the Kingdom of Poland.

The position of the integrationists, both Polish and Jewish, appeared to be strengthened by the industrialization of the Kingdom of Poland. The collapse of the 1863 uprising did not interrupt the industrial upsurge there. Jews played a major role in the industrial revolution in this area, and their percentage of the population of the two largest cities, Warsaw and Łódź, increased rapidly, the result not only of natural increase and immigration from the small towns of the Congress Kingdom, but also of the movement to Warsaw of Jews from the former eastern parts of the Polish–Lithuanian Commonwealth, which was legalized after 1868. This movement became even greater following the introduction in the tsarist empire after 1881 of new anti-Jewish laws which did not apply in the Congress Kingdom. In all, there arrived in the Kingdom of Poland perhaps as many as 200,000 'Litvaks', as Jews from these areas, formerly part of the Grand Duchy of Lithuania (Litwa), were called.[105] Indeed, one consequence of the rapid industrial development of the Kingdom was that there was much less emigration from there than from the other parts of partitioned Poland–Lithuania.

The belief that integration would provide an easy and rapid solution to the Jewish problem was always misplaced, as was the hope that a Polish-dominated secular system of education could be created in the Congress Kingdom under conditions of political repression and Russian rule. Jewish society was also much slower to respond to change than the rather naive integrationists believed it would be. In addition, on the Polish side even the most committed assimilationists were convinced of the superiority of Polish culture and Catholicism over what they saw as the 'backward' and 'medieval' Jewish religion. Among the various Polish words used to describe the process of Jewish integration, one of the most common was *ucywilizowanie*: the 'civilizing' of the Jews. A man as committed to granting equality to the Jews and to their incorporation in the developing Polish

[105] This is the estimate of Kaplun-Kogan, *Die jüdische Sprach- und Kulturgemeinschaft in Polen*, 4.

middle class as Wielopolski had very little understanding of Jewish society, seeing the Jews as a passive body capable of fundamental remoulding. His approach to them was above all instrumental. In a speech which he drafted but never delivered to the clerks of the Governing Committee of Internal Affairs, he even envisaged the possibility of a pro-reform dictatorship based on townspeople and Jews which would overcome the resistance to his plans of the more conservative nobility.[106] There is a great deal of truth in the judgement of Nathan Gelber, who wrote, 'For Wielopolski, the Jews were merely a mass that once they had been granted legal equality could be totally transformed. He did not know the Jewish people at all and was not aware of the obstacles in the way of their assimilation.'[107] The next two decades were sadly to expose the shallowness of the process of establishing a religiously neutral, secular society in which the Jews could find their appropriate place.

CONCLUSION

The process of integration in the Kingdom of Poland had some similarities to that in Prussia and, to a lesser degree, in the Habsburg empire and contrasts significantly with what took place in the remainder of the tsarist empire. The constitution of 1815 laid down that the Kingdom of Poland was a state 'based on the principles of order, freedom, and justice'. Although the struggle to achieve full legal equality was to be protracted and to encounter strong opposition, as was also the case in the German states, the method by which Jews could obtain their citizenship once they had 'demonstrated their fitness' was clear.

Jews constituted a major part of the urban society of the Kingdom of Poland. In the period after 1795 a Jewish bourgeoisie emerged, made up of army contractors and suppliers to the government who later became bankers and industrialists. Without them, the emergence of a Polish bourgeois class would have been very difficult. Christian–Jewish hostilities in the towns must be seen as one of the reasons for the slow development of such a class and for the weakness of Western-style liberalism in the Kingdom of Poland.

Within the Jewish community there was a mixed response to the problems and opportunities created by the call for the Jews to acculturate themselves and to seek to integrate themselves into Polish society. The Orthodox and now largely hasidic majority of the community opposed integration, referring to those in favour of the transformation of the Jews as *apikorsim* (apostates) or *shebselim* (supporters of Sabbatianism). As in Galicia, there were many differences between the supporters of integration. These included followers of the Haskalah, who were primarily interested in the reform of Judaism through a revived and purified Hebrew; men like Hayim Selig Slonimski, or the editor of *Izraelita*, Samuel Hirsh

106 Janowski, *Polish Liberal Thought before 1918*, 123.

107 Gelber, *Die Juden und der polnische Aufstand 1863*, 99–100.

Peltyn, who sought to transform the Jews into 'Poles of the Mosaic persuasion'; and radical integrationists, who in many cases, like Leopold Kronenberg and Jan Bloch, converted to Catholicism. As in Galicia, the integrationists were strong mainly in the cities, principally Warsaw, Łódź, and Zamość, while the Orthodox were mostly to be found in small towns and townlets. However, the conflict between the Orthodox and the integrationists was not nearly as bitter as in Galicia, or as it was to be in the rest of the tsarist empire.

The triumph of the integrationists in the third quarter of the nineteenth century was more apparent than real. It was always going to be difficult to integrate the Jews into Polish society. This process was made much more difficult by the repression which followed the uprising of 1863 and by the policies of Russification which accompanied it. There was far less chance than in Galicia of using the educational system to create a large group of Polish-speaking Jews, and no chance of realizing the Positivists' dream of creating a secular and scientifically based society through universal education. Capitalism was also to make slow and uneven progress in the Kingdom of Poland. Its initial stages were accompanied by great disruption and hardship for the majority, and it was certainly not the panacea for Poland's ills sought by both the Positivists and the Jewish elite.

Finally, as we have seen, those on the Polish side who favoured Jewish integration had both a strong sense of the inferiority of Jewish to Polish society and unrealistic expectations of how rapidly the Jews could be transformed. They also greatly overestimated the ability of the Jewish elite to carry through such a transformation. Nevertheless, the assumption that Jewish integration could not have succeeded in the Kingdom of Poland and that its supporters were hopelessly naive should be rejected. It is another of the implicit assumptions of the now discredited nationalist grand narrative of Jewish history and an example of what E. P. Thompson has described as the 'boundless contempt' exhibited in the present for those whose aspirations in the past were not fulfilled. The history of the Jews in the Kingdom of Poland is a story of lost opportunities for which subsequent generations were to pay a high price.

TEN

THE JEWS IN THE TSARIST EMPIRE, 1772–1825

Transformations brought about by governmental force will generally not be stable and will be especially unreliable in those cases where this force struggles against centuries-old habits, with ingrained errors and with unyielding superstition; it would be better and more opportune to direct the Jews towards improvement; to open the path to their own benefit, overseeing their progress from afar and removing anything that might lead them astray, not employing any force, not setting up any particular institution, not acting in their place, but enabling their own activity. As few restrictions as possible, as much freedom as possible. This is a simple formula for any organization of society.

MIKHAIL MIKHAILOVICH SPERANSKY, *Minutes of the Committee for the Amelioration of the Jews*, 20 September 1803

In the conception of the Great Russian people, the tsar is the embodiment of the state . . . He is not the chief of the army, nor the people's choice, nor the head of state or the representative of the administration, nor even the sentimental *Landesvater* or *bon père du peuple* . . . The tsar is the state itself—ideal, benevolent, and at the same time its stern expression.

KONSTANTIN DMITRIEVICH KAVELIN, *Thoughts and Remarks about Russian History*, 1866

SPECIFIC FEATURES OF THE INTEGRATIVE PROCESS IN THE TSARIST EMPIRE

As a result of the partitions of Poland the tsarist empire came to control the destinies of a large majority of the Jews of the Polish–Lithuanian Commonwealth. Under the terms of the first partition (1772), Russia annexed an area of Belarus, including Polotsk, Mogilev, and Vitebsk, with a Jewish population of over 50,000. The second and third partitions (1793, 1795) brought the boundaries of the empire up to the rivers Bug and Niemen and incorporated almost the entire Grand Duchy of Lithuania, including major Jewish centres such as Minsk, Vilna, Grodno (today Hrodna), and Novogrudok, and much of right-bank Ukraine including Zhitomir, Bratslav, and Kamenets-Podolsky (Kamyanets-Podilsky). This brought under the sway of the Romanovs a Jewish population which was estimated by the Polish census of 1764 at nearly 290,000. By the end of the eighteenth century this figure had grown to around 600,000, approximately

1.5 per cent of the empire's inhabitants.[1] As we have seen, after 1815 the Kingdom of Poland, which was united dynastically with the tsarist state, was added to these possessions. By 1820 the Jews numbered 1.6 million, of whom 400,000 lived in the Congress Kingdom. This constituted nearly 3.5 per cent of the empire's 46 million. By 1880 the Jewish population had risen to 4 million, the largest concentration of Jews in the world, with 1.1 million in the Congress Kingdom. This constituted 4.7 per cent of the empire's population of 86 million.

Before the partitions of Poland–Lithuania only a very small number of crypto-Jews lived within the borders of the Grand Duchy of Muscovy and of its successor, the Russia of Peter the Great (r. 1682–1725). The dominant Russian Orthodox Church, like the Western Christian Church, had a strong tradition of anti-Judaism and supersessionism. The eastern Mediterranean was the area where the Christian faith had originated, and its first centuries were marked by strong competition with, and hostility to, its Jewish rival. The tradition of hostility to Judaism was absorbed by the Russian Orthodox Church, which saw itself as the inheritor of Byzantium, the Third Rome, which, unlike the first two, pagan Rome and Christian Constantinople, would last until the end of the world.

Jews were certainly present in Kievan Rus (see Chapter 1). The Russian Primary Chronicle records that in 986 Jews from the Khazar khanate tried unsuccessfully to convert the pagan ruler of Kiev, the grand duke Vladimir. After the adoption of Orthodoxy by the rulers of the Grand Duchy in the late tenth century, local churchmen such as Hilarion of Kiev and Cyril of Turov set out in their works the standard themes of Christian supersessionism—the antithesis of the Old and New Testaments, of Law and Grace, and of the Jewish synagogue and the Christian Church.[2] The saints' lives in the *Paterikon* of the Kievan crypt, which dates back to the thirteenth century but was expanded until the end of the fifteenth century, contain a number of anti-Jewish motifs, including that of the abbot Theodosius, who unsuccessfully sought martyrdom at the hands of the Jews, and the monk Eustathius, who was allegedly crucified by a Jewish slave trader for failing to adopt Judaism.[3] Similarly, the ecclesiastical charter issued by Yaroslav the Wise in the thirteenth century, with its prohibition on sexual relations between Christians and Jews, is clearly derived from Byzantine precedents.[4]

[1] R. Mahler, *Jews in Old Poland in the Light of Figures* (Yid.). Mahler's estimates are based on the statistics contained in 'Perepisi evreiskogo naseleniya v yugo-zapadnom krae v 1765–1791', in *Arkhiv Yugo-Zapadnoi Rossii*, pt. 5, vol. ii, books 1 and 2 (Kiev, 1890). See also Eisenbach, 'Żydzi w dawnej Polsce w świetle liczb', and Stampfer, 'The 1764 Census of Polish Jewry', 41–59.

[2] On this, see Fedotov, *The Russian Religious Mind*, 69–93.

[3] For details, see *Kyyevo-pechers'kyi pateryk*, 106–8; Prestel, 'A Comparative Analysis of Two Patericon Stories'; and Chekin, 'Turks, Jews and the Saints of the Kievan Caves Monastery'.

[4] Birnbaum, 'On Some Evidence of Jewish Life and Anti-Jewish Sentiments in Medieval Russia', 235–8.

However, Kievan Rus did not participate in the Crusades, and accusations against the Jews of spreading the plague, desecrating the host, and murdering Christian children to obtain their blood for ritual purposes seem to have been absent here. The identification of Jews with the Devil, which became common in Western Christendom from the thirteenth century, and the anti-Jewish stereotypes which are a feature of medieval mystery plays and religious iconography also do not seem to have been present in Kievan Rus. According to John Klier: 'in the absence of tangible evidence of the type found in Western Europe only a tenuous case can be made for the argument that anti-Jewish feeling was a vital ingredient of Kievan culture, or that the concerns of the clerical elite were communicated to a wider popular audience'.[5]

Judaeophobia seems to have been much more prevalent in Muscovite Rus. There are very few contemporary references to Jews during the period when most of the Russian lands were ruled by the Mongol Golden Horde. With the rise of Muscovy, the situation changes. When, in 1550, the Polish king Zygmunt August requested Ivan IV 'the Dread' (r. 1547–84) to permit Jewish merchants to trade in Muscovy as in the past, he refused on the grounds that 'It is not appropriate to allow Jews to come to Russia with their goods, since many evils result from them. For they import poisonous herbs into our realm and lead Russians astray from Christianity.'[6] The brutal treatment received by Jews who found themselves in Muscovite hands as a consequence of the wars of the sixteenth and early seventeenth centuries is well documented.[7] When Muscovite armies took Polish–Lithuanian cities during the Livonian War, for instance, they offered the Jews they found there the choice of baptism or death, and the same occurred in Polotsk in 1563.[8]

The increased hostility to Jews seems, at least in part, to have arisen out of the belief that they were responsible for the Judaizing heresy which emerged in Novgorod in the 1480s and spread to Moscow before it was brutally suppressed. Although there is little evidence that Jews were significantly involved in this movement, some of the churchmen responsible for its repression were convinced that they were combating Jewish influence, a claim which echoed the earlier assertion that the Khazars had tried to convert the grand duke of Kiev.[9] The fear that the Jews were a religious threat to Holy Russia was strengthened by the bitter

5 Klier, *Russia Gathers her Jews*, 24–61.

6 *Pamyatniki diplomaticheskikh snoshenii Moskovskogo gosudarstva s Pol'sko-Litovskim*, ii. 21, 341–2.

7 On this, see the numerous examples in Ettinger, 'The Muscovite State and its Attitudes towards the Jews' (Heb.).

8 Baron, *A Social and Religious History of the Jews*, xvi. 175, 398 n. 11.

9 There is a large literature on the Judaizing heresy. See Golubinsky, *Istoriya russkoi tserkvi*, ii; Kazakova and Lurie, *Antifeodal'nye ereticheskie dvizheniya na Rusi XIV–nachala XVI veka*; Klibanov, *Reformatsionnye dvizheniya v Rossii v XIV–pervoi polovine XVI v.*; Vernadsky, 'The Heresy of the Judaizers and the Policies of Ivan III of Moscow'; Halperin, 'The Heresy of the Judaizers and the Image of the Jew in Medieval Russia'; Klier, 'Judaizing without Jews?'; and De Michelis, *La Valdesia di Novgorod*. For the view that Jews were involved with the Judaizers, see Ettinger, 'Vliyanie evreev na eres' zhidovstvuyushchikh v moskovskoi Rusi'.

conflict with Polish–Lithuania, with its large Jewish population, which culminated in the attempt by a group of boyars to place Prince Władysław, the son of Zygmunt III of Poland–Lithuania, on the throne of Muscovy during the 'Time of Troubles' in the early seventeenth century. Attempts were also made to discredit another of the pretenders to the throne, the second 'false Dmitry', by asserting that he was a 'Jew by birth' (*rodom zhidovin*) surrounded by heretics and deicidal Jews (*bogoubits zhidov*).[10]

Hostility to the Jews persisted into the eighteenth century. While Peter the Great may have tolerated some crypto-Jews at his court and may have toyed with the idea of allowing Jews to settle in Russia, his successor, Catherine I, reverted to the earlier policy, expelling all Jews from the area of Ukraine under Russian rule. As late as July 1738 a retired naval officer, Aleksandr Voznitsyn, who converted to Judaism, and Borokh Leibov, a Jew from the Smolensk district held responsible for his conversion, were burned at the stake in St Petersburg.

Small numbers of Jews did manage to penetrate Russia, both in the Baltic area and in Ukraine. Thus, at the beginning of the reign of Peter the Great's daughter Elizabeth (r. 1741–62), the Russian senate responded favourably to petitions from the authorities in Riga and Ukraine requesting that Jews be granted at least temporary residence and be allowed to attend the fairs which were a vital element of Ukrainian economic life. However, Elizabeth overruled the senate on the grounds that 'I desire no profit from the enemies of Jesus Christ.'[11]

One new influence on Russian attitudes was the anti-Judaic tradition of the Polish–Lithuanian Commonwealth, whose attitudes were also to be found in the area of Ukraine that was now part of the Russian state. However, suspicion that the Orthodox Church in that area might be tainted by Greek Catholicism led to a marked reluctance to accept alleged martyrs of ritual murder whose cults were celebrated by the Orthodox Church in Poland–Lithuania. Gabriel Zabludovsky was one such case: he was allegedly killed by the Jews for ritual purposes in the late seventeenth century and his cult is celebrated to this day in the Orthodox Cathedral in Białystok.[12] However, the belief that it was the Talmud that was at the root of Jewish evil failed to penetrate Russia at this time.

In spite of this unfavourable background, the Russian tsars from the time of Catherine the Great (r. 1762–96) did attempt, like governments almost everywhere in Europe, to 'transform' their Jewish population into 'useful subjects'. However, the process in Russia had some specific features which made it different from what occurred elsewhere. In the first place, Russia was not an estate society, like the countries which had been part of Western Christendom, but an autocracy, which derived its political ideas and institutions from Byzantium and from the

[10] Gessen, 'Evrei v moskovskom gosudarstve XV–XVII veka', 153, and Perrie, *Pretenders and Popular Monarchism in Early Modern Russia*, 158–61.

[11] *Polnoe sobranie zakonov Rossiiskoi Imperii* (*PSZ*), 1/ii, no. 8840 (16 Dec. 1743).

[12] Dubnow, 'Tserkovnye legendy ob otroke Gavriile Zabludovskom', 309.

two centuries of Tatar rule to which the Grand Duchy of Muscovy had been subjected.

Under Peter the Great and later under the empress Catherine, an attempt had been made to transform Russia into an estate society on Western lines, with four main estates (*sosloviya*) made up of nobles, merchants, townspeople, and peasants, in accordance with Catherine's belief in a society 'in which each legally-defined category of the population possessed its own clearly enunciated and exclusive rights, privileges and obligations'.[13] The problem of where to place the Jews in this hierarchy constantly perplexed tsarist administrators.

Of these estates only the nobility was granted rights, albeit limited, by Catherine's Charter of the Nobility in 1786, and even these did not seriously compromise the autocratic nature of the government. However, the ineffectiveness of the tsarist bureaucracy meant that these estates were self-administered, and it has often been argued that the attempt to impose the concept of an estate society on Russia, where the patrimonial model was so firmly established, met with very little success. Yet the division into estates did correspond to some Russian social realities. Even after 1861, when serfdom was abolished, elements of the privileges of the nobility and of the separate status of the peasantry were retained.

The tsarist empire was also not a nation state, a characteristic it shared with the Habsburg empire and even, to some degree, with Prussia. Yet it differed further from the European states not only in that it was multi-national but also in that it was a land empire extending over much of Eurasia. During the eighteenth century and into the first half of the nineteenth, it was not government policy to Russify the heterogeneous population, and groups like the Old Believers, who had rejected the church reforms of Peter the Great, the Muslims, and the Karaites were allowed, in many respects, to administer themselves. As regards the Jewish population which it had incorporated, the Russian bureaucracy was constantly looking for an element within Jewish society which it could use to reform the Jews in the Russian interest. Tsarist bureaucrats, very much under the influence of the philosophy of the Enlightenment, which had begun to influence Russia during the reign of Catherine the Great, and impressed by Napoleon's calling of an Assembly of Jewish Notables in 1807 as a means of 'reforming' the Jews, wanted to do something similar in Russia (on this, see Chapter 9).

With St Petersburg as the imperial capital, the Jews were far away from the bureaucrats who drew up regulations for them and were very much on the periphery of the empire. The areas they inhabited were almost entirely agricultural with very little industrial development, and there was very little in the way of a Christian bourgeoisie or proto-bourgeoisie. The importance of Odessa in the history of the Jews in this region was that it was the only town that had a largely middle-class character, at least until the second half of the nineteenth century. A

[13] Kamendrowsky and Griffiths, 'The Fate of the Trading Nobility Controversy in Russia'.

primary goal for the Russian bureaucrats in this area was to make sure that it was firmly incorporated into the empire. The conservative character of the tsarist policy preserved the dominance of the Polish nobility in these parts until at least the middle of the nineteenth century, though the bureaucrats were suspicious of the long-standing links between the Polish nobility and the Jews.

For much of the period the empire remained largely agrarian, with society divided between a small group of landowners and, until 1861, a mass of serfs. Although there was some industrial and commercial development in Russia during the first three-quarters of the nineteenth century, it was primarily agriculture-related. Most important was the export of grain, which was now relocated from Danzig to Odessa and was responsible for the prosperity of Volhynia and Podolia in the first part of the nineteenth century. Between 1820 and 1860 the value of grain exports from the tsarist empire rose from 7 million to 37 million roubles. There was some commercialization of agriculture in Ukraine, but it was impeded by the persistence of serfdom. With its abolition in 1861, sugar refining became a major industry. Other agriculturally linked industries, such as tobacco production and brewing and distilling, also grew significantly throughout the century.

The railways were also developed, particularly in the 1860s and 1870s. In 1860 there were barely 1,010 miles of railways in the empire, but by 1880 this had grown to 19,011 miles. As in the Kingdom of Poland (and elsewhere in Europe), Jews, such as the entrepreneurs Samuel Polyakov and the Guenzburg family, played a key role in constructing the Russian railway network. The two mainstays of the first industrial revolution, textiles and metallurgy, developed more slowly. Apart from the major textile centre around Łódź, textile production was mostly to be found around Moscow, while metallurgical production was located in the Urals, St Petersburg, and eastern Ukraine.

In general, industry was still very undeveloped. Throughout the middle decades of the nineteenth century there was a major debate between the Ministry of the Interior and the minister of finance over whether industrial development was indeed desirable. One of Nicholas I's finance ministers, Egor Frantsevich Kankrin, described railways as 'the invention of the devil'. It was only in 1881, when Nikolay Khristianovich Bunge became minister of finance, that a concerted policy to encourage industrialization was embarked upon.

THE TSARITSA CATHERINE AND THE JEWS

The Jewish community of the tsarist empire has a long and distinguished historiography. Its original historians, such as Yuly Gessen, Simon Dubnow, and Ilya Orshansky, who emerged in Russia in the late nineteenth century, were preoccupied with the worsening condition of the Jewish population there, and were committed to a Jewish identity based not on religion but on peoplehood. They found the origins of what they saw as the deep-rooted and ineradicable Russian Judaeophobia in the Byzantine religious inheritance of Muscovy. In Dubnow's view, the 'European mask' of St Petersburg was merely a cover for Russia's 'Muscovite face'.[14] In their view this explained why the Jewish issue was central to the thinking of the tsarist government, which was prey to a 'Jewish obsession'. Gessen, whose work was notable for his meticulous investigation of the Russian government archives, also saw the fears of Jewish economic exploitation of the peasantry as a key factor in explaining the attitudes of the tsarist bureaucracy. Dubnow, in order to provide historical underpinning for his autonomist ideology, also laid great stress on Jewish autonomous institutions such as the Council of Four Lands and the Council of Lithuania, and on the self-government which the Jews enjoyed in the Polish–Lithuanian Commonwealth. Their successors in recent years in the West, such as Michael Stanislawski, Steven Zipperstein, John Klier, Hans Rogger, Heinz-Dietrich Loewe, and Benjamin Nathans, have been concerned to revise these views, demonstrating that Russian bureaucrats were frequently motivated by ideas drawn from the European Enlightenment with its belief that Jews could be transformed by the appropriate policies into useful subjects. Jewish issues were more often than not peripheral to their concerns and affected overwhelmingly those areas of the empire annexed as a result of the partitions of Poland–Lithuania.

There was considerable continuity in the policies pursued by the tsarist government towards the Jews from the first incorporation of significant numbers of Jews into the empire in 1772 until 1881. These policies were part of an attempt to transform the empire into a 'properly governed state', in the style of eighteenth-century Austria and Prussia.[15] Two main principles underlay the actions of the government in relation to the Jews. In the first place there was the belief that they were a harmful element. By their oppressive behaviour, they disrupted relations between landlords and peasants in the sensitive western provinces of the empire, and action needed to be taken in order to limit their deleterious influence. This was the product of their 'fanatical' religious beliefs. Jews despised non-Jews and kept themselves separate from non-Jewish society, feeling no loyalty to the country in which they lived, or to its sovereign. They disdained physical labour, which they felt should be performed by the 'inferior' peasantry, and concentrated themselves in unproductive and parasitical occupations which depended on exploitation of the surrounding society.

Secondly, the leading tsarist officials, for the most part men of the Enlightenment, shared the general European view that the faults of the Jews were not innate, but the consequence of their unfortunate history. Although the negative behaviour of the Jews had to be curbed, Jewish society could be made over by 'rational' reforms, which in the autocratic tsarist empire would transform them, not into citizens, but into useful subjects.

[14] Quoted in Klier, *Russia Gathers her Jews*, p. xv.

[15] On this, see Raeff, 'The Well-Ordered Police State and the Development of Modernity in Seventeenth and Eighteenth Century Europe', and id., *The Well-Ordered Police State*.

The first Russian ruler who had seriously to confront this issue was the empress Catherine II (r. 1762–96). A member of a minor German princely family, she was a convinced believer in the principles of the Enlightenment, which she sought to apply in the reorganization of her empire, whose extent had increased enormously during the eighteenth century. These principles were the basis for the *Instructions* which she wrote in 1766 for the commission she convened to elaborate a new system of laws. Russian realities and her fear of French revolutionary ideas meant that she had relatively little real success in transforming the country, although she was more effective in this than her nineteenth-century successors. In relation to the Jews she strongly opposed religiously motivated restrictions, which she held were responsible for the negative aspects of Jewish behaviour. She also had a high regard for Jewish commercial acumen, which she believed could benefit Russia. At the same time, like some of the philosophers of the Enlightenment she admired most, above all Voltaire and Diderot, she saw the Jews as the adherents of a primitive and obscurantist religion which taught contempt for non-Jews and overvalued financial gain. Writing to Diderot in 1773, she observed that Jews 'swarmed' all over Belarus and that 'their entry into Russia could cause great harm to our petty tradesmen, since these people draw everything to themselves and as a consequence it might be that their return would be more of a hurt than a help'.[16] Her freedom to act in this area was also severely circumscribed. As a woman and a foreigner who had usurped the Russian throne, she was determined not to offend Russian religious sensibilities, as had been done by her deposed husband, Peter III. In the manifesto justifying her *coup d'état*, she listed defence of Orthodoxy as her primary reason for seizing power.

Catherine was quickly confronted by the Jewish issue when, shortly after her accession, she had to deal with a petition submitted to the empress Elizabeth before her death in 1761 asking her to relax her ban on Jewish settlement within the empire. According to Catherine's own account of this issue, when the proposal was submitted to the senate it was 'unanimously recognized as useful'. Catherine was, however, unwilling to jeopardize her position by antagonizing public opinion. Accordingly, she reaffirmed the ban on Jewish settlement, citing Elizabeth's remark that she did not wish to obtain profit from 'the enemies of Jesus Christ'.[17]

Catherine confirmed her decision on 14 October 1762, when she directed the senate to append to a draft invitation to all foreigners who might wish to settle in Russia a specific exclusion for Jews, which was duly promulgated on 4 December. At the same time she was not above surreptitiously encouraging Jewish settlement. She was primarily concerned to promote the settlement of 'New Russia', the area she was in the process of seizing from the Turks on the northern shore of the Black Sea. In 1763 she secretly encouraged Polish and other European Jews to

[16] Golitsyn, *Istoriya russkogo zakonodatel'stva o evreyakh*, 61.

[17] 'O sostoyanii Rossii pri Ekaterine velikoi', 3.

settle in this area in return for permission to their co-religionists to establish themselves again in Riga. Few Jews were induced to settle in New Russia, but a number did move to Riga, where by 1780 there were enough to open a synagogue. A very small number of Jews were also allowed to establish themselves in St Petersburg. In a letter to Diderot, Catherine wrote that 'they are tolerated in spite of the law; their presence is simply ignored'.[18]

The first partition, with the significant number of Jews which this brought into the empire, meant that more active policies had to be adopted. Following the Russian entry into the newly acquired territories, Field Marshal Zakhar Chernyshev, the first governor-general of the area, issued a proclamation on 16 August 1772 which guaranteed the religious freedoms of inhabitants of whatever faith and promised that all groups, without exception, would retain the 'rights, freedoms, and privileges' they had enjoyed under Polish rule. 'From this day onward . . . every estate . . . of the incorporated territories shall enjoy throughout the entire expanse of the Russian empire the advantages appropriate to it.' A special section of the proclamation assured the Jews that their traditional communal rights would be maintained, as would their title to their properties. It guaranteed that 'the Jewish communities [*evreiskie obshchestva*] dwelling in the towns and on the lands joined to the Russian empire [will] retain and preserve those freedoms which they now enjoy by law regarding the control of their property . . . as long as they, for their part, with the appropriate compliance of loyal subjects, live and pursue their present trades and business according to their callings [*po zvaniyam svoim*]'.[19]

There has been some dispute over the meaning of these assurances, but it does seem that the authorities intended to permit Jews to carry out the same occupations they had followed under Polish–Lithuanian rule.[20] The reference to the Jewish community probably implied that the Jewish communal structure would be maintained, which went against the more usual tsarist policy of curtailing such autonomous jurisdictions, as was done with the privileges of the German nobles in the Baltic or the freedoms of the Ukrainian Cossacks. Certainly, the contrast with the actions of the empress Elizabeth is striking.

The primary concern of Chernyshev was to incorporate the area, which was now divided into two provinces, Mogilev and Polotsk (later Vitebsk), into the tsarist empire as smoothly as possible. Even before the annexation of the region, the government seems to have decided to treat the Jews collectively as a 'mercantile' people and place them in the same tax category as the merchant estate.[21] Chernyshev, for his part, counselled the government to follow Polish precedents in its treatment of the Jews. As a result the responsibility of the *kehilot* for the

[18] 'O sostoyanii Rossii pri Ekaterine velikoi', quoted in Pipes, 'Catherine II and the Jews', 6.

[19] Gessen, *Istoriya evreiskogo naroda*, 129–30.

[20] For the controversy on this issue between Golitsyn and Gessen, see Klier, *Russia Gathers her Jews*, 60–1.

[21] On this, see Anishchenko, *Cherta osedlosti*.

collection of taxes was retained, and Chernyshev gave instructions 'to have all Jews affiliate with the *kahals* and institute such [*kahals*] as the governors may suggest or as necessity for them may arise'.[22] The poll tax on Jews, soon nicknamed the 'soul tax', was fixed at 1 rouble, as against the 70 copecks levied on each peasant and the 1 rouble 20 copecks levied on merchants. The *kehilot* were now also to issue internal passports to control the movement of the Jewish population. The sale of liquor, a major Jewish activity, would be controlled by the city magistrates, but for the moment the authorities lacked the administrative resources to effect this change. In practice the initial transition from Polish to Russian rule had little effect on the position of the Jews.

From the mid-1770s, partly in response to the Pugachev rebellion, a major peasant uprising in the south-east, Catherine attempted to tighten her hold over the provinces of her rapidly expanding empire in order to make her administration more effective. She saw the provinces annexed from Poland–Lithuania as a laboratory in which reforms could be tested. In November 1775 she issued a Statute for the Administration of the Provinces, dividing the empire into provinces similar to those which had been created in Mogilev and Polotsk.

Catherine was particularly concerned by the situation in provincial towns. In her Charter for the Towns of April 1775 she divided the urban population into estates, which were later given a degree of self-government as 'municipal communities' (*gorodskie obshchestva*). Merchants who had capital of 500 roubles or more were enrolled formally into the estate of merchants (*kuptsy*). This estate was divided into three guilds. To belong to the first guild one needed to possess capital worth at least 10,000 roubles, for the second, between 1,000 and 10,000, and for the third, between 500 and 1,000. Merchants were exempted from the soul tax and were no longer responsible collectively for the taxes liable to be paid by a particular community. Merchants paid an annual tax of 1 per cent on their declared capital. They constituted only a small minority of the urban population. The remainder, mostly traders and artisans, were classified as 'townspeople' (*meshchane*) and remained liable to the soul tax. One could move up and down this social hierarchy provided one could demonstrate that one possessed the requisite wealth. At the same time Catherine reduced the power of the noble owners in sixteen towns in the recently annexed areas of Poland–Lithuania, transforming them into local administrative centres, as was envisaged in her provincial reform.[23]

Catherine also began to reform the composition of local government in the towns. A separate judicial structure was created to dispense justice to the two newly established estates of merchants and townspeople. In urban settlements which were designated as cities (*goroda*) these were called municipal magistracies

[22] Quoted in Dubnow, *History of the Jews in Russia and Poland*, i. 308, from *PSZ* 1/xix, no. 13865 (13 Sept. 1772).

[23] Anishchenko, *Cherta osedlosti*, 65. These sixteen towns had a total population of 7,093 Christians and 2,873 Jews.

(*gorodovye magistraty*); in other settlements they were called councils (*ratushi*). The magistracy was headed by an elected mayor (*burgomistr*) and two to four councillors (*ratmany*), all elected by their constituents. They were subsequently given additional responsibilities, most importantly the collection of taxes, and were regarded as part of the imperial bureaucracy.

These reforms were extended to the newly acquired Belarusian territories, and the question of how the Jews could be made part of the new local government organizations soon arose, and whether these organizations were compatible with the existing Jewish communal structures. As we have seen, initially the Jewish communal structure was maintained, and by a decree of the senate in 1776 the existence of the *kehilah* and its fiscal and administrative responsibilities was confirmed. Chernyshev insisted that the Jews in Belarus be set apart as a separate tax unit and entered on special registers. Their poll tax was to be collected by the *kehilah*, which also retained some judicial functions. Only cases between Jews and non-Jews were to come before the general courts of the district and provincial councils; the latter were also to function as courts of appeal.[24]

The decision to retain and expand the Jewish autonomous institutions was above all the consequence of the administrative weakness of the tsarist empire, which meant that it was in no position to dispense with the *kehilot* as tax-collecting and law-enforcing agencies. This situation was also desired by most Jews, although some members of the Jewish elite saw advantages in being inscribed into the merchant estate which was being set up in Belarus. Certainly, by the end of 1778 Catherine had received a number of petitions from Jews who wished to be inscribed as merchants. She granted permission and sent an instruction to Chernyshev that Jews who qualified were to be allowed to join the merchant estate, as laid down in the law of April 1775. Very soon 10 per cent of all Jews in Polotsk province and 6.5 per cent in Mogilev province had been enrolled into the merchant guilds. The remaining Jewish population was subsequently inscribed into the ranks of townsmen. This had drastic consequences for the structure of Jewish communal autonomy, since the wealthiest element in the community was now no longer subject to the tax regime of the *kehilot*.

The positive side of this development was made clear in the imperial government's reply to queries from local administrators asking whether Jews were in fact to be incorporated fully into the new structure. On 2 May 1783 it confirmed that 'Jews [*Evrei*] living in the Belarusian provinces are to be taxed according to the estate in which they inscribe themselves, without distinction of origin and religion.'

There were, however, a number of negative consequences. One of the most serious was that all Jews were now classed as urban and, as members of the two estates of merchants and townspeople, were barred from residence in the countryside, where they might 'enrich themselves' at the expense of the peasants. This

[24] Dubnow, *History of the Jews in Russia and Poland*, i. 309.

caused great hardship to a large number of the Jews of the area who lived either in small noble towns or in villages where they acted as agents or factors of the local nobility. As members of urban communities they were also now barred from dealing in alcohol. In the Belarusian provinces in May 1783 Chernyshev's successor, P. B. Passek, not only barred Jews from distilling or selling liquor, but forbade landlords to lease them taverns, distilleries, or breweries. He also ordered the expulsion of Jews from the villages into the towns, a measure which affected thousands of Jewish families.

The rights of Jews to vote for the new municipal councils also proved illusory in the face of the opposition of the Christian burghers in the area. Towns here were small, and Jews were a significant proportion of the population in most (all twelve towns in Mogilev province, seven out of eleven in Polotsk province). In the first elections held in the 1780s they won control of the mayoralties in eight towns. They were unable to take office since both merchants and townspeople now came under the jurisdiction of magistrates and Jews could not swear the Christian oath required in town courts.

The governors in the provinces of Mogilev and Polotsk, M. V. Kakhovsky and M. N. Krechetnikov, were also suspicious of the Jews, whom they saw as dishonest and exploitative.[25] They were particularly concerned for the local Orthodox population, which the administration felt it had a special duty to protect since this was one of the motives given for the Russian participation in the first partition of Poland–Lithuania. They saw the *kehilah* in its existing form as an oppressive agency within the Jewish community, but they hoped to gain its cooperation in introducing the reforms the government wanted. Krechetnikov was particularly influenced by Benjamin Shpier, a Jewish merchant from Mogilev who advocated a radical reform of Jewish communal structures. Under his influence Krechetnikov convened a Jewish assembly in Polotsk between 26 August and 6 September 1773, which did little more than maintain the existing structures, although it did give them some government legitimacy. In April 1774 Kakhovsky ordered the establishment of *kehilot* at the local, regional, and provincial levels, giving them wide powers, which they used in the conflict with the hasidic movement. (On this, see Volume II, Chapter 8.)

In response to this situation, in November 1785 the Jews of the two provinces sent a delegation to St Petersburg, headed by the Vitebsk merchant Lavka Faybishovich, which submitted eighteen petitions from different communities to the Russian senate. In their submissions, the Jews asked for Jewish expulsions from the countryside to be stopped, and for Jews to be allowed to lease the right to distil and sell alcohol, or even purchase such rights from the authorities. Jews should be guaranteed their electoral rights in the towns of the area and permitted to plead in the municipal courts. They should also retain their own courts for the

[25] Kakhovsky's report is found in Derzhavin, *Sochineniya*, vii. 312.

settlement of civil cases between Jews, and the *kehilah* should retain the right to apportion taxes among its members.[26]

Before this, in March 1785 Catherine asked the senate to discuss the issue, stating that since Jews had been placed by her decrees 'in the same position as the others', it was necessary to observe the rule that everyone was 'entitled to the advantages and rights appertaining to his calling or estate without distinction of religion or nationality'.[27] This led the senate on 7 May 1786 to issue an edict Concerning the Protection of the Rights of Jews in Russia in Respect of their Legal Responsibility, which affirmed unequivocally that, since Jews had already been 'accorded a status equal to that of others', all 'Jews must be able to enjoy the privileges and rights appropriate to their calling and fortune, without distinction of origin and religion.'[28]

Some concessions were made to the Jewish demands, but the senate refused to make an exception for the Jews and maintained the magistrates' monopoly on the sale of liquor in the towns. Jews could seek to obtain leases to sell alcohol from them. Those Jews who held valid leases, even if they were members of an urban estate, should retain their rights under such agreements. In the countryside only landowners were entitled to the right of distillation, but Jews could lease distilleries and taverns in the countryside and 'temporarily' reside there. 'Premature' expulsions from the countryside should be halted, and Jews with valid permission from the *kahal* were granted 'temporary residence' there provided they fulfilled their fiscal obligations. There should be no discrimination against Jews in municipal elections. They were not to be allowed their own courts, but were to be permitted to swear a Hebrew oath. Jewish complaints that they were being discriminated against in the magistrates' courts were led to an assurance that all members of a given estate were equally entitled to the rights granted to it. The rights of the *kehilot* to settle purely religious disputes, to issue passports, to administer schools, and to apportion taxes were affirmed.[29]

This decree certainly bears the mark of Enlightenment thinking. However, a comparison with the decrees of Joseph II in Austria (see Chapter 8) makes clear its limitations. The ability of the bureaucracy to establish an administration which would take into account the interests of the Jews was very limited in Russia, and no provision was made to enable the Jews to modernize their educational system or move out of the traditional occupations on which they had long been dependent. The desire to maintain order and to avoid antagonizing Christian townspeople and the peasantry also meant that the grandiloquent phraseology of the edict remained on paper, while the Jewish population continued to be subjected to harassment, often by ignorant and prejudiced local officials. The edict also aroused considerable local opposition in Belarus, and it was largely ignored in later legislation.

[26] For these petitions, see Anishchenko, *Cherta osedlosti*, 92–3.

[27] Dubnow, *History of the Jews in Russia and Poland*, i. 312.

[28] *PSZ* 1/xxii, no. 16391.

[29] Dubnow, *History of the Jews in Russia and Poland*, i. 313.

The limitations of the edict were revealed on 23 December 1791, when an imperial government decree, based on a report by the president of the commercial court, A. P. Vorontsov, rejected a claim by some Jewish traders submitted in September 1790 that they should be allowed to establish themselves as merchants in Smolensk and Moscow. Yuly Gessen commented on this edict that 'unexpectedly there emerged the so-called Pale (or region) of Permanent Jewish Settlement'.[30] It is certainly true that Jews were denied the right of free movement or settlement within the empire. In this respect, however, they were in the same position as everyone else in Russia, with the exception of the nobility (*dvoryanstvo*), who had only acquired this right in 1785, as part of the Charter of the Nobility. The edict embodied one of the basic facts of Russian constitutional life. The fact is that, as Richard Pipes has pointed out, with the exception of the nobility, no estate possessed any generalized freedoms or rights:

> These are notions derived from a feudal tradition of which Russia knew nothing. In Russia, freedoms and rights, such as they were, came by royal favour and were attached to duties borne on behalf of the state; they were inevitably granted to specific individuals and for limited periods of time (never in hereditary possession). In the patrimonial regime of Russia, which was still entrenched in the eighteenth century, nothing was permitted that was not permitted explicitly; or to put it in other words, whatever was not specifically allowed was deemed forbidden. Hence the Crown had no need legally to limit the 'right' of persons or groups, such as the Jews, to do anything, such as move freely throughout the Empire.[31]

Certainly, until the revolution of 1905 there were no citizens in Russia, only subjects. They had no rights even to choose their employment.

At the root of the prohibition to settle freely was probably Catherine's awareness of the weakness of the native Muscovite merchant class and its hostility to any foreign competition, in which was included Jewish competition. In February 1790, for instance, the Moscow merchants lodged a formal complaint with the city's governor-general against Jewish 'commercial malpractices'. In their view, the ability of the Jews (they used the now pejorative word *zhidy*[32]) to undercut native merchants showed that they had smuggled in their goods and had not paid customs duties. They appealed to the governor-general to expel those Jews who had established themselves in Moscow and to prohibit future settlement. The prohibition on settlement may also have been related to Catherine's fears, inspired by the French Revolution, of encouraging any popular discontent. It is characteristic that the decree of 23 December 1791 did allow Jews to settle in the Black Sea area, recommending that they be allowed to join urban communities on the territories of Ekaterinoslav and Tavrida (Crimea), which had just been conquered from the Turks.

The basic outlines of Catherine's policies on her Jewish subjects had already

[30] Gessen, *Istoriya evreiskogo naroda v Rossii*, i. 77.

[31] Pipes, 'Catherine II and the Jews', 14.

[32] On this, see Klier, 'Zhid'.

been laid down by the time of the second and third partitions of Poland–Lithuania, which increased the Jewish population of the empire nearly tenfold. In her instructions on these territories, she did not introduce any new regulations concerning Jews, merely reaffirming that all new subjects would retain their rights and privileges. The Pale of Settlement was now given a much clearer definition. By the edict of 23 June 1794, the area in which Jews were permitted to enrol in the ranks of merchants and townsmen was delineated as including the two Belarusian provinces, the territories opened to them officially in 1791 (Ekaterinoslav and Tavrida), and the provinces of Minsk, Podolia, and Volhynia (taken from Poland in the second partition). After the third partition the two Lithuanian provinces of Vilna and Slonim were also added. At the same time, primarily because of fiscal difficulties and out of a desire to force Jews to move out of the more crowded north-eastern provinces into the newly opened territories north of the Black Sea, the government, by a tax statute of 23 June 1794, imposed a double tax on them (2 rather than 1 per cent on capital for merchants, and 4 against 2 roubles for townsmen).[33] Those who were unwilling to pay this tax could, on payment of a lump sum, leave the tsarist empire. At the same time Jews were explicitly exempted from military service in return for payment of a special tax.

Some attempt was still made to exclude Jews from the countryside, and in 1795 a decree laid down that Jews living in rural areas should be registered in towns and that efforts should be made to induce them to live where they were registered.[34] In the same year the powers of the *kehilot* were restricted so that they lost their administrative and judicial functions and were henceforth only to concern themselves with 'the ceremonies of religion and divine service'.[35] In practice the usefulness of the *kehilot* as tax-collecting agencies was so great that the government was unable to dispense with them.

It is difficult to discern in the actions taken by Catherine in relation to her Jewish subjects anything more than a series of random responses to her own political situation and to local conditions in the annexed territories. Financial considerations—the need to pay for the wars of the eighteenth century and the attendant imperial expansion—were also a constant factor in determining her policies. Because of the weakness of the Russian bureaucratic structures, her attempt to impose on her empire a more centralized and effective administration was largely unsuccessful. This was even more the case in the newly annexed provinces, where for the most part the political and social structure inherited from Poland–Lithuania was left untouched. Essentially, the authorities seem to have pursued two contradictory goals: the incorporation of the Jews into the existing social estates and the maintenance of the autonomous structures which

[33] For the decree, see *PSZ* 1/xxiii, no. 17224 (23 June 1794). On the government's motives, see Rest, *Die russische Judengesetzgebung von der ersten polnischen Teilung bis zum 'Položenie dlja Evreev' (1804)*, 123. [34] Dubnow, *History of the Jews in Russia and Poland*, i. 319. [35] Ibid. 320.

had been established in Poland–Lithuania. Pressure from those hostile to the Jews, whether in the annexed territories or in Moscow, Smolensk, and Riga, also led to measures undermining their equal treatment.

THE JEWS UNDER PAUL AND ALEXANDER I (1796–1825)

The short reign of Catherine's son Paul (r. 1796–1801) saw little in the way of innovation in Jewish policy. Unlike the situation after the first partition, the Jews were not specifically mentioned in the guarantees of religious and other freedoms issued after the second and third partitions, confirming the principle established during Catherine's reign that everything not explicitly permitted to them was forbidden. The principle of double taxation for Jews was maintained, as was the Pale of Settlement. The government stopped intervening to ensure the Jewish right to vote in municipal elections, although it did on occasion defend Jewish rights. Thus in 1800 the senate resolved that landowners no longer had the right to try Jews on their estates, which included the towns over which they still enjoyed proprietary rights.[36] This period saw the beginnings of significant migration from the areas of Lithuania and Belarus to Ukraine, principally to the provinces of Novgorod-Seversky and Poltava.

By now the imperial administration was increasingly conscious that it could no longer resort to ad hoc improvisation in making policy for its Jewish subjects, with its greatly increased population following the second and third partitions. Accordingly, aware of its own ignorance of the issue, it began to gather information to help in the formulation of a coherent policy. Since Russian policy in the territories annexed from Poland was, for the moment, to leave unchanged the dominant position of the nobility, it made sense to consult with them, soliciting their opinions through the marshals of the nobility in the different provinces. This decision was strengthened by concern for the welfare of the local peasantry, whose position had worsened as a result of the political unrest of the 1790s and by an outbreak of disease among animals.

The issue was first raised in the province of Minsk, where the local governor, Zakhar Karneev, in the face of a serious local famine, was ordered by the central government to consult the local nobility so that he could provide 'an explanation of the causes of the impoverished condition of the peasants' and suggest means for improving their situation. The marshals of the nobility who convened in Minsk in the spring of 1797 were obviously concerned, in the first instance, to justify themselves and protect their privileges. They explained that conditions in the province were partly the result of external factors, such as 'the changes and revolutions in the area', poor weather conditions, and the inadequate state of local communications. In addition, the difficulties of the area were, they alleged, caused by Jewish

[36] Gessen, *Istoriya evreiskogo naroda v Rossii*, i. 92.

tavern-keepers (who were, of course, their own agents), 'who are proprietors of taverns and inns in circumvention of the legal obligation that they live in the towns and who lead the peasants into debt and drunkenness to the detriment of agriculture'. Leasing of both whole estates and services such as milling, often to Jews, was also attacked, as was the disproportionate number of priests, whose poverty led them to charge excessive fees for baptisms, weddings, and funerals.[37]

Although 'Jewish exploitation' was only one of the factors adduced by the report in explaining the famine, this aspect was seized upon by the central government. Paul sent the material to the procurator-general of the senate, A. B. Kurakin, and instructed him to inform Governor Karneev that 'he, through his office, should take actions similar to those measures proposed by the marshals regarding the limitation of the rights of the Jews, who ravaged the peasants, and the clergy, who oppressed them by their immoderate extortions, and regarding the terms of leases'.[38]

The following April the governors of the remaining provinces annexed from Poland–Lithuania were asked by the senate to submit recommendations on how the situation of the peasants could be ameliorated. Like Governor Karneev, they sought the opinion of the local nobility. The marshals of the nobility of Podolia met in Kamenets-Podolsky and repeated the claims of their counterparts in Minsk that a major factor in agricultural backwardness was Jewish control of the liquor trade. They expressed their appreciation to the tsar 'for his imperial benevolence in leaving us the franchise of selling liquor' and requested that 'the right to distil and sell liquor not be granted to Jews, or even to Christians', but that nobles should have the right to employ people to undertake these activities at their own discretion since they alone by their careful control of the trade had prevented its worst effects on the peasantry from being realized. Echoing physiocratic arguments, they also called for Jews to be barred from engaging in 'uneconomic foreign trade'. This was opposed by the deputy governor of the province, Aleksey Yuzefovich, who suggested instead that the nobles themselves should be encouraged to take part in the export of agricultural produce, which at this time was being diverted from its previous routes to the Baltic to the newly established Russian ports on the Black Sea, particularly the new town of Odessa.[39]

The final set of consultations involved the nobility of Lithuania, a large province created in 1796, which was made up of nineteen districts with Vilna as its capital. (In 1802 some of these were assigned to the province of Grodno.) These discussions were more protracted than the earlier ones, and the different marshals only submitted their reports in 1800, after being chided by the senate for their delay in doing so. The delay seems to have arisen because the Baltic German governor of the province, I. G. Friesel, wished to obtain more information on which

[37] This report was published in Bershadsky, 'Polozhenie o evreyakh 1804 goda', *Voskhod*, 15 (1895), no. 1, 87–8.

[38] Gessen, *Evrei v Rossii*, 20.

[39] Bershadsky, 'Polozhenie o evreyakh 1804 goda', *Voskhod*, 15 (1895), no. 1, 94–5.

to base his own report to the senate, which was submitted with those of the nineteen local marshals of the nobility.

Of the latter, three favoured retaining pre-partition conditions on the grounds that the Jews were too deeply involved in the rural economy to be displaced. All agreed that the involvement of the Jews in the liquor trade should be curtailed, and most proposed that Jews be barred from distilling and inn-keeping and from the sale of liquor in noble-owned taverns. This would inevitably create a large class of 'superfluous' Jews. Those who could not be absorbed into the towns should be settled on public and private land as free agricultural labourers not bound to the soil (i.e. not as serfs). Sixteen marshals proposed that Jews should also be barred from distilling and inn-keeping and from the sale of liquor in manorial taverns. Some of those who were made unemployed in this way should be sent to the towns, and the rest should 'be scattered over the Crown and noble estates, where they could farm and could provide finance for the nobility'. In addition, the marshals called for 'the abolition of specific Jewish forms of dress and the introduction among the Jews of the form of dress customary among other inhabitants'. The goal was to end the 'separatism' of the Jews, who 'constitute a people who isolate themselves, to which end they have their own administration . . . in the form of synagogues and *kahal*s, which not only arrogate to themselves spiritual authority, but also meddle in civil affairs and in matters appertaining to the police'.[40]

The final form of the submission owed a considerable amount to the intervention of Friesel, who was probably influenced by the legislation dealing with Jews which had been introduced in Prussia and Austria (on this, see Chapters 7 and 8). His own comprehensive memorandum also reflected some of the debates which had just taken place in Poland–Lithuania during the Four Year Sejm. In Friesel's view, a 'general reform' of the Jews was necessary, such as was being implemented elsewhere in Europe. This should take education as its starting point, since 'the education of the Jewish people must begin with their religion'. He had probably been in touch with the mitnagdic opponents of hasidism, since he then asserted that it was necessary 'to wipe out all Jewish sects with their superstitions and to forbid strictly the introduction of any innovations which might plunge them into greater ignorance'. Jews should be compelled to send their children to state schools, to conduct all their business dealings in Polish, and to abandon Jewish dress, and should be forbidden to marry below the age of 20. He divided Jews into four occupational categories: merchants, craftsmen, innkeepers, and others. Jewish merchants could certainly be made into useful subjects of the empire provided their deep-rooted dishonesty could be controlled by strict supervision. The same was true of Jewish artisans, but here action needed to be taken against the usually shoddy and substandard character of their work. Jewish tavern-keeping

[40] Dubnow, *History of the Jews in Russia and Poland*, i. 325–6; Bershadsky, 'Polozhenie o evreyakh 1804 goda', *Voskhod*, 15 (1895), no. 3, 75–7.

was entirely deleterious in its impact on society and should be prohibited by law. So too should the activities of factors, money-changers, and those receiving public charity, who should be compelled to take up agriculture. To facilitate their success in this they should be exempt from taxation for ten years. As a consequence of these occupational reforms, Jews would be divided into three categories, merchants, artisans, and farmers, which would enable them to be placed in the estate structure of the wider society. The *kahal* and the whole structure of Jewish self-government could then be abolished, ending the ability of the Jewish elite to exploit the ignorant Jewish masses, 'prisoners of fear and ignorance without any morality, without any dignity, without any education'.[41]

All these different opinions were placed before the senate in the spring of 1800, with the aim of establishing a new and comprehensive policy for the Jews. One of the senators, Gavriil Derzhavin (1743–1816), sometimes described as Russia's greatest eighteenth-century poet, decided to take upon himself the task of preparing the guidelines for such a policy. Born in Kazan to an impoverished noble family, and having spent most of his life first in the army and then as a civil servant in St Petersburg and as governor of the provinces of Olonets and Tambov, both far from the Pale of Settlement, he had little direct knowledge of Jews. The only contact which he had with organized Jewish life was when, in 1799, he was sent to investigate conditions in the town of Shklov, in the area incorporated into the empire in the partition of 1772 (on Shklov, see Volume II, Chapter 6). Shklov was a private town and had passed into the hands of an autocratic and self-willed Russian nobleman, Semen Gavrilovich Zorich, whose arbitrary exactions and oppressive behaviour were much resented by the local Jewish population, among whom maskilic ideas had gained something of a foothold. The Jews had appealed to the emperor against what they claimed was Zorich's attempt to transform them into serfs, and Derzhavin was dispatched to investigate. His view was that the Jews were at least in part responsible for the problems which had befallen them, and the incident left him with a strong distrust of Jews both individually and as a collective.

In June 1800, by virtue of the experience he had gathered in Shklov, Derzhavin was again sent to Belarus to investigate the recurrence of famine conditions there. He was given wide-ranging powers by the emperor to punish those responsible for the disaster and to impose sanctions on nobles who, 'moved by unprecedented greed, leave their peasants without assistance'. If necessary, their estates could be confiscated and placed under state administration.[42]

The emperor's letter of instruction contained no reference to Jews. However, after it was conveyed to Derzhavin by the procurator-general of the senate, P. I. Obolyaninov, a supplementary statement was added, which may have reflected Derzhavin's own preoccupations:

[41] For Friesel's report, see Bershadsky, 'Polozhenie o evreyakh 1804 goda', *Voskhod*, 15 (1895), no. 3, 85–96.

[42] Paul I to Derzhavin, in Derzhavin, *Sochineniya*, vi, no. 1201 (16 June 1800), 385.

> Since, according to our information, a major cause of the exhaustion of the Belarusian peasantry is the Jews [*zhidy*], who extract their profits from them, the Most High will is that you deliver a personal opinion and report on their pursuits, in order to prevent this general harm, and that you give your opinion on the general conditions there.[43]

Once in Belarus, Derzhavin proceeded to draft an elaborate memorandum, characteristically entitled 'The Opinion of Senator Derzhavin regarding the avoidance of the grain shortage in Belarus by curbing the mercenary trade of the Jews and concerning their reform'. In preparing it, Derzhavin took advice from local burghers, from Jesuits at the local Jesuit college in Vitebsk, and from two Jewish maskilim, one of the first examples of the negative synergy created by the interaction of Russian autocracy and the Haskalah. One of them, Nata Notkin (sometimes known as Nota Khamovich Notkin or Nathan Shklover), served as a purveyor to Potemkin and lived in St Petersburg. He suggested to the administration that the Jews should be resettled in agricultural and cattle-breeding colonies 'in the neighbourhood of the Black Sea ports'. The other, Dr Ilya Frank, a physician from Kreslovka in the province of Vitebsk, favoured radical religious reform, which would restore Judaism to 'its original purity, [which] rested on unadulterated deism and the postulates of pure morality', but which had in the course of time been distorted by 'the absurdities of the Talmud'. Jews should be admitted to state schools and learn Russian and German in addition to Hebrew.[44] Derzhavin also had at his disposal the recommendations of the various marshals of the nobility in the newly acquired territories as well as the legislation introduced in neighbouring Prussia.

Derzhavin's memorandum examined social conditions in Belarus and the reasons for the famine, and gave an account of the history of the Jews in Poland–Lithuania and of how they could be 'reformed'. It opens with a characteristic preamble:

> Inasmuch as Supreme Providence, in order to attain its unknown ends, leaves this people, despite its dangerous characteristics, on the face of the earth, and refrains from destroying it, the governments under whose sceptre it takes refuge must also suffer it to live; assisting the decree of destiny, they are in duty bound to extend their patronage even to the Jews, but in such wise that they [the Jews] may prove useful both to themselves and to the people in whose midst they are settled.

Derzhavin saw the Jews as the principal cause of the unsatisfactory state of Belarus, although he was also strongly critical of the local peasants and their Polish landlords. He attacked the 'laziness' of the peasants and contrasted them unfavourably with Russian serfs, a contrast he saw as the consequence of the excessive 'freedom' they had enjoyed under Polish rule. Referring to the Polish

[43] Obolyaninov to Derzhavin, ibid., no. 1202 (16 June 1800), 385–6.

[44] For Notkin's opinion, see 'Mnenie', in Derzhavin, *Sochineniya*, vii. 306–29; for Frank's, ibid. 259. See also Gessen, *Evrei v Rossii*, 8, 447, and Dubnow, *History of the Jews in Russia and Poland*, i. 330–1.

nobility, he distinguished between the magnates, to whom he was particularly hostile, and the bulk of the nobility, who treated their peasants improperly but who were merely following the lead of the magnates. All the nobility were at fault in failing to administer their estates themselves (as was the case, he claimed, in central Russia) and leaving them in the hands of factors and agents. Leaseholding should be strictly controlled and magnates should only be allowed to lease estates to other magnates, and then for periods of not less than nine years. The liquor trade should be strictly controlled and reserved to magnates; it should not be leased out, and especially not to Jews.

This led him to his principal target. In his view, most Jewish economic activity—trading, leasing of land, inn-keeping, and brokerage—was nothing more than means 'to squeeze out the wealth of their neighbours under the pretext of offering them benefits and favours'. The Jewish religion had nothing to recommend it. The education provided for Jewish children was 'a hotbed of superstition', while moral sentiments were entirely absent among the Jews—'they have no concept of lovingkindness, disinterestedness, and other virtues'. All they did was 'to amass riches in order to erect a new temple of Solomon or to satisfy their earthly desires'.

What was needed was a radical transformation of Jewish society. The Jews should be placed under 'supreme [i.e. imperial] protection and tutelage' and should be supervised by a special Christian official, called a 'protector', who, with the assistance of committees appointed by the provincial administrations, would be responsible for implementing the necessary transformation. They would take a census and require all Jews to take family names. The Jews would then be divided into four categories: merchants, urban townspeople, rural townspeople, and agricultural settlers. They would be evenly spread over Belarus, and any surplus population would be transferred to other provinces.

To further the transformation, the *kehilot* should be abolished and replaced by 'synagogues' with rabbis and 'schoolmen' who in the different provinces would be responsible for the spiritual affairs of the Jews. A supreme ecclesiastical tribunal, the 'Sendarin' (*sic*), presided over by the chief rabbi, or 'patriarch', and modelled on the Muslim mufti of the Tatars, should be established in St Petersburg.

Various restrictions were also proposed. The Jews should be forbidden to employ Christian domestics, deprived of the right to participate in town government, and forced to abandon Jewish dress and to execute all their business documents in Russian, Polish, or German. Children should attend Jewish religious schools only to the age of 12, after which they would be transferred to state schools. A government printing press should be established, which would publish Jewish religious books 'with philosophic annotations'.

If these proposals were implemented, Derzhavin concluded, 'the stubborn and cunning tribe of Hebrews will be properly set to rights'. By carrying out these reforms, the tsar Paul would earn great fame since he would have fulfilled the command of the Gospels: 'Love your enemies, bless them that curse you, do good to them that hate you.'[45]

The deposition and murder of Paul in March 1801 meant that no action was taken on this far-reaching plan, which has some similarities to the reforms later to be introduced by Nicholas I. Paul's successor, Alexander (r. 1801–25), was much more influenced by liberal views in the early years of his reign before the war with Napoleon and was also much better informed about Jewish matters, partly because of his close relationship with Adam Czartoryski (on this, see Chapter 9). The first two years of his reign saw important administrative reforms, with the establishment of a Council of State and individual ministries, and the senate, as a consequence, losing its executive functions. Proposals were also mooted for a constitution and for the abolition of serfdom.

The Jewish issue soon demanded the attention of the new administration because of a series of disputes over what electoral rights Jews should enjoy in the towns acquired in the second and third partitions of Poland–Lithuania. This led to a ruling by the senate on 15 December 1803 that Jews possessed the same rights as other townspeople in the areas acquired by the second partition, but that in the lands incorporated by the third partition (which included the province of Vilna), Magdeburg law, which denied the Jews representation in municipalities, should continue to operate. In addition, concerns were expressed by the governor of Kiev province, P. Pankratiev, on the adverse consequences of the expulsion of the Jews from the countryside.[46]

This confused situation clearly needed clarification, and it was for this purpose that Alexander created on 9 November 1802 the Committee for the Organization of Jewish Life, the first of many such bodies in both the tsarist empire and the Kingdom of Poland. It included among its members Derzhavin himself, now minister of justice, and Catherine's last lover, Count V. A. Zubov, who was sympathetic to his views, which led Derzhavin to claim later that it had been set up to implement his memorandum on the Jews. This seems to be belied by the more liberal opinions of its remaining members, Count Viktor Kochubey, who in September 1802 had been appointed to the newly created post of minister of the interior, and two Poles now in the service of the tsarist administration, Adam Czartoryski and Seweryn Potocki. Count Zubov, who died on 21 June 1804, played little part in the discussions of the committee and Derzhavin was dismissed as minister of justice on an unrelated issue and replaced on the committee by his successor as minister of justice, P. V. Lopukhin.

Kochubey was a close associate of the tsar and a member of his Secret Committee together with Nikolay Novosiltsev, Count P. A. Stroganov, and

[45] For the opinion, see Derzhavin, 'Mnenie', in *Sochineniya*, vii. 231–305; see also Dubnow, *History of the Jews in Russia and Poland*, i. 329–34, and Klier, *Russia Gathers her Jews*, 95–115.

[46] These issues are discussed in Bershadsky, 'Polozhenie o evreyakh 1804 goda', *Voskhod*, 15 (1895), no. 6, 55–63, and in Klier, *Russia Gathers her Jews*, 116–20.

Czartoryski. He was a man of the Enlightenment who believed that the defects of the Jews could be cured by appropriate government policies, above all in education, a view shared by Czartoryski and Potocki, who had been involved in the attempts at 'Jewish reform' during the Four Year Sejm. During that period Potocki was also a strong supporter of the rights of burghers and the constitution of 3 May. All three were actively involved in educational reform in the tsarist empire, Kochubey as a member of the Committee of Education for New Russia and Astrakhan from 1801, Czartoryski as director of the school system in Vilna province, and Potocki as a member of the special commission on schools in the Ministry of Public Enlightenment from 1802, and as head of the Kharkov educational district from 1803.

The Jews in Belarus and Lithuania, having some idea of the contents of Derzhavin's original report, reacted with alarm to the setting up of the committee, and responded with their traditional resort to lobbying. In response, the minister of the interior tried to allay Jewish disquiet. On 21 January 1803 he sent a circular to provincial governors in the north-west instructing them to inform the *kehilot* that 'in appointing the Committee for the Investigation of Jewish Matters' the government had 'no intention whatsoever of impairing their status or curtailing any substantial advantage enjoyed by them'. On the contrary, the aim was to 'offer them better conditions and greater security'.[47] The removal of Derzhavin, who was out of sympathy with the reformist aspirations of Alexander's government, both from the position of minister of justice and from his membership of what became popularly known as the Jewish Committee, may also have reduced Jewish anxiety.

At the beginning of 1803, in a further attempt to reassure Jewish opinion, the committee itself resolved to invite representatives from the *kehilot* to send deputies to St Petersburg to inform them of their views on the proposed reforms. Accordingly, Jewish deputies from the provinces of Minsk, Podolia, Mogilev, and Kiev made their way to the capital. Deputies may also have been sent from other provinces, but concrete evidence for this is lacking. In the capital the deputies made contact with the small group of Jews who had established themselves there and who understood Russian political conditions. These included Nata Notkin, who, as we have seen, had submitted a memorandum to Derzhavin and had been asked to submit an opinion to the committee; Abraham Perets, a wealthy merchant and contractor linked with Mikhail Mikhailovich Speransky, Kochubey's assistant; and the protomaskil Judah Leib Nevakhovich (Judah Leib b. Noah).[48]

[47] Shugurov, 'Doklad o evreyakh imperatoru Aleksandru Pavlovichu', 255. As John Klier has pointed out, material from the First Jewish Committee, which otherwise would have been lost, can be extracted from this report of the Third Jewish Committee, which was created in 1809 and submitted its report to the Tsar in 1812.

[48] On these developments, see Gessen, *Istoriya evreiskogo naroda v Rossii*, i. 140, and Klier, *Russia Gathers her Jews*, 125–7.

The committee does seem to have been aware of the need for reform to be carried out slowly and with a degree of consent. According to an entry in its journal of 20 September 1803, probably written by Speransky:

> Transformations brought about by governmental force will generally not be stable and will be especially unreliable in those cases where this force struggles against centuries-old habits, with ingrained errors and with unyielding superstition; it would be better and more opportune to direct the Jews towards improvement, to open the path to their own benefit, overseeing their progress from afar and removing anything that might lead them astray, not employing any force, not setting up any particular institution, not acting in their place, but enabling their own activity. As few restrictions as possible, as much freedom as possible. This is a simple formula for any organization of society![49]

The committee, after some discussion, came up with a general programme for 'Jewish reform', which it submitted to the Jewish deputies. This could not have been to their liking, as they responded by claiming that they could not give their opinion until they had consulted their own *kehilot* and asking for a six-month delay to make this possible. The committee was unwilling to delay and decided to submit its plan directly to the *kehilot*. The goal was not consultation, since it was made clear that no changes in the proposals would be entertained, but rather to ensure the smooth implementation of the proposed reforms. The local *kehilot* were even less enthusiastic, calling for the implementation of a number of proposed provisions, most notably those relating to the involvement of Jews in the liquor trade and in leasing in general, to be delayed 'for fifteen to twenty years'.

As a consequence of the opening of the Russian archives, we now have a better idea of what the Jewish leaders found objectionable in the proposed legislation. In their replies, the *kehilot* of Minsk and Kiev attempted to bring home to the committee the economic realities which prevailed in their provinces and the inextricable links of the Jews to the manorial economy. The Minsk *kehilah* warned of the severe consequences of the expulsion of Jews from the countryside, while that of Kiev (which included Jewish representatives from Kiev province) underlined the implications of the removal of the large number of Jewish innkeepers. They pointed out that the tavern was the principal link between the peasants and the wider market, to which they brought their agricultural surpluses and where they bought goods which could not be produced in the villages. The breaking of this nexus would only further impoverish the villages. Both responded to nobles' criticism of Jewish behaviour by attacking the arbitrary rule of the nobility and calling for legal safeguards against arbitrary action.[50] These objections were brushed aside and the report was submitted to Alexander in October 1804. It stressed the harmful character of much of the Jews' economic activity and their separate status. Although they had been made subject to the general courts and the local

[49] Shugurov, 'Doklad o evreyakh imperatoru Aleksandru Pavlovichu', 254–5.

[50] TsDIAU, Kiev, f. 533, op. 1, d. 1690 for Minsk, and d. 433 for Kiev. These are discussed in Klier, *Rossiya sobiraet svoikh evreev*.

administration of the towns, they had managed to preserve their separateness and govern themselves through their *kehilot*. Their most common means of earning a living was the sale of liquor, which was the source of much abuse and complaints from the surrounding population. In order to deal with these issues, the committee drafted a Statute Concerning the Organization of the Jews, which was promulgated by the tsar on 9 December 1804.[51]

The members of the committee were very satisfied with their labours, observing that, 'if one compares the present statute for the Jews with all those which in other states have been drafted for them, the committee is convinced that, if one takes local conditions into account, nowhere have measures been designed for them that are more moderate or more lenient'.[52] The statute itself was less impressive. It combined Enlightenment-derived ideas for the transformation of the Jews with the now traditional Russian preoccupation with the need to limit their 'harmful impact' on the peasantry of the areas acquired from Poland–Lithuania, claiming that it was motivated by 'solicitude for the true welfare of the Jews' as well as by 'the advantage of the native population in those provinces in which these people are permitted to reside'.

The first section dealt with education (in Russian: 'enlightenment'). Its ten articles allowed Jewish children free access to state schools and universities and granted Jews the right to open their own secular schools in which the language of instruction could be German, Polish, or Russian. After a period of six years all Jewish public and commercial documents would have to use one of these languages. Jews who were elected to municipalities, who served as *kahal* members, or who were elected as rabbis were to demonstrate after a similar period their written and spoken knowledge of one of these languages. Jewish members of municipalities were required to wear European-style clothes.

The statute attempted to delineate the respective spheres of competence of the civic authorities and the Jewish autonomous institutions. Jews were subject to the authority of the towns, the police, and the common law courts. At the same time, in spite of the attacks on the system of Jewish self-government, it did not abolish the *kehilah*. This may have been dictated by a desire to avoid excessive confrontation or by awareness of the inadequacy of the state's administrative and tax-gathering apparatus. By article 50 Jews were given the right to elect rabbis and members of the *kehilah*, who were to be replaced every three years and whose election had to be ratified by the provincial administration. The *kehilot* were to be responsible for ensuring the payment of state taxes and were to submit an annual report of what they had done 'to the municipal councillors in the towns, to the administrator on state properties, and to the landowners on private estates' (article 54).

Rabbis were responsible for 'all ceremonies of the Jewish faith and the deciding of all disputes of a religious character', but were expressly forbidden to make use

51 For the statute, see *PSZ* 1/xxviii, no. 21547 (9 Dec. 1804).

52 Golitsyn, *Istoriya russkogo zakonodatel'stva o evreyakh*, 441.

of the sanction of excommunication. A 'dissident' sect had the right to establish its own synagogue and elect its own rabbi in any community, giving a legal sanction to the expansion of hasidism (article 53). Perhaps under the impact of Jewish lobbying, the statute did not include the creation of an overriding religious authority, the 'Sendarin' proposed by Derzhavin. The Minsk and Kiev *kehilot* had strongly attacked this concept, pointing out that the Sanhedrin was a phenomenon of the Jewish past and had no place in the modern era.[53]

Jewish economic life was to be radically transformed and all Jews were to be placed in one of four categories: merchants, townspeople, manufacturers and artisans, and farmers. Accordingly, inn-keeping and all types of leasing linked with agriculture were to be barred to Jews (article 34). Although this clause seems to have been intended solely to prohibit Jewish involvement in the liquor trade, on 21 December 1805 the government made it clear that it was to apply to all agricultural leases. Given the close involvement of the Jews in the agricultural economy, this was a savage blow. A second Jewish Committee, established in August 1806, estimated that approximately 60,000 families were dependent on agriculture-related activities for their livelihood and would have to be resettled.[54] The statute proposed that some of the people who would lose their occupations as a result of this legislation should move to the towns and the remainder should be absorbed into farming, for which purpose two additional provinces, Astrakhan and Caucasia, were to be opened to Jewish settlement.

In addition, the statute aimed to encourage industry and handicrafts among the Jews, and those who established factories which were 'in particular demand' were eligible for state loans in line with the physiocratic assumptions of the statute. Trading, although not positively discouraged as a Jewish occupation, was certainly regarded as less worthy than farming, manufacturing, or artisanry. Manufacturers, artisans, and merchants were now given the right to reside temporarily for business purposes in 'the interior provinces, not excluding the capitals, but only if they possess passports issued by the provincial authorities', such as were required for foreign travel. The statute abolished the oppressive double taxation of the Jews, and by 1807 this seems to have ceased.[55] At the same time, the limitations on Jewish residence imposed by the Pale of Settlement, whose boundaries were now set down, were retained, although there were exemptions for merchants, artisans, and manufacturers.

The statute was not well received by the bulk of Jewish society. As we have seen, the representatives of the *kehilot* asked the government to delay 'for fifteen to twenty years' its economic provisions, particularly those relating to the sale of liquor and rural leasing. Petitions asking for the abrogation of these clauses were also sent to

53 On this, see Klier, *Rossiya sobiraet svoikh evreev*.

54 *PSZ* 1/xxviii, no. 21967 (21 Dec. 1805). See also Klier, *Russia Gathers her Jews*, 146–8.

55 *PSZ* 1/xxix, no. 22678 (8 Nov. 1807). In the course of setting out tax rates, this decree notes that Jews no longer pay the double tax. See also Klier, *Russia Gathers her Jews*, 139–40.

St Petersburg by individual *kehilot* as well as from landowners, who were dependent on Jewish leaseholders to administer their estates. They may also have feared prosecution for continuing to make use of Jewish leaseholders, as was envisaged under article 35 of the statute, but there is no evidence of any such prosecutions.

The Russian government was alarmed by the strength of these protests, particularly since they coincided with Napoleon's summoning of the Assembly of Jewish Notables in Paris in May 1806. There was also the fear that, in the event of war between France and Russia, which seemed imminent with the formation of the anti-Napoleonic coalition of Great Britain, Prussia, and Russia in the same year, the loyalty of the Jewish population could not be relied on. Fears of French subversion were strengthened by Napoleon's transforming the assembly into a 'Sanhedrin', which in October 1806 invited all Jewish communities in Europe to send representatives to its meeting held between February and March 1807. As a consequence, in February, Kochubey, as minister of the interior, advised governors in the western provinces to take steps to prevent any contact between local Jews and the Sanhedrin and to spread rumours of its intentions to 'reform' the Jewish religion.[56] In addition, the second Jewish Committee, established in August 1806, whose members included Kochubey, the foreign minister, A. Budberg, Czartoryski, Potocki, Lopukhin, Novosiltsev, and another Pole, Tadeusz Czacki, who had been a member of the Committee for the Transformation of the Jews in the Four Year Sejm (see Chapter 6), advised the tsar of the need 'to delay the resettlement of the Jews from the country into cities and towns and of the need to treat this nation carefully in the light of the schemes of the French government'.[57]

Kochubey also attempted to conciliate Jewish opinion directly, inviting the Jewish *kehilot* in the affected provinces to send deputies to their provincial capitals to make their views known. The deputies, or, as they were referred to by the Russian authorities, 'the attorneys of the Jewish communes', did not confine themselves to attacking the disastrous consequences of the ban on agricultural leases for the economic well-being of their communities. They called for an end to the double taxation of Jews, as had been promised by the statute, requested that the scope of rabbinic tribunals be widened, and asked for a modification of the requirement that commercial records be kept in a European language. Delegates pointed out the difficulties which Jewish town councillors or *kehilah* members faced in acquiring Russian in the short period allowed them. They also questioned the requirement to abandon Jewish dress for those serving as magistrates or outside the Pale of Settlement. In order to avoid having to shave their beards, it was suggested that Russian dress was more suitable for Jews than German. There was no point in sending Jewish children to Russian schools until they had some knowledge of the Russian

[56] Golitsyn, *Istoriya russkogo zakonodatel'stva o evreyakh*, 5–55, and Klier, *Russia Gathers her Jews*, 148–9.

[57] Shugurov, 'Doklad o evreyakh imperatoru Aleksandru Pavlovichu', 257–8, and Klier, *Russia Gathers her Jews*, 149.

language. The more practicable course would be for Russian to be taught in Jewish schools, where children would also acquire Hebrew and the 'dogmas of the faith'.

However, with the defeat of the Prussians at the battle of Eylau on 14 June 1807, the threat of a Franco-Russian conflict seemed for the moment to have subsided, and the government decided to proceed with the proposed expulsion of Jews from the countryside. On 19 October 1807 the tsar instructed the governors of the western provinces to begin the resettlement on 1 January of the following year.[58] The Jews were to be divided into three groups, to be resettled in 1808, 1809, and 1810. Lists of those to be resettled were to be drawn up by provincial governors and marshals of the nobility, who were first to take a census of the Jews in their area. Those Jews too poor to pay for their resettlement should seek assistance from their local *kehilah*. If this was not available, they were to be settled on landed estates, whose owners were to build factories for them, or to work in factories which would be established by Jewish manufacturers. These plans reflected the étatist conceptions which dominated Russian economic policy in relation to factory production, particularly of woollen textiles needed for military uniforms, and echoed the proposals made by Nata Notkin to Derzhavin. They were also in accord with article 21 of the statute, which provided 20,000 roubles for this purpose for each of the provinces annexed from Poland.

These resources were not forthcoming, and very few factories were in fact established. The bulk of the Jews would thus have to be settled on agricultural land, particularly in New Russia, Astrakhan, and the Caucasus. The proposal for agricultural resettlement was the first of a large number of attempts, which continued under the Soviets, to convert the Jews into farmers.[59] A number of Jews took advantage of this offer, and by 1807 four colonies of Jewish farmers had established themselves in the province of Kherson, numbering nearly 300 families, or altogether 2,000 people. As the expulsion proceeded, more Jews sought to relocate themselves in this way.[60]

The expulsions began as planned, inflicting considerable hardship on the hapless Jewish population; indeed the hardship was so great that on 29 December 1808 a new decree was issued suspending the expulsions and allowing the Jews to remain where they were until the question had been fully discussed.[61] The issue was accordingly referred to a third Jewish Committee, which was appointed in January 1809 with a mandate to examine all aspects of the problem of how the Jews could be diverted from the rural economy and the liquor trade to other economic activities. It was headed by V. I. Popov (the deputy minister of the interior), and included Potocki, Senator Alekseev, Zakhar Karneev (the assistant minister of the interior), and I. A. Druzhinin (the former governor of the province of Minsk

58 Dubnow, *History of the Jews in Russia and Poland*, i. 351.

59 For a history of these schemes until the 1880s, see Nikitin, *Evrei-zemledel'tsy*.

60 Dubnow, *History of the Jews in Russia and Poland*, i. 364.

61 *PSZ* 1/xxx, no. 23424 (29 Dec. 1808).

and state councillor). The tsar wrote a letter to the committee's chairman admitting the impossibility of removing the Jews from the countryside because of the destitution of most of those who had been barred from pursuing their previous occupations, particularly in the supply of alcohol.[62]

In addition, arrangements for the absorption of Jewish settlers into the area north of the Black Sea were rudimentary. The Emigration Bureau for New Russia and the governor of the province of New Russia, the duc de Richelieu (a French revolutionary émigré), in their reports to St Petersburg stressed that the emigrants who had already arrived were having difficulty establishing themselves and there was no accommodation for further newcomers. By the beginning of 1810 the settled immigrants numbered 600 families with 3,640 members. Three hundred additional families had requested resettlement. They were waiting to be accommodated, and, because of their unsatisfactory living conditions, were falling prey to disease. As a result, by a decree of 6 April 1810 the government temporarily suspended the settlement of Jews in the area.

The new Jewish committee finally reported in March 1812. Its conclusions were a damning commentary on everything which had been done since the first consultation with the Belarusian nobility in 1797. It argued that the removal of the Jews from the liquor trade would not end drunkenness and would only increase Jewish poverty. Jews performed valuable economic functions in the countryside, and the belief that they could be transformed overnight into factory workers was without foundation. All that the government had achieved was to reduce an already impoverished group 'to even greater destitution'. Accordingly, the authorities should 'put a resolute stop to the methods of interference at present being applied by allowing the Jews to remain in their present places of residence' and permitting them to engage in agricultural leasing.[63]

The government accepted the committee's recommendations, partly since war with France was now imminent. However, this meant that the more positive of the recommendations were never implemented and the committee was formally dissolved in 1818. A similar fate befell many of the provisions of the statute itself, which demonstrated once again the huge gulf between Russian theory and practice. The government lacked both the will and the resources to implement the educational provisions of the statute. Government primary schools were few in number and Christian in character, whether Roman Catholic or Greek Orthodox, and so were unacceptable to almost all Jewish parents. By 1808 only one Jewish pupil was attending such a school in the province of Vitebsk and nine in the province of Mogilev. The requirement that Jewish schools (which meant essentially *ḥeders*) should teach Russian, German, or Polish proved impossible to implement given the lack of a system of inspection. Thus, almost no Jews were able to obtain the qualifications necessary to attend university and the very few who did could not subsequently find appropriate employment. For example,

[62] Dubnow, *History of the Jews in Russia and Poland*, i. 352–3.

[63] Ibid. 353–4.

Simon Wolf, who graduated from the Faculty of Law at Dorpat, was briefly employed in the Justice College for Livland and Kurland Affairs, but was soon dismissed on the grounds that he could not be allowed to work on ecclesiastical cases. The language requirements for rabbis and for the conduct of business proved impossible to implement, as did the limitations on traditional Jewish dress, although they were to appear again in subsequent legislation.

In the war which finally broke out with Napoleon in 1812 the Jews, by and large, remained loyal to the tsarist government. Some, like the leader of Habad hasidism, Rebbe Shneur Zalman of Lyady, did so because of their fear that French revolutionary ideas would undermine Jewish religious belief. Others were impressed by the apparent willingness of the tsar's government to consult Jewish opinion or did not take seriously the prospect of a Napoleonic victory and the return of Polish rule. They may also have been affected by the wave of anti-French and patriotic feeling which swept through the tsarist empire. According to the Russian irregular fighter Denis Davydov, 'the frame of mind of the Polish inhabitants of Grodno was very hostile. The Jews living in Poland were, on the whole, all so devoted to us that they refused to serve the enemy as scouts and often gave us most valuable information concerning him.'[64]

Alexander encouraged the Jews to trust in his benevolence. He received a delegation from the local *kehilah* in Kalisz, in the western part of the Duchy of Warsaw, following which appeals were circulated in the area in Yiddish calling on the local Jews to offer up prayers for his victory. Two Jewish agents, Zundel Sonnenberg of Grodno and Leyser Dillon of Nesvizh, were attached to the headquarters of the Russian army between 1812 and 1815 as purveyors and military suppliers. They also acted as a conduit for the transmission of Jewish views to the emperor. In June 1814 Alexander asked them to assure 'the Jewish kahals of his most gracious favour'. He promised that he would soon promulgate 'an ordinance concerning their wishes and requests for the immediate amelioration of their present condition'.[65]

When he returned to Russia after the Congress of Vienna, Alexander introduced a number of changes in the way Jewish matters were administered by his government. On 18 January 1817 he issued a decree transferring responsibility for all matters connected with the *kehilot*, except for legal issues, to the head of the Central Administration of the Religious Affairs of Foreign Creeds, a post which had been held from 1810 by Alexander's close associate Prince Aleksandr Golitsyn, who also held the office of director-general of the Most Holy Synod of the Russian Orthodox Church and who shared the tsar's growing religious mystical propensities. Later in 1817 a combined Ministry for Ecclesiastical Affairs and Public Instruction was established, which was also headed by Golitsyn, and the document setting it up stipulated that all 'Jewish matters which are now the

[64] Ibid. 357. [65] Ibid. 359.

responsibility of the senate and the ministers' would be handled by this new ministry.[66]

It was also decided to create a permanent advisory council of elected Jewish representatives which would be attached to the ministry. A delegation of Russian Jews was also granted an audience with Alexander at Bruchtal, in Baden, in 1814, where they were given assurances that the Jews would be better treated in future in the tsarist empire. After the war Sonnenberg and Dillon settled in St Petersburg, where they continued to advise the government. However, they were aware of their lack of legitimacy and appealed to the government to instruct the *kahal*s to elect delegates who could be consulted on matters affecting the Jewish community. This was accepted by the authorities, and in the instructions to the newly established ministry was appended a term requiring that 'the [names of the] deputies shall after their election be submitted by the Minister to His Majesty for ratification'.[67]

In autumn 1817 all the larger *kehilot* received instructions from provincial governors to choose an electoral college, which would be made up of two electors from every province. In August 1818 the twenty-two electors representing eleven provinces assembled in Vilna and elected in turn three delegates and three alternatives who were to be sent to St Petersburg. Apart from Sonnenberg and Dillon, Michael Eisenstadt, Benish Lapkovski, and Marcus Veitelson from the province of Vitebsk, and Samuel Epstein from the province of Vilna, were chosen. They were described as the Deputation of the Jewish People and continued to function until 1825. In March 1819, with Golitsyn's authorization, Sonnenberg informed local *kehilot* that this body was to be the sole avenue for complaints to the central authorities.[68] It did prove effective as a lobby and a means for transmitting the views of local Jewish communities to the central authorities, but the hopes of its members that they would be permanently consulted by the authorities were disappointed and in 1825 it was abolished by Golitsyn's successor as minister of public enlightenment, A. S. Shishkov.

The growing mystical inclinations of Alexander and Golitsyn manifested themselves in their hope that they would become the instruments of Divine Providence and accomplish the conversion of the Jews, something which Alexander had also discussed with Czartoryski. Golitsyn, as president of the Russian Bible Society, was eager to follow the course established by the body on which it was modelled, the Missionary Bible Society of London. On 25 March 1817 Alexander decreed the founding of a Society of Israelite Christians, whose goal would be to prepare Jews for conversion, whether to Russian Orthodoxy, Catholicism, or Lutheranism, and assist those who had already converted. Its preamble illustrates well the tone which now pervaded the tsarist government:

[66] On these developments, see Klier, *Russia Gathers her Jews*, 164–9.

[67] Dubnow, *History of the Jews in Russia and Poland*, i. 393.

[68] Pen, 'Deputatsiya evreiskogo naroda'.

We have learned of the difficult situation of those Jews who, having by Divine Grace perceived the light of the Christian truth, have embraced the same, or are making ready to join the flock of the good Shepherd and the Saviour of souls. These Jews, whom the Christian religion has severed from their brethren of the flesh, lose every means of contact with them, and not only have forfeited every claim of assistance, but are also exposed to all kinds of persecutions and oppressions on their part. Nor do they readily find shelter among Christians, their new brethren in the faith, to whom they are as yet unknown . . . For this reason, We, taking to heart the fate of the Jews converted to Christianity, and prompted by reverent obedience to the Voice of Bliss which calleth unto the scattered sheep of Israel to join the faith of Christ, have deemed it right to adopt measures for their welfare.[69]

Among the measures which were adopted were the granting of free Crown land, with the right to found all kinds of settlements. They were granted full equality, extensive communal self-government, and reductions in taxation. The colonies established were to be part of the Society of Israelite Christians, which was to be managed by a special committee to be set up in St Petersburg under the patronage of the emperor. One unexpected consequence of Alexander's conversionary zeal was that, having enlisted the support of Lewis Way of the London Bible Society, he was confronted by the latter's submission of a memorandum to the international congress which met in Aachen in autumn 1818 calling for the civil emancipation of the Jews of Russia, without which their conversion could not be accomplished. Alexander, like the other European sovereigns at the conference, failed to respond in any effective manner.[70]

Although a fair amount of land was made available for future 'Israelite Christians', very few converts in fact materialized, and in 1824 Golitsyn advised the tsar to dissolve the society which was to supervise their welfare. Alexander refused, and the body dragged on until 1833. A greater problem was caused by the resurgence of 'Judaizing' sects among the peasantry in the provinces of Voronezh, Saratov, and Tula, which called for a religion based on the Jewish Bible. The government took draconian measures to extirpate these groups. In 1823 the Council of Ministers resolved to conscript those of its members able to serve, and to deport the rest to Siberia. To discredit the movement, it was to be described as 'a Jewish [*zhidovskaya*] sect' and its members as actual Jews (*zhidy*).[71]

These years also saw the enactment of a number of restrictive anti-Jewish measures. In 1816 efforts were made to end the practice whereby Jews purchased crops in the fields from landowners on the understanding that they would be harvested by the landowners' serfs. Astrakhan and the Caucasus were removed from the Pale of Settlement. Jews were now forbidden in a decree of 22 April 1820 to employ Christian domestics because of their alleged propensity for proselytism. Jews were also barred from entering into leases in which, in return for a lump sum

[69] Dubnow, *History of the Jews in Russia and Poland*, i. 396.

[70] On Way, see ibid. 397–8; Kohler, 'Jewish Rights at the Congresses of Vienna (1814–1815) and Aix-La-Chapelle (1818)', and Parkes, 'Lewis Way and his Times'.

[71] Dubnow, *History of the Jews in Russia and Poland*, i. 402–3.

paid to the landowner, they were responsible for the gathering in and sale of the harvest. The recurrence in the early 1820s of famine conditions in Belarus led to renewed attempts to expel them from the villages and to forbid them from holding leases or managing inns in the countryside. Once again, in 1824 and 1825 perhaps 20,000 Jews were forced to leave their places of residence and give up their sources of livelihood before resettlement was halted. It was replaced by a proposal envisaging the expulsion of one-eighth of the Jewish population every year for eight years, a plan which was soon abandoned.[72]

On 1 May 1823 a new Committee for the Amelioration of the Jews was established, including the ministers of the interior, finance, justice, and ecclesiastical affairs and public enlightenment. Its functions were broadly defined as:

> to examine the enactments concerning Jews passed up to date and point out the way in which their presence in the country might be rendered more comfortable and useful and also what obligations they are to assume towards the government; in a word, to indicate all that may contribute towards the amelioration of the civil status of this people.[73]

In practice the objectives of the administration were considerably less benevolent, and one of its principal tasks remained to render the Jews 'harmless' to the population among whom they lived.

In an attempt to reduce smuggling, at the suggestion of the viceroy of the Kingdom of Poland, the grand duke Constantine, Jews not residing in towns were forbidden to live within 50 versts (about 30 miles) of the frontier, with the exception of those owning immovable property. Jews from neighbouring countries, especially the Habsburg empire, were forbidden to move to the tsarist empire.

CONCLUSION

Most of the far-reaching legislation introduced for the transformation of the Jewish community in the first half-century of Russian rule remained unimplemented. In this respect, the period came to be remembered widely in Jewish collective memory as a golden age in which the Jews were largely left alone and allowed to manage their own affairs. At the same time the basic tenets which were to dominate Jewish policy under Nicholas I and his successors were formulated in these years. They were characterized by a strong belief in the negative impact of the Jews on the surrounding population, summed up in the view that Jewish 'exploitation' was responsible for the miserable state of the peasantry. At the same time, while, in accordance with Enlightenment principles, Russian bureaucrats did accept that Jews could be transformed into useful subjects, they were also convinced that this would require substantial effort on the part of the government. Both these principles were at the root of the way in which the 'Jewish problem' was to be handled by Nicholas I over the next thirty years.

72 On these developments, see Gessen, *Istoriya evreiskogo naroda v Rossii*, i. 207–8.

73 Dubnow, *History of the Jews in Russia and Poland*, i. 408.

ELEVEN

NICHOLAS I AND THE JEWS OF RUSSIA, 1825–1855

You wrongly reproach me
For opposing union with you;
You yourselves are to blame
For the sinful rupture of fraternal ties . . .

I do not excuse my prejudices,
I am ready to improve myself,
But I recognize a hostile voice
No matter how sweet it sounds . . .

It is time to abandon these quarrels
And hateful words.
You should better turn
Your attention to my rights;
Then you yourselves will see
That I am in no way worse than you.

REUBEN KULISHER, 1849

NICHOLAS I AND THE JEWS

NICHOLAS I has an unenviable reputation. By most historians of Russia he is seen as unimaginative, chauvinist, militaristic, and repressive, a man whose reign was characterized by thirty years of stagnation, the gloom of which was only alleviated by a literary flowering which he did his best to suppress. According to one of them, his reign was the 'apogee of autocracy'.[1] In Jewish eyes, he was a man motivated by the most primitive anti-Judaism, and initiated the heartless conscription of Jewish children. In the words of the Yiddish folk song:

Az Nikolai Pavlovich iz keyzer gevorn
Zaynen yidishe hertser umetik gevorn.

When Nikolay Pavlovich became tsar,
Jewish hearts grew sad.

There is considerable truth in these judgements. According to Michael Stanislawski: 'To Nicholas, the Jews were an anarchic, cowardly, parasitic people, damned perpetually because of their deicide and heresy; they were best dealt with

[1] Presnyakov, *Apogei samoderzhaviya*. See also Riasanovsky, *Nicholas I and Official Nationality in Russia, 1825–1855*.

by repression, persecution, and, if possible, conversion.'[2] At the same time, Nicholas was in some ways the last of the enlightened despots. A leading scholar of the period, while conceding the all-pervasive étatism and bureaucratic centralization which characterized his rule, has also argued that this was a time of 'pre-reforms' which paved the way for the changes introduced by Alexander II.[3] Nicholas was determined to reorganize and systematize the administration of his empire and transform it into a 'properly governed state' of the sort desired by eighteenth-century enlightened autocrats.[4] His goal was to establish effective methods of state administration and control which would unify his multi-confessional and ethnically diverse empire. As a consequence, his reforms were characterized by the creation of new administrative agencies and the reform and centralization of existing ones. Through them he aimed to rebuild and control the state's infrastructure from above. Thus Pavel Kiselev, who from 1840 chaired the re-established Committee for the Reform of the Jews, in his capacity as minister of state domains from 1837 to 1856, embarked on a major attempt to transform the situation of the state peasantry (those directly subject to the tsar) by reforming the village infrastructure, building schools, which became known as Kiselev schools, encouraging the growth of agricultural productivity, and attempting to improve moral and religious life.[5]

Certainly it was in Nicholas's reign that the government began to intervene on a substantial scale in Jewish life, with the objective of 'moulding the Jews in ways consistent with the emperor's overall aims and ideology'[6] and turning them into loyal subjects of the tsar by establishing direct state supervision of the life and religious activity of the Jewish community and eliminating the traditional mediators between the state and the Jews. In carrying out this goal, however, Nicholas was forced to take into account some inescapable realities and also to convince his own civil servants. Some of them shared his views and preoccupations, but others, like Kiselev, were more pragmatic, and some, like Count Mikhail S. Vorontsov, governor-general of New Russia between 1823 and 1854, and Sergey S. Uvarov, minister of public enlightenment (education) between 1833 and 1849, who were influential in the middle years of Nicholas's reign, were reformers inspired by the ideas of the Enlightenment. Kiselev, in addition, had some connections with the territories of the Polish–Lithuanian Commonwealth through his marriage to Countess Sofia, the daughter of Stanisław Szczęsny Potocki, a prominent eighteenth-century pro-Russian politician who had been marshal of the Targowica Confederation[7] (see pp. 199–200 above).

Nicholas's reformist aspirations also gained some Jewish support. In her autobiography Pauline Wengeroff gives a favourable account of the 'beginning of the

[2] Stanislawski, *Tsar Nicholas and the Jews*, 10.
[3] On this, see Lincoln, *Nicholas I*.
[4] On this, see Ch. 10, n. 15.
[5] See Druzhinin, *Gosudarstvennye krest'yane i reforma P. D. Kiseleva*.
[6] Stanislawski, *Tsar Nicholas and the Jews*, p. xii.
[7] On Nicholas's ministers, see Lincoln, 'The Ministers of Nicholas I'.

era of enlightenment', referring to the 'great reforms under Tsar Nicholas I [that] brought about the spiritual, yes, even the physical regeneration of the Jews in Lithuania'. In her words:

whoever, like me, lived between the years 1838 and today, took part in all the religious battles in the family life of Lithuanian Jewry and finally observed the great progress made, must express his admiration for the idea of that reform legislation and bless it. Indeed, you must speak of it enthusiastically if you compare the generally uncultivated, poor Jews of the 'forties with Lithuanian Jewry of the 'sixties and 'seventies, among whom today there are so many men of such perfect European refinement, who have outstanding accomplishments in the most diverse fields of literature, science and art, and who do not lack honours and titles from the outside world.[8]

THE FIRST YEARS OF NICHOLAS'S REIGN

One of Nicholas's first acts as emperor was to reappoint the Jewish Committee which had been established by Alexander with instructions to review and codify all legislation in effect regarding the Jews. The legal position of the Jews at the beginning of his reign was certainly marked by many contradictions. As a result of the legislative changes in their situation since 1772, all Jews were both members of an estate—merchants, townspeople, or farmers—and at the same time still subject to a *kehilah* which retained significant powers in spite of the attempts to undermine its influence. The executive agency of the *kehilah*, the *kahal*, was responsible to the local police and treasury officials, who were, in turn, responsible to the governor of the province.

According to the terms of Alexander's statute of 1804, Jews were considered subjects of the tsarist empire, with the right to own land, except for estates settled with peasants. However, their right to reside in the countryside in any capacity other than as farmers was to be ended, although practical considerations meant that this had never been implemented. Their children were to be allowed to attend Russian government schools or specific Jewish schools, and they were free to engage in any form of trade and commerce except for the production and sale of liquor, another area where theory and practice diverged. They could enrol in artisan guilds, and participate, subject to some restrictions, in the institutions of urban self-government.

The principal body in the central government responsible for dealing with Jewish issues was the rapidly growing Ministry of the Interior, where such matters were the responsibility of the 'fourth section' of the Department of Spiritual Affairs for Foreign Confessions, which was created on 8 February 1832 from an earlier institution, the Chief Administration of Spiritual Affairs of Foreign Faiths. It was made up of three divisions: the first handled Catholic affairs; the second

[8] Wengeroff, *Memoiren einer Grossmutter*, i. 118.

Protestants and non-Christians, including Muslims, Jews, Buddhists, and others; the third, cases brought before the senate and other ministries.[9]

When Nicholas promulgated a new Statute on the Jews in 1835, an order of the senate laid down that those matters concerning Jews 'which by their nature require the decisions of that ministry' be referred to the Ministry of the Interior as a whole, while the Department of Spiritual Affairs for Foreign Confessions was to be responsible for strictly religious concerns. However, other ministries also retained some responsibilities concerning the Jews.

In addition to the Jewish Committee, Nicholas instructed the Committee for the Western Provinces to examine the position of the Jews and propose any reforms that it considered appropriate. Later, in 1840, he convened a new Jewish Committee, now renamed the Committee for Reorganizing the Jews, under the chairmanship of Pavel Kiselev, which continued into the reign of Alexander II. The members of these committees were typical tsarist bureaucrats, recruited from the landed aristocracy and educated in the elite schools of St Petersburg. They were also almost all members of the State Council which, in its General Assembly and Department of Laws, frequently discussed and elaborated policy on the Jews and was responsible for the initiation of legislation. Some sat on the Committee of Ministers, which also dealt with Jewish issues, although it declined in significance during Nicholas's reign.

Given the multiplicity of influences affecting Jewish policy, it is perhaps not surprising that it was not wholly consistent. The first major measure promulgated by the tsar, the imposition of military conscription on the Jews, reflected his own militarism. As we have seen, the induction of Jews into the army, whether in revolutionary France, in Austria under Joseph II, in Prussia after 1811, or in the Kingdom of Poland during the revolution of 1830, was part of the process of transforming them into citizens. This was not the case in Russia. Here, as Stanislawski has pointed out, military service was not 'a duty borne equally by all citizens in exchange for the protection of the state and its laws but a burden selectively imposed by the government for social and economic reasons'.[10] This had the paradoxical consequence that, whereas Russia was the first country to introduce compulsory military service, it was one of the last to implement universal conscription. In Stanislawski's words:

> Until 1874, each category of Russian subjects was liable to a different set of military regulations. The nobility after 1762, and the clergy were exempt from any compulsory service; the guild merchants were permitted to pay a special tax in lieu of personal service, the peasants were drafted not personally but by commune, at the discretion of their landlord.[11]

Jews had initially been exempt from military service after the incorporation into the empire of the areas where they lived. They were all classed as merchants

[9] On the bureaucratic structure, see *Gosudarstvennost' Rossii*.
[10] Stanislawski, *Tsar Nicholas and the Jews*, 13. [11] Ibid. 14.

from the point of view of conscription and were required to pay a 500-rouble exemption tax. There were occasional discussions over whether they should be drafted, but they were generally felt to be unsuitable as recruits. This was not the view of Nicholas. He was a convinced believer in the value of the army as a school for virtue. He summed up his view of the army as follows:

> Here there is order . . . All things logically flow from one another. No one commands without first learning to obey. No one rises above anyone else except through a clearly defined system. Everything is subordinated to a single, defined goal and everything has its precise designations. That is why I shall always hold the title of soldier in high esteem. I regard all human life as being nothing more than service because everyone must serve.[12]

In the words of an astute observer, Astolphe de Custine, writing in 1839, 'The government of Russia is camp discipline substituted for the order of the city, a state of emergency transformed into the normal state of society.'[13] It was axiomatic to Nicholas that most of the ills of Jewish society could be cured by forcing its young men to spend a period in the army. This would also make them much more responsive to conversionary initiatives. Some of his advisers had doubts. The Jewish Committee attempted by delay to frustrate such an initiative, and a similar attempt may also have been made by Nikolay Novosiltsev, the principal adviser to the viceroy of the Kingdom of Poland, the grand duke Constantine.

Nicholas was not to be baulked in a matter which was so important to him; he had his own chief of staff draft the legislation, which was promulgated on 26 August 1827.[14] It did not stipulate a specific Jewish quota. (The common claim that the Jewish quota was double the norm is incorrect.) The quota varied from year to year, but generally the Jews were required to furnish four to eight recruits for every 1,000 tax souls. This increased somewhat in the last four years of Nicholas's reign because of the Crimean War. Jews were inducted into the army between the ages of 12 and 25. Those over 18 served for twenty-five years in the regular army; those under 18 served in special cantonist battalions (a 'canton' is an army camp) until they reached the age of 18, when they commenced their twenty-five-year service. Cantonist battalions had existed for other categories of recruit, such as criminals and vagabonds under 18, or the minor sons of Polish and Ukrainian nobles who had participated in the uprising of 1830. Those who served in them were educated in special boarding schools attached to army camps which had first been created in 1805 for the sons of Russian private soldiers.

Some categories of Jews were exempt, among them rabbis, members of the merchant estate, and those who had completed courses in state-sponsored

[12] Cited in Presnyakov, *Apogei samoderzhaviya*, 1.

[13] Marquis de Custine, *La Russie en 1839*, i. 50.

[14] *PSZ* 2/ii, no. 1329. Laws dealing with Jews are also cited in V. O. Levanda, *Polnyi khronologicheskii sbornik zakonov i polozhenii, kasayushchikhsya evreev* (hereafter Levanda).

educational institutions. Those living on Jewish agricultural colonies and, later, pupils in government-run Jewish schools or rabbinical seminaries were also excluded. As was the case with all groups liable to the draft, the local community was collectively responsible for its implementation and it was to be supervised by specially elected members of the *kehilah*. Jews were to enjoy religious freedoms while serving, but were to be billeted only in Christian homes during their travels, and were forbidden contact with local Jews. Jews who completed their military term were eligible to serve in the civil service.

This was a punitive law and had none of the compensatory elements which made military service acceptable in the West. Its introduction was the cause of appalling suffering and of major disruption to Jewish life. In all, in the reign of Nicholas I, around 70,000 Jews served in the Russian army. According to the figures of the Ministry of the Interior (which may not have been complete), the Jewish population of the Pale of Settlement in 1849 was 1,041,000 (out of a total of 16,697,000).[15] Figures for 1865 from the same source give 1,430,643 Jews in the Pale of Settlement (out of 18,222,538).[16] In all, between 4.5 and 6.5 per cent of Jews there were affected by the draft.

One reason why service in the army was so hated by the large majority of the Jewish community was that the provision for religious freedom was disregarded and, as implied above, conversion was openly encouraged. The conversion rate was personally supervised by Nicholas, who expressed dissatisfaction that more was not achieved. We do not know how many Jews in Nicholas's army finally converted, but Stanislawski estimated that at least half of the cantonists, who numbered around 50,000, and a substantial number of adult recruits did so between 1827 and 1854.[17] In the years 1842 and 1843 over 2,250 Jewish soldiers were converted. Although more recent studies, which have made use of the Russian archives now available, have shown that some efforts were made to satisfy the religious needs of adult Jewish recruits, and that local factors rather than central government policy were critical in the pressure on them to convert, this new material has not significantly undermined the view that cantonists were subject to enormous pressures, both moral and physical, to adopt Russian Orthodoxy.[18]

Another matter which caused great bitterness was the fact that the majority of the recruits were minors. This was primarily the result not of government policy but of the way in which the *kehilah* leadership implemented the law. Since most Jews married very young, most 18-year-olds were married (on this, see Volume II, Chapter 9). Given the choice between conscripting fathers or children, the communal leadership opted for the latter. Since Jewish births were not systematically registered, a substantial number of the recruits were younger than the minimum

[15] Gessen, *Istoriya evreiskogo naroda v Rossii*, ii. 102.

[16] *PSZ* 2/xxv, no. 24298.

[17] Stanislawski, *Tsar Nicholas and the Jews*, 25.

[18] On this, see Petrovsky-Shtern, 'Jews in the Russian Army'.

age. The appalling consequences of this have been described by Herzen, who in 1835, when he was exiled to Vyatka, encountered a group of Jewish cantonists:

They brought the children and formed them into regular ranks: it was one of the most awful sights I have ever seen, those poor, poor children! Boys of twelve or thirteen might somehow have survived it, but little fellows of eight and ten . . . Not even a brush full of black paint could put such horror on canvas.

Pale, exhausted, with frightened faces, they stood in thick, clumsy, soldiers' overcoats, with stand-up collars, fixing helpless, pitiful eyes on the garrison soldiers who were roughly getting them into ranks. The white lips, the blue rings under their eyes, bore witness to fever or chill. And these sick children, without care or kindness, exposed to the raw wind that blows unobstructed from the Arctic Ocean, were going to their graves.[19]

The *kehilah* leadership also tended to select recruits from the weakest and most defenceless sections of the community. Indeed, this was encouraged by the government as a means of social control, since the *kahal* could recruit anyone who did not pay taxes or who could be held guilty of any sort of anti-social behaviour. In addition, because of resistance to the draft, the *kehilah* leadership often found itself obliged to hire special officials (graphically named *khapper*s—grabbers) to enforce the draft.

The involvement of the communal leadership in enforcement of the draft caused enormous shock, undermining deep-rooted traditions of social solidarity. The Hebrew writer Buki b. Yogli (pseudonym of Judah Leib Katzenelson, 1846–1917) has described his grandmother's response to the *khapper*s. She was convinced that such oppressors could only be Philistines or Amalekites. But she soon discovered that this was not the case:

No, my child, to our great horror, all *khapper*s were in fact Jews, Jews with beards and side-locks. And that is indeed our greatest problem. We Jews are accustomed to attacks, libels, and evil decrees from the non-Jews—such have happened from time immemorial and such is our lot in Exile. In the past, there were gentiles who held a cross in one hand and a knife in the other, and said: 'Jew, kiss the cross or die', and Jews preferred death to apostasy. But now there come Jews, religious Jews, who capture children and send them off to apostasy. Such a punishment was not even listed in the Bible's list of the most horrible curses. Jews spill the blood of their brothers, and God is silent, the rabbis are silent . . .[20]

The involvement of the *kehilah* in conscription precipitated a breakdown of communal solidarity which manifested itself in a number of ways, including violent protests against the *khapper*s and the *kahal*, denunciations to the government, and attempts to leave the community. Thus, in Minsk a poor widow whose son had been seized by *khapper*s adopted the traditional method of protest and attempted to prevent the Torah from being removed from the ark during the sabbath service. When her protest proved unavailing, she burst out: 'Lord of the Universe! You took pride in the Patriarch Abraham who agreed to sacrifice his

[19] Herzen, *My Past and Thoughts*, 170.

[20] Buki b. Yogli [Katzenelson], *What my Eyes Saw and my Ears Heard* (Heb.), 14.

son. Order me to kill my son, and I will do so. But you could hardly have obtained Abraham's permission for the conversion of his son!'[21]

Jews rarely attempted to attack recruiting columns to liberate children. They knew only too well the repressive character of the tsarist government. They turned their anger rather against the *kahal* and its servants, the *khappers*. In his memoirs Yekhezkel Kotik has described attempts to resist the latter:

> When they heard the police knocking at the door, the family was seized by mortal terror. Occasionally they even resisted the kidnappers with axes, knives, iron bars, and hammers prepared in advance, and as soon as the kidnappers entered the house, all the members of the family attacked them with murderous blows. Both sides fought until their strength gave out, and victory went to the one that held out longest. Naturally that was usually the kidnappers.[22]

Anti-*kehilah* rioting took place in the autumn of 1827 in Bershad in Podolia, and subsequently in Starokonstantinov in Volhynia and in Minsk. These actions were sometimes encouraged by religious leaders. When conscription was intensified in the early 1850s, Rabbi Elijah Shik of Grodno attacked the communal leadership's complicity in government oppression:

> [He] called on everyone to revolt against the heads of the community, and to tear the kahal building to shreds . . . With an axe in his hands, he ran in front of the crowd that had gathered, each man armed with an axe; before they were stopped, they had broken the iron bolts on the door of the kahal building and freed the three prisoners incarcerated there.[23]

The government could have chosen no more effective method of breaking the influence of the *kehilah* in Jewish life and undermining communal solidarity, as was probably its intention.

During the first decade of his rule Nicholas introduced few other changes to the policies towards the Jews which had been laid down by his predecessors. It was only on 13 April 1835 that the attempt of the Jewish Committee to systematize the legislation on the Jews led to the promulgation of a statute on the Jews. It formally established the borders of the Pale of Settlement (see Map 8), which were to remain until the First World War. Within this area the forced resettlement of the Jews from the countryside was ended, and Jews had the right to buy, work, or lease land, with the exception of settled estates, gentry properties on which Christian serfs lived and worked. They were also given the right to live on such land and to establish factories there. In addition, Jews were given permission to lease rural enterprises such as taverns, inns, or mills.

Jews could reside outside the area of the Pale of Settlement through the acquisition of an inheritance, in order to secure rights at courts in the interior, by studying at academic institutions, and in some commercial affairs. First-guild

21 Quoted in Stanislawski, *Tsar Nicholas and the Jews*, 128.

22 Kotik, *Journey to a Nineteenth-Century Shtetl*, 237–8.

23 Quoted in Stanislawski, *Tsar Nicholas and the Jews*, 129.

merchants (those paying the most tax) were permitted to travel to both capitals and to seaports and to reside in Moscow for periods of up to six months. In terms of this statute the Jews, like other 'Eastern' peoples, though subjects of the empire, were defined as aliens (*inorodtsy*) because of their separate way of life and allegedly lower level of civilization.[24] Some attempts, not for the most part implemented, were made to ensure Jewish participation in municipal self-government in the Pale. Most other aspects of the 1804 statute were retained, including the farming of taxes. The power, authority, and obligations of the *kehilot* were kept intact, although efforts were made to reorganize the *korobka*, the kosher meat tax, their most important source of revenue.

Attempts were also made to systematize the censorship of Jewish books. One of the first acts of Nicholas after his accession and following the unsuccessful Decembrist revolt was to tighten censorship in a new code of June 1826. It included a provision that one member of the Vilna Censorship Committee should be able to read Yiddish and Hebrew.[25] In October 1836 the minister of the interior, Dmitry Bludov, spurred on by maskilic denunciations of the burgeoning hasidic literature, introduced a new censorship law for books printed using Hebrew characters.[26] All books in Jewish possession published without censorship or imported without permission were to be presented within a year to the local police for examination by a special commission of rabbis which was to report those which were objectionable to the Ministry of the Interior. It would henceforth be illegal to possess any uncensored work. In addition, all presses using Hebrew type were to be shut down with the exception of two, one in Vilna and another in Kiev, which was subsequently moved to Zhitomir, and their publications were to be vetted by specially appointed censors.[27] In fact, so many books were submitted to the police that the proposed vetting could not take place, and subsequent years saw a further expansion of the production of books in Hebrew and Yiddish, as a result of which this form of censorship was no more effective than the other attempts of the tsarist government to control publications, yet another example of the ineffectiveness of tsarist censorship.

PAVEL KISELEV, SERGEY UVAROV, AND THE REFORM OF THE JEWS

The need in the aftermath of the Polish uprising of 1830 to consolidate the government's hold over the former Polish provinces, and the recurrence of famine there in the late 1830s, led Nicholas to undertake a new initiative in relation to the

[24] On this, see Slocum, 'Who, and When, Were the *Inorodtsy*?'

[25] *PSZ* 2/i, no. 403.

[26] For examples of the maskilic denunciations, see Ginzburg, *Historical Writings* (Yid.), i. 50–3, and in Zinberg, *A History of Jewish Literature*, vol. x. One of these denunciations came from Isaac Baer Levinsohn and is reprinted in his *Shorshei halevanon*, 295. There is also an important anonymous article on this topic, 'Tzenzura v tsarstvovanii Nikolaya I'.

[27] *PSZ* 2/xi, no. 9649.

Jews. He requested Pavel Kiselev to review what had been done in the area and to report whether changes were necessary. Kiselev was a pragmatist with some sympathy for the views of the Enlightenment and particularly admired the way Napoleon had dealt with the Jewish issue. He was also much struck by the transformation of the Jews in Germany, telling the maskil Max Lilienthal (1815–82): 'Believe me, if we had such Jews as I met in the different capitals of Germany, we would treat them with the utmost distinction, but our Jews are entirely different.'[28]

Kiselev set out his views in a memorandum which he submitted to the emperor in 1840 entitled 'On the Ordering of the Jewish Nation in Russia'.[29] It started by repeating the usual clichés on why it was so difficult to deal with the Jews: the religious teachings of the Talmud preserved their isolation and sense of superiority, the *kahal* acted as a sort of dictatorship within the Jewish community, which was entrenched as a result of the way the kosher meat tax was collected, while the special dress which the Jews wore underlined their separateness from the rest of the population.

Kiselev then adopted a radically new tack. There was no point in repressing the Jews since they were well acquainted with persecution and it only strengthened their distinctive characteristics. One should rely rather 'on the example of other states . . . [and] begin the fundamental transformation of this nation . . . [by] the removal of those harmful factors that obstruct its path to the general civil order'. This was to be achieved by the moral and religious re-education of the Jews and the abolition of those legal impediments to the 'rapprochement' (*sblizhenie*) of the Jews with the rest of the population. A network of schools for Jewish children should be set up in which particular emphasis would be placed on the teaching of the Russian language and history and which would also inculcate loyalty to the state and the importance of taking up 'useful' occupations. All rabbis should be certified by the new schools, and provincial rabbis appointed throughout the Pale. Separate Jewish dress should be forbidden. Finally, the government should abolish the *kahal* and the kosher meat tax.

Kiselev recognized that these changes would obviously require time to allow the emergence of a new generation of Westernized and enlightened Jews. He was therefore prepared, in order to accelerate the 'productivization' of the Jews, to have recourse to those very police measures whose inefficacy he had acknowledged. Jews were to be divided into 'productive' and 'non-productive', and be given five years to establish their usefulness, either by proving stable residence through the ownership of property or by becoming artisans, farmers, or guild merchants. Those who did not establish themselves as 'productive' would be liable to conscription and forcible retraining.

[28] Quoted in Dubnow, *History of the Jews in Russia and Poland*, ii. 45.

[29] The memorandum was published by Dubnow in 'Istoricheskie soobshcheniya', although he fails to attribute it to Kiselev, which was established by Gessen, *Istoriya evreiskogo naroda v Rossii*, ii. 78.

For all its coercive elements, this was a very different approach from that inherent in the introduction of conscription, although these dissonances do not seem to have been perceived by Kiselev or, indeed, by anyone in the imperial circle. Nicholas duly approved the proposals and established a Committee for Reorganizing the Jews (Komitet dlya opredeleniya mer korennogo preobrazovaniya evreev v Rossii), which became popularly known as the Jewish Committee, headed by Kiselev himself and made up of a number of leading Russian bureaucrats in St Petersburg including Sergey Uvarov, the minister of public enlightenment, to consider how to achieve 'a complete transformation of Jewish life'.[30] In the early 1840s the committee obtained the approval of Nicholas for a series of measures with this aim. These included the establishment of state-sponsored Jewish schools, the abolition of the *kahal* and the reorganization of the tax on kosher meat, the creation of a nationwide Rabbinic Commission, the strengthening of the position of the official or Crown rabbinate, and the imposition of 'order' on what was seen as the chaotic state of Jewish marriage law. The Jews would be rendered more productive by encouragement of their settlement on state lands and by division of their economic activities into useful and non-useful categories, while their integration into the wider society would be facilitated by the abolition of traditional Jewish dress.

These were radical measures and Kiselev was well aware that they were likely to arouse opposition from the majority of Jews in the Pale of Settlement. In a circular which he issued to provincial governors-general about his objectives in April 1845, he stated: 'All the regulations alluded to have been issued and will be issued separately, in order to conceal their interrelation and common aim from the fanaticism of the Jews. For this reason, his Imperial Majesty has been graciously pleased to command me to communicate all the said plans to the Governors-General confidentially.'[31]

The first major initiative to be put into practice was the establishment of a network of state-sponsored Jewish schools. This led to the development of the de facto alliance between the maskilim and the tsarist government already noted. When Nicholas ascended the throne in 1825, supporters of the Haskalah had been an insignificant minority in the areas directly annexed into the empire from Poland. There was, in addition, a larger group within the mitnagedim who were not hostile to the study of secular subjects, provided this could be introduced within the framework of normative Judaism. Their views also converged with those of the maskilim as regards their belief in the need for change in Jewish educational practice, calling for more emphasis on the study of Hebrew and the Bible in addition to the Talmud, scepticism of the hair-splitting interpretative technique of *pilpul*, and a willingness to accept foreign languages and secular subjects into the school curriculum.

[30] Quoted in Dubnow, 'Istoricheskie soobshcheniya', 3.

[31] Dubnow, *History of the Jews in Russia and Poland*, ii. 66.

At this stage the Russian government, unlike those in Prussia, Austria, and the Kingdom of Poland, did not distinguish between the maskilim and the rest of Jewish society. Thus in 1836 Dmitry Bludov, the minister of the interior, when asked by the maskilim to counteract the spread of hasidism by exercising some control over the large mass of hasidic devotional and hagiographic literature, explained to Uvarov that he could see no difference between the hasidim and their opponents—they were all fanatical, ignorant Jews.[32] The result of this was Bludov's placing the more stringent censorship of books in Hebrew and Yiddish in the hands of a special commission of rabbis, much to the chagrin of the maskilim.

This did not undermine the conviction of the leaders of traditional society, generalizing from what had occurred elsewhere in the Polish lands, that the maskilim had an especially privileged relationship with the authorities. Thus, when Rabbi Nahman b. Simhah of Bratslav (1772–1810), who was much preoccupied by the threat to normative belief of rationalism and the ideas of the Enlightenment, met three maskilim in Uman in 1810, the account given by his followers included the observation that 'these heretics were important men close to the government'.[33] The perception by the leaders of Jewish traditional society of close links between the maskilim and the government was intensified when one of them, Isaac Baer Levinsohn (1788–1860), a maskil who had spent time in Brody and Tarnopol and became friendly with leading Galician maskilim, was able to obtain a subsidy from the Jewish Committee in 1828 to publish his book *Te'udah beyisra'el* (Education in Israel). This book expressed the basic ideology of the Haskalah, calling for reform of the teaching of Hebrew, the introduction of secular subjects into the Jewish educational system, and the 'productivization' of Jewish economic life. This subsidy was not the result of any conscious decision by the government to support the maskilim, and a request by Levinsohn for a second subsidy in 1836 was refused.[34] Nevertheless, it greatly increased the prestige both of the Haskalah in general and of Levinsohn in particular. In a letter to him, written in 1834, the Vilna scholar Mathias Strashun wrote:

From the day that your book appeared, I read it from beginning to end and could not put it down. I read it twice and thrice and could not have my fill: I wished that I were a dove, that I could fly to you, to be with you and embrace you, to be your dutiful servant for ever. . . . Your book alone made me into a man.[35]

Another maskil, Abraham Baer Gottlober (1810–99), described the book as follows:

The book appeared at a propitious time and became very popular, its readership increasing from day to day. Countless young people began to study Hebrew systematically, and also Russian. They were courageous and unafraid of the fanatics who tried to hinder them.[36]

[32] Correspondence between Uvarov and Bludov in the Hebrew University, Rivkind Archive, Saul Ginsburg Material, file 22/3, no. 2, items i–v, quoted in Stanislawski, *Tsar Nicholas and the Jews*, 41.

[33] Stanislawski, *Tsar Nicholas and the Jews*, 52.

[34] Ibid. 52–3, 58.

[35] Quoted in Nathanson, *A Book of Remembrance* (Heb.), 49.

[36] Gottlober, 'Memoirs' (Yid.), quoted in Dawidowicz (ed.), *The Golden Tradition*, 117.

Small circles of maskilim now began to establish themselves in Vilna, Berdichev, and elsewhere. The developing grain port of Odessa, on the Black Sea, became another centre of enlightened views. There a community of grain dealers from the Galician town of Brody had brought with them the maskilic ideas they had imbibed in their native town. They came to a town without an established Jewish community and were able to create one based on the Haskalah. Odessa became notorious within the Pale for religious laxity. In the words of a Yiddish proverb, 'The fires of hell burn around Odessa up to a distance of fifty versts.' (For more detail on developments in Odessa, see Volume II, Chapter 6.)

The maskilim were still a small and largely insignificant minority within the Jewish community. By 1840 they had managed to publish only eleven original works, five translations, and a handful of poems.[37] They had been able, however, to set up some schools in which they implemented their educational ideas. Of these the most important was that established in Odessa in 1826. Under its able and energetic director, the Galician maskil Bezalel Stern, the school flourished. By 1835 it had 289 pupils, while its sister girls' school created in the same year had sixty. Its curriculum followed those of the reformed Jewish schools in Galicia, with the addition of Russian. It comprised Hebrew grammar and composition; the Bible with Mendelssohn's translation and commentary; selected tractates of the Talmud; Jewish moralistic literature; German, French, and Russian language and literature; mathematics; physics; rhetoric; Russian and world history; geography; calligraphy; and mercantile law.[38]

In 1838 Stern was able to help in establishing a similar school in Kishinev (today Chişinău) in Bessarabia, which had come under Russian rule in 1812. The attempt to create a reformed school in Uman was prevented by the local authorities concerned about the reaction of the traditional majority of the Jewish community there. Finally, in 1838, the small Germanized community in the town of Riga received permission from the Ministry of Public Enlightenment to invite the German Jewish rabbi Max Lilienthal, now 23 years old, from Munich to establish a modern Jewish school there.

The emergence of these schools convinced Kiselev and his committee that the government could use education to remould the Jewish community. The key role in the implementation of this new policy was entrusted to Sergey Uvarov, the minister of public enlightenment. Uvarov was a typical Europeanized Russian aristocratic bureaucrat of his generation. He was a supporter of the moderate Enlightenment of the eighteenth century, but was also strongly under the influence of the conservative Romanticism of post-1815 Europe, taking as his mentors Jean-Victor Moreau, Karl vom Stein, and Charles André Pozzo di Borgo. It was he who in a report to the tsar in 1833 had claimed that education must be conducted 'with faith in the . . . principles of orthodoxy, autocracy, and nationality'. Although this phrase was to become the catchword of reactionary politicians in

[37] Stanislawski, *Tsar Nicholas and the Jews*, 58. [38] Ibid.

the later nineteenth century, Uvarov understood it very differently, arguing that for a political system to function effectively it had to take into account the religion, patriotic feelings, and national honour of the nation in which it operated.[39]

In his general educational policy Uvarov sought to blend European civilization with the Russian spirit, 'to efface for ever any antagonism between European enlightenment and the needs of our situation'.[40] As regards the Jews, he believed they could be transformed and saw the goal of educational policy towards them as 'their gradual rapprochement with the Christian population and the eradication of the superstitions and harmful prejudices instilled by the study of the Talmud'.[41] In a report he delivered to Nicholas on 17 March 1841 entitled 'On the Transformation of the Jews and on the Opinion on this Subject Abroad', he claimed, on the basis of his contacts with 'educated Jews in Germany' and those running the reformed schools in Russia, that 'the best Jews' accepted that study of the Talmud was only necessary for the training of rabbis. Other Jews should instead study the Bible and Judaism's ethical and moral teaching. In this way one could counter what he regarded as the 'negative influence of the Talmud'.[42]

Uvarov set out his aims in a memorandum, 'On the Education of the Jews',[43] in which he argued that although the goal was the reduction of the deleterious effect of the Talmud, this should be kept secret. Describing the reaction of traditional Jewish society to the success of the schools in Odessa, Kishinev, and Riga he observed:

> the Jewish elders say: 'These schools are fine, their spirit is pure Jewish, but learning leads to Christianity.' In the language of these inveterate adherents of Jewish prejudices and superstitions, these words mean: 'The teaching in the newly established schools may slowly destroy in the Jews the fanaticism of separation and introduce them to the general principle of civic patriotism [*grazhdanstvennost'*].' In this they are not mistaken, for is not the religion of the Cross the purest symbol of universal civility?[44]

The similarity of his views to those of Czartoryski in 1817 is obvious. They also reveal the deep-rooted mismatch in the alliance between the maskilim and the authorities. What the maskilim envisaged was a much less far-reaching transformation of Jewish life, which would not involve all-out confrontation with traditional Jewish society. The failure of the maskilim to go along with such a transformation inevitably led to accusations of bad faith by the Russian officials

[39] He set out these views in an account of why Napoleon had failed: Uvarov, *L'Empereur Alexandre et Buonaparte*. This issue is fully discussed in Riasanovsky, *Nicholas I and Official Nationality in Russia, 1825–1855*.

[40] Uvarov, *Extrait du compte-rendu du Ministère de l'instruction publique pour l'année 1837*, 27.

[41] *Sbornik postanovlenii po Ministerstvu narodnogo prosveshcheniya* (St Petersburg, 1876), ii, sect. 2, 521, quoted in Stanislawski, *Tsar Nicholas and the Jews*, 67.

[42] *Sbornik postanovlenii po Ministerstvu narodnogo prosveshcheniya*, ii, sect. 2, 227–43, quoted in Stanislawski, *Tsar Nicholas and the Jews*, 65–6.

[43] Memorandum on the Education of the Jews, quoted in Stanislawski, *Tsar Nicholas and the Jews*, 66–7.

[44] Ibid.

with whom they dealt, while at the same time the suspicion on the part of most Jews that the goal of the authorities was merely conversion under another name undermined the credibility of the maskilim in Jewish society as a whole. As in so many areas of Jewish life, the ill-informed and far-reaching interventions of Russian officialdom destroyed the stability of traditional Jewish society. Given the absence of any real possibility of integration or of finding an appropriate place for a transformed Jewish society in the tsarist empire, it created ultimately not stability, but disruption and radicalization.

This was all still in the future. For the moment, Uvarov was preoccupied with his task of setting up a network of reformed Jewish schools to achieve his goal of the transformation of the next generation of Jews. However, his attempt to introduce committees of local bureaucrats and Jewish figures to implement the reform was frustrated by Jewish passive resistance. This led him to take a step which displayed his poor political judgement and his contempt for Jewish public opinion. In January 1841 he summoned Max Lilienthal to St Petersburg to discuss how to use German Jews to implement his reform. Lilienthal obtained the support of many leading figures in Germany and Italy for this project. He was, however, a disastrous choice for the important task that had been entrusted to him. He was young and inexperienced, knew no Russian, and his only contact with Russian conditions had been in the Baltic city of Riga, which was quite untypical. (On developments in Riga, see Volume II, Chapter 6.)

Lilienthal's attempt to persuade the Jewish communities of Vilna and Minsk that the new schools were not intended to undermine traditional Jewish belief ended in total failure. Convinced that a voluntary implementation of the reform was impossible, he persuaded Uvarov that Jewish education should be placed under the control of the Ministry of Public Enlightenment. A rabbinical synod on the model of Napoleon's Sanhedrin should be convoked, which would give Jewish approval for the changes envisaged.

On 22 June 1842 Nicholas gave his approval to this law. All Jewish schools, including the *ḥeder*s and the yeshivas as well as 'any others of whatever sort in which Jews either study the interpretations of their Law and Scripture, or teach children', were placed under the supervision of the Ministry of Public Enlightenment. In order to achieve the 'swift implementation of the goals of the government', a commission, to be entitled the Imperial Commission for the Education of the Jews of Russia and composed of four rabbis, one from each of the areas in which the Jews lived, would be convened in St Petersburg.[45]

Lilienthal was now sent round the Pale to select suitable members for the commission. Since he clearly enjoyed the support of the authorities, he was given a respectful hearing in the various Jewish communities and was welcomed in Odessa, Berdichev, and Kishinev. He even obtained qualified approval for the reform from Rabbi Isaac b. Hayim, son of the founder of the Volozhin yeshiva,

[45] *PSZ* 2/xvii, no. 15771.

who agreed to serve on the commission. So too did the Lubavitcher Rebbe, Menahem Mendel Schneersohn (the grandson of Shneur Zalman of Lyady, 1789–1866), but he only took part in order to make plain his opposition to what was being proposed. Its other members were Jacob Joseph Halpern, a wealthy Jewish financier from Berdichev with traditional views, Bezalel Stern, the Galician maskil who was director of the Odessa Jewish school, Lilienthal himself, as well as Uvarov and some of his civil servants.

The commission met in St Petersburg between 6 May and 27 August 1843. The hostility of the traditional Jewish members of the commission to what was envisaged was quickly revealed, while the alliance between the government and the maskilim was cemented. On 13 November 1844 the government finally promulgated its law On Establishing Special Schools for the Education of Jewish Youth. In the accompanying circular it was explained that 'the goal of the education of the Jews consists in their gradual rapprochement with the Christian population, and in the eradication of the superstitions and harmful prejudices instilled by the study of the Talmud'.[46] The law itself, while still permitting Jewish children to attend Christian schools and universities, established a network of Jewish primary schools, which were to correspond to the Christian parish schools, and secondary schools, as well as two rabbinic schools, which, like the Warsaw Rabbinic School, would train rabbis and Jewish teachers (on these, see below, in this chapter, pp. 376–8). Students who attended the Jewish secondary schools and the rabbinic schools would effectively be exempt from the draft. The ministry would collect the funds necessary for establishing the schools by imposing a new Jewish tax on sabbath candles. At the same time private Jewish schools and home tutoring would now fall under the remit of the Ministry of Public Enlightenment.

Lilienthal did not remain long in Russia to supervise the implementation of this reform, departing in mid-1845 first for his native Bavaria and then for the United States. His departure was caused partly by the opposition of his wife's family to her moving to Russia, but perhaps more by his realization that he had alienated not only traditional opinion but most of the maskilim. Bezalel Stern, in particular, was convinced from his experience in both Galicia and Odessa that only slow and moderate reform which carried the community with it could succeed.

Nevertheless, the state-sponsored Jewish school system expanded rapidly. By 1855 seventy-one schools had been established. There is some dispute about the numbers of students enrolled, which range in different sources between 3,363 and 3,708. This should be compared with the estimate of the Jewish Committee that the Jewish private school system, mostly composed of traditional *ḥeder*s and yeshivas, was made up of 5,361 institutions with 10,861 teachers and 69,464 students.[47] The schools attempted to combine general and Jewish instruction,

[46] *PSZ* 2/xix, no. 18240.

[47] A. Beletsky, *Vopros ob obrazovanii russkikh evreev v tsarstvovanie Imperatora Nikolaya I* (St Petersburg, 1894), 90, 147, quoted in Klier, *Imperial Russia's Jewish Question, 1855–1881*, 225.

teaching both Hebrew and Russian, as well as arithmetic, geography, history, and calligraphy. Six hours a week were devoted to religion, and on Friday afternoons the pupils were prepared for the weekly Torah portion, which was taught from the Mendelssohn *Biur*, the translation of the Bible into German written in Hebrew characters, which was reissued in a new edition by the Vilna maskilim Abraham Dov Lebensohn (Adam Hakohen, 1794?–1878) and Isaac Benjacob.[48]

The schools strongly emphasized loyalty to the authorities. The text employed in the classes on Jewish religion were written by a young maskil, Leon Mandelstamm, who was Lilienthal's successor as 'Jewish expert' (*uchenyi evrei*) at the Ministry of Public Enlightenment. He expanded as follows on the rabbinic distinction between contemporary non-Jews and ancient idolaters, claiming that 'the nations under whose protection we live' could not be classed as idolaters, since they obeyed not only the seven laws laid down by Noah but most of the Jewish commandments. They therefore had a place 'in the World to Come' and 'we are commanded and obligated to love them, to wish them well, and to thank them for their generosity and mercy, for we shall live for ever in their country'.[49]

After 1848, when Uvarov was dismissed as part of Nicholas's reaction to the revolutions of that year in Europe, the Jewish primary and secondary schools became rather more practical and commercial in their educational emphasis. The secondary school in Vilna was now transformed into a technical high school, including among its subjects of instruction bookkeeping, geometry, mechanics, physics, and chemistry.

Although at first many wealthy traditional families were suspicious of the Jewish school system, this hostility seems to have diminished with time. Stanislawski has concluded that, while a large percentage of the students in the new schools came from the poorer families in the community, who may have hoped in this way to avoid conscription, they were also attended by the children of more prosperous and 'enlightened' families.[50] They also provided employment for a number of maskilim, including Kalman Schulman, Abraham Mapu, Abraham Baer Gottlober, and Judah Leib Gordon.

Within just over a month of the promulgation of the law on Jewish schools, Kiselev introduced the second of his measures to revolutionize Jewish life further. On 19 December 1844 a new law was issued abolishing the *kahal*, the executive agent of each *kehilah* (in Russian, *evreiskoe obshchestvo*). The *kahal*, which was usually composed of between three and five members, was responsible for taxation, the administration of justice, and internal policing. Under the new law, as one official put it, 'No special Jewish governance would continue to exist'[51]—the *kahal* would be abolished and its place would be taken by the local municipal authority,

[48] On these developments, see Stanislawski, *Tsar Nicholas and the Jews*, 97–109, and E. Tsherikover, 'Kazennye evreiskie uchilishcha', in *Evreiskaya entsiklopediya*, ix. 110–15.

[49] Quoted in Stanislawski, *Tsar Nicholas and the Jews*, 103.

[50] Ibid. 106.

[51] Milyutin, *Ustroistvo i sostoyanie evreiskikh obshchestv v Rossii*, 41.

which would also exercise jurisdiction over Jews living in the surrounding countryside.[52]

In fact, the responsibilities of the *kahal* were taken over by the Jewish communal officials responsible for collecting taxes (*sborshchiki*), who were also responsible for conducting censuses and ensuring that conscription quotas were met. The Jews still did not pay taxation directly to the government, and local Jewish communities continued to participate in the apportionment of the tax burden, both national and local. The communal officials were responsible for the collection of money to support philanthropic and other communal services and had the same legal responsibilities as the elders of communes established by artisans or townspeople. They were to be assisted in their duties by elected assistants. Together with the officers elected under the 1827 conscription statute, they would be directly subordinate to the local authorities.

Jewish taxation was maintained, but modified to serve Kiselev's reforming objectives. The main internal Jewish tax, the tax on kosher meat, was retained, and the auxiliary levy on immovable property, business activities, and bequests was now made compulsory. The taxes on ritual baths and other religious rites were abolished.[53]

This measure neither integrated the Jews into the larger administrative system nor abolished all aspects of Jewish communal organization or abrogated the status of rabbinic courts, since Russia lacked the administrative resources fully to subordinate Jews to the estate structure which had been established by Catherine. Moreover, to do so would have meant writing off the substantial arrears in taxation which were owed by the Jewish *kehilot*. In the conflict between the government's desire to reform the Jews and its interest in taxation and recruitment it was the latter which took precedence. Thus, for instance, in Vilna the administration of the community now became the responsibility of the wardens of the Great Synagogue, the *tsedakah gedolah*.

However, although Jewish autonomous structures did continue to exist, the new legislation contributed further to undermine their legitimacy within the Jewish community. In the 1830s there had been many protests against the unfairness of the recruitment and taxation policies of the *kehilot*. Now a new phenomenon began to emerge: Jews began to take the drastic step of petitioning the authorities to be allowed to secede from the community. Thus, in 1850 and 1851 the artisans of Dubno complained to the government that they bore an unfair proportion of the burden of recruitment and taxation and accordingly asked to be considered a separate unit for these purposes, with the right to send a representative to the town council.[54] Similar requests were made by the Jewish artisans of

52 *PSZ* 2/xix, no. 18545, art. 1.

53 On the function of Jewish autonomous institutions after the abolition of the *kahal*, see Shohat, 'The Administration of the *Kehilot* in Russia after the Abolition of the *Kahal*' (Heb.).

54 Margolis, *The History of Jews in Russia* (Yid.), doc. 92, 353–8.

Belaya Tserkov and Vladimir-Volynsky. The members of the Jewish artisans' guild in Belaya Tserkov justified their petition by claiming that they wished

> to throw off the yoke of the Jewish community which—according to its ancient traditions—looks with contempt upon artisans, and takes too large a share of taxes and recruits from them. If they are permitted to establish their own community [*obshchestvo*], the artisans will promptly and punctiliously pay all their duties and will not be so oppressed.[55]

Similar secessionist aspirations were expressed by those at the other pole of the social scale: merchants who had succeeded in entering the merchant estate and who resented the fact that they were still liable for the debts of the *kehilot*, which carried with them a liability to the draft. From 1852 on, merchants began to petition to secede from the *kehilah*. Such petitions were submitted in Indura, in the province of Grodno, in Minsk, and in Kremenchug. In 1854 eleven first-guild merchants and honorary citizens, led by one of the richest Jews in Russia, Joseph Yozel (Evzel) (later Baron) Guenzburg, also appear to have sought exemption from the tax liabilities of the *kehilah*.[56]

By and large, the government did not support these moves, being more concerned to use the *kehilot* for the purposes of tax collection and recruitment, but they showed how strong centrifugal forces had become within the Jewish community, which had always prided itself on its social cohesion.[57] The undermining of the legitimacy of the *kahal* affected all sectors of Jewish society, from the maskilim to the observant. Thus, according to the maskil Abraham Shalom Fridberg (Har Shalom, 1838–1902): 'The leaders of the Jews were at that time in no way deserving of consideration as descendants of Abraham, for they were as far from the qualities of mercy as heaven is from earth. This was the "sin of the kahal", whose evil reached to the heavens and whose iniquity knew no bounds.'[58] This was also the view of a leading traditionalist, Rabbi Baruch Halevi Epstein (1860–1942): 'This was the period known by that frightful and shocking name, the "time of the Cantonists", or, more to the point, the "time of the sins of the kahal", for indeed our fathers, the leaders of our communities, committed a grave sin, a travesty inscribed in blood and tears . . . for which there is no expiation.'[59]

The government also intervened in Jewish religious life. When dealing with non-Orthodox, non-Christian, and non-Russian groups within the empire, the tsarist bureaucracy, like that of other empires, usually sought to co-opt local elites for the purposes of control and transformation. In the case of the Jews this proved difficult. The members of the Jewish Committee recognized the central role

[55] S. Rombakh, 'Jewish Artisans in Russia in the First Half of the Nineteenth Century' (Yid.), *Tsaytshrift*, 1 (1926), 29, quoted in Stanislawski, *Tsar Nicholas and the Jews*, 131.

[56] Margolis, *The History of Jews in Russia* (Yid.), 113–14; Tsherikover, 'From the Russian Archives' (Yid.).

[57] Stanislawski, *Tsar Nicholas and the Jews*, 133.

[58] A. Fridberg, 'Memoirs from my Youth' (Heb.), *Sefer hashanah*, 3 (1901), 84, quoted in Stanislawski, *Tsar Nicholas and the Jews*, 133.

[59] Quoted in Stanislawski, *Tsar Nicholas and the Jews*, 123.

which religion played in Jewish life, concluding that it was 'the principal, and possibly the sole, force shaping the social and family position of this people'. Its influence was all-pervasive, and governments in western and central Europe had made it into an effective 'instrument by which to transform the Jewish people'.[60] The committee members were thus frustrated by the absence in Jewish life in the tsarist empire of a central religious body with executive power like Napoleon's Assembly of Jewish Notables and the Paris Sanhedrin, and the consistory system which had subsequently been established. This system had not only consolidated authority into one central institution susceptible to state directives, but was an important means to eliminate 'previous biases that alienated the Jews from the rest of civil society'.[61] Similarly, the bureaucrats on the committee believed that a major obstacle to their reformist plans lay in the lack of a Jewish clergy (*dukhovenstvo*), either in the legal sense or with defined modern professional qualifications of the type which was emerging in western and central Europe.[62] Certainly, as we have seen in Chapter 5, although the rabbinate had become increasingly institutionalized from the sixteenth century, the qualifications for rabbinic ordination were not of the type recognized as useful by the Russian bureaucrats, with their deeply entrenched anti-talmudic prejudices. In addition, many religious functions, including the solemnization of marriage and the granting of divorce, could be performed by any man properly versed in Jewish law.

To remedy these 'defects' in Jewish society, the committee proposed in 1847 the creation of a central Rabbinic Commission, which would be assisted by a provincial rabbinate operating under the supervision of the Ministry of the Interior. This would establish a 'special central institution, which would have a moral influence on the Jews', and which would 'give force to the decrees promulgated by the government to reform this people' and 'direct the Jewish masses to merge with civil society and to engage in useful labour'. Its religious character was necessary because 'the Jews, given the tenets of their religion, cannot respect civil authority in religious matters'.[63] The model seems to have been the French consistory system admired by Kiselev.

At the local level, the committee sought to consolidate the institution of officially recognized 'state rabbis' (*kazennye ravviny*—literally Treasury rabbis, although they were, in fact, paid for by the Jewish community through special Jewish taxes). This state rabbinate had not emerged as the result of any specific reform but was the product of tsarist attempts in the first decades of the nineteenth century to

[60] Report of P. D. Kiselev to Personal Section of His Imperial Majesty's Chancellery regarding the reasoning behind the creation of the state rabbinate and Rabbinic Commission, 26 Nov. 1855; Rossiiskii gosudarstvennyi istoricheskii arkhiv, St Petersburg (RGIA), f. 1269, op. 1, d. 15, l. 30, quoted in Freeze, *Jewish Marriage and Divorce in Imperial Russia*, 53.

[61] RGIA, f. 821, op. 8, d. 283, l. 28, quoted in Freeze, *Jewish Marriage and Divorce in Imperial Russia*, 53.

[62] On this, see Schorsch, 'Emancipation and the Crisis of Religious Authority'.

[63] RGIA, f. 1269, op. 1, d. 15, ll. 31, 33, 36, quoted in Freeze, *Jewish Marriage and Divorce in Imperial Russia*, 83.

lay down the required qualifications and functions of rabbis.[64] According to Alexander I's 1804 Statute Concerning the Organization of the Jews, 'by 1812, anyone who is not literate in one of the aforementioned languages [Russian, Polish, and German] cannot be appointed to a communal post or to the rabbinate'.[65] In 1826 rabbis, like the clergy of other confessions, were made responsible for maintaining registers of births, deaths, and marriages.[66] These Jewish 'metrical' records of vital statistics differed in two significant respects from those kept by other confessions: they were to be in Hebrew as well as Russian, and they were also to record divorces, which was not the case with Russian Orthodox metrical books, the result of the fact that, while rabbis had the right to grant divorces, in the Orthodox Church this was the prerogative of the central Church authorities. They took the form of published, bound volumes with individual entry numbers, a format which made it all but impossible to doctor the records by tearing out or inserting pages. Falsification was made still more difficult by the requirement that the rabbi deposit annually a copy of the metrical books with the provincial board. The imposition on the state rabbi of this obligation was the consequence of the attempt of the bureaucracy to administer the Jews more effectively by establishing proper records.[67] Already in the 1804 statute Jews had been required to adopt surnames which would, the bureaucrats hoped, facilitate the control of property and the placing of Jews in the appropriate socio-legal categories (*sostoyaniya*). Similarly, the establishment of metrical records was seen as a way of obtaining a more accurate record of the number of Jews than the various poll tax censuses which had been taken between 1808 and 1822. The Jewish Committee estimated in 1840 that more than a quarter of the Jewish population went unrecorded, which affected both the number of recruits sent to the army and the level of taxation paid by individual communities.[68]

The statute of 1835 went still further in defining the role of state rabbis, who were described both as 'the supervisors and interpreters of Jewish law' and as state servants. They were to be elected by the Jews in a given community for a three-year period, and their election had to be confirmed by the provincial governor. They were to supervise the conduct of religious services, rule on questions of Jewish law, and instruct their congregants on 'the true meaning of the law'. In doing so they were to rely on 'persuasion and exhortation', and the use of excommunication was implicitly denied them. In addition, only the official rabbi or his assistant had the right to perform marriages, divorces, circumcisions, and burials.[69] This power was entrenched in 1853, when it was laid down that

[64] Shohat, *The Office of Crown Rabbi in Russia* (Heb.), and also id., 'The Attitude of Society to Rabbis from Rabbinical Schools' (Heb.), and Greenbaum, 'The Russian Rabbinate under the Czars'.

[65] Levanda, 53–9.

[66] Shohat, *The Office of Crown Rabbi in Russia* (Heb.), 9.

[67] On this, see Kabuzan, *Narodonaselenie Rossii v XVIII–pervoi polovine XIX v.*, and Avrutin, 'The Politics of Jewish Legibility'.

[68] RGIA, f. 1269, op. 1, d. 69, l. 4, quoted in Avrutin, 'The Politics of Jewish Legibility', 141.

[69] Levanda, 303; Derzhavnyi arkhiv mista Kyyeva (DamK), f. 16, op. 469, d. 9, quoted in Freeze, *Jewish Marriage and Divorce in Imperial Russia*, 97.

'marriages and divorces not performed by the rabbi and his assistant will be considered illegal'.[70]

As a state servant the rabbi was made responsible for ensuring that 'the Jews observe their moral obligations and obey general state laws and appointed authorities'.[71] This was made explicit in the official oath sworn by state rabbis, which was similar to that required of Orthodox parish priests. It read:

I will direct all the Jews, using all the means at my disposal, to fulfil their obligations: obedience to civil authorities and the preservation of social order and peace . . . I will not permit or hide anything harmful or contrary to the laws of the empire and I will act to support the interests and needs of the supreme authorities. I will preserve strictly all secrets entrusted to me and, in general, will conduct myself and behave in a way appropriate to a good and loyal subject.[72]

The government's hope that it would be able to create a professional rabbinate on the French or German model was not fulfilled. Initially there was an absence of suitably trained individuals. Thus, according to the maskil Isaac Baer Levinsohn, the first generation of state rabbis consisted of Jews who knew enough Russian to maintain the metrical books but were not viewed as actual rabbis by their communities. There were even cases where existing rabbis took the post after learning to sign their names in Russian.[73]

It was partly in order to create a cadre to meet this demand that in 1847 the government, after some delay, established two state rabbinical seminaries on the model of that in Warsaw, one in Vilna and one in Zhitomir, as was mandated by the law of November 1844. In addition to training rabbis, these schools were to produce the educated laymen who would transform Russian Jewish life. They provided a seven-year secondary education. During the first three years students took the same secular subjects as students in a Russian pre-gymnasium, including Russian, arithmetic, and geography, as well as traditional Jewish subjects such as the Pentateuch with the commentaries of Rashi, the early prophets, and the book of Proverbs. In the next four years the secular subjects included history, physics, and foreign languages, and the Jewish curriculum included basic halakhic texts. At the end of these seven years students could choose between a three-year pedagogical course and a three-year course of rabbinical training.[74]

The rabbinic schools provided employment for the cream of the Russian Haskalah. The poet Adam Hakohen Lebensohn taught Hebrew at the Vilna Rabbinic School; Wolf Tugendhold, who had also been associated with the Warsaw Rabbinic School, taught Jewish history; Samuel Joseph Fuenn and Judah

[70] Levanda, 800.

[71] DamK, f. 16, op. 469, d. 9, l. 12, quoted in Freeze, *Jewish Marriage and Divorce in Imperial Russia*, 97–8.

[72] Levanda, 445.

[73] Shohat, *The Office of Crown Rabbi in Russia* (Heb.), 9, 12.

[74] Derzhavnyi arkhiv Zhytomyrs'koyi oblasti, f. 396, op. 1, d. 1, l. 1, quoted in Freeze, *Jewish Marriage and Divorce in Imperial Russia*, 340. On these rabbinic schools, see also Dohrn, 'The Rabbinical Schools as Institutions of Socialization in Tsarist Russia, 1847–1873', and Melamed, 'The Zhitomir Rabbinical School'.

Behak taught the Jewish religion; while Samuel b. Joseph Strashun (Zaskovitzer) and Hirsh Kliaczko taught Mishnah and Talmud. Among those who taught at Zhitomir were the Warsaw maskil Hayim Selig Slonimski, son-in-law of Abraham Stern and later editor of the Warsaw Hebrew paper *Hatsefirah*; the poet Jacob Eichenbaum (Gelber); and the Brody maskil Mordecai Sukhostaver.

Like that in Warsaw, the schools did not achieve what Uvarov had expected them to do, which was to create a German-style professional rabbinate which, with a new enlightened elite, would carry out the transformation of Russian Jewry. Given the conservative nature of the Jewish community in the Pale and the fact that the Crown rabbinate was elected, the graduates of the schools found great difficulty in gaining such posts, even in the more propitious climate of the early years of the reign of Alexander II (on this, see Chapter 12). Neither did they enjoy high prestige in Jewish society. Lev Osipovich Levanda attacked their students as 'riffraff—the most loathsome of Jewish youths in all the districts of this land',[75] while Shalom Jacob Abramowitsch (Mendele Mokher Seforim, 1835–1917) described the schools as 'shelters for the sons of the poor, for young men who live a life of suffering in the yeshivas, for grooms who sneak out and run away from the house of the fathers-in-law, for married men who become tired of their wives and leave them and their children'.[76]

Nevertheless, they were relatively well attended. There were 251 students at the Vilna Rabbinic School in 1855 and 271 at that in Zhitomir, and they made up many of the members of the first generation of the Russian Jewish intelligentsia, who developed a strong loyalty to these bodies and who were to play a significant role in the following decades. Their graduates included Abraham Goldfaden, Lev Levanda, Mikhail Morgulis, Abraham Jacob Paperna, and Leon Pinsker.

Increasing numbers of Jewish students were also attending Russian schools and universities. In the early 1840s there were 230 Jewish students attending Russian elementary schools and between 100 and 120 in secondary education. Nearly forty were at universities, mostly in medical faculties. These are considerable numbers: in 1847 there were only 18,911 students in Russian gymnasiums and 4,566 at Russian universities, and enrolment fell by a quarter after 1848.[77]

These students saw themselves, like the Polish and Russian intelligentsias which were also forming at this time, as an elite with a special mission: they would carry what they had learnt to the benighted masses of their people. In the words of Mikhail Morgulis, every student in these schools

> regarded himself as no less than a future reformer, a new Mendelssohn, and therefore, on the quiet, worked out a plan of action which he jealously guarded from his friends. . . . [They] were thoroughly convinced that they were going to bring about a complete revolution in the world-view of the Jewish people, and impatiently awaited their moment of

[75] L. Levanda, 'Tipy i siluety', *Voskhod*, 1 (1881), no. 4, 86.

[76] Abramowitsch, *The Complete Works of Mendele Mokher Seforim* (Heb.), 237, quoted in Shohat, *The Office of Crown Rabbi in Russia* (Heb.), 23.

[77] Stanislawski, *Tsar Nicholas and the Jews*, 108, 208.

action. They were like military commanders standing at the ready for the approaching enemy attack, waiting only for the moment when they would be able to display the wonders of their courage and to distinguish themselves for their fatherland.[78]

The views held by the developing Russian Jewish intelligentsia were not uniform. In the first place, there was a marked distinction between the first generation, that of Isaac Baer Levinsohn, who were rather cautious and aware of their isolation and weakness in Jewish society, and the generation which followed, the product of the heady years of the establishment of the Jewish school system, who were much more radical. They differed also in the extent to which they wished to retain elements of Jewish tradition, in particular the Talmud and kabbalistic sources. The sort of religious reform which should be favoured—whether one should go beyond the moderate changes which had been introduced into the modern synagogues in Odessa, Riga, and Vilna in the 1840s—was also a matter of some controversy.

Language also occasioned dispute. The maskilim all hoped that a reformed and purified Hebrew language would lie at the heart of any transformation of Jewish life. But they differed on whether the goal was to create a new poetic language or a language which could be used in education. They all despised Yiddish as a debased 'jargon', but some, notably Israel Aksenfeld, saw Yiddish as the only way to reach the unenlightened Jewish masses. Although German was the initial language of the Haskalah, Russian quickly displaced it as the language the maskilim thought should be the principal foreign language taught in the Russian Jewish schools. Indeed, these schools proved very successful at expanding the use of Russian within the Jewish community.

As we have seen, many maskilim had highly naive views of the benevolence of the tsarist government. Levinsohn dedicated his book *Te'udah beyisra'el* to 'God's anointed one [*mashiaḥ*], His Majesty Nicholas Pavlovich, for all the good he has done my nation'. He went on to explain that all of the tsar's actions were motivated by an overwhelming love for the Jews and a desire for their happiness and success.[79] A similar view was held by Abraham Baer Gottlober. Describing the introduction of the draft, he wrote:

No doubt the government meant no harm to the Jews, but wanted to make them equal with the other inhabitants of the country. Had the Jewish leaders had the sense to accept this decree in good grace and thank the government for accepting the Jews for military service along with the other nationalities under its protection, the government would have watched over the Jews. But the Jews could not understand that the government meant well; they considered the decree a calamity and marked it as a fast day, weeping and wailing at their misfortune.[80]

78 Morgulis, 'Iz moikh vospominanii', *Voskhod*, 15 (1895), no. 2, 116.

79 Levinsohn, *Testimony in Israel* (Heb.), unpaginated preface.

80 Gottlober, 'Memoirs' (Yid.), quoted in Dawidowicz (ed.), *The Golden Tradition*, 117.

At the same time there was a growing awareness among the maskilim of the deleterious effect on the Jews of their lack of rights. In 1842 a group of Jewish leaders in Odessa submitted a petition to Mikhail Vorontsov, the governor-general of the province, calling on the authorities to improve the civil status of the Jews. In the absence of 'material rights and privileges', they argued, education would 'ruin the sons of Jacob'.[81]

The Rabbinic Commission also failed to achieve the objectives set for it by the government. In February 1847 Kiselev, in the name of the Jewish Committee, had submitted a comprehensive proposal to create such a commission, which was established by imperial decree on 1 July 1848.[82] Its principal tasks were to serve as an advisory organ and overseer for local state rabbis, and to operate as a higher 'court of appeals' in Jewish divorce cases, in which capacity it was to examine cases involving ambiguities in Jewish law or complaints by one party against a local rabbi for an unjust decision in a divorce suit.[83] Yet at the same time it was laid down that the commission was not to treat private divorce suits 'because these cases have hitherto been decided definitively by local rabbis, who have been selected by the agreement of both spouses'. It was, in addition, to carry out any other duties which the Ministry of the Interior 'considers necessary to impose on it'. It was barred from intervening against the hasidim on the grounds that 'the state is not obliged to support any single interpretation of the Jewish religion', and was also not to concern itself with the censorship of books.[84]

Since 'the Jews will not have confidence in people who are appointed [by the state]', the Jewish Committee recommended that each provincial governor in the Pale be made responsible for finding three 'loyal' candidates, who would then participate in an election in which the franchise would be restricted to rabbis, honorary citizens (*pochetnye grazhdane*, a status established in 1832 partly to reduce massive ennoblement by creating an intermediate category whose members, like the nobility, were exempt from poll tax, conscription, and corporal punishment), and merchants (*kuptsy*). The list of candidates elected in each province was then to be sent to the Ministry of the Interior, which would select the five members of the commission and which would supervise its activities and confirm its decisions. It was to have its seat in St Petersburg, and not in the town of Zhitomir, the capital of Volhynia, in the heart of the Pale, as was originally proposed by the Jewish Committee.[85]

81 Lerner, *Evrei v novorossiiskom krae*, 40.

82 RGIA, f. 1269, op. 1, d. 15, quoted in Freeze, *Jewish Marriage and Divorce in Imperial Russia*, 85.

83 Decree of His Imperial Majesty on the Statutes of the Rabbinical Commission, 1 July 1848, RGIA, f. 821, op. 8, d. 280, quoted in Freeze, *Jewish Marriage and Divorce in Imperial Russia*, 85.

84 RGIA, f. 1269, op. 1, d. 14, l. 18–18 ob.; f. 821, op. 8, d. 293, l. 16*b*, quoted in Freeze, *Jewish Marriage and Divorce in Imperial Russia*, 84, 86.

85 RGIA, f. 1269, op. 1, d. 15, ll. 19 ob.–20, and report of Count P. D. Kiselev, 'Regarding the Proposal for the Location of the Rabbinic Commission in Zhitomir', n.d., quoted in Freeze, *Jewish Marriage and Divorce in Imperial Russia*, 84–5.

The Rabbinic Commission met only once in the reign of Nicholas I, and not until four years after its establishment, probably because of the increasingly reactionary climate after 1848 and the difficulty of selecting appropriate members. Officials complained that the Jews 'chose people who did not meet the expectations of the state', while one Russian official was compelled to admit subsequently that the members of the commission who held views typical of the moderate Haskalah had 'no status in religious and social matters with the Jews of Russia'.[86] Nevertheless, the meeting aroused considerable interest in Jewish society in the hope that its members could act in defence of Jewish interests. According to one report from the Ministry of the Interior, its meetings 'not only stirred up the general interest of the Jews (generally in the western provinces), but [also] attracted many of them to come to St. Petersburg, under the pretext of [bringing] private matters [to the Rabbinic Commission]'.[87]

The commission was given a broad agenda by the ministry, which saw it essentially as a source of information on the Jewish community. Its brief included queries about the censorship of Jewish books (including *midrashim*, Passover *hagadot*, prayer books, and commentaries), 'secret rabbis' (probably a reference to non-official rabbis) and hasidic sects, the Jewish oath, the administration of metrical books, recording births, deaths, and marriages, and the question of the right of Jewish soldiers to marry, which had ostensibly been granted by a decree of 1834. The ministry was disappointed with the results of its deliberations, and an official complained that its members had been 'completely unprepared to deal with the questions presented to them'.[88]

One reason why the government had systematized the laws on the Crown rabbinate and created the Rabbinic Commission was its desire to 'bring order' to the Jewish family. In an 1854 memorandum on the question of why attempts to transform Jews into 'productive agricultural producers' had so little success, the Jewish Committee also raised the more general question of the lack of control over Jewish marriage practices, especially the question of under-age marriages and what they perceived as the very high rate of divorce. The early age at which marriages were entered into put a severe burden on young couples and, although the legal age for marriage had been set at 18 in the Jewish statute of 1835, it was clear that this provision was being evaded. With regard to the high divorce rate, the committee claimed that 'divorces among the Jews occur without proper grounds [and] so frequently that out of one hundred Jews, perhaps twenty divorce their wives', an estimate which was borne out later by official statistics. However, while it is true that the breakdown of communal authority and the stresses to which the Jews were subject had significantly increased the breakdown of marriage and that

86 RGIA, f. 821, op. 8, d. 293, l. 16*b*, quoted in Freeze, *Jewish Marriage and Divorce in Imperial Russia*, 87.

87 Memorandum from Sergey Lanskoy to P. D. Kiselev, RGIA, f. 1269, op. 1, d. 15, ll. 28–9, 8 Nov. 1853, quoted in Freeze, *Jewish Marriage and Divorce in Imperial Russia*, 88.

88 RGIA, f. 821, op. 8, d. 293, l. 16*b*, quoted in Freeze, *Jewish Marriage and Divorce in Imperial Russia*, 87.

Jewish law did make divorce relatively easy, the extent of the problem was probably exaggerated in the minds of the committee members because it contrasted so strikingly with the virtual prohibition on divorce which was the norm in Russian Orthodoxy.[89]

Nevertheless, the Jewish Committee was so concerned by these issues that they were prepared to abandon the usual tsarist practice of leaving matters of family law to individual religious denominations and contemplate that of European governments, which, since the Enlightenment, had intervened in these matters. Intervention in Russia was planned to be through the state rabbinate and the Rabbinical Commission, but this proved ineffective partly because of the limited powers and jurisdiction of both these institutions. The Crown rabbinate had been denied the right of excommunication, the general practice of European governments since the end of the eighteenth century, while the powers of the commission over marriage were very ambiguous. These limited powers reflected the authorities' ambivalence about creating a separate 'Jewish officialdom' within the state bureaucracy. In addition, the understanding of bureaucrats in St Petersburg of the nature of the crisis which the Jewish family was undergoing was extremely limited (on this, see Volume II, Chapter 9).

In their search to find Jews who could assist in their project of transforming Jewish society the imperial bureaucrats created an additional institutional nexus between it and the state in the form of the 'Jewish expert' (*uchenyi evrei*).[90] From the 1840s such experts were recruited both for the Department of Spiritual Affairs for Foreign Confessions of the Ministry of the Interior and for the offices of provincial governors. They were usually adherents of the Haskalah and were to advise the government on the implementation of the ambitious plans it had initiated from 1840. In this first phase of their recruitment they appear to have been intelligent and able, vigorously advancing the maskilic agenda through the highest offices of the empire. They were primarily responsible for providing information, and wrote reports on many matters, including the oath of allegiance for Jewish military recruits and Crown rabbis, traditional Jewish education, and the rites and customs of Judaism. They were also responsible for the translation of material in Jewish languages into Russian, and for providing digests of the Hebrew and Yiddish press.

The position of the Jewish experts also placed them in the role of mediators between the government and the Jewish community, since they were required to justify these reforms, although they were specifically barred by the law from direct negotiations with the community leadership, being servants rather than agents of the government. As with the Crown rabbinate and the Rabbinic Commission, this

[89] Report of the Jewish Committee to the MVD [Ministry of the Interior] Department of Agriculture, 15 May 1854, RGIA, f. 1269, op. 1, d. 48, l. 2–2 ob., quoted in Freeze, *Jewish Marriage and Divorce in Imperial Russia*, 73–4. The question of the high Jewish divorce rate is discussed at length in Freeze.

[90] On this, see the doctoral thesis which is being prepared by V. Schedrin, Brandeis University, with the title 'Jewish Bureaucracy in Late Imperial Russia: The Phenomenon of Expert Jews'.

undermined their position in the eyes of most Jews. Among them were also some of the first secular historians of Russian Jewry. Thus in 1854 Moisey Iosifovich Berlin, who served as a Jewish expert in the Ministry of the Interior, wrote an unpublished history of hasidism, one of the first sympathetic maskilic accounts, and also produced his valuable *Ocherk etnografii evreiskogo narodo-naseleniya* (Essay on the Ethnography of the Jewish Population, St Petersburg, 1861).

In December 1844, the same month as the promulgation of the law abolishing the *kahal*, Kiselev attempted to press forward on another of the six areas of his blueprint for the reform of Jewish life, passing a law increasing the inducements to Jews to take up farming. In practice, neither sufficient land nor adequate finance was made available, and Jewish agricultural settlement did not take place on a significant scale.

The government also legislated, in accordance with Kiselev's recommendations, to ban specific forms of Jewish dress, both to diminish Jewish 'separateness' and as part of its drive to reduce corporate and religious isolation and strengthen the imperial polity.[91] The issue had first been raised in the Jewish statute of 1804, which had laid down that, when Jews travelled from the Pale of Settlement to the interior provinces of the empire, they were to wear 'German' dress (this was modified to 'Russian' dress in 1809), which would facilitate their 'rapprochement' with the rest of the population. However, like many of the laws of Alexander I's reign, it was not enforced. In the 1835 statute the requirement was repeated, and Jews travelling outside the Pale were required to wear clothing similar to that of individuals of their legal status.[92]

It was in the 1840s that the issue was first seriously addressed. This was another example of the negative synergy produced by the interaction of government policy and the maskilic drive to reform Jewish life. In 1843 a group of maskilim in Vilna sent a petition to the Ministry of Public Enlightenment which claimed that 'the first obstacle to the enlightenment of the Jewish people is their distinct dress . . . All attempts to enlighten the Jewish people will be in vain until they change their dress.' According to them, the more civilized Jews wanted to abandon separate ways of dressing but were afraid to do so because of communal pressure.[93] According to another petition,

> In no country does a particular style of dress exist for my co-religionists: not in Europe, not in Asia, and not in Africa. Only we Jews who live in Poland and Lithuania distinguish ourselves from our neighbors to our own detriment . . . Yet when Polish and Lithuanian Jews travel to our capital [St Petersburg], they do not count wearing German or Russian

[91] On Nicholas's reforms of Jewish dress, see Gessen, 'Bor'ba pravitel'stva s evreiskoi odezhdoi v Imperii i Tsarstve Pol'skom'; id., 'Russkoe zakonodatel'stvo ob odezhde evreev'; Rubens, *A History of the Jewish Costume*, 104–8; Klausner, 'The Decree on Jewish Clothing' (Heb.); Penkalla, 'The Socio-Cultural Integration of the Jewish Population in the Province of Radom', 220–4, and Avrutin, 'The Politics of Jewish Legibility', 149–55.

[92] *PSZ* 2/x, no. 8054 (13 Apr. 1835).

[93] Gessen, 'Bor'ba pravitel'stva s evreiskoi odezhdoi v Imperii i Tsarstve Pol'skom', 12.

clothing a sin. From this, it is evident that these Jews continue to wear their dress only by custom, and do not see it as a religious obligation.[94]

When this issue was taken up by the Jewish Committee, its report declared that

in Western Europe, where Jews did not distinguish themselves from the other inhabitants by their costume, they had merged with the majority culture. But in the western provinces of Russia, where dress distinguished Jews from their neighbors, they formed a distinct caste and remained steeped in their prejudices despite the best efforts of the government. The specific style of dress had no religious significance for Jews but was rather 'a marker of their insularity' and was only maintained by communal pressure.[95]

As a consequence, a comprehensive set of decrees was enacted banning Jewish costume. This was defined as 'silk hoods, belts, fur hats and other so-called coverings without peaks, yarmulkes, short trousers and boots . . . [for Jewish women] wigs of any sort that match their hair color'.[96] These changes were to be introduced in stages. In the first stage only Jews in larger provincial towns would be required to change their clothing, and the reform would then be extended to small towns and shtetls. By 1 January 1851 the changes would be obligatory everywhere, with an exception provided for those over 60. The ban on items of clothing was also introduced incrementally. From 1845 it was forbidden on pain of a fine of 3 to 5 roubles to wear yarmulkes in public; three years later Jews were prohibited from wearing sidelocks, and from 1851 women were forbidden to shave their heads upon marriage.[97]

The authorities were convinced that these measures would be popular. Shortly after the promulgation of the decree, one police official reported confidently that 'the majority of Jews, including the followers of the hasidic sect, will dutifully fulfill His Majesty's wishes, and change their national costume, especially the younger ones . . . who can't wait to change their costumes'.[98] In fact, the ban was bitterly resented by the bulk of Jewish society. According to Pauline Wengeroff, the reform was a 'catastrophe' for the majority of Jews: 'The ukase was called "the gzeyreh" (the harsh edict)—not one of the many gzeyros that overcame the Jewish people, but simply "the gzeyreh".'[99] The bitterness it occasioned was increased by the brutal way it was sometimes enforced. According to a petition from the Jewish community of Zhitomir: 'On the streets, district inspectors tear the wigs off Jewish women's heads, bonnets, and other head attire; they pull them by their hair to the police station and pour a few buckets of cold water on them;

94 RGIA, f. 1269, op. 1, d. 36, l. 7, quoted in Avrutin, 'The Politics of Jewish Legibility', 151.

95 RGIA, f. 1269, op. 1, d. 7, l. 13, quoted in Avrutin, 'The Politics of Jewish Legibility', 152.

96 Gessen, 'Russkoe zakonodatel'stvo ob odezhde evreev', 49.

97 RGIA, f. 1269, op. 1, d. 36, l. 29*b*, quoted in Avrutin, 'The Politics of Jewish Legibility', 152.

98 Gosudarstvennyi arkhiv Rossiiskoi Federatsii (GARF), f. 109, folder 1, op. 20, d. 186, ll. 5*b*, 25*b*, 27*b*, quoted in Avrutin, 'The Politics of Jewish Legibility', 152–3.

99 Wengeroff, *Rememberings*, 94–5.

they keep them under arrest for 48 hours; and then finally make them sweep the streets in public.'[100]

Many Jews refused to observe the decree. Thus in 1845 Shmuil Lezinsky, a merchant of the second guild, refused to take off his yarmulke when ordered to do so by local police. When they failed to arrest him, a number of other Jews exclaimed: 'If we had more Jews like him then we would continue to adhere to our traditions and [wear] our clothing.' Many Jews also preferred to pay fines rather than comply, and they were often supported by communal leaders. This indeed was one of the intentions of the authorities, who hoped in this way to supplement the taxes they collected from the Jews. The Jewish philanthropist Jacob Joseph Halpern of Berdichev reportedly donated at least 1,000 roubles to help pay the tax on wearing yarmulkes for the poorer Jews.[101]

As a result, the impact of the new regulations in the 1840s and 1850s was quite limited. Travellers in the Pale of Settlement confirm the persistence there of traditional Jewish dress: 'a long coat or frock coat in black cloth edged in front with velvet and fastened from the neck to the waist; a wide belt, socks, shoes or slippers; a skull cap; a hat with a wide brim most of which is shaped like a sugar loaf or cut off with a deep edge of sable or other fur'.[102] Even when Jews complied with the law, as Abraham Paperna observed, their beards and sidelocks grew back in time and 'things returned to their old ways'.[103]

The one reform where Kiselev encountered significant opposition from within the bureaucracy, and which was only implemented partially and with some delay, was his call, following Prussian precedents, to divide the Jews into 'productive' and 'unproductive' categories, which was described in Russian as the *razbor* (classification). Kiselev's view was that it was irrational to class most Jews as townspeople, when a large number neither lived in towns nor worked in urban occupations. As we have seen, he accepted the general Russian official view that the Jews exercised a harmful influence on the economic and moral life of the peasantry in the former Polish provinces. He opted for a typically bold, if misguided, solution, looking to Prussia for his model. In his opinion, entry into the estate of townspeople should be restricted to Jewish traders with substantial economic resources. The remainder should be compelled to become guild merchants, artisans, or farmers. To achieve this goal, he proposed that the Prussian division of Jews into 'productive' and 'unproductive' be applied. All Jews who were not guild merchants, licensed artisans, townspeople who could demonstrate that they lived

[100] The full petition is reprinted in Dubnow et al. (eds.), 'Goneniya na zhenskie golovnye ubory (1853 g.)', 400–1.

[101] Quoted in Avrutin, 'The Politics of Jewish Legibility', 153. On Halpern's activities as a spokesman for the Jewish communities in the south-western region of the empire, see *Evreiskaya entsiklopediya*, vi. 117–18, and Khiterer, 'Iosif Galperin'.

[102] Hollaenderski, *Les Israélites de Pologne*, 224–5. For other examples, see Lvovich (ed.), *Narody Russkogo Tsarstva*, 584; Alekseev, *Ocherki domashnei i obshchestvennoi zhizni evreev*; and Berlin, *Ocherk etnografii evreiskogo narodo-naseleniya*.

[103] Paperna, 'Iz nikolaevskoi epokhi', 54.

in a town, or farmers would be classed as 'unproductive'. They would be given five years in which to transform themselves and take up a 'productive' occupation, abandoning their rural dwelling places. Those who failed to comply would be severely punished, mainly by becoming liable for conscription.[104]

Nicholas, not surprisingly, approved this proposal, but it encountered strong bureaucratic opposition, particularly from Mikhail Vorontsov, governor-general of New Russia. He argued that it was ridiculous to class Jewish petty traders as 'non-productive' since they performed valuable economic functions which benefited all sections of the population, including those in the countryside. The proposed reform would do serious damage to the economic structure of the areas concerned, and the principal problems of the Jews—their own poverty and lack of skills—would only be exacerbated by forcing them into the towns, where most of them would have no means of support.[105]

It took over a year to overcome the opposition to the proposal, but in 1846 reclassification became official government policy. Its official promulgation concluded that, in spite of the many benefits Russian rule had conferred on the Jews, 'they have not been willing to avail themselves of the opportunities presented to them and have avoided any amalgamation with the society under whose protection they live, existing as before, for the most part, off the work of the rest of the population, which justifiably complains of this'.

To 'improve' the Jews, acting on the advice of the best-educated of them, the government had abolished the *kahal*s, established special Jewish schools, created opportunities for Jews to become farmers, and would in the future ban Jewish forms of dress.

> Since the government has provided all the means for the moral and material well-being of the Jews, it is justified in hoping that the Jews will finally abandon any undertaking that endangers the interests of the rest of the population, and will choose for themselves, like their compatriots, more sound modes of living. It is entirely justified that the refractory and disobedient be punished as idlers who are a burden to the society of which they are a part. Therefore, in order to make a just distinction between those Jews who have already sought to make themselves useful and those who have no trade or other legal occupation, the government requires the latter to declare themselves in one of the following categories:
>
> 1. one of the three merchant guilds
> 2. the ranks of townspeople owning property in any city or town
> 3. any artisan guild to which they bring the requisite knowledge of a craft
> 4. farmers.

Financial support would be provided for those who wished to become farmers. By 1 January 1850 all Jews were required to register themselves in the required categories. After that date any Jew who had not done so, or who had not attained an academic degree or the rank of honorary citizen, would be listed in a special

[104] On this, see Stanislawski, *Tsar Nicholas and the Jews*, 155–60.

[105] Quoted in Lerner, *Evrei v novorossiiskom krae*, 53.

category and subjected to punitive measures, which would be spelled out in due course. 'So warned in advance, the Jews have the choice of taking up the means offered to them to conduct an honest and secure life, or to suffer the unpleasant consequences which their persistence on the path of evil must lead to.'[106]

Not surprisingly, the proposal, sometimes described as the 'classification' (*razryad*), provoked consternation among the Jews. In the words of the folk song, 'Ah, a tsore, a gzeyre mit di razryaden!' ('Alas! What misfortune and persecution there is in the classification!'). In fact the government had not been able to implement the reclassification by the due date, and the outbreak of the Crimean War and Nicholas's death meant that it had still not been implemented by the accession of his successor, Alexander II, in 1855.

Yet although the official attempt to restructure Jewish economic life had little to show for it, the reign of Nicholas did see a far-reaching economic transformation of the Jews, which is partly masked by the incompleteness of Russian official statistics. In the first place, there was a significant increase in the number of guild merchants. According to official statistics, the number of guild merchants increased from nearly 5,000 in 1830 to almost 27,500 in 1851. This growth was most marked in those areas linked with the grain trade, the provinces of Chernigov, Kherson, Poltava, Kiev, Ekaterinoslav, Podolia, and Volhynia. Most of these merchants were not wealthy—over 95.6 per cent belonged to the third, poorest, guild of merchants. The movement into the merchant guild must therefore be seen as a consequence not only of Jews taking up new occupations, but also of the desire of many to benefit from the privileges of the merchant guild, especially exemption from the draft. The attempt to encourage agricultural settlement, half-baked though it was, also had some effect. The number of Jewish farmers grew from 3,600 in 1830 to nearly 15,500 in 1851, almost half of whom were located in the province of Kherson. However, neither of these developments was on a scale sufficient to alleviate the economic pressures in the Pale of Settlement.

There were other significant changes in Jewish economic activity. From the end of the eighteenth century (and probably much earlier), the most important Jewish occupation in the Pale of Settlement was agriculture-related leasing of estates, mills, and, especially, inns and taverns, and the petty moneylending activities linked with it. The government saw the position of the Jews in the countryside primarily in terms of the liquor trade, and tsarist policy had fitfully attacked their role in the agricultural economy in the first fifty years of Russian rule, seeing them as one of the principal causes of the impoverishment of the peasantry. Thus, as we have seen, under Alexander's statute of 1804 Jews were forbidden to engage in distilling or to run inns or taverns.

At the same time the government was heavily dependent on the liquor trade to finance its own operations. In the period to 1855 the revenue which the govern-

106 This memorandum was published in the *Allgemeine Zeitung des Judenthums*, 10 (1846). It is discussed in Stanislawski, *Tsar Nicholas and the Jews*, 157–9.

ment derived from distilling and the sale of alcohol equalled and sometimes surpassed all direct taxation.[107] The optimum solution was for the government to establish a state liquor monopoly. To do so, however, would undermine one of the most important economic bases of the nobility in the formerly Polish areas. It was also probably beyond the administrative ability of the tsarist bureaucracy. Instead, the empire was divided into two parts, 'privileged' provinces, which included the formerly Polish areas, in which landlords were permitted to retain the right to distil and sell alcohol on their estates (*propinacja*) and to continue to lease out these activities to Jewish leaseholders, and 'non-privileged' provinces, in which the sale and production of alcohol was the monopoly of the state, but was farmed out to large entrepreneurs.

The clearly negative consequences for the state of the expulsion of the Jews from the countryside had meant that it was implemented only very slowly in the last years of Alexander's reign and ended in the early years of the reign of Nicholas. The law barring Jews from involvement in the liquor trade became a dead letter, and under the 1835 statute all Jews in the Pale were specifically permitted to lease inns and taverns, along with land, mills, and other aspects of the rural economy, with the exception of estates settled by peasants.

It very soon became apparent that the existence of two different regimes for the sale of alcohol had created a situation in which the cheaper products of the western provinces were being smuggled on a large scale into the rest of the empire. The government ruled out the proposed solution that free trade in alcohol should be established throughout the empire. Instead, it sought to replace the large number of small-scale liquor producers in the western provinces by large-scale commercial distillers and distributors, as were emerging in the rest of the empire. As a consequence, restrictions were now introduced on the distillation and sale of alcohol by Jews in the countryside, while Jewish businessmen were encouraged to become large-scale leaseholders and were even allowed to take leases in areas outside the Pale.

Government policy was set out in a regulation of 15 August 1845, which made a clear distinction between Jewish guild merchants, who were permitted to sell liquor anywhere they chose, and Jewish townspeople, who could take leases only in economic ventures not linked with the liquor trade. Jews were forbidden to live in inns or taverns in the countryside or to engage in distilling. However, the law was widely evaded, and in June 1853 the government issued a further decree ordering that all leases concluded with Jews should contain a clause explicitly forbidding the sale of alcohol. The prohibition on Jews living in the countryside was reinforced, and was only relaxed after the accession of Alexander II.

Because of the widespread corruption which characterized the tsarist bureaucracy, these measures did not wipe out Jewish inn-keeping. They did, however, concentrate the sale of alcohol in the hands of a much smaller number of

[107] Ibid., n. 33.

individuals. In 1860 the first report on the excise duties owed by the leaseholders of alcohol concessions was published. Fourteen Jewish honorary citizens and guild members were responsible to the Treasury for over 6.7 million roubles annually. One, the honorary citizen Evzel Guenzburg, alone paid the Treasury nearly 3.8 million.

The same process of stratification could also be observed in another major Jewish activity, trading. Jewish small traders were adversely affected not only by the disruption occasioned by government policy but also by the replacement of seasonal fairs by permanent markets and by the barriers created by the new borders to their traditional trading links. It was this which lay behind the tsarist obsession with 'Jewish smuggling' and with the renewed ban on Jewish settlement within 50 versts (about 30 miles) of the frontier in 1843.

The consequences were the impoverishment of most Jewish merchants and the emergence of a small group of prosperous traders. The Slavophile Ivan Aksakov has left a description of a fair in Ukraine in the 1850s: 'around each Jewish wholesale merchant a hundred petty, poor Jews crowd, who secure goods from the wholesale store to sell . . . lending commerce a certain feverish vitality'.[108] This scene was immortalized in the early 1870s in music by Modest Mussorgsky in the piece 'Samuel Goldenburg and Schmuyle' from *Pictures at an Exhibition*, based on two paintings by Victor Hartman.

Some Jews found employment in the small-scale textile and sugar-refining industries which were created in the second half of Nicholas's reign by Jewish entrepreneurs, but this was not sufficient to absorb the enormous increase in *luftmenshn* with almost no means of earning a living. More moved into artisan trades. Between 1789 and 1849 the percentage of Jews claiming to be artisans in Berdichev grew from 15.3 to 29.6 per cent and in Minsk between 1812 and 1851 from 13.1 to 22.8 per cent. Jewish artisans had to belong to craft guilds if they wished to hire assistants or take on apprentices, but could work on their own without restriction. They were, in addition, permitted to join craft guilds by the legislation of 1804 and 1835, provided this did not contravene local privileges. Because of Christian opposition to admitting Jewish artisans to their guilds, from the beginning of Nicholas's reign a number of Jews petitioned the authorities to be allowed to establish their own guilds. The reclassification legislation further encouraged this development, since only those artisans who were members of a guild were to be classified as 'productive'. The growing number of Jewish artisans led to the introduction on 16 April 1852 of restrictions on the number of Jewish artisans. At the same time special 'non-artisan' guilds were to be set up for those Jews who could not be accommodated within the established guilds. None of this was able to stem the flow of Jews into artisan trades.

Economic restructuring was accompanied by important changes in the social geography of the Jewish community. Jews moved from the north to the south,

[108] Quoted in Blackwell, *The Beginnings of Russian Industrialization 1800–1860*, 232.

especially the south-east of the Pale of Settlement. Thus, Jewish population grew most rapidly in the provinces of Chernigov, Kherson, and Poltava, areas which were benefiting from the expansion of the grain trade, where some Jewish agricultural settlement was possible and where the *kehilot* were weaker, which meant that conscription weighed less heavily on the poorer parts of the population.

Urbanization also proceeded rapidly in the area. We do not have specific figures for Jews, but they probably made up at least half of the population of the towns in the Pale of Settlement. Between 1825 and 1856 the Jewish urban population of the western provinces rose from over 491,000 to nearly 877,000. Jews were also moving out of the Pale. Those who had permission to do so, particularly former soldiers, began to establish themselves in the central Russian provinces, and especially in Moscow and St Petersburg.[109] Jews also moved to areas in the tsarist empire where fewer people were conscripted or where, when they were conscripted, it was less onerous, such as the Kingdom of Poland and Bessarabia, and began to emigrate illegally, moving mainly to Prussia and Austria.

THE LAST YEARS OF NICHOLAS I

The last years of Nicholas's reign were difficult ones for the Jews of Russia. The revolutionary upheavals of 1848–9, in which Nicholas eventually became involved when he intervened to crush Hungary's attempt to achieve independence, pushed the emperor towards an even more reactionary position. Kiselev's influence waned, and Uvarov was dismissed as too liberal. From early 1850 Nicholas again turned to Jewish matters, concentrating on his favoured area of conscription. His anger was aroused by what he saw as the widespread Jewish attempt to evade the law and, to counter this, he ordered all Jewish communities to provide three additional recruits for each one who failed to report. An additional recruit was also to be levied for every 2,000 roubles which a community owed in back taxes. In June 1851 Nicholas further increased the Jewish draft, and two years later decided to punish Jewish recruiting officials if they failed to fulfil their quotas. By 1853, in a war situation, he went so far as to decree that any Jewish community could arrest any Jew found travelling without a passport and present him to the authorities for conscription. These measures had such devastating consequences, setting community against community and individual against individual, that relaxations had to be introduced in 1854. Their effect was not really felt before Nicholas's death on 18 February 1855.

These years also saw the resurgence of accusations of ritual murder, the bane of the Jewish communities of Poland–Lithuania. Such accusations had not ended with the Enlightenment and with their condemnation by the Pope. In 1816 a member of the Grodno *kahal*, Shalom Lapin, was accused, partly on the basis of evidence provided by a Jewish convert, of murdering a 4-year-old girl shortly

[109] On this, see Kleinmann, *Neue Orte—neue Menschen*.

before Easter. On this occasion, Tsar Alexander intervened decisively, making it clear that he did not believe that Jews engaged in ritual killing and ordering that the 'secret investigation be cut short and the murderer found'.[110] After this and some similar accusations in the Kingdom of Poland, Alexander's close associate Prince Golitsyn issued a circular to provincial governors on 6 March 1817 condemning such accusations and ordering that 'henceforward the Jews shall not be charged with murdering Christian children, without any evidence and purely as a result of the superstitious belief that they are in need of Christian blood'.[111]

The strength of this statement did not prevent Jews from being accused of murdering a 3-year-old boy at Easter in the town of Velizh in the province of Vitebsk. Two prominent Jews, a merchant, Shmerka Berlin, and a *kahal* elder, Yevzik Zetlin, were named as the perpetrators. Initially, they were found not guilty, but when one of their accusers succeeded in petitioning the tsar, the case was reopened and a tissue of lies was constructed describing how the Jews had extracted blood for their Passover rituals from the murdered boy. Altogether forty-two Jews were arrested by the provincial governor, convinced of the truth of the accusations. He was able to win the backing of the new tsar, Nicholas, who was perfectly willing to believe that the Jews engaged in practices of this sort. On 16 August 1826 Nicholas wrote to the provincial governor, Khovansky: 'Whereas the above occurrence demonstrates that the Kikes make wicked use of the religious toleration accorded to them, therefore, as a warning and as an example to others, let the Jewish schools [i.e. the synagogues] of Velizh be sealed up until further notice, and let services be forbidden, whether in them or near them.'[112] In the end, on 18 January 1835 the Jews were exonerated by the Council of State and their accusers punished, one by exile to Siberia and the other by being 'turned over to a priest for admonition'. After nine years the synagogues were reopened and those falsely accused finally released. When signing the verdict, Nicholas justified his action by the absence of proof. He continued:

> I do not have, and, indeed, cannot have the inner conviction that the murder has not been committed by the Jews. Numerous examples of similar murders . . . go to show that among the Jews there probably exist fanatics or sectarians who consider Christian blood necessary for their rites. This appears the more possible, since unfortunately even among us Christians there sometimes exist such sects which are no less horrible and incomprehensible. In a word, I do not for a moment think that this custom is common among all Jews, but I do not deny this possibility that there may be among them fanatics just as horrible as among us Christians.

As a consequence, Nicholas refused to sign a decree stating that provincial governors should abide by the ruling of 1817 and not pursue cases of this sort 'from prejudice only'.[113]

110 Dubnow, *History of the Jews in Russia and Poland*, ii. 74.
111 Ibid. 75.
112 Ibid. 78.
113 Ibid. 83.

Over twenty-five years later a new accusation of ritual murder surfaced. In the town of Saratov, which lay outside the Pale and where the Jewish community consisted of about forty soldiers and a few merchants and artisans, two Christian boys were found murdered, bearing traces of circumcision. Two Jews, a soldier named Shlieferman, who was a 'circumcision expert', and a furrier, Yankel Yushkevich, were arrested. In the course of the investigation, a special judicial commission was appointed by Nicholas, not only to solve the crime, but to 'investigate the dogmas of the religious fanaticism of the Jews'.[114] This special commission was set up under the auspices of the Ministry of the Interior, to which the Jewish convert Daniel Khvolson, an eminent Hebraist, gave evidence refuting the idea that the Jews needed Christian blood for their rituals. The following year the judicial commission, having failed to find any evidence against the accused, decided to set them at liberty, but 'to leave them under strong suspicion'. The Council of State did not accept this determination. Its members refused to enter into a discussion of the 'still unsolved question of the use of Christian blood by the Jews', while affirming that they 'unhesitatingly recognized the existence of the crime [at Saratov] itself'. The accused were sentenced to penal servitude. All except one were released on grounds of the deleterious effect on them of the eight years' incarceration they had suffered. The furrier Yankel Yushkevich served another seven years, only to be pardoned after a petition by Adolphe Crémieux, the prominent French Jewish politician, in 1867.

CONCLUSION

The three decades of Nicholas's rule had disastrous consequences for the Jews of the tsarist empire. The many initiatives undertaken in these years, whether punitive or reforming, did not achieve their objectives. They neither succeeded in creating a body of modernized Jews on the French or German model who could lead their community forward and make those changes necessary for adaptation to the modern world, nor did they transform the mass of Jews into what the tsarist bureaucrats could regard as 'useful subjects'. Rather, the ill-thought-out and poorly conceived initiatives undermined the authority of the traditional Jewish leadership without putting much in its place. They greatly increased social stratification in the community, with devastating consequences for communal solidarity. They also created a huge gulf between the small group of Westernizers and integrationists, who trusted naively in the good faith of the authorities, and the overwhelming majority, who saw the government as deeply hostile, persecuting, and conversionary. The rifts in the community, which were later to become still more profound, made an easy transition to modernity, always unlikely under tsarist autocracy, even more difficult.

[114] Ibid. 151.

TWELVE

THE REIGN OF ALEXANDER II 1855–1881

Education is the slogan of our age and in its embrace the mass of poor Jews find freedom from the abnormality and humiliation of their lives.

O. GURVICH, overseer of a Vilna Jewish primary school, 1865

THE GOVERNMENT AND THE JEWS IN THE ERA OF THE 'GREAT REFORMS'

THE ACCESSION of Alexander II in February 1855 was greeted with high expectations. After the stagnation and repression of the last years of Nicholas I's reign it was believed that his successor would introduce the radical reforms whose necessity had been made obvious by Russia's poor performance in the continuing Crimean War.

Initially, Alexander seemed both eager and able to fulfil these expectations. He brought the war to an end and re-established Russia as a significant member of the European concert. He proceeded to plan for the long-overdue abolition of serfdom on the grounds that 'It is better to abolish serfdom from above than to await the day when it will begin to abolish itself from below',[1] and also proposed a number of other major reforms, including the introduction of a more representative system of local government, the establishment of a new legal system with trial by jury and much more scope for legal advocacy, and the reorganization of the army. In addition, he promised to reintroduce a measure of self-government in the Kingdom of Poland.[2]

The Jewish elite placed similar hopes in the 'reforming tsar'. Shortly after his accession, on 31 March 1856, Alexander called on Pavel Kiselev as chairman of the government Committee for the Transformation of the Jews to conduct a comprehensive review of Russian legislation dealing with the Jews so as to facilitate 'the merger of this people [*narod*] with the native population insofar as the moral status of the Jews makes this possible'.[3] In his Coronation Manifesto of 26 August

[1] Emmons, *The Russian Landed Gentry and the Peasant Emancipation of 1861*, 51.

[2] On the reforms of Alexander II, see Lincoln, *The Great Reforms*, 24–60; Saunders, *Russia in the Age of Reaction and Reform, 1801–1881*, 204–77; Emmons, *The Russian Landed Gentry and the Peasant Emancipation of 1861*; and Rieber (ed.), *The Politics of Autocracy*.

[3] *PSZ* 2/xl, no. 42264 (28 June 1865), quoted in Klier, *Imperial Russia's Jewish Question, 1855–1881*, 15.

1856 Alexander announced his intention of reforming the way in which the draft was applied to the Jewish community.

There also appeared to be a significant change in the attitude of educated Russians to the 'Jewish question', epitomized in an exchange that took place in the press in 1858. On 26 July and 4 September V. R. Zotov published in the St Petersburg magazine *Illyustratsiya* two anti-Jewish articles, one attacking the banker Joseph Yozel (Evzel) Guenzburg (whom he referred to as 'Mr N') and a second describing the failings of 'the west Russian Yids' (*Zhidy*). These articles were denounced by two Jewish journalists, Isaak Andreevich Chatskin in *Russkii vestnik* on 17 September and M. Gorvitz in *Atenei* for September–October. Zotov responded in *Illyustratsiya* on 23 and 30 October by claiming that those who attacked him were 'without any doubt the agents of the well-known N, who obviously does not spare gold for the praise of his name and there thus appeared in print two Jewish littérateurs, a certain Reb Chatskin and a Reb Gorvits'. This provoked a public protest. On 18 November *Russkii vestnik* published a response entitled 'The Conduct of *Illyustratsiya* and a Protest', which attacked Zotov's behaviour and was signed by forty-eight people, including a number of well-known writers and publishers. It was amended in the next issue to include ninety-nine signatories as well as a letter from Ivan Turgenev expressing the hope that the protest would deter those who wished to emulate Zotov.[4] On 25 November *Sanktpeterburgskie vedomosti* published a further protest signed by eleven important literary figures, including Konstantin Kavelin, Vladimir Spasovich, Nikolay Chernyshevsky, Pavel Annenkov, and Ivan Turgenev, which concluded that 'We do not know Messrs Chatskin and Gorvits personally, and have no ties with them. But recognizing the high calling of literature, we consider it an obligation to protest against such an abuse of the printed word by a periodical which allows itself to become a weapon of personal insult.' In the Russian 'thick periodicals' a number of articles now appeared calling for the complete emancipation of the Jews.

The heady atmosphere of the time is captured in the poem 'Awake, My People', by one of the leading members of the Russian Jewish intelligentsia, the Hebrew poet Judah Leib Gordon (1831–92), which appeared in the Vilna Hebrew weekly *Hakarmel* in 1866:

> Awake my people! How long will you sleep?
> The night has passed, the sun shines through.
> Awake, cast your eyes hither and yon.
> Recognize your time and place.
>
> The land where we live and are born,
> Is it not thought to be part of Europe?
> Europe, the smallest of continents
> But the mightiest of all in wisdom and knowledge.

[4] On this, see Klier, *Imperial Russia's Jewish Question, 1855–1881*, 51–65.

This land of Eden is now open to you.
Its sons now call you 'brothers'.
How long will you dwell among them as a guest
Why do you reject their hand?

They have already removed the burden from your back
And lifted the yoke from around your neck.
They have erased from their hearts hatred and folly.
They stretch out their hands to you in peace.

So raise your head high, stand up straight,
Look at them with loving eyes.
Open your hearts to wisdom and reason.
Become an enlightened nation, speaking their tongue.

Everyone capable of learning should study.
Labourers and artisans should take to a craft.
The strong and the brave should be soldiers.
Farmers should buy fields and ploughs.

To the treasury of the state bring your wealth,
Bear your share of its riches and bounty,
Be a man in the streets and a Jew at home,
A brother to your countryman and a servant to your king.

There was some basis for these hopes. Even before Alexander's accession Count Kiselev, as head of the Jewish Committee, had prepared a memorandum in 1854 explaining why Nicholas's hope that conscription could be used to 'reform' the Jews was misplaced. He claimed that the Jews made bad soldiers and that the fines on Jewish communities for failing to fulfil their draft quotas made it impossible for them to pay their taxes. During the last months of the Crimean War the committee had also recommended a modification of the way in which the conscription law was being applied to the Jews, arguing that the number of conscripts demanded was too high.[5] This modification constituted part of the Coronation Manifesto, which laid down that Jews were to be conscripted in the same way as members of other estates, as had been requested in a petition to the Jewish Committee by a group of twenty leading Jewish merchants and 'honorary citizens'.[6] If there were a shortage of recruits, the general laws would be applied and additional recruits (three for every one who did not report) would no longer be exacted from Jewish communities as a penalty. The practice introduced in 1853, whereby individuals or communities could substitute Jews without passports for those conscripted, was abolished.

Cantonist schools were abolished for the general population in the Coronation Manifesto and, as a consequence, child soldiers, including Jewish cantonists, were now returned to their parents or relatives. The one exception was in the case of

5 On this, see Stanislawski, *Tsar Nicholas and the Jews*, 184–8.

6 Gessen, *Istoriya evreiskogo naroda v Rossii*, ii. 140–1.

converts, who were to be placed with Christian families. Jews who did not convert were still barred from military promotion. Only in 1861 was permission given to promote a Jew to sergeant for general merit, rather than for distinction on the battlefield as had previously been the case. Promotion to a higher rank was ruled out.

On 14 March 1856, shortly after Alexander's accession, Kiselev had submitted a memorandum to him pointing out that 'the attainment of the goal indicated in the imperial decree of 1840 of bringing about the merger (*sliyanie*) of the Jews with the general population is hampered by various restrictions introduced on a provisional basis which, taken in conjunction with the general laws, contain contradictions and engender confusion'. He enumerated the issues which he felt hindered this aim. The government had failed to exercise effective control over Jewish religious life and was losing the struggle against 'fanaticism'. It had pursued inconsistently the goal of fostering progressive education among the Jews, and problems had arisen because for Jews who had been through higher education there were few career openings outside the civil service, which was still barred to them. Jews were, in addition, prevented from participating in local government on an equal footing with Christians and were still subject to a series of restrictions on their place of residence, their right to own property, and their freedom to choose a trade or profession.[7]

In response to this memorandum, on 31 March 1856 Alexander called on the Jewish Committee to conduct a thorough review of all legislation concerning Jews. This led to a prolonged debate, concluded only in 1865, on how far the existing restrictions on Jewish residence and choice of occupation should be relaxed. During this review the minister of the interior, Sergey S. Lanskoy, canvassed the opinion of the governors and governors-general of provinces which might be affected. Among them there were a number who favoured the abolition of the Pale of Settlement and of all other restrictions imposed on Jews. This was the view of the governor-general of New Russia and Bessarabia, Count A. G. Stroganov, who wrote to Lanskoy on 22 January 1858 advocating the immediate granting of civil rights to the Jews and allowing them freedom of both residence and choice of occupation. In his opinion the Jews should be allowed 'to live in all places in the empire and engage without any restrictions and on equal terms with all Russian subjects in such crafts and industries as they themselves may choose, in accordance with their habits and abilities'. The adoption of such a policy would accord with the 'law of justice' and would benefit the national economy as well as undermine Jewish 'fanaticism'.[8] A similar position was adopted by Prince I. I. Vasilchikov, governor (later governor-general) of Kiev, Podolia, and Volhynia,

[7] Dubnow, *History of the Jews in Russia and Poland*, ii. 157–8; Gessen, *Istoriya evreiskogo naroda v Rossii*, ii. 142.

[8] Gessen, 'Popytka emansipatsii evreev v Rossii', 158–62; Dubnow, *History of the Jews in Russia and Poland*, ii. 169.

who argued that the surplus of Jewish master craftsmen in his region would be relieved by allowing them to move to the interior of Russia.[9] In 1861 Lanskoy himself, who had earlier argued that it was discrimination which had been responsible for the failure of the government's attempts to transform the Jews into useful citizens, together with the minister of public enlightenment, E. P. Kovalevsky, submitted a report to the Jewish Committee advocating the abolition of the Pale of Settlement.[10] Similar calls were made in 1862 by Count A. K. Sievers, the governor of the province of Kharkov, adjacent to the Pale of Settlement, and in the following year by the minister of finance, M. K. Reitern.[11]

These views were rejected in favour of more gradual and limited measures by the Jewish Committee, chaired from 1856 by Count Dmitry Bludov after Kiselev's appointment as Russian ambassador to France. In Bludov's view, Jewish emancipation would have to be an incremental process and could only be fully implemented when the Jews had reformed their communal life, acquired Western-style education, and become engaged in 'useful' occupations.[12] This view was shared by the majority of the committee and by the administration, including the tsar. On 17 February 1861 the committee rejected Stroganov's call for the immediate granting of civil rights to the Jews on the grounds that 'the equalization of the Jews in rights with the native population cannot be carried out other than gradually, by means of disseminating among them true enlightenment, by changing their internal life, and by directing them towards useful pursuits'. Alexander minuted 'I quite agree'.[13] It was the tsar who had stressed in his 1856 instructions to the Jewish Committee that the granting of rights was conditional on the moral transformation of the Jews, something of which he saw relatively little sign.

The main reason why the government was unwilling to abolish the Pale of Settlement and allow unrestricted Jewish emigration into the interior of Russia seems to have been the widespread conviction within its ranks that the recently emancipated peasantry would be unable to cope with its new freedom and would lose its land to outsiders. It was to preserve the stability of village life that the peasant commune (*mir*, or *obshchina*) was retained and that after 1862 the chief official in a rural district, the *ispravnik*, was no longer elected by the local nobility but appointed by the Ministry of the Interior. The peasant commune, which retained the power to redistribute village land periodically and to determine crop rotation, was now entrusted with the collection of taxes and could employ the sanction of

[9] *PSZ* 2/xl, no. 42264 (28 June 1865).

[10] For their views, see ibid., cited in Levanda, 1036–8; and Rogger, 'Government, Jews, Peasants and Land after the Liberation of the Serfs', 122. See also Gessen, 'Popytka emansipatsii evreev v Rossii', 158–62, and id., *Istoriya evreiskogo naroda v Rossii*, ii. 148.

[11] Gessen, *Zakon i zhizn'*, 130–1, and id., *Istoriya evreiskogo naroda v Rossii*, ii. 158–60.

[12] Gessen, *Zakon i zhizn'*, 111.

[13] Gessen, *Istoriya evreiskogo naroda v Rossii*, ii. 147–8; Klier, *Imperial Russia's Jewish Question, 1855–1881*, 20–1.

collective responsibility to ensure their payment. It also continued to administer justice at the local level and was able to grant permission to leave or join its ranks.[14]

The belief that the village had to be protected from Jewish exploitation was widespread in the administration. Thus the governor-general of the North-West, Vladimir I. Nazimov, who had been a key figure in drafting the proposals for peasant emancipation ultimately enacted in the decree of 19 February 1861, rejected the abolition of all restrictions on Jewish activities, which, in his view, would only reinforce 'parasitism' and harmful middleman activities.[15] Similarly, the new governor-general of New Russia and Bessarabia, Count P. E. Kotzebue, argued in 1862 that the Pale of Settlement should only gradually be abolished and that Jews should first be given the right to settle, conduct trade, and obtain land only in the urban areas of the empire. 'Permission for the Jews to settle in the villages and the countryside would place them in direct contact with our agricultural population, which in its present material and moral condition would be more likely to fall victim to the speculative activities of the Jews than to derive benefit from close relations with them.'[16]

Accordingly, the government was not prepared to abolish all restrictions on the Jews. Its policy has been described as one of 'selective integration', the rewarding of those sections of Jewish society which had succeeded in transforming themselves on the lines advocated by the authorities, 'a process by which the tsarist state hoped to disperse certain categories of Jews into the Russian social hierarchy'.[17] It was premised on the assumption that there were groups within the Jewish community which would respond to incentives of the sort offered by the government and who, 'once "merged", would cease to constitute a separate estate, or even a distinct social and legal entity'.[18] This can be seen as a late example of an approach to the Jews widely adopted in the late eighteenth and early nineteenth centuries, in which governments rewarded those Jews willing to acculturate, while offering a grudging toleration to the rest (normally the majority). As we have seen, this policy was first implemented in revolutionary France, where the national assembly emancipated the French Sephardi communities before those of Alsace, and was later adopted in the Prussian emancipatory legislation of 1812 and 1833.

The government ultimately decided to ease the restrictions on three groups of Jews, who it was thought would contribute to the economy and who were unlikely to come into conflict with the peasantry: merchants of the first guild, university graduates, and artisans belonging to a guild. The matter was considered by the Jewish Committee throughout the early years of Alexander's reign.

14 On the terms of the emancipation, see Emmons, *The Russian Landed Gentry and the Peasant Emancipation of 1861*, Field, *The End of Serfdom*, and Zaionchkovsky, *Otmena krepostnogo prava v Rossii*.

15 RGIA, f. 1282, op. 2, ed. khr. 64 (1860–1), 60–7, quoted in Klier, *Imperial Russia's Jewish Question, 1855–1881*, 21.

16 Gessen, *Zakon i zhizn'*, 128–9.

17 Nathans, *Beyond the Pale*, 78.

18 Ibid.

After protracted discussion, a resolution on merchants was adopted and enacted as a law by the tsar on 16 March 1859, laying down that approximately 100 Jewish merchants who had belonged to the first guild for not less than two years prior to the enactment of the law were to be permitted to settle permanently in the interior provinces, accompanied by their families and a limited number of servants and clerks. They were to be entitled to live and trade on equal terms with Russian merchants, with the proviso that after their settlement they should continue their membership of the first guild, which included paying the appropriate membership dues, for no less than ten years, failing which they would be sent back to the Pale. Jewish merchants and bankers from abroad 'noted for their social position' were to be allowed to trade in Russia under a special permit to be secured in each case from the ministers of the interior and finance.[19]

As regards those who had been through higher education, it was resolved to deny the right of residence in the interior to gymnasium graduates, limiting it to graduates of universities and other institutions of higher learning who had received the degrees of doctor, master, or candidate (equivalent to a bachelor's degree). Such individuals, according to the decree of 27 November 1861, were permitted not only to settle anywhere in the empire but also to enter the civil service.[20]

Towards the end of Alexander's reign, by a decree of 19 January 1879, this privilege was extended to all Jews who had received higher education, regardless of the type of diploma, so that the categories now covered included pharmacists, dentists, feldshers (physicians' assistants), and midwives.

These relaxations on the restrictions on Jewish settlement only affected a small minority of the Jewish community. Nevertheless, one of their consequences was the development of the Jewish community of St Petersburg. Jewish notables such as Samuel Polyakov and Joseph Guenzburg established themselves there and became effective advocates of the Jewish cause.

Within the Jewish Committee considerable discussion was devoted to the question of how much further the privileges should be extended. As we have seen, there was a fair amount of support among the governors and governors-general of the western provinces for allowing Jewish artisans to settle in the interior of Russia. Only the governor-general of the North-West region thought the existing regime should be maintained. In the end the Jewish Committee decided to allow artisans to settle throughout the empire, but under strict conditions. When, shortly before its dissolution in 1863, the committee referred the matter to the Committee of Ministers and the Council of State, the new minister of the interior, Petr Valuev, cautioned against allowing Jewish artisans to settle in the interior with Jewish domestics, on the ground that this would

> enable Jewish businessmen of all kinds to reside in the interior provinces under the guise of employees of their coreligionists . . . The Jews will endeavour to transfer their activity to a

[19] Dubnow, *History of the Jews in Russia and Poland*, ii. 162.

[20] Ibid. 166; *PSZ* 2/xxxvi, no. 37684 (27 Nov. 1861).

field more favourable to them, and it goes without saying that they will not fail to seize the first opportunity of exploiting the places of the Empire hitherto inaccessible to them.[21]

As a result, the legislation of 28 June 1865 which permitted Jewish master craftsmen and craftsmen, mechanics, distillers, and brewers to leave the Pale of Settlement imposed significant restrictions on this privilege. In the view of those who drafted this legislation, 'recognizing the need to proceed with changes to a long-established order, it should be accomplished with caution and gradually, especially in the present case where it might mean the rapid flood into the interior of a long-alien element'.[22] An artisan who wished to move outside the Pale had to produce a certificate from his guild attesting to his qualifications and a document from the police confirming that he was not accused of any crime. At specified intervals he had to obtain a passport from his native town in the Pale, since his status in the interior was that of temporary resident. He was allowed to deal only with goods he produced himself, and if he was out of work had to return to his original home. Given the restrictions, relatively few people availed themselves of the new privilege, while some who did without the requisite qualifications were constantly at the mercy of the police, whom they had to bribe in order to remain in their new places of residence.[23]

One final category of people allowed to reside outside the Pale was that of retired soldiers. This concession was only reluctantly conceded. In response to a proposal of the Jewish Committee in 1858 that these soldiers be allowed to live in the interior, the tsar responded, 'I decidedly refuse to agree.' However, on 3 June 1862 a group of retired soldiers who had served in the guards battalions were allowed to remain in St Petersburg. It was only in 1867 that this privilege was extended to all former soldiers.[24]

With the large majority of Jews still confined to the Pale of Settlement, the emancipation of the serfs created a new situation for them, closely connected as most were with the manorial system as the agents of the nobility in the Pale and the principal commercial link between the village and the small town. For some Jews the commercialization of agriculture provided great economic opportunities, but most were not in a position to profit from the new situation. In August 1869, writing in the Russian Jewish weekly *Den'* (this paper should be distinguished from that with the same name edited by the Slavophile Ivan Aksakov), Ilya Orshansky warned of the need to adapt to the new conditions, which were having a devastating impact on Jewish life in the Pale: 'the impoverished situation of our co-religionists in Russia . . . is a transitory phenomenon, a temporary one, and will be eliminated to the degree that Jewry adapts itself to new structures of life, forgetting old trades and occupations which are now obsolete, and learning new ones'.[25]

21 Dubnow, *History of the Jews in Russia and Poland*, ii. 170.

22 Gessen, *Zakon i zhizn'*, 128–9.

23 *PSZ* 2/xl, no. 42268 (28 June 1865).

24 *PSZ* 2/xxxvii, no. 38444 (3 June 1862); Gessen, *Istoriya evreiskogo naroda v Rossii*, ii. 144.

25 *Den'*, 22 Aug. 1869.

A decade later the situation had worsened. An article in the Russian Jewish newspaper *Nedel'naya khronika Voskhoda* drew attention to the impoverishment of the Jews of Pinsk by the construction of a railway from Brest to Kiev, which had left redundant those who had previously been involved in transporting grain from Pinsk to Kiev by river.[26]

Jewish poverty was not new in eastern Europe, but the massive impoverishment of the late nineteenth century, which was exacerbated by the increase in the Jewish population of the tsarist empire from around 1 million in 1800 to over 5.2 million in the census of 1897, created the new phenomenon of the *luftmenshn* desperately seeking employment wherever they could, and lay at the root of both the massive emigration which began even before the assassination of Alexander and the radicalization of much of Jewish life.

Jewish poverty was exacerbated by the desire of tsarist bureaucrats to protect the peasantry in their unaccustomed new freedom and to guard against Jewish 'exploitation'. They thus attempted to reconcile 'what the government of the tsars had so far found irreconcilable: subsistence for several hundred thousand Jews lacking in skills, capital or regular employment; the well-being of several million peasants; the interests of their Polish and Russian landlords and those of the exchequer'.[27] A number of regulations on Jewish residence were now relaxed. Jews were permitted to live in Nikolaev (today Mykolayiv), Sevastopol, and parts of Kiev, from which they had been excluded although these towns were technically within the Pale and were important trading centres. They were also able to live in all parts of towns like Vilna and Zhitomir, where they had previously been forbidden to live on certain streets.

In 1857, even before the abolition of serfdom, the Council of State had abrogated the 1853 regulation which laid down that only Jewish farmers or manufacturers could acquire rural parcels of land. The following year those who owned property in the frontier zone from which Jews had been expelled in 1843 in order to combat smuggling were allowed to return, and in 1859 Jews were permitted to lease and settle on mortgaged estates on which there was a serf population, a measure intended above all to assist landowners and those to whom they owed money.[28]

The abolition of serfdom raised the question of whether Jews should have the right to acquire that part of the land which had passed outright into noble hands. Initially, the emancipation decree forbade Jews to acquire such land even in the case of mortgage default. The shortage of capital in the Pale of Settlement led to a change in policy, and in 1862 the Jewish Committee agreed to grant a petition from Jewish first-guild merchants that Jews in the Pale be allowed to buy noble

[26] Quoted in Klier, 'From "Little Man" to "Milkman"', 220.

[27] Rogger, 'Government, Jews, Peasants and Land after the Liberation of the Serfs', 123–4.

[28] *PSZ* 2/xxxii, no. 31400, cited in Levanda, 857; *PSZ* 2/xxxiii, no. 33659, cited in Levanda, 901–3; *PSZ* 2/xxxiv, no. 35016, cited in Levanda, 925–6. See also Rogger, 'Government, Jews, Peasants and Land after the Liberation of the Serfs', 124.

lands on which there were no longer any obligations between peasants and owners.[29]

Jews also benefited from the reform of local government in 1864 which saw the establishment of district and provincial assemblies (*zemstva*) with executive committees in all except the nine formerly Polish provinces and some provinces in the north and far east. They were given the right to levy taxes and to spend the proceeds on schools, public health, roads, and other social services, although they were also required to carry out tasks deputed to them by the authorities. Jews who satisfied the requirements of the property-qualified franchise were able to vote and be elected to these assemblies. In Ukraine, in particular, Jews began to participate in rural assemblies and were also sometimes appointed to rural offices.

Even more important was the judicial reform of 1864, which established a system of courts based on European models with irremovable judges and a system of appeal. While it did leave to the Ministry of the Interior the right to banish individuals without trial, and left the settlement of disputes between peasants to the peasant courts which had been established in the 1840s, it marked a clear step towards the establishment of the rule of law. One aspect of this was the emergence of the Russian bar as an independent organization which Jews were allowed to join. A number of Jews soon became eminent members of the legal profession, including Maksim Vinaver, Oskar Gruzenberg, and Genrikh Sliozberg.[30] In Michael Stanislawski's words:

> Beyond the social pressure that encouraged Jews to study law and the governmental pressure which inadvertently encouraged research by restricting Jews from fully-fledged legal practice, there was a basic ideological confluence between the Russian bar and the Jewish historians (as well as the 'juridical' wing of Russian historians). All had at their core a profound belief in Western, mostly Anglo-Saxon, concepts of equality, justice and the rule of law which would liberate all Russians including the Jews, in an imminent *Rechtstaat*.[31]

The Jewish lawyers also saw their role as defending Jews unjustly accused of crimes. The first major case of this type was a ritual murder trial in the eastern Caucasus in 1878. Here a team of Jewish lawyers succeeded in obtaining the acquittal of the Jews accused of killing a child for ritual purposes, but were unable, as they had hoped, to persuade the court to hold that there was no such a crime as ritual murder.

As in Poland, a variety of terms were employed to describe what was involved in the government's main goal to transform the Jews. These included emancipation (*emansipatsiya*), Europeanization (*evropeizatsiya*), assimilation (*assimilyatsiya*), and Russification (*obrusenie*). All of these were vague and, with the exception of

[29] *PSZ* 2/xxxvii, no. 38214 (26 Apr. 1861), cited in Levanda, 980–1. Before emancipation the position of the serfs was summed up in the peasant assertion 'We are yours but the land is ours'.

[30] For an account of the connection between the study of Russian Jewish history and the legal circles in St Petersburg, see Vinaver, 'Kak my zanimalis' istoriei'.

[31] Stanislawski, *Tsar Nicholas and the Jews*, 6.

Russification, did not correspond to Russian realities. The three words most favoured by the bureaucracy were union (*soedinenie*), rapprochement (*sblizhenie*), and merger (*sliyanie*).[32] All implied a reform of the Jews so as to weaken the 'deleterious effect' on them of the Talmud, which was seen as anti-Christian and the root of Jewish separatism, and to strengthen Russian cultural influences.

This was also the goal of the educational reforms of Uvarov. The Jewish Committee believed that these would weaken the role of the Talmud as the basis of Jewish national identity (*natsional'nost'*) and promote a knowledge of the Russian language and Russian history, since 'nothing unites an individual people [*plemya*] with the dominant nationality like the spread of information about its history and literature'.[33] (On these reforms, see Chapter 11.)

After 1855 the term 'merger' became more usual than 'rapprochement'. When Kiselev wrote to Alexander describing the failures of Nicholas's reforms, he described their goal as 'merger', a term also employed by Alexander in his instructions to the Jewish Committee. It differed from the earlier terms in that some of those who used it saw it as linked with the creation of a society in which some Jews would meet with Christians on equal terms. The superiority of Christian values was taken for granted. Thus, in a report to the Ministry of Public Enlightenment on 22 January 1858 Count Stroganov called for Jews to be granted civil rights. 'By this path the West has moved forward to the attainment of the lofty goal of the merger of Jews with Christians, a goal tied closely with the divine truths of Christianity.'[34] When Sergey Lanskoy, the minister of the interior, wrote to the Jewish Committee advocating Jewish equality on 25 October 1858, he used both terms:

> the merger or, to put it more precisely, the rapprochement of the Jewish people with the native population in education, occupation and the like . . . can be attained only by the equalization of the Jews in rights with the other inhabitants of the Empire and therefore special enactments of any sort for them, excepting those treating of religion, and assorted restrictions and limitations, must be seen as absolute obstacles to their rapprochement with the rest of the population and virtually the one and only cause of the wretched condition in which they are still found among us.[35]

Conversion to Russian Orthodoxy was no longer as actively fostered as in Nicholas's reign. In 1864 the government abandoned one of its incentives to conversion by discontinuing the practice of paying special allowances to Jewish converts serving in the army. It also repealed the law whereby a convicted criminal could obtain a lighter sentence by conversion to Christianity.

'Union' and 'rapprochement' had been among the principal goals of the state-run Jewish school system established under Nicholas in 1842. As is clear from

[32] On this question, see Klier, *Imperial Russia's Jewish Question, 1855–1881*, 66–83.

[33] Quoted ibid. 74.

[34] 'Aleksandr II', *Evreiskaya starina*, 1 (1909), 814, quoted ibid. 75.

[35] Ibid.

Kiselev's memorandum of March 1856, the authorities were now not at all satisfied with the achievements of this system. However, Russian officials remained confident of the value of this school system to draw Jews out of their traditional isolation, and some steps were taken in the early years of Alexander's reign to strengthen it. On 3 May 1855 a law laid down that after a period of twenty years only graduates of the state secondary-school system or the rabbinical seminaries could be employed as rabbis or teachers.[36] Efforts were also made to increase supervision over *ḥeder*s, whose reform was also the concern of the maskilim and the Jewish intelligentsia.

One of the reasons why the system was unpopular with most Jews was because it was seen as part of the oppressive system established by Nicholas, and because they believed that one of its goals was to convert the Jews to Christianity. The government required that school heads be Christian, like many of the teachers of secular subjects, and many of these individuals were unsympathetic to Jewish concerns. There was some awareness within the bureaucracy of the defects of the system, and some attempts were made to make it more effective and popular. On 12 March 1859 the minister of public enlightenment, E. P. Kovalevsky, observed:

> the spread of humane knowledge among the Jews by itself can shake and ultimately eradicate the moral–religious prejudices which are rooted in them. Therefore, it seems to me, every means should be used to encourage subjects necessary for a humane education, not only in state, but in private Jewish schools, and at the same time [we should] meddle as little as possible in the religious teaching of children, leaving that to the responsibility of their parents.[37]

This was followed on 6 September 1862 by a law permitting Jews to serve as headmasters of Jewish primary and secondary schools.[38]

There was also a broader debate within the bureaucracy and among both Russians and Jews over the utility of the system. Within the Jewish world there were those, many of them graduates of the system, who wished to retain and reform it. Others called instead for admission of Jews to the general educational system, now in the process of substantial reform, with the enactment of a University Statute on 18 June 1863 and a new law on primary schools on 14 July 1864. In September 1858 Joseph Guenzburg had sent a petition to the minister of public enlightenment calling for 'religion-free' education to be available for Jews.[39]

In 1864 the Ministry of Public Enlightenment commissioned a report from one of its inspectors, F. Postels, on all aspects of Jewish education, both state and

[36] *PSZ* 2/xxxii, no. 31831 (3 May 1855).

[37] Tsherikover, *Istoriya Obshchestva dlya rasprostraneniya prosveshcheniya mezhdu evreyami v Rossii, 1863–1913 gg.*, 14, quoted in Klier, *Imperial Russia's Jewish Question, 1855–1881*, 228.

[38] *PSZ* 2/xxxviii, no. 38641 (6 Sept. 1862).

[39] On this, see Alston, *Education and the State in Tsarist Russia*; Tsherikover, *Istoriya Obshchestva dlya rasprostraneniya prosveshcheniya mezhdu evreyami v Rossii, 1863–1913 gg.*, 33–4.

private. His findings confirmed the unsatisfactory state of most *ḥeder*s but did not make clear recommendations either for their reform or for the expansion of the state system.[40] Three years later the new minister of public enlightenment, Count Dmitry Tolstoy, himself investigated the problem. While impressed with the achievements of the state system in Odessa, he felt that it was working badly everywhere else. This led him to recommend that it be closed down and the resources used to improve existing district schools, where Jews could acquire 'useful trades' alongside Christians. He set up a committee to examine the question. His view that the system had outlived its usefulness was supported by those who believed that 'merger' would be fostered by a single school system. Chief among them was the Kiev paper *Kievlyanin*, noted for its hostility to Jews.

It took some six years for the decision finally to be taken. On 16 March 1873 a decree of the Ministry of Public Enlightenment drastically reduced the number of Jewish primary schools, which now offered only a one-year course. Jewish secondary schools were abolished and the state rabbinical seminaries transformed into teacher training colleges (that in Zhitomir was closed in 1885, while that in Vilna lasted until the end of tsarist rule). Count Tolstoy justified his decision on the grounds that the system was no longer necessary because of the significant increase in Jewish enrolment in the general schools system. This was certainly now occurring on a larger scale, so that by 1875 the Committee of Ministers could express concern that Jews were denying gymnasium places to Christians and abolish the scholarship programme which had been established to encourage Jewish entry into these schools.[41] The entry of Jews into the Russian school system accelerated in the 1870s. According to Ministry of Public Enlightenment statistics, by 1880 Jews made up nearly 7,000 of the 66,000 enrolled in secondary education, and their representation as a percentage of this group was rising. This was a reversal of the long-standing fear of general education within the Jewish community, but soon aroused fears that 'The Yid is on the move [*zhid idet*]'. According to a letter from an Orthodox priest published on 5 August 1881 in Ivan Aksakov's periodical *Rus'*, 'It is hard to live with the Jews now, and it will be still harder when they become the intelligentsia of our region, something that apparently cannot be avoided.'[42]

Jews not only began to enter gymnasiums but also sought university education, both for its own sake and to acquire professional skills and the unrestricted residential rights granted to Jewish university graduates in 1861.[43] Medicine was one of the first areas of higher learning in which the Russian government began to loosen restrictions. The Medical–Surgical Academy in St Petersburg contained the greatest concentration of Jewish male students of any Russian institution of

[40] 'Otchet chlena Soveta ministra narodnogo prosveshcheniya Postel'sa, po obozreniyu evreiskikh uchilishch s 7 maya po 7 sentyabrya 1864 goda', *Zhurnal Ministerstva Narodnogo Prosveshcheniya*, 125 (1865), quoted in Klier, *Imperial Russia's Jewish Question, 1855–1881*, 230–1.

[41] Klier, *Imperial Russia's Jewish Question, 1855–1881*, 238.

[42] Quoted ibid. 405.

[43] Nathans, *Beyond the Pale*, 214–15.

higher learning in the early part of the nineteenth century.[44] Over the course of the nineteenth century government decrees made medical service more attractive to Jews, so that by the 1880s, one observer maintained, 'there was almost no occasion when a (male) Jewish gymnasium student applied to anything but a medical faculty'.[45] Jews were drawn to medicine for both practical and moral reasons, and medicine came to be seen as one of the most effective means for Jews both to contribute to the general welfare and to transform Jewish society.[46]

The government also continued the attempts begun during the reign of Nicholas I to restructure Jewish religious life. In November 1855, shortly after Alexander's accession, Kiselev wrote to Sergey Lanskoy, requesting permission to reconvene the Rabbinic Commission, stressing the 'lofty' goals which this body could serve in reforming Jewish religious and family life.[47] As before, it proved difficult to select suitable 'enlightened' candidates for the commission, and Prince Vasilchikov, governor-general of Kiev, Podolia, and Volhynia, in particular, stressed the difficulties he faced since, in contrast to Lithuania, 'the Jewish masses here have the lowest level of general education . . . those who devote the entire or vast part of their lives to studying Jewish spiritual books, religious laws and Talmudic interpretations are venerated among the Jews, defining all the conditions of family, social and civil life', while people with general education were rare and did not enjoy the respect of fellow Jews, who 'scornfully' dismissed them as 'Frenchmen or Germans'.[48]

The five members of the Rabbinic Commission selected by the Ministry of the Interior were all moderate maskilim and included Dr Abraham Neumann, a Bavarian-born Jew who had served as a state rabbi and the director of a Jewish school in Riga and was later appointed rabbi in St Petersburg; the Odessa maskil Marcus Gurovich, who had already undertaken a field mission in 1854 to assess the impact of government policies on the Jews in New Russia; the merchant Yekutiel-Zisl Rapoport of Minsk, a prominent Jewish notable and intercessor; and Jacob Barit (1797–1883), a leading figure in Vilna religious life.[49]

Much of the deliberation of this Rabbinic Commission was devoted to how to encourage the education of Jewish women, a reflection of how women's education

44 Approximately forty Jewish men matriculated between 1835 and 1854: Nathans, *Beyond the Pale*, 60.

45 Sliozberg, *Dela minuvshikh dnei*, i. 110–11, as quoted in Epstein, 'Caring for the Soul's House', 48.

46 The hope that modern medicine would help reform the Jews is well discussed in Epstein, 'Caring for the Soul's House', 1–2.

47 Memorandum from P. D. Kiselev to the Ministry of the Interior, 'Regarding the Rabbinic Commission and Provincial Rabbinate', 26 Nov. 1855, RGIA, f. 821, op. 8, d. 281, ll. 8–11 ob., quoted in Freeze, *Jewish Marriage and Divorce in Imperial Russia*, 89.

48 Letter of the military governor of Kiev, Podolia, and Volhynia to the Minister of the Interior, 3 July 1856, RGIA, f. 821, op. 1, d. 281, l. 53 ob., quoted in Freeze, *Jewish Marriage and Divorce in Imperial Russia*, 89.

49 On Neumann, see *Evreiskaya entsiklopediya*, xi. 656; on Gurovich, Rapoport, and Barit, see Lederhendler, *The Road to Modern Jewish Politics*, 77–9, 94, 143–4.

had become part of the political climate of the time.[50] (For more detail on Jewish women's education, see Volume II, Chapter 9.) The ministry entrusted the commission with the task of 'propagating a healthier understanding of this subject among the Jews [and] transmitting it through educated rabbis',[51] hoping in this way to increase support in the Jewish community for the education of girls at communal expense. Aware of the hostility in traditional circles to education for women, the commission proposed that rabbis, preachers, and teachers of Jewish law in state schools should seek 'to inspire, in the hearts of the young and in their parents, an aspiration to educate their children, regardless of sex'. They should preach the importance of education and that 'daughters, between the ages of eleven and twelve years, attend sabbath and religious holidays, and also be present at ceremonies to hear these edifying sermons'.[52] This somewhat naive approach was attacked by the Odessa maskil Mikhail Morgulis (1837–1912), who stressed that it was, above all, economic stringency, rather than the teachings of the Talmud, which limited the spread of education for Jewish girls.[53] Nevertheless, the commission's deliberations are a testimony to its commitment to moderate reform and to the role which the government at this stage envisaged for it.

The next Rabbinic Commission, which met between November 1861 and March 1862, was also dominated by moderate maskilim, although for the first time it included a hasidic representative, Avraham Madievsky from Poltava province, a follower of the Lubavitcher Rebbe. By now the government was becoming disillusioned with the reforming potential of the commission, which, as a result, was now transformed into a body whose principal responsibility was to review rabbinic decisions in divorce cases, a development which increased its legitimacy and importance in Orthodox circles.[54]

The government's attempt to use the state rabbinate to transform Jewish life was also largely unsuccessful. As we have seen, according to the decree of 3 May 1855, candidacy for the post of state rabbi was open not only to graduates of 'rabbinic seminaries [and] secondary Jewish state schools' but also to those who had completed a degree in 'secular institutions of higher, secondary, and primary education'.[55] This probably reflected a desire on the part of the authorities to encourage the selection of those with secular education who could combat Jewish 'fanaticism', but it clearly made the position of graduates of the two rabbinic schools more difficult. There were those in the administration, most notably the governor-general of the North-West, Vladimir Nazimov, who wanted the authorities to favour graduates of state-sponsored rabbinic schools. In a lengthy

[50] On this, see Stites, *The Women's Liberation Movement in Russia*, 29–63.

[51] RGIA, f. 821, op. 8, d. 282, l. 39 ob., quoted in Freeze, *Jewish Marriage and Divorce in Imperial Russia*, 90.

[52] Cited in Morgulis, 'K istorii obrazovaniya russkikh evreev', first pub. in *Evreiskaya biblioteka*, i–iii (St Petersburg, 1872–3), i. 330.

[53] Ibid. 331.

[54] On this meeting of the commission, see Freeze, *Jewish Marriage and Divorce in Imperial Russia*, 91–5.

[55] *PSZ* 2/xxxii, no. 31831, cited in Levanda, 880.

memorandum to the Ministry of the Interior in 1861 he emphasized that reform could be achieved only by 'uprooting the influence of backward and fanatical rabbis' and by replacing them with enlightened minds versed in both secular and religious subjects.[56]

Local communities had the right to select their state rabbi, and most were strongly resistant to graduates of the rabbinic schools. Thus in the elections for 236 rabbinic positions supervised by Nazimov in 1859 and 1860, there were only fifteen candidates from these schools and none were elected.[57] Like their counterparts in the emerging Russian intelligentsia, the schools' graduates saw themselves as having a mission to transform Jewish life. In the words of a letter addressed by students at the Vilna School to the authorities: 'Joyously, we take our posts because we have been presented with the opportunity (in consort with the will of the state) to further the education and to raise the morals of our co-religionists.'[58]

Similarly, with the support of the faculty at the Zhitomir Rabbinic School, the students, in a petition of 1 April 1859, urged the state to annul the elections and simply appoint them as state rabbis: 'Given the aversion of the majority of Jews toward European education and toward those with a European education, it is impossible to wait for the new rabbi to be elected voluntarily by the community.'[59]

Those who ran the rabbinic schools were aware how difficult it would be to replace the spiritual rabbinate and envisaged a more limited role for their alumni. Writing in *Kievskii telegraf* on 31 November 1865, Hayim Selig Slonimski, head of the Zhitomir Rabbinic School, argued that the spiritual rabbi would not disappear soon. The role of the state rabbis was to act as a countervailing force, checking the spread of fanaticism and preparing the way for enlightenment.[60]

Certainly even enlightened communities like that in Odessa regarded the graduates of the schools as callow and inexperienced, voting in 1859 for the German-trained rabbi Simeon Aryeh Schwabacher, who had previously served in Landsberg, Bavaria, and in Lviv. Fearful of the government desire to impose graduates of the schools on them as rabbis, a group of Vilna Jews sent a petition on 11 October 1859 to the minister of the interior explaining why they had rejected the state rabbinical students. They claimed that, 'in contrast to other Jewish communities', Vilna had always had the most renowned rabbis of each century, famous for their 'erudite scholarship, high merit, and other qualities'. Rather than

[56] Memorandum from the governor-general of Vilna, Grodno, and Kovno provinces to the Ministry of the Interior, n.d., RGIA, f. 821, op. 8, d. 408, l. 510–510 ob., quoted in Freeze, *Jewish Marriage and Divorce in Imperial Russia*, 99.

[57] Letter from the governor-general of Vilna, Grodno, and Kovno provinces to the Ministry of the Interior, 17 Nov. 1859, RGIA, f. 821, op. 8, d. 408, l. 1, quoted in Freeze, *Jewish Marriage and Divorce in Imperial Russia*, 100.

[58] RGIA, f. 821, op. 8, d. 408, ll. 5 ob.–6, 13–13 ob., quoted in Freeze, *Jewish Marriage and Divorce in Imperial Russia*, 101.

[59] Petition organized by Feitel Blyumendfeld to the Ministry of the Interior, 1 Apr. 1859, RGIA, f. 821, op. 8, d. 405, quoted in Freeze, *Jewish Marriage and Divorce in Imperial Russia*, 102.

[60] Quoted in Klier, *Imperial Russia's Jewish Question, 1855–1881*, 241.

accept inexperienced students, they proposed to select Jacob Barit, 'an erudite scholar educated in Europe' and a prominent member of the Rabbinic Commission in St Petersburg.[61]

These fears were somewhat misplaced. The Jewish Committee was not particularly eager to impose graduates of the rabbinic schools on unwilling communities. In its view, depriving Jewish communities of the right to free elections would 'fail, like other coercive measures applied to the Jews'. It had little desire to repeat the scandal caused by the imposition of an unsuitable candidate in Vilna in 1860, which had been commented on in the Austrian and Polish press. At the same time it did urge local government officials to 'exert a proper influence and to do what they could to arrange for the selection of rabbinic school graduates'.[62]

Educated opinion in Russia was also becoming less sympathetic to Jewish concerns. As we have seen, Jews were greatly encouraged by the way in which many Russian literary figures had come to their defence in the *Illyustratsiya* affair. Those debates on the Jewish question were part of a new openness following the relaxation of censorship after the death of Nicholas I. Alexander's government abolished the Censorship Committee created in response to the fears provoked by the 1848 revolution in Europe, and after some delay established in 1865 a set of regulations which ended pre-publication censorship in Moscow and St Petersburg.[63] In addition, the prohibition established in the 1840s by the censors on advocating the granting of civil rights to the Jews on the grounds that this showed a lack of confidence in the government's benevolence was now abrogated.[64] As was the case with peasant emancipation, the government encouraged discussion of the Jewish issue as an aid to policy-making. Although it would have preferred to keep this debate within strict limits, this proved impossible and a wide range of opinions was expressed. The level of these discussions, in which some Jews participated, was not, for the most part, particularly high and was marked not only by calls for the Jews to be granted equal rights, but also by quite primitive expressions of Judaeophobia.[65]

One of the principal advocates of relaxing the restrictions imposed on the Jews was the editor of *Odesskii vestnik*, N. I. Pirogov, the administrator of the educational district of Odessa from 1857 to 1858, where he was also the newspaper censor. He persuaded the governor-general, Count Stroganov, to transfer publication of this paper from his office to an editorial board made up of teachers

[61] Petition of the Vilna Jewish Community to S. S. Lanskoy, Ministry of the Interior, 11 Oct. 1859, RGIA, f. 821, op. 8, d. 408, l. 8, quoted in Freeze, *Jewish Marriage and Divorce in Imperial Russia*, 101.

[62] RGIA, f. 821, op. 8, d. 408, l. 7, quoted in Freeze, *Jewish Marriage and Divorce in Imperial Russia*, 101. On the Vilna incident, first reported in *Kolokol*, see Klier, *Imperial Russia's Jewish Question, 1855–1881*, 238–9.

[63] Yu. Gerasimova, *Iz istorii russkoi pechati v period revolyutsionnoi situatsii kontsa 1850-kh–nachala 1860-kh gg.* (Moscow, 1974), 15, quoted in Klier, *Imperial Russia's Jewish Question, 1855–1881*, 32.

[64] Gessen, 'Smena obshchestvennykh techenii, ii', 37, quoted in Klier, *Imperial Russia's Jewish Question, 1855–1881*, 32.

[65] On these debates, see Lukashevich, *Ivan Aksakov, 1823–1886*, 76–95, and Klier, *Imperial Russia's Jewish Question, 1855–1881*, 32–65, 122–43.

at the local Richelieu Lyceum, of whom two, A. Bogdanovsky and A. I. Georgievsky, were to become editors. One of the first articles to appear under their editorship was one by the local Jewish writer Osip Aronovich Rabinovich. Entitled 'Concerning Moshkas and Ioshkas', it called on the Jewish masses to recover the dignity which had been lost under the rule of the Polish nobility:

> You were happy to have special quarters and special streets: you were happy that you were named Mairoki and Moshka; you were very happy not to have to furnish soldiers nor to be responsible for municipal government . . . But subsequently, things appeared differently; you could not leave your special quarters; you wished to bear arms but couldn't; you wished to hold office, but they were closed to you; you cried out that you were named Moisei or Moses, Ber or Bernhard, but they still called you Moshka or Berka.[66]

In response an anonymous article in the St Petersburg *Russkii invalid* on 19 November 1858 argued that both Jews and Russians had obligations in the new era. The Jews needed to regain their dignity. The Russians would

> be worthy of our age if we reject the wretched habit of permitting into Russian history things which expose the Jews to shame and mockery; rather, we recall the reasons which led them to such a state; we will not forget the aptitude of the Jews for science, art and knowledge and, giving them a place amongst us, we will use their energy, resourcefulness and cleverness as a new means of satisfying the needs of society, which grow every day.

Rabinovich's article was followed by one in *Odesskii vestnik* on 6 March 1858 by Pirogov himself entitled 'The Odessa Talmud Torah' in which he praised the transforming effect of the modern education provided to the children there.

Even at this date, these expressions of philosemitism did not go unchallenged. Another native of Odessa, N. B. Gersevanov, argued in several articles in *Sanktpeterburgskie vedomosti* (15 May 1858) and *Severnaya pchela* (21 and 23 March 1859) that, unlike the Christian nations who were of Indo-German race and whose temperament was lymphatic and sanguine so that their national characteristics were kind-heartedness and humanitarianism, the Jews were Semites from Asia. Their temperament was choleric and erotic, their national characteristics were hard-heartedness, hot temper, and voluptuousness. They could not be good citizens because they saw their stay in any country as temporary. They despised their neighbours and exploited them through their dishonest trading practices. Their reform could only result from a very long process of moral education and intermarriage with Europeans, which in the Russian context could only mean conversion to Russian Orthodoxy.

Similarly, some of those who signed the protest letters against Zotov, including Ivan Aksakov, S. S. Gromyka, I. K. Babst, and A. Kraevsky, the editor of the liberal newspaper *Golos*,[67] soon emerged as leading Judaeophobes, and *Severnaya pchela*,

[66] Quoted in Klier, *Imperial Russia's Jewish Question*, 37.

[67] For an account of the Judaeophobia of *Golos*, the leading liberal newspaper during the reign of Alexander II, sometimes described as the Russian *Times*, which the paper abandoned after 1878, see Klier, *Imperial Russia's Jewish Question, 1855–1881*, 370–83.

which had close ties to the central administration, continued to publish strong attacks on Jews. Old-style religious anti-Judaism was for the moment regarded within the intelligentsia as the survival of a medieval prejudice, but was part of the stock-in-trade of *Domashnyaya beseda dlya narodnogo chteniya*, a weekly established in 1858 for ordinary Orthodox believers, which appears to have had links with the upper echelons of the Russian Orthodox Church. The paper described Jews on 7 February 1859 as 'a race cast out by God', and in an editorial on 4 April on the advance of the Jews in Europe commented, 'What a flexible thing this civilization is . . .! How little human civilization demands of the Jewish people, who willingly shouted before the indecisive Pilate, "His blood be upon us, and upon our children".'[68]

A key role in the formulation of a religiously based but modern Judaeophobia was played by the Slavophile publicist Ivan Aksakov, one of the signatories of the 1858 protest against Zotov.[69] When a law was proposed (it was promulgated on 27 November 1861) permitting Jews to enter the civil service, he argued in the journal *Den'* on 16 November that the law did not take into account that some positions would inevitably have to be barred to the Jews because of the Christian character of the state. Even if Christian principles were only imperfectly applied in Russian public life, it was around the 'Christian banner' that the Russian nation rallied. Although the Russian state had offered the Jews a refuge, it could not permit them to be in authority over Christians, particularly when they continued to be guided by their own moral principles, their 'Jewish banner', which was a negation of Christian ideals. The two religions constituted mutually exclusive moral systems, a fact which the Russian state could not ignore.

Echoing conservative German thinkers and also reflecting the Slavophile view that Russian Orthodoxy was an essential element in Russian communal life, he claimed that one could seek the extension of Jewish rights only on the basis of Christian principles, not through their negation. Jews should be allowed to practise their religion; they should be freed from restrictive legislation and granted full communal autonomy. However, they should have no role in the administration of the state.

In response to criticism of his views, Aksakov published in *Den'* on 31 March 1862 an article by 'A. Aleksandrov'[70] entitled 'A Few Words about the Talmud', which repeated the usual claims that the Talmud was the central text of Judaism and established a moral code fundamentally different from and hostile to Christianity. This led to a prolonged polemic, at the end of which Aksakov summed up his views in *Den'* on 8 August 1864 under the heading 'What Is the "Jew" as Regards Christian Civilization?' What was needed in relation to the

[68] On *Domashnyaya beseda*, see Klier, *Imperial Russia's Jewish Question, 1855–1881*, 124–5.

[69] On Aksakov's views, see ibid. 126–43.

[70] A. Aleksandrov was the pseudonym of A. N. Aksakov, a relative of Aksakov's, but his identity was unknown to Aksakov when he received the article.

'Jewish question', he claimed, was 'to muffle the dissonance and eliminate the dissension arising from the existence of the Jewish race in Christian society'. There could be no 'neutral society' in which Jews and Christians could meet as equals, ignoring their religious differences. Echoing Schleiermacher and Hegel, he argued that Judaism and Christianity were successive stages in the spiritual development of mankind. Contemporary Jews were a historical fossil,

> a congealed moment of human development, for ever hostile to its subsequent stages . . . The Jews, denying Christianity and putting forth the pretensions of Judaism, deny the logic of the year 1864, the successes of human history, and wish to return humanity to that level, to that moment of consciousness, which it had reached prior to the appearance of Christ on earth.

Even apparently enlightened Jews had not abandoned the 'Jewish banner'. Their 'negative and comfortable way' of ceasing to be Jews while neither rejecting Judaism nor converting to Christianity had made them 'moral and intellectual amphibians', devoid of any principles, unaffected by the moral climate which in a Christian state influences even atheists. They could have no place in a modern Christian society.

Aksakov also came to argue in the short-lived paper *Moskva*, which he edited after the collapse of *Den'*, that the Jews were an economically privileged group. On 15 August 1865 he asserted:

> One of the most privileged races [*plemena*] in Russia is undoubtedly the Jews in our western and southern provinces . . . The contemporary structure of the Jews constitutes a *status in statu* in the western region, where the wisdom of the Polish kings and the Polish nobility long ago strengthened Jewish domination. They agitate for the emancipation of the Jews. The question should be put differently—it is not a question of the emancipation of the Jews, but of the emancipation of the Russian population from the Jews, of the freeing of the Russian people in the west and partly in the south of Russia from the Jewish yoke.

JEWISH RESPONSES

The policy of 'selective integration' was certainly attractive to important sections of Russian Jewry. Among those who responded favourably were those who had profited from the economic changes of the first half of the nineteenth century. The first generation of Russian Jewish financiers made their fortunes primarily as military contractors. Their successors owed their wealth mainly to the enormously lucrative state liquor monopoly but soon moved into new fields such as banking and railway construction. Most prominent in their ranks was the Guenzburg family. Joseph Guenzburg came from Kamenets-Podolsky, where he made his fortune as a tax farmer and was succeeded by his son Horace, who established a banking house in St Petersburg.[71] Other prominent Jewish financiers

[71] On the Guenzburgs, see Ananich, *Bankirskie doma v Rossii, 1860–1914 gg.*, 37–71.

were the railway magnates Samuel Polyakov and Abraham Varshavsky, and the Kiev sugar magnate Josif Brodsky. This group saw themselves as inheriting the mantle of the *shtadlanim*, the advocates who had represented the Jews to the authorities in Poland–Lithuania and hoped by intercession with the authorities, with whom they were well acquainted, to improve the lot of the Jews. They were conscious that this could only be done gradually. In June 1856 a group of St Petersburg first-guild merchants, led by Joseph Guenzburg, submitted a characteristically worded petition to the government:

> Should the government differentiate by the extension of rights between those who have failed to distinguish themselves by their attitude, usefulness, and industry, and the young generation who have been educated by and in the spirit of the government, as well as the upper levels of the merchant class, who have for many years developed the economic life of the region, and the conscientious craftsmen who earn their bread by the sweat of their brow, then all the Jews, seeing in these select few the focus of the government's justice and good will and the exemplar of what it wishes to be done, will happily aspire to the ends indicated by the government. We request that the Benevolent Monarch welcome us, and deign, separating the wheat from the chaff, to encourage our good and commendable activities by granting moderate privileges to those of us who are deserving and enlightened.[72]

The petition then proposed that such rights should be granted to honorary citizens, merchants of the first and second guild, soldiers with an honourable discharge, and artisans who could produce special commendations of merit.

It certainly had some impact. When, on 16 March 1859, after protracted debate, the government gave first-guild merchants the right to reside outside the Pale, the wording of the decree closely followed Guenzburg's petition.[73] Having achieved partial success, Guenzburg continued to press the authorities. In September 1858, together with eleven other Jewish merchants, he called again for the relaxation of restrictions on those who had received higher education, and in July 1862 called for similar concessions to gymnasium students, artisans, and army veterans.[74]

The maskilim and the emerging Jewish intelligentsia also responded enthusiastically to the hopes engendered in the initial years of Alexander's reign. Simon Dubnow has commented on this phenomenon:

> as far as [this group] is concerned, the rapidity and intensity of its spiritual transformation may well be compared with the stormy eve of Jewish emancipation in Germany. This wild rush for spiritual regeneration was out of all proportion to the snail-like tardiness and piecemeal character of civil emancipation in Russia. However, the history of Western

[72] Gessen, *Zakon i zhizn'*, 113.

[73] RGIA, f. 1149, op. 5, ed. khr. 7 (1858–9), ll. 11–18, quoted in Klier, *Imperial Russia's Jewish Question, 1855–1881*, 24.

[74] RGIA, f. 796, op. 144, ed. khr. 159 (1863–5), ll. 1–180, quoted in Klier, *Imperial Russia's Jewish Question, 1855–1881*, 24.

> Europe has shown more than once that such pre-emancipation periods, including those that evidently prove abortive, offer the most favourable conditions for all kinds of mental and cultural revolutions. Liberty as a hope invariably arouses greater enthusiasm for self-rejuvenation than liberty as a fact, when the romanticism of the unknown has vanished.[75]

There was, as we have already observed, a significant difference between the older generation and younger generation of maskilim. The first generation, men like Isaac Baer Levinsohn, Abraham Baer Gottlober, and Bezalel Stern, were interested mostly in moderate reform through the medium of a modernized and reformed Hebrew language. The second generation, mostly younger graduates of the Russian Jewish school system, were often Russified and enamoured of the rapidly developing radical Russian culture of the 1860s. They felt a strong sense of mission to bring enlightenment to what they saw as the backward Jewish society of the Pale of Settlement. What the majority of both groups shared was a belief in the good faith of the authorities and a desire to work with them to impose necessary reforms on Jewish society. As a small radical elite they were very conscious of their isolation and their unpopularity in the eyes of the conservative majority of Jewish society, which they were quite willing to flout. As we have seen, they encouraged the government to institute more zealous censorship of hasidic books and to exercise greater control over Jewish religious life. The younger generation also sought the support of the government in obtaining nomination to the position of state rabbi over the objection of local communities.

The two groups were beginning to coalesce in what was to become the Jewish intelligentsia. In both Russia and the Polish lands the absence of a coherent and self-confident bourgeoisie led to the emergence of what came to be described as the intelligentsia, a social group made up of those possessing academic higher education—principally doctors, lawyers, teachers, and literary figures. Members of the intelligentsia were not always to be identified as those with a high school diploma; more important was that one's manners and language be those of the educated class and that one have some familiarity with the humanities. In Poland the intelligentsia adopted many of the attitudes of the nobility, from which a significant proportion of its members were derived, above all the belief that it was the embodiment of the nation, its conscience and driving force. It also inherited the noble disdain for trade and manufacturing. These characteristics were shared by the Russian intelligentsia, derived partly from the nobility and partly from the children of the married parish clergy of the Russian Orthodox Church. Richard Pipes has pointed out that this group seems to emerge 'wherever there exists a significant discrepancy between those who represent or believe they represent public opinion and the authorities'. As a consequence, both in Poland and Russia, the intelligentsia was made up of those 'not wholly preoccupied with [their] personal well-being but at least as much and preferably much more concerned with that of society at large'.[76]

[75] Dubnow, *History of the Jews in Russia and Poland*, ii. 206.

[76] Pipes, *Russia under the Old Regime*, 253.

The emerging Jewish intelligentsia acquired some of these traits and in the 1860s began to debate the difficult problem of the nature of Jewish identity. This was complicated by the fact that Russian identity itself was a matter of dispute between Slavophiles and Westernizers, and that the question of what was 'Russian' (*russkii*) in the context of the multinational (*rossiiskii*) empire was never to be resolved satisfactorily. In addition, the Pale of Settlement had been part of the Polish–Lithuanian Commonwealth, and the majority of the population was composed of people who were beginning to see themselves as Lithuanians, Ukrainians, and, more slowly, Belarusians. The Jewish intelligentsia was also well aware of the inadequacies of the maskilic view of the world and began to seek alternatives. Mostly they were less committed to Hebrew than their predecessors, and some developed a passionate interest in the Russian language and Russian culture.

There were also those who sought to distance themselves from the Jews and the restrictions imposed on them by total immersion in Russian society, what has been called 'radical assimilation'. Some were converts, like Daniel Khvolson, who, when asked whether he had converted out of conviction, responded, 'Yes, out of the conviction that it was better to be a professor in St Petersburg than a melamed [a *ḥeder* teacher] in Shnipishok.' Others were determined to obtain the opportunities available in the tsarist empire. Their attitude is reflected in the petition submitted to Count Kiselev in 1856 by thirty-four students at the Medical–Surgical Academy, seeking the modification of a secret instruction of Tsar Nicholas I which restricted the admission of Jews to state service against the letter of the Jewish statute of 1804:

> Not daring to judge the reason for such a restriction, we dare only to pray our Fatherland not to confuse us, who have been educated in its spirit and under its eyes, with the mass of our unhappy race. It was not the Talmud which we studied, and it is not to Palestine that we belong any longer, but to Holy Russia . . . From all our soul we thank the government for giving us the highest good education. But our people judge education by its actual utility; the eyes of all our young generation are upon us, who first scorned its prejudices.[77]

The principal means available to the Russian Jewish intelligentsia for exchanging and propagating their views was the developing Russian Jewish press, which emerged in the 1860s. It published in Hebrew, Yiddish, and Russian, and although the circulation of most of the papers was quite small, it played an enormous role in developing the ideas of the reforming minority with Russian Jewry. It should be remembered that, small though its circulation was, this was also true of contemporary Russian periodicals. During the early years of the reign of Alexander II the 'thick journals', which were the principal voice of educated public opinion, had no more than 30,000 subscribers. The sixty-seven newspapers of the empire had a total circulation of barely 65,000.[78]

[77] YIVO, Elias Tcherikower Archives, file 755, fos. 63218–19, quoted in Klier, *Imperial Russia's Jewish Question, 1855–1881*, 28.

[78] McReynolds, *The News under Russia's Old Regime*, table 6.

The most important of the Hebrew newspapers were the weeklies *Hamagid* (The Preacher), published from 1856 in Lyck, East Prussia, but intended for the Russian market; *Hakarmel* (Mount Carmel), which appeared from 1860 in Vilna; *Hamelits* (The Intercessor), which had a Yiddish supplement, *Kol mevaser* (The Voice of the Herald), which was published from 1860 in Odessa; and the monthly *Hashaḥar* (The Dawn), founded in Vienna in 1869. *Hamagid* and *Hakarmel* were quite similar in character. Edited by old-style maskilim, Eliezer Lipmann Silbermann and David Gordon in Lyck and Samuel Joseph Fuenn in Vilna, they expressed in somewhat platitudinous language the principal ideas of the original Russian maskilim: the importance of education in the vernacular of the country, the value of secular culture, and the importance of moderate Jewish religious reform. Their circulations were small, 1,000 for *Hamagid* and probably about the same for *Hakarmel*. *Hakarmel* ceased publication in 1871, although it continued to appear in occasional form with issues devoted to literary or scientific subjects, while *Hamagid* did not appear after 1881. *Hamelits* was rather different. Its editor, Alexander Tsederbaum, was a very gifted journalist who succeeded not only in increasing the circulation of the paper to over 5,000, but also in making it a lively and courageous defender of the reform of Jewish life and scourge of Jewish obscurantism. Although he shared the general maskilic scorn for Yiddish, he also developed the Yiddish supplement, *Kol mevaser*, which created a place where the newly developing Yiddish literature could reach a wide audience.

Hashaḥar, which was published by Perets Smolenskin (1840/2–1885) in Vienna between 1869 and 1878, was of a much higher intellectual calibre and soon had a cadre of devoted readers in the tsarist empire and a circulation which has been estimated at between 800 and 2,000. It saw its goal as twofold: to fight against Jewish religious fanaticism on the one hand and against the growing Russification and indifference to Jewish matters of the Jewish intelligentsia on the other. In Dubnow's words: '*Hashahar* was the staff of life for the generation of that period of transition which stood on the border-line dividing the old Judaism from the new.'[79]

The Russian Jewish press was part of a new phenomenon, the emergence of a Jewish press in vernacular languages, and is comparable to the German Jewish weekly press or *Izraelita* in Warsaw.[80] The failure of the *Odesskii vestnik*, whose sympathy for the Jews had waned with Pirogov's transfer to Kiev in 1858, to respond sympathetically to Jewish concerns aroused by an anti-Jewish riot in Odessa in April 1859, as well as the failure of the Russian press generally to react to this incident, led to renewed calls for the establishment of a Jewish publication in Russian. On 23 December 1856 the Odessa-based writer Osip Rabinovich and

[79] Dubnow, *History of the Jews in Russia and Poland*, ii. 218.

[80] On the Russian Jewish press, see Klier, *Imperial Russia's Jewish Question, 1855–1881*; Orbach, *New Voices of Russian Jewry*; L. Levanda, 'K istorii vozniknoveniya pervogo organa russkikh evreev'; and Gessen, 'Smena obshchestvennykh techenii, ii'.

the merchant and communal activist Joachim Hayim Tarnopol had submitted a formal request to Pirogov for permission to publish such a newspaper.[81] In Pirogov's view this would acquaint Jews with the Russian language, popularize the government's policy of 'merger', and counteract the influence of Jewish 'fanatics'. With the support of the governor-general, Count Stroganov, the proposal was submitted to A. S. Norov, the minister of public enlightenment, and the Jewish Committee. The committee rejected the proposal because of its opposition to the discussion of Jewish religious matters in Russian.[82] It was prepared to allow a paper in a 'Jewish' language, which was unacceptable to Rabinovich and Tarnopol since, as they wrote to Pirogov on 12 June 1858, one of their principal goals was to encourage the spread of Russian among Jews. Further discussions followed, and when Rabinovich and Tarnopol informed the Jewish Committee that they were willing to exclude religious matters from the paper, they were granted the appropriate permission on 22 October 1859.[83]

This led to the founding of the weekly *Rassvet* (Dawn).[84] Its place of publication was Odessa, the seat of the largest acculturated and Russified Jewish community in the tsarist empire. Like other Jewish publications in the vernacular, it had a dual goal, both to inform the general public about the nature of Jewish society and advocate their civil rights and to spread 'European' values among the Jews, while also exposing abuses and obscurantism within the community.

Rassvet appeared for the first time on 27 May 1860, under the motto 'And God said: "Let there be light!"' It was jointly edited by Rabinovich and Tarnopol, but in practice Tarnopol ceased to be involved after the first issue and the paper was run by Rabinovich together with the novelist Lev Levanda, who was also a 'Jewish expert' in the office of the governor-general of Vilna province. (For Levanda's literary works, see Volume II, Chapter 7.) The criticism of Jewish life and encouragement of educational and religious reform was left to Levanda, while Rabinovich would inform the Russian public about the true character of Jewish life and belief and would argue for the alleviation of Jewish restrictions in Russia.

The paper was controversial from its inception. In its first issue it published an unsigned article by Levanda entitled 'A Few Words about the Jews of Western Russia', which described the poverty of the Jews of Minsk province and its devastating consequences for Jewish family life. This was felt by many of the paper's subscribers as giving ammunition to the Judaeophobes, and it led to Tarnopol's withdrawal from involvement with the paper. He formally resigned as editor after

[81] Gessen, 'Smena obshchestvennykh techenii, ii', 40–1.

[82] RGIA, f. 821, op. 8, ed. khr. 256 (1857), ll. 3, 38–9, quoted in Klier, *Imperial Russia's Jewish Question, 1855–1881*, 70–1.

[83] Klier, *Imperial Russia's Jewish Question, 1855–1881*, 46, 48–50.

[84] On *Rassvet*, see ibid. 84–101; Zinberg, *Istoriya evreiskoi pechati v Rossii v svyazi s obshchestvennymi techeniyami*, 40–62; Slutsky, *The Russian Jewish Press in the Nineteenth Century* (Heb.), 37–55; Orbach, *New Voices of Russian Jewry*, 22–53; Shohetman, 'The First *Rassvet*' (Heb.).

the twentieth issue, and supported those who attacked the paper for 'blackening the name of Israel', particularly in *Hamagid*.[85]

While the paper allowed a number of different opinions to be voiced in its columns on such subjects as how Jewish religious life should be reformed, editorial policy remained in Rabinovich's hands. Like Levanda, he was a strong critic of hasidism and what he saw as religious obscurantism. He considered the adoption of Russian a key element in the achievement of equal rights. On 19 August 1860 he argued that Yiddish was 'incapable of expressing any enlightened belief' and that, while Hebrew had served the Jews in the diaspora as 'the monument of their past glory', it was now a dead language. 'Our Fatherland is Russia; therefore its language, like its air, should be ours.'

Rabinovich strongly opposed the view that Jews needed to demonstrate that they were worthy of equal rights. On 1 July 1860 he wrote:

> We do not agree with those who tie the question of our moral regeneration to the question of our emancipation. History shows that full civil rights for us never depended upon the level of our education but on the higher or lower development of people among whom we live. In this respect, our private problem depends upon the resolution of a general problem.

He also tried to demonstrate how much the Jews had sought to bring themselves closer to the society in which they lived, writing on 28 April 1861:

> They have adopted the clothes of Russians and their style of life is more and more like theirs; they are increasing the number of their educational institutions; increasingly they speak Russian among themselves; they engage in philanthropy; they shed their blood for their fatherland; they value state decorations as sacred things and pledge their service; they contribute to the treasury of national literature; they assist national life and amusement.

Rassvet lasted barely a year. Its strong advocacy of the Jewish right to equal treatment caused problems with the censors, but it was for the most part able to deal with them. Its circulation never reached more than 640 subscribers, significantly below its break-even point of 800. What seems to have induced Rabinovich to close it was a blistering attack to which he was subjected by Governor-General Stroganov after the paper published several articles on the fate of Tsipka Mendak, a young Jewish girl allegedly kidnapped and forcibly baptized in Lithuania. Stroganov told Rabinovich bluntly, 'If something appears in your paper that does not please me, or if it should bore me while I read it, or if I just feel like it, or perhaps if my stomach aches, I will close your paper down immediately.'[86] Stroganov, who was otherwise sympathetic to Jewish issues, may have been subjected to strong criticism from the central authorities because of the coverage of the case in Russia and abroad, particularly in the Belgian journal *Le Nord*. It is also possible that Stroganov's displeasure may have been a reflection of the central administration's anger at the paper's keen advocacy of equal rights.[87]

[85] Orbach, *New Voices of Russian Jewry*, 38; Lederhendler, *The Road to Modern Jewish Politics*, 126.
[86] Gessen, 'Smena obshchestvennykh techenii, ii', 57.
[87] Ibid. 58–9.

Those who had supported the establishment of *Rassvet* were unwilling to see it disappear, and it was soon succeeded by *Sion*, edited by Emmanuel Soloveichik and Leon Pinsker, who was later to be one of the earliest Russian Zionists.[88] It stressed its links with its predecessor. The distinctive typeface was retained, as was its motto, 'Let there be light!', and in the first issue the editors praised Rabinovich and claimed that this was the new paper's second year of publication. At the same time it adopted a less critical posture in relation to the Jewish community and its need for reform, attempting rather to answer antisemitic criticisms of the Jews and to acquaint the Russian public with the positive side of Jewish life and Jewish history. The editors also sought to avoid outright confrontation with the hasidim. The paper's goal was to enable Jews 'to be sons of their time and of their nation, while still remaining Jews'. It took the name *Sion* because the title *Rassvet* had now been adopted by a publication in St Petersburg, but its choice also reflected a more positive attitude to the Jewish past. At one level this could be seen as a rejection of the policy of *Rassvet* of openly discussing the faults of Jewish society, which it was now felt had merely given ammunition to those hostile to the extension of Jewish rights.

Sion soon found itself plunged into a bitter controversy with the emerging Ukrainian national movement and its monthly *Osnova*, published in St Petersburg from 1861 to 1862.[89] This led *Sion* to define more clearly its view of what constituted Jewish identity. While still advocating 'merger' with the Russian people, it claimed that some specific aspects of Jewishness would survive this. It was much more sympathetic to Hebrew than Rabinovich, opening its columns to the poet Judah Leib Gordon, who, in an article on 27 October 1861, argued that Hebrew should be the medium through which the Jewish intelligentsia—especially graduates of the state rabbinic schools—brought modern civilization to the rest of the community. It was also a link with Jews elsewhere. 'In the interests of our religion and our nationality [*natsional'nost'*], in opposition to the growth of indifference, should we not wish to preserve the means of spiritual unity for all our brothers who are scattered around the globe?'

The paper rejected what it described as 'radical assimilationism'. It argued that the failure of 'rapprochement' on the Jewish side was partly the result of the late development of Russian culture, while Ukrainian culture seemed to offer even less. A modern Jewish identity would need to retain Hebrew as a language of study and prayer and a link with the literature of the past. Jews could become patriots while retaining their own identity, as was demonstrated in western Europe, where common links, which the paper defined as 'Jewish cosmopolitanism', coexisted with a strong sense of affinity with the nations among whom the Jews lived. The paper's definition of Jewish identity was deliberately ambiguous:

[88] On *Sion*, see Klier, *Imperial Russia's Jewish Question, 1855–1881*, 102–22.

[89] On this, see Serbyn, 'The *Sion–Osnova* Controversy of 1861–1862'.

We again note that we never say that the Jews should try to preserve their peculiarities save for their religion; we only say that nobody has the right to demand of the Jews that they reject their harmless national peculiarities only because they are peculiarities and thus displeasing to him . . . The question of precisely what are these national characteristics and how long the Jews might preserve them in the midst of the dominant local population we are careful not to answer.

Just as the conflict with Ukrainian nationalism led *Sion* to formulate more sharply its commitment both to some form of Jewish ethnic identity which could be reconciled with Russification and to equal rights for Jews in a reformed Russian empire, so the Polish revolt of 1863–4 forced similar rethinking in the principal Hebrew-language journals.[90]

Sion also ran into difficulties with the censors, and on 27 April 1862 it announced that it was suspending publication because of its inability to refute 'baseless charges' made against the Jews and Judaism by the Russian press. This seems to be a reference to the fact that the censors were unwilling to allow any discussion in the press of religious matters. According to the editor, Soloveichik, the polemics with *Osnova* led the Odessa censor to reaffirm a rule, consistently circumvented by *Rassvet* and *Sion*, that all items dealing with the religious life of the Jews had to be passed by the spiritual censor, under the control of the Holy Synod, which would have made the publication of such material impossible. It may also be that the paper was in financial difficulties because of its small circulation.[91]

The fact that the two main centres of integrationist ideas within the Jewish community were Odessa and St Petersburg was also highlighted by the establishment in October 1863 of the Society for the Promotion of Culture among the Jews of Russia (Obshchestvo dlya rasprostraneniya prosveshcheniya mezhdu evreyami v Rossii, ORPE), with its two main branches in these cities. The St Petersburg branch included in its members Joseph Guenzburg, who provided most of its financial support, Leon Rosenthal, and Rabbi Abraham Neumann, and two converts who were sympathetic to the alleviation of Jewish restrictions, Daniel Khvolson and the court physician I. Berthenson.

Leon Rosenthal described the goal of the society as follows:

Highly placed individuals, with whom we came in contact and to whom we turned with our petitions and reports about improving the welfare of our co-religionists, continually reproached us that the Jews were sunk in darkness and fanaticism, stood aloof from everything Russian, and were given to harmful and degrading pursuits. These high officials told us: 'How can you hope that we will open the country before the Jews in their present condition?' 'Why', they asked, 'don't you undertake anything to help your people escape from their low moral condition?' . . . Each time that we spoke about civil rights for the Jews, high officials demanded of us a practical demonstration that the Jews had changed for the better

[90] Baker, 'The Reassessment of Haskala Ideology in the Aftermath of the 1863 Polish Revolt'.
[91] Slutsky, *The Russian Jewish Press in the Nineteenth Century* (Heb.), 47.

and deserved these rights. Activated by this motive, we have organized a league of educated men for the purpose of eradicating our above-mentioned shortcomings by disseminating among the Jews the knowledge of the Russian language and other useful subjects.[92]

The society was regarded with some suspicion by the authorities, and it took two years before it was given permission to function. It was only in 1867 that it was allowed to establish a branch in Odessa, and it was more than twenty-five years before a second branch was created, in Riga. The organization had an elite character, as was shown by its high subscription fee, and its membership never rose above 500. It made strong efforts to attract as honorary members liberal Russian journalists and sympathetic bureaucrats.

It saw itself as having two goals: defending the Jews against unjust accusations and advocating the Jewish cause on the one hand, and advancing knowledge of the outside world and encouraging modern knowledge and education among the Jews, especially in the Russian language, on the other. The hope that the society would emerge as a spokesman for the Jewish community proved misplaced. Russian officials did not trust its members, particularly when they refused to acknowledge and denounce Jewish ritual murders or the existence of a secret Jewish *kahal* controlling all Jewish life in Russia. It did succeed in publishing between 1874 and 1876 a three-volume work entitled *Mirovozzrenie talmudistov* (The World-View of the Talmudists), intended to dispel some of the Judaeophobic myths about this work.

The society was thus compelled to limit its objectives to fostering 'education for the sake of emancipation', providing financial assistance for Jewish students, and translating a number of works of history and the natural sciences into Russian. In Odessa, where there was a much larger community, the society saw its goal as 'the enlightenment of the Jews through the Russian language and in the Russian spirit'. It sought to translate the Bible and prayer book into Russian, although it stressed at the same time the importance of Hebrew in Jewish culture.

The society also attempted to assist the Jewish press with subsidies. This often created difficulties. Its agreement with Alexander Tsederbaum for him to publish a supplement on education and scholarship in *Hamelits* quickly broke down, as did the society's attempt to persuade Tsederbaum to Germanize the Yiddish of *Hamelits*'s supplement, *Kol mevaser*.[93] The subsidy granted to *Den'* by the Odessa branch of the society did not prevent the paper from attacking strongly what it saw as the craven and assimilationist stance of the society's St Petersburg leadership.

As the situation of Russian Jewry deteriorated, the society began to widen its activities. At its annual meeting in 1880 it established two sections: one to encourage Jewish involvement in agriculture, the other to assist Jewish artisans. These

[92] This quotation comes from a useful history of the society, published on the fiftieth anniversary of its foundation, Tsherikover, *Istoriya Obshchestva dlya rasprostraneniya prosveshcheniya mezhdu evreyami v Rossii, 1863–1913 gg.*, 30–1.

[93] Ibid. 121.

were to be the nuclei of the Society for Artisan and Agricultural Labour (Obshchestvo dlya remeslennogo i zemledel'cheskogo truda).[94]

The emergence of the Jewish press in Hebrew, Yiddish, and Russian also formed the basis for the rapid development of literature in these languages, which is discussed in Volume II, Chapter 7. Among the writers whose work appeared at this time were the Hebrew novelists Abraham Mapu and Perets Smolenskin, the poet Judah Leib Gordon, the essayist Moses Leib Lilienblum (1843–1910), and Shalom Jacob Abramowitsch (Mendele Mokher Seforim), who wrote in both Hebrew and Yiddish. Jewish writers producing work in Russian include Osip Rabinovich, Ilya Orshansky, one of the principal contributors to *Den'*, Lev Levanda, and Grigory Isaakovich Bogrov, the pioneers of the later development of Russian Jewish literature in Russian.

THE POLISH INSURRECTION OF 1863–1864 AND THE GROWING SOCIAL CRISIS

From the late 1860s it became increasingly apparent that Alexander was not going to introduce a constitution or a consultative assembly, which was opposed not only by conservatives in his entourage but also by liberals such as Nikolay Milyutin and Yury Samarin, who believed that reform was only possible through the exercise of the unlimited power of the tsar. He also seemed to have no intention of lifting any of the remaining restrictions on the Jews.

The Polish Uprising of 1863–4, which elicited substantial support in the nine formerly Polish provinces of the empire, particularly the provinces of Vilna and Kovno, led to an outpouring of Great Russian chauvinism and a desire to Russify the affected area. In the north-west the repression of the Poles was particularly severe. It was carried out by the 'hangman' General Mikhail Muravev, who held the office of military governor of the provinces of Vilna, Grodno, Kovno, Vitebsk, Minsk, and Mogilev until 1865, replacing Vladimir Nazimov, who had been removed on 3 May 1863 for 'excessive leniency' to the rebels. Muravev implemented a ruthless policy, suppressing revolutionary activity and weakening Polish influence while strengthening the local peasantry, who were granted land under more liberal conditions than in the Russian interior in an attempt to undermine the position of the nobility, who were given significantly worse terms than landlords elsewhere in an effort to force them to sell their land, which could also not be bought in this region by Poles.

Initially the Jews were not much affected by this repression since, with some exceptions, they had not supported the revolt in either Lithuania or Ukraine, where the local Poles had also largely ignored calls to rebel.[95] Indeed some Jews

[94] On its history, see Shapiro, *The History of ORT*.

[95] On this, see Nadel, 'O stosunkach Żydów na wileńszczyźnie do powstania styczniowego', 41, and Klier, 'The Polish Revolt of 1863 and the Birth of Russification'.

felt that the situation in the aftermath of the revolt would make the local authorities more sympathetic to their interests. Accordingly, the pedagogical council of the rabbinic school in Vilna voted to end its 'long-established servitude to foreign enlightenment' and replaced German with Russian for the teaching of the Bible, morals, Hebrew grammar, and Jewish history.[96]

One aspect of the repression was confiscation of the lands of those who had supported the uprising, and the determination of the government to strengthen Russian landholding in the region. There were those in the local administration of the area, such as Prince Vasilchikov, who held the view that Jews could be used to weaken Polish landholding provided adequate safeguards for the interests of the peasants could be established. On 25 November 1863, even before the uprising was over, he wrote to the Ministry of the Interior:

> In Jewry, numerous, educated, and liberated from restrictions, the government may find an oppositionist force against the tempestuous Poles. Polish nationalism, which is strong in the state not because of numbers but because of education, the privileges of birth, and chiefly because of the restrictions placed on the rights of other estates, cannot be neutralized and balanced by physical force alone . . . The whole secret consists in bestowing an advantage on the other, apparently insignificant, Jewish element, which contains resources of vital strength which can be nurtured and strengthened at the expense of other forces hostile to the government.[97]

This was also the view both of conservative journalists such as M. N. Katkov, the editor of *Moskovskie vedomosti*, and of liberals such as V. F. Korsh, the editor of *Sanktpeterburgskie vedomosti* and also, for a time, of the principal Russian newspaper in Vilna, *Vilenskii vestnik*, while it was under the editorship of M. F. De-Pule.[98] It was ultimately rejected by the central government, partly under the influence of Muravev himself, who in his memoirs wrote acidly that 'the Jews played a double game: they feigned joy [on the occasion of Russian victories] but this was a sham because they helped the insurgents everywhere and gave them money'.[99] Thus, by decree on 5 March 1864, Jews, like 'persons of Polish origin', were excluded from the tax exemptions and financial assistance created for Russian purchasers of land in the formerly Polish provinces.

Properties acquired with this assistance could not be leased, managed, bought, or inherited by Jews or persons of Polish origin, although Jews were still permitted to lease distilleries and taverns on such land. In addition, to strengthen the Orthodox peasantry the holdings they received were somewhat larger than elsewhere, and their obligation to perform labour services or make payments to their landlords was immediately ended.[100]

[96] *Istoricheskie svedeniya o vilenskom ravvinskom uchilishche* (Vilna, 1873), 36–7, quoted in Klier, *Imperial Russian's Jewish Question, 1855–1881*, 162.

[97] Quoted in Sliozberg, *Dela minuvshikh dnei*, ii. 147.

[98] For their views, see Klier, *Imperial Russia's Jewish Question, 1855–1881*, 153–8, 165–6.

[99] Shatskin, 'K istorii uchastiya evreev v pol'skom vosstanii 1863 g.', 29–30.

[100] Mysh (ed.), *Rukovodstvo k russkim zakonam o evreyakh*, 354–5, 371; *PSZ* 2/xxxix, no. 40656, cited in Levanda, 1013–14. See also Zaionchkovsky, *Otmena krepostnogo prava v Rossii*, 225–31.

This prohibition on acquiring land with government assistance was soon widened, both in order to strengthen Russian landowning and because of the fears of many bureaucrats in the region that Jewish ownership of land would threaten the welfare of the local peasantry. The terms of the emancipation had not resolved the 'peasant problem', and rural unrest was a feature of life in the tsarist empire throughout the second half of the nineteenth century, often blamed on Jewish 'exploitation'. When the governor-general of Kiev called for restrictions to be imposed on the growing number of Jews purchasing agricultural property settled by peasants in the region, his call met with a sympathetic response from the newly formed Western Committee, which was responsible for formulating policy for the formerly Polish provinces. The committee had been responsible for the law of 5 March 1864 giving incentives to Russian purchasers of land there, and it was also determined to strengthen the position of the Orthodox peasantry as a counterweight to the nobility, issuing a regulation requiring landlords to terminate the obligations of their former serfs and to agree to redemption of their holdings. It was feared that Jews, who disposed of significant amounts of capital and to whom the local landowners were frequently indebted, would frustrate the committee's objectives, outbidding potential Russian bidders for land and using their financial power to establish a hold over the peasantry. As a result, the committee resolved, on 10 July 1864, that the right granted to Jews in 1862 to acquire estate lands 'was not extended to provinces where mandatory redemption has been carried out', depriving the Jews of landholding rights in the nine formerly Polish provinces but not in the rest of the Pale.[101] Even when economic necessity led the Committee of Ministers in 1867 to relax the prohibitions on the leasing of mills, distilleries, sugar beet refineries, and other agricultural enterprises to Jews, it upheld the provisions of the law of 5 March 1864 on the sale of land to them.[102]

Certainly these years did see some Jews adapting to the new and more commercial situation in agriculture and establishing themselves both as bailiffs (in Bessarabia) and leaseholders (in Ukraine) and as owners of estates in those areas where they were allowed to purchase them. According to one estimate, in 1868 Jews had leased 701 out of 5,143 noble estates in Kiev, Volhynia, and Podolia. A contemporary study by the geographer P. P. Chubinsky claimed that by 1872 Jews controlled one-sixth of the agricultural land in the south-western provinces and one-tenth of the noble estates. These figures aroused fear that this process would gather speed and would lead to these individuals giving employment to many more Jews in the countryside, while also increasing alarm that the attempts of the

[101] *PSZ* 2/xxxix, no. 41039, cited in Levanda, 1016; 'Otnoshenie ministra vnutrennikh del ot 12 iyulya 1864 g.', in *Materialy Komissii po ustroistvu byta evreev* (hereafter *Materialy*), i. 1–2; Rogger, 'Government, Jews, Peasants and Land after the Liberation of the Serfs', 125–6.

[102] *Materialy*, i. 4–5; *PSZ* 2/xlii, no. 45257, cited in Levanda, 1092–3; Rogger, 'Government, Jews, Peasants and Land after the Liberation of the Serfs', 126.

authorities to preserve the Russian nobility as an effective and coherent social force were failing.[103]

Jews also moved into some aspects of manufacturing. Josif Brodsky made a fortune in sugar-refining, Samuel Polyakov and Abraham Varshavsky were active in railway-building, and Jews played a large part in the textile industries of Łódź and Białystok. Although Jews were only a small part of the nascent Russian capitalist class, they soon came to be seen as responsible for the ills of industrialization and for the development of industrial society as another source of Jewish power.

Not only was there growing unease about Jewish 'exploitation' of the peasantry, but Russian bureaucrats were increasingly convinced that the Jews were not transforming themselves in the way that was expected of them, in spite of what they saw as their generous treatment. The inability of the educated minority to impose reform on the community undermined the belief within bureaucratic circles in the value of even the partial measures of emancipation which had been embarked upon.

The fundamental lack of understanding between significant sections of the Russian bureaucracy and the Jewish intelligentsia became painfully obvious during the Brafman affair. As we have seen, one of the most deleterious consequences of Nicholas's policies had been drastically to undermine Jewish solidarity and to encourage among Jews a very strong (and in many cases justified) sense of grievance against the *kehilah* elite. Jacob Brafman had such a sense of grievance. He was born in Kletsk, in the province of Minsk, and clashed with the *kehilah* over the debts he had incurred during the illness and death of his baby daughter. His poverty and defiance of communal authority made him a prime target for conscription, and he fled the town, ultimately converting to Russian Orthodoxy. As a result of a petition to Alexander II, he was appointed instructor in Hebrew at the Minsk Russian Orthodox seminary and entrusted with the task of facilitating Jewish conversion.[104]

Brafman's activities in this area were markedly unsuccessful, but while on leave in Vilna he became acquainted with A. I. Zabelin, who had taken over as the editor of *Vilenskii vestnik* and who on 25 January 1866 initiated a discussion on the 'Jewish question' with the goal of discovering 'the most hopeful course for the improvement of the life of the Jewish race, in order to liberate the people of West Russia from the harmful influence of Jewry in the economic–political–moral life of the whole region'. He published four articles by Brafman in August 1866 enti-

[103] Orshansky, *Evrei v Rossii*, 123–5; Weinryb, *Neueste Wirtschaftsgeschichte der Juden in Russland und Polen*, 56–61, 217–18; Chubinsky, *Materialy i issledovaniya*, vii. 6, 182–4. On the 'decline of the nobility', see Hamburg, *Politics of the Russian Nobility, 1881–1905*, and Becker, *Nobility and Privilege in Late Imperial Russia*.

[104] There is a large literature on Brafman. See L. Levanda, 'Iz perepiski L. O. Levandy', ed. Landau; 'Iz perepiski L. O. Levandy', ed. Druyanov, 279–80; Ginzburg, *Converts in Tsarist Russia* (Heb.); Levitats, 'On the Consequences of Brafman's *Book of the Kahal*' (Heb.); L. O. Gordon, 'Otryvki vospominanii'; Klier, *Imperial Russia's Jewish Question, 1855–1881*, 169–81, 263–83.

tled 'The View of a Jewish Convert to Orthodoxy on the Jewish Question in Russia', which attempted to explain the failure of his conversionary activities in terms of the success of the Jews in obstructing their 'merger' with the majority of the population. In his view, although the *kahal* had been abolished by government decree in 1844, in fact it continued to exist as the dominant factor in Jewish life, with a judiciary which still controlled the life of individual Jews with its powers of excommunication and control of economic life. The *kahal* was part of an 'international Jewish organization' led by the recently established Alliance Israélite Universelle which incited the Jewish masses against the authorities and the Christian religion, and was responsible for Jewish 'fanaticism' and 'separatism'. Its influence could only be rooted out by destroying this 'secret Jewish government'. All Jewish communal bodies should be dissolved and the Jews included in the estates established by Catherine the Great.

Brafman's articles occasioned a protest by the Society for the Promotion of Culture among Jews and, along with his attacks on the Roman Catholic Church in the north-east, probably led to Zabelin's dismissal. On 1 November 1866 he was replaced as editor by M. F. De-Pule, who was more sympathetic to the Jews and who encouraged the literary activity of Lev Levanda, serializing his novel *Samuil Gimpel's* in the pages of *Vilenskii vestnik*. This did not end the influence of Brafman, who had gained the support of a number of individuals in the local bureaucracy, in particular I. P. Kornilov, director of the educational district of Vilna, who recommended him both to the assistant minister of public enlightenment, I. D. Delyanov, and to K. P. von Kaufman, who had replaced Muravev as governor-general in 1866. He was accordingly appointed censor of Jewish books in Vilna.

By now the Jews of Vilna were sufficiently worried by Brafman's influence to request von Kaufman to convene a special commission to examine his claims. It met under the chairmanship of a local bureaucrat and included a number of prominent Jews, including Jacob Barit and Levanda, as well as Brafman himself. This initiative soon backfired. Von Kaufman, who was sympathetic to Jewish concerns, was replaced as governor-general on 9 October 1866 by E. T. Baranov, who accepted without question the tissue of half-truths advanced by Brafman and argued that Jewish 'isolation' was furthered by 'the preservation, in secret, of the kahal institution of the Jews which has been abolished by the government'.[105] This 'isolation' should be ended by making Jews in the countryside and in small towns part of the peasant *volost'*, the administrative system of self-government established after emancipation.

In the event, on 2 March 1868 Baranov was replaced by the much more liberal A. L. Potapov, who, aware of the unease which the commission's proceedings

[105] Quoted in Klier, *Imperial Russia's Jewish Question, 1855–1881*, 171–2. On this commission, see Gessen, 'Iz letopisi minuvshego'; Ansky [Rapoport], 'Evreiskaya delegatsiya v Vilenskoi komissii 1869 goda'; and RGIA, f. 821, op. 9, ed. khr. 164 (1881–2), ll. 63, 76, quoted in Klier, *Imperial Russia's Jewish Question, 1855–1881*, 171–81. See also Lederhendler, *The Road to Modern Jewish Politics*, 144.

were arousing among Jews, on 13 September 1869 invited the Jewish communities of the region to elect deputies to review its work. This led to the establishment of a common front of maskilim and more traditional Jews who were able, when they met in October, to persuade the authorities not only to abandon the plan to make Jews subject to the peasant *volost'*, but to abolish most restrictions on Jewish settlement outside the Pale of Settlement and to grant Jews full electoral rights in municipalities.

This proved something of a false dawn. When these proposals were forwarded to the newly formed Commission for the Reorganization of Jewish Life in 1872, their principal reaction was to criticize the work of the commission for not sufficiently investigating the survival of the secret system of Jewish self-government.[106] No action was taken on the other recommendations. Brafman also continued from strength to strength. In 1868–9 he was able, with a stipend of 2,500 roubles from the governor-general, to publish in two books an expanded version of his articles, based on the minutes of the Minsk *kahal* in the first half of the nineteenth century supplemented by selected passages of an 'anti-Christian' character from the Talmud and rabbinic literature. These two books, *Evreiskie bratstva, mestnye i vsermirnye* (Jewish Brotherhoods, Local and International; Vilna, 1868) and *Kniga kagala* (The Book of the Kahal; first edition, Vilna, 1869; second, enlarged, edition, St Petersburg, 1875; third edition, including *Evreiskie bratstva*, St Petersburg, 1882–8), were sent to government offices in the Pale to assist those dealing with Jewish issues. Certainly, the concept of a secret Jewish world government was enthusiastically taken up by Vitaly Yakovlevich Shulgin, who became editor of the main Kiev paper, *Kievlyanin*, from July 1864 until his death in 1878, and by many other bureaucrats and journalists. In Shulgin's words in *Kievlyanin* on 31 March 1870: 'In the midst [of the Jewish people] many horrendous things flourish—the obscurantism of diabolical superstition and fanaticism—and many thousands of Jewish heads are crammed with perverted conceptions, but the moral responsibility for all this mess falls exclusively upon Jewish institutions and on the Jewish government.'

All efforts of the Jews to point out the bogus and unfounded character of Brafman's accusations proved vain. Indeed, in Shulgin's view they only demonstrated the bad faith of the Jewish reformers and integrationists. As he wrote on 23 April 1870:

> At last the progressives, who accuse us of intolerance and bigotry when we talk about the realities of life in our area, can see the facts of Jewish life. The publicists of *Razsvet*, *Den* and *Sion* could hardly have failed to know about these abuses, so why have they never said anything about them? Is it because they were more concerned with protecting their personal interests by speaking patriotic lies?[107]

Brafman himself enjoyed the patronage of the Imperial Geographic Society, which published the second edition of his book. In 1870 he was promoted to the

106 *Materialy*, i. 4.

107 Quoted in Klier, *Imperial Russia's Jewish Question, 1855–1881*, 276.

post of censor of Jewish books in the Chief Office for Press Affairs in St Petersburg, and in 1872 served on the committee which drafted the law on military service enacted in 1874. He was also a frequent commentator on Jewish affairs in the St Petersburg daily *Golos*.

Attacks on the bad faith of the Russian Jewish intelligentsia now became more frequent. It became much more difficult for their voices to be heard in the Russian press, unlike the situation in the early 1860s, when a significant number published articles in papers like *Moskovskie vedomosti*, *Russkii vestnik*, *Golos*, *Domashnyaya beseda*, *Vilenskii vestnik*, and *Odesskii vestnik*. As early as 12 May 1866 *Vilenskii vestnik* attacked this group as 'a *magnum nihil*, neither Russian nor Jew'. By March 1874 the 'thick journal' *Delo* could claim:

> In taking up the defence of their nationality, Jewish publicists resort to absurdities and to outrageous falsehoods, denying even criticisms of the dark side of Jewish life which are fully justified . . . At the very beginning of public discussion on the Jewish question, public opinion was apparently quite favourable to the fate of the Jews, but by the end it completely rejects the assumptions of the silly defences of Jewish publicists.

The formerly liberal *Golos* on 4 April 1875 wrote in an editorial:

> Defending what are in effect illegal institutions, whenever the question concerns the Jews, Jewish publicists don't answer the question, but start to defend the Jewish religion, to speak about the great worth of talmudic study, about the fanaticism of Christians and their medieval prejudices, about the talents and extraordinary abilities of the Jews, and conclude with speeches about humanity, liberalism, and the other fruits of contemporary civilization which, however, will only mature when the Jews are granted full and universal rights.

Jewish 'separatism' was increasingly seen by the authorities as the root of their problems with the Jews. After a visit to the Kingdom of Poland, where he was shocked by the sight of hasidim in traditional Jewish dress, Alexander ordered the laws forbidding the wearing of such clothing to be strictly enforced. At a subsequent discussion in the Council of State it was concluded that 'the prohibition of external differences in dress is yet far from leading to the goal sought by the Government, that is to destroy the exclusiveness of the Jews and the almost hostile attitude of the Jewish communities towards Christians, these communities forming in our land a secluded religious and civil caste or, one might say, a state within a state'.[108] As a consequence, the council proposed in December 1870 the establishment of a special commission whose task would be to 'consider ways and means to weaken as far as possible the communal cohesion among the Jews'. This Commission for the Reorganization of Jewish Life was set up the following year under the chairmanship of the assistant minister of the interior, Lobanov-Rostovsky.

Increasingly the government's commitment to abolishing the restrictions under which the Jews laboured seemed to be weakening. In 1870 a committee was

[108] Dubnow, *History of the Jews in Russia and Poland*, ii. 191.

established within the Ministry of the Interior to decide whether the restriction of Jewish representation on municipal councils to one-third of the total number of councillors should be maintained. Only one member of the committee, Novoselsky, the mayor of Odessa, was for total repeal provided educational qualifications were established. A minority favoured increasing the proportion of Jews to a half, but most called for the maintenance of the existing regulations. As a consequence, the new municipal statute retained the norm of one-third and reaffirmed that Jews were not eligible for the office of mayor.

The worsening situation was highlighted by the outbreak of a pogrom in Odessa, the main centre of acculturation in the south, in March 1871, which followed an earlier anti-Jewish riot in April 1859. The Odessa pogrom was the consequence of growing commercial rivalry between the Greek community, previously dominant in the grain trade, and the Jews, who were increasingly taking a more important role. Even more disturbing than the three days of rioting and destruction, in which eight people died and twenty-one were seriously injured, was the response of the authorities. According to the governor-general of New Russia and Bessarabia, Count Kotzebue, the Jews were themselves responsible for the violence, 'having started first'. In a report to the Ministry of the Interior, he wrote:

> The recent events showed that the [religious] antipathy of Christians, primarily from the lower classes, is reinforced by bitterness arising from the exploitation of their labor by the Jews, and the latter's ability to get rich and to dominate all commercial and mercantile operations. From the crowds of Christians were often heard the words, 'The Jews mock Christ, they get rich and they suck our blood.'[109]

Widespread disillusion followed. In the words of the president of the Odessa branch of the Society for the Promotion of Culture among Jews:

> [One cannot help] losing heart and becoming rather doubtful as to whether the goal pursued by [the society] is in reality a good one, seeing that all the endeavours of our brethren to draw nearer to the Russians are of no avail as long as the Russian masses remain in their present unenlightened condition and harbour hostile sentiments towards the Jews.[110]

When the Committee for the Amelioration of the Condition of the Jews met, it discussed two issues: 'the amelioration of the spiritual life of the Jews' and the feasibility of resettling Jews in the rest of the empire. There were other pressures on the authorities, in particular the fears of bureaucrats in the formerly Polish provinces that Jews were taking over the economic life of the area. One of those most exercised by the problem was Prince A. M. Dondukov-Korsakov, the governor-general of Kiev between 1869 and 1877.

Dondukov-Korsakov seems to have been influenced by Shulgin, under whose editorship *Kievlyanin* became increasingly hostile to the Jews and to their

109 Quoted in Klier, *Imperial Russia's Jewish Question, 1855–1881*, 359.

110 Dubnow, *History of the Jews in Russia and Poland*, ii. 215–16.

allegedly deleterious economic impact in Ukraine. In response to an article in *Den'* by the young Jewish lawyer Mikhail Morgulis, defending the economic role of Jews in the south-west, Shulgin responded in *Kievlyanin* on 14 August 1865, arguing that the increasing role of Jews in economic life would mean the surrender of 'our brothers united in blood and faith, flesh of our flesh, blood of our blood' into the hands of aliens (*inoplemenniki*) who were 'enemies of Christianity in principle'. He concluded:

> Yes, Mr Morgulis, your plan is very good: the Jews, to be sure, will dislodge the Polish element from western Russia sooner than we can. Nonetheless, it seems to us that we will not sin against the wishes of Russian society if we refuse the honour granted to Kiev of being the new Jerusalem, and to western Russia, the second Promised Land. History shows that Poland paid too dearly for this honour.

In 1869 *Kievlyanin* undertook a major campaign against the evils of Jewish leaseholding, which probably induced Dondukov-Korsakov early the following year to propose that a regulation forbidding Jews to lease or purchase estates acquired with government assistance be extended to all noble property in the provinces of Kiev, Volhynia, and Podolia which were under his authority. In addition, he proposed the reintroduction of the restrictions on Jewish trading in liquor in the rural areas of the Pale which had been relaxed in 1863 and 1865. Although no action was taken, Alexander's favourable response led Dondukov-Korsakov to submit to the tsar, on 26 October 1872, an extensive Memorandum Concerning the Most Important Questions in the Administration of the South-West Region. This was submitted by Alexander to the Committee for the Amelioration of the Condition of the Jews.[111]

Dondukov-Korsakov began with an account of how the Jews were playing an increasing role in the agricultural life of the three provinces. In this area 721,000 Jews made up nearly 13 per cent of the population. In the towns they made up 32 per cent of the inhabitants, in the small towns 53 per cent, and in rural settlements 14 per cent. Jews rented 819 estates on the basis of formal and legal contracts and many more on the basis of informal or camouflaged arrangements, 'so that it can be said that one-sixth of all estates are in their hands'. They owned 27 out of 108 sugar refineries, 500 out of 564 distilleries, 99 out of 148 breweries, 5,700 out of 6,353 mills, 527 other manufacturing establishments, 15,000 shops, and 190,000 inns and taverns. They dominated the trade in lumber and grain, and the export business in these and other commodities, and frequently worked for the government as contractors.

The growing economic power of the Jews was all the more dangerous because of the links between them and their political influence outside Russia. Echoing Brafman, Dondukov-Korsakov claimed that 'The cause of every last Jew is also

[111] 'Vypiska iz vsepoddanneishei zapiski o bolee vazhnykh voprosakh po upravleniyu yugozapadnym kraem 1872 g.', in *Materialy*, i. 1, quoted in Rogger, 'Government, Jews, Peasants and Land after the Liberation of the Serfs', 127–9.

the cause of the worldwide Jewish *kahal* . . . that powerful yet elusive association' which had shown its power in the past when its agents Sir Moses Montefiore and Adolphe Crémieux had intervened in St Petersburg in a ritual murder case and when Jews were accused of evading military service. The Odessa pogrom of 1871 had been an instinctive protest of the masses against growing Jewish power and government inaction. In the provinces under his control, the police and the peasantry's dependence on the Jews had prevented similar violence, but urgent action was needed to defuse the situation. 'The principal endeavours of the government must be concentrated on the Jewish question.' In the long run, the problem could be solved by the dispersal of the Jews throughout the empire, but in the meantime it was necessary to maintain the prohibition on the Jewish purchase of land and extend it to leasing.

These proposals were, for the moment, rejected by the Jewish Committee.[112] It opposed extending the rules forbidding the leasing or purchase of estates originally purchased with government assistance and upheld the Jewish right to lease other land. It took this position both because of the need to protect the rights of private property and because, in its view, there was no evidence that Jewish leaseholders managed their estates worse than others. It also rejected Dondukov-Korsakov's antisemitic view of the Jewish world conspiracy. It was reluctant, given the situation in the formerly Polish provinces, to alienate a numerous group in the region and add to the empire's enemies. The problems of the Jews in the south-west could not be separated from this issue in the country as a whole, which the Jewish Committee was reviewing.

Among the reports which were submitted to it, there were several which echoed Dondukov-Korsakov's views and thus, in its report, the commission stressed the role of the Talmud in preserving Jewish 'separatism'. In addition, it called for an end to what remained of Jewish autonomy, and its views may have had something to do with the ending in 1873 of the government-sponsored Jewish school system. However, the commission fell prey to the usual Russian procrastination and had still not issued its recommendations when Alexander II was assassinated in March 1881.

One striking sign of the hopes invested in Alexander is the fact that when the question of whether the Jews should serve in the military was again debated in the Ministry of War in the early 1860s, Joseph Guenzburg lobbied successfully in favour of military service, convinced that in this way Jews could prove their devotion to the state and achieve civil rights by performing civil obligations.[113] Jews had already erected a monument to those of their faith who had died in the Crimean War, and Osip Rabinovich's stories 'The Penalty Recruit' and 'The Inherited Candlestick' had highlighted the contrast between the sacrifices demanded of Jewish soldiers and the lack of rights enjoyed by the Jews of the empire.

[112] *Materialy*, i. 1–7, quoted in Rogger, 'Government, Jews, Peasants and Land after the Liberation of the Serfs', 129–30.

[113] Sliozberg, *Dela minuvshikh dnei*, i. 93.

The introduction of universal military service and the creation of a modern army based on a system of reservists was the last of the reforms to be introduced by Alexander, and it was obviously crucial if the tsarist empire was to remain a great power. It took a long time to prepare, but by the 1860s the draft system had already been modified to enable those liable for service to hire a replacement, a system widely employed by Jews and used by those hostile to them to prove their lack of civic virtue.[114]

The new army law introduced in 1874 after long debate ended this system. It established a uniform draft system for Christians and Jews with provisions to discourage Jewish evasion. If there were insufficient Jews of draft age, local recruiting offices were empowered to draft Jews up to the age of 30 (the usual cut-off being 21). Christians and Jews were to form a common pool for the assignment of numbers in the draft, being placed on the same list, but if a Jew was exempted from the draft for family reasons he was to be replaced by the next Jew on the list, not the next person, to ensure that Jews would not benefit from a disproportionate number of exemptions.[115]

Although the committee drafting the bill decided, on a majority vote (the casting vote being that of the chief of the General Staff), that Jews could not be officers on the grounds that their authority would not be accepted, this was overruled by the State Council. However, the minister of war retained the right to veto the promotion of Jews in those areas of the army where this might prove harmful.[116]

Given their experience of the draft under Nicholas and the fact that the army had not greatly changed in spite of the reforms, it is not surprising that Jews continued to evade military service. The extent of this evasion was hotly debated and almost certainly exaggerated by the Judaeophobe press. It reinforced the army high command in its view that the Jews had not responded appropriately to the concessions which had been made to them. Accordingly, on 3 February 1876 recruitment boards were ordered to place the Jews in a separate category for recruitment purposes, and two years later the recruitment rules for Jews were further tightened when the State Council decreed that, in the event of a shortage of Jewish recruits without exemptions, or with family exemptions of the second or third class, recruitment boards could draft Jews with a first-class exemption. The measure was to remain in force until such time 'as the need should pass, as a consequence of a better fulfilment of their obligations to the state by the Jewish population'.[117]

Jews now began to serve in considerable numbers in the army, and some served with distinction in the Russo-Turkish War of 1877–8. Several Jews participated in

[114] For the army reform, Zaionchkovsky, *Voennye reformy 1860–1870 godov v Rossii.*

[115] Ibid. 313–14.

[116] Ibid. 323–4.

[117] Mysh (ed.), *Rukovodstvo k russkim zakonam o evreyakh*, 505–6, quoted in Klier, *Imperial Russia's Jewish Question, 1855–1881*, 342.

the Russian volunteer force which fought in Serbia in the initial stages of the crisis, and some Jewish journalists were among those who were part of the campaign to force Russia to declare war on Turkey. Rabbi Simeon Schwabacher in Odessa collected funds for war relief, and similar appeals were made in Vilna. This did not prevent attacks on the Jews for allegedly siding with the Turks, and a campaign was launched against the abuses of the military purveyors to the Russian army, many of whom were Jews. The difficulties in the campaign increased the atmosphere of chauvinism. Russia's humiliation at the Congress of Berlin in June–July 1878, which overturned the Treaty of San Stefano between Russia and Turkey and reduced in size the large Bulgarian state closely linked with Russia which it had established, was attributed to Disraeli's 'racial predisposition towards the Turks'.[118] Dubnow was almost certainly correct in claiming in *Voskhod* in January 1891 that 'the roots of contemporary Russian antisemitism were established in the epoch of the last Russo-Turkish War'.

The late 1870s saw further restrictions on Jewish economic activity. In 1877 the prohibition on Jews buying land in the provinces of Mogilev and Vitebsk which had been relaxed in 1865 was reintroduced, and in May 1880 the Don Cossack Territory was closed to almost all Jews, who were also forbidden to buy or lease landed property there in response to fears that the taking over of the local railway by Samuel Polyakov would constitute a threat to the existence of the Cossack military caste.[119]

Fears of the negative impact of Jewish leasing in the countryside became more common. In April 1880 the Ministry of the Interior requested confidential information on the extent of Jewish leasing of peasant land in Mogilev and possibly in other provinces. The report submitted by the governor of Mogilev argued that most leaseholders were not engaged in agriculture and had a negative impact on the peasantry. In April 1880 and May 1881 the Office of Peasant Affairs in Vilna province reported in a similar fashion and requested that Jewish leasing of peasant land be halted.[120]

These views were also echoed in the press. A good example is the article by V. Varzer, 'Jewish Leaseholders in Chernigov Province', published in October 1879 in the prestigious 'thick journal' *Otechestvennye zapiski*, edited by M. E. Saltykov-Shchedrin and N. A. Nekrasov. The article made the exaggerated claim that Jewish leaseholders, 'accidental people, with no ties to or respect for the land', already controlled 40 per cent of the land in the province, and accused them of exploiting the peasants under their control. In much of the public discourse of this period Jews were either identified with or compared to kulaks, originally petty traders but increasingly, in the post-emancipation era, seen as rapacious

118 Quoted in Kaufman, 'Evrei v russko-turetskoi voine 1877 g.', 65. On the Jews and the Balkan crisis of 1875–8, see ibid. 52–72, 176–82, and Klier, *Imperial Russia's Jewish Question, 1855–1881*, 390–6.

119 On these developments, see Rogger, 'Government, Jews, Peasants and Land after the Liberation of the Serfs', 130–2.

120 Ibid. 133.

peasants (sometimes described as *miroedy*—commune eaters) intent on acquiring land at the expense of their neighbours.[121]

The long-standing Jewish involvement in the liquor trade was also attacked. By the middle of the nineteenth century a dual system had evolved. In the Russian interior the right to sell vodka was auctioned by the state to suppliers who purchased it from distilleries belonging to the nobility and sold it through their own network of taverns. In the Pale of Settlement the trade was in the hands of tax farmers, as in the interior, but production and sale in the countryside were noble monopolies.[122] As part of the Great Reforms, a law of 4 July 1861 replaced leasing of the sale of liquor by an excise tax on spirits. This obviously ended the role of the great Jewish tax farmers, but left most inns in the Pale of Settlement in the hands of Jewish innkeepers, who were specifically excluded from the decrees forbidding Jewish ownership or leasing of land. Jewish skills in brewing and distilling also proved indispensable, and, as we have seen, the law of 1865, which opened the Pale to Jewish craftsmen, specifically included Jewish distillers and brewers.[123]

While the government was willing enough to permit the Jews to produce alcohol, it remained reluctant to allow them to sell it. The new regulations on the liquor trade, promulgated on 4 July 1861, initially permitted the Jews inside the Pale of Settlement to trade only in towns and small towns (shtetls). On 18 March 1863 the State Council reinterpreted the law to allow Jews to trade on an equal basis with all other citizens, but a law of 14 May 1874 limited the right of Jews to sell liquor wherever they had the right of residence in the Pale by requiring that they own the taverns or inns where the sale took place. The law was also vague in that it specified that this trade could take place only 'in their own homes'. It was not specified that such taverns or inns had to be on Jewish land, but it was frequently interpreted in this way, a view finally upheld by the senate in 1882. None of these regulations ended the role of the Jewish innkeepers, who were widely attacked for evading the law of 1874 and as the cause of peasant drunkenness, despite the fact that in the Russian interior, where Jews played no role in the liquor trade, the problem of abuse of alcohol was even more acute than in the Pale of Settlement.[124]

Jews were also attacked for their participation in the various revolutionary movements which burgeoned in Russia at the end of the reign of Alexander II. They played no part in the first socialist groups organized in the tsarist empire, and few participated in the initial 'going to the people' in the mid-1870s. However, recent research has shown that there was greater Jewish participation in the later Populist movement than previously believed, and that some 20 per cent of the Populist activists in Ukraine were Jews. Jewish revolutionaries such as

[121] On this, see Klier, *Imperial Russia's Jewish Question, 1855–1881*, 300–21.

[122] Christian, *Living Water*, 117–54.

[123] *PSZ* 2/xxxvi, no. 37197 (4 July 1861); xxxviii, no. 39386 (18 Nov. 1863); xlix, no. 53524 (14 May 1874).

[124] On this, see the article by I. Orshansky, *Den'*, 4 Oct. 1869.

Mark Natanson also seem to have played a significant role in shaping the basic doctrines of the movement.[125] The first Jewish socialist grouping was also established in Vilna in the early 1870s. One of its leaders, Aaron Samuel Liebermann, escaped arrest when his comrades were taken into custody in 1875 and established a Jewish socialist organization first in Austria and Prussia and finally in London. Jews were involved in the socialist demonstration in Kazan on 6 December 1876, for which three were arrested and convicted, and a young Jewish terrorist, I. O. Mlodetsky, attempted to assassinate Count M. T. Loris-Melikov, the minister of the interior, in February 1880.

Jewish participation in the revolutionary movement was thus on a relatively small scale. Nevertheless, it was commented on by a number of government officials. In their memorandum calling for a relaxation of the restrictions under which Jews laboured, two members of the government Commission for the Amelioration of the Condition of the Jews, Neklyudov and Karpov, remarked, 'The rising generation of Jews has already begun to participate in the revolutionary movement to which they had hitherto been strangers.'[126] Jewish involvement in revolutionary activity was also commented on by those hostile to the Jews. In a letter to V. M. Putsykevich, the editor of the reactionary newspaper *Grazhdanin*, Fedor Dostoevsky wrote in September 1878:

> Apropos: when will people finally realize how much the Yids (by my own observation) and perhaps the Poles are behind this nihilist business? What a collection of Yids were involved in the Kazan Square incident, and then [the negative role played by] the Yids throughout the history of Odessa. Odessa, the city of Yids, is the center of our rampant socialism. In Europe, the very same situation: the Yids are terribly active in the socialist movement, and I'm not speaking about the Lassalles and Karl Marxes. And understandably so: the Yid has everything to gain from every radical cataclysm and coup d'état because it is he himself, *status in statu*, that constitutes his own community, which is unshakable and only gains from everything that undermines non-Yid society.[127]

Rhetoric of this sort soon became the stock-in-trade of the Judaeophobe press. After the arrest of Mlodetsky, *Novoe vremya*, one of the most respected conservative newspapers in St Petersburg, published an article in March 1880 claiming that 'the Yids are the firm allies of Nihilism . . . from times of old these Yids have been representative of the revolutionary spirit'. In response to criticism the paper attempted on 18 March to explain how Jews could simultaneously be supporters of capitalism and of socialism. In the paper's view the essence of Judaism was 'cosmopolitanism'. Since the whole world existed for Jews as an object of exploitation, capitalism and socialism were simply parallel paths to the same goal.

The last years of Alexander's reign also saw the resurgence of blood libel accusations. That some Jews engaged in such practices was widely believed within

125 Haberer, *Jews and Revolution in Nineteenth-Century Russia*.

126 Dubnow, *History of the Jews in Russia and Poland*, ii. 197.

127 Quoted in Goldstein, *Dostoyevsky and the Jews*, 151–2.

Russian educated opinion. Thus, the otherwise liberal daily *Golos* on 23 July 1863 could assert:

> All religions not yet cleansed of superstition show examples of [human sacrifice] and since all religions have their fanatics, it is in no way unbelievable that among the followers of the teachings of Moses are to be found their own brand of fanatics. It is likely that these people don't know the Talmud very well, but having heard of the superstition about Christian blood, resolved upon cruelty and murder.

From the early 1870s the idea that Jews engaged in ritual murder was propagated by N. P. Gilyarov-Platonov, the editor of the Moscow daily *Sovremennye izvestiya*, who was close to conservative circles, especially the Aksakov family and Konstantin Pobedonostsev. He was followed as editor by Hipolit Lutostański (Lyutostansky), a former Roman Catholic priest who had been defrocked for sexual misconduct in 1867 and who then briefly became an Orthodox monk. He left the Orthodox clergy in 1876 and then published a book accusing 'Jewish sectarians' of ritual murder, which he republished in an enlarged version in 1880.[128] Lutostański was a highly disreputable character and was sentenced to two weeks in jail after a dispute with his publisher. He also lost a libel action against Alexander Tsederbaum after a public disputation. In spite of this, and his repudiation of his views in 1882 (a repudiation he in turn repudiated in 1902), his works were given a serious hearing. Some of the discussion of his work was hostile, but others accepted his main thesis and all treated it as a serious scholarly work. No amount of advocacy on the part of the Jews could dispel the myths which were now increasingly widespread. When Daniel Khvolson republished his refutation of the blood libel in 1879, he was attacked in the newspaper *Novoe vremya* by the historian Nikolay Kostomarov, who had, as a result of a case in Saratov in 1860, become convinced that 'some' Jews engaged in ritual murder, and who now not only claimed that there was ample evidence that 'Jewish sectarians' engaged in ritual murder but also gave Lutostański's work his scholarly imprimatur.[129]

In this climate of opinion, it is not surprising that on 5 March 1879, in the province of Kutais, in Georgia, nine local Jews should have been charged with the murder for ritual purposes of a young Georgian girl. The Jewish leadership in St Petersburg recognized the importance of the trial and engaged two leading non-Jewish attorneys, P. I. Aleksandrov and L. Kupernik, to defend the accused.

[128] Lyutostansky [Lutostański], *Vopros ob upotreblenii evreyami-sektatorami khristianskoi krovi dlya religioznykh tselei, v svyazi s voprosami ob otnosheniyakh evreistva k khristianstvu voobshche* [The Question of the Use by Jewish Sectarians of Christian Blood for Religious Purposes, in connection with Questions of the General Attitudes of Jewry to Christianity]. The title of the 2nd edn. is *Ob upotreblenii evreyami (talmudistskimi sektatorami) khristianskoi krovi dlya religioznykh tselei v svyazi s voprosom ob otnosheniyakh evreistva k khristianstvu voobshche* [On the Use by the Jews (Talmudic Sects) of Christian Blood for Religious Purposes, in connection with Questions of the General Attitudes of Jewry to Christianity].

[129] Khvolson, 'O nekotorykh srednevekovykh obvineniyakh protiv evreev'. The work was also issued in book form in 1861, and a 2nd edn. was produced in 1880 during the Kutais Affair. A shorter version appeared in 1879 as a pamphlet, *Upotreblyayut li evrei khristianskuyu krov'?*

They not only succeeded in securing the acquittal of the accused but were also able to call into question the claim that the Jews needed Christian blood for their rituals.

By the end of Alexander's reign, Judaeophobia had become a central element in the ideology of Russian conservatism. The Jews were seen as the embodiment of the capitalist system, whose inevitable consequences were parliamentary rule and the undermining of the agrarian social structure and the landed nobility. Jewish revolutionaries were the embodiment of 'nihilism' and threatened the social order. This 'conservative utopianism' was strengthened by the simultaneous emergence of political antisemitism in central Europe, and a negative synergy between the two movements was established which was to intensify in subsequent decades.[130]

JEWISH RESPONSES TO THE WORSENING SITUATION

In May 1869, nearly ten years after the demise of the first *Den'* and of *Sion*, a new Russian Jewish newspaper with the ambitious title of *Den': organ russkikh evreev* (The Day: The Organ of Russian Jewry) began to appear in Odessa, headed by a three-man editorial committee made up of Mikhail Morgulis, Mikhail Kulisher, and Ilya Orshansky, who were nominated by the Odessa branch of the Society for the Promotion of Culture among Jews, which financed the venture. All three, in addition to their journalistic experience, were law graduates, Morgulis and Kulisher of the University of St Vladimir in Kiev and Orshansky of the University of New Russia in Odessa.

The paper reflected the views of the new generation of Jewish university graduates. It called for Russification and 'complete fusion of the interests of the Jewish population with those of other citizens', but regarded as a prerequisite for these developments the unconditional granting of complete legal equality to the Jews. In the view of its editors, the 'Jewish problem' was not a national but a social and economic issue and would be resolved only when this 'section of the Russian people' enjoyed complete equality of rights with the remainder of the population. In accordance with this view, a number of its articles, particularly those by Orshansky and Morgulis, examined the economic situation in the Pale and defended the Jewish role there. The paper also attempted to demonstrate the falsehood of Brafman's assertions, publishing the recantations of his Jewish collaborators and a set of historical articles on the origin and nature of the Jewish system of communal autonomy by Morgulis.[131]

Den' ceased publication in just over two years. It was subject to persistent intervention by the censors because of its advocacy of complete emancipation for the Jews, and when Orshansky's proposed leading article on the Odessa pogrom,

130 On this, see Klier, 'Russian Judeophobes and German Antisemites'.

131 For these, see *Den'*, 1 Aug. 1870, 30 Jan., 12 and 26 Mar., 6 Apr., 29 May 1871.

which saw its origins in the 'general moral condition of contemporary Russian society' and castigated those involved in the administration of justice and education as Judaeophobic, was banned, its editors decided to close the paper. It appeared for the last time on 8 June 1871.[132]

Even before the collapse of *Den'* the indefatigable entrepreneur Alexander Tsederbaum had attempted to establish a rival Russian-language weekly, *Vestnik russkikh evreev*. In its first issue on 3 January 1871 it took a more conservative position than *Den'*. Jews, it argued, would like to pursue rapprochement with Russians in civil and social relations, while retaining the religion of their forefathers. The successful accomplishment of the process would make a separate Jewish newspaper superfluous, but, because of the alienation caused by the specific conditions of Jewish civil, social, and economic life, this was still far off. Its general quality was significantly below that of *Den'*, and it ceased publication in 1883.

When a new group of Russian Jewish newspapers began publication in the late 1870s, it was under very different conditions. The optimism of the early years of Alexander's reign had by now largely evaporated and there was a growing climate of Judaeophobia. In addition, the rapid Russification of the educated minority of Russian Jewish youth was causing considerable alarm among the older Jewish integrationists. The weeklies *Russkii evrei* and the revived *Rassvet*, and the 'thick journal' *Voskhod*, established in 1879 in St Petersburg, where the Jewish community had grown considerably in the 1860s and 1870s, were much less naive in their expectations of the authorities and much more concerned about the corrosive effects of Russification in conditions where the Jews as a whole, like the majority of Russians, did not enjoy civil rights.

One of the issues which these papers took up was the question of whether Jews were evading military service to a greater extent than the rest of the population. According to A. E. Landau, writing in *Voskhod* in March 1881, rights and obligations should be given simultaneously since 'a rightless person cannot be under obligation'. Despite their understandable reluctance to undertake military service, Jews served at a rate one and a half times greater than that of the non-Jewish population. Attempts were also made to defend the Jews against the charge of 'nihilism'. According to *Russkii evrei* on 5 December 1879, 'We boldly and directly declare that there is not a single Jew who, loving his country and concerned with its interests, has anything in common with those who wish to change the world by means of murder and robbery.'

The last years of Alexander's reign also saw a new political activism on the part of the Orthodox section of the Jewish community. As we have seen, the creation of the commission to investigate Brafman's claims in Vilna marked a new willingness to cooperate among those old foes the maskilim and the Orthodox. When the Rabbinic Commission next met, after a gap of seventeen years, between February and April 1879, the maskilim were on the defensive and the Orthodox mounted a

[132] On this, see Zipperstein, *The Jews of Odessa*, 114–28.

concerted campaign to have their candidates appointed to it. This provoked considerable alarm in the maskilic camp. According to Moses Leib Lilienblum, writing in *Hakol* number 22 (1878), the fate of the Jews could not be left to the narrow-minded rabbis:

> Anyone acquainted with the spirit of our rabbis knows how ill-equipped they are to comprehend what is in the Jews' best interest; they do not know the suffering of their own people . . . I have no doubt whatsoever that the rabbis would be satisfied if the Jews did not win equal rights, just as long as every iota of the prayers inherited from our ancestors could be preserved . . . The word 'exile' [*galut*] is for them like a toy in the hands of a child: They do not want it to be taken away from them. In their eyes the Jews without their *galut* are like a body without a soul.[133]

The Orthodox aggressively campaigned for influence. A key role was played by Rabbi Jacob Halevi Lipschitz (1838–1921) of Kovno, a staunch supporter of the Orthodox position, who, in response to Lilienblum, asserted that the Orthodox spiritual rabbis were the real leaders of the Jewish community. 'To whom does an anguished and distressed man turn first [as do] the poor and wounded in spirit, every widow and orphan, every oppressed and discouraged individual, and so on—but to the local rabbi?' The function of the Rabbinic Commission was not to secure equal rights for the Jews but rather to address religious questions involving marriage and divorce. Lipschitz was therefore outraged at 'the foolish wickedness of the Jewish intelligentsia, who elect their own—those who are distant from the Torah'. They should limit their role in Jewish religious life to the registration of Jewish vital statistics in the metrical books, leaving religious questions to genuine rabbis learned in Torah and halakhah.[134]

The change in the popular mood was reflected in the widespread support garnered by the Orthodox. 'The elections were a plebiscite against the state rabbis and those who upheld the banner of acculturation and russification. And the result was a resounding defeat for the non-Orthodox camp.'[135] In the event, however, the Ministry of the Interior appointed to the Rabbinic Commission only maskilim and reformers, many of them with no religious qualifications, like Baron Horace Guenzburg. This led Rabbi Isaac Elhanan Spektor, the influential rabbi of Kovno, to write to one member of the commission, Avraham Elijah Harkavy (1835–1919), a well-known orientalist from Vilna. Pointing out that the authorities had not selected 'any of the great geonim' (religious authorities) to serve on the commission, he questioned the moral integrity and ability of its members to address issues involving Jewish law.[136] In the event the struggle for control of the commission was not justified by its subsequent meagre activity, which consisted of an examination of seven divorce cases. However, this did not discourage the

[133] Cited in Lederhendler, *The Road to Modern Jewish Politics*, 150.

[134] Lipschitz, *Zikhron ya'akov*, ii. 203.

[135] Freeze, *Jewish Marriage and Divorce in Imperial Russia*, 246.

[136] Lipschitz, *Zikhron ya'akov*, ii. 207.

Orthodox, who were now convinced that a Rabbinic Commission in their hands could play an important role in Jewish life.

CONCLUSION

The situation of the Jews in the Russian empire in the last years of Alexander II's reign was highly ambivalent. Civil rights had been extended to an important section of the community, and Russification and secularization were proceeding rapidly. At the same time, the impact of the ending of serfdom and the commercialization of agriculture had worsened the economic situation of the bulk of the Jews in the Pale of Settlement. Within the government and in educated public opinion there was also growing scepticism about the commitment of the Jewish elite to the processes of 'merger' and 'reconciliation', while Judaeophobia was increasingly widespread in conservative circles.

It has often been argued that it was only in the reign of Alexander III that a new policy was introduced in relation to the Jews, based on the assumption that they could never be transformed into useful subjects and that the goal of the authorities should be only to limit their harmful impact on the population among whom they lived. As we have seen, already in the second decade of Alexander's reign such views were increasingly widespread in official circles. The Jewish elite still harboured the hope that the government would lift the remaining restrictions on the Jews if the Jews educated and Russified themselves. But they too were becoming disillusioned, and the seeds of the 'new Jewish politics' which took ethnicity rather than religion as the main marker for Jewish difference had already begun to sprout in the last years of Alexander's reign.

*

The wave of pogroms of 1881–2 is widely held to have marked a new period in the history of the Jews of the former Polish–Lithuanian Commonwealth. In the view of the tsarist authorities, the Jews themselves were responsible for the wave of unrest because of their 'exploitation' of the surrounding population. Their consequent disillusionment with, and rejection of, their own policy of transforming the Jews into useful subjects led to a crisis among the supporters of integrationist principles within the Jewish elite. Many now adopted proto-nationalist positions while others looked to the socialist movement and the abolition of capitalism to create the conditions in which the Jews would be able to achieve equality with their neighbours.

Yet already in the last decade of Alexander II's reign there had been, within the Russian bureaucracy, growing doubts about the feasibility of transforming the Jews so as to enable their merger with the wider population. Judaeophobia became increasingly common within the bureaucracy, while the negative consequences of the half-measures involved in the abolition of serfdom soon led to a social crisis in which the Jews assumed their familiar role as scapegoats.

In the remaining areas of north-eastern Europe integrationist principles still seemed securely established. Yet everywhere there were clear signs of future problems. In Prussian Poland the growing bitterness of the Polish–German conflict undermined the liberal version of the German national idea, to which most Jews in the province adhered. Chauvinist views became more prevalent within the German administration, while the beleaguered Poles came to resent bitterly what they saw as the collusion of local Jews in their oppression. In Galicia the links between the ruling landed classes and the Jewish elite came under pressure with the emergence of new political forces: the more mature and sophisticated Ukrainian national movement in the east and the emerging peasant movement in the west. In the Kingdom of Poland the pro-integrationist position of the Positivists and their Jewish allies was coming under more intense fire as the attempt to work within the framework of Russian rule came to seem increasingly craven, and as antisemitism in its modern form began to infiltrate from Germany.

These challenges to the view that the Jews should be transformed into citizens or useful subjects, which had informed the various attempts to deal with the 'Jewish question' since the middle of the eighteenth century, were to become ever more powerful in the last decades of the nineteenth century, and they form the core of the second volume of this work.

GLOSSARY

arenda Lease of monopoly rights, usually of an estate.

arendator Holder of an arenda.

Ashkenaz, Ashkenazi Although in its narrowest sense 'Ashkenaz' denotes German lands, the term 'Ashkenazi' is generally used to denote Jews who share in the cultural legacy that derived initially from northern France and Germany and spread eastward to include Poland–Lithuania and other lands of east central Europe.

av beit din (Hebrew) Head of a Jewish religious court.

ba'al shem, pl. ***ba'alei shem*** (Hebrew; literally 'Master of the Divine Name') The title given in popular usage and in Jewish literature, especially kabbalistic and hasidic works from the Middle Ages onwards, to one who possessed secret knowledge of the Tetragrammaton and other 'Holy Names' and who knew how to work miracles by the power of these names.

ban (Hebrew: *ḥerem*) Denotes the various degrees of religious and social ostracism imposed by rabbinical courts. Frequently used as a deterrent; transgressors would be threatened with the ban when an edict was promulgated.

beit midrash (Hebrew; literally 'house of study'; Yiddish: *besmedresh*) A building attached to a synagogue where Jewish men assemble to study the Torah.

cantonists Jewish children who were conscripted into the army in tsarist Russia during the reign of Nicholas I, in which they served for twenty-five years.

chamber of deputies (Polish: *izba poselska*; literally 'house of deputies') The lower house in the Sejm, containing representatives from each province (*województwo*) in Poland (the Crown) and the Grand Duchy of Lithuania. It was elected by the nobility (*szlachta*) of each province, meeting in the local *dietine (Polish: *sejmik*).

Commonwealth (Polish: *rzeczpospolita*) The term *rzeczpospolita* is derived from the Latin *res publica*. It is sometimes translated as 'Commonwealth' and sometimes as 'republic', often in the form 'Noblemen's Republic' (Rzeczpospolita szlachecka). After the Union of Lublin in 1569, it was used officially in the form Rzeczpospolita Obojga Narodów (Commonwealth of Two Nations) to designate the new form of state which had arisen. In historical literature this term is often rendered as 'the Polish–Lithuanian Commonwealth'.

confederation (Polish: *konfederacja*) A union of nobles called together to defend the country or obtain certain defined political objectives. After 1652, but mainly in the eighteenth century, the indiscriminate use of the **liberum veto* regularly paralysed the *Sejm; confederations, which were not subject to the veto, were the only means available for achieving political objectives in an emergency.

Congress Kingdom (otherwise Kingdom of Poland, or Congress Poland) A constitutional kingdom created at the Congress of Vienna (1814–15), with the tsar of Russia as hereditary monarch. After 1831 it declined to an administrative unit of the Russian empire in all but name. After 1864 it lost the remaining vestiges of the autonomy it had been granted at Vienna and was now officially referred to as 'Privislinskii krai' (Vistula Territory).

Council of Four Lands (Hebrew: Va'ad Arba Aratsot) The principal body through which the Jews governed themselves autonomously in the Polish–Lithuanian *Commonwealth. It lasted from the late sixteenth century to 1764.

Crown (Polish: Korona) The Polish part of the Rzeczpospolita (Republic, or *Commonwealth), as distinct from the Grand Duchy of Lithuania, with which it was dynastically linked from the fourteenth century and constitutionally linked in 1569 by the Union of Lublin. In addition to its Polish core territories, it included Royal Prussia and Ukraine, which, after 1569, was transferred from the Grand Duchy to the Crown.

devekut (Hebrew; literally 'cleaving, attachment') A term which became central to hasidism, although it was also in use previously. It denotes communion with God, achieved mainly through prayer or meditation, using the appropriate mystical interpretations and meanings given to the words of prayer.

Diet See 'Sejm' ('Seym' in eighteenth-century Polish spelling).

dietine (Polish: *sejmik*) A local assembly of the nobility operating in each province of the *Commonwealth. It elected deputies to the *Sejm and provided them with instructions governing their conduct there.

Duchy of Warsaw State created in 1807 on the basis of the Treaty of Tilsit and enlarged after the French defeat of the Austrians in 1809. Its constitutional structure was laid down by the Constitution of 1807 and its duke was Frederick Augustus I, king of Saxony. It was abolished by the peacemakers at Vienna.

Four Year Sejm (diet) This *Sejm, which was transformed into a *confederation in order to avoid being bound by the **liberum veto*, met in Warsaw from 6 October 1788 to 2 May 1792 under the leadership of the marshal of the Sejm, Stanisław Małachowski. Making use of the favourable international situation (the involvement of Austria and Russia in a war with Turkey), the 'Patriotic' Party introduced a number of reforms in the social and political system of the *Commonwealth which aimed to free it from the hegemony of the tsarist empire and re-establish its independence.

Frankists Followers of Jacob Frank (1726–91), the head of a mystical antinomian sect among Polish Jews, who hailed him as the messiah.

galut (Hebrew; literally 'exile') The Diaspora. *Galut* (Ashkenazi pronounciation: *golus*) embodies a sense of the pain of the Jewish condition, which in traditional Jewish thinking will only be brought to an end by the coming of the messiah.

gaon, pl. ***geonim*** (Hebrew; literally 'genius') A term originally used to designate the heads of the academies of Sura and Pumbeditha in Babylon from the sixth to the middle of the eleventh centuries. Later used to describe a man who had acquired a phenomenal command of the Torah. One *gaon* was Rabbi Elijah b. Solomon Zalman, the Vilna Gaon.

Gemara Another name for the Talmud.

Gemeinde (German; literally 'community') The term used in Prussia for the reformed *kehilah*.

gmina, pl. ***gminy*** (Polish; commune) The Polish term for the local communal institution which administered synagogues, schools, cemeteries, and *mikvaot*. The Hebrew term was **kahal*, but the Polish term was frequently used in the nineteenth century.

goy, pl. ***goyim*** (Hebrew; literally 'person', 'people') Term used by Jews for non-Jews, sometimes with pejorative overtones.

Great Emigration (Polish: Wielka Emigracja) After the failure of the Polish insurrection of 1830–1, between 8,000 and 9,000 of those who had participated in it went into emigration. Because of its political and cultural significance, this group became known as the Great Emigration.

Habad Acronym derived from the Hebrew words *ḥokhmah*, *binah*, *da'at* (wisdom, understanding, knowledge). It was applied to a sect of *hasidism, also known as the Lubavitch hasidim, founded in the Grand Duchy of Lithuania by Shneur Zalman of Lyady (Liozna).

halakhah (Hebrew; literally 'the way') A word used to describe the entire prescriptive part of Jewish tradition. It defines the norms of behaviour and religious observance.

Hasidei Ashkenaz (Hebrew: pietists of Ashkenaz) Groups of hasidim (pietists) who appeared chiefly in the Rhineland in the twelfth and thirteenth centuries. They followed a highly ascetic regimen, and their doctrines stressed humility and the pursuit of esoteric knowledge. Except in terms of their general and profound influence on Ashkenazi culture, these hasidim are not connected to the hasidism that arose in Poland–Lithuania in the second half of the eighteenth century.

hasidism A mystically inclined movement of religious revival consisting of distinct groups with charismatic leadership which arose in the borderlands of the Polish–Lithuanian Commonwealth in the second half of the eighteenth century. The movement soon spread rapidly and became particularly strong in Ukraine, southern Poland (Małopolska or Galicia), and central Poland (the Kingdom of Poland).

Haskalah (Hebrew; literally 'wisdom' or 'understanding' but used in the sense of 'the Jewish Enlightenment') A rationalistic movement which emerged in the Jewish world under the impact of the European Enlightenment in the second half of the eighteenth century and continued to the second half of the nineteenth century. It first became important in Germany under the influence of Moses Mendelssohn and soon spread to the rest of European Jewry. Its followers were called maskilim.

ḥavurot (Hebrew) See *ḥevrah*.

Haydamaks The name used to describe armed groups which were active in Polish Ukraine in the eighteenth century. The Haydamaks included both ordinary bandits and peasant insurrectionaries.

ḥazan (Hebrew) Cantor officiating in a synagogue.

ḥeder (Hebrew; literally 'room') Colloquial name for a traditional Jewish elementary school in which teaching is carried on by a *melamed*.

ḥerem (Hebrew) See 'ban'.

ḥevrah, pl. ***ḥevrot*** or ***ḥavurot*** (Hebrew) A mutual benefit society made up of people in the same occupation or who were devoted to performing some social or religious task (charity, burial, early morning prayer, etc.).

ḥiluk (Hebrew; literally 'dividing') A method of talmudic analysis which examined specific texts in detail.

intelligent (Russian; Polish: *inteligent*) Member of the intelligentsia. In both Russia and the Polish lands the absence of a coherent and self-confident bourgeoisie led to the emergence of what came to be described as the intelligentsia, a social group made up of those possessing academic higher education—principally doctors, lawyers, teachers, and literary figures.

January insurrection The ill-fated insurrection against the tsarist monarchy which began in January 1863. After its defeat, the Russian government embarked on a determined effort to Russify not only the Kresy (the western provinces of the empire which had been part of the Polish–Lithuanian *Commonwealth) but also the *Congress Kingdom.

jurydyki (Polish) Areas within towns not subject to the legal control of the municipal administration, but owned by noble or ecclesiastical dignitaries.

kabbalah Jewish mysticism, the search for an inner spiritual meaning to the Torah and its commandments.

kahal, ***kehilah*** (Hebrew; Yiddish: *kehile*) Although both terms mean 'community', *kahal* is used to denote the institution of Jewish autonomy in a particular locality, while *kehilah* denotes the community of Jews who live in the town.

Karaite Follower of a heretical sect of Judaism who recognized the validity of the written (Hebrew *kara*: read) but not the Oral Law (the Talmud). In Poland many of the Karaites were descended from Tatars who had converted to this form of Judaism.

kashrut (Hebrew) The system of maintaining the Jewish dietary laws. Hence *kosher: conforming to Jewish dietary law.

kest (Yiddish) Arrangement by which men supported their Torah scholar sons-in-law for a number of years after marriage.

kidush hashem (Hebrew; literally 'sanctification of God's Name') Martyrdom, the sacrifice of one's life rather than be forced into idolatry, immorality, or unjustified homicide.

kloyz, pl. ***kloyzn*** (Yiddish) Small prayer hall.

kosher (Ashkenazi pronunciation; Hebrew: *kasher*) Term originally used in the Bible in the sense of 'fit' or 'proper' and later ritually correct or faultless. Usually used to denote food that is permitted, in contrast to that which is not kosher (treif). See also *kashrut*.

liberum veto The right of every deputy in the Sejm to overturn legislation of which he did not approve or for which his dietine had not provided him with instructions. In the sixteenth century, and even in the seventeenth century, decisions were still taken by majority vote, but in 1652 Władysław Siciński exercised his veto as an individual to 'explode the Sejm'; thenceforth there was continuous and irresponsible use of the veto, rendering normal parliamentary activity impossible.

Litvak A Jew from the territories of the Grand Duchy of Lithuania (Litwa). In terms of Jewish stereotypes, the Litvak was a rationalist, an opponent of hasidism, often a social radical, and also a miser.

luftmensh (Yiddish; literally 'a man with his head in the air') One of the many impoverished inhabitants of the *Pale of Settlement who hoped to secure his livelihood by various far-fetched schemes. The archetypal *luftmensh* was Shalom Aleichem's Menahem Mendel.

magid, pl. ***magidim*** (Hebrew) Itinerant preacher, skilled as a narrator of stories.

magistrat The name for the municipal administration in pre-*partition Poland.

Maimonides Moses b. Maimon (1135–1204), the outstanding figure of medieval Jewish theology and *halakhah. Also known by the acronym Rambam, he was the author of numerous works, including the theological work *Moreh nevukhim* (Guide of the Perplexed) and the compendious halakhic code *Mishneh torah*.

Małopolska (Polish; literally 'Lesser Poland' or 'Little Poland') Southern Poland, the area around Kraków. Also referred to under the Habsburgs as (western) Galicia.

maskilim (Hebrew) See 'Haskalah'.

matzah (Hebrew) Unleavened bread eaten during the Jewish festival of Passover.

melamed (Hebrew: teacher) Teacher in a **ḥeder*.

mezuzah (Hebrew) A parchment scroll on which are written two biblical passages (Deut. 6: 4–9 and 11: 13–21), inserted into a case and fixed to the doorpost of rooms in a Jewish home, in fulfilment of a biblical commandment.

mikveh, pl. ***mikvaot*** (Hebrew) Pool or bath of clear water, immersion in which renders ritually clean a person who has become ritually unclean through contact with the dead or any other defiling object or through an unclean flux from the body, especially menstruation.

minyan, pl. ***minyanim*** (Hebrew) A quorum of ten adult Jewish men, aged 13 years and over, needed for certain public prayers and other religious ceremonies; can be used more generally to refer to prayer groups.

mitnaged, pl. **mitnagedim** (Hebrew; literally 'opposer') The rabbinic opponents of hasidism.

Nahmanides Moses b. Nahman (1194–1270), also known by the acronym Ramban. A Spanish rabbi and scholar who wrote influential works in the areas of halakhah, biblical commentary, and kabbalah.

November uprising The unsuccessful Polish insurrection against Tsar Nicholas I, which began in November 1830 and which was followed by the *Great Emigration.

Pale of Settlement (Russian: Cherta [postoyannoi evreiskoi] osedlosti) Area within the borders of tsarist Russia in which the residence of Jews was legally permitted.

pan (Polish) Lord, master, or noble. Also used today as the polite form of the second person singular.

partition The dividing up of the Polish–Lithuanian Commonwealth, which led to its disappearance as a state at the end of the eighteenth century. The first partition, which was carried out by Russia, Prussia, and Austria, took place in 1772. The second partition, in which only Russia and Prussia took part, occurred in 1793, and the third after the Kościuszko rebellion in 1795.

pilpul (Hebrew; derived from *pilpel* pepper) A method of detailed textual analysis which involves examining all the arguments presented in the large corpus of the Talmud in order to obtain a logical basis for the interpretation of halakhah; the method was also used to sharpen the wits of the student.

Podolacy The east Galician aristocracy.

Polish–Lithuanian Commonwealth See 'Commonwealth'.

powiat The basic administrative unit in pre-*partition Poland–Lithuania, subordinate to the province (*województwo*). It remained a basic administrative unit in the various parts of partitioned Poland and in the independent state which emerged after 1918.

propinacja (Polish) The monopoly on the sale of alcohol on a noble estate. From the sixteenth century the *propinacja* had formed an important part of the estate owners' income from their lands, particularly in those regions where the export of grain to the international market of Danzig was not practical.

Purim Jewish festival, usually sometime in March, which celebrates the defeat of the Persian minister Haman in his attempt to massacre the Jews of that country, as told in the book of Esther. It has the atmosphere of a carnival.

Rashi Acronym for Rabbi Solomon b. Isaac (1040–1105). An outstanding halakhic scholar, he was the author of the standard commentaries on the Bible and Talmud.

Realschule Secondary school in German-speaking Europe for modern subjects, particularly the sciences.

rebbe (Hebrew) Leader of a hasidic group. See also 'tsadik'.

Rosh Hashanah Jewish New Year.

rosh yeshivah (Hebrew) Head of a *yeshiva.

royal (free) town A town directly dependent on the king and subsequently on the government of the different parts of *partitioned Poland. Burghers in royal or 'government' towns had greater rights than those in towns controlled by the nobility ('private towns'). The reverse was for the most part the case with the Jews.

Rzeczpospolita (Polish) Republic, or *Commonwealth.

sefirot (derived from Hebrew *safor*, to numerate, because of its relationship to the ten primordial numbers) A fundamental term of the kabbalah used to describe the ten stages of emanation that emerged from Ein Sof (literally 'the Infinite'), the name given in kabbalah to God transcendent, in His pure essence, and which form the realm of God's manifestations in His various attributes.

Sejm The central parliamentary institution of the Polish–Lithuanian *Commonwealth, composed of a senate and a chamber of deputies; after 1501 both of these had a voice in the introduction of new legislation. Until the middle of the seventeenth century the Sejm functioned reasonably well; after that, the use of the **liberum veto* began to paralyse its effectiveness. Also used for the local parliament in Galicia, as in 'Sejm Galicyjski'.

sejmiki, sing. ***sejmik*** (Polish) See 'dietine'.

senate The upper house of the Sejm. It was composed of all the great officials of the government, the provincial governors, hetmans, marshals, and treasurers, headed by the archbishop of Gniezno, who also served as *interrex* on the death of the king.

Shekhinah (Hebrew: 'dwelling' or 'resting') Usually refers in rabbinic literature to the numinous immanence of God in the world. In kabbalistic thought the Shekhinah represents the feminine principle.

shofar Animal's horn (usually that of a ram) prepared for use as a musical instrument. During the month of Elul (the last month of the Hebrew year) the shofar is blown from the second day of the month to usher in the penitential season.

shtadlan, pl. ***shtadlanim*** (Aramaic; from the root *shtadal*, 'to intercede on behalf of') Representative of the Jewish community with access to high dignitaries and legislative bodies.

shtetl (Yiddish: 'small town') The characteristic small town of central and eastern Poland, Ukraine, Belarus, and Lithuania, with a substantial Jewish population which sometimes amounted to the majority of the population. These were originally 'private' towns under the control of the **szlachta*. See 'royal (free) town'.

Shulḥan arukh (Hebrew; literally 'The Set Table') The last comprehensive code of *halakhah, it was written by Joseph Caro (1488–1575) in Palestine. The custom arose of publishing it together with the *Mapah* ('Tablecloth'), the commentary of Moses Isserles (1525–72) of Kraków, who supplemented the work of the Sephardi author by adding reference to Ashkenazi practice.

starosta (Polish) Royal administrator, holder of the office of *starostwo*.

Sukkot Jewish harvest festival which takes place five days after the Day of Atonement in early autumn.

szlachta (Polish) The Polish nobility. A very broad social stratum making up nearly 8 per cent of the population in the eighteenth century. Its members ranged from the great magnates, like the Czartoryskis, Potockis, and Radziwiłłs, who dominated political and social life in the last century of the Polish–Lithuanian *Commonwealth, to small landowners (the *szlachta zagrodowa*), and even landless retainers of the great houses. What distinguished members of this group from the remainder of the population was their noble status and their right to participate in political life in the dietines, the Sejm, and the election of the king.

takanah, pl. ***takanot*** (Hebrew) Edict or directive enacted by halakhic authorities or the leaders of a *kahal* acting together with rabbinical judges that has the force of law within the Jewish community. Its authority is derived from that of the body or individual who issues it and does not depend on the interpretation of a scriptural verse or talmudic passage.

tosafot (Hebrew) Collections of talmudic commentary deriving mainly from French and German lands in the twelfth to fourteenth centuries. The tosafists in their comments generally took as their point of departure not a talmudic passage but the comments on it of *Rashi and other earlier commentators.

tovim (Hebrew; literally 'the good ones') One of the titles of those who held office in the **kahal*.

treif Not *kosher.

tsadik (Hebrew; literally 'the just one' or 'a pious man') The leader of a hasidic sect (or community). Hasidim often credited their tsadikim or *rebbe*s with miraculous powers, seeing them as mediators between God and man.

tsitsit (Hebrew; literally 'fringes') Tassels consisting of eight threads knotted in a prescribed manner attached to each corner of a four-cornered ritual garment worn by Jewish men.

Va'ad Arba Aratsot (Hebrew) *Council of Four Lands.

voivode (Polish: *wojewoda*) Initially this official acted in place of the ruler, especially in judicial and military matters. From the thirteenth century the office gradually evolved into a provincial dignity; between the sixteenth and eighteenth centuries the voivode conducted the local dietine, led the *pospolite ruszenie* (general mobilization) of the *szlachta* in times of danger to the *Commonwealth, and occasionally governed cities and collected certain dues.

voivodeship (Polish: *województwo*) A province governed by a *voivode.

Wielkopolska (Polish; literally 'Great Poland' or 'Greater Poland') Western Poland, the area around Poznań.

Wissenschaft des Judentums Literally, the Science of Judaism, or in today's terminology 'Jewish studies', as opposed to traditional Jewish learning.

wójt (Polish; German: *Vogt*) During the medieval establishment of towns, the *wójt* was the official who organized the new town and occupied the leading place in its local administration as the head of the town's court. By the eighteenth century the *wójt* was generally the chief administrator of a group of villages.

yarmulke (Yiddish; Hebrew: *kipah*) Skull-cap worn for prayer and by religious Jewish men at all times.

yeshiva Rabbinic college, the highest institution in the traditional Jewish system of education.

Yom Kippur The Day of Atonement.

Zohar (Hebrew; literally '[The Book of] Splendour') The fundamental work of kabbalistic literature comprising various related compositions in Aramaic and dating mainly from the last decades of the thirteenth century in Spain. Scholars consider that the main author was Moses b. Shem Tov de León.

BIBLIOGRAPHY

ABRAMOWITSCH, SHALOM JACOB, *The Complete Works of Mendele Mokher Seforim* [Kol kitvei mendele mokher sefarim] (Jerusalem, 1952).

AGNON, S. Y., and A. ELIASBERG (eds.), *Das Buch von den polnischen Juden* (Berlin, 1916).

ALEKSEEV, A. A., *Ocherki domashnei i obshchestvennoi zhizni evreev: ikh verovaniya, bogosluzhenie, prazdniki, obryady, talmud, i kagal*, 3rd edn. (St Petersburg, 1896).

ALSTON, PATRICK, *Education and the State in Tsarist Russia* (Stanford, Calif., 1969).

ALVIS, ROBERT, *Religion and the Rise of Nationalism: A Profile of an East-Central European City* (Syracuse, NY, 2005).

ANANICH, B. V., *Bankirskie doma v Rossii, 1860–1914 gg.* (Leningrad, 1991).

ANDERSON, MATTHEW, *Britain's Discovery of Russia 1553–1815* (London, 1958).

ANICH, E., *Vosstanie i voina 1794 goda v litovskoi provintsii* (Moscow, 2001).

ANISHCHENKO, EVGENY KONSTANTINOVICH, *Cherta osedlosti* (Minsk, 1998).

ANSKY, S. A. [SOLOMON ZAINWIL RAPOPORT], 'Evreiskaya delegatsiya v Vilenskoi komissii 1869 goda', *Evreiskaya starina*, 5 (1912), no. 2, 187–201.

Arkhiv Yugo-Zapadnoi Rossii, pt. 5, vol. ii (Kiev, 1890).

ASHKENAZI, ELIEZER, *Seliḥot ufizmonim* [penitential prayers and hymns] (Lublin, 1614).

ASHTON, THOMAS SOUTHCLIFFE, *The Industrial Revolution in England 1760–1830* (London, 1948; many reprints).

ASKENAZY, SZYMON, *Książe Józef Poniatowski* (Warsaw, 1920).

——'Z dziejów Żydów polskich w dobie Księstwa Warszawskiego i Królestwa Polskiego', *Kwartalnik poświęcony badaniu przeszłości Żydów w Polsce*, 1/1 (1912–13), 1–14.

——'Ze spraw żydowskich w dobie kongresowej', *Kwartalnik poświęcony badaniu przeszłości Żydów w Polsce*, 1/3 (1913), 1–36.

ASSAF, DAVID, 'Hasidism and its Expansion: The Effectiveness of the Rabbi Nehemiah Yehiel of Bychow, the Son of the Holy Jew' (Heb.), in Israel Bartal et al. (eds.), *Studies of Jewish Culture in Honor of Chone Shmeruk/Keminhag ashkenaz upolin: sefer yovel le ḥone shemeruk* (Jerusalem, 1993), 269–98.

——*Poland: Chapters in the History of the Jews of Eastern Europe and their Culture*, nos. 5–6: *Torah and Learning: The World of the Torah in Poland* [Polin: perakim betoledot yehudei mizraḥ eiropah vetarbutam, nos. 5–6: Torah ute'udah: olam hatorah bepolin] (Tel Aviv, 1990).

——'Polish Hasidism or Hasidism in Poland: On the Question of the Geography of Hasidism' (Heb.), *Gal-ed*, 14 (1995), 197–206.

——*The Regal Way: R. Israel of Ruzhin and his Place in the History of Hasidism* [Derekh hamalkhut: r. yisra'el meruzin umekomo betoledot haḥasidut] (Jerusalem, 1997); trans. as *The Regal Way: The Life and Times of Rabbi Israel of Ruzhin* (Stanford, Calif., 2002).

AUGUSTINE, *On the City of God* (London, 2003).

AVRON, DOV (ed.), *Minute Book of the Electors of the Community of Poznań* [Pinkas hakesherim shel kehilat pozna] (Jerusalem, 1966).

AVRUTIN, EUGENE, 'The Politics of Jewish Legibility: Documentation Practices and Reform during the Reign of Nicholas I', *Jewish Social Studies*, 11/2 (2005), 136–69.

BADZIAK, KAZIMIERZ, 'The Great Capitalist Fortunes in the Polish Lands before 1939 (The Case of the Poznański Family)', *Polin*, 6 (1991), 57–87.

BAKER, MARK, 'The Reassessment of Haskala Ideology in the Aftermath of the 1863 Polish Revolt', *Polin*, 5 (1990), 221–49.

BAŁABAN, MAJER, *Dzieje Żydów w Galicyi i w Rzeczypospolitej Krakowskiej 1772–1868* (Lwów, 1914).

——*Historia lwowskiej synagogi postępowej* (Lwów, 1937).

——*Historja Żydów w Krakowie i na Kazimierzu, 1304–1868*, 2 vols. (Kraków, 1931; repr. 1991).

——*Die Judenstadt von Lublin* (Berlin, 1919).

——'Die Krakauer Judengemeinde-Ordnung von 1595 und ihre Nachträge', pt. 1: *Jahrbuch der jüdisch-literarischen Gesellschaft*, 10 (1912), 296–360; pt. 2: *Jahrbuch der jüdisch-literarischen Gesellschaft*, 11 (1916), 88–114.

——'Pravovoi stroi evreev v Pol'she v srednie i novye veka', *Evreiskaya starina*, 3 (1910), no. 1, 39–69; no. 2, 161–91; no. 3, 324–45; 4 (1911), no. 1, 40–54; no. 2, 180–96.

——'Sabataizm w Polsce (Ustęp z "Dziejów mistyki żydowskiej w Polsce" z trzema rycinami)', in Bałaban (ed.), *Księga jubileuszowa ku czci profesora Dr. M. Schorr* (Warsaw, 1935), 35–90.

——*Żydzi lwowscy na przełomie XVI i XVII wieku* (Lwów, 1906).

——(ed.), *Księga pamiątkowa ku czci Berka Joselewicza pułkownika wojsk polskich w 125-letnią rocznicę jego bohaterskiej śmierci (1809–1934)* (Warsaw, 1934).

BAMBERGER, MOSES LÖB, *Geschichte der Juden in Schönlanke* (Berlin, 1912).

BAR-ITZHAK, HAYA, *Jewish Poland: Legends of Origin. Ethnopolitics and Legendary Chronicles* (Detroit, 2001).

BARNAI, Y., *Letters of Hasidim from Erets Israel* [Igerot ḥasidim me'erets yisra'el] (Jerusalem, 1980).

BARNAVI, ELI (ed.), *A Historical Atlas of the Jewish People* (New York, 1992).

BARON, SALO, 'The Impact of the Revolution of 1848 on Jewish Emancipation', *Jewish Social Studies*, 11/3 (1949), 195–248.

——*The Jewish Community* (New York, 1942).

BARON, SALO, *The Russian Jew under Tsars and Soviets*, 2nd edn. (New York, 1987).

——*A Social and Religious History of the Jews*, xvi: *Poland–Lithuania 1500–1650* (Philadelphia, 1976).

BARTAL, ISRAEL, *The Jews of Eastern Europe, 1772–1881*, trans. Chaya Naor (Philadelphia, 2005).

——and ISRAEL GUTMAN (eds.), *Broken Chain: Polish Jewry through the Ages* [Kiyum veshever: yehudei polin ledoroteihem], 2 vols. (Jerusalem, 1997).

BARTEL, WOJCIECH M., *Ustrój i prawo Wolnego Miasta Krakowa 1815–1846* (Kraków, 1976).

BARTOSZEWICZ, KAZIMIERZ, *Wojna żydowska w roku 1859* (Warsaw, 1913).

BARTOSZEWSKI, WŁADYSŁAW, and ANTONY POLONSKY (eds.), *The Jews in Warsaw* (Oxford, 1991).

BARTYS, JULIAN, 'The Grand Duchy of Poznań under Prussian Rule: Changes in the Economic Position of the Jewish Population 1815–48', *Leo Baeck Institute Yearbook*, 17 (1972), 191–204.

BARZILAY, ISAAC, 'The Jew in the Literature of the Enlightenment', *Jewish Social Studies*, 18/4 (1956), 243–61.

BAUER, KRZYSZTOF, *Wojsko koronne powstania kościuszkowskiego* (Warsaw, 1981).

BAUMGART, PETER, 'Die Stellung der jüdischen Minorität im Staat des aufgeklärten Absolutismus: Das friederizianische Preussen und das josephinische Österreich im Vergleich', *Kairos*, 22 (1980), 226–45.

BEALES, DEREK, *Joseph II: In the Shadow of Maria Theresa, 1741–1780* (Cambridge, 1987).

BEAUJEU, CHEVALIER DE, *Mémoires* (Amsterdam, 1700).

BEAUVOIS, DANIEL, *Lumières et société en Europe de l'Est: L'Université de Vilna et les écoles polonaises de l'Empire Russe, 1803–1832* (Lille, 1977).

——'Polish–Jewish Relations in the Territories Annexed by the Russian Empire in the First Half of the Nineteenth Century', in Chimen Abramsky, Maciej Jachimczyk, and Antony Polonsky (eds.), *The Jews in Poland* (Oxford, 1986), 78–90.

——*Trójkąt ukraiński: Szlachta, carat i lud na Wołyniu, Podolu i Kijowszczyźnie, 1793–1914* (Lublin, 2005).

BECKER, SEYMOUR, *Nobility and Privilege in Late Imperial Russia* (DeKalb, Ill., 1985).

BEIZER, MICHAEL, *The Jews of St Petersburg: Excursions through a Noble Past* (Philadelphia, 1989).

BEN-SASSON, HAIM HILLEL, *Thought and Conduct: Social Views of Polish Jews in the Late Middle Ages* [Hagut vehanhagah: hashkefoteihem shel yehudei polin beshilhei yemei habeinayim] (Jerusalem, 1959).

BER OF BOLECHÓW, DOV, *The Memoirs of Ber of Bolechow (1723–1805)*, ed. and trans. M. Vishnitzer (London, 1922).

BERLIN, MOISEY IOSIFOVICH, *Ocherk etnografii evreiskogo narodo-naseleniya* (St Petersburg, 1861).

BERNSTEIN, LAURIE, *Sonia's Daughters: Prostitutes and their Regulation in Imperial Russia* (Berkeley, 1995).

BERO, J., 'Z dziejów szkolnictwa żydowskiego w Królestwie Kongresowym 1815–1830', *Minerwa Polska*, 2 (1929), 77–106.

BERSHADSKY, SERGEY, 'Polozhenie o evreyakh 1804 goda', *Voskhod*, 15 (1895), no. 1, 82–104; no. 3, 69–96; no. 4, 86–96; no. 6, 33–63.

——(ed.), *Russko-evreiskii arkhiv: Dokumenty i materialy dlya istorii evreev v Rossii*, 2 vols. (St Petersburg, 1882).

BIALE, DAVID, *Eros and the Jews: From Biblical Israel to Contemporary America* (New York, 1992).

——'A Journey between Worlds: East European Jewish Culture from the Partitions of Poland to the Holocaust', in Biale (ed.), *Cultures of the Jews: A New History* (New York, 2002), iii: *Modern Encounters*, 77–134.

BIALIK, HAYIM NAHMAN, *The Letters of H. N. Bialik* [Igerot h. n. bialik], ed. F. Lachower, 5 vols. (Tel Aviv, 1937–9).

BIAŁYNIAK [KAROL RZEPECKI], *W półwiekową rocznicę: Rok 1848-my. Opis wypadków w Berlinie i W. Księztwie Poznańskiem* (Poznań, 1898).

BIENIARZÓWNA, JANINA, JAN M. MAŁECKI, and JÓZEF MITKOWSKI (eds.), *Dzieje Krakowa*, ii: *Kraków w wiekach XVI–XVIII* (Kraków, 1984); iii: *Kraków w latach 1796–1918* (Kraków, 1979).

BIRNBAUM, H., 'On Some Evidence of Jewish Life and Anti-Jewish Sentiments in Medieval Russia', *Viator*, 4 (1973), 225–55.

BISKUPSKI, MIECZYSŁAW B., and JAMES PULA (eds.), *Polish Democratic Thought from the Renaissance to the Great Emigration* (New York, 1990).

BLACKWELL, WILLIAM J., *The Beginnings of Russian Industrialization 1800–1860* (Princeton, 1968).

BLANKE, R., *Prussian Poland in the German Empire* (Boulder, Colo., 1981).

BLANNING, TIM, *Joseph II* (London, 1994).

BLEJWAS, STANISLAUS, 'Polish Positivism and the Jews', *Jewish Social Studies*, NS 46/1 (1984), 21–36.

——*Realism in Polish Politics: Warsaw Positivism and National Survival in Nineteenth-Century Poland* (New Haven, 1984).

BLOBAUM, ROBERT, 'Criminalizing the "Other": Crime, Ethnicity, and Antisemitism in Early Twentieth-Century Poland', in Blobaum (ed.), *Antisemitism and its Opponents in Modern Poland* (Ithaca, NY, 2005), 81–102.

BLOCH, PHILIPP, 'Die ersten Culturbestrebungen der jüdischen Gemeinde Posen unter preussischer Herrschaft', in *Jubelschrift zum siebzigsten Geburtstage des Professor Graetz* (Breslau, 1887), 194–217.

——*Die General-Privilegien der polnischen Judenschaft* (Poznań, 1892).

——'Judenwesen', in R. Prümers (ed.), *Das Jahr 1793: Urkunden und Aktenstücke zur Geschichte der Organisation Südpreussens* (Poznań, 1895), 591–628.

BOBIŃSKA, CELINA (ed.), *Studia z dziejów młodzieży Uniwersytetu Krakowskiego od Oświecenia do połowy XX w.*, 3 vols. (Kraków, 1964–70).

BOBRZYŃSKI, MICHAŁ, WŁADYSŁAW LEOPOLD JAWORSKI, and JÓZEF MILEWSKI (eds.), *Z dziejów odrodzenia politycznego w Galicji 1859–1873* (Warsaw, 1905).

BOGUCKA, MARIA, 'Polish Towns between the Sixteenth and Eighteenth Centuries', in Jan K. Fedorowicz, Maria Bogucka, and Henryk Samsonowicz (eds.), *A Republic of Nobles: Studies in Polish History to 1864* (Cambridge, 1982), 135–52.

——and HENRYK SAMSONOWICZ, *Dzieje miast i mieszczaństwa w Polsce przedrozbiorowej* (Wrocław, 1986).

BORTNOWSKI, WŁADYSŁAW, *Kaliszanie: Kartki z dziejów Królestwa Polskiego* (Warsaw, 1970).

BORZYMIŃSKA, ZOFIA, 'Przyczynek do dziejów szkolnictwa w XIX wieku, czyli jeszcze o Szkole Rabinów', *Biuletyn Żydowskiego Instytutu Historycznego*, 131–2/3–4 (1984), 183–92.

——*Szkolnictwo żydowskie w Warszawie 1831–1870* (Warsaw, 1994).

BRAFMAN, YAKOV, *Kniga Kagala: Vsemirnyi evreiskii vopros* (St Petersburg, 1888).

BRANN, MARCUS, *Geschichte des jüdisch-theologischen Seminars (Fränckelsche Stiftung) in Breslau: Festschrift zum fünfzigjährigen Jubiläum der Anstalt* (Breslau, 1904).

BRAWER, ABRAHAM JACOB, *Galicia and its Jews: Studies in the History of Galicia in the Nineteenth Century* [Galitsiyah viyehudeiha: meḥkarim betoledot galitsiyah bame'ah hashemoneh-esreh] (Jerusalem, 1964).

BRESLAUER, B., *Die Abwanderung der Juden aus der Provinz Posen: Denkschrift im Auftrage des Verbandes der Deutschen Juden* (Berlin, 1909).

BREUER, MORDECHAI, 'The Jewish Minority in the Enlightened Absolutist State', in Michael A. Meyer and Michael Brenner (eds.), *German Jewish History in Modern Times*, 4 vols. (New York, 1996), i. 144–64.

——'The Status of the Rabbinate in the Administration of the *Kehilot* of Ashkenaz in the Sixteenth Century' (Heb.), *Tsiyon*, 41 (1976), 47–66.

BRISTOW, EDWARD, *Prostitution and Prejudice: The Jewish Fight against White Slavery, 1870–1939* (New York, 1983).

BUJAK, FRANCISZEK, *Galicya*, 2 vols. (Lwów, 1908–10).

BUKI B. YOGLI [JUDAH LEIB KATZENELSON], *What my Eyes Saw and my Ears Heard* [Mah shera'u einai veshameru oznai] (Jerusalem, 1947).

BUMBLAUSKAS, ALFREDAS, *Senosios Lietuvos istorija 1009–1795* (Vilnius, 2005).

BUSZKO, JÓZEF, 'The Consequences of Galician Autonomy after 1867 for Jews, Poles and Ukrainians', *Polin*, 12 (1999), 86–99.

——*Dzieje ruchu robotniczego w Galicji Zachodniej, 1848–1918* (Kraków, 1986).

CACKOWSKI, STEFAN, *Gospodarstwo wiejskie w dobrach biskupstwa i kapituły chełmińskiej w XVII–XXVIII w.*, 2 vols. (Toruń, 1961–3).

CAŁA, ALINA, *Asymilacja Żydów w Królestwie Polskim (1864–1897)* (Warsaw, 1989).

——*Wizerunek Żyda w polskiej kulturze ludowej* (Warsaw, 1992).

CARSTEN, FRANCIS LUDWIG, 'The Court Jews: A Prelude to Emancipation', *Leo Baeck Institute Yearbook*, 3 (1958), 140–56.

CHEKIN, L. S., 'Turks, Jews and the Saints of the Kievan Caves Monastery', *Jews and Slavs*, 3 (1995), 127–34.

CHRISTIAN, DAVID, *Living Water: Vodka and Russian Society on the Eve of Emancipation* (Oxford, 1990).

CHUBINSKY, P. P., *Materialy i issledovaniya*, vii (St Petersburg, 1872).

COHEN, ISRAEL, *Vilna* (Philadelphia, 1943).

COHEN, TOVA, 'From Private Sphere to Public Sphere: The Writings of Nineteenth-Century Enlightened Women' (Heb.), in David Assaf et al. (eds.), *From Vilna to Jerusalem: Studies in East European Jewish History in Honour of Professor Shmuel Werses* [Mivilna liyerushalayim: meḥkarim betoledoteihem uvetarbutam shel yehudei mizraḥ eiropah mugashim leprofesor shemu'el verses] (Jerusalem, 2002), 235–58.

——'Key to the "Learned" (Lamdani) Technique: A Code of Haskalah Literature' (Heb.), *Mehkarei yerushalayim besifrut ivrit*, 13 (1992), 138–69.

——'Maskilot: Feminine or Feminist Writing?', *Polin*, 18 (2005), 57–86.

——*One Beloved and the Other Hated: Between Reality and Fiction in the Depiction of Women in Haskalah Literature* [Ha'aḥat ahuvah veha'aḥat senuah: bein metsiut ledimyon beteurei ha'ishah besifrut hahaskalah] (Jerusalem, 2002).

CORRSIN, STEPHEN D., 'Political and Social Change in Warsaw from the January 1863 Uprising to the First World War: Polish Politics and the "Jewish Question"', Ph.D. thesis (University of Michigan, 1981).

——*Warsaw before the First World War: Poles and Jews in the Third City of the Russian Empire 1880–1914* (Boulder, Colo., 1989).

——'Warsaw: Poles and Jews in a Conquered City', in Michael F. Hamm (ed.), *The City in Late Imperial Russia* (Bloomington, Ind., 1986), 123–76.

COXE, WILLIAM, *Travels into Poland, Russia, Sweden and Denmark Interspersed with Historical Relations and Political Inquiries* (London, 1784).

CROSS, FRANK LESLIE (ed.), *The Oxford Dictionary of the Christian Church* (London, 1961).

CUSTINE, MARQUIS DE, *La Russie en 1839*, 2 vols. (Brussels, 1843).

CYGIELMAN, SHMUEL A., 'The Basic Privileges of the Jews of Great Poland as Reflected in Polish Historiography', *Polin*, 2 (1987), 116–49.

CZACKI, TADEUSZ, *O Żydach* (Vilna, 1807).

——*Rozprawa o żydach i karaitach* (Kraków, 1860).

CZAPLICKA, JOHN (ed.), *Lviv: A City in the Crosscurrents of Culture* (Cambridge, Mass., 2005).

CZARTORYSKI, PRINCE ADAM, *Memoirs of Prince Adam Czartoryski*, i, ed. Adam Gielgud (London, 1888).

DAREVSKY, I. A., *K istorii evreev v Kieve ot poloviny VIII v. do kontsa XIX v.* (Kiev, 1907).

DAVIES, NORMAN, *God's Playground: A History of Poland*, 2 vols. (New York, 1981–4).

DAVIS, JOSEPH, *Yom Tov Lipmann Heller: Portrait of a Seventeenth-Century Rabbi* (Oxford, 2004).

DAVITT, MICHAEL, *Within the Pale* (London, 1903).

DAWIDOWICZ, LUCY (ed.), *The Golden Tradition: Jewish Life and Thought in Eastern Europe* (New York, 1984).

DE MICHELIS, CESARE G., *La Valdesia di Novgorod: 'Giudaizzanti' e prima riforma* (Turin, 1993).

DELPECH, F., 'L'Histoire des Juifs en France de 1780 à 1840', in Bernhard Blumenkranz and Albert Soboul (eds.), *Les Juifs et la Révolution française* (Paris, 1976), 3–70.

DEMBKOWSKI, HARRY E., *The Union of Lublin: Polish Federalism in the Golden Age* (Boulder, Colo., 1982).

DERZHAVIN, GAVRIIL, *Sochineniya Derzhavina*, 9 vols. (St Petersburg, 1864–83).

Diarjusze sejmowe z wieku XVIII, ed. Władysław Konopczyński, ii: *Diarjusz Sejmu z r. 1746* (Warsaw, 1912); iii: *Diarjusze Sejmów z lat 1750, 1752, 1754, 1758* (Warsaw, 1937).

DINUR, BENZION, *As Generations Change* [Bemifneh hadorot] (Jerusalem, 1955).

——'The Origins of Hasidism', in Gershon Hundert (ed.), *Essential Papers on Hasidism* (New York, 1991), 86–208.

DOHM, CHRISTIAN WILHELM VON, *Über die bürgerliche Verbesserung der Juden* (Berlin, 1781).

DOHRN, VERENA, 'The Rabbinical Schools as Institutions of Socialization in Tsarist Russia, 1847–1873', *Polin*, 14 (2001), 83–104.

DOKTÓR, JAN, 'The Non-Christian Frankists', *Polin*, 15 (2002), 135–44.

——(ed.), *Rozmaite adnotacje, przypadki, czynności i anekdoty Pańskie* (Warsaw, 1966).

DRESNER, SAMUEL H., *The Zaddik* (New York, 1960).

DRUZHININ, NIKOLAY MIKHAILOVICH, *Gosudarstvennye krest'yane i reforma P. D. Kiseleva*, 2 vols. (Moscow, 1946–58).

DUBIN, LOIS, *The Port Jews of Habsburg Trieste: Absolutist Politics and Enlightenment Culture* (Stanford, Calif., 1999).

DUBNOW, SIMON [SHIMON DUBNOV], *Evrei v Rossii i zapadnoi Evrope v epokhu antisemitskoi reaktsii*, 3 vols. in 1 (Moscow, 1923).

——*The History of Hasidism* [Toledot haḥasidut] (Tel Aviv, 1930–1).

——*History of the Jews*, trans. Moshe Spiegel, 5 vols. (South Brunswick, NJ, 1967–73); 1st published as *Istoriya evreiskogo naroda na Vostoke* (Berlin, 1930; new edn., Moscow, 2006).

——*History of the Jews in Russia and Poland from the Earliest Times until the Present Day*, 3 vols. (Philadelphia, 1916).

——'Istoricheskie soobshcheniya: Podgotovlenie raboty po istorii russkikh evreev', *Voskhod*, 21 (1901), no. 4, 25–40; no. 5, 3–21.

——*Noveishaya istoriya evreiskogo naroda*, 3rd edn., 3 vols. (Berlin, 1923).

——'Tserkovnye legendy ob otroke Gavriile Zabludovskom', *Evreiskaya starina*, 9 (Apr.–Sept. 1916), 309–16.

——(ed.), *The Minute Book of the Council of Lithuania* [Pinkas hamedinah o pinkas va'ad harashiyot bimedinat lita] (Berlin, 1925).

——et al. (eds.), 'Goneniya na zhenskie golovnye ubory (1853 g.)' (with preface), *Evreiskaya starina*, 8 (1915), nos. 3–4, 399–403.

DUKER, ABRAHAM, 'The Polish Political Émigrés and the Jews in 1848', *Proceedings of the American Academy for Jewish Research*, 24 (1955), 69–102.

DUPAQUIER, J., 'Population', in P. Burke (ed.), *The New Cambridge History*, xiii (Cambridge, 1979), 80–114.

DYŁĄGOWA, HANNA, *Towarzystwo Patriotyczne i Sąd Sejmowy 1821–1829* (Warsaw, 1970).

DYNNER, GLENN, '"Men of Silk": The Hasidic Conquest of Polish Jewry, 1754–1830', Ph.D. diss. (Brandeis University, 2002).

——*'Men of Silk': The Hasidic Conquest of Polish Jewry, 1754–1830* (New York, 2006).

DZIEDZIC, JÓZEF, *Żyd we wsi: Z zagadnień przyszłości narodowej* (Lwów, 1913).

EBERHARDT, PIOTR, *Przemiany narodowościowe na Litwie* (Warsaw, 1997).

ECHT, SAMUEL, *Die Geschichte der Juden in Danzig* (Leer, 1973).

EDWARDS, JOHN, *The Jews in Christian Europe 1400–1700* (London, 1988).

EISENBACH, ARTUR, 'Les Droits civiques des Juifs dans le Royaume de Pologne', *Revue des Études Juives*, 123 (Jan.–June 1964), 19–84.

——*The Emancipation of the Jews in Poland, 1780–1870* (Oxford, 1991).

——*Kwestia równouprawnienia Żydów w Królestwie Polskim* (Warsaw, 1972).

——'Mobilność terytorialna ludności żydowskiej w Królestwie Polskim', in Witold Kula and Janina Leskiewiczowa (eds.), *Społeczeństwo Królestwa Polskiego: Studia o uwarstwieniu i ruchliwości społecznej*, 8 vols. to date (Warsaw, 1965–), iii. 177–316.

——'Prawo obywatelskie i honorowe Żydów (1790–1861)', in Witold Kula and Janina Leskiewiczowa (eds.), *Społeczeństwo Królestwa Polskiego: Studia o uwarstwieniu i ruchliwości społecznej*, 8 vols. to date (Warsaw, 1965–), i. 237–300.

——'Le Problème des Juifs polonais en 1861 et les projets de réforme du Marquis Aleksander Wielopolski', *Acta Poloniae Historica*, 20 (1969), 138–62.

——*Wielka Emigracja wobec kwestii żydowskiej, 1832–1849* (Warsaw, 1976).

——'Wokół świadomości roli politycznej mieszczaństwa polskiego na przełomie XVIII i XIX w.', *Kwartalnik Historyczny*, 95 (1988), 173–96.

——*Z dziejów ludności żydowskiej w Polsce w XVIII i XIX wieku* (Warsaw, 1983).

——'Żydzi w dawnej Polsce w świetle liczb', *Kwartalnik Historyczny*, 66 (1959), 511–20.

EMDEN, JACOB, *Megilat sefer: korot ḥayav vezikhronotav shel ya'akov emden* [autobiography], ed. A. Bik [Shauli] (Jerusalem, 1979).

——*Zot torat hakenaot* [anthology of documents on Sabbatianism] (Altona, 1752).

EMMONS, TERENCE, *The Russian Landed Gentry and the Peasant Emancipation of 1861* (Cambridge, 1968).

Encyclopaedia Judaica (1st edn., Jerusalem, 1971–2; 2nd edn., 2007).

Encyclopedia of Ukraine, ed. Danylo Husar Struk (Toronto, 1993).

ENGELBRECHT, HELMUT, *Geschichte des österreichischen Bildungswesens: Erziehung und Unterricht auf dem Boden Österreichs*, iv (Krems, 1985).

EPSTEIN, LISA RAE, 'Caring for the Soul's House: The Jews of Russia and Health Care, 1860–1914', Ph.D. thesis (Yale University, 1995).

ETKES, IMMANUEL, *The Besht: Magician, Mystic and Leader* (Hanover, NH, 2005).

——*The Gaon of Vilna: The Man and his Image*, trans. J. M. Green (Berkeley and Los Angeles, 2002).

——*Lithuania in Jerusalem* [Lita biyerushalayim] (Jerusalem, 1991).

——'The Study of Hasidism: Past Trends and New Directions', in Ada Rapoport-Albert (ed.), *Hasidism Reappraised* (London, 1996), 446–64.

ETTINGER, SHMUEL, 'The Council of the Four Lands', in Antony Polonsky, Jakub Basista, and Andrzej Link-Lenczowski (eds.), *The Jews in Old Poland* (London, 1993), 93–109.

——'Moses of Kiev', in *Encyclopaedia Judaica*.

——'The Muscovite State and its Attitudes towards the Jews' (Heb.), *Tsiyon*, 18 (1953), 136–68.

——'The Role of the Jews in the Colonization of Ukraine (1569–1648)' (Heb.), *Tsiyon*, 21/3–4 (1956), 110–24.

——'Vliyanie evreev na eres' zhidovstvuyushchikh v moskovskoi Rusi', *Jews and Slavs*, 4 (1995), 9–27.

EVANS, ROBERT J., *Austria, Hungary and the Habsburgs: Essays on Central Europe c.1683–1867* (Oxford, 2006).

——*The Making of the Habsburg Monarchy, 1550–1700: An Interpretation* (Oxford, 1979).

Evreiskaya entsiklopediya, 16 vols. (St Petersburg, 1906–13).

FEDOR, THOMAS STANLEY, *Patterns of Urban Growth in the Russian Empire during the Nineteenth Century*, University of Chicago Department of Geography Research Paper 163 (Chicago, 1975).

FEDOROWICZ, JAN K., MARIA BOGUCKA, and HENRYK SAMSONOWICZ (ed. and trans.), *A Republic of Nobles: Studies in Polish History to 1864* (Cambridge, 1982).

FEDOTOV, GEORGII PETROVICH, *The Russian Religious Mind* (New York, 1960).

FEINER, SHMUEL, *Haskalah and History*, trans. Chaya Naor and Sondra Silverston (Oxford, 2002).

FELDMAN, WILHELM, *Asymilatorzy, syjoniści i Polacy: Z powodu przełomu w stosunkach żydowskich* (Kraków, 1893).

——*Bismarck a Polska*, 2nd edn. (Kraków, 1947).

——*Stronnictwa i programy polityczne w Galicji 1841–1906*, 2 vols. (Kraków, 1906).

FIELD, DANIEL, *The End of Serfdom: Nobility and Bureaucracy in Russia 1855–1861* (Cambridge, Mass., 1976).

FINKELSTEIN, LUDWIK, 'History of the Rabbinical School of Warsaw from its Establishment in 1826 to its Closure in 1863', Ph.D. thesis (Open University, 2006).

FISCHER, HORST, *Judentum, Staat und Heer in Preussen im frühen 19. Jahrhundert: Zur Geschichte der staatlichen Judenpolitik*, Schriftenreihe wissenschaftlicher Abhandlungen des Leo Baeck Instituts 20 (Tübingen, 1968).

FISHMAN, DAVID, 'Rabbi Moshe Isserles and the Study of Science among Polish Rabbis', *Science in Context*, 10 (1997), 571–88.

——*Russia's First Modern Jews: The Jews of Shklov* (New York, 1995).

FISHMAN, S. (ed.), *Follow my Footprints: Changing Images of Women in American Jewish Fiction* (Hanover, NH, 1992).

FISZMAN, SAMUEL (ed.), *The Polish Renaissance in its European Context* (Bloomington, Ind., 1988).

FRAENKEL, P., 'The Memoirs of B. L. Monasch of Krotoschin', *Leo Baeck Institute Yearbook* (1979), 195–223.

FRAM, EDWARD, *Ideals Face Reality: Jewish Law and Life in Poland 1550–1655* (Cincinnati, 1997).

FRANKE, B. (ed.), *Die Residenzstadt Posen und ihre Verwaltung im Jahre 1911* (Poznań, 1911).

FRANKEL, JONATHAN, *Prophecy and Politics: Socialism, Nationalism, and the Russian Jews, 1862–1917* (Cambridge, 1981).

FREEZE, CHAERAN, *Jewish Marriage and Divorce in Imperial Russia* (Hanover, NH, 2002).

FREEZE, GREGORY, *The Parish Clergy in Nineteenth Century Russia: Crisis, Reform, Counter-Reform* (Princeton, 1983).

FREUDENTHAL, MAX, *Leipziger Messgäste: Die jüdischen Besucher der Leipziger Messen in den Jahren 1675 bis 1764* (Frankfurt am Main, 1928).

FREUND, ISMAR, *Die Emanzipation der Juden in Preussen unter besonderer Berücksichtigung des Gesetzes vom 11. März 1812*, 2 vols. (Berlin, 1912).

FRIEDMANN, FILIP, 'Dzieje Żydów w Galicji 1772–1914', in Ignacy Schiper, Arieh Tartakower, and Aleksander Hafftka (eds.), *Żydzi w Polsce odrodzonej*, 2 vols. (Warsaw, 1932–3), i. 377–412.

——*Dzieje Żydów w Łodzi, od początków osadnictwa Żydów do r. 1863: Stosunki ludnościowe, życie gospodarcze, stosunki społeczne* (Łódź, 1935).

——*Die galizischen Juden im Kampfe um ihre Gleichberechtigung 1848–1869* (Frankfurt am Main, 1929).

FRIEDMANN, FILIP, 'Die Judenfrage im galizischen Landtag', *Monatsschrift für Geschichte und Wissenschaft des Judenthums*, 72/5 (1928), 457–77.

FRIEDRICH, KAREN, *The Other Prussia: Royal Prussia, Poland and Liberty, 1569–1772* (Cambridge, 2000).

FUENN, SAMUEL JOSEPH, *Kiryah ne'emanah* [monograph on the Vilna Jewish community] (Vilna, 1860).

FUKS, LAJB, 'Simon de Pool—faktor Króla Jana Sobieskiego w Holandii', *Biuletyn Żydowskiego Instytutu Historycznego*, 21 (1957), 3–12.

GALANT, I., 'Zadolzhennost' evreiskikh obshchin v XVII veke', *Evreiskaya starina*, 5 (Jan.–Mar. 1913), 129–32.

GALAS, MICHAŁ, 'Duchowość Żydów polskich w pracach Gershoma Scholema', *Ruch Biblijny i Liturgiczny*, 3 (1995), 186–91.

——'Die Mystik der polnischen Juden in Gershom Scholems Arbeiten: Ein forschungsgeschichtlicher Überblick', *Judaica: Beiträge zum Verstehen des Judentums*, 2 (1995), 97–102.

——'Sabbatianism in the Seventeenth Century Polish–Lithuanian Commonwealth', in R. Elior (ed.), *The Sabbatian Movement and its Aftermath: Messianism, Sabbatianism and Frankism*, Jerusalem Studies in Jewish Thought 17 (Jerusalem, 2001), 51–63.

GARNCARSKA-KADARY, B., 'The Family and Socio-economic Situation of the Jews of Kraków, 1796–1868', in E. Reiner (ed.), *Kroke, Kazimierz, Kraków: Studies in the History of the Jews of Kraków* [Kroke, kazimierz, krakov: meḥkarim betoledot yehudei krakov] (Tel Aviv, 2001).

GĄSOWSKI, TOMASZ, 'From *Austeria* to the Manor: Jewish Landowners in Autonomous Galicia', *Polin*, 12 (1999), 120–36.

GEIGER, A. (ed.), *Melo Chofnajim* [collection of Hebrew documents with German translation] (Berlin, 1840).

GEKKER, E., 'Proekty reformy evreiskogo byta v Pol'she v kontse XVIII veka', *Evreiskaya starina*, 7 (Apr.–June 1914), 206–19; (July–Sept.), 328–40.

GELBER, NATHAN M., *Aus zwei Jahrhunderten: Beiträge zur neueren Geschichte der Juden* (Vienna, 1924).

——'The History of the Jews in Poland from the First Partition to the Second World War' (Heb.), in Israel Halpern (ed.), *The House of Israel in Poland* [Beit yisra'el bepolin], 2 vols. (Jerusalem, 1948–53), i.

——*The History of the Zionist Movement in Galicia, 1875–1918* [Toledot hatenuah hatsiyonit begalitsiyah, 1875–1918] (Jerusalem, 1958).

——'The Jewish Problem in Poland in the Years 1815 to 1830' (Heb.), *Tsiyon*, 13–14 (1948–9), 123–44.

——*Die Juden und der polnische Aufstand 1863* (Vienna, 1923).

——*Major Jewish Towns* [Arim ve'imahot beyisra'el], ed. Judah Leib Maimon, vi: *Brody* (Jerusalem, 1955).

——'Żydzi a zagadnienie reformy Żydów na Sejmie Czteroletnim', *Miesięcznik Żydowski*, year 1, 2/10 (Oct. 1931), 326–44; 2/11 (Nov. 1931), 429–40.

——(ed.), *The Jews and the Polish Revolt: The Memoirs of Ya'akov Halevi Levin from the Polish Revolt of 1830–31* [Hayehudim vehamered hapolani: zikhronotav shel ya'akov halevi levin mimei hamered hapolani bishenat 1830–31] (Jerusalem, 1953).

GELLNER, ERNST, *Nations and Nationalism* (Ithaca, NY, 1983).

GESSEN, YULY, 'Bor'ba pravitel'stva s evreiskoi odezhdoi v Imperii i Tsarstve Pol'skom', *Perezhitoe*, 2 (1910), 10–18.

——'Evrei v moskovskom gosudarstve XV–XVII veka', *Evreiskaya starina*, 8 (Apr.–June 1915), 153–72.

——*Evrei v Rossii* (St Petersburg, 1906).

——*Istoriya evreiskogo naroda* (St Petersburg, 1916).

——*Istoriya evreiskogo naroda v Rossii*, 2 vols., repr. of the 1916 edn. with additions (Leningrad, 1925–7).

——'Iz letopisi minuvshego: Vilenskaya komissiya po ustroistvu byta evreev (1866–1869 gg.)', *Perezhitoe*, 2 (1910), 306–11.

——'Popytka emansipatsii evreev v Rossii', *Perezhitoe*, 1 (1909), 144–63.

——'Russkoe zakonodatel'stvo ob odezhde evreev', in *Evreiskaya entsiklopediya*, xii. 46–50.

——'Smena obshchestvennykh techenii, II: Pervyi russko-evreiskii organ', *Perezhitoe*, 3 (1911), 37–59.

——'V efemernom gosudarstve: Evrei v Varshavskom gertsogstve (1807–1812)', *Evreiskaya starina*, 3 (1910), no. 2, 3–38.

——*Zakon i zhizn': Kak sozidalis' ogranichitel'nye zakony o zhitel'stve evreev v Rossii* (St Petersburg, 1911).

GIEROWSKI, JÓZEF, 'The Jews in the Kościuszko Insurrection', in Heiko Haumann and Jerzy Skowronek (eds.), *'Der letzte Ritter und erste Bürger im Osten Europas': Kościuszko, das aufständische Reformpolen und die Verbundenheit zwischen Polen und der Schweiz* (Basel, 1996), 192–9.

——*Sejmik Generalny księstwa mazowieckiego na tle ustroju sejmikowego Mazowsza* (Wrocław, 1948).

GIERSZEWSKI, STANISŁAW, *Struktura gospodarcza i funkcje rynkowe mniejszych miast województwa pomorskiego w XVI i XVII w.* (Gdańsk, 1966).

GIEYSZTOR, ALEKSANDER, et al., *History of Poland*, 2nd edn. (Warsaw, 1979).

GIEYSZTOROWA, IRENA, 'Research into the Demographic History of Poland: A Provisional Summing-Up', *Acta Poloniae Historica*, 18 (1968).

GIL, MORDECHAI, 'The Rhadanite Merchants and the Land of Radhan', *Journal of the Economic and Social History of the Orient*, 17 (1974), 299–328.

GILLER, AGATON, *Historia powstania narodu polskiego w 1861–1864*, 4 vols. (Paris, 1864).

GINZBURG, SHAUL M., *Converts in Tsarist Russia* [Meshumodim in tsarishn rusland] (New York, 1946).

——*Historical Writings* [Historishe verk], 3 vols. (New York, 1937).

GLASSL, HORST, *Das österreichische Einrichtungswerk in Galizien (1772–1790)* (Wiesbaden, 1975).

GOLB, NORMAN, and OMELJAN PRITSAK, *Khazarian Hebrew Documents of the Tenth Century* (Ithaca, NY, 1982).

GOLDBERG, JACOB, 'De non tolerandis Iudaeis', in S. Yeivin (ed.), *Studies in Jewish History Presented to Professor Raphael Mahler on his Seventy Fifth Birthday* (Merhavia, 1974), 39–52.

——'From Intercession to Citizenship: The Representatives of the *Kehilot* during the Four Year Sejm' (Heb.), in Goldberg, *Jewish Society in the Polish–Lithuanian Commonwealth* [Haḥevrah hayehudit bemamlekhet polin-lita] (Jerusalem, 1999), 217–31.

——'The Jew and the Rural Tavern' (Heb.), in Goldberg, *Jewish Society in the Polish–Lithuanian Commonwealth* [Haḥevrah hayehudit bemamlekhet polin-lita] (Jerusalem, 1999), 232–40.

——*Jewish Privileges in the Polish Commonwealth: Charters of Rights Granted to Jewish Communities in Poland–Lithuania in the Sixteenth to Eighteenth Centuries* (Jerusalem, 1985).

——'The Jewish Sejm: Its Origins and Functions', in Antony Polonsky, Jakub Basista, and Andrzej Link-Lenczowski (eds.), *The Jews in Old Poland* (London, 1993), 147–64.

——*Jewish Society in the Polish–Lithuanian Commonwealth* [Haḥevrah hayehudit bemamlekhet polin-lita] (Jerusalem, 1999).

——'Julian Ursyn Niemcewicz on Polish Jewry', *Polin*, 18 (2005), 323–36.

——'Pierwszy ruch polityczny wśród Żydów polskich: Plenipotenci żydowscy w dobie Sejmu Czteroletniego', in J. Michalski (ed.), *Lud żydowski w narodzie polskim: Materiały sesji naukowej w Warszawie 15–16 września 1992* (Warsaw, 1994), 45–63.

——'Poles and Jews in the Seventeenth and Eighteenth Centuries: Rejection or Acceptance', *Jahrbücher für Geschichte Osteuropas*, NS 22 (1974), 248–82.

GOLDSTEIN, DAVID I., *Dostoyevsky and the Jews* (Austin, Tex., 1981).

GOLDSZTEJN, A., 'Służba wojskowa a Żydzi w Cesarstwie Rosyjskim i Królestwie Polskim do roku 1874', MA thesis (Warsaw University, n.d.).

GOLITSYN, NIKOLAY NIKOLAEVICH, *Istoriya russkogo zakonodatel'stva o evreyakh* (St Petersburg, 1886).

GOLUBINSKY, EVGENY EVSIGNEEVICH, *Istoriya russkoi tserkvi*, 2 vols. (Moscow, 1906).

GORDON, JUDAH LEIB, *The Works of Judah Leib Gordon: Poetry* [Kitvei yehudah leib gordon: shirah] (Tel Aviv, 1956).

——*The Works of Judah Leib Gordon: Prose* [Kitvei yehudah leib gordon: prozah] (Tel Aviv, 1960).

GORDON, L. O., 'Otryvki vospominanii', *Evreiskii vestnik* (Leningrad, 1928), 38–51.

GÓRSKI, KAROL, 'The Origins of the Polish Sejm', *Slavonic and East European Review*, 44 (1966), 122–38.

——'Some Aspects of the Polish Reformation in the XVI and XVII Centuries', *Slavonic and East European Review*, 9 (1931), 598–611.

Gosudarstvennost' Rossii, 2 vols. (Moscow, 1990).

GOTTLOBER, ABRAHAM BAER, 'Memoirs' (Yid.), in A. Fridkin, *Gotlober and his Epoch* [Gotlober un zayn epokhe] (Vilna, 1925).

GRAETZ, HEINRICH, 'The Structure of Jewish History', in Graetz, *The Structure of Jewish History, and Other Essays*, trans., ed., and introd. Ismar Schorsch (New York, 1975).

GRAETZ, MICHAEL, 'Autobiography: On the Self-Understanding of the Maskilim', in Michael A. Meyer and Michael Brenner (eds.), *German Jewish History in Modern Times*, 4 vols. (New York, 1996), i. 324–32.

GRAHAM, H. F., 'Peter Mogila, Metropolitan of Kiev', *Russian Review*, 14/4 (1955), 345–56.

Le Grand Sanhédrin de Napoléon, ed. Bernhard Blumenkranz and Albert Soboul (Toulouse, 1979).

GREEN, ARTHUR, 'Early Hasidism: Some Old/New Questions', in Ada Rapoport-Albert (ed.), *Hasidism Reappraised* (London, 1996), 441–6.

GREENBAUM, AVRAHAM, 'The Russian Rabbinate under the Czars', in L. J. Greenspan, R. A. Simpkins, and Brian Horowitz (eds.), *The Jews of Eastern Europe: Studies in Jewish Civilization*, xvi (Lincoln, Nebr., 2003), 1–8.

——'The Spread of Hasidism in the Nineteenth Century: A First Socio-Geographic Study' (Heb.), unpublished.

GREENBERG, LOUIS, *The Jews in Russia: The Struggle for Emancipation*, 2 vols. (New York, 1944–5).

GROCHULSKA, BARBARA, *Księstwo Warszawskie* (Warsaw, 1966).

GRONIOWSKI, KRZYSZTOF, *Uwłaszczenie chłopów w Polsce* (Warsaw, 1976).

GROT, ZDZISŁAW, *Orężny czyn poznańskiej Wiosny Ludów* (Poznań, 1948).

GRÖZINGER, KARL E., 'The Names of God and the Celestial Powers: Their Function and Meaning in the Hekhalot Literature', in J. Dan (ed.), *Proceedings of the First International Conference on the History of Early Jewish Mysticism* (Jerusalem, 1987), 53–69.

——'Tsadik and Ba'al Shem in East European Hasidism', *Polin*, 15 (2002), 159–68.

GRUDZINSKI, TADEUSZ, *Boleslaus the Bold, Called also the Bountiful, and Bishop Stanislaus: The Story of a Conflict* (Warsaw, 1985).

GRUENBAUM, YITZHAK, '*Haint*: Memoirs and Evaluations', in Yehuda Gotthelf and A. Bar (eds.), *The Jewish Press That Was: Accounts, Evaluations, and Memories of Jewish Papers in Pre-Holocaust Europe* (Tel Aviv, 1980), 17–33.

GRZEŚ, B., J. KOZŁOWSKI, and A. KRAMSKI, *Niemcy w Poznańskiem wobec polityki germanizacyjnej 1815–1920*, ed. L. Trzeciakowski (Poznań, 1976).

GUESNET, FRANÇOIS, *Polnische Juden im 19. Jahrhundert: Lebensbedingungen, Rechtsnormen und Organisation im Wandel* (Cologne, 1998).

GULDON, ZENON, and WALDEMAR KOWALSKI, 'Jewish Settlement in the Polish Commonwealth in the Second Half of the Eighteenth Century', *Polin*, 18 (2005), 308–21.

—— —— 'Osadnictwo żydowskie w województwach poznańskim i kaliskim w XVI–XVII wieku', *Biuletyn Żydowskiego Instytutu Historycznego*, 162–3/2–3 (1992), 66–73.

—— —— and JACEK WIJACZKA, 'The Accusation of Ritual Murder in Poland', 1500–1800', *Polin*, 10 (1997), 99–140.

GUMOWSKI, MARIAN, *Hebräische Münzen im mittelalterlichen Polen* (Graz, 1975).

GUMPLOWICZ, LUDWIK, *Prawodawstwo polskie względem Żydów* (Kraków, 1867).

GURLAND, H. J., *On the History of Anti-Jewish Decrees* [Lekorot hagezerot al yisra'el], vii (Odessa, 1892).

GUTERMAN, ALEXANDER, *From Assimilation to National Self-Assertion: Chapters in the History of the the Great Synagogue in Warsaw 1806–1943* [Mehitbolelut leleumiut: perakim betoledot hakeneset hagadol hasinagogah bevarshah 1806–1943] (Jerusalem, 1993).

——'The Origins of the Great Synagogue on Tłomackie Street', in Władysław Bartoszewski and Antony Polonsky (eds.), *The Jews in Warsaw* (Oxford, 1991), 181–211.

——'Żydzi sefardyjscy na ziemiach polskich', *Kwartalnik Historii Żydów*, 1/209 (Mar. 2004), 7–24.

HABERER, ERICH, *Jews and Revolution in Nineteenth-Century Russia* (Cambridge, 1995).

HABERMAN, A., *Anti-Jewish Decrees in Germany and France* [Gezerot ashkenaz vetsarefat] (Jerusalem, 1956).

HAGEN, WILLIAM W., *Germans, Poles, and Jews: The Nationality Conflict in the Prussian East* (Chicago, 1980).

HAKARO, DAVID B. ISAAC, *Ohel raḥel* [homiletic work] (Shklov, 1790).

HAKOHEN, D., *Shpola* [Shepolah] (Haifa, 1965).

HALECKI, OSKAR, *From Florence to Brest* (New York, 1958).

——*Jadwiga of Anjou and the Rise of East Central Europe* (New York, 1991).

HALEVI, DAVID B. SAMUEL, *Turei zahav* [commentary on the *Shulḥan arukh*] (Lublin, 1646).

HALPERIN, C. J., 'The Heresy of the Judaizers and the Image of the Jew in Medieval Russia', *Canadian-American Slavonic Studies*, 9 (1975), 141–55.

HALPERN, ISRAEL, *The House of Israel in Poland* [Beit yisra'el bepolin], 2 vols. (Jerusalem, 1948–53).

——*Jews and Jewry in Eastern Europe: Studies in their History* [Yehudim veyahadut bemizraḥ eiropah: meḥkarim betoledoteihem] (Jerusalem, 1968).

——(ed.), *Minutes of the Council of Four Lands: Compilation of Regulations, Notes and Resolutions* [Pinkas va'ad arba aratsot: likutei takanot ketavim ureshumot] (Jerusalem, 1945); 2nd, rev., edn., ed. Israel Bartal (Jerusalem, 1990).

HAMBURG, GARY M., *Politics of the Russian Nobility, 1881–1905* (New Brunswick, NJ, 1984).

HAMBURGER, ERNEST, *Juden im öffentlichen Leben Deutschlands: Regierungsmitglieder, Beamte und Parlamentarier in der monarchischen Zeit 1848–1918* (Tübingen, 1968).

HAMM, MICHAEL F. (ed.), *The City in Late Imperial Russia* (Bloomington, Ind., 1986).

HANDELSMAN, MARCELI, *Napoleon a Polska* (Warsaw, 1911).

——'Prośba Żydów do Fryderyka Augusta', *Kwartalnik poświęcony badaniu przeszłości Żydów w Polsce*, 1/3 (1912–13), 174–6.

HANNOVER, NATHAN NATA, *Abyss of Despair*, trans. A. Mesch (New Brunswick, NJ, 1950); previously published as *Yeven metsulah: gezerot taḥ vetat* [Miry Pit: The Decrees of 1648–9], ed. Y. Fikhman and I. Halpern (En Harod, 1944).

HÄUSLER, WOLFGANG, 'Toleranz, Emanzipation und Antisemitismus: Das österreichische Judentum des bürgerlichen Zeitalters (1782–1918)', in N. Vielmetti (ed.), *Das österreichische Judentum* (Vienna, 1974), 84–96.

HAVELOCK, H., 'The Cossacks in the Early Seventeenth Century', *English Historical Review*, 13 (1898), 242–60.

HEN, JÓZEF, *Mój przyjaciel król: Opowieść o Stanisławie Auguście* (Warsaw, 2003).

HEPPNER, AARON, and I. HERZBERG, *Aus Vergangenheit und Gegenwart der Juden und der jüdischen Gemeinden in den Posener Landen*, 2 vols. (Koschmin, 1904–9).

HERLIHY, PATRICIA, *Odessa: A History 1794–1914* (Cambridge, 1985).

——'Odessa, Staple Trade and Urbanization in New Russia', *Jahrbücher für Geschichte Osteuropas*, 21 (1973), 184–95.

HERZEN, ALEXANDER, *My Past and Thoughts* (New York, 1974).

HESCHEL, ABRAHAM JOSHUA, *The Earth Is the Lord's: The Inner World of the Jew in East Europe* (New York, 1986).

HIMKA, JOHN-PAUL, 'Dimensions of a Triangle: Polish–Ukrainian–Jewish Relations in Austrian Galicia', *Polin*, 12 (1999), 25–48.

——'Ukrainian–Jewish Antagonism in the Galician Countryside during the Late Nineteenth Century', in P. J. Potichnyj and H. Aster (eds.), *Ukrainian–Jewish Relations in Historical Perspective* (Edmonton, 1988), 111–58.

HINZ, HENRYK, 'The Philosophy of Polish Enlightenment and its Opponents', *Slavic Review*, 30 (1971), 340–9.

HISDAI, YA'AKOV, 'The "Servant of the Lord" in the Generation of the Fathers of Hasidism' (Heb.), *Tsiyon*, 47 (1982), 253–92.

HOLLAENDERSKI, LEON, *Les Israélites de Pologne* (Paris, 1846).

HORAK, STEPHAN M., 'The Kiev Academy—a Bridge to Europe in the Seventeenth Century', *East European Quarterly*, 2 (1968), 117–37.

HORN, ELŻBIETA, 'Problem żydowski w twórczości Dragomanowa', *Biuletyn Żydowskiego Instytutu Historycznego*, 57/1–3 (1966), 3–37.

HORODECKY, SAMUEL ABA, *Hasidism and Hasidim* [Haḥasidut veḥasidim], 4 vols. (Tel Aviv, 1928–43).

HORSZOWSKI, S., *Ekonomiczny rozwój Lwowa w latach 1772–1914* (Lwów, 1935).

HUNDERT, GERSHON D., 'The Contexts of Hasidism', in Waldemar Kowalski and Jadwiga Muszyńska (eds.), *Żydzi wśród chrześcijan w dobie szlacheckiej Rzeczypospolitej* (Kielce, 1996), 171–84.

——'The Implications of Jewish Economic Activities for Christian–Jewish Relations in the Polish Commonwealth', in Chimen Abramsky, Maciej Jachimczyk, and Antony Polonsky (eds.), *The Jews in Poland* (Oxford, 1986), 55–63.

——'Jewish Children and Childhood in Early Modern East Central Europe', in D. Kramer (ed.), *The Jewish Family: Metaphor and Memory* (New York, 1989), 81–94.

——'Jewish Popular Spirituality in the Eighteenth Century', *Polin*, 15 (2005), 93–104.

——'Jews in Poland: Materials for Brandeis in Kraków, 1998', unpublished.

——*Jews in Poland–Lithuania in the Eighteenth Century: A Genealogy of Modernity* (Berkeley and Los Angeles, 2004).

——*The Jews in a Polish Private Town: The Case of Opatów in the Eighteenth Century* (Baltimore, 1992).

——'Population and Society in Eighteenth Century Poland', in Jerzy Michalski (ed.), *The Status of the Jews in the Polish Nation* (Warsaw, 1994), 12–19.

——'The Role of the Jews in Commerce in Early Modern Poland–Lithuania', *Journal of European Economic History*, 16 (Fall 1987), 245–75.

——'Security and Dependence: Perspectives on Seventeenth-Century Polish–Jewish Society Gained through a Study of Jewish Merchants in Little Poland', Ph.D. thesis (Columbia University, 1978).

——'Some Basic Characteristics of the Jewish Experience in Poland', *Polin*, 1 (1986), 28–34.

HUSIK, ISAAC, *A History of Mediaeval Jewish Philosophy* (London, 1916; repr. Philadelphia, 1940).

IBN KHURDADHBE, *Kitab al-masalik wa'l-mamalik*, ed. M. J. De Goeje, Bibliotheca Geographorum Arabicorum 6 (Leiden, 1889).

IDEL, MOSHE, *Hasidism: Between Ecstasy and Magic* (Albany, NY, 1995).

In Praise of the Ba'al Shem Tov [Shivḥei habesht] (Kopys, 1814), trans. Dan Ben-Amos and Jerome R. Mintz (Bloomington, Ind., 1970); with introduction and annotations by A. Rubinstein (Jerusalem, 1991).

ISSERLES, MOSES, *Responsa* (Sudyłków, 1835; repr. Jerusalem, 1971).

JACOB ISRAEL OF KREMENETS, *Shevet miyisra'el* [ethical work] (Żółkiew, 1772).

JACOB JOSEPH OF POLONNOYE, *Toledot ya'akov yosef* [fundamental hasidic work] (Korets, 1780).

JACOBSON, J., 'Das Naturalisationsverzeichnis der Stadt Posen', *Zeitschrift für die Geschichte der Juden in Deutschland*, 8 (1938), 1–40.

——*Zur Geschichte der Juden in Rogasen* (Berlin, 1935).

JAFFE, MORITZ, *Die Stadt Posen unter preussischer Herrschaft: Ein Beitrag zur Geschichte des Ostens*, Schriften des Vereins für Sozialpolitik 119, pt. 2 (Leipzig, 1909).

JANCZAK, JULIAN K., 'The National Structure of the Population of Łódź in the Years 1820–1939', *Polin*, 6 (1991), 20–6.

JANOWSKI, MACIEJ, *Polish Liberal Thought before 1918*, trans. Danuta Przekop (Budapest, 2004); Eng. trans. of *Polska myśl liberalna do 1918 roku* (Kraków, 1998).

JAWORSKI, RUDOLF, *Handel und Gewerbe im Nationalitätenkampf: Studien zur Wirtschaftsgesinnung der Polen in der Provinz Posen (1871–1914)* (Göttingen, 1986).

——and BLANKA PETROW-ENNKER (eds.), *Women in Polish Society* (New York, 1992).

JEDLICKI, JERZY, *Nieudana próba kapitalistycznej industrializacji: Analiza państwowego gospodarstwa przemysłowego w Królestwie Polskim XIX w.* (Warsaw, 1964).

——*A Suburb of Europe: Polish Nineteenth Century Approaches to Western Civilization* (Budapest, 1999); Eng. trans. of *Jakiej cywilizacji Polacy potrzebują: Studia z dziejów idei i wyobraźni XIX wieku* (Warsaw, 1998).

JERSCH-WENZEL, STEFI, 'Conflicts in the Years before 1848', in Michael A. Meyer and Michael Brenner (eds.), *German Jewish History in Modern Times*, 4 vols. (New York, 1996), ii. 42–9.

——'Juden zwischen Germanisierung und Polonisierung im 19. Jahrhundert in Posen', paper presented at the International Congress on the History of Jews in Poland, Jerusalem, 1988.

——*Jüdische Bürger und kommunale Selbstverwaltung in preussischen Städten 1808–1848* (Berlin, 1967).

——'The Prussian Edict of 1812', in Michael A. Meyer and Michael Brenner (eds.), *German Jewish History in Modern Times*, 4 vols. (New York, 1996), ii. 24–7.

——'Zur Geschichte der jüdischen Bevölkerung in der Provinz Posen im 19. Jahrhundert', in G. Rhode (ed.), *Juden in Ostmitteleuropa: Von der Emanzipation bis zum Ersten Weltkrieg* (Marburg, 1989), 73–84.

The Jewish Encyclopedia (New York, 1901–16).

KABUZAN, VLADIMIR MAKSIMOVICH, *Narodonaselenie Rossii v XVIII–pervoi polovine XIX v.* (Moscow, 1963).

——*Narody Rossii v XVIII v.: Chislennost' i etnicheskii sostav* (Moscow, 1990).

KALEMBKA, SŁAWOMIR, *Towarzystwo Demokratyczne Polskie w latach 1832–1846* (Toruń, 1966).

——*Wielka emigracja: Polskie wychodźstwo polityczne w latach 1831–1862* (Warsaw, 1971).

KALIK, YEHUDIT [JUDITH KALIK], 'The Catholic Church and the Jews in the Polish–Lithuanian Commonwealth in the Seventeenth and Eighteenth Centuries' (Heb.), Ph.D. thesis (Hebrew University, Jerusalem, 1998).

KALIK, YEHUDIT [JUDITH KALIK], 'Polish Attitudes towards Jewish Spirituality in the Eighteenth Century', *Polin*, 15 (2002), 77–86.

KALINKA, WALERIAN, *Dzieła* (Kraków, 1892).

——*Ostatnie lata panowania Stanisława Augusta*, 2 vols. (Poznań, 1868).

KALLAS, MARIAN, *Konstytucja Księstwa Warszawskiego* (Toruń, 1970).

KAMENDROWSKY, V., and D. M. GRIFFITHS, 'The Fate of the Trading Nobility Controversy in Russia: A Chapter in the Relationship between Catherine II and the Russian Nobility', *Jahrbuch für Geschichte Osteuropas*, 26 (1978), 198–221.

KAMIŃSKI, ANDRZEJ, 'The Cossack Experiment in Szlachta Democracy in the Polish–Lithuanian Commonwealth: The Hadiach (Hadziacz) Union', *Harvard Ukrainian Studies*, 1/2 (June 1977), 178–97.

KANDEL, DAWID, 'Hymn do Napoleona', *Kwartalnik poświęcony badaniu przeszłości Żydów w Polsce*, 1/2 (1912–13), 121–7.

KANN, ROBERT A., *A History of the Habsburg Empire, 1526–1918* (Berkeley, 1974).

——*The Multinational Empire: Nationalism and National Reform in the Habsburg Monarchy, 1848–1918*, 2 vols. (New York, 1950; repr. 1977).

KAPLAN, HERBERT H., *The First Partition of Poland* (New York, 1962).

KAPLAN, MARION, *The Making of the Jewish Middle Class* (New York, 1991).

KAPLUN-KOGAN, WLADIMIR WOLF, *Die jüdische Sprach- und Kulturgemeinschaft in Polen: Eine statistische Studie* (Berlin, 1917).

KARNIEL, JOSEF, 'Fürst Kaunitz und die Juden', *Jahrbuch des Instituts für Deutsche Geschichte, Tel-Aviv*, 12 (1983), 15–27.

——'Das Toleranzpatent Josephs II für die Juden Galiziens und Lodomeriens', *Jahrbuch des Instituts für Deutsche Geschichte, Tel-Aviv*, 11 (1982), 55–71.

——*Die Toleranzpolitik Kaiser Josephs II* (Gerlingen, 1986).

KATZ, JACOB, *Between Jews and Gentiles* [Bein yehudim legoyim] (Jerusalem, 1960).

——*Divine Law in Human Hands: Case Studies in Halakhic Flexibility* (Jerusalem, 1998).

——*The 'Shabbes Goy': A Study in Halakhic Flexibility* (Philadelphia, 1989).

——*Tradition and Crisis: Jewish Society at the End of the Middle Ages* (New York, 1991).

KAUFMAN, A., 'Evrei v russko-turetskoi voine 1877 g.', *Evreiskaya starina*, 8 (1915), 52–72, 176–82.

KAZAKOVA, NATALIYA ALEKSANDROVNA, and I. S. LURIE, *Antifeodal'nye ereticheskie dvizheniya na Rusi XIV–nachala XVI veka* (Moscow, 1955).

KAŹMIERCZYK, ADAM, 'The Case of Jakub Becal, King Jan III Sobieski's Jewish Factor', *Polin*, 15 (2002), 249–66.

——'The Problem of Christian Servants as Reflected in the Legal Codes of the Polish–Lithuanian Commonwealth during the Second Half of the Seventeenth Century and in the Saxon Period', *Gal-ed*, 15–16 (1997), 23–40.

——*Żydzi w dobrach prywatnych w świetle sądowniczej i administracyjnej praktyki dóbr magnackich w wiekach XVI–XVIII* (Kraków, 2002).

——(ed.), *Żydzi polscy 1648–1772: Źródła*, Studia Judaica Cracoviensia 6 (Kraków, 2001).

KELLENBENZ, HERMANN, *Sephardim an der unteren Elbe: Ihre wirtschaftliche und politische Bedeutung vom Ende des 16. bis zum Beginn des 18. Jahrhunderts*, Vierteljahrschrift für Sozial- und Wirtschaftsgeschichte, Beiheft 40 (Wiesbaden, 1958).

KEMLEIN, SOPHIE, 'The Jewish Community in the Grand Duchy of Poznań under Prussian Rule, 1815–1848', *Polin*, 14 (2001), 49–67.

——*Die Posener Juden 1815–1848: Entwicklungsprozesse einer polnischen Judenheit unter preussischer Herrschaft*, Hamburger Veröffentlichungen zur Geschichte Mittel- und Osteuropas 3 (Hamburg, 1997); trans. into Polish as *Żydzi w Wielkim Księstwie Poznańskim 1815–1847: Przeobrażenia w łonie żydostwa polskiego pod panowaniem pruskim* (Poznań, 2001).

——'Zur Geschichte der Juden in Westpreussen und Danzig (bis 1943)', in Akademie für Lehrerfortbildung in Dillingen, *Danzig/Gdańsk: Deutsch-polnische Geschichte, Politik und Literatur* (Dillingen, 1996), 94–109.

KHITERER, VICTORIA, 'Iosif Galperin: A Forgotten Berdichev Shtadlan', *SHVUT: Studies in Russian and East European Jewish History and Culture*, 7/23 (1998), 33–47.

——'The Social and Economic History of Jews in Kiev before February 1917', Ph.D. diss. (Brandeis University, 2008).

KHVOLSON, DANIEL A., 'O nekotorykh srednevekovykh obvineniyakh protiv evreev', *Biblioteka dlya chteniya* (1861), nos. 164–5; also issued as *O nekotorykh srednevekovykh obvineniyakh protiv evreev* (1861; 2nd edn., 1880); shorter version published as *Upotreblyayut li evrei khristianskuyu krov'?* (St Petersburg, 1879).

KIENIEWICZ, STEFAN (ed.), 'Assimilated Jews in Nineteenth-Century Warsaw', in Władysław Bartoszewski and Antony Polonsky (eds.), *The Jews in Warsaw* (Oxford, 1991), 171–80.

——*The Emancipation of the Polish Peasantry* (Chicago, 1969).

——'The Jews of Warsaw, Polish Society and the Partitioning Powers', in Władysław Bartoszewski and Antony Polonsky (eds.), *The Jews in Warsaw* (Oxford, 1991), 151–70.

——*Między ugodą a rewolucją: Andrzej Zamoyski w latach 1861–1862* (Warsaw, 1962).

——*Powstanie styczniowe* (Warsaw, 1972).

——*Społeczeństwo polskie w powstaniu poznańskim 1848 roku* (Warsaw, 1960).

——(ed.), *History of Poland* (Warsaw, 1986).

——(ed.), *Rok 1848 w Polsce: Wybór źródeł* (Wrocław, 1948).

KIERSZNOWSKI, R., *Wstęp do numizmatyki polskiej wieków średnich* (Warsaw, 1964).

KITOWICZ, JĘDRZEJ, *Opis obyczajów za panowania Augusta III*, ed. Roman Pollak (Wrocław, 1950).

KLAUSNER, ISRAEL, 'The Decree on Jewish Clothing, 1844–1850' (Heb.), *Gal-ed*, 6 (1982), 11–26.

KLAUSNER, ISRAEL, *Vilna during the Period of the Gaon: The Spiritual and Social Conflict within the Vilna Kehila during the Period of the GRA* [Vilna bitekufat hagaon: hamilḥamah haruḥanit veḥevratit bikehilat vilna bitekufat hagr"a] (Jerusalem, 1942).

KLEINMANN, YVONNE, *Neue Orte—neue Menschen: Jüdische Lebensformen in St. Petersburg und Moskau im 19. Jahrhundert* (Göttingen, 2006).

KLIBANOV, ALEKSANDR ILICH, *Reformatsionnye dvizheniya v Rossii v XIV–pervoi polovine XVI v.* (Moscow, 1960).

KLIER, JOHN, 'The Concept of "Jewish Emancipation" in a Russian Context', in Olga Crisp and Linda Edmondson (eds.), *Civil Rights in Imperial Russia* (Oxford, 1989), 121–44.

——'From "Little Man" to "Milkman": Does Jewish Art Reflect Jewish Life?', in L. J. Greenspan, R. A. Simpkins, and Brian Horowitz (eds.), *The Jews of Eastern Europe: Studies in Jewish Civilization*, xvi (Lincoln, Nebr., 2003), 217–32.

——*Imperial Russia's Jewish Question, 1855–1881* (Cambridge, 1995).

——'The Jewish *Den* and the Literary Mice, 1869–1871', *Russian History*, 10/1 (1983), 31–49.

——'Judaizing without Jews? Moscow–Novgorod, 1470–1504', in A. M. Kleimola and G. D. Lenhoff (eds.), *Culture and Identity in Muscovy, 1359–1584* (Moscow, 1997), 336–49.

——'The Polish Revolt of 1863 and the Birth of Russification: Bad for the Jews?', *Polin*, 1 (1986), 95–110.

——*Rossiya sobiraet svoikh evreev: Proiskhozhdenie evreiskogo voprosa v Rossii, 1772–1825* (Moscow, 2000).

——*Russia Gathers her Jews: The Origins of the 'Jewish Question' in Russia 1772–1825* (DeKalb, Ill., 1986); enlarged Russian edn.: *Rossiya sobiraet svoikh evreev: Proiskhozhdenie evreiskogo voprosa v Rossii, 1772–1825* (Moscow, 2000).

——'Russian Judeophobes and German Antisemites: Strangers and Brothers', *Jahrbücher für Geschichte Osteuropas*, 37/4 (1989), 524–40.

——'Zhid: The Biography of a Russian Epithet', *Soviet and East European Review*, 50 (Jan. 1982), 1–15.

KNOLL, PAUL W., *The Rise of the Polish Monarchy: Piast Poland in East Central Europe, 1320–1370* (Chicago, 1972).

KOCHAN, LIONEL, *The Making of Western Jewry, 1600–1819* (Basingstoke, 2004).

KOCHANOWICZ, J., 'The Polish Economy and the Evolution of Dependency', in Daniel Chirot (ed.), *Origins of Backwardness in Eastern Europe: Economics and Politics from the Middle Ages until the Early Twentieth Century* (Berkeley, 1989), 92–130.

KOHLER, M., 'Jewish Rights at the Congresses of Vienna (1814–1815) and Aix La Chapelle (1818)', *Publications of the American Jewish Historical Society*, 26 (1918), 16–25.

KOHTE, WOLFGANG, *Deutsche Bewegung und preussische Politik im Posener Lande 1848–49* (Poznań, 1931).

KOIDONOVER, ZEVI HIRSCH, *Kav hayashar* [ethical work] (Frankfurt am Main, 1705).

KOŁŁĄTAJ, HUGO, *Listy anonima, i Prawo polityczne narodu polskiego*, 2 vols., ed. B. Leśnodorski and H. Wereszycka (Kraków, 1954).

KÖLLMANN, W., 'Bevölkerungsgeschichte 1800–1920', in *Handbuch der deutschen Wirtschafts- und Sozialgeschichte*, ii: *Das 19. und 20. Jahrhundert*, ed. Hermann Aubin and Wolfgang Zorn (Stuttgart, 1976).

KONOPCZYŃSKI, WŁADYSŁAW, *Le Liberum Veto: Étude sur le développement du principe majoritaire* (Paris, 1930).

Korespondencja namiestników Królestwa Polskiego z 1861 roku, ed. S. Kieniewicz and I. Miller (Wrocław, 1964).

KOSIM, JAN, *Losy pewnej fortuny: Z dziejów burżuazji warszawskiej w latach 1807–1830* (Wrocław, 1972).

KOŚKA, MAŁGORZATA, and DOROTA LEWANDOWSKA, *Materiały do dziejów Żydów na ziemiach polskich w XIX wieku w zbiorach AGAD* (Warsaw, 1994).

KOSTROWICKA, IRENA, ZBIGNIEW LANDAU, and JERZY TOMASZEWSKI, *Historia gospodarcza Polski XIX i XX wieku* (Warsaw, 1975).

KOT, STANISŁAW, *Socinianism in Poland: The Social and Political Ideas of the Polish Anti-Trinitarians of the 16th and 17th Centuries* (Boston, 1955).

KOTIK, YEKHEZKEL [YISROEL KOTIK], *Journey to a Nineteenth-Century Shtetl: The Memoirs of Yehezkel Kotik*, ed. David Assaf (Detroit, 2002).

KOVALINSKY, VITALY, *Metsenaty Kieva* (Kiev, 1998).

KOWALSKI, TADEUSZ (ed.), *Relacja Ibrahima ibn Jakuba*, Monumenta Poloniae Historica, 2nd ser., 1 (Kraków, 1946).

KOZIEBRODZKI, WŁADYSŁAW, *Repertorium czynności galicyjskiego Sejmu Krajowego od 1861 po rok 1883* (Lwów, 1885).

KOZIK, JAN, *Ukraiński ruch narodowy w Galicji* (Kraków, 1973); trans. Andrew Gorski and Lawrence D. Orton as *The Ukrainian National Movement in Galicia, 1815–1849*, ed. Lawrence D. Orton (Edmonton, 1986).

KOZIŃSKA-WITT, HANNA, 'Die Krakauer jüdische Reformgemeinde 1864–1874', doctoral diss. (University of Tübingen, 1996).

KRANNHALS, DETLEF, *Danzig und der Weichselhandel in seiner Blütezeit vom 16. zum 17. Jahrhundert* (Leipzig, 1942).

KRASICKI, IGNACY, *The Adventures of Mr. Nicolas Wisdom* (Evanston, Ill., 1992).

KRASIŃSKI, Z., *Listy do Adama Sołtana* (Warsaw, 1970).

KRASNOWOLSKI, BOGUSŁAW, 'Architektura krakowskiego Kazimierza jako świadectwo historii', paper presented at the Judaica Centre, Kazimierz, May 2006.

KRASZEWSKI, JÓZEF IGNACY, *Latarnia czarnoksięska* (Kraków, 1977).

——*Z roku 1868: Rachunki* (Poznań, 1869).

KRAUS, E., 'Marcus Mosse: A Jew in the Prussian Province of Posen', *Leo Baeck Institute Yearbook*, 42 (1997), 3–28.

KRAUSHAR, ALEKSANDER, *Historia Żydów w Polsce* (Warsaw, 1867).

KRINSKY, CAROL, *Synagogues of Europe: Architecture, History, Meaning* (Mineola, Tex., 1985).

KROCHMAL, NAHMAN, *The Writings of Rabbi Nahman Krochmal* [Kitvei renak], ed. S. Rawidovich, 2nd edn. (London, 1961).

KRYSIŃSKI, D., *Wybór pism* (Warsaw, 1956).

KUKIEL, MARIAN, *Dzieje Polski porozbiorowe, 1795–1921* (Paris, 1983).

KULA, WITOLD, *An Economic Theory of the Feudal System: Towards a Model of the Polish Economy, 1500–1800* (London, 1976).

——and J. LESKIEWICZOWA (eds.), *Przemiany społeczne w Królestwie Polskim 1814–1864* (Wrocław, 1979).

KULCZYCKI, JOHN J., *School Strikes in Prussian Poland, 1901–1907: The Struggle over Bilingual Education* (distributed from Boulder, Colo., 1981).

KULIK, ALEXANDER, 'The Earliest Evidence on the Jewish Presence in Western Rus', unpublished.

KUPFER, EFRAIM F., and TADEUSZ LEWICKI, *Źródła hebrajskie do dziejów Słowian i niektórych innych ludów środkowej i wschodniej Europy* (Wrocław, 1956).

Kyyevo-pechers'kyi pateryk, ed. Dmytro Abramovych (Kiev, 1930).

LAUBERT, MANFRED, 'Die Judenfrage auf den Posener Provinziallandtagen von 1827 und 1845', *Zeitschrift für die Geschichte der Juden in Deutschland*, 4/1 (1932), 30–46.

——'Zur Entwicklung des jüdischen Schulwesens in der Provinz Posen', *Zeitschrift für die Geschichte der Juden in Deutschland*, 1/4 (1930), 304–21.

LAZUTKA, STANISLOVAS, and EDVARDAS GUDAVIČIUS, *Privilege to Jews Granted by Vytautas the Great in 1388* (Moscow, 1993).

LEDERHENDLER, ELI, 'The Jews in Imperial Russia', in J. Wertheimer (ed.), *The Modern Jewish Experience: A Reader's Guide* (New York, 1993), 18–24.

——*The Road to Modern Jewish Politics: Political Tradition and Political Reconstruction in the Jewish Community of Tsarist Russia* (New York, 1989).

LEESON, DANIEL, 'The Tarnobrzeg Blood Libel', unpublished.

LEIMAN, SID, 'Rabbi Jonathan Eibeschuetz's Attitude to the Frankists', *Polin*, 15 (2003), 144–51.

LELEWEL, JOACHIM, *Polska, dzieje i rzeczy jej*, 20 vols. (Poznań, 1851–68).

LENOWITZ, HARRIS, 'The Struggle over Images in the Propaganda of the Frankist Movement', *Polin*, 15 (2002), 105–30.

LERNER, O. M., *Evrei v novorossiiskom krae* (Odessa, 1901).

LESLIE, ROBERT F., *Polish Politics and the Revolution of November 1830* (London, 1956).

——*Reform and Insurrection in Russian Poland 1856–1865* (London, 1963).

——(ed.), *The History of Poland since 1863* (Cambridge, 1980).

LEŚNODORSKI, BOGUSŁAW, *Dzieło Sejmu Czteroletniego* (Wrocław, 1951).

LEVANDA, LEV, 'Iz perepiski L. O. Levandy', ed. A. Druyanov, *Evreiskaya starina*, 6 (1913), no. 2, 279–81.

——'Iz perepiski L. O. Levandy', ed. A. E. Landau, in *Evreiskaya biblioteka*, ix (St Petersburg, 1901), 1–64.

——'K istorii vozniknoveniya pervogo organa russkikh evreev', *Voskhod*, 1 (1881), no. 6, 132–52.

——'Tipy i siluety (vospominaniya shkol'nika kontsa sorokovykh godov)', *Voskhod*, 1 (1881), no. 1, 32–59; no. 2, 120–9; no. 3, 1–23; no. 4, 49–94.

LEVANDA, V. O., *Polnyi khronologicheskii sbornik zakonov i polozhenii, kasayushchikhsya evreev* (St Petersburg, 1874).

LEVINE, HILLEL (ed.), *The Chronicle: A Document on the History of Jacob Frank and his Movement . . . translated into Hebrew and edited by Hillel Levine* [Hakronikah: te'udah letoledot ya'akov ferank utenuato . . . betseruf targum le'ivrit, mavo vehe'arot bidei hilel levin] (Jerusalem, 1984).

LEVINSOHN, ISAAC BAER, *Shorshei halevanon* (or *Beit ha'otsar*) [collection of studies] (Vilna, 1871).

——*Testimony in Israel* [Te'udah beyisra'el] (Vilna, 1828).

LEVITATS, ISAAC, *The Jewish Community in Russia, 1772–1844* (Jerusalem, 1943; repr. 1970).

——*The Jewish Community in Russia, 1844–1917* (Jerusalem, 1981).

——'On the Consequences of Brafman's *Book of the Kahal*' (Heb.), *Tsiyon*, 3 (1938), 170–8.

LEVYTSKY, K., *Istoriya politychnoyi dumky halyts'kykh ukrayintsiv, 1848–1914*, 2 vols. (Lviv, 1926).

——*Ukrayins'ki polityky: Syl'vety nashykh davnikh posliv i politychnykh diyachiv*, 2 vols. (Lviv, 1936–7).

LEWALSKI, KRZYSZTOF, 'Szkic do dziejów misji chrześcijańskich wśród Żydów na ziemiach polskich w XVIII–XX wieku', *Studia Historyczne*, 36 (1993), 185–202.

LEWANDOWSKI, W., 'Materiały do udziału Żydów w Gwardii Narodowej, Gwardii Miejskiej i Straży Bezpieczeństwa', *Biuletyn Żydowskiego Instytutu Historycznego*, 18–20 (1956), 114–38.

LEWIN, ISAAC, 'The Protection of Jewish Religious Rights by Royal Edicts in Pre-Partition Poland', in M. Giergielewicz (ed.), *Polish Civilization: Essays and Studies* (New York, 1979), 115–34.

LEWIN, L., 'Ein Judentag aus Süd- und Neuostpreussen', *Monatsschrift für Geschichte und Wissenschaft des Judenthums*, NS 23 (1915), no. 4, 180–92; no. 5, 278–300.

LEWIN, SABINA, 'The First Elementary Schools for Children of the Mosaic Faith in Warsaw 1818–1830' (Heb.), *Gal-ed*, 1 (1973), 63–100.

——'Pierwsze szkoły elementarne dla dzieci wyznania mojżeszowego w Warszawie w latach 1818–1830', *Przegląd Historyczno-Oświatowy*, 8 (1965), no. 2, 157–96.

LEWIN, SABINA, 'The Warsaw Rabbinical Academy', *Gal-ed*, 11 (1989), 35–58.

LEWITTER, LUCJAN, 'Poland under the Saxon Kings', in J. O. Lindsey (ed.), *The New Cambridge Modern History*, vii (Cambridge, 1957), 365–90.

LEYB B. OZER, *An Account of Sabbatai Zevi* [Sipur ma'asei shabetai tsevi: beshraybung fun shabetai tsevi] (Jerusalem, 1978).

LICHTEN, JOSEPH, 'Notes on the Assimilation and Acculturation of Jews in Poland, 1863–1943', in Chimen Abramsky, Maciej Jachimczyk, and Antony Polonsky (eds.), *The Jews in Poland* (Oxford, 1986), 106–29.

LINCOLN, W. BRUCE, *The Great Reforms: Autocracy, Bureaucracy and the Politics of Change in Imperial Russia* (DeKalb, Ill., 1990).

——'The Ministers of Nicholas I: A Brief Enquiry into their Backgrounds and Service Careers', *Russian Review*, 34/3 (July 1975), 308–23.

——*Nicholas I: Emperor and Autocrat of All the Russias* (London, 1978).

LIPSCHITZ, JACOB HALEVI, *Zikhron ya'akov* [historical notes and personal memories], 3 vols. (Frankfurt am Main, 1924–30).

LOCKE, JOHN, *A Letter Concerning Toleration* (Indianapolis, 1955).

LOMBARD, MAURICE, *Espaces et réseaux du haut Moyen Âge* (Paris, 1972).

LOWENSTEIN, S., 'The Shifting Boundary between Eastern and Western Jewry', *Jewish Social Studies*, NS 4/1 (1997), 60–78.

LUKASHEVICH, STEPHEN, *Ivan Aksakov, 1823–1886* (Cambridge, Mass., 1965).

LUKOWSKI, JERZY, *Liberty's Folly: The Polish–Lithuanian Commonwealth in the Eighteenth Century, 1697–1795* (London, 1991).

——*The Partitions of Poland: 1772, 1793, 1795* (London, 1999).

LURIA, SOLOMON, *Responsa* (Lublin, 1574).

——*Yam shel shelomoh* [commentary on the Talmud] (many edns., incl. Prague 1616–18; Kraków, 1633–5).

LVOVICH, V. (ed.), *Narody Russkogo Tsarstva: Kniga dlya chteniya doma i v shkolakh* (Moscow, 1901).

LYUTOSTANSKY [LUTOSTAŃSKI], IPPOLIT, *Ob upotreblenii evreyami (talmudistskimi sektatorami) khristianskoi krovi dlya religioznykh tselei v svyazi s voprosom ob otnosheniyakh evreistva k khristianstvu voobshche*, 2 vols. (St Petersburg, 1880).

——*Vopros ob upotreblenii evreyami-sektatorami khristianskoi krovi dlya religioznykh tselei, v svyazi s voprosami ob otnosheniyakh evreistva k khristianstvu voobshche* (Moscow, 1876).

MACARTNEY, CARLILE AYLMER, *The Habsburg Empire, 1790–1918* (London, 1968).

——*Maria Theresa and the House of Austria* (London, 1969).

MCCAGG, WILLIAM O., *A History of Habsburg Jews, 1670–1918* (Bloomington, Ind., 1989).

MCREYNOLDS, LOUISE, *The News under Russia's Old Regime* (Princeton, 1991).

MAGOCSI, PAUL R., *Galicia: A Historical Survey and Bibliographic Guide* (Toronto, 1983).

MAHLER, RAPHAEL, 'The Economic Background of Jewish Emigration from Galicia to the United States', *YIVO Annual of Jewish Social Science*, 7 (1952), 257–64.

——*Hasidism and the Jewish Enlightenment: Their Confrontation in Galicia and Poland in the First Half of the Nineteenth Century* (Philadelphia, 1985), trans. Aaron Klein and Jenny Machlovitz from *Ḥasidut vehaskalah* (Merhavia, 1961).

——*The History of the Jews in Poland: Economy, Community, Social Conditions* [Toledot hayehudim bepolin: kalkalah, ḥevrah, hamatsav hamishpati] (Merhavia, 1946).

——*A History of Modern Jewry 1780–1815* (London, 1971).

——*Jews in Old Poland in the Light of Figures* [Yidn in amolikn poyln in likht fun tsifern], 2 vols. (Warsaw, 1958).

——'Z dziejów Żydów w Nowym Sączu w XVII i XVIII wieku', *Biuletyn Żydowskiego Instytutu Historycznego*, 55 (1965), 3–32.

MAHLER, T., 'Walka między ortodoksją a postępowcami w Krakowie w latach 1843–1868', Master's thesis (Archiwum Żydowskiego Instytutu Historycznego, n.d.).

MAIMON, SOLOMON, *Salomon Maimon: An Autobiography*, trans. J. Clark Murray (Paisley, 1888; repr. London, 1954); trans. from *Salomon Maimon's Lebensgeschichte, mit einer Einleitung und mit Anmerkungen neu herausgegeben von Dr. Jakob Fromer* (Munich, 1911).

MAKOWSKI, KRZYSZTOF A., 'Between Germans and Poles: The Jews of Poznań in 1848', *Polin*, 14 (2001), 68–82.

——'Das Grossherzogtum Posen im Revolutionsjahr 1848', in R. Jaworski and R. Luft (eds.), *1848/49: Revolutionen in Ostmitteleuropa* (Munich, 1996), 149–72.

——*Siła mitu: Żydzi w Poznańskiem w dobie zaborów w piśmiennictwie historycznym* (Poznań, 2004).

MAŁECKI, JAN, 'Lwów i Kraków—dwie stolice Galicji', *Roczniki Dziejów Społecznych i Gospodarczych*, 50 (Kraków, 1989), 119–31.

——'Le Rôle de Cracovie dans l'économie polonaise aux XVIe, XVIIe et XVIIIe siècles', *Acta Poloniae Historica*, 21 (1970), 108–22.

MALINO, FRANCES, *A Jew in the French Revolution: The Life of Zalkind Hourwitz* (Cambridge, Mass., 1996).

MANEKIN, RACHEL, 'The Expansion and Consolidation of Jewish Orthodoxy in Galicia: Mahazikei Hadat 1867–1888' (Heb.), Ph.D. thesis (Hebrew University, 2000).

——'Politics, Religion and National Identity: The Galician Jewish Vote in the 1873 Parliamentary Elections', *Polin*, 12 (1999), 100–19.

MANIKOWSKI, ADAM, 'Zmiany czy stagnacja? Z problematyki handlu polskiego w drugiej połowie XVII wieku', *Przegląd Historyczny*, 64 (1973), 771–89.

MANN, JACOB, *Texts and Studies in Jewish History and Literature*, ii: *Karaitica* (New York, 1972).

MANTEUFFEL, TADEUSZ, *The Formation of the Polish State: The Period of Ducal Rule, 963–1194* (Detroit, 1982).

MAREK, P., 'Belorusskaya sinagoga i ee territoriya', *Voskhod*, 23 (1903), no. 5, 71–82.

MARGOLIN, ARNOLD, *The Jews of Eastern Europe* (New York, 1926).

MARGOLIS, O., *The History of Jews in Russia (1772–1861)* [Geshikhte fun yidn in rusland (1772–1861)] (Moscow, 1930).

MARKIEWICZ, HENRYK (ed.), *Żydzi w Polsce: Antologia literacka* (Kraków, 1997).

MARKIEWICZ, MARIUSZ, *Historia Polski 1492–1795* (Kraków, 2002).

MARTEL, A., *La Langue polonaise dans les pays ruthènes: Ukraine et Russie Blanche, 1569–1667* (Lille, 1938).

Materiały do dziejów Sejmu Czteroletniego, 6 vols., ed. Janusz Woliński et al. (Wrocław, 1955–69).

Materialy Komissii po ustroistvu byta evreev, 2 vols. (St Petersburg, 1872).

Matricularum Regni Poloniae summaria, excussis codicibus, qui in Chartophylacio Maximo Varsoviensi asservantur, contexuit indicesque adiecit Theodorus Wierzbowski, ed. Teodor Wierzbowski, pt. 1 (Warsaw, 1905).

MAY, ARTHUR J., *The Hapsburg Monarchy, 1867–1914* (Cambridge, Mass., 1951; repr. 1968).

MEIR, NATHAN, 'The Jews in Kiev, 1859–1914: Community and Charity in an Imperial Russian City', Ph.D. thesis (Columbia University, 2004).

MELAMED, EFIM, 'The Zhitomir Rabbinical School: New Materials and Perspectives', *Polin*, 14 (2001), 105–15.

MENAHEM MENDEL OF VITEBSK, *Likutei amarim* [hasidic work] (Lwów, 1811).

MENCEL, TADEUSZ, 'Prawa wyborcze ludności miejskiej w Księstwie Warszawskim i Królestwie Polskim (1807–1830)', in Tadeusz Cieślak (ed.), *Naród i państwo: Prace ofiarowane Henrykowi Jabłońskiemu w 60 rocznicę urodzin* (Warsaw, 1969), 271–87.

MENDELSOHN, EZRA, *The Jews of East-Central Europe* (Bloomington, Ind., 1983).

——*On Modern Jewish Politics* (Oxford, 1993).

MENDES-FLOHR, PAUL, and JEHUDA REINHARZ (eds.), *The Jew in the Modern World: A Documentary History*, 2nd edn. (New York, 1995).

MERUNOWICZ, TEOFIL, *Żydzi: Studium społeczne* (Lwów, 1879).

MICHAŁOWSKA-MYCIELSKA, ANNA, 'Jan Achacy Kmita: An Anti-Jewish Writer of the First Half of the Seventeenth Century', *Scripta Judaica Cracoviensia*, 4 (2006), 11–16.

MICHALSKI, JERZY, 'Sejmowe projekty reformy położenia ludności żydowskiej w Polsce w latach 1789–1792', in Michalski (ed.), *Lud żydowski w narodzie polskim: Materiały sesji naukowej w Warszawie 15–16 września 1992* (Warsaw, 1994), 20–44.

MICZYŃSKI, SEBASTIAN, *Zwierciadło Korony Polskiey, urazy ciężkie, y utrapienia wielkie, które ponosi od Żydów* (Kraków, [1618]).

MILLER, J., 'The Polish Nobility and the Renaissance Monarchy: The "Execution of Laws Movement"', *Parliaments, Estates and Representation*, 3/3 (Dec. 1983), 65–87; 4/1 (June 1984), 1–24.

MIŁOSZ, CZESŁAW, *The History of Polish Literature* (Berkeley, 1983).

MILYUTIN, B., *Ustroistvo i sostoyanie evreiskikh obshchestv v Rossii* (St Petersburg, 1849–50).

MINCZELES, HENRI, *Vilna, Wilno, Vilnius: La Jérusalem de Lituanie* (Paris, 1993).

MISSALOWA, GRYZELDA, *Studia nad powstaniem łódzkiego okręgu przemysłowego*, i (Łódź, 1964).

MORAWSKA, EWA, 'Polish–Jewish Relations in America, 1880–1940: Old Elements, New Configurations', *Polin*, 19 (2006), 71–86.

MORDECAI B. SAMUEL, *Sha'ar hamelekh* [ethical kabbalistic work] (Zhovkva, 1762).

MORGENSZTERN, JANINA, 'O osadnictwie Żydów w Zamościu na przełomie XVI–XVII w.', *Biuletyn Żydowskiego Instytutu Historycznego*, 43–4 (1962), 3–17.

——'Operacje kredytowe Żydów w Zamościu w XVII w.', *Biuletyn Żydowskiego Instytutu Historycznego*, 64 (1967), 3–32.

——'Pośrednictwo Żydów w nawiązywaniu nieoficjalnych kontaktów dyplomatycznych między dworem polskim i tureckim w 1590 r.', *Biuletyn Żydowskiego Instytutu Historycznego*, 40 (1961), 37–49.

——'Uwagi o Żydach sefardyjskich w Zamościu w latach 1588–1650', *Biuletyn Żydowskiego Instytutu Historycznego*, 38 (1961), 69–82.

——'Z dziejów Żydów w Kraśniku do połowy XVII w.', *Biuletyn Żydowskiego Instytutu Historycznego*, 34 (1960), 71–90; 36 (1960), 3–40.

MORGULIS, MIKHAIL, 'Iz moikh vospominanii', *Voskhod*, 15 (1895), no. 2, 108–29; no. 4, 21–35; no. 7, 140–54; no. 9, 97–122; nos. 11–12, 81–103; 16 (1896), nos. 5–6, 169–90; 17 (1897), no. 4, 65–87; no. 6, 86–100.

——'K istorii obrazovaniya russkikh evreev', in Morgulis, *Voprosy evreiskoi zhizni: Sobranie statei* (St Petersburg, 1899).

MSTISLAVSKY, S. [SIMON DUBNOW], 'Oblastnye kagal'nye seimy v voevodstve volynskom i v Belorussii (1666–1764)', *Voskhod*, 14 (1894), no. 4, 24–42.

MUELLER, WIESŁAW, 'Jews in the *ad limina* Reports of the Polish Bishops of the Seventeenth and Eighteenth Centuries', paper presented at the International Conference on the History of the Jews in Poland, Jerusalem, Feb. 1998.

MÜLLER, MICHAEL G., *Polen zwischen Preussen und Russland: Souveränitätskrise und Reformpolitik 1736–1752* (Berlin, 1983).

MUSTEIKIS, ANTANAS, *The Reformation in Lithuania: Religious Fluctuations in the Sixteenth Century*, Boulder East European Monographs (Boulder, Colo., 1988).

MYSH, MIKHAIL IGNATEVICH (ed.), *Rukovodstvo k russkim zakonam o evreyakh*, 4th edn. (St Petersburg, 1914).

NADAV, M., 'The History of the Pinsk *Kehilah*, 1506–1880' (Heb.), in Z. Rabinowitsch (ed.), *Pinsk* (Tel Aviv, 1973).

NADEL, B., 'O stosunkach Żydów na wileńszczyźnie do powstania styczniowego', *Biuletyn Żydowskiego Instytutu Historycznego*, 28 (1958), 39–64.

NADEL GOLOBIC, E., 'Armenians and Jews in Medieval Lvov: Their Role in Oriental Trade 1400–1600', *Cahiers du monde russe et soviétique*, 20/3–4 (July–Dec. 1979), 345–88.

NADLER, ALAN, *The Faith of the Mithnagdim: Rabbinic Responses to Hasidic Rapture* (Baltimore, 1997).

NAMIER, LEWIS, *1848: The Revolution of the Intellectuals* (London, 1946).

NATHANS, BENJAMIN, *Beyond the Pale: The Jewish Encounter with Late Imperial Russia* (Berkeley, 2002).

NATHANSON, B., *A Book of Remembrance: An Account of the Life of the Ribal (Isaac Baer Levinsohn)* [Sefer hazikhronot: divrei yemei ḥayei ribal] (Warsaw, 1878).

NEUMAN, ABRAHAM A., *The Jews in Spain*, i (Philadelphia, 1942).

NIKITIN, VIKTOR NIKITICH, *Evrei-zemledel'tsy* (St Petersburg, 1887).

'O sostoyanii Rossii pri Ekaterine velikoi: Voprosy Diderot'a i otvety Ekateriny', *Russkii arkhiv*, 18/3 (1880), 1–29.

OLSZEWSKI, HENRYK, *Sejm Rzeczypospolitej epoki oligarchii 1652–1763* (Poznań, 1966).

OPPMAN, A., 'Berek Jawor', in J. Tuwim (ed.), *Księga wierszy pisarzy polskich 19-go wieku* (Warsaw, 1954), 483–4.

ORBACH, ALEXANDER, *New Voices of Russian Jewry: A Study of the Russian-Jewish Press of Odessa in the Era of the Great Reforms, 1860–1871* (Leiden, 1980).

ORSHANSKY, ILYA G., *Evrei v Rossii: Ocherki ekonomicheskogo i obshchestvennogo byta russkikh evreev* (St Petersburg, 1877).

ORTON, LAWRENCE D., 'The Formation of Modern Kraków, 1866–1914', *Austrian History Yearbook*, 19–20 (1983–4), 105–17.

ORZESZKOWA, ELIZA, *O Żydach i kwestyi żydowskiej* (Vilna, 1882).

ÖSTREICH, C., *'Des rauhen Winters ungeachtet . . .': Die Auswanderung Posener Juden nach Amerika im 19. Jahrhundert*, Hamburger Veröffentlichungen zur Geschichte Mittel- und Osteuropas 4 (Hamburg, 1997).

Pamyatniki diplomaticheskikh snoshenii Moskovskogo gosudarstva s Pol'sko-Litovskim, ii, ed. G. F. Karpov, Sbornik Imperatorskogo Russkogo Istoricheskogo Obshchestva 59 (St Petersburg, 1887).

PAPERNA, A. I., 'Iz nikolaevskoi epokhi', in V. E. Kelner (ed.), *Evrei v Rossii: XIX vek* (St Petersburg, 2000).

PAPROCKI, FRANCISZEK, *Wielkie Księstwo Poznańskie w okresie rządów Flottwella 1830–1841* (Poznań, 1970).

PARKER, W. H., *A Historical Geography of Russia* (London, 1968).

PARKES, JAMES, 'Lewis Way and his Times', *Transactions of the Jewish Society of England*, 20 (1964), 189–201.

PARTYKA, JOANNA, 'Szlachecka silva rerum jako źródło do badań etnograficznych', *Etnografia Polska*, 32 (1988), 67–94.

PASEK, JAN, *Memoirs of the Polish Baroque: The Writings of Jan Chryzostom Pasek, a Squire of the Commonwealth of Poland and Lithuania*, ed. Catherine Leach (Berkeley, 1976).

Das Paterikon des Kiever Höhlenklosters, ed. D. I. Abramovich and D. Tschiževskij (Munich, 1964).

PAVLENKO, YURY VITALIIOVYCH, *Narys istoriyi Kyyeva* (Kiev, 2003).

PELEŃSKI, JAROSŁAW, 'The Incorporation of the Ukrainian Lands of Old Rus' into Crown Poland (1569): Socio-Material Interest and Ideology—A Reexamination', in *American Contributions to the Seventh International Congress of Slavists* (The Hague, 1973), iii: *History*, ed. Anna Cienciała, 19–52.

PEN, S., 'Deputatsiya evreiskogo naroda', *Knizhki Voskhoda*, 25 (1905), no. 1, 62–84; no. 2, 50–65; no. 3, 56–71.

PENKALLA, ADAM, 'The Socio-Cultural Integration of the Jewish Population in the Province of Radom', *Polin*, 3 (1988), 214–37.

PERRIE, MAUREEN, *Pretenders and Popular Monarchism in Early Modern Russia* (Cambridge, 1995).

PETROVSKY-SHTERN, YOHANAN, 'The Drama of Berdichev: Levi Yitshak and his Town', *Polin*, 17 (2004), 83–95.

——'Hasidism, Havurot and the Jewish Street', *Jewish Social Studies*, NS 10/2 (2004), 20–54.

——'Jews in the Russian Army: Through the Military towards Modernity', Ph.D. thesis (Brandeis University, 2001).

PHILIPSON, DAVID, *The Reform Movement in Judaism*, rev. S. B. Freehof (New York, 1967).

PIETRZAK-PAWŁOWSKA, IRENA (ed.), *Uprzemysłowienie ziem polskich w XIX i XX wieku* (Wrocław, 1970).

PIKULSKI, GAUDENTY, *Złość żydowska przeciwko Bogu i bliźniemu, prawdzie i sumieniu na objaśnienie przeklętych talmudystów na dowód ich zaślepienia i religii daleko od Prawa Boskiego przez Mojżesza danego* (Lwów, 1758).

PILARCZYK, KRZYSZTOF, 'Printing the Talmud in Poland in the Sixteenth and Seventeenth Centuries', *Polin*, 15 (2002), 59–64.

PILAT, TADEUSZ, 'Własność tabularna w Galicji', *Wiadomości statystyczne o stosunkach krajowych*, 12 (1891), pp. i–liii, 1–67.

PIPES, RICHARD, 'Catherine II and the Jews: The Origins of the Pale of Settlement', *Soviet Jewish Affairs*, 5 (1975), 3–20.

——*Russia under the Old Regime* (London, 1974).

POCIECHA, WŁADYSŁAW (ed.), *Acta Tomiciana*, 17 vols. (Poznań, 1852–).

PODHORODECKI, LESZEK, *Dzieje Lwowa* (Warsaw, 1993).

PODLASKI, KAZIMIERZ, *Białorusini, Litwini, Ukraińcy* (London, 1985).

PODRAZA, ANTONI, 'Jews and the Village in the Polish Commonwealth', in Antony Polonsky, Jakub Basista, and Andrzej Link-Lenczowski (eds.), *The Jews in Old Poland* (London, 1993), 299–321.

Podręcznik statystyki Galicyi. See *Rocznik statystyki Galicyi wydany przez Krajowe Biuro Statystyczne*.

POLANYI, KARL, *The Great Transformation: The Political and Economic Origins of our Time* (New York, 1944).

POLLARD, ALFRED FREDERICK, *The Jesuits in Poland* (Oxford, 1982).

Polnoe sobranie zakonov Rossiiskoi Imperii, 1st collection: 1649–1825, 45 vols. (St Petersburg, 1830–43); 2nd collection: 1825–81, 62 vols. (St Petersburg, 1830–84).

POLONSKY, ANTONY, 'The Revolutionary Crisis of 1846–1849 and its Place in the Development of Nineteenth-Century Galicia', in Zvi Gitelman, Lubomyr Hajda, John-Paul Himka, and Roman Solchanyk (eds.), *Culture and Nations of Central and Eastern Europe* (Cambridge, 2000), 443–70.

——'Warszawska Szkoła Rabinów: Orędowniczka narodowej integracji w Królestwie Polskim', in M. Galas (ed.), *Duchowość żydowska w Polsce* (Kraków, 2000), 287–307.

——JAKUB BASISTA, and ANDRZEJ LINK-LENCZOWSKI (eds.), *The Jews in Old Poland* (London, 1993).

POPPE, ANDRZEJ, 'Khazarian Hebrew Documents of the Tenth Century', *Polin*, 3 (1988), 332–42.

POTOCKI, STANISŁAW KOSTKA, *Podróż do Ciemnogrodu* (Warsaw, 1820; repr. Wrocław, 1955).

POTOCKI, WACŁAW, *Ogród fraszek niewypłewionny*, ed. Alexander Brückner (Kraków, 1907).

PRESNYAKOV, ALEKSANDR EVGENEVICH, *Apogei samoderzhaviya: Nikolai I* (Leningrad, 1925); trans. J. C. Zacek, with an introduction by Nicholas V. Riasanovsky, as *Emperor Nicholas I of Russia: The Apogee of Autocracy, 1825–1855* (Gulf Breeze, Fla., 1974).

PRESTEL, DAVID KIRK, 'A Comparative Analysis of Two Patericon Stories', *Russian History*, 7 (1980), 11–20.

PRIBRAM, ALFRED FRANCIS, *Urkunden und Akten zur Geschichte der Juden in Wien*, 2 vols. (Vienna, 1918).

PRUS, B., *Kroniki tygodniowe*, ed. Jan Baculewski, 20 vols. to date (Warsaw, 1953–).

PRUSZYŃSKI, KSAWERY, *Podróż po Polsce* (Warsaw, 1937).

PTAŚNIK, JAN, *Miasto i mieszczaństwo w dawnej Polsce*, 2nd edn. (Warsaw, 1949).

PURCHLA, JACEK, *Jak powstał nowoczesny Kraków*, 2nd edn. (Kraków, 1990).

PUŚ, WIESŁAW, 'The Development of the City of Łódź (1820–1939)', *Polin*, 6 (1991), 3–19.

——*Dzieje Łodzi przemysłowej* (Łódź, 1987).

——*Przemyśł Królestwa Polskiego w latach 1870–1914* (Łódź, 1984).

——*Żydzi w Łodzi w latach zaborów 1793–1914* (Łódź, 2001).

PYTLAS, STEFAN, 'The National Composition of Łódź Industrialists before 1914', *Polin*, 6 (1991), 37–56.

RAEFF, MARC, 'The Well-Ordered Police State and the Development of Modernity in Seventeenth and Eighteenth Century Europe: An Attempt at a Comparative Approach', *American Historical Review*, 80 (1975), 1221–43.

——*The Well-Ordered Police State: Social and Institutional Change through Law in the Germanies and Russia, 1600–1800* (New Haven, 1983).

RAKOWSKI, KAZIMIERZ, *Powstanie poznańskie w 1848 roku* (Lwów, 1900).

RAN, LEIZER (ed.), *The Jerusalem of Lithuania*, 2 vols. (New York, 1974).

RAPOPORT-ALBERT, ADA, introduction to Rapoport-Albert (ed.), *Hasidism Reappraised* (London, 1996), pp. xvii–xxiv.

REDDAWAY, WILLIAM F., J. H. PENSON, OSKAR HALECKI, and ROMAN DYBOSKI (eds.), *The Cambridge History of Poland*, 2 vols. (Cambridge, 1941–50; repr. 1971).

REINER, ELHANAN, 'The Ashkenazi Elite at the Beginning of the Modern Era: Manuscript versus the Printed Book', *Polin*, 10 (1997), 85–98.

——'Changes in the Yeshivas of Poland and Germany in the Sixteenth and Seventeenth Centuries: The Dispute about *Pilpul*' (Heb.), in Israel Bartal, Chava Turniansky, and Ezra Mendelsohn (eds.), *Studies of Jewish Culture in Honor of Chone Shmeruk* [Keminhag ashkenaz upolin: sefer yovel leḥone shmeruk] (Jerusalem, 1993), 9–80.

——'Wealth, Social Position and the Study of Torah: The Status of the *Kloyz* in East European Society in the Early Modern Period' (Heb.), *Tsiyon*, 58 (1993), 287–328.

——(ed.), *Kroke, Kazimierz, Kraków: Studies in the History of the Jews of Kraków* [Kroke, kazimierz, krakov: meḥkarim betoledot yehudei krakov] (Tel Aviv, 2001).

REST, MATTHIAS, *Die russische Judengesetzgebung von der ersten polnischen Teilung bis zum 'Položenie dlja Evreev' (1804)* (Wiesbaden, 1975).

RIASANOVSKY, NICHOLAS V., *Nicholas I and Official Nationality in Russia, 1825–1855* (Berkeley, 1959).

RICHARZ, MONIKA, *Der Eintritt der Juden in die akademischen Berufe: Jüdische Studenten und Akademiker in Deutschland 1678–1848*, Schriftenreihe wissenschaftlicher Abhandlungen des Leo Baeck Instituts 28 (Tübingen, 1974).

RIEBER, ALFRED (ed.), *The Politics of Autocracy: Letters of Alexander II to Prince A. I. Bariatinskii, 1857–1864* (Paris, 1966).

RINGELBLUM, EMANUEL, 'A Debate about Jews in the Polish Sejm of 1775' (Yid.), in Ringelblum, *Chapters in the History of Former Jewish Life in Poland* [Kapiteln geshikhte fun amolikn yidishn lebn in poyln], ed. Jacob Shatzky (Buenos Aires, 1953), 118–25.

——'Dzieje zewnętrzne Żydów w dawnej Rzeczypospolitej', in Ignacy Schiper, Arieh Tartakower, and Aleksander Hafftka (eds.), *Żydzi w Polsce odrodzonej*, 2 vols. (Warsaw, 1932–3), i. 37–80.

——'An Echo of the French Revolution' (Yid.), in Ringelblum, *Chapters in the History of Former Jewish Life in Poland* [Kapiteln geshikhte fun amolikn yidishn lebn in poyln], ed. Jacob Shatzky (Buenos Aires, 1953), 573–9.

——*Polish Jews and the Kościuszko Uprising, 1794* [Di poylishe yidn in oyfshtand fun koshtsyushko—1794] (Vilna, 1937); trans. into Polish as *Żydzi w powstaniu kościuszkowskiem* (Warsaw, 1938).

——'Projekty i próby przewarstwowienia Żydów w epoce stanisławowskiej', *Sprawy Narodowościowe*, 1 (1934), 3–9; 2–3 (1934), 18–26.

Rocznik statystyczny stołecznego miasta Poznania (Poznań, 1935).

Rocznik [later *Podręcznik*] *statystyki Galicyi wydany przez Krajowe Biuro Statystyczne*, ed. T. Rutkowski until 1897 and subsequently by T. Pilat (Lwów, 1887–1913).

ROGALL, JOACHIM (ed.), *Land der grossen Ströme: Von Polen nach Litauen* (Berlin, 1996).

ROGGER, HANS, 'Government, Jews, Peasants and Land after the Liberation of the Serfs', in Rogger, *Jewish Policies and Right-Wing Politics in Imperial Russia* (Berkeley and Los Angeles, 1996), 113–75.

ROMANCHUK, YU., 'Die kulturellen Bestrebungen der Ruthenen in Galizien', *Ruthenische Revue*, 3 (1903), 66–73.

——'Tovarystvo "Prosvita" v pershykh chasakh svoho rozvytku', *Narodnyi ilyustr. kalendar tov. 'Prosvita'* (Lviv, 1927), 31–44.

RÖNNE, LUDWIG VON, and HEINRICH SIMON, *Die früheren und gegenwärtigen Verhältnisse der Juden in den sämmtlichen Landestheilen des Preussischen Staates* (Breslau, 1843).

ROSE, WILLIAM J., *Stanislaw Konarski, Reformer of Education in 18th Century Poland* (London, 1929).

ROSENTHAL, J. M., 'Marcin Czechowic and Jacob of Bełżyce: Arian–Jewish Encounters in 16th Century Poland', *Proceedings of the American Academy for Jewish Research*, 34 (1966), 77–98.

ROSMAN, MOSHE, *Founder of Hasidism: A Quest for the Historical Ba'al Shem Tov* (Berkeley and Los Angeles, 1996).

——'The History of Jewish Women in Early Modern Poland: An Assessment', *Polin*, 18 (2005), 25–56.

——'Images of the House of Israel as a Centre of Torah after the Catastrophes of 1648' (Heb.), *Tsiyon*, 51/4 (1986), 435–48.

——'Innovative Tradition: Jewish Culture in the Polish–Lithuanian Commonwealth', in D. Biale (ed.), *Cultures of the Jews: A New History* (New York, 2002), ii. 217–68.

——'Jewish Perceptions of Insecurity and Powerlessness in 16th–18th Century Poland', *Polin*, 1 (1986), 19–27.

——*The Lords' Jews: Magnate–Jewish Relations in the Polish–Lithuanian Commonwealth during the Eighteenth Century* (Cambridge, Mass., 1990).

——'A Minority Views the Majority: Jewish Attitudes towards the Polish–Lithuanian Commonwealth and Interaction with Poles', *Polin*, 4 (1989), 31–41.

——'Polish Jews in the Gdańsk Trade in the Late 17th and Early 18th Centuries', in Isidore Twersky (ed.), *Danzig between East and West: Aspects of Modern Jewish History* (Cambridge, Mass., 1985), 111–20.

ROSSET, EDWARD, *Prostytucja i choroby weneryczne w Łodzi* (Łódź, 1931).

ROSTWOROWSKI, EMANUEL, 'Miasta i mieszczanie w ustroju Trzeciego Maja', in Jerzy Kowecki (ed.), *Sejm Czteroletni i jego tradycje* (Warsaw, 1991), 138–51.

ROTH, CECIL (ed.), *The Ritual Murder Libel and the Jew: The Report by Cardinal Lorenzo Ganganelli (Pope Clement XIV)* (London, 1935).

ROWELL, S. C., *Lithuania Ascending: A Pagan Empire within East-Central Europe, 1295–1345* (Cambridge, 1994).

RUBASHOV, SHNEUR ZALMAN, 'K istorii sabbatianstva v Pol'she (O knige, tsitiruemoi I. Galyatovskim)', *Evreiskaya starina*, 5 (1912), no. 2 (Apr.–June), 219–21.

RUBENS, ALFRED, *A History of the Jewish Costume*, rev. edn. (London, 1973).

RUBINSTEIN, AVRAHAM, 'Between Hasidism and Sabbatianism' (Heb.), in Rubinstein, *Chapters in the History and Ideas of Hasidism* [Perakim betorat haḥasidut vetoledoteiha] (Jerusalem, 1978), 182–97.

RUDNYTSKY, IVAN L., 'Mykhailo Drahomanov and the Problem of Ukrainian Jewish Relations', *Canadian Slavonic Papers*, 11 (Summer 1969), 182–98; repr. in Rudnytsky, *Essays in Modern Ukrainian History* (Cambridge, Mass., 1987), 283–97.

——'Polish–Ukrainian Relations: The Burden of History', in Rudnytsky, *Essays in Modern Ukrainian History* (Cambridge, Mass., 1987), 49–76.

——'The Ukrainians in Galicia under Austrian Rule', *Austrian History Yearbook*, 3/2 (Houston, 1967), 394–429.

Russkii biograficheskii slovar' (St Petersburg, 1908).

RUSSOCKI, STANISŁAW, 'Le Système représentatif de la république nobiliaire de Pologne', in Karl Bosl (ed.), *Der moderne Parlamentarismus und seine Grundlagen in der ständischen Repräsentation* (Berlin, 1977), 279–96.

RYABININ, I. S., *Rada miejska lubelska w XVII w.* (Lublin, 1931).

RYBARSKI, ROMAN, *Handel i polityka handlowa Polski w XVI stuleciu* (Poznań, 1928).

SALMONOWICZ, STANISŁAW, 'Protestanci i katolicy w jednym mieście: Casus Torunia XVI–XVIII wieku', in Adam Kaźmierczyk et al. (eds.), *Rzeczpospolita wielu wyznań* (Kraków, 2004), 65–78.

SAMSONOWICZ, HENRYK, 'Dom zboża', *Polityka*, 31 May 1997.

SAMUŚ, PAWEŁ (ed.), *Polacy—Niemcy—Żydzi w Łodzi w XIX–XX wieku* (Łódź, 1997).

SASPORTAS, J., *Tsitsat novel tsevi* [collection of letters and pamphlets on the Sabbatian movement] (Jerusalem, 1975).

SATLOW, MICHAEL S., *Creating Judaism: History, Tradition, Practice* (New York, 2006).

SAUNDERS, DAVID, *Russia in the Age of Reaction and Reform, 1801–1881* (London, 1992).

SAWICKI, ARON, 'Szkoła Rabinów w Warszawie (1826–1863)', *Miesięcznik Żydowski*, 3 (1933), 244–74.

SCHEDRIN, VASSILI, 'Jewish Bureaucracy in Late Imperial Russia: The Phenomenon of Expert Jews'. Uncompleted Ph.D. diss. (Brandeis), in possession of the author.

SCHIPER, IGNACY, *Dzieje handlu żydowskiego na ziemiach polskich* (1937; repr. Kraków, 1990).

——*Istoriya evreiskogo naroda*, 2 vols. (Moscow, 1921).

SCHIPER, IGNACY, *Studya nad stosunkami gospodarczymi Żydów w Polsce podczas średniowiecza* (Lwów, 1911).

——*Żydzi Królestwa Polskiego w dobie Powstania Listopadowego* (Warsaw, 1932).

——'Żydzi pod zaborem pruskim (1772–1807, 1815–1918)', in Ignacy Schiper, Arieh Tartakower, and Aleksander Hafftka (eds.), *Żydzi w Polsce odrodzonej*, 2 vols. (Warsaw, 1932–3), i. 551–3.

——ARIEH TARTAKOWER, and ALEKSANDER HAFFTKA (eds.), *Żydzi w Polsce odrodzonej*, 2 vols. (Warsaw, 1932–3).

SCHMIDT, HANS, *Die polnische Revolution des Jahres 1848 im Grossherzogtum Posen* (Weimar, 1912).

SCHMITT, H., *Rzut oka na projekt bezwarunkowego równouprawnienia Żydów oraz odpowiedź na zarzuty z którymi dzisiejsi ich obrońcy przeciw narodowi polskiemu występują* (Lwów, 1859).

SCHNEE, JOHANNES HEINRICH AUGUST, *Die Hoffinanz und der moderne Staat*, 6 vols. (Berlin, 1953–67).

SCHOLEM, GERSHOM, *Major Trends in Jewish Mysticism* (New York, 1946).

——*Sabbatai Sevi: The Mystical Messiah 1626–1676* (Princeton, 1973).

——'Understanding the Internal Processes', in Scholem, *On the Possibility of Jewish Messianism in our Time and Other Essays*, trans. Jonathan Chipman (repr. Philadelphia, 1997), 45–8.

——'What Is Judaism?', in Scholem, *On the Possibility of Jewish Messianism in our Time and Other Essays*, trans. Jonathan Chipman (repr. Philadelphia, 1997), 114–17.

SCHORR, MOJŻESZ, 'Krakovskii svod statutov i privilegii', *Evreiskaya starina*, 1 (1909), no. 1, 247–64; no. 3, 76–100; no. 4, 223–45.

——'Zasadnicze prawa Żydów w Polsce przedrozbiorowej', in Ignacy Schiper, Arieh Tartakower, and Aleksander Hafftka (eds.), *Żydzi w Polsce odrodzonej*, 2 vols. (Warsaw, 1932–3), i. 191–9.

——'Zur Geschichte des Josef Nasi', *Monatsschrift für Geschichte und Wissenschaft des Judenthums*, NS 5/4 (1897), 169–77, 228–37.

——*Żydzi w Przemyślu do końca XVIII wieku: Opracowanie i wydawnictwo materyału archiwalnego* (Lwów, 1903; repr. Warsaw, 1991).

SCHORSCH, ISMAR, 'Emancipation and the Crisis of Religious Authority: The Emergence of the Modern Rabbinate', in Schorsch, *From Text to Context: The Turn to History in Modern Judaism* (Hanover, NH, 1984), 9–50.

SCHREINER, STEFAN, 'Isaac of Troki's Studies of Rabbinic Literature', *Polin*, 15 (2002), 65–76.

SCHWARZFUCHS, SIMON, *A Concise History of the Rabbinate* (Oxford, 1991).

SEDLAR, JEAN W., *East Central Europe in the Middle Ages, 1000–1500* (Seattle, 1994).

SEGEL, HAROLD B., *Renaissance Culture in Poland: The Rise of Humanism, 1470–1543* (Ithaca, NY, 1989).

SEIDLER, G. L., *The Polish Contribution to the Age of Enlightenment* (Lublin, 1972).

SERBYN, R., 'The *Sion–Osnova* Controversy of 1861–1862', in Peter J. Potichny and Howard Aster (eds.), *Ukrainian–Jewish Relations in Modern Perspective* (Edmonton, 1988), 85–110.

SHABANOVA, A., 'Zhenskoe vrachebnoe obrazovanie v Rossii', *Istoricheskii vestnik*, 131 (1913), no. 3, 952–61.

SHACHAR, Y., *Criticism of Society and Leadership in the Musar and Drush Literature in Eighteenth-Century Poland* [Bikoret haḥevrah vehanhagat hatsibur besifrut hamusar vehaderush bepolin bame'ah hashemoneh-esreh] (Jerusalem, 1992).

SHAPIRO, LEON, *The History of ORT* (New York, 1980).

SHATSKIN, I., 'K istorii uchastiya evreev v pol'skom vosstanii 1863 g.', *Evreiskaya starina*, 8 (1915), no. 1, 29–37.

SHATZKY, JACOB, 'Abraham Jaakov Stern 1768–1842' (Yid.), in *The Joshua Starr Memorial Volume*, Jewish Social Studies Publications 6 (New York, 1953), 203–19.

——*The History of Jews in Warsaw* [Di geshikhte fun yidn in varshe], 3 vols. (New York, 1947–53).

——'Jews in the Polish Uprising of 1831' (Yid.), *Historishe shriftn*, 2 (1937), 353–89, 617.

——'Sephardim in Zamość' (Yid.), *YIVO bleter*, 35 (1931), 93–120.

SHILO, SHMUEL, 'The Individual versus the Community in Jewish Law in Pre-Eighteenth Century Poland', in Antony Polonsky, Jakub Basista, and Andrzej Link-Lenczowski (eds.), *The Jews in Old Poland* (London, 1993), 219–34.

SHLOEGEL, K., 'W poszukiwaniu "Ziemi Obiecanej"', *Tygiel Kultury*, 4 (1997), 10–17.

SHMERUK, CHONE, 'Students from Germany in Polish Yeshivas' (Heb.), in Shmuel Ettinger, Salo Baron, Ben-Zion Dinur, and Yitshak Halpern (eds.), *Festschrift for Yitshak Baer* [Sefer hayovel leyitsḥak ba'er] (Jerusalem, 1960), 304–17.

——'Yiddish Literature and Collective Memory: The Case of the Chmielnicki Massacres', *Polin*, 5 (1990), 173–83.

SHOCHET, ELIJAH JUDAH, *The Hasidic Movement and the Gaon of Vilna* (Northvale, NJ, 1994).

SHOHAT, AZRIEL, 'The Administration of the *Kehilot* in Russia after the Abolition of the *Kahal*' (Heb.), *Tsiyon*, 42 (1979), 143–233.

——'The Attitude of Society to Rabbis from Rabbinical Schools' (Heb.), in *Religion and Life* [Hadat vehaḥayim] (Jerusalem, 1993), 240–68.

——*The Office of Crown Rabbi in Russia* [Mosad 'harabanut mita'am' berusiyah] (Haifa, 1975).

SHOHETMAN, B., 'The First *Rassvet*' (Heb.), *He'avar*, 2 (1954), 61–72.

SHUGUROV, MIKHAIL, 'Doklad o evreyakh imperatoru Aleksandru Pavlovichu', *Russkii arkhiv*, 41/1 (1903), 253–73.

SHULMAN, NISSON E., *Authority and Community: Polish Jewry in the Sixteenth Century* (New York, 1986).

SIEGELBAUM, LEWIS, 'The Odessa Grain Trade: A Case Study in Urban Growth and Development in Tsarist Russia', *Journal of European Economic History*, 9 (1980), 113–51.

SIKORSKA-KULESZA, JOLANTA, 'Prostitution in Congress Poland', *Acta Poloniae Historica*, 83 (2001), 123–33.

SILBERGLEIT, HEINRICH, *Die Bevölkerungs- und Berufsverhältnisse der Juden im deutschen Reich*, i (Berlin, 1930).

SILBERSZTEJN, S., 'Postępowa synagoga na Daniłowiczowskiej w Warszawie: Przyczynek do historii Żydów polskich', Master's thesis (University of Warsaw, n.d. [1933–4]); repr. in *Biuletyn Żydowskiego Instytutu Historycznego*, 74 (1970), 31–57.

SINKOFF, NANCY, 'Benjamin Franklin in Jewish Eastern Europe: Cultural Appropriation in the Age of the Enlightenment', *Journal of the History of Ideas*, 61 (2000), 133–52.

——'Strategy and Ruse in the Haskalah of Mendel Lefin of Satanow', in Shmul Feiner and David Sorkin (eds.), *New Perspectives on the Haskalah* (London, 2001), 86–102.

SKINNER, F. W., 'Odessa and the Problem of Urban Modernization', in Michael F. Hamm (ed.), *The City in Late Imperial Russia* (Bloomington, Ind., 1986), 209–48.

SLIOZBERG, GENRIKH, *Dela minuvshikh dnei: Zapiski russkogo evreya*, 3 vols. (Paris, 1934).

ŚLIWOWSKI, JERZY, 'Zagadnienie tzw. Projektu Nowosilcowa Kodeksu Karzącego Królestwa Polskiego', *Czasopismo Prawno-Historyczne*, 1 (1957), 114–30.

SLOCUM, J. W., 'Who, and When, Were the *Inorodtsy*? The Evolution of the Category of "Aliens" in Imperial Russia', *Russian Review*, 57/2 (1998), 173–90.

SLONIK, BENJAMIN AARON, *Responsa* (Vilna, 1894).

SŁONIMSKI, ANTONI, *138 wierszy* (Warsaw, 1984).

SLUTSKY, Y., *The Russian Jewish Press in the Nineteenth Century* [Ha'itonut hayehuditrusit bame'ah hateshaesreh] (Jerusalem, 1970).

SMOLEŃSKI, W., *Ostatni rok Sejmu wielkiego* (Kraków, 1897).

SOMBART, WERNER, *Die Juden und das Wirtschaftsleben* (Leipzig, 1911); trans. M. Epstein as *The Jews and Modern Capitalism*, introd. Samuel Z. Klausner (New Brunswick, NJ, 1982).

Sovetskaya istoricheskaya entsiklopediya, 16 vols. (Moscow, 1961–76).

STAMPFER, SHAUL, 'Patterns of Internal Jewish Migration in the Russian Empire', in Yaacov Ro'i, *Jews and Jewish Life in Russia and the Soviet Union* (London, 1995) 28–47.

——'The 1764 Census of Polish Jewry', in G. Bacon and M. Rosman (eds.), *Annual of Bar-Ilan University*, Studies in the Humanities 24–5 (1989), 41–147.

——'Social Attitudes towards Early Marriage in Eastern Europe in the Mid-Nineteenth Century' (Heb.), in Ezra Mendelsohn and Chone Shmeruk (eds.),

Studies on Polish Jewry: Paul Glikson Memorial Volume [Kovets meḥkarim al yehudei polin: sefer lezikhro shel paul gelikson] (Jerusalem, 1987), 65–77.

Stańczycy: Antologia myśli społecznej i politycznej konserwatystów krakowskich, ed. Marcin Król (Warsaw, 1982).

STANISLAWSKI, MICHAEL, *'For Whom Do I Toil?' Judah Leib Gordon and the Crisis of Russian Jewry* (New York, 1988).

——'The State of the Debate over Sabbatianism in Poland: A Review of the Sources', in John Micgiel, Robert Scott, and Harold B. Segel (eds.), *Poles and Jews: Myth and Reality in the Historical Context* (New York, 1986), 58–69.

——*Tsar Nicholas and the Jews: The Transformation of Jewish Society in Russia* (Philadelphia, 1983).

STANKOWA, MARIA, 'Zmierzch znaczenia Lublina', in Stankowa, *Dzieje Lublina* (Lublin, 1965).

STANLEY, J., 'The Politics of the Jewish Question in the Duchy of Warsaw, 1807–1813', *Jewish Social Studies*, 44/1 (1982), 47–62.

STASZIC, STANISŁAW, *O przyczynach szkodliwości Żydów i o środkach usposobieniu ich aby się społeczeństwu użytecznymi stali*, 1st published in *Pamiętnik Warszawski* in 1816; repr. in *Dzieła* (Warsaw, 1818), iv. 217 ff.; repr. in August Rohling, *Zgubne zasady Talmudyzmu do serdecznej rozwagi Żydom i Chrześcijanom wszelkiego stanu, podał A. Rohling*, trans. from *Der Talmudjude*, 2nd edn. (Lwów, 1875).

——*Pisma filozoficzne i społeczne*, ed. B. Suchodolski, 2 vols. (Kraków, 1954).

——*Przestrogi dla Polski*, ed. S. Czarnowski (Kraków, 1926).

Statistisches Jahrbuch für den Preussischen Staat, 16 vols. (Berlin, 1904–20).

STAUTER-HALSTEAD, KEELY, 'Jews, Anti-Semitism, and the Sex Trade in Turn-of-the-Century Poland', unpublished.

——'Jews as Middleman Minorities in Rural Poland: Understanding the Galician Pogroms of 1898', in R. Blobaum (ed.), *Anti-Semitism and its Opponents in Modern Poland* (Ithaca, NY, 2005), 39–59.

——*The Nation in the Village: The Genesis of Peasant National Identity in Austrian Poland, 1848–1914* (Ithaca, NY, 2001).

STEFAŃSKI, KRZYSZTOF, 'The Synagogues of Łódź', *Polin*, 11 (1998), 154–67.

STEGNER, TADEUSZ, *Liberałowie Królestwa Polskiego* (Gdańsk, 1990).

STEINLAUF, MICHAEL, 'Mr Gelhab and Sambo in *Peyes*: Images of the Jew on the Polish Stage, 1863–1914', *Polin*, 4 (1989), 98–128.

STERN, SELMA, *The Court Jew: A Contribution to the History of Absolutism in Central Europe* (Philadelphia, 1950).

STEUART, A. FRANCIS (ed.), *Papers Relating to the Scots in Poland 1576–1793* (Edinburgh, 1915).

STITES, RICHARD, *The Women's Liberation Movement in Russia: Feminism, Nihilism and Bolshevism* (Princeton, 1968).

STÖKL, GÜNTHER, *Die Entstehung des Kosakentums* (Munich, 1953).

STONE, DAN, *The Polish–Lithuanian State, 1386–1795* (Seattle, 2001).

STRAUSS, H., 'Liberalism and Conservatism in Prussian Legislation for Jewish Affairs, 1815–1847', in Herbert A. Strauss and Hanns G. Reissner (eds.), *Jubilee Volume Dedicated to Curt C. Silberman* (New York, 1969), 114–32.

——'Pre-Emancipation Prussian Policies towards the Jews 1815–1847', *Leo Baeck Institute Yearbook*, 9 (1966), 107–37.

STREITER, KARL HEINK, *Die nationalen Beziehungen im Grossherzogtum Posen (1815–1848)* (Bern, 1986).

STRUVE, K., 'Gentry, Jews, and Peasants: Jews as the Other in the Formation of the Modern Polish Nation in Rural Galicia', in N. Wingfield (ed.), *Creating the Other: Ethnic Conflict and Nationalism in Habsburg Central Europe* (New York, 2003).

SUCHENI-GRABOWSKA, ANNA, *Monarchia dwu ostatnich Jagiellonów a ruch egzekucyjny* (Warsaw, 1974).

SUCHODOLSKI, STANISŁAW, *Początki mennictwa w Europie środkowej, wschodniej i północnej* (Wrocław, 1971).

SUROWIECKI, WAWRZYNIEC, *Wybór pism* (Warsaw, 1957).

ŚWIĘTOCHOWSKI, ALEKSANDER, 'Klasyfikacja wyznaniowa', *Prawda*, 4 (1883).

——*Liberum Veto*, ed. Samuel Sandler, 2 vols. (Warsaw, 1976).

——'Nie tędy', *Przegląd tygodniowy*, 7 (1877).

——'Wskazania polityczne', in Świętochowski, *Ognisko: Księga zbiorowa wydana dla uczczenia dwudziestopięcioletniej pracy T. T. Jeża* (Warsaw, 1882).

——*Wspomnienia* (Warsaw, 1966).

SYSYN, FRANK, *Between Poland and the Ukraine: The Dilemma of Adam Kysil, 1600–1653* (Cambridge, Mass., 1985).

SZABO, FRANZ A. J., 'Austria's First Impressions of Ethnic Relations in Galicia: The Case of Governor Anton von Pergen', *Polin*, 12 (1999), 49–60.

——*Kaunitz and Enlightened Absolutism, 1753–1780* (Cambridge, 1995).

SZCZEPANOWSKI, STANISŁAW, *Nędza Galicji w cyfrach: Program energicznego rozwoju gospodarstwa krajowego* (Lwów, 1888).

SZTERENKAC, I., 'Zniesienia kahałów i utworzenie dozorów bóżniczych (w pierwszych latach Królestwa Polskiego)', MA thesis (Warsaw University, n.d.).

TA-SHEMA, ISRAEL M., 'New Sources on the History of the Jews in Poland in the Twelfth and Thirteenth Centuries' (Heb.), *Tsiyon*, 54 (1989), 205–8.

——'On the History of the Jews in Poland in the Twelfth and Thirteenth Centuries' (Heb.), *Tsiyon*, 53 (1988), 347–69.

——'On the History of the Jews in Twelfth- and Thirteenth-Century Poland', *Polin*, 10 (1997), 287–317.

TAWNEY, RICHARD HENRY, *Religion and the Rise of Capitalism: A Historical Study* (London, 1926).

TAYLOR, A. J. P., *The Habsburg Monarchy, 1809–1918: A History of the Austrian Empire and Austria-Hungary*, new edn. (London, 1948; repr. Harmondsworth, 1976).

TAZBIR, JANUSZ, 'Images of the Jew in the Polish Commonwealth', *Polin*, 4 (1989), 18–30.

——*A State without Stakes: Polish Religious Toleration in the Sixteenth and Seventeenth Centuries* (Warsaw, 1973).

——'Żydzi w opinii staropolskiej', in Tazbir, *Świat panów Pasków* (Łódź, 1986).

TEIMANAS, DAVID BENCIONAS, *L'Autonomie des communautés juives en Pologne aux XVIe et XVIIe siècles* (Paris, 1933).

TELLER, ADAM, *A Confined Life: The Jewish Quarter of Poznań in the Mid-Seventeenth Century* [Ḥayim betsavta: harova hayehudi shel poznan bamaḥatsit hasheniyah shel hame'ah ha-17] (Jerusalem, 2003).

——'General Arenda and the General *Arendarz* in Eighteenth Century Lithuania', in R. Aharonsohn and S. Stampfer (eds.), *Jewish Entrepreneurship in Modern Times: Eastern Europe and Erets Yisra'el* [Yazamut yehudit ba'et haḥadashah: mizraḥ eiropah ve'erets yisra'el] (Jerusalem, 2000), 48–78.

——'"In the Land of their Enemies"? The Duality of Jewish Life in Eighteenth-Century Poland', *Polin*, 19 (2006), 431–46.

——'The Laicization of Early Modern Jewish Society: The Development of the Polish Communal Rabbinate in the 16th Century', in M. Graetz (ed.), *Schöpferische Momente des europäischen Judentums in der frühen Neuzeit* (Heidelberg, 2000), 333–49.

——'The Legal Status of the Jews on the Magnate Estates of Poland–Lithuania in the Eighteenth Century', *Gal-ed*, 15–16 (2000), 41–63.

——'"Radziwiłł, Rabinowicz and the Rabbi of Świerz: The Magnates' Attitude towards Jewish Regional Autonomy in 18th Century Poland–Lithuania', in Teller (ed.), *Studies in the History of the Jews in Old Poland: In Honor of Jacob Goldberg* (Jerusalem, 1998), 246–76.

——'The Shtetl as an Arena for Polish Jewish Integration in the Eighteenth Century', *Polin*, 17 (2004), 25–40.

TETER, MAGDALENA, *Jews and Heretics in Catholic Poland: A Beleaguered Church in the Post-Reformation Era* (Cambridge, 2006).

——'The Legend of Ger Zedek of Wilno as Polemic and Reassurance', *AJS Review*, 29/2 (2005), 237–63.

THACKERAY, FRANK, *Antecedents of Revolution: Alexander I and the Polish Kingdom* (Boulder, Colo., 1980).

THON, OZJASZ, 'Wstęp', in Ignacy Schiper, Arieh Tartakower, and Aleksander Hafftka (eds.), *Żydzi w Polsce odrodzonej*, 2 vols. (Warsaw, 1932–3), i. 7–18.

TOKARZ, WACŁAW, 'Miscellanea: Z dziejów sprawy żydowskiej za księstwa warszawskiego', *Kwartalnik Historyczny*, 16 (1902), 262–76.

TOKARZ, WACŁAW, *Sprzysiężenie Wysockiego i Noc Listopadowa* (Warsaw, 1980).

TOLLET, DANIEL, 'Les Manifestations anti-juives dans la Pologne des Wasa (1588–1668)', *Revue d'Histoire Moderne et Contemporaine*, 33 (July–Sept. 1986), 427–39.

——'Marchands et hommes d'affaires juifs dans la Pologne des Wasa (1588–1668)', Ph.D. diss. (University of Paris, 1985).

——'Merchants and Business-men in Poznań and Kraków, 1588–1668', in Chimen Abramsky, Maciej Jachimczyk, and Antony Polonsky (eds.), *The Jews in Poland* (Oxford, 1986), 22–30.

TOMASZEWSKI, JERZY (ed.), *Żydzi w obronie Rzeczypospolitej* (Warsaw, 1996).

TOPOLSKI, JERZY, *Gospodarka polska a europejska w XVI–XVIII wieku* (Poznań, 1977).

——'Sixteenth-Century Poland and the Turning Point in European Economic Development', in J. K. Fedorowicz (ed. and trans.), *A Republic of Nobles* (Cambridge, 1982), 74–90.

——'Wpływ wojen połowy XVII wieku na sytuację ekonomiczną Podlasia', in Aleksander Gieysztor, Gerard Labuda, Tadeusz Manteuffel, and Tadeusz Zawadzki (eds.), *Studia historica w 35-lecie pracy naukowej Henryka Łowmiańskiego* (Warsaw, 1958), 309–50.

——(ed.), *Dzieje Poznania* (Warsaw, 1988).

TOPOROV, V. N., 'K russko-evreiskim kul'turnym kontaktam i literaraturno-tekstovym svyazyam', in Toporov, *Svyatost' i svyatye v russkoi dukhovnoi kul'ture*, i (Moscow, 1995), 340–412.

TOURY, JACOB, *Soziale und politische Geschichte der Juden in Deutschland 1847–1871: Zwischen Revolution, Reaktion und Emanzipation* (Düsseldorf, 1977).

TROTSKY, I., 'Jewish Institutions of Social Welfare, Education, and Mutual Assistance', in Jacob Frumkin, Gregor Aronson, and Alexis Goldenweiser (eds.), *Russian Jewry, 1860–1917*, trans. Mirra Ginsburg (New York, 1966), 416–33.

TRUNK, ISAIAH, 'The Council of the Lands of Russia' (Yid.), *YIVO bleter*, 40 (1956), 63–85.

TRZECIAKOWSKA, MARIA, and LECH TRZECIAKOWSKI, *W dziewiętnastowiecznym Poznaniu* (Poznań, 1982).

TRZECIAKOWSKI, LECH, *The Kulturkampf in Prussian Poland*, trans. K. Kretkowska (Boulder, Colo., 1990).

——*Walka o polskość miast Poznańskiego na przełomie XIX i XX wieku* (Poznań, 1964).

TSHERIKOVER, ELIYAHU, 'From the Russian Archives' (Yid.), *Historishe shriftn*, 1 (1929), 779–92.

——*Istoriya Obshchestva dlya rasprostraneniya prosveshcheniya mezhdu evreyami v Rossii, 1863–1913 gg.* (St Petersburg, 1913).

TURNIANSKY, CHAVA, 'Yiddish "Historical Songs" as Sources for the History of the Jews in Pre-Partition Poland', *Polin*, 4 (1989), 42–52.

'Tzenzura v tsarstvovanii Nikolaya I', *Russkaya starina*, 107 (1903), 658–63.

Universal Jewish Encyclopedia, 10 vols. (New York, 1939–43).

Ustawodawstwo Księstwa Warszawskiego, i, ed. W. Bartel, J. Kosim, and W. Rostocki (Warsaw, 1964).

UVAROV, SERGEY SEMENOVICH, *L'Empereur Alexandre et Buonaparte* (St Petersburg, 1813).

——*Extrait du compte-rendu du Ministère de l'instruction publique pour l'année 1837* (St Petersburg, 1837).

VENTURI, FRANCO, *Roots of Revolution: A History of the Populist and Socialist Movements in Nineteenth Century Russia* (New York, 1960).

VERETE, MEIR, 'Polish Proposals for the Territorial Solution of the "Jewish Question" 1788–1850' (Heb.), *Tsiyon*, 6 (1941), 148–55, 203–13.

VERNADSKY, GEORGE, 'The Heresy of the Judaizers and the Policies of Ivan III of Moscow', *Speculum*, 8 (Oct. 1933), 436–48.

VINAVER, MAKSIM, 'Kak my zanimalis' istoriei', *Evreiskaya starina*, 1 (1909), 41–54.

VINOGRAD, YESHAYAHU, *Thesaurus of the Hebrew Book* [Otsar hasefer ha'ivri], ii: *Places of Print* [Reshimat hasefarim arukhah lefi mekomot hadefus] (Jerusalem, 1993).

VÖLKER, KARL, *Kirchengeschichte Polens* (Berlin, 1930).

WALICKI, ANDRZEJ, *Philosophy and Romantic Nationalism: The Case of Poland* (Oxford, 1982).

WANDYCZ, PIOTR S., *The Lands of Partitioned Poland 1795–1918* (Seattle, 1974).

——'The Poles in the Habsburg Monarchy', in A. Markovits and F. Sysyn (eds.), *Nationbuilding and the Politics of Nationalism: Essays on Austrian Galicia* (Cambridge, Mass., 1982), 68–93.

WANGERMANN, ERNST, *The Austrian Achievement, 1700–1800* (London, 1973).

WĄSICKI, JAN, *Ziemie polskie pod zaborem pruskim: Wielkie Księstwo Poznańskie 1815–1848* (Poznań, 1980).

WEEKS, THEODORE W., 'Assimilation, Nationalism, Modernization, Antisemitism: Notes on Polish Jewish Relations, 1855–1905', in R. Blobaum (ed.), *Antisemitism and its Opponents in Modern Poland* (Ithaca, NY, 2005), 20–38.

——*From Assimilation to Antisemitism: The Jewish Question in Poland, 1850–1914* (DeKalb, Ill., 2006).

——*Nation and State in Late Imperial Russia: Nationalism and Russification on the Western Frontier 1863–1914* (De Kalb, Ill., 1996).

——'Russians, Poles and Jews 1862–1905: The Death of the Ideal of Assimilation in the Kingdom of Poland', *Polin*, 12 (1999), 242–56.

WĘGRZYNEK, HANNA, 'Ludność żydowska wobec powstania listopadowego', in J. Tomaszewski (ed.), *Żydzi w obronie Rzeczypospolitej* (Warsaw, 1996), 31–42.

——'Sixteenth-Century Accounts of Purim Festivities', *Polin*, 15 (2003), 87–92.

WEINRYB, BERNARD, 'The Beginnings of East European Jewry in Legend and Historiography', in M. Ben-Horin, Bernard Weinryb, and Solomin Zeitlin (eds.), *Studies and Essays in Honor of Abraham A. Neuman* (Leiden, 1962), 443–502.

WEINRYB, BERNARD, *Jews of Poland: A Social and Economic History of the Jewish Community in Poland from 1100 to 1800* (Philadelphia, 1976).

——*Neueste Wirtschaftsgeschichte der Juden in Russland und Polen*, i: *Das Wirtschaftsleben der Juden in Russland und Polen von der ersten polnischen Teilung bis zum Tode Alexanders II (1772–1881)* (Breslau, 1934).

——'Studies in the Communal History of Polish Jewry II', *Proceedings of the American Academy for Jewish Research*, 12 (1942), 121–40; 15 (1945), 93–129.

WEINTRAUB, WIKTOR, 'Tolerance and Intolerance in Old Poland', *Canadian Slavonic Papers*, 13 (1971), 21–43.

WENGEROFF, PAULINE, *Memoiren einer Grossmutter: Bilder aus der Kulturgeschichte Russlands im 19. Jahrhundert*, 2 vols. (Berlin, 1908).

——*Rememberings: The World of a Russian-Jewish Woman in the Nineteenth Century*, trans. H. Wenkart (Bethesda, Md., 2000).

WETTSTEIN, FEIVEL, *Treasures from the Minute Book of the Kraków Kahal* [Divrei ḥefets mipinkasei hakahal bekraka] (Kraków, 1902).

WETTSTEIN, P., 'The Past Revealed through Old Minute Books' (Heb.), in Wettstein, *The Treasure House of Literature* [Otsar hasifrut] (Kraków, 1892).

WIDMAN, KAROL, *Franciszek Smolka, jego życie i zawód publiczny* (Lwów, 1886).

WIERZBIENIEC, WACŁAW, 'An Attempt at the Evaluation of Jewish Life in Przemyśl in the Times of the Autonomous Galicia', unpublished.

——'The Processes of Jewish Emancipation and Assimilation in the Multiethnic City of Lviv during the Nineteenth and Twentieth Centuries', in J. Czaplicka (ed.), *Lviv: A City in the Crosscurrents of Culture* (Cambridge, Mass., 2005), 223–50.

WILENSKY, MORDECAI, 'Hasidic–Mitnaggedic Polemics in the Jewish Communities of Eastern Europe: The Hostile Phase', in Gershon Hundert (ed.), *Essential Papers on Hasidism* (New York, 1991), 244–71.

——*Hasidim and Mitnagedim: The History of the Conflict between Them 1772–1815* [Ḥasidim umitnagedim: letoledot hapolmus shebeineihem bashanim 5532–5575], 2 vols. (Jerusalem, 1970).

WINGFIELD, NANCY (ed.), *Creating the Other: Ethnic Conflict and Nationalism in Habsburg Central Europe* (New York, 2003), 1–18.

WISCHNITZER, MARK, *A History of Jewish Crafts and Guilds* (New York, 1965).

——'Proekty reformy evreiskogo byta v Gertsogstve Varshavskom i Tsarstve Pol′skom (po neizdannym materialam)', *Perezhitoe*, 1 (1909), 164–222.

WISCHNITZER, RACHEL, *The Architecture of the European Synagogue* (Philadelphia, 1964).

WODZICKI, STANISŁAW, *Wspomnienia z przeszłości od 1768 do roku 1840* (Kraków, 1873).

WODZIŃSKI, MARCIN, '"Cywilni chrześcijanie": Spory o reformę Żydów w Polsce, 1789–1830', in G. Borkowska and M. Rudkowska (eds.), *Kwestia żydowska w XIX wieku: Spory o tożsamość Polaków* (Warsaw, 2004), 9–42.

——'Jakub Tugendhold and the First Maskilic Defence of Hasidism', *Gal-ed*, 18 (2002), 463–77.

——*Oświecenie żydowskie w Królestwie Polskim wobec chasydyzmu: Dzieje pewnej idei* (Warsaw, 2003); trans. Sarah Cozens and Agnieszka Mirowska as *Haskalah and Hasidism in the Kingdom of Poland: A History of Conflict* (Oxford, 2005).

——' "Sprawa chasydymów": Z materiałów do dziejów chasydyzmu w Królestwie Polskim', in K. Matwijowski (ed.), *Z historii ludności żydowskiej w Polsce i na Śląsku* (Wrocław, 1994), 227–42.

WOLAŃSKI, MARIAN, *Związki handlowe Śląska z Rzeczypospolitą w XVII wieku* (Wrocław, 1961).

WOLF, G., 'Die Versuche zur Errichtung einer Rabbinerschule in Österreich', *Zeitschrift für die Geschichte der Juden in Deutschland*, 5 (1892), 27–53.

WOLF, HILLEL B. ZE'EV [Hillel of Kovno], *Heikel ben shaḥar* [mitnagdic homiletic work] (Warsaw, 1804).

WURM, DAWID, *Z dziejów żydostwa brodzkiego za czasów dawnej Rzeczypospolitej Polskiej (do r. 1772)* (Brody, 1935).

WUTTKE, HEINRICH, *Städtebuch des Landes Posen* (Leipzig, 1877).

WYROBISZ, ANDRZEJ, 'Functional Types of Polish Towns in the 16th–18th Centuries', *Journal of European Economic History*, 12/1 (1983), 69–103.

——'Materiały do dziejów handlu w miasteczkach polskich na początku XVIII wieku', *Przegląd Historyczny*, 62 (1971), 703–16.

——'Rola miast prywatnych w Polsce w XVI i XVII wieku', *Przegląd Historyczny*, 65 (1974), 19–45.

——'Small Towns in 16th and 17th Century Poland', *Acta Poloniae Historica*, 34 (1976), 153–63.

WYROZUMSKA, BOŻENA, 'Did King Jan Olbracht Banish the Jews from Kraków?', in A. Paluch (ed.), *The Jews in Poland*, i (Kraków, 1992), 27–37.

YERUSHALMI, YOSEF, *Zakhor: Jewish History and Jewish Memory* (Seattle, 1996).

Z dziejów gminy starozakonnych w Warszawie w XIX stuleciu, i: *Szkolnictwo* (Warsaw, 1907; repr. 1983).

ZAIONCHKOVSKY, PETR ANDREEVICH, *Krizis samoderzhaviya na rubezhe 1870–1880-kh godov* (Moscow, 1964).

——*Otmena krepostnogo prava v Rossii*, 3rd edn. (Moscow, 1968).

——*Voennye reformy 1860–1870 godov v Rossii* (Moscow, 1952).

ZAKRZEWSKI, ANDRZEJ J., '*Złość żydowska* . . . Gaudentego Pikulskiego, czyli XVIII-wieczna encyklopedia antysemityzmu', in Jerzy Mizgalski (ed.), *Żydzi Częstochowianie: Współistnienie, Holocaust, pamięć* (Częstochowa, 2006), 108–17.

ZAKRZEWSKI, Z., *O brakteatach z napisami hebrajskimi* (Kraków, 1909).

ZAMOYSKI, ADAM, *The Polish Way: A Thousand-Year History of the Poles and their Culture* (London, 1987; repr. 1994).

ZAWADZKI, HUBERT W., *A Man of Honour: Adam Czartoryski as a Statesman of Russia and Poland 1795–1831* (Oxford, 1993).

ŻBIKOWSKI, ANDRZEJ, *Żydzi krakowscy i ich gmina w latach 1869–1919* (Warsaw, 1994).

ZIELIŃSKA, ZOFIA, *Walka 'Familii' o reformę Rzeczypospolitej 1743–1752* (Warsaw, 1983).

ZIENKOWSKA, KRYSTYNA, 'Citizens or Inhabitants? The Attempt to Reform the Status of the Polish Jews during the Four Years' Sejm', *Acta Poloniae Historica*, 76 (1997), 31–52.

——'The Jews Have Killed a Tailor', *Polin*, 3 (1988), 78–101; 1st published as 'Tumult w Warszawie w maju 1790 roku', *Kwartalnik Historyczny*, 95 (1988), 121–48.

——'Reforms Relating to the Third Estate', in S. Fiszman (ed.), *Constitution and Reform in Eighteenth-Century Poland: The Constitution of May 1791* (Bloomington, Ind., 1997), 329–55.

——*Sławetni i urodzeni: Ruch polityczny mieszczaństwa w dobie Sejmu Czteroletniego* (Warsaw, 1976).

——'Spór o Nową Jerozolimę', *Kwartalnik Historyczny*, 93 (1986), 351–76.

——'W odpowiedzi profesorowi Arturowi Eisenbachowi', *Kwartalnik Historyczny*, 95 (1988), 197–201.

ZIENTARA, BENEDYKT, ANTONI MĄCZAK, IRENEUSZ IHNATOWICZ, and ZBIGNIEW LANDAU, *Dzieje gospodarcze Polski do 1939* (Warsaw, 1973).

ZINBERG, ISRAEL, *A History of Jewish Literature*, 12 vols. (Cincinnati, 1978).

——*Istoriya evreiskoi pechati v Rossii v svyazi s obshchestvennymi techeniyami* (St Petersburg, 1915).

ZIPPERSTEIN, STEVEN, *Imagining Russian Jewry: Memory, History, Identity* (Seattle, 1999).

——*The Jews of Odessa: A Cultural History, 1794–1881* (Stanford, Calif., 1985).

——'Remapping Odessa: Rewriting Cultural History', *Jewish Social Studies*, NS 2/2 (1996), 21–37; repr. in Zipperstein, *Imagining Russian Jewry: Memory, History, Identity* (Seattle, 1999).

ZÖLLNER, ERICH (ed.), *Österreich im Zeitalter des aufgeklärten Absolutismus* (Vienna, 1983).

ŻYCHLIŃSKI, LUDWIK, *Historia sejmów Wielkiego Księstwa Poznańskiego do r. 1847*, 2 vols. (Poznań, 1867).

INDEX

A

T

Y

Z